World Space-Economy

World Space-Economy

Anthony R. de Souza
J. Brady Foust
University of Wisconsin—Eau Claire

Charles E. Merrill Publishing Company
A Bell & Howell Company
Columbus   Toronto   London   Sydney

Published by
Charles E. Merrill Publishing Company
A Bell & Howell Company
Columbus, Ohio 43216

This book was set in Optima.
The Production Editor was Ann Mirels.
The cover was prepared by Will Chenoweth.

Copyright ©, 1979, by Bell & Howell Company. All rights reserved. No part of this book may be reproduced in any form, electronic or mechanical, including photocopy, recording, or any information storage and retrieval system, without permission in writing from the publisher.

International Standard Book Number: 0-675-08292-7
Library of Congress Catalog Card Number: 78-65767
8 9 10—86 85

Cover Photographs:
Left— SOURCE Ford Motor Company
Right—SOURCE Tomas Sennett for World Bank Group

Printed in the United States of America

Preface

This book represents a new type of economic geography text; it encompasses alternative and controversial views about the world's space economy. Today's students are unhappy with materials that make of them "institutional fodder" at the expense of their own personalities and development. They want a deeper understanding of what is going on in the world. This book is designed to explore the organization of world space and political economy so that students can find their own way in the world without necessarily subscribing or submitting to a dominant set of values. Education should, above all, encourage intellectual freedom.

In this text we do survey orthodox models and theories, but we also include some radical critiques and theories. The orthodox category consists of conservative and liberal ideas that take the present capitalist system for granted. Radicals (on the left) recognize Western culture-boundness, expose traditional prejudices and assumptions, and subject the existing world order to scrutiny. We hope that the issues and ideas reviewed here will provide a large number of students with an opportunity to re-examine their own world view.

We prepared the text for a one-semester or one-quarter course. With plentiful use of supplementary readings, it may also be used for a one-year course. Supplementing the text are twelve audio-visual modules that can be arranged to function in a variety of ways.

We are grateful to Ingolf Vogeler, Robert Wiseman, Earl Scott, and Dennis Lord who wrote productive reviews of the entire manuscript. Their thoughtful suggestions and recommendations served us well. Most of our many sources for materials are acknowledged in the citations and bibliography. We want to extend a special word of gratitude to all those individuals and institutions that permitted reproduction of their photographs and illustrations free of charge. We thank them warmly for their generosity.

We are particularly indebted to Yvonne Plomedahl for carrying the burden of typing the manuscript. Gratitude is due

Alice Thiede, of Owen Ayres and Associates, for her efficiency and skill in drafting the cartographic illustrations, and Publications, Illustrations and Presentations, Inc. for noncartographic art. Thanks go to Nadia de Souza for designing some of the illustrations, and for preparing the bibliography and index. Finally, our sincere thanks to Greg Spatz and Ann Mirels at Charles E. Merrill for initiating and bringing the project to its completion. Responsibility for any errors and omissions, however, remains ours alone. For the future we invite constructive criticisms and ideas for improvements. Please write to us and we will take your recommendations seriously.

Anthony R. de Souza

J. Brady Foust

Contents

1
Introduction

IDEAS OF ECONOMISTS   3
    Smith's Vision of Progress | The Ricardian View | Marx's Vision of Capitalist Development | Marxists and Imperialism | Keynes and the Fall of Economic Liberalism

COMPETING MINDSETS   14
    The Conservative Mindset | The Liberal Mindset | The Radical Mindset

ECONOMIC PROBLEMS   17
    The Resource Allocation Problem | The Development Problem

MACROECONOMICS AND MICROECONOMICS   19

FUNDAMENTAL GEOGRAPHICAL CONCEPTS   20
    Properties of Space | Spatial Process and Spatial Structure | Spatial Interaction

PERSPECTIVES ON ECONOMIC GEOGRAPHY   27
    Commercial Geography | Man-Environment Relations | Areal Differentiation | Spatial Organization | The Dialectical Approach

SUMMARY AND PLAN   32

2
Population

POPULATION DISTRIBUTION   39
    Population Size | Population Density | Influences upon Population Distribution | Urbanism

POPULATION COMPOSITION   49
    Demographic Structure | Cultural Traits | Economic Characteristics

MIGRATION   62
    Migration Process | Patterns of Migration

POPULATION GROWTH   71
    Rates of Growth | Malthus' Principle of Population | Marx and the Population-Resources Problem | The Demographic Transition | Population Growth and Underdeveloped Countries | A Solution? Three Views
SUMMARY   88

3
Resources

RESOURCES AND POPULATION   94
    Carrying Capacity and Overpopulation | Optimum Population and the Quality of Life
TYPE OF RESOURCES AND THEIR LIMITS   97
    Resources and Reserves | Renewable and Nonrenewable Resources | Limits of Natural Resources
FOOD RESOURCES   100
    Food Problems | Proposals to Increase Food Production | A Solution to the World Food Supply Situation
NONRENEWABLE MINERAL RESOURCES   115
    Depletion Curves and Depletion Rate Estimates | Projected Reserves of Key Minerals | Ocean Mineral Resources and Recycling | Environmental Impact of Mineral Extraction
ENERGY   120
    The Energy "Crisis" | Adequacy of Fossil Fuels | Energy Options | From a Cowboy to a Spaceship Life-style
SUMMARY   139

4
Agriculture and Rural Land Use

TRANSFORMING NATURE: AGRICULTURE   145
    The Emergence of Agriculture | The Diffusion of Agriculture | Human Impact on the Land
FACTORS AFFECTING RURAL LAND USE   156
    Site Characteristics | Cultural Preferences and Perception of Environment | Systems of Production | Relative Location
THÜNEN'S MODEL   166
    The Law of Diminishing Returns and the Concept of Rent | The Isolated State | Evaluation of Thünen's Model
EVIDENCE IN SUPPORT OF THÜNEN'S MODEL   182
    Agricultural Locations at Local Scales | Agricultural Locations at Regional Scales | Agricultural Locations at National and International Scales
SUMMARY   189

CONTENTS ix

5
Cities and Urban Land Use

CITIES AND SOCIETIES   198
  Basic Forms of Society | Transformation of Market Exchange | Relative Importance of Different Modes of Exchange
PROCESS OF CITY BUILDING   202
  Production and Cost Behavior of the Single Firm | Scale Economies and Diseconomies of the Single Firm | Transport Costs of the Single Firm | Economic Costs and City Building
LOCATION OF LAND USES INSIDE CITIES   207
  The Competitive Bidding Process | Ceiling Rents | The Residential Location Decision | Site Demands of Firms | Market Outcomes
SPATIAL MODELS OF URBAN LAND USE   217
  The Concentric Zone Model | The Sector Model | The Multiple-Nuclei Model | Evaluation of Land Use Models | The Spread City | Sources of Change | Polarization of Urban Areas
SUMMARY   240

6
Urban Hierarchies and Hinterland Trade

CENTRAL PLACES AND THEIR HINTERLANDS   245
  Locational Patterns of Cities | Central Places | Hinterlands | The Law of Retail Gravitation
AN ELEMENTARY CENTRAL PLACE MODEL   251
  Threshold and Range | Order of a Good | Order of a Center | Emergence of a Central Place Hierarchy
THE CHRISTALLER CENTRAL PLACE MODEL   255
  The Marketing Principle | The Traffic Principle | The Administrative Principle | Southern Germany
EXTENSIONS OF THE CHRISTALLER MODEL   261
  Lösch's Economic Landscape | City-Rich and City-Poor Sectors | Economic Regions in Reality | Christaller and Lösch Compared | Isard's Modifications | Wholesaling and the Mercantile Model of Settlement
EVIDENCE IN SUPPORT OF CENTRAL PLACE THEORY   269
  Trade Centers of the Upper Midwest | Rank-Size Rule | Structural Elements of the Central Place Hierarchy | Consumer Travel as a Mirror of the Hierarchy
SUMMARY   298

7
Manufacturing

SPATIAL FORCES INFLUENCING MANUFACTURING   308
  Phases of Manufacturing | Uneven Distribution of Raw Materials

THE SIMPLE WEBERIAN MODEL: ASSEMBLY COSTS 310
Weber's Raw Material Classes | Ubiquities Only | Localized Raw Materials | Weight-Losing Raw Materials

EXTENSIONS OF WEBER'S MODEL: TRANSPORTATION COSTS 318
Space-Cost Curves | Distortions of the Isotropic Surface: The Effects of Localized Resources | Secondary Sector vs. Tertiary Sector

CHANGES IN COST 321
Production Costs | The Cost of Labor: Locational Impacts | Locational Impacts of the Cost of Capital | Entrepreneurship and Technical Skills

A VARIABLE COST MODEL 330

THE LOCATIONAL EFFECTS OF TECHNIQUE 336

SCALE CONSIDERATIONS IN INDUSTRIAL LOCATION 339
Principles of Scale Economies | Possible Scale Economies | Spatial Implications of Scale Economies | Vertical and Horizontal Integration | Scale and the Modern Corporation | Inter-Firm Scale Economies: Agglomeration

DEMAND AND INDUSTRIAL LOCATION 348
A Demand Potential Surface | A Transport Cost Surface

THE COST OF COMPETITION: LOCATIONAL INTERDEPENDENCE 354
The Ice Cream Vendor Analogy

CASE STUDIES 357
Copper Manufacturing | Iron and Steel | The Cotton-Textile Industry | Soft Drinks | Ready Mixed Concrete

INDUSTRIAL REGIONS 367

SOCIAL CONSEQUENCES OF CHANGES IN THE LOCATION OF MANUFACTURING 369

SUMMARY 371

8
Transportation

NETWORK ANALYSIS 378
Networks as Graphs | Network Density and Shape | Location of Routes and Networks

TRANSPORT COSTS 397
Terminal Costs and Transport Gradients | Variations in Transport Rates | Transport Costs and Location

TRANSPORT IMPROVEMENTS 415
Improved Transport Facilities | Cost-Space Convergence | Time-Space Convergence | Idealized Model of Network Change

SUMMARY 423

9
Decision-Making

THE BEHAVIORAL MATRIX 428

AGRICULTURE 429
Environmental Space: A Game Theory Approach | The Diffusion of Technological Innovations | Catastrophy Theory: Possible Applications

CONTENTS

THE SIZE AND SPACING OF CITIES   444
MANUFACTURING   454
SUMMARY   460

10
Underdevelopment

FROM PRIMITIVE TO UNDERDEVELOPED   465
STATISTICAL INDEX NUMBERS AND UNDERDEVELOPMENT   467
  Single and Multiple Measures of Underdevelopment | Importance of Qualitative Differences
LIMITING FACTORS AND UNDERDEVELOPMENT   469
  Leibenstein's List of Attributes of Underdevelopment | Rapid Population Growth | Climate and Resources | Capital and Labor | Vicious Cycles of Poverty
SOCIOLOGICAL THEORIES OF UNDERDEVELOPMENT   479
  The Idea of a "Stagnant, Traditional Society" | The Idea of Social and Economic Dualism
HISTORICAL EXPLANATIONS OF UNDERDEVELOPMENT   482
  Rostow's Historical Scheme | A Closer Look at Rostow's Second Stage | Development: Evolutionary or Revolutionary? | Marxists and Rostow's Version of History | A Global World View
THE GEOGRAPHER'S PERSPECTIVE ON UNDERDEVELOPMENT AND MODERNIZATION   491
  The World View in Western Geography | The Dialectical Historical View
UNDERDEVELOPMENT-AS-PROCESS: THE COLONIAL DIVISION OF LABOR   501
SUMMARY   509

11
International Trade and Aid

THE CONVENTIONAL CASE FOR TRADE   516
  Direct Gains from Trade | Indirect Gains from Trade | Costs of Protection
LIMITED GAINS FROM TRADE   521
  The World Division of Labor | Structure of Trade | Fluctuations of Commodity Prices | Share of World Trade | Terms of Trade | Protection and Preferences | Import Substitution
IMPROVING THE STATUS OF TRADE   541
  GATT and UNCTAD | The EEC and the Lomé Convention | A New International Economic Order | Trade Among Underdeveloped Countries | Trade Prospects
AID   551
  Origins and Amount of Aid | The Classical Model and Private Investment | Aid and National Development
SUMMARY   563

12
Urban and Regional Differences in Income and Welfare

CENTER-PERIPHERY RELATIONS   569
    The Center-Periphery Concept | Neo-Classical Theories of Regional Development | Polarized Development: Models of Myrdal and Hirschman | Friedmann's Models of Regional Development

THE PROTO-PROLETARIAT   585
    Urban Growth with Dependent Industrialization | A Neglected Occupational Element | Defining the Proto-Proletariat | Economic, Ecological, and Political Features of Urban Third World Masses | Policy Issues

TANZANIA'S DEVELOPMENT STRATEGY   604

SUMMARY   612

Bibliography

Index

List of Maps

1.8 Hudson-Mohawk corridor and the relative location (situation) of New York   **24**

2.1 World population distribution   **42**

2.3 The spread of urbanization in the United States   **46**

2.10 Sex ratios of the United States   **57**

2.13 (A) World income potential and (B) World population potential for the early 1960s   **63**

2.14 United States: net migration by states, 1960–1970   **70**

2.15 Average annual population growth rates, 1970–75   **72**

3.5 Geography of hunger and malnutrition   **102**

3.7 Continents sized in proportion to their potentially arable land   **107**

3.16 Movement of petroleum, 1975   **128**

3.20 Nuclear power reactors in the United States, 1974   **133**

4.1 The Fertile Crescent   **146**

4.2 Origins of domesticated plants and animals   **149**

4.3 World patterns of land use, AD 1500   **150**

4.4 World agriculture   **157**

4.19 Theoretical land use rings in the United States   **187**

List of Maps

4.20	Average value (dollars) per hectare of cropland	**188**
4.21	Major agricultural regions of the United States	**190**
4.22	Yields of wheat in metric tons per hectare	**191**
4.23	Average caloric yield from arable land as measured by yields from small grains and potatoes	**192**
5.11	Urbanization in the Detroit region	**228**
5.12	Extent of commuting fields in the United States in 1960	**229**
5.13	Megalopolis as defined by Gottman	**229**
5.14	Projected growth of United States urban regions with a population of one million or more by the year 2000	**230**
5.16	Internal economic geography of the suburban minicity: King of Prussia, Pennsylvania	**235**
6.2	Service areas of Mobile, Alabama	**247**
6.3	U.S. metropolitan trade areas based on newspaper circulation, 1933	**248**
6.5	Wholesale trade areas in Wisconsin based on the break-point model	**250**
6.14	The distribution of central places in South Germany	**260**
6.21	Distribution of farms in the Upper Midwest	**272**
6.22	Hexagonal lattice conforming to the underlying rural population pattern in the Upper Midwest	**272**
6.24	Distribution of trade centers in the Upper Midwest	**276**
6.25	Dispersed cities	**279**
6.26	Higher-order trade centers and trade areas in the United States	**280**
6.38	Purchase movements of urban and rural consumers for clothing in southwestern Iowa	**296**
6.39	Purchase movements of urban and rural consumers for furniture in southwestern Iowa	**298**
6.40	Purchase movements of urban and rural consumers for dry cleaning in southwestern Iowa	**299**
6.41	Purchase movements of urban and rural consumers for foodstuffs in southwestern Iowa	**300**

List of Maps

7.13	Variations in average hourly wages of production workers	**325**
7.14	Corporate headquarters: 500 largest corporations, 1976	**327**
7.27	Market potential, United States	**350**
7.29	Transport cost to the national market	**351**
7.30	Manufacturing potential	**352**
7.31	Transport cost to the national manufacturing market	**352**
7.37	Copper mining and concentrating	**358**
7.38	Copper smelting	**359**
7.39	Copper refining	**359**
7.40	Steel manufacturing	**363**
7.41	Location pattern of bottled and canned soft drink manufacturing, 1963	**366**
7.42	Location pattern of ready-mixed concrete production, 1963	**368**
7.43	Major world industrial regions	**369**
7.44	The pattern of manufacturing in the U.S.	**370**
8.5	Evolution of Ghana's primary and secondary road system, 1910–1959	**382**
8.9	Road density in Tanzania	**386**
8.12	The railroad pattern of the United States	**390**
8.15	Effect of the U.S.-Canadian border on railroad networks, and effect of the Ontario-Quebec border on road patterns	**393**
8.16	Development of the East African transport network	**394–95**
10.2	GNP per capita by major regions, 1975	**468**
10.7	The "mad" scramble for Africa	**489**
10.8	Land allocations in Kenya, 1957	**490**
10.9	The diffusion of "modernization in Tanzania"	**495**
10.10	Daily intake of animal protein, 1962	**497**
10.11	Earnings of U.S. investments, 1960	**498**
11.5	"Islands of development" in Africa	**523**

12.5	Percentage of families below low income level in the United States, 1969	**579**
12.6	Extent of commuting fields in the United States in 1960	**580**
12.13	Tanzanian growth centers	**607**

INTRODUCTION

KEY TERMS

- abstract space
- accessibility
- agglomeration
- areal differentiation
- capitalism
- capital accumulation
- complementarity
- concrete space
- connectivity
- demand and supply
- dependence
- dialectical approach
- direction
- distance
- division of labor
- intervening opportunity
- iron law of wages
- isotropic surface
- labor theory of value
- law of comparative costs
- location (absolute and relative)
- macroeconomics and microeconomics
- man-environment approach
- market
- spatial interaction approach
- spatial organization
- spatial process
- spatial structure
- surplus value
- transferability

1

Economic geography deals with the spatial organization of economic activities. Specifically, it is concerned with patterns of production, exchange, and consumption, and the processes that create such patterns. The understanding of these patterns and processes usually begins with the adoption of a single viewpoint for the selection and organization of facts. However, this book is a review and, therefore, lacks a single perspective. It recognizes controversy where it exists and shows how different viewpoints provide different interpretations of our economic world. A consideration of different viewpoints is very important. Different perspectives guide the way questions are asked about observed reality, and influence research findings.

All approaches to economic geography are, therefore, "theory-laden" or "value-laden." Like other social scientists, geographers think of the economic world in their own value terms. This is true whether they claim to be critics or defenders of a particular economic system. Geographers who claim to be uncommitted in their research and teaching are not. "To be uncommitted is not to be neutral, but to be committed—consciously or not—to the status quo" (Dowd, 1964:63).

This book is confined to the world's capitalist system. *Capitalism* is the political economic system based on private property and profit. The capitalist system over the last 200 years has drawn nearly the whole world into a single system of dominant and dominated countries. Dominant countries include the developed countries of North America, non-communist Europe, Australia, Japan and a few other scattered jurisdictions which are often called the "First World." Dominated countries are the underdeveloped, ex-colonial colonies of Africa, Asia, and Latin America (the "Third World").

Attention is focused on two problems of the capitalist system: *resource allocation* and *development*. The allocation problem revolves around mechanisms which allocate and redistribute scarce resources of land, labor, and capital. The development problem is more difficult to clarify because there exist many, sometimes conflicting, views of what is meant by development. If a holistic, goal-free definition is adopted, development is the whole process of change. Such a comprehensive definition implies that development has both positive and negative dimensions. There is, however, some broad agreement that development means change for the better. In this case, the purpose of development is to raise the standard of living of people especially in underdeveloped countries as rapidly as feasible—to

Ideas of Economists

provide secure jobs, adequate nutrition and health, clean water and air, cheap transport, and education. Whether development takes place depends on the extent to which social and economic changes help or hinder in meeting the basic needs of the majority of the people.

This introductory chapter provides a background for materials presented later; it introduces the concepts that provide a bridge between geography and economics. The first section of the chapter deals with the ideas proposed by great economists that have molded capitalism. Ideas play a central role in shaping the activities of the economic world and influence the views and actions of individuals, groups, and governments. In general, the ideas that defend or promote vested interests dominate. Thus in the First World, the ideas that defend ruling interests have prevailed. This section is followed by an outline of conservative, liberal, and radical world views, and by a preliminary discussion of two pervasive economic problems which the rest of this book considers in more detail. A short discussion on the distinction between macroeconomics and microeconomics is also provided. The last two sections are geographical in orientation. A section is devoted to key words and concepts used by geographers to study the spatial organization of economic activities. The final section traces the changing nature of economic geography. Attention is given to the grand themes of man-environment relations, areal differentiation, and spatial organization. Another approach, dialectical economic geography, is also explored. The dialectical approach, which juxtaposes contradictory explanations of our economic world, is used in some parts of this text.

OBJECTIVES

By the end of this chapter you should be able:

1. To compare and contrast the visions and theories that interpret capitalism.
2. To differentiate conservative, liberal, and radical perspectives.
3. To identify two central economic problems.
4. To define fundamental geographical concepts.
5. To review the grand themes of economic geography.

Ideas of Economists

The world space-economy is a reflection of its political economy. World economy has been shaped partly by vested interests and historical circumstances, and partly by the ideas of economists. Although we must never ignore the role of vested interests and circumstances, most scholars would agree that the ideas of economists like Adam Smith and David Ricardo have played a central role in the evolution of the world space-economy. A review of the ideas that have interpreted *capitalism* from the age of mercantilism through monopoly capitalism follows.

Smith's Vision of Progress

In the sixteenth century, an age of nascent capitalism, rulers of most European states were *mercantilists*. According to *mercantilism*, the first task of government was the central direction of the economy and the rapid accumulation of gold and silver in the royal exchequer. The economic landscape was cluttered with obstacles to the free-play of European economies. Guilds limited entry into craft industries. Tariffs, exclusive trade treaties, and quotas checked international trade. Policies of government intervention, particularly those related to foreign trade, aimed at securing substantial profits for large trading companies, and raising revenues for national governments. Opposition to mercantilism increased in the late eighteenth century and a climate of *economic liberalism* gradually emerged, especially in Britain where economic life was being transformed by improvements in farming techniques and by the Industrial Revolution. As an ideology, the term "economic liberalism" is used synonymously with the "classical approach" to economics. Classical liberalism pictured people as egoistic, coldly calculating, and independent of the society of which they were a part.

The principal origin of the classical model is Adam Smith's *Wealth of Nations*, published in 1776. His book extolled the ideology of economic liberalism and refuted the doctrine of mercantilism. Smith believed that economic liberty promised rising per capita and real income, and could fulfill individual aspirations. Economic liberty would allow people to follow their own self-interests and reap the resulting rewards.

At the heart of Smith's vision of progress was a world of free enterprise capitalism. Central control of the economy should be vested in the "invisible hand of the market." Production should be in the hands of small entrepreneurs and independent artisans. People should be freed from the shackles of meddling governments and from joint-stock companies, now called corporations, which work to limit competition.

Smith emphasized the factors that led to the wealth of a nation. He said that labor established the relative value of things, but that actual commodity prices were determined by *supply* and *demand* in the *market*. The "market" is an abstract term that refers, in general, to the negotiation of exchange transactions that generally involve money, and the determination of the prices at which these exchanges are transacted. Smith stressed that the wealth of a nation was a function of the skill of the labor force and the proportion of productive labor to unproductive labor.

Smith said that the skill of the labor force was keyed to the *division of labor*. To illustrate the division of labor, he quoted the example of the manufacture of pins:

> One man draws out the wire, another straights it, a third cuts it, a fourth points it, a fifth grinds it at the top for receiving the head; to make the head requires two or three distinct operations; to put it on, is a peculiar business, to whiten the pins is another; it is even a trade by itself to put them into the paper . . . (1950, Vol. I:8).

Ideas of Economists

The first economist: Adam Smith (1723–90). A Scotsman, born in the small port town of Kirkaldy, he became a student at Glasgow University at the age of 14, and won a scholarship to Oxford in 1740. After Oxford, Smith returned to Scotland to lecture at Edinburgh University from 1748 to 1751. His major work on economics, *An Inquiry into the Nature and Causes of the Wealth of Nations,* was published in 1776. The work became the foundation upon which classical economics was constructed. SOURCE: *Scottish National Portrait Gallery.*

DEMAND AND SUPPLY

In a competitive market economy, prices are determined by conditions of demand and supply. *Demand* for a good refers to the amount of a good buyers would like to purchase during a given period and at a given price. *Supply* of a good is the quantity of a good sellers would like to sell during a given period at a given price. When a particular market price is established, a specific quantity of the good will be supplied and demanded. If these two quantities are equal, both sellers and demanders will be able to conduct business in the desired quantities, and the market is said to be in equilibrium. A change in supply or demand will force the equilibrium price to change. Defenders of the market mechanism claim that this system of production for private profit is efficient and impersonal. Critics of the market mechanism argue that it results in an inequitable, unfair, and unjust allocation of scarce goods. A free enterprise economy results in a lopsided concentration of income and purchasing power. Thus it is suggested that the private enterprise economy emphasizes production for the wealthy.

If ten people divided the labor, they could produce 48,000 pins a day, or 4,800 apiece. If one worker, however, were set the task of carrying out all the operations, pin output would be minimal. Smith also pointed out that with labor specialization the size of the output—for pins or whatever—need only be limited by the the size of its market.

Smith said that the rate of *capital accumulation* determined the proportion of productive labor to unproductive labor. Capital not only facilitated the creation of plants and machinery to assist labor, but enabled labor to be employed. Smith's ideas were developed in the first half of the nineteenth century by several British economists, particularly David Ricardo (1772–1823). Except for the addition of marginal analysis in the 1870s, which led to the substitution of the term "neoclassical" for "classical" model, few changes were made to the accepted interpretation of the capitalist system until the 1930s. Until then, the economic system was assumed to be self-regulating or self-righting.

The Ricardian View

In contrast to Smith, Ricardo had a pessimistic view of the prospects for humankind. Along with Thomas Malthus (1776–1834), Ricardo believed that it was natural for population to eventually increase faster than production. In an "improving" free enterprise economy, Ricardo thought that this dismal outcome might be postponed.

With David Ricardo (1772–1823) economics became known as the "dismal science." A Londoner, he had little formal education. Yet at the age of 14, Ricardo was making money on the stock exchange, and succeeded in accumulating a fortune, sufficient for him to "retire" at 42. He began to publish works on money and banking in 1810. His works on monetary economics did not exert the influence comparable to *The Principles of Political Economy and Taxation*, which appeared in 1817 and dominated classical economics for the following half-century. SOURCE: *The Bettmann Archive, Inc.*

Ideas of Economists

Ricardo developed his ideas on what the world should be like in an abstract equilibrium model of capitalist society. His model of the market system was constructed in the image of an idealized social harmony achieved through the economic rationality of people. To keep his system harmonious and in equilibrium, Ricardo introduced the notion of the equilibrium wage rate. Wages, he said, were determined by scarcity and the costs of subsistence. An increased demand for labor brings forth a supply so that, in the long run, workers receive a "natural wage" set by the costs of subsistence. This was the *iron law of wages*, which led to the conclusion "that not only was compassion wasted on the working man, but it was damaging. It might raise hopes and income in the short run. But it accelerated the population increase by which both [employers and employees] were brought down. And any effort by government or trade unions to raise wages and rescue people from poverty would similarly be in conflict with economic law, be similarly frustrated by the resulting increase in numbers" (Galbraith, 1977:35).

Ricardo's world was dominantly agricultural, and therefore the landlord was the principle figure in his growth model of the market system. Ricardo argued that during the early stages of national growth, population is small and only the most fertile land is cultivated. Under these conditions, rent paid by farm workers to landlords is a small proportion of national income. Landlords make fat profits. As demand for labor increases in an expanding economy, workers increase their numbers. To feed the larger population, more less-fertile land is brought into cultivation. Food prices go up because of the higher costs of food production on the less favored land. Landlords raise the rents charged on the older, more fertile lands, because the higher food prices charged could bear higher rents. Meanwhile, higher food costs force employers to pay higher money wages to maintain wage rates at the subsistence level. Since labor establishes the value of things, manufactured goods increase in price, and industrial entrepreneurs obtain reduced profits. Less capital is available for industrial expansion. This process of economic growth continues, with capital accumulation and growth gradually slowing down until, after many years of expansion, the economy enters a dismal stationary state.

In Ricardo's largely rural world, the beneficiaries of growth were the landlords, who increased rents as more and more land of decreasing fertility was brought into cultivation to feed a growing population. Consequently, "the more numerous the people, the richer the landlords. They fattened, their people starved" (Galbraith, 1977:35).

There were at least two differences of opinion between Ricardo and Malthus on matters of economic growth. First, Ricardo criticized Malthus' defense of landlords. He believed that they were a barrier to progress and social harmony. For example, landlords in early nineteenth century England protected their interests with tariffs on imported grains. Ricardo admired the industrial entrepreneur, who in his model system epitomized economic rationality.

Second, Ricardo and Malthus disagreed over what would happen to the large profits accruing to landlords. Ricardo insisted "that it would either be spent or it would be saved and used for investment in land improvement, building, industrial development, in which case it would also be spent" (Galbraith, 1977:36). Thus there could never be a shortage of purchasing power. Malthus, however, argued that profits may not always be spent, and therefore "the economy would, on occasion, falter and break down. There would be depressions resulting from a shortage of purchasing power as part of the natural order of things" (Galbraith, 1977:36). Until the Great Depression and Keynes, however, Ricardo's ideas on purchasing power ruled supreme.

Ricardo's analytics were not confined to a domestic economy. He showed two ways in which an analysis of the domestic economy could be applied to the international economy. First, Ricardo argued that in a *laissez-faire* environment, international specialization and division of labor between the center (metropolitan countries) and the periphery (satellite countries) was advantageous to both areas. *Laissez-faire* is the classical philosophy that opposes government interference in economic affairs if such interference is inimical to the interests of capitalists. Support for the liberal doctrine of free international trade was embodied in Ricardo's *law of comparative costs*. This law can best be illustrated by means of the example of two countries (United States and the United Kingdom) producing two commodities, wheat and cloth. Assume that the United States can produce wheat and cloth more cheaply than the United Kingdom, and the difference between American and British costs is greater for wheat than for cloth, as follows:

	Per Unit Production Costs	
	Cloth	Wheat
United Kingdom	130	120
United States	110	60

Although the United Kingdom has an absolute advantage in neither good, it does have a comparative advantage in cloth. The United Kingdom would benefit if it specialized in the production and export of cloth. Conversely, the United States would be better off if it concentrated on wheat. Moreover, specialization in time would drive down the selling price of British cloth and American wheat. As price changes took place, increasing import-export trade between the United States and the United Kingdom would establish a market equilibrium of prices and trade.

Second, Ricardo showed how his doctrine of economic growth could be applied internationally. He suggested that under free enterprise conditions, *capital flows into areas where it is most needed*. The classical model assumed that international investment "leads to the movement of capital from countries where its marginal value productivity is low to countries where it is high, and this tends to exercise an equalizing effect throughout the world inducing a rise in the world's capital resources, thereby acting as an accelerator in boosting the world's real income" (Clairmonte, 1960:163–164).

Marx's Vision of Capitalist Development

Most followers of Ricardo sanctified the capitalist system. Even Wisconsin economist Thorstein Veblen (1857–1929), who ridiculed the rich for their habits of conspicuous consumption and leisure, did not inveigh against capitalism.

Ideas of Economists

Karl Marx (1818–1883). He was born in Trier at the head of the Moselle Valley, and studied philosophy at Bonn University, Berlin University and Jena. In 1843 he settled in Paris, and after a brief return to Germany, he moved to London in 1849 where he remained until his death. Marx's economics was essentially that of the classical school, especially the ideas of Ricardo. SOURCE: *The Bettmann Archive, Inc.*

Thorstein Veblen (1857–1929), the son of Norwegian immigrant parents, was born in Wisconsin and educated at Carleton College, Minnesota. He is best known for his analysis of conspicuous consumption (the consumption of goods which is ostentatious and intended to impress) in the *Theory of the Leisure Class* published in 1899. SOURCE: *The Bettmann Archive, Inc.*

Karl Marx was the first economist to assail an economic society in which capitalists owned the means of production. He attacked the economic order which Ricardo described and interpreted. Marx believed that capitalism was doomed.

His argument was on three levels: moral (injustices of capitalism), sociological (class conflict), and economic (accumulation of capital in private hands leading to economic abundance and the breakdown of capitalism). At each level of his discussion, *conflict* is emphasized. Out of conflict comes change, and change is a "dialectical process" by which socialism was to replace capitalism. Marx believed that change had an economic basis in the class division of society into workers and capitalists. He said that conflict between workers and capitalists would build until the fabric of society was torn asunder by revolution.

Marx's evolutionary model of the tendencies of capitalist development begins with a *labor theory of value* and ends with the doctrine of periodic business crises, unemployment, class conflict, and transition to socialism (Figure 1.1). Marx noted that the value of a good is determined by the amount of socially necessary labor embodied in it. In a pre-capitalist society, relative values of commodities are readily calculated. If good A entails 10 hours of labor and good B, 20 hours, then B has twice the value of A; that is, the two goods can be traded at the rates of 2A:1B. In such a society, all exchange is of equivalent value.

In a capitalistic society, on the other hand, *surplus value* is created. Surplus value or *exploitation* is the difference between the value produced by the worker (value of units of labor produced) and the worker's wage (value of labor

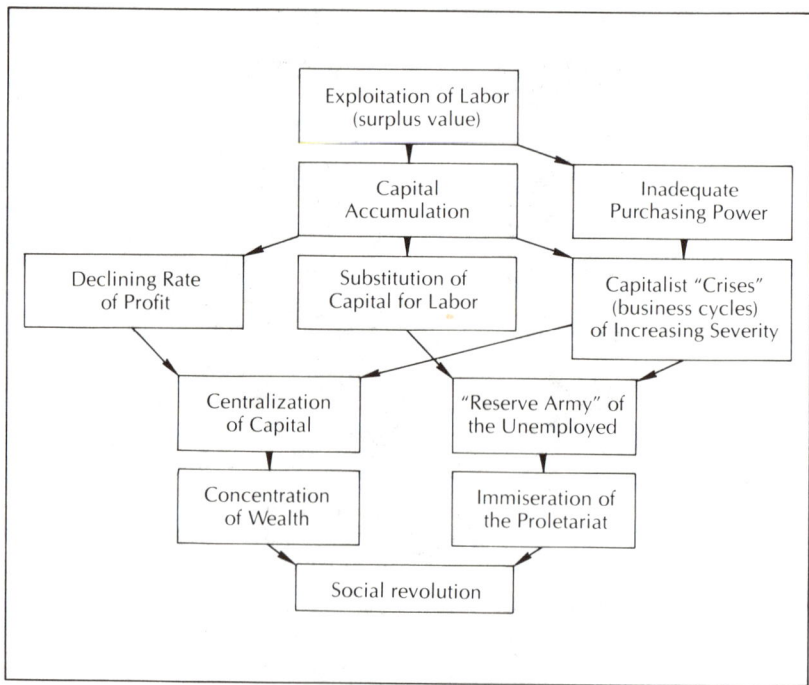

FIGURE 1.1 Model of Marx's theory of capitalist development.
SOURCE: Daniel R. Fusfield, 1966, *The Age of the Economist*, Glenview: Scott, Foresman and Company, p. 58, Fig.1.

Ideas of Economists

power). Marx asked: How can one class of people, capitalists, get something for nothing? How do they acquire a portion of produced value for themselves without contributing any labor in return? Marx said that labor is a commodity, and its value is determined in just the same way as the value of any other commodity. It is determined by the amount of socially necessary labor required to produce it, which is nothing more than a worker's subsistence wage. For example, if a laborer has to work six hours to obtain a subsistence income, then that is the socially necessary amount of labor time required to "produce" a worker. Suppose a worker has to work 12 hours instead of six hours to gain a job in a factory. In this case, Marx said, the worker creates surplus value for the capitalist. He works six hours for himself, and another six hours for his master, and the rate of surplus value is six hours divided by six hours, or 100 percent. Another example may clarify Marx's conception of exploitation of workers by capitalists. If a worker labors for 10 hours but uses only five hours to produce the value of his wage good, then that worker is exploited because he works five surplus hours for the capitalist.

Exploitation of the worker can be intensified, and the surplus value appropriated by the capitalist increased, by an employer who stretches the working day of his laborers. If the work week were stabilized, an employer could expand surplus value by substituting capital for labor. The gains of an employer are short-lived however. His competitors imitate his method of production. His rate of surplus value is driven down to its former level. The capitalist is back where he started. He is compelled to introduce more labor-saving machinery and the cycle begins again. Marx argued that the process of introducing even more labor-saving equipment is inimical to workers. Displaced laborers form a "reserve army" of the unemployed, which keeps wages at minimal levels.

The essence of Marx's theory is that the engine which drives economic growth is capital accumulation. Economic growth is always unbalanced. The capitalist mode of production fails to achieve equilibrium because of the contradictory nature of competitive production. As a result, there are short-run cyclical crises (unemployment and declining rates of profit) which are corrected by increasing rates of accumulation through concentration (the trend toward larger, more efficient factories in each industry) and geographical extension (imperialism). Marx argued that periodic crises become more frequent and catastrophic over time. In each crisis big capitalists devour little capitalists, and individual capitalism becomes monopoly capitalism. Capitalists seek larger outputs and bigger profits, and they deploy bigger and better machines which replace more and more laborers, whose work generally consists of small, insignificant, and tedious operations that are repeated for hours. The misery of workers intensifies and conditions ripen for the movement from capitalism to socialism which, according to Marx, is a higher stage of historical evolution. Thus the search for surplus value through labor exploitation leads to the growth, stagnation, and demise of capitalism.

Marxists and Imperialism

Most nineteenth century economists had little to say about colonialism and underdeveloped countries. The colonial world earned their attention only as it affected economic progress in Europe and North America. Marx was a partial exception.

Although he focused attention on the advanced capitalist state, he also made the underdeveloped world an integral part of his system. He regarded underdeveloped countries as extensions of the capitalist core (Europe-North America) and thought that their destiny was to trace the path mapped out by modern industrial nations. Thus he believed colonial world capitalism to be a progressive force. Capitalism was needed to develop a revolutionary proletariat in underdeveloped countries.

In the early twentieth century, followers of Marx had much more to say about underdeveloped countries. Rosa Luxemburg and Lenin elaborated theories of imperialism that explain how capitalism in the age of monopoly must find new space for continued expansion. Luxemburg argued, for example, that consumption cannot increase in a closed capitalist system and thus accumulation is impossible. She argued that it is the invasion of underdeveloped countries by capitalism which keeps the system alive. She described the "manner in which the capitalist system, by trade, conquest, and theft, swallowed up the pre-capitalist economies—some reduced to colonies of capitalist nations, some remaining nominally independent—and fed itself upon their ruins" (Robinson, 1951:26). As Joan Robinson has said, "few would deny that the extension of capitalism into new territories was the mainspring of . . . the 'vast secular boom' of the last two hundred years, and many academic economists account for the uneasy condition of capitalism in the twentieth century largely by the 'closing of the frontier' all over the world" (1951:28).

In recent years, neo-Marxists have shown how an intensifying and expanding industrial capitalism integrated societies unevenly into a single net of world market and resource exploitation (Baran and Sweezy, 1966; Frank, 1970; Arrighi

Lenin.

Ideas of Economists

and Saul, 1973; and Poulantzas, 1975). They pay special attention to a complement to the theory of imperialism, a theory of *dependence,* which considers the effects of imperialism on underdeveloped countries. "Dependence" means a conditioning situation in which the economies of one group of countries are underdeveloped by the development and expansion of others. Forms of dependency vary from country to country, and they change from one historical period to another. They vary and change according to: (1) the characteristics of the international system, and (2) the nature and degree of an underdeveloped country's ties to that system.

According to neo-Marxists, world political economy does not cause underdevelopment directly, but by generating and reinforcing an infrastructure of dependency which includes institutions, social classes, and processes such as urbanization and industrialization. Thus dependency is not merely an external matter. Foreign exploitation is possible only when it finds support among local interest groups who profit by it. To break out of dependency, neo-Marxists argue that underdeveloped countries must isolate themselves from foreign domination and, even more important, transform their socio-economic structures.

Keynes and the Fall of Economic Liberalism

The heyday of economic liberalism was the period 1850–1875 when Britain virtually succeeded in controlling world economy. Economic liberalism was agreeable to British conditions only after Britain became the "workshop of the world" and her industries were in no fear of foreign competition. But British hegemony was short-lived. Britain's competitive status was shaken after the onset of a world economic crisis in the 1870s. As a consequence, liberalism was gradually abandoned. The retreat of British liberalism can be explained superficially by the international trade practices of other powers, particularly Germany and the United States. More than any other factor, however, the drift from individual capitalism to "monopoly" capitalism made the idea of a *laissez-faire* economic environment untenable (see box). Not until the world depression of the 1930s did economic liberalism come to be rejected; and not until the acceptance of J. M. Keynes' *General Theory* did the belief that the economic system was self-righting come to be discredited

Keynes' *General* Theory is an analysis of the causes of unemployment. He argued that employment depends on the level of national production which is governed by the volume of demand for consumer goods and the volume of private and public investments. He introduced the concept of equilibrium at less than full employment, which may be explained as follows: a decline in total spending caused by reduced investment reduces incomes, which in turn causes savings to decline until the desire to save is brought into balance with the desire to invest. Keynes did not think that a modern capitalist economy could sustain a high enough level of investment to maintain full employment. He advocated government control of the level of economic activity in the national interest *(state capitalism),* but he advised that the economy in general be left free to respond to the decisions of welfare-maximizing consumers and profit-maximizing producers.

Keynes presented an alternative to socialism for the First World. His theory, which permitted government to borrow and spend the proceeds to cure an

John Maynard Keynes (1883–1946). Born the year that Karl Marx died, he was educated at Eton, and then at Cambridge, where he studied philosophy under Alfred Whitehead and economics under Alfred Marshall. SOURCE: *The Bettmann Archive, Inc.*

economic depression, did not amend the neoclassical paradigm to any great degree. It was designed less to alter market exchange economies than to preserve and revitalize them. Keynesian economics became the mainstream until the 1970s when state capitalism appeared incapable of dealing with the twin problems of inflation and high unemployment.

Competing Mindsets

Economists like Smith, Marx, and Keynes identified economic problems and analyzed them in their own value terms. Smith was a capitalist, Marx a socialist, and Keynes advocated state capitalism. The way we think about and analyze economic problems also depends on *our* world view. We can recognize three competing viewpoints: conservative, liberal, and radical (Table 1.1). Conservative and liberal viewpoints are widely accepted by western social scientists including geographers, but at the present time the liberal mindset dominates.

The Conservative Mindset

The conservative view of the world is inherited from the ideas of Smith, Ricardo, and their followers. Conservatives are convinced that a capitalist free enterprise economy allows individuals to achieve maximum personal liberty and material

Competing Mindsets

> **MARKET STRUCTURE**
>
> In the text, we used the term "monopoly" rather loosely. The word *monopoly* comes from the Greek *mono* meaning one. Thus a monopolistic market is one with only one seller. There were few if any pure monopolies in late nineteenth century Britain. It is more accurate to say that a competitive (individual) market system was replaced, particularly in the industrial sector, by an *oligopolistic* market structure. *Oligopoly* comes from the Greek *oligo* meaning a few. Thus an oligopolistic market is a market structure consisting of a few dominant sellers. The table describes the major characteristics of competitive, monopolistic, and oligopolistic market structures.
>
> | Market Structure | Number of Firms | Type of Product | Degree of Competition Price | Degree of Competition Nonprice |
> |---|---|---|---|---|
> | Pure competition | Many of small size | Homogeneous | Great | None |
> | Pure monopoly | One | Homogeneous (only one) | None | None* |
> | Oligopoly | A few large firms dominate the industry†† | Usually differentiated† | Little | Great |
> | Monopolistic competition | Many of small size | Differentiated | Great | Great |
>
> *May be some advertising and product changes.
> †May be homogeneous in some few cases.
> ††May be small firms constituting a "competitive" fringe.
>
> SOURCE: L. A. Dow, 1974, *Economics*. Columbus, Ohio: Charles E. Merrill Publishing Company, Table 21–6, p. 368.

well-being. Market mechanisms of demand and supply work to satisfy consumer preferences. The role of government in society should be limited to the maintenance of law and order so that capitalism can operate freely. Fewer government regulations and programs would solve many national and international problems.

The Liberal Mindset

Liberals share with conservatives a faith in capitalism. Unlike conservatives, however, they place great emphasis on individual equality and social justice. The state must intervene on behalf of every citizen whenever market mechanisms fail to meet

TABLE 1.1 Alternative Paradigms

Alternative Viewpoints	Human Nature	Work Incentives	Unit of Analysis	Analysis Based on	Human Goals	Nature of Market Economy	Nature of Societal Problems	Role of State	Social Change
Conservative	Humans are naturally unproductive & individualistic	Essentially material: (1) positive: raise in income (2) negative: unemployment	Individuals, persons or companies	Classical & marginal economics: competition & individuals maximizing profits	Maximum personal liberty & material well-being	Harmonious state of equilibrium: created by supply & demand forces	(1) Individuals: lack of motivation, culture of poverty, racial inferiority (2) Government interference in the economy	Only police power to maintain law & order so that the market can work freely	Gradual change results from individuals' interactions in the market place
Liberal	Humans are naturally unproductive, but of goodwill	Essentially material: (1) positive: raise in income (2) negative: unemployment	Individuals and groups in society	Keynesian economics: competition & individuals maximizing profits with government assistance	Individual equality & social justice (equal opportunity)	State of equilibrium, achievable with government involvement in the economy	(1) Monopolistic tendencies in major economic sectors (2) Insufficient & inappropriate government programs	Police power & offsetting inadequacies in the economy whenever basic human needs & social justice are not achieved	Rapid change through government actions
Radical	Humans are naturally productive, & cooperative	None really necessary: social awards valuable	Classes in society	Marxist economics: labor theory of value, theory of surplus value, theory of class struggle & revolution	Social equality: from each according to their ability, to each according to their need	Contradictions & crises of production & consumption; exploitation of workers; irrational allocation of natural & human resources	Capitalism which creates unemployment, poverty, hunger, regional inequality	Police & economic power used to maintain & enhance capitalism	Revolutionary change through mass movement to transform society's structure and values

SOURCE: Ingolf Vogeler and Anthony R. de Souza, *Dialectics of Third World Development*. Montclair, New Jersey: Allanheld, Osmun & Co. Publishers, Inc. (in press).

basic human needs. Western powers must be prepared to assist the world's poor. Rich, developed industrial nations should provide aid and technical assistance as gifts and loans.

The Radical Mindset

Radicals maintain that scholars must look at Marxist theory to interpret economic problems. This does not mean, however, that classical economic theory cannot be employed to gain insights into particular social situations. Radicals criticize conservatives and liberals because their analyses do not go the root of problems. They argue that the dynamics of socio-economic organization in capitalist societies produce particular kinds of class and institutional structure. Classes and institutions formed by the capitalist mode of production "explain" a particular set of social problems that cannot be solved without changing the form of socio-economic organization at national and international levels.

Economic Problems

Two economic problems persist: (1) the problem of resource allocation, and (2) the problem of development. One's world view guides the manner in which these problems are analyzed (see box).

SCIENTIFIC INQUIRY AND MODELS

No matter whether social scientists classify themselves as conservatives, liberals, or radicals, they usually use the same *scientific method* to analyze problems. A *scientific method* consists of three steps: (1) the selection of a set of variables and relationships which are assumed to be important forces controlling or structuring an event; (2) the development of hypotheses about the selected variables and relationships that can be tested by observable facts; and (3) the testing of the hypotheses with empirical data.

Initial or rough hypotheses are called *models*. The modeling process is an attempt to discover key variables controlling an event. The stages of model building are illustrated (see figure, top following page). It is important to remember that models are abstractions from reality. They are built in order to demonstrate some properties of the real world. Models based on imaginary constraints are called *normative* models; those based on existing conditions are called *descriptive* models.

Empirical testing of observable facts is called *validation* (see figure, bottom following page). The diagram suggests that the validation process is never ending. In a sense this is so, but if our hypotheses are supported continuously by evidence from observations and require no modifications, they become *laws*. Interrelated sets of laws which represent observed regularities become *theories*.

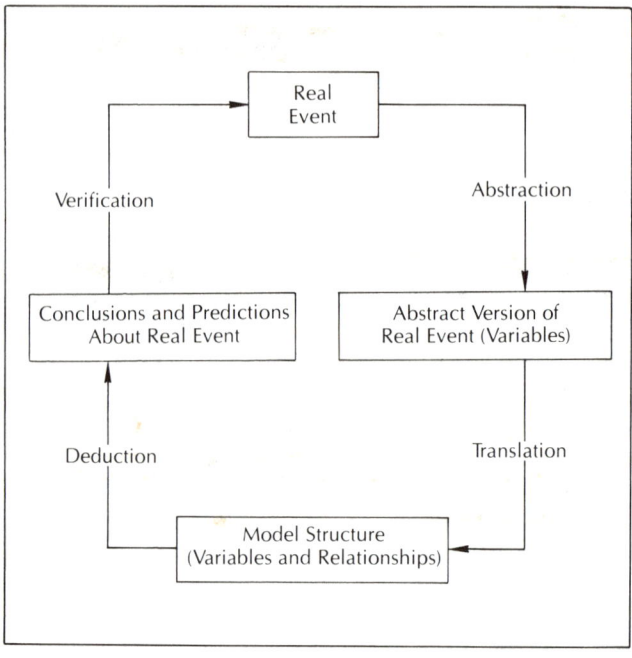

Stages in model building. SOURCE: R. J. Chorley, 1964, "Geography and Analog Theory," *Annals* of the Association of American Geographers, **54,** p. 129, Fig. 1.

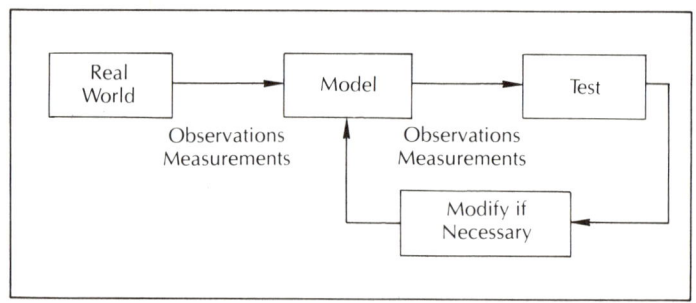

The model validation process.

The Resource Allocation Problem

Societies must decide how to allocate scarce resources among alternative and competing uses. They must make choices and trade-offs. For example, if a society wants to use resources to produce automobiles, then the same resources are not available to construct houses.

The allocation problem revolves around three interrelated issues:

1. What kinds of goods and services should be produced, and in what quantity and quality? For example, should scarce resources be used to produce more milk or more soft drinks?
2. How are goods and services to be produced? For example, should goods be produced by methods that emphasize labor or capital equipment?
3. Who should get and consume the goods and services produced? In other words, how should the Gross National Product be divided and distributed among the members of an economic society?

The Development Problem

Since World War II, development has become an important issue. Rich industrial nations are engaged in a powerful "growth race" that has significant military, political, and environmental overtones. Poor countries are trying to crack the walls of underdevelopment. The problem of development is serious and complex, and it has excited an immense amount of interest in the academic world, especially among American social scientists. Although researchers generally agree on the nature of underdevelopment, few agree on what causes it, or how it might be eliminated. For example, is underdevelopment the result of internal obstacles and physical isolation from the West, or is it the result of the historical process by which capitalist countries gained control of the whole world's economy? Would a judicious mix of state planning and *laissez-faire* capitalism enable the economies of poor countries to develop their resources to the point where growth becomes a self-sustaining and transforming process, as happened in Western economies? Or would a collectively owned and collectively governed economic system that allocates resources according to need, not private profit, stimulate the development of underdeveloped countries?

Macroeconomics and Microeconomics

When discussing the private enterprise, or capitalist, system, economists make a distinction between *macroeconomics* and *microeconomics*. Macroeconomics deals with the operation of an economy as a whole. It considers aggregate issues such as business cycles, unemployment and inflation, and economic growth and development. Microeconomics is the economics of individual enterprises and individual workers and consumers. It considers, among other things, how firms either under individual or corporate ownership set prices and make profits under competition and monopoly. Of particular interest is the question of *efficiency* versus *equity* in the allocation of resources. It is generally agreed that the market is much more convenient and efficient than nonmarket allocative mechanisms such as rationing coupons that limit the quantity of scarce goods people can purchase regardless of the amount of cash they have to spend. On the other hand, the market is frequently criticized because the allocation of scarce resources is inequitable. It is biased in favor of those with plenty of cash. For example, it is charged that the private enterprise system attaches "more importance on psychiatric care for the neurotic pets of the wealthy than it does in the provision of minimal health services for the children of the poor" (Hunt and Sherman, 1978:172). In remaining chapters of this text much of what we will be concerned with links macroeconomic and microeconomic views with geographic views.

Fundamental Geographical Concepts

Economic geographers and economists analyze the same problems, but their emphases differ. Economists think of the economic system as a machine that transforms raw materials into finished products for exchange and consumption. Economists think of this process in "spaceless" terms. Geographers emphasize the spatial nature of economic processes. In this section, fundamental concepts for a spatial point of view are identified and defined. The major concepts are grouped under three headings: (1) properties of space, (2) spatial process and spatial structure, and (3) spatial interaction.

Properties of Space

Geographers divide space into *abstract* and *concrete space*. Abstract space is homogeneous in all respects and movement is equally easy in all directions. On a plane, abstract space is called an *isotropic surface* and allows geographers to develop simple normative models of economic behavior. Concrete or environmental space is the actual surface of the earth in all its geographical complexity.

A set of terms is required to discuss the properties of space. Only a limited number of *dimensional primitives* are necessary to characterize geographical phenomena. *Primitives are undefined terms* that may be used to describe things in the real world. Each primitive is independent of the other, and is essential for a complete description. In geography, the main primitive elements are point, line, and area. Points may represent cities or other foci of human activity, lines may represent transportation routes, and areas may represent nations, regions, or any other two dimensional features. When spatial elements interact, the primitives involved will shape the geographical pattern that results. Figure 1.2 provides examples of relations between dimensional primitives.

The spatial elements of point, line, and area may be used to define basic spatial concepts of *distance, direction, and connectivity*. Figure 1.3A shows two points randomly placed on a blank piece of paper. Point A can be discussed in terms of its distance from Point B and vice versa. If Point A is chosen as an arbitrary starting place, all other points can be defined in terms of their distance and direction from Point A. A line can be defined as a series of points or a given distance from a point in a specific direction (Figure 1.3B). A series of defined lines describes a bounded area (Figure 1.3C).

Fundamental Geographical Concepts

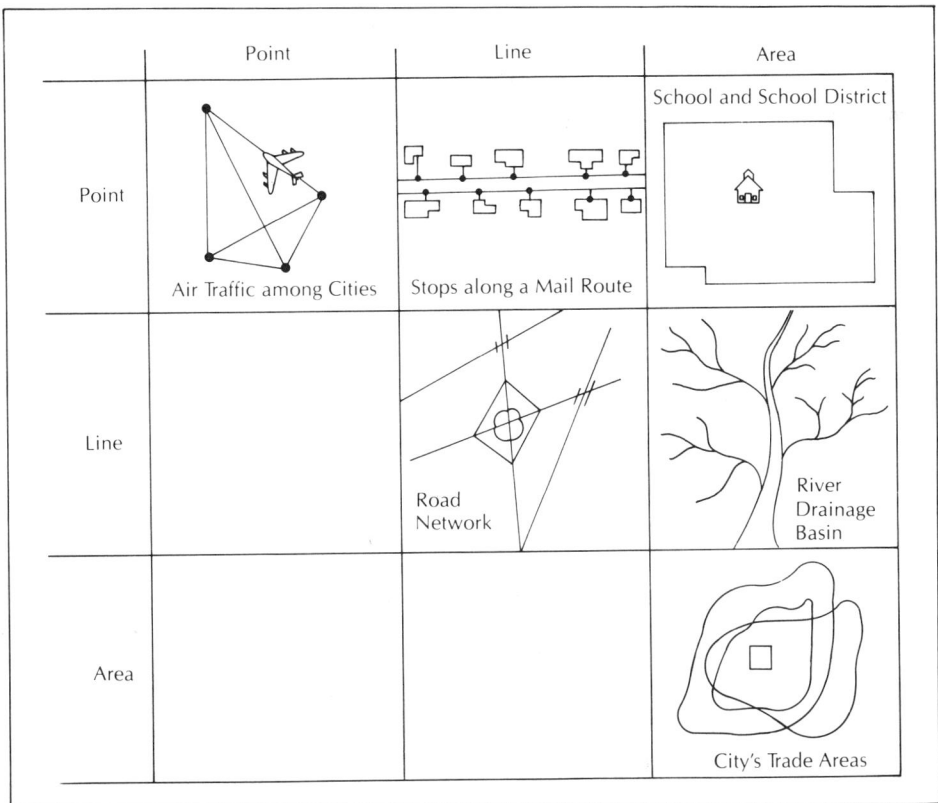

FIGURE 1.2 Relations between dimensional primitives.

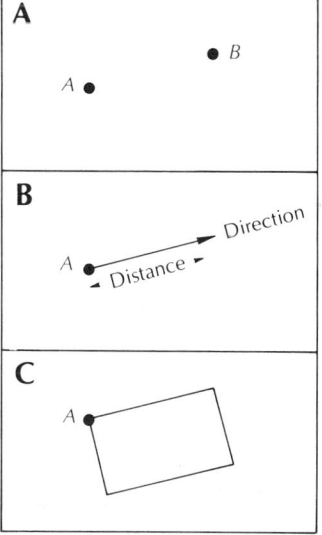

FIGURE 1.3 Abstract space: area, point, and line defined by distance and direction.

The concept of connectivity is illustrated in Figure 1.4. Point A is connected to many other points by lines, whereas B is connected to only a few points. The points might represent cities and the lines scheduled air passenger flights. Point A has a higher degree of connectivity than B.

FIGURE 1.4 Abstract space: connectivity.

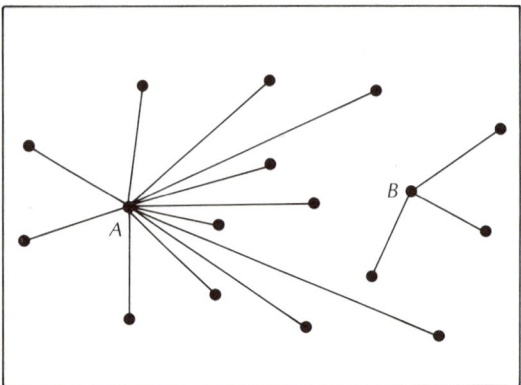

Other measures of space such as *agglomeration* and *accessibility* are extensions of the concepts of distance, direction, and connectivity. Figure 1.5 illustrates two clusters. Points in Cluster A are closer together than those in Cluster B. Cluster A represents greater agglomeration or lower *aggregate distance*. A shopping center, for example, reduces the distance consumers must travel to purchase goods by concentrating or clustering many stores at any one point. A city itself is a clustering strategy reducing aggregate distance among residential, employment, retailing, recreational, and other functions.

FIGURE 1.5 Abstract space: agglomeration.

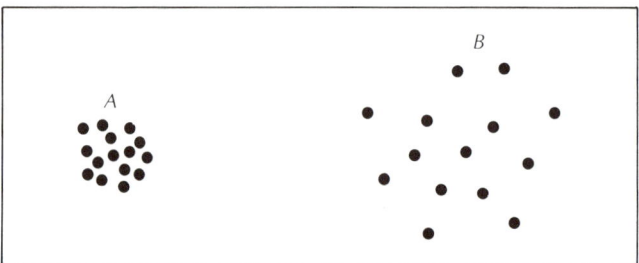

Figure 1.6 illustrates the idea of accessibility. Point X has a high degree of accessibility and Point Y a low degree of accessibility. Accessibility is another measure of aggregate nearness. Agglomeration refers to total aggregate nearness among a number of points, whereas accessibility refers to the nearness of a given point to other points. Points in space such as retail outlets in a city with a high degree of accessibility have a tremendous advantage over inaccessible locations. The failure of a retailing operation is often correctly blamed on a "poor location." This implies that the location has a low degree of accessibility to potential customers.

Basic spatial concepts and their extensions are absolute concepts when applied to an abstract space such as an *isotropic surface* which is a "mathematically

Fundamental Geographical Concepts

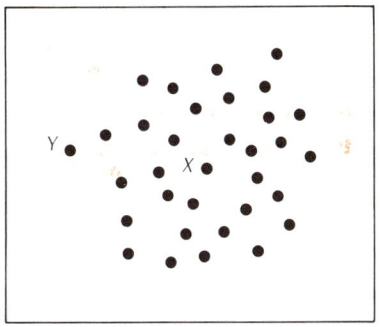

FIGURE 1.6 Abstract space: accessibility.

flat" plain over which movement is equally easy in all directions. *Absolute distance*, for example, is measured in standard units such as kilometers. An important property of absolute space is symmetry. For example, if it is ten kilometers between City A and City B, then the distance between City B and City A is also ten kilometers.

Geographers frequently assume an abstract space when they develop idealized patterns. Advantages of an abstract approach include simplicity and clarity. An abstract approach concentrates on the effects of space alone without the influence of other variables. Idealized patterns that result from the absolute measures of space may be used as a norm against which real world patterns are compared.

Absolute measures of space apply to concrete space. A kilometer on the earth's surface is the same as any other kilometer. However, the use of relative measures of distance, direction, and connectivity very often provides a more meaningful view of concrete space.

Relative distance, for example, is measured in terms of cost, time, and/or effort. It is an important variable in geography because economic landscapes represent strategies that attempt to minimize the relative *friction of distance*. Figure 1.7 illustrates the concept of relative distance with reference to a point on the periphery of a city. A ten kilometer trip from Point A on a rural highway may require much less cost, time, or effort than a ten kilometer trip from Point A to the center of the city. Note that the property of distance symmetry that holds in abstract space does not hold in the example of concrete space.

Concrete qualities of space must be referenced to specific points or areas on the earth's surface. Any location, for example, requires a fixed reference point.

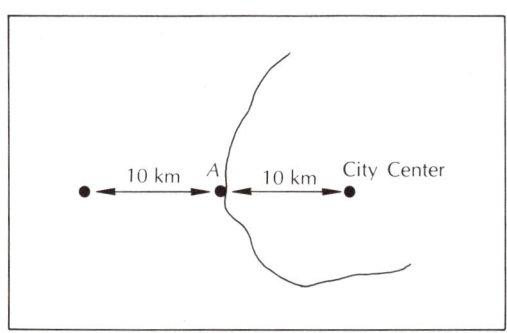

FIGURE 1.7 Relative distance.

Geographers deal with two kinds of location. Absolute location refers to a point's location in terms of a standard grid system. Latitude and longitude are the most common means of describing absolute location. Relative location is position with respect to other locations. It is a measure of connectivity and accessibility and usually changes over time. The concept of relative location is of greater interest to economic geographers than absolute location.

To illustrate the importance of relative location, let us consider the position of New York City. The absolute location of New York (latitude and longitude) does not tell us why it became the largest city and port in the nation. In 1820, Boston, New York, Philadelphia, and Baltimore were competing ports of similar size, but after 1825 New York surpassed its rivals. Why? Geographers find the answer in the relative location of New York. The Appalachian Highlands represented a cost and time barrier (high friction of distance) between the resources of the American interior and the return flow of manufactured goods from Europe. Notice New York's location at the mouth of the Hudson River (Figure 1.8). The Hudson River is almost at sea level all the way to Albany where it is joined by the Mohawk River which cuts through the Appalachians. In 1825, the Erie Canal was completed linking the Hudson-Mohawk corridor with Lake Erie. An advantageous location relative to a primary traffic artery provided a major impetus for New York's growth.

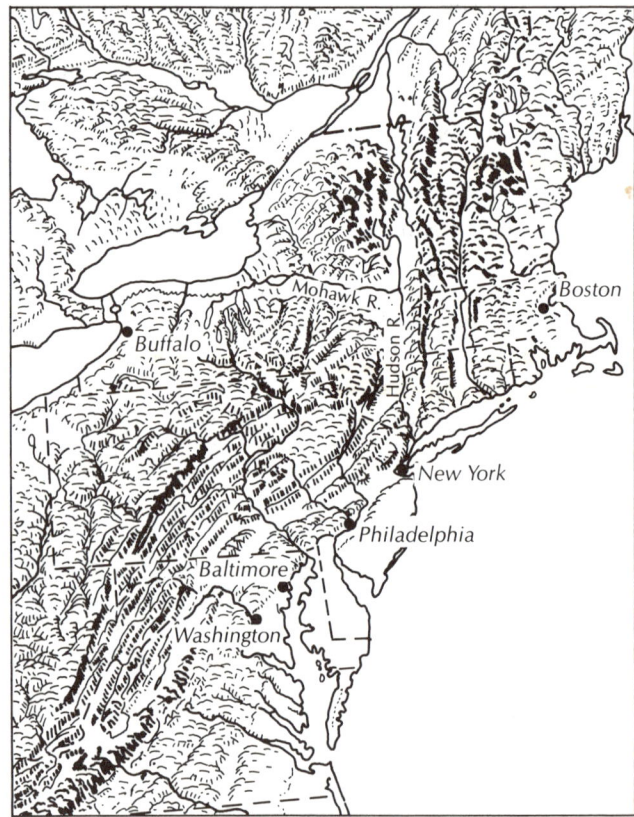

FIGURE 1.8 Hudson-Mohawk corridor and the relative location (situation) of New York.

Fundamental Geographical Concepts

Spatial Process and Spatial Structure

A *spatial process* is a movement or locational strategy. Locational strategies may involve the best locations for manufacturing plants, or the optimal arrangement of retail outlets. *Spatial structure* is the internal organization of a distribution, and it limits, channels, or controls a spatial process. Spatial process and spatial structure are circularly causal. For example, the existing distribution of regional shopping centers in a city will influence the success of any new regional shopping center in the area.

Figure 1.9 illustrates the influence of spatial structures. Two cities, A and B, have a trade relationship (Figure 1.9A). What will influence the spatial nature of this process? In abstract space, a straight line route will minimize the distance between the two cities (Figure 1.9B). In concrete space, the route has been distorted by the presence of a physical barrier (Figure 1.9C). The costs of cutting through the mountain barrier outweigh the costs of using an indirect route. Another effect of concrete space is shown in Figure 1.9D. The ideal straight-line route between cities C and D has been distorted to connect existing center A.

Although natural routeways are very important, they may be overemphasized. Spatial structures channel, but do not generate movement. If either city in Figure 1.9C were removed, trade through the pass would cease. If the pass did not exist, trade could still take place if the benefits of interaction exceeded movement costs.

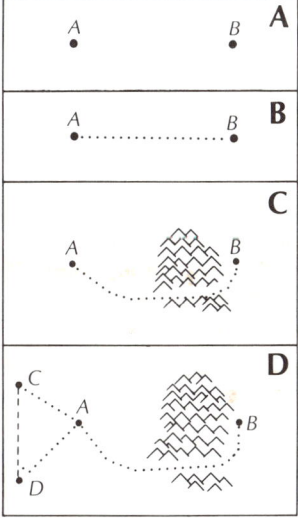

FIGURE 1.9 Spatial structures: (A) abstract space; (B) ideal trade route minimizing cost; (C) distortion by physical barrier; (D) distortion of route between C and D to connect existing center A.

Spatial Interaction

Flows of goods, people, and information are collectively known as *spatial interaction*. Three conditions inhibit or promote interaction—*complementarity, transferability,* and *intervening opportunity.*

Complementarity is the first requirement for spatial interaction. In order for movement to occur between two places, there must be a supply of some item in one place and a demand for it in another, and the demand and the supply must be specifically complementary. For example, petroleum is moved great distances from oil fields in the Middle East to the industrialized nations of North America, Europe, and Japan. Since supply and demand complement each other, a condition of complementarity exists.

Second, the condition of transferability must be met for exchanges to occur. All movement incurs costs, and costs increase with distance. An item must be transferable at acceptable costs from a supply area to a demand area. The condition of transferability is illustrated in Figure 1.10. The cost of producing electricity is shown from three different locations (A, B, and C). Transfer costs are given from A. The product is transferable between A and B, but not between A and C.

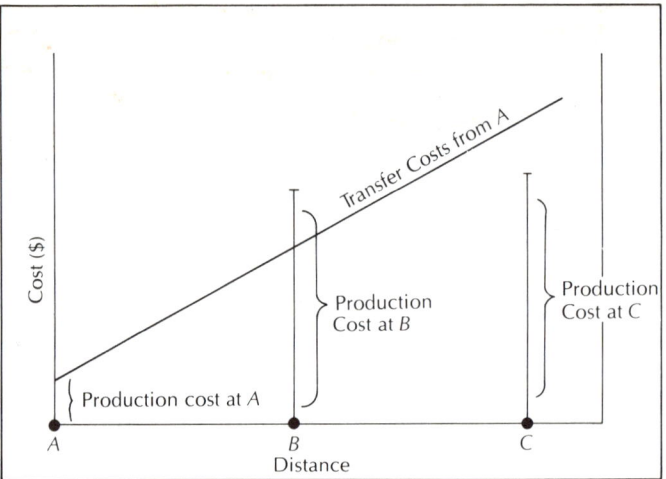

FIGURE 1.10 Transferability.

Third, the presence of intervening opportunities inhibits interaction between places. Intervening opportunity is a negative concept and emphasizes the importance of relative location. Figure 1.11A shows the location of three cities. A major department store is located in City A. The conditions of transferability and complementarity hold. Consumers from B and C travel to City A to shop. A second store is opened in City B and the flow stops (Figure 1.11B). City B is an intervening opportunity for both B and C.

FIGURE 1.11 Intervening opportunities: (A) shopping patterns before intervening opportunities introduced at B; (B) shopping patterns after intervening opportunities introduced at B.

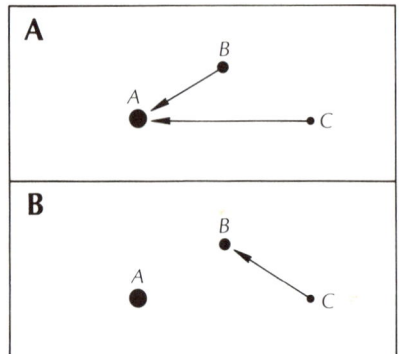

Perspectives on Economic Geography

Economic geography occupies a middle position between economics and geography. Although the core of economic geography is concerned with spatial patterns of economic phenomena and the processes that create such patterns, at any one time a variety of views of the economic geographer's task exist.

Economic geography emerged from commercial geography as a distinct field of study in the late nineteenth century. Subsequently, economic geography was affected by three major themes or paradigms of geography in general: man-environment relations, areal differentiation, and spatial organization. Although all three approaches have always been present, a man-environment emphasis flourished largely by itself until the 1930s, areal differentiation was influential from the late 1930s to the late 1950s, and spatial organization emerged as a dominant approach in the 1960s and 1970s. In the last few years still another view, historical and dialectical, has been developing.

Commercial Geography

The development of economic geography dates from the era of European exploration and discovery in the fifteenth through the nineteenth centuries, when geography meant excitement and adventure. Geographers were on the voyages and their reports to geographical societies were the big news of the day. They helped bring to merchants and government officials information about populations and resources found in other lands.

Probably the best known commercial geography was G. G. Chisholm's *Handbook of Commercial Geography* published in 1899. Chisholm was an English scholar who wrote that the purpose of commercial geography was to stimulate "an intellectual interest in the study of geographical facts relating to commerce." Virtually all of his book was an inventory of commodity and trade statistics for different regions. Such a treatment was not highly regarded by those who wanted to see an analytical rather than a descriptive explanation of the facts of trade and commerce.

Man-Environment Relations

The term *economic geography* was used in the United States for the first time in 1888 and twelve years later the American geographer Ellen Semple (1900) authored a book with that title. By the end of World War I, economic geography was firmly established as a discipline, and in 1925 a new journal, *Economic Geography,* began publication.

At least some economists hoped that the new field of economic geography would be closely tied to economics and would apply principles of classical economic theory in a spatial context. Events turned out otherwise. Early economic geography studies were concerned with theory, but not economic theory. They drew on the principles of environmentalism that permeated social science. Environmentalism was derived from nineteenth century natural philosophy.

We need not concern ourselves with the nineteenth century origins of environmentalism, only the *man-environment* theme in geography during the first quarter of the twentieth century. The man-environment theme emphasizes the importance of site, the links people have with the soil, sun, and rain. Geographers believed that physical environments molded human affairs. For example, a cool temperate climate fostered inventive, industrious West Europeans, whereas the humid tropics produced docile Africans (see box).

THE CONCEPT OF ENVIRONMENTALISM AND UNDERDEVELOPED LANDS

The environmental dictum was idealogically acceptable during the years of twentieth century colonial expansion, and it helped to shape the modern viewpoint of the nature and causes of economic "backwardness" in Africa, Asia, and Latin America. A dominant belief was that "unfavorable" climates resulted in low levels of productivity among indigenous people. Disease, climate, and the "colored races" were also seen as major obstacles to white settlement in the tropics. Many of the American Geographical Society's Special Publications from the 1920s to the early 1950s were devoted to environmental questions about human physiology and European residence in the tropics (Jefferson, 1921; Price, 1939; Pelzer, 1945). Perhaps the most influential work to have shaped the geographer's understanding of tropical developmental problems was P. Gourou's highly pessimistic book, *The Tropical World,* published in 1946 (in English in 1953). His book emphasized that the tropical environment poses nearly insurmountable problems at every turn.

Ellen Semple played a major role in spreading the idea of environmentalism. In *Influences of Geographical Environment* she wrote:

> Man is a product of the earth's surface. This means not merely that he is a child of the earth, dust of her dust; but that the earth has mothered him, fed him, set him tasks, directed his thoughts, confronted him with difficulties that have strengthened his body and sharpened his wits, given him his problems of navigation or irrigation, and at the same time whispered hints of their solution (1911:1).

The environmentalist concept exemplified by Semple was adhered to in numerous economic geographies. One example is R. N. Brown's *Principles of Economic Geography* (1920). Each chapter developed a picture of people being molded by climate, vegetation, and animal life. Few, if any, geographers who study man-environment relations now would claim that the physical environment is the sole determinant of human economic behavior. Geographers now place emphasis on adaptation and adjustment to potentialities in the environment, and attempt to discover how particular groups of people, especially at the local scale, organize their thoughts about the environment and how it might be used (Porter, 1965).

Areal Differentiation

Economic geographers were badly "burnt" by their encounter with environmental determinism and its underlying preoccupation with race. Reactions to the period of excessive determinism were essentially two-fold. The retreat from environmentalism led a few economic geographers to look for their explanations in economics. They said that economic geography should analyze universally applicable economic principles that underlie our whole industrial life.

Most economic geographers, however, rejected theory altogether. They emphasized the *areal differentiation* concept. They concerned themselves with region construction and the variation of economic activities on the earth's surface. They agreed with R. Hartshorne who said that " . . . no universals need be evolved, other than the general law of geography that all its areas are unique" (1939:468).

The "unique" approach resulted in detailed descriptions of production, exchange, and consumption. At the teaching level, textbooks were organized by regions or topics, and they contained masses of factual data. Indeed they resembled, in some respects, nineteenth century commercial geographies. At the research level, scholarly papers and monographs became increasingly specialized, and as a consequence the field of economic geography became less unified.

Areal differentiation dominated economic geography until the decade of the 1960s, when spatial organization came to the fore. The spatial organization approach has done a great deal to help geographers think in new ways about spatial distributions and space relations, and to resolve the problem of increasing disunity in the field. Moreover, it has brought economic geography into a closer relationship with other social sciences, especially economics.

Spatial Organization

The *spatial organization* theme in modern economic geography provides a framework for analyzing the location of economic activities and the spatial structure and behavior of economic systems. It emphasizes the importance of relative location or situation in a mobile and interconnected world. The popularity of the organization of space theme during the last twenty years was influenced by the "quantitative revolution" (Figure 1.12). One element of that revolution was quantification and experimentation with a wide range of statistical techniques, but another, more important element was an emphasis on the formulaton of hypotheses and search for theory. Economic geographers found the theories they were looking for not in geography, but in economics and the biological and behavioral sciences, including location and general systems theory.

Location theory attempts to explain and predict the spatial decisions of firms that result from aggregates of individual decision-making. The main aim of locational theorists has been to integrate the space dimension into classical economic theory. The origins of location theory stem from the work of Thünen on agricultural location in the 1820s, and subsequent contributions to industrial and settlement theory by Alfred Weber and William Christaller. They developed norma-

FIGURE 1.12 Quantifiers tearing geography away from its qualitative traditions. SOURCE: L. Curry, 1967, "Quantitative Geography," *Canadian Geographer*, **11**, p. 266, Fig. 1.

tive models of firms in a world of pure competition and assumed that entrepreneurs are completely rational and attempt to maximize profits with perfect knowledge of the cost characteristics of all locations. They explained location decisions deterministically and solely in terms of differences in production and transport costs between sites.

General systems theory provides a framework for explaining the interrelatedness of places and activities in the world space-economy. A system is "a set of objects together with relationships between the objects and their attributes" (Hall and Fagen, 1956:18). Objects in spatial economic systems, for example, perform a role in the operation of an economy such as cities, towns, villages, and rural farmsteads. Relationships are transport and communications connections that tie the system of places and their economic activities together.

Major principles of systems theory of interest to economic geographers are organization, interaction, hierarchy, and growth. *Organizations* are arrangements for substituting the more specialized effort or knowledge of several or many individuals for that of one. Specialization requires *interaction* for efficient production, distribution, and consumption of standardized goods and services. The concept of *hierarchy* is perhaps the most important concept relating to system organization and interaction. It is linked to the idea of threshold, which is the minimum size or scale necessary to support a specialized function. Low order functions have small thresholds and higher order functions have bigger thresholds.

Over time, systems change in *size* and *complexity*. If a system increases in size, it may be able to attain thresholds for higher-order, more specialized functions.

In recent years, geographers have devoted much attention to the problems of the growth and expansion of economic systems. Supported through grants from government agencies and private foundations, they have concerned themselves with such issues as resource-use inequalities, ecological damage, and development. The task of clarifying these issues has sparked an interest in the nature of decision-making.

Geographers who have studied *decision-making* have demonstrated the determinism of classical normative models of human behavior and have stressed the *indeterminancy* principle. They have been attracted to the theory of *stochastic processes*, which emphasizes that we live in a world that is a probabilistic mixture of choice, calculation, and chance. Their behavioral studies, however, have been restricted to descriptions of individual rather than group decision-making. Yet the behavior of many modern institutions can only be understood with reference to collegial decision-making.

The Dialectical Approach

Since the 1950s a whole generation of economic geographers, who may be described as either conservatives or liberals, have used theories of spatial organization to study the geography of the world political economy. In recent years, a small group of radical geographers has charged that traditional theories of spatial organization obscure more than they reveal. In their view, these theories are narrowly conceived, blind to historical facts, and serve the goals of those who wield power in the economic system. They believe that a *dialectical approach,* based on ideas flowing from Marxist analysis, implants a more precise set of ideas about the world's political economy.

The dialectical approach achieves understanding of the world by drawing attention to the power-relations of society. This mindset sees the relations of places in the context of the world's political economy. It recognizes a contemporary reality, the disadvantageous situation of most people with respect to the control and use of resources, and exposes the structure of relations in the world's political economy which preserves and intensifies that disadvantageous situation.

For the radical geographer, the dialectical world view is the context for critiquing existing theories of spatial organization. Classical location theory, for example, is criticized for its inappropriate assumptions, lack of historical perspective, and *status quo* orientation. Based on nineteenth century free enterprise capitalism, it draws attention to producers and consumers, but not to capitalists and workers. It analyzes different market structures, but fails to provide any understanding of the dynamics of capitalist evolution.

A major virtue of the work of radical geographers is that it acknowledges and analyzes prevailing value systems. It inquires deeply into processes of social and economic organization. Traditionally, economic geographers have avoided the question of values. They treated economic problems either in descriptive and verbal ways or within a quantitative-theoretic framework. Reluctant to accept that we live in an ideological world, they ignored the fact that the world space-economy is a reflection of its political economy.

Summary and Plan

We began this chapter with a brief account of the highlights of economic thought and the evolution of the private enterprise system. One of the purposes of that sketch was to impress upon the reader that there are at least three views on how the capitalist system functions. *Conservatives* believe that the market allocates resources in the most efficient and reasonable manner. *Liberals* believe in the market mechanism, but that government intervention is necessary to maximize social welfare. *Radicals* (of the left) criticize the market economy as well as traditional accounts of how it functions. All these approaches analyze the same problems: the market allocation of resources and development.

When economists study resource allocation, they concentrate on *microeconomic* problems of individual firms, workers, and consumers, and when economists deal with development, they concentrate on *macroeconomic* problems of the economic system as a whole. Economic geographers link macroeconomic and microeconomic views with spatial views.

We introduced some fundamental geographical concepts, included a brief discussion of scientific methodology and the use of models, and commented on the three geographical traditions of *man-environment relations, areal differentiation,* and *spatial organization*. All three themes are present in today's literature which reflects the continuity of these traditions and the personalities of geographers themselves. Such variety is a sign of a vigorous field of scholarship, and to reduce it all to one *paradigm* (or super concept) would be misleading. Nonetheless, most geographers would agree that the spatial organization theme flourishes in economic geography today. Consequently this book has made the paradigm of spatial organization the main basis for organizing and presenting material. Traditionally, geographers have examined the spatial organization of economic activities from either a conservative or a liberal viewpoint. However, in recent years a few geographers have offered a radical perspective. The radical mindset insists on a *global* world view that sees the spatial organization of activities in the context of the world's political economy. This book includes all three views of the space-economy.

We have tried to present conservative, liberal, and radical views impartially, but of course this is not completely possible. Moreover, the coverage of traditional and radical views varies from chapter to chapter. In general, traditional views are more fully developed than radical views. Some geographers will complain that either traditional or radical views are all wrong, and therefore should not have been included. For example, some radicals will charge that the classical location models reviewed in Chapters 4, 5, 6, and 7 reveal more about the thinking of many geographers than they do about the functioning of the economy, and also reveal their conservative or liberal ideology in support of capitalism. But other radicals will point out that the world space-economy has evolved subject to the conditions specified by orthodox theories.

We believe that exposure to a variety of views is healthy, and that the individual must decide whether a given approach is "good or bad" or "right or wrong." For example, do conservative and liberal approaches deliberately distort reality by assuming a "harmonious" society and ignoring such problems as imperialism and class conflict? Does the radical approach provide a true picture of the space-economy in its national and international dimensions?

This book includes most of the usual topics and some neglected ones—population, poverty, pollution, aid, and imperialism—in a traditional arrangement. Chapters 2 and 3 consider population and resources, important ingredients in the determination of demand and supply in a market exchange economy. Chapter 4 examines agriculture. About one-half of the chapter is devoted to a classical model of rural land use. This model begins with an abstract geographical system and proceeds to more factual descriptions of agricultural patterns. Chapter 5 concerns the developed capitalist city, its land use patterns and its problems. Chapters 6 and 7 study the geography of retailing and services and the location of manufacturing. Chapter 8 is devoted to transportation, especially transport costs. Spatial decision-making is discussed in Chapter 9. Instead of considering, as in Chapter 7, how people could or should make decisions in a "harmonious" free enterprise economy, it illustrates some of the ways in which individuals engaged in agricultural, manufacturing, and service activities might make sub-optimal locational choices. We assume that people are *satisficers;* they make sub-optimal decisions because they have imperfect knowledge about present and future events. The final three chapters examine the theme of *unequal* development with special reference to the underdeveloped world. Are there pervasive relationships of dominance and servitude throughout the world space-economy? What prevents poor people in underdeveloped countries (and in developed countries) from developing? Chapter 10 surveys the phenomena of underdevelopment. It describes the nature of underdevelopment, and provides some views on what causes and perpetuates it. The controversial topics of international trade and aid are discussed in Chapter 11. Attention in Chapter 12 is given to differences in income and welfare inside underdeveloped countries.

Numerous illustrations and tables will aid the reader in studying the material in the book. Technical information as well as ideas and accounts from different points of view are contained in boxes. At the beginning of each chapter is a set of objectives and a list of key terms. The reader also will benefit by looking at the works cited in the text and following the suggestions for further reading.

DISCUSSION QUESTIONS

1. "Economic geography is a value-oriented science." Do you agree?
2. Discuss: The ideas of economists have had a decisive influence on the world's spatial economy.

3. Why are models useful even if they do not describe perfectly the facts they try to explain?
4. Why must geographers take into account the effects of the world's political economy on resource allocation and development in both rich and poor nations?
5. Distinguish between conservative, liberal, and radical viewpoints.
6. Define the concepts of distance, direction, and connectivity.
7. Provide examples of point, line, and area relationships.
8. Define and illustrate the relationship between complementarity, intervening opportunity, and transferability.
9. Discuss the idea that as mobility increases, relative location increases in importance.
10. "The difference between the man-environment theme and the organization of space theme is one of scale and level of inquiry." Comment.
11. Write an essay on the changing nature of economic geography.

SUGGESTED READINGS

Ideas of Economists

Galbraith, J. K., *The Age of Uncertainty.* Boston: Houghton Mifflin Company, 1977.

Conservative, Liberal, and Radical Mindsets

Gordon, D., *Problems in Political Economy.* Lexington, Mass.: D. C. Heath, 1971.

Central Economic Problems

Brookfield, H., *Interdependent Development.* Pittsburgh: University of Pittsburgh Press, 1975.

Heilbroner, R. L., *The Economic Problem.* Englewood Cliffs, N.J.: Prentice-Hall, Inc., 1972.

Fundamental Geographical Concepts

Abler, R., J. S. Adams and P. Gould, *Spatial Organization.* Englewood Cliffs, N.J.: Prentice-Hall, Inc., 1971.

Nystuen, J. D., "Identification of Some Fundamental Spatial Concepts" in B. J. L. Berry and D. F. Marble, eds., *Spatial Analysis: A Reader in Statistical Geography.* Englewood Cliffs, N.J.: Prentice-Hall, Inc., 1968, pp. 35–41.

Ullman, E. L. "The Role of Transportation and Bases for Interaction" in W. L. Thomas, ed., *Man's Role in Changing the Face of the Earth.* Chicago: The University of Chicago Press, 1956, pp. 862–880.

Suggested Readings

CHANGING NATURE OF ECONOMIC GEOGRAPHY

Berry, B. J. L., E. C. Conkling, and D. M. Ray, *The Geography of Economic Systems*. Englewood Cliffs, N.J.: Prentice-Hall, Inc., 1976, pp. 3–11.

King, L. J., "Alternatives to a Positive Economic Geography," *Annals* of the Association of American Geographers, **66** (1976):293–308.

Population

KEY TERMS

- birth rate
- components of population change
- composition
- death rate
- demographic transition
- dependency ratio
- deterministic
- labor force
- law of diminishing returns
- migration
- natural increase
- population density
- population distribution
- population pyramids
- "push-pull" model
- resources
- scarcity
- sex ratio
- subsistence
- urbanization

2

Today the world economy can produce cars, washing machines, and televison sets faster than population, but does not distribute enough food for rapidly growing numbers of people, especially in underdeveloped countries. Although the speed of world population growth is one of the most frequently debated issues of recent times, there is more to population than numbers. Populations have particular distributions. They have varying propensities to migrate. They also have particular characteristics: age composition, sex ratio, income and educational levels, and social attitudes. In an examination of economic activities, the qualities of a population are important.

This chapter introduces basic population concepts, and raises controversial issues concerning the population "problem." The chapter is divided into four parts. In it we consider, first, population numbers and their distribution over the earth; second, population characteristics; third, migration; and finally, population growth trends and theories. Throughout the discussion, we stress the theme of world and regional patterns of population.

OBJECTIVES

By the end of this chapter you should be able:

1. To describe gross patterns of world population distribution.
2. To account for the variable distribution of people over the earth.
3. To describe the relationship between urbanization and economic growth.
4. To identify and describe demographic, cultural, and economic aspects of population composition.
5. To demonstrate how migration redistributes population.
6. To measure rates of natural increase, and to summarize the relationship between population growth rates and doubling times.

Population Distribution

7. To discuss Malthus' theory of population.
8. To discuss Marx's conception of the population-resources relationship.
9. To describe and evaluate the theory of the demographic transition.
10. To consider solutions to the population problems of underdeveloped countries.

Population Distribution

Human populations are unevenly distributed over the earth. *Population distribution* means arrangement, spread, and density. Contrasts in population distribution are studied at different scales of observation. At the macro-scale, broad geographical areas, continents, countries, or regions within countries are compared. At the micro-scale, local variations, particularly within cities, are examined. In this discussion, we will emphasize gross patterns of population distribution.

Population Size

A comparison of continental population figures shows that Asia's population is the largest. Asia contains slightly more than 50 percent of the world's population. Europe, including the Soviet Union, is home to 19 percent of all people, Africa to 10 percent, North America to 9 percent, South America to 5 percent, and Australia and the Pacific Islands to 0.5 percent. Populations of three continents, Africa, Asia (excluding Japan and the Soviet Union), and Latin America, that are called underdeveloped, account for 75 percent of all people. Of the three billion people in the underdeveloped world, 75 percent live in Asia; Africa's share is 14 percent, and Latin America's is 11 percent.

Given such large variations among continents, it is not surprising that national figures show even more variability. Ten out of two hundred countries account for over 60 percent of the world's people (Table 2.1). Four countries, China, India, Soviet Union, and the United States contain about 50 percent of the world's population. Approximately 21 percent of all people live in China, 15 percent in India, 6.5 percent in the Soviet Union, and 5.5 percent in the United States. Six of the "top ten" nations in population size, China, India, Indonesia, Japan, Bangladesh and Pakistan, are located in South and East Asia.

Population Density

National population statistics do not tell us anything about the area available for human habitation. Consequently, we often relate population to land area. This ratio is called *population density*—the average number of people per unit of area, usually a square kilometer.

TABLE 2.1 Ten countries with largest populations (1975)

Country	Population (000)	Population as % of World Total	Area Km² (000)	Density (Population per Km²)
China	822,800	21	9,562	86
India	608,072	15	3,137	194
USSR	254,393	6	22,274	11
USA	213,540	5	9,363	23
Indonesia	132,112	3	1,906	69
Japan	111,570	3	370	302
Brazil	106,996	3	8,521	13
Bangladesh	78,600	2	143	550
Nigeria	75,023	2	925	81
Pakistan	69,229	2	803	86

SOURCE: *World Book Atlas,* The World Bank, Washington, D.C., 1977.

Table 2.1 shows population densities for the most populous countries. Note that the continental United States has a relatively low population density of only 23 persons per square kilometer. If the entire world population were placed inside the United States, its population density would be just about that of England now. The United States is one of the sparsely populated areas of the world.

Table 2.2 ranks the world's most crowded nations. Five of these countries, the Netherlands, Belgium, Japan, West Germany, and the United Kingdom, maintain high living standards. Contrary to popular opinion, not all crowded nations are poor. But what explains the fact that people in a densely populated country like Belgium enjoy a high standard of living? What part of the explanation lies in its industrious population and its ability to adopt technological advances? What part of the explanation lies in its history of trade and colonial exploitation in the last four centuries?

TABLE 2.2 Ten most densely populated countries (1975)

Country	Population (000)	Area Km² (000)	Density (Population per Km²)
Bangladesh	78,600	143	550
Taiwan	16,000	32	500
Netherlands	13,650	33	414
South Korea	35,280	98	360
Belgium	9,799	31	316
Lebanon	3,164	10	316
Japan	111,570	370	302
West Germany	61,830	249	248
United Kingdom	55,960	244	229
Trinidad and Tobago	1,082	5	216

SOURCE: *World Bank Atlas,* The World Bank, Washington, D.C., 1977.

Population Distribution

The world's population is spread unevenly over the earth's surface: (A) land and no people, Svartisen Glacier, Norway; (B) land and few people, Wisconsin (SOURCE: *University of Wisconsin—Extension*); (C) crowded city-state of Singapore (SOURCE: *World Bank Photo* by Edwin G. Huffman); and (D) cramped tenements of Genoa, Italy.

Population density is a valuable abstraction, but its usefulness is inversely related to size of area. It conceals too much variation. For instance, Egypt has only 20 persons per square kilometer, a density less than the United States. But 96 percent of the population is concentrated along the Nile Valley, where densities exceed 1,000 per square kilometer. Similarly, in the United States, large areas are essentially devoid of people, whereas others are densely settled. The island of Manhattan has a density of 30,000 people per square kilometer.

Figure 2.1, a dot-and-circle map, illustrates the varying distribution of population throughout the world. It shows that most of the human race is concentrated in but few parts of the earth, whereas large areas are nearly empty. Four major

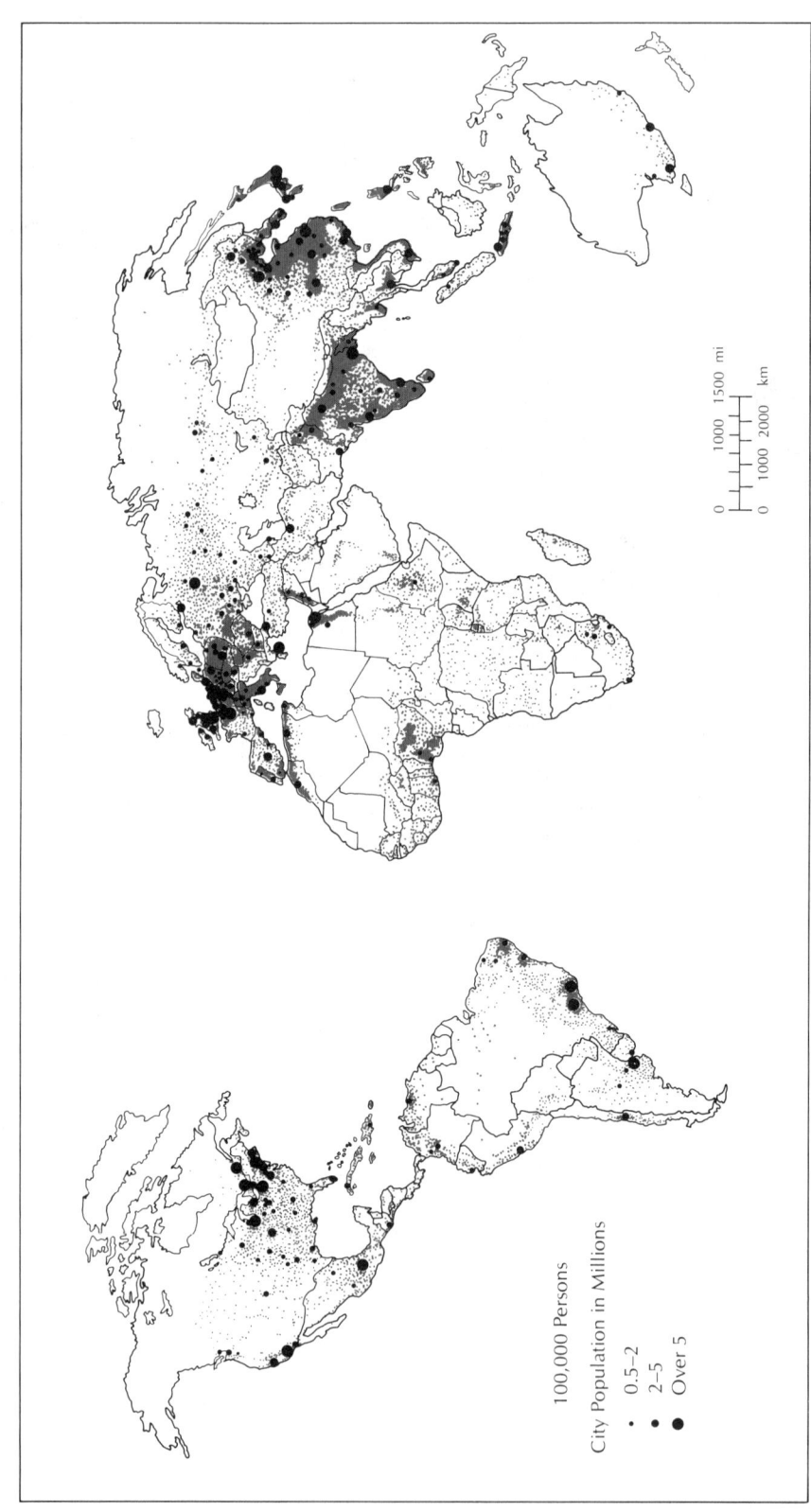

FIGURE 2.1 World population distribution. SOURCE: Jan O. Broek and John W. Webb, 1973, *A Geography of Mankind*. New York: McGraw-Hill, pp. 38–39, Fig. 2.3.

Population Distribution

areas of dense settlement are East Asia, South Asia, Europe, and Eastern North America. In addition, there are minor clusters in Southeast Asia, Africa, Latin America, and along the Pacific Coast of the United States. More than 80 percent of the world's population lives in major and minor areas of dense settlement.

Influences upon Population Distribution

Is there a reason for the massing of population in some areas? One possible explanation is physical environment. People concentrate along edges of continents, live at low elevations, and in humid mid-latitude and sub-tropical climates. Rugged mountainous areas and regions deficient in moisture and heat pose obstacles for dense settlement and agriculture. Yet there are many exceptions to these generalizations. For example, the British Isles and Japan support the view that insularity assists population concentrations, but the low densities in Tasmania and Iceland refute it.

Natural elements provide only a partial explanation for population distribution. Furthermore, it is *deterministic* to hold that natural elements control population distribution. Climatic extremes such as insufficient rainfall may present difficulties for human habitation and cultivation; but given the forces of technology, air-conditioning, water storage, and irrigation, the deficiencies of nature can be overcome.

If physical elements alone do not explain population distribution, what other factors are involved? Human distributions are molded by the organization, technology and development of economic systems. They are strongly influenced by cultural traits, which also affect demographic components of fertility, mortality, and migration. Social disasters, like war, may alter population distribution at any scale. Social and political decisions, such as tax policies or zoning and planning ordinances, are eventually reflected on the population map. Time or inertia has a profound impact on distribution. We must always consider historical circumstances when we are trying to interpret the variable distribution of people over the earth.

No single factor can explain the areal distribution of population worldwide. Factors are complex and interrelated. They operate directly or indirectly in almost every situation and always in the context of time. It is seldom easy to demonstrate the degree to which a single factor has shaped population distribution.

Urbanism

The modern city is the most impressive and forceful expression of humankind's struggle with nature. It has little regard for the physical environment. Cities spread in tentacular fashion into the countryside, and seem to cover the earth in asphalt and concrete. Yet in the United States only 1.5 percent of the nation's land is occupied by urban populations.

Population concentration reaches its greatest intensity in cities. Cities generate and support, through employment and consumption opportunities, much higher population densities than rural areas.

The modern metropolis: downtown Chicago.

Agricultural surplus is needed for urban growth. Before the Industrial Revolution, urban settlements in Europe and North America were small. The Industrial Revolution marked a major change in the social organization of production—from simple mercantilist accumulation to the expanded reproduction of industrial capitalism. With the Industrial Revolution, cities not only accumulated surpluses from beyond their own confines, but generated even larger surpluses from their own industrial activities.

The shift in the mode of production was accompanied by the movement of people off the land and into urban industrial and service occupations. Rural–urban migration was a feature of the nineteenth century in developed countries, and it is now a characteristic of underdeveloped countries. A large part of total urban growth in almost every country is occurring in great metropolitan cities. Although "millionaire cities" (i.e. cities with more than one million people) long have been common in Europe-North America, they are now almost as numerous in underdeveloped countries (Figure 2.2). In 1975 there were 91 and 90 million cities in developed and underdeveloped countries, respectively.

The amount of urbanization varies considerably in time and space. *Urbanization is the proportion of total population in urban places.* In the United States, urban population is usually defined as people living in places that have at least 2,500 inhabitants. Until recently, the United States was predominantly a rural nation. In 1790 only 5 percent of the population was urbanized. During the nineteenth century, urbanization increased with national economic growth and industrial development. By 1920 more than 50 percent of all Americans lived in

Population Distribution

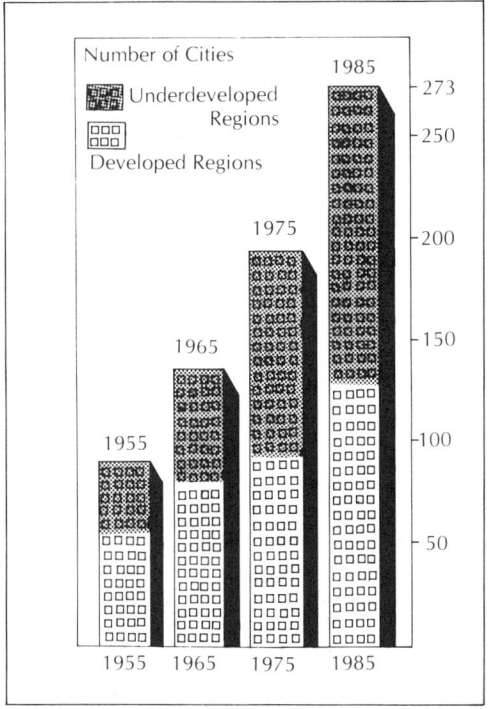

FIGURE 2.2 Million-cities. SOURCE: *Development Forum,* 1975, Vol. 3, Number 9, p. 5.

cities. The pace of urbanization slowed in the economic depression of the 1930s, but increased rapidly thereafter. In 1960, urban population was 69.9 percent, expanding to 73.5 percent a decade later. State-by-state percentages show that California was 90 percent urbanized in 1970 (Figure 2.3). Only five states, Vermont, West Virginia, Mississippi, North Dakota, and South Dakota, had less than 50 percent of their populations living in urban places.

In recent decades, underdeveloped countries have experienced an urban transformation as profound as that in nineteenth century North America. The proportion of world urban population in underdeveloped countries was 27 percent in 1920, 44 percent in 1960, and expected to reach 66 percent by 1980. The speed of urban growth in underdeveloped countries is a striking feature of the twentieth century. During the 1950s and 1960s, urban population increased at an average rate of about 5 percent annually, doubling every 14 years. Urban growth is occurring more rapidly in the underdeveloped world than in the developed world, and is concentrated in the larger cities. Compared with developed countries, rates of large-city growth are very rapid (Table 2.3).

What is exceptional about urbanization in underdeveloped countries is not so much an increased proportion of urban to total population (urbanization), but an unprecedented absolute growth of urban population (urban growth). In the period 1960–65, the average annual growth rate of urban population was 5.8 percent, 4.6 percent, and 3.8 percent in Latin America, Africa, and Asia, respectively. In Western Europe during its period of fastest urban population growth (late nineteenth century) the rate was only 2.1 percent. The rate of urbanization is half that of urban growth. In other words, urban growth is being paralleled by high growth rates in rural areas.

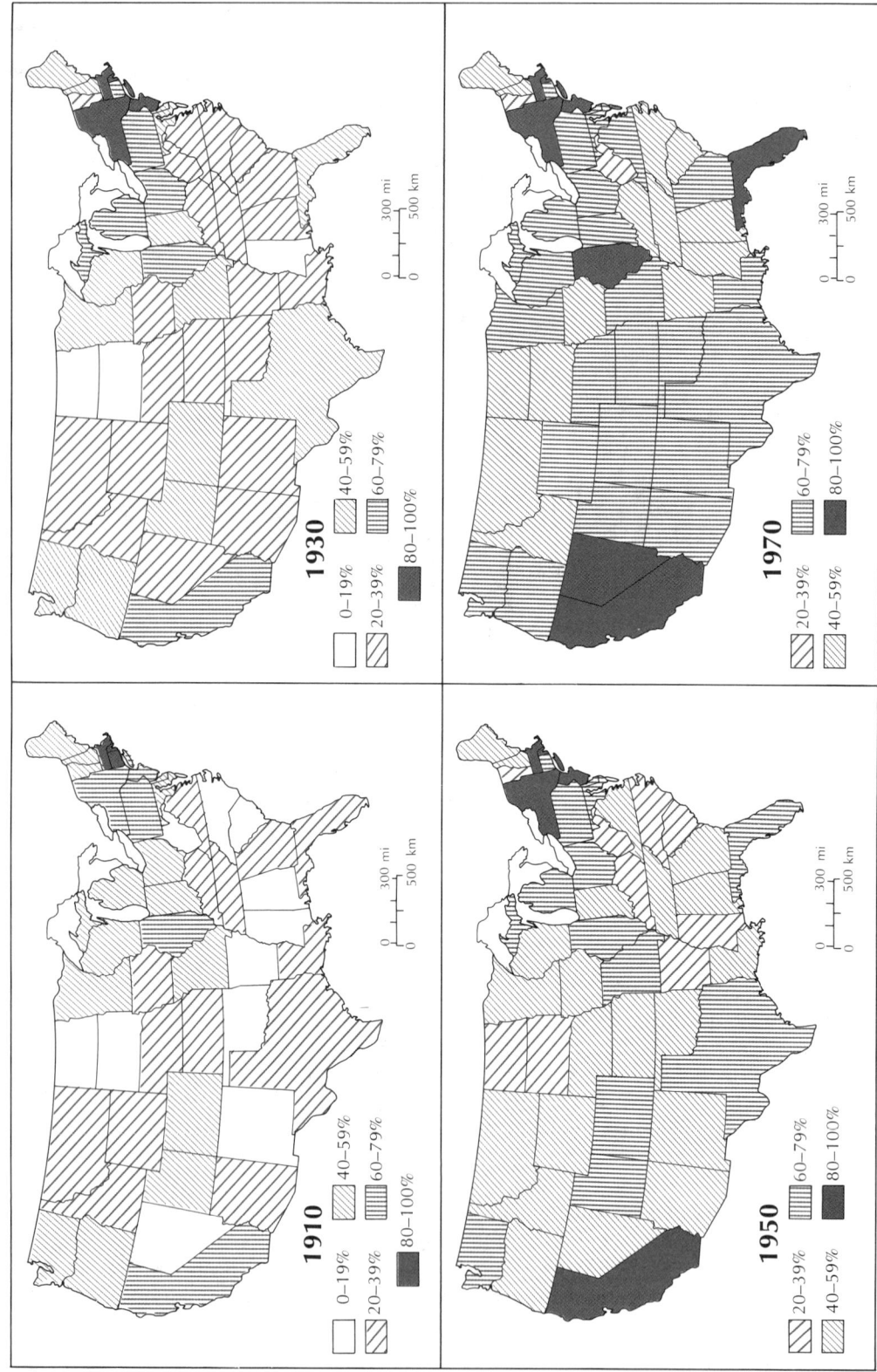

FIGURE 2.3 The spread of urbanization in the United States. SOURCE: *U.S. Census of Population.*

Population Distribution

TABLE 2.3 Population (millions) residing in large cities (more than 500,000) in the underdeveloped world and three selected regions (1920–1960)

	1920	1930	1940	1950	1960	Absolute Increase	Percentage Increase
World total	106.6	143.3	181.1	228.2	353.6	247.0	231
Europe	51.7	62.4	68.4	71.3	82.8	31.1	60
Other more developed regions*	41.2	60.3	77.3	101.5	140.2	99.0	241
Underdeveloped world	13.7	20.6	35.4	55.4	130.6	116.9	836

*These include Japan, North America, Soviet Union, temperate South America, Australia and New Zealand.

SOURCE: United Nations, *Growth of the World's Urban and Rural Population, 1920–2000*. New York, 1969.

A   B

Third World cities are growing but not developing: (A) downtown São Paulo, Brazil (SOURCE: *Brazilian Embassy*, Washington, D.C.); and (B) squatter settlement, Guatemala City, Guatemala.

The underdeveloped world was about 25 percent urbanized in 1975. By contrast, most of the industrialized nations were about 70 percent urbanized (Table 2.4). Figure 2.4 emphasizes that rich industrial countries are the most intensively urbanized. It shows a strong relationship between town-dwelling population and level of income per person. The graph in Figure 2.4 does not imply that urbanization equals development. For one thing, the "gap" in the level of urbanization between the developed and the underdeveloped world is closing. Second, urbanization in the underdeveloped world is not being accompanied by increased prosperity. Instead, the urbanization of the Third World is paralleled by increasing inequality in income and amenities. This contradiction can be explained easily: Underdeveloped countries are urbanizing under a world economy created and controlled by developed nations.

TABLE 2.4 Percentages of urban in total population (1950 and 1975) in eight major areas and 24 regions of the world

Area or Region	Percentage of Urban in Total Population	
	1950	1975
Northern America	63.6	76.5
Oceania	64.5	71.6
Europe	54.8	67.2
Soviet Union	39.4	60.5
Latin America	40.9	60.4
East Asia	16.6	30.7
Africa	13.2	24.4
South Asia	15.5	23.0
Developed Regions	53.4	69.2
Australia and New Zealand	78.7	85.5
Temperate South America	62.8	80.8
Western Europe	63.2	77.1
Northern America	63.6	76.5
Japan	50.3	75.2
Northern Europe	70.8	75.1
Soviet Union	39.4	60.5
Southern Europe	44.9	59.2
Eastern Europe	42.2	56.6
Underdeveloped Regions	15.6	27.3
Tropical South America	36.5	59.3
Middle America	39.5	57.1
Other East Asia*	23.2	50.0
Caribbean	33.0	48.2
Southern Africa	36.5	46.2
Western South Asia	23.3	43.7
Northern Africa	23.2	39.5
Micronesia and Polynesia	20.6	32.1
Middle Africa	8.1	24.6
China	11.1	23.5
Eastern South Asia	13.4	22.1
Middle South Asia	15.6	21.1
Western Africa	9.6	18.5
Melanesia	2.0	13.7
Eastern Africa	5.3	12.3

*East Asia other than China or Japan.

SOURCE: United Nations Population Division. Table reprinted from HABITAT: United Nations Conference on Human Settlements, Global Review of Human Settlements, Item 10 of the Provisional Agenda A/CONF.70/A/1, pp. 21–22.

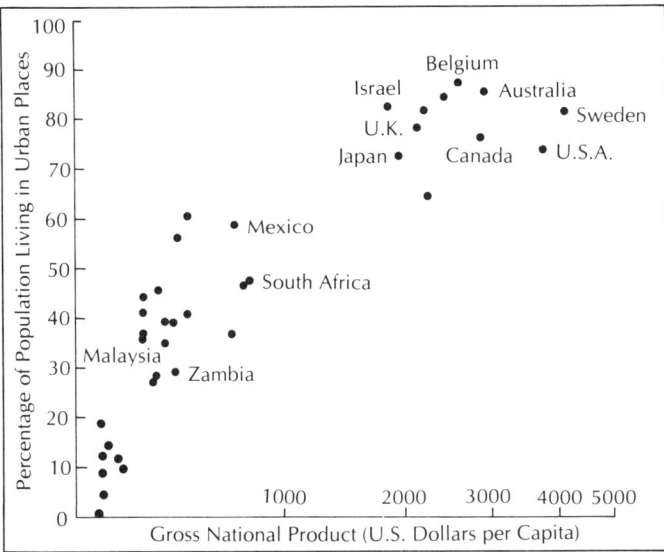

FIGURE 2.4 The relationship between urbanization and gross national product. SOURCE: *U.N. Statistical Yearbook*, 1974, and *U.N. Demographic Yearbook*, 1973.

Population Composition

So far we have dealt with numbers and distributions of people, but not with population composition. By *population composition* we mean *demographic, cultural, and economic characteristics*. Population characteristics differ between rich and poor nations, between cities and rural areas, and between cities and suburbs.

Demographic Structure

Age Composition One measure of age composition is the *dependency ratio*. It compares the percentage of people in the economically active age class (15–64) with those in relatively non-productive age groups. The ratio is higher in underdeveloped than in developed countries, primarily because in underdeveloped countries a large proportion of the population is under 15 years (Table 2.5). Nations with large proportions of their populations under 15 or above 64, or both, have, other things being equal, greater service needs and lower productive capacities than those with populations mostly in working-age groups. Table 2.5 suggests that compared to developed countries, underdeveloped countries have a smaller proportion of their population in the active age group. But the age group classification employed by the United Nations is based on Western experience. In the underdeveloped world, many young and old people are economically active.

For more careful study of age-structure, we construct *population pyramids*. They are built up in five-year age groups or age cohorts, males on one side, females on the other, with the base representing the youngest group, the apex the

A youthful population is a problem for an underdeveloped country when schools and medical services are in short supply. SOURCE: *World Bank Photo* by Edwin G. Huffman.

oldest. Population pyramids are compared by expressing male and female age groups as percentages of total population.

Population pyramids reflect trends in mortality and migration, but the most important influence on population age structure is *fertility*. High fertility produces a structure in which the proportion of young people is relatively high, and elderly relatively low. Conversely, low fertility forms a structure weighted in favor of the elderly. Africa, Asia, and Latin America illustrate the former situation, and Europe the latter.

TABLE 2.5 Population in different age groups for selected countries (about 1970, percent)

Country	Young (Under 15)	Adult (15–64)	Aged (65 and Over)	Young & Aged
Developed:				
Sweden	20.78	65.01	14.21	34.99
United Kingdom	23.72	62.73	13.55	37.27
United States	28.49	61.64	9.87	38.36
Underdeveloped:				
India	40.42	56.41	3.16	43.58
Brazil	42.06	54.80	3.14	45.20
Kenya	48.37	48.06	3.57	51.94

SOURCE: *United Nations Demographic Yearbook*, 1973.

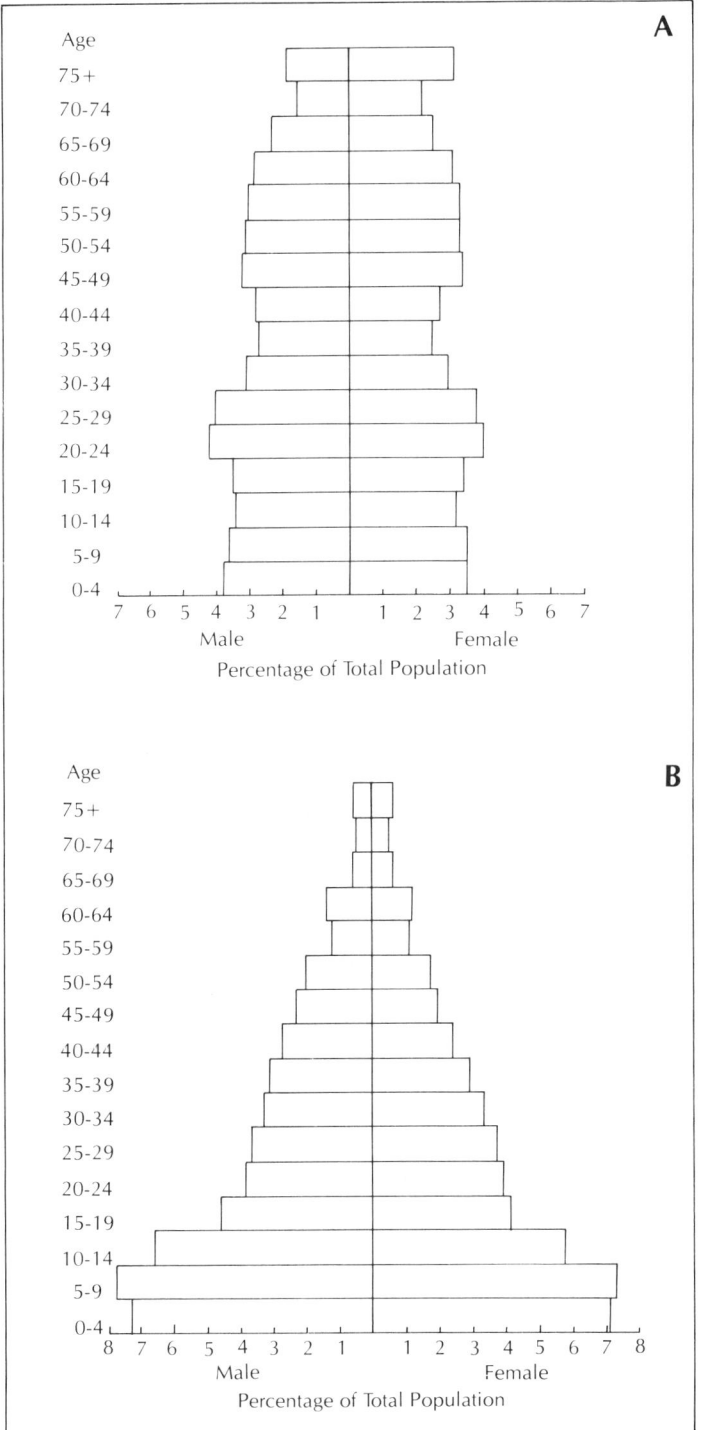

FIGURE 2.5 Population pyramids: (A) Sweden (1970); (B) India (1970). SOURCE: *U.N. Demographic Yearbook,* 1972.

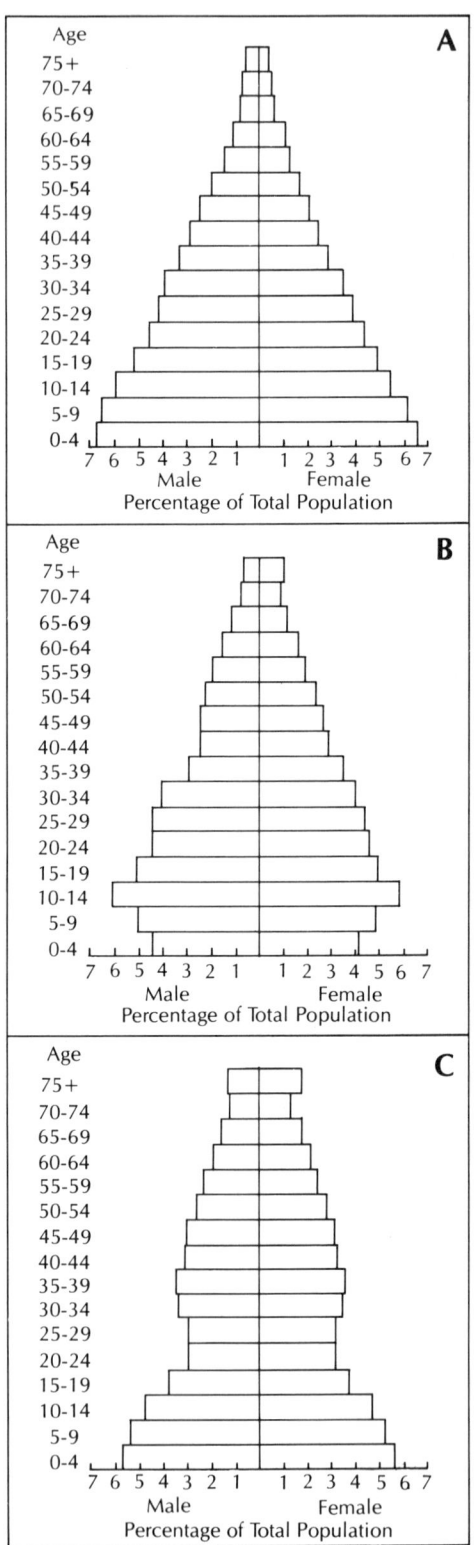

FIGURE 2.6 Population pyramids: (A) India (1951); (B) Japan (1960); (C) United States (1960). SOURCE: *U.N. Demographic Yearbook,* 1970.

Population Composition

Two different types of population pyramids are: (1) the squat triangular profile with a broad base, concave sides, and narrow tip reflecting a young population, and (2) the elongated profile with a narrow base reflecting an old population (Figure 2.5). The elongated profile, where population is quite evenly distributed over the age spectrum, exemplifies some West European countries such as Sweden and the United Kingdom. The broad-base profile is characteristic of fast-growing countries with high birth and declining death rates; for instance, India and Mexico.

In addition to the two basic types, three intermediate population profiles, reflecting different demographic histories, are commonly found (Figure 2.6). First, if a population has high birth and death rates, and low life expectancy (under 60 years), the profile is shaped like an equilateral triangle, as in the United States in 1900 and India in 1951. Second, a sharp decrease in the birth rate produces a population profile that is restricted at the base, like that of Japan in 1960. Third, if a population once had low birth and death rates, and then experiences a rise in birth rate, the resulting profile is bell-shaped. Such is the shape of the United States' 1960 profile. The pyramid's "waist" reflects the "baby dearth" of the Depression years when total births dropped to about 2.5 million from an average of close to 3 million a year. At the time, the fertility rate—the number of children born to the average woman in her lifetime—dropped close to 2.1, which is the level that would lead to a stable population if maintained indefinitely. The bulge at the base of the 1960 pyramid is a consequence of the "baby boom" that followed World War II. In the mid-1950s the fertility level increased to 3.8 and the number of births each year exceeded 4 million. In the decade of the 1960s, however, there was a "baby bust." Fertility levels plunged, so the 1970 pyramid has a narrower base (0-4, and 5-9 age classes). In 1976 the fertility rate had fallen to 1.76, a level below the replacement level.

The extent to which age composition may differ within regions can be seen in Figure 2.7, where urban and rural populations of the Upper Midwest are compared. Urban areas exceed rural areas in the proportion of population between ages 15 and 39; but rural population is higher before age 15. A shift occurs in the age group 15 to 19. High school graduates leave rural areas seeking employment or going to college. Females leave earlier and in greater numbers than males, probably because males find more job opportunities in the countryside.

Although a high proportion of young adults is a striking feature of many American cities, we could overgeneralize. For instance, compare the extreme cases of Florissant, Missouri, a fast growing suburb of St. Louis, with St. Petersburg, Florida, a popular retirement community (Figure 2.8). In St. Petersburg 30 percent of the residents are over age 65 and 25 percent under 19, whereas in Florissant 3 percent are over 65 and 47 percent are under 19.

Substantial differences in age-composition also exist within metropolitan areas (Figure 2.9). Families with children in the Twin Cities urbanized area tend to locate in the suburbs, and the elderly, young single people, and childless married couples concentrate near the downtowns of Minneapolis and St. Paul. The proportion of persons over age 60 is about three times as high in the central cities as in the suburbs.

Sex Ratio Another way in which populations differ is the proportion of males to females. This ratio, the *sex ratio,* is expressed as the number of males per 100 females in a population. The mean world sex ratio is about 98. It is less than 100

FIGURE 2.7 Superimposed urban and rural population pyramids of the Upper Midwest. SOURCE: *U.S. Census of Population*, 1970.

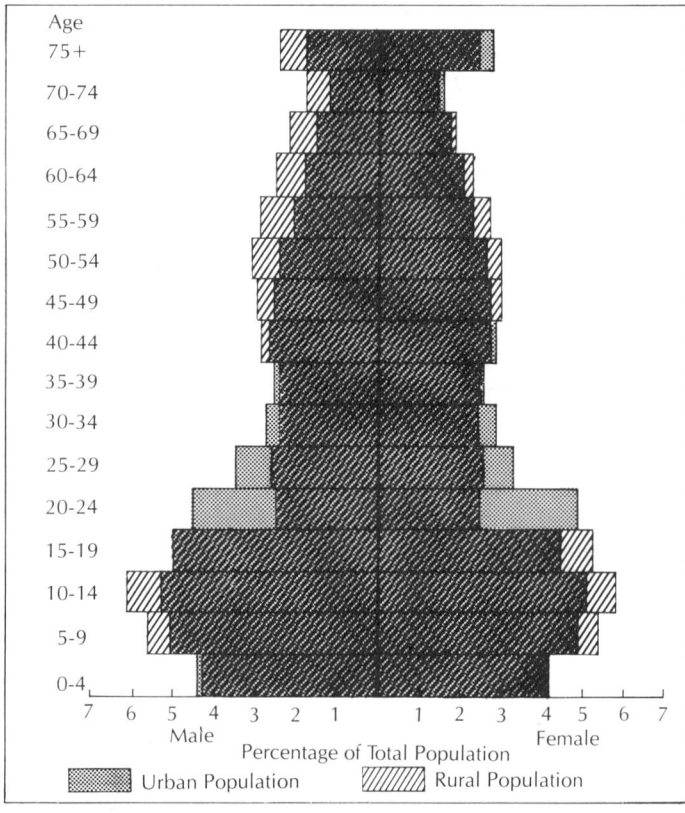

because males in most societies have a shorter life-span than females. Sex ratios below 90 and over 110 are considered unbalanced. The balance of the sexes is a rough index of the source, volume, and destination of migratory flow.

Long distance migration tends to be male selective; strong in-migration raises the sex ratio, and out-migration lowers it by leaving behind a surplus of females. Immigrant countries—Australia, Canada, and the United States—had male surpluses in the nineteenth and early twentieth centuries (Figure 2.10). High sex ratios are a feature of "frontier" areas, for instance Alaska today, where the ratio is about 130. As time passes, Alaska's ratio will probably decrease, just as it did from east to west in the United States during this century (Figure 2.11).

Short-distance migration in developed countries is less sex selective than in the past. Female rural-to-urban migrants are becoming more and more numerous. They predominate in cities specializing in political, commercial, and service activities. However, the proportion of males still tends to be higher in heavy industrial, mining, and military towns.

Cultural Traits

Nationality, language, race, religion, and literacy rank high in importance among the various qualities of a population. These cultural traits not only influence demographic composition, but also economic and social behavior.

Population Composition

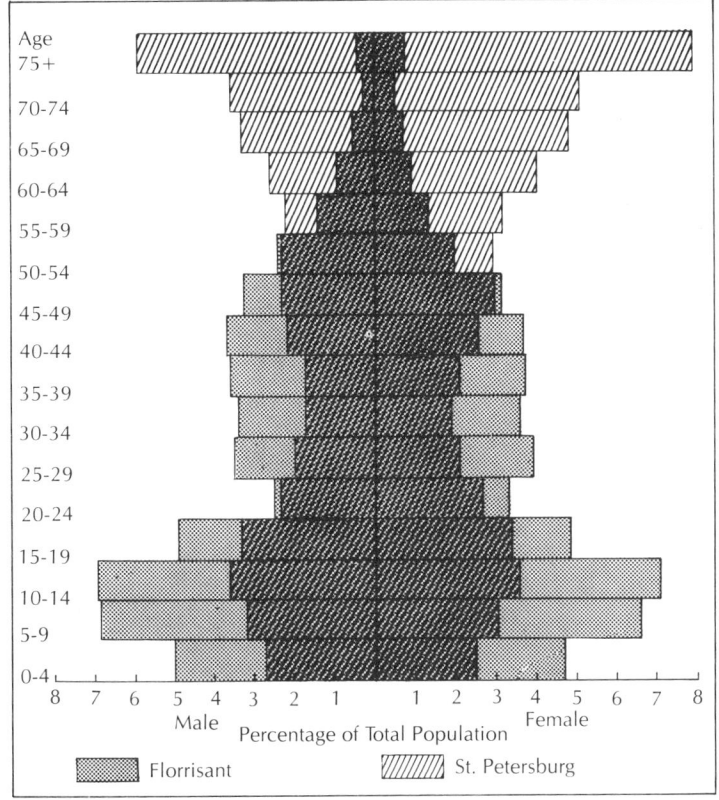

FIGURE 2.8 Superimposed pyramids: Florrisant, Missouri and St. Petersburg, Florida. SOURCE: *U.S. Census of Population,* 1970.

Nationality Membership in a nationality group provides people with a sense of identity and unity. Differences between nationality groups can produce internal and external economic and social problems. Internal conflicts and tensions are prevalent in Europe, such as, the antagonism between the Flemings and French-speaking Walloons in Belgium. Ethnic conflict commonly occurs and thwarts development in Africa. Before independence, people united willingly to support the fight against colonial rule; but the task of building a nation in the years following the granting of independence did not command such unity of purpose. Economic and political fragmentation is a major external problem of African and European countries. In Western Europe, the Common Market is a post Second World War attempt to overcome the throttling effects of fragmentation.

Language Like nationality, language fosters group unity, but reduces communications with outsiders. In Kenya, communication problems engendered by tribal linguistic diversity are considered handicaps to development. The government is promoting Swahili as a national language. Language differences can promote territorial segregation and spawn separatist movements, as in India and Canada. Yet Switzerland is a cohesive nation, despite its German, French, Italian, and Romansch-speaking populations.

Race Some racial groups have achieved higher status than others. Many problems are created by attitudes of racial superiority. Subjugated races suffer psychological rejection and economic and social discrimination. Africans, long

FIGURE 2.9 Superimposed pyramids: center cities and suburban population of the Twin Cities urbanized area. SOURCE: *U.S. Census of Population,* 1970.

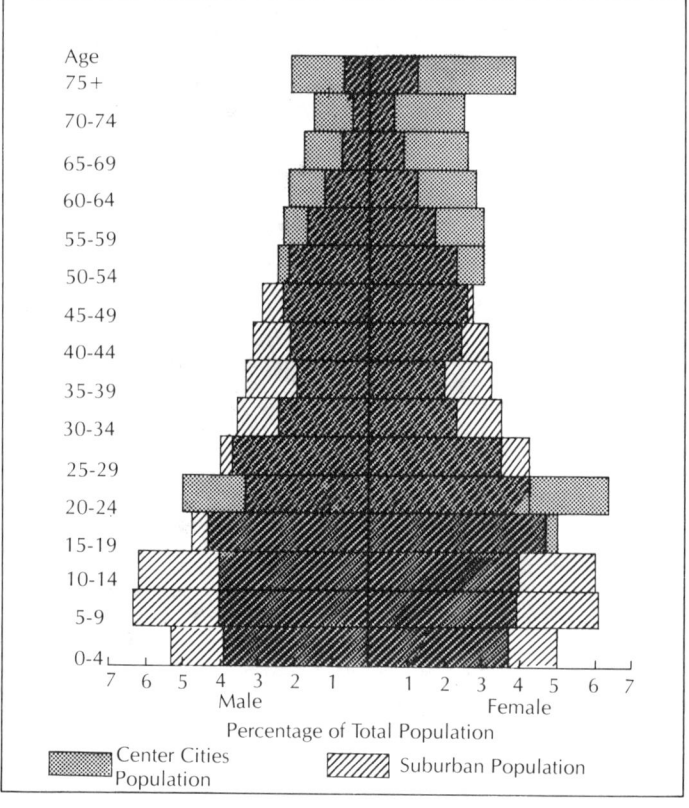

FIGURE 2.10 Sex ratio of the population of the United States, 1820–1966. SOURCE: *U.S. Bureau of the Census,* 1960 and *Current Population Reports,* Series P-25, No. 352, 1966.

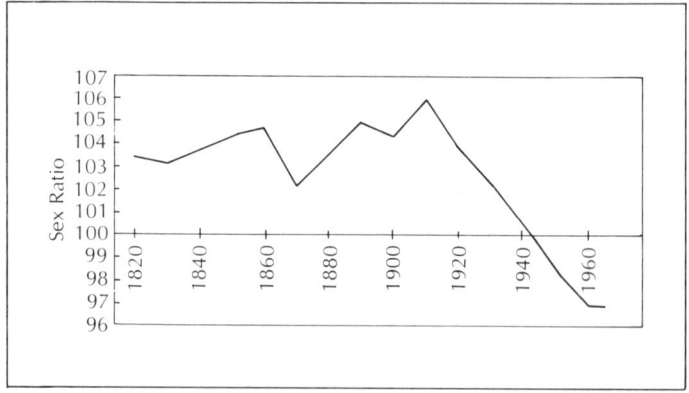

denied their status under apartheid policies in the Republic of South Africa, are severely disadvantaged. A greater part of Canada's native population lives outside the mainstream of society on reservations. American blacks experience residential and occupational discrimination.

Religion Religious differences can disrupt national economic systems. Recent examples are the effects of rivalries between Moslems and Christians in Beirut, and hatred between Catholics and Protestants in Belfast.

Population Composition

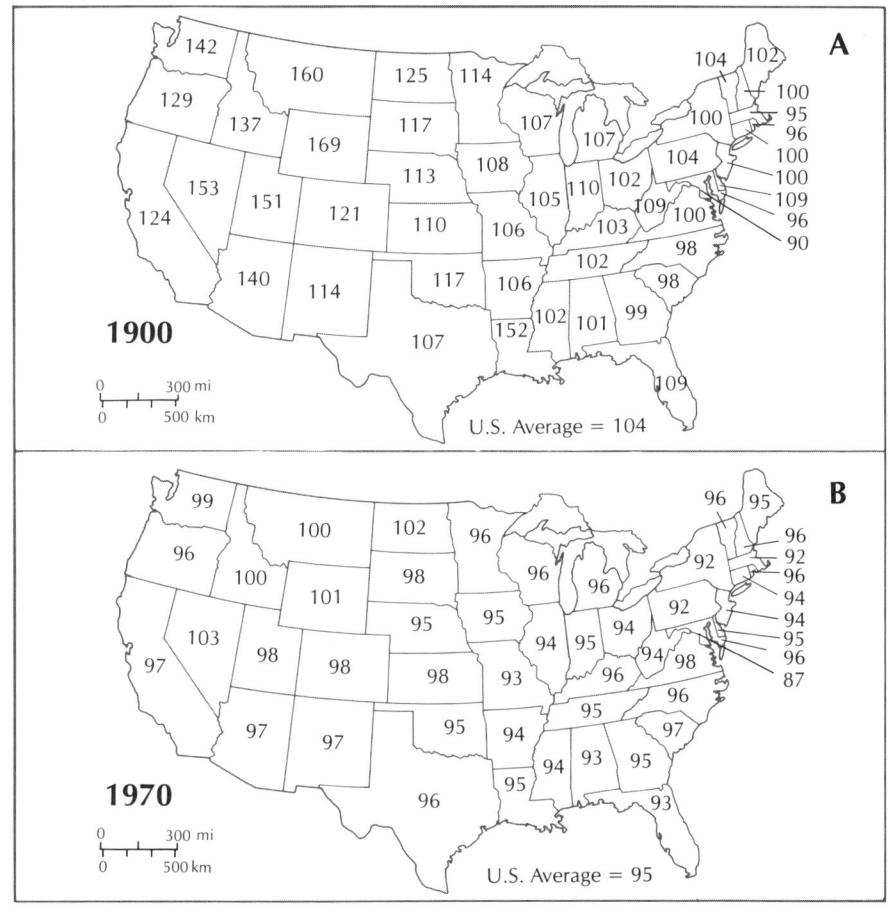

FIGURE 2.11 Sex ratios of the United States: (A) 1900 and (B) 1970. SOURCE: *U.S. Bureau of the Census,* 1900 and 1970.

Literacy Educational attainment is a population trait associated with economic development. The minimum measure of educational attainment is the degree of illiteracy. Lowest illiteracy rates occur in the urban-industrial countries of Western Europe-North America (0-5 percent), while over much of Africa, the illiteracy level exceeds 70 percent. A low degree of literacy is an obstacle to national economic development.

Economic Characteristics

Active Population The total population of a country may be divided into two parts: one, that which is economically active; the other, that which is inactive. Economically active refers to productively employed and temporarily unemployed people. The economically active population is known as the *labor force*. Size of population is the most important determinant of the size of the labor force, but the proportion of the population which is economically active, known as the activity rate, varies considerably from 25-50 percent. Major factors influencing activity rates are age structure and female participation. Activity rates are higher in Communist countries of Eastern Europe (52-54 percent) than in the industrial West (40-45 percent), because of women's more extensive participation in the labor force. In underdeveloped countries activity rates vary from 20-40 percent. They would be higher if the age structure were not so heavily tilted in favor of very young age groups.

Unemployment Unemployment, which means willing and able workers with no jobs, varies widely nationally and internationally. In the industrial West, unemployment rates are low, except during major downturns in the cycle of business activities (see box). Nonetheless, some areas are more prone to unemployment than others. Pockets of unemployment are the result of many forces including unequal distributions of natural and human resources, and business contractions in areas of economic specialization. In underdeveloped countries, the problem of unemployment and underemployment is serious, and in most countries is a more serious problem than the food supply. High levels of unemployment exist in urban areas, especially among young people. As an example, in the late 1960s in urban areas of Sri Lanka, the rate of unemployment was 36 percent for males and 48 percent for females in the 15–24 age group.

Industrial Composition The active population engages in many kinds of economic activity. The United States *Standard Industrial Classification* lists thousands of industries. The United Nations adopts a nine-division classification, which facilitates the study of international comparisons:

1. Agriculture, forestry, hunting, and fishing;
2. Mining and quarrying;
3. Manufacturing;
4. Construction;
5. Production of electricity and gas;
6. Commerce;
7. Transport, storage, and communications;
8. Services; and
9. All others.

These nine groups may be simplified still further into three crude sectors, as follows:

1. Primary activities including agriculture, mining, quarrying, forestry, hunting, and fishing;
2. Secondary activities including manufacturing, construction, and electricity, gas and water workers; and
3. Tertiary activities including commerce, transportation, storage, communication, and other service workers.

UNEMPLOYMENT IN THE UNITED STATES

The United States economy is subject to periods of expansion (boom) and contraction (depression or recession). In each contraction period the amount of unemployment rises to high levels:

Depression or Recession Years	Officially Reported Maximum Unemployment
1926–1927	4%
1929–1933	25
1937–1938	20
1945–1946	4
1948–1949	8
1953–1954	6
1957–1958	8
1960–1961	7
1969–1970	6
1974–1975	9%

SOURCE: U.S. Department of Labor, all except last reported in Geoffrey Moore, "Recession?" *Economic Outlook USA*, 1974 (Summer), Vol. 1, p. 4.

But even in recent periods of expansion such as 1977, levels of unemployment have been quite high. As a further point, unemployment rates have varied greatly by race, sex, and age. Young workers, women, and blacks suffer the highest unemployment rates in the United States.

Category	All Workers, 16 and Over	Young Workers, 16–19 Years
All	9.4%	23.6%
All whites	8.4	—
All blacks	15.4	—
All men	8.4	—
All women	10.2	—
White men	7.6	20.8
White women	9.4	21.4
Black men	15.4	42.8
Black women	15.5%	43.0%

SOURCE: U.S. Department of Labor, *Employment and Earnings* (July 1975).

Conservative economists and geographers in the United States tend to blame the unemployed for unemployment. For example, they may claim that anyone who really wants a job can get one. Radicals do not believe that workers are themselves responsible for unemployment. They say unemployment occurs when saving is greater than planned investment, and that it is an unsolvable problem within capitalism.

Table 2.6 illustrates for a number of developed and underdeveloped countries the percentage share of economically active males by industrial sectors. Note the low share in primary employment in developed countries. In the underdeveloped world, the proportion in primary activities is high, and employment in the tertiary sector often exceeds the secondary.

TABLE 2.6 Percentage distribution of economically active males by industrial sectors (about 1970)

Country	Primary	Secondary	Tertiary
Developed:			
England and Wales	3.27	53.12	43.61
United States	5.17	40.13	54.70
Australia	8.87	40.41	50.72
Underdeveloped:			
Argentina	18.49	32.58	48.93
India	69.84	12.22	17.94
Tanzania	85.33	4.23	10.44

SOURCE: *United Nations Demographic Yearbook,* 1973.

Economic growth alters labor force composition. The changing composition of the labor force in the United States and New York State are shown in Figure 2.12. As the economy grew, the proportion of the labor force in secondary and tertiary activities increased at the expense of primary activities, particularly agriculture. New York State experienced a drop in its primary sector and a rise in its secondary and tertiary sectors about fifty years earlier than the United States as a whole. The high level of employment in the tertiary sector in New York State probably will be attained by the United States as a whole in the years ahead.

Income Perhaps the most familiar index to measure a population's relative development, its economic well-being, and capacity to consume is per capita income. Table 2.7 shows the enormous disparity among major regions. In 1975 the wealth produced by North America alone was about one and one-half times greater than the combined gross national products of the Middle East, South America, Central America, Africa, and Asia, which had more than eleven times the population of North America. There is also inequality within the Third World: in 1975 Asia had a gross national product of $556 billion for nearly two billion people; Africa, $163 billion for 414 million people; and Central and South America, $327 billion for 319 million people.

The geographical distribution of the world's wealth in relation to population is shown in Figure 2.13. The income map depicts the twin peaks of North America and Western Europe, each encircled by a steep gradient merging into an essentially homogeneous region representing the more remote economic backwaters of the world. This pattern contrasts with the population map where the highest numbers are located in South and Southeast Asia.

Futurologists have predicted that the income gap between the developed and the underdeveloped world will widen from the present ratio of 12:1 to around 18:1 by the year 2000 (Kahn and Wiener, 1967). Data in Table 2.8 indicate that the

Population Composition

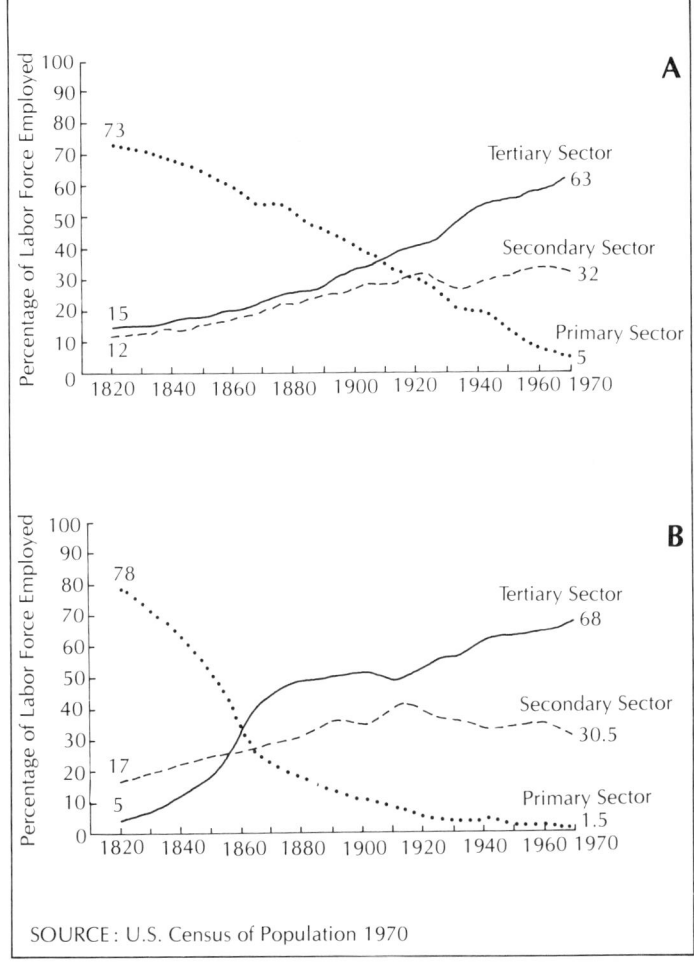

FIGURE 2.12 Economic sector—employment relationships for (A) the United States and (B) New York State. SOURCE: *U.S. Bureau of the Census.*

disparity in income between developed and underdeveloped countries is not just enormous and becoming larger but virtually inevitable. The table shows that the absolute gap in per capita income between the United States and three Latin American countries with different rates of growth is widening.

However well income per capita may seem to reflect international disparities, its use should be treated with caution. First, it fails to indicate ways in which incomes are distributed through the strata of societies. In most underdeveloped countries wealth is concentrated in a small elite. Even within developed countries major inequities in the internal distribution of income exist. A second problem is that variations exist in ways countries measure income per capita. Finally, the per capita income indicator fails to take into account economic activities outside national monetized accounting systems in underdeveloped countries. Activities such as street trading, which may play an important role in the lives of many people in the Third World, never find their way into national accounting systems. For these reasons, per capita income has only limited utility, and often serves only to publicize the problem of poverty.

TABLE 2.7 Gross National Product, by major regions, 1975

Region or Country	GNP Per Capita (US $)	GNP (US $000 Millions)	Percentage of Total GNP	Population (Millions)	Percentage of Total Population
North America	7100	1678	28	236	6
Oceania	4480	94	1	21	1
Japan	4450	496	8	112	3
Europe (excluding USSR)	3830	1971	32	515	13
USSR	2550	649	11	254	7
Middle East	1990	153	2	77	2
South America	1050	224	4	213	5
Central America	970	103	2	106	3
Africa	390	163	3	414	10
Asia (excluding Japan)	280	556	9	1957	50

SOURCE: *World Bank Atlas,* The World Bank, Washington, D.C., 1977.

TABLE 2.8 The widening gap between the United States and selected Latin American countries

	1974 Income per Capita (US $)	Average Annual Growth Rate (1970–75)	1975 Income per Capita (US $)
U.S.	6680	1.6	7120
Haiti	170	1.5	190
Absolute Gap	6510		6930
U.S.	6680	1.6	7120
Brazil	940	6.2	1030
Absolute Gap	5740		6090
U.S.	6680	1.6	7120
Chile	1070	−2.7	990
Absolute Gap	5610		6230

SOURCE: *World Bank Atlas,* The World Bank, Washington, D.C., 1977.

Migration

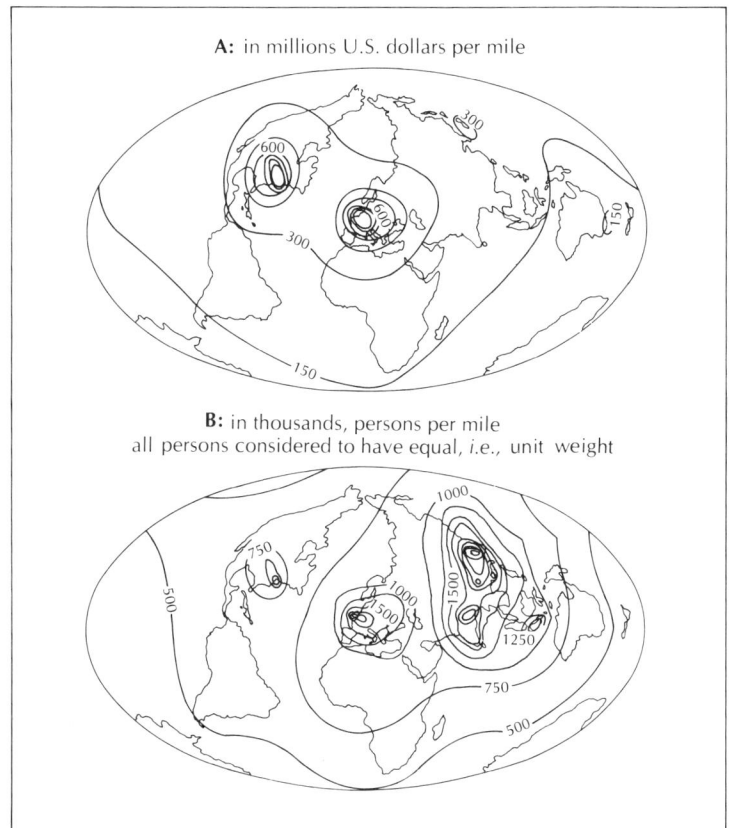

FIGURE 2.13 (A) World income potential and (B) World population potential for the early 1960s. SOURCE: William Warntz, 1965, *Macrogeography and Income Fronts*. Philadelphia: Regional Science Institute, pp. 92, 111, Figs. 19, 24.

Migration

The main *components of population change are migration and natural change*. Population growth is influenced by differences between birth and death rates, and differences between immigration and emigration. The first component to be considered is human migration.

Geographers disagree about the meaning of *migration*, though many define it as *a movement involving a change of residence of substantial duration*. On the basis of this arbitrary definition, we consider permanent migrations of say, a year or more, and exclude from this discussion temporary movements of tourists, seasonal movements of people with more than one home and daily movements of commuters.

THE WIDENING GAP

Simple arithmetic shows why developed and underdeveloped countries continue to diverge. Assume there is a developed country with an income of $800 per capita and an underdeveloped country with an income of $25 per capita, both growing at the same rate, say 5 percent per annum. What is the effect after one year?

Per Capita Income

	Year 1		Year 2
Developed Country	$800.00	plus 5% growth	$840.00
Underdeveloped Country	25.00	plus 5% growth	26.25
Absolute Gap	$775.00		$813.75

The initial gap of $775 widens to $813.75 after one year. The *absolute* gap between the developed and the underdeveloped country would continue to diverge, for a while at least, even if the underdeveloped country managed to grow at twice the rate of the developed country.

Per Capita Income

	Year 1	Year 2
Developed Country	$800.00 plus 2.5% growth	$820.00
Underdeveloped Country	25.00 plus 5% growth	26.25
Absolute Gap	$775.00	$793.75

In this situation, the *relative* gap between the two countries has narrowed, but the absolute gap continues to widen. Of course, if the underdeveloped country continued to grow at twice the rate of the developed, the absolute income gap would eventually be eliminated.

One can argue that the satisfaction of increased income for an individual is more important than the gap among people. An added hundred dollars, which an American might regard as "mad" money to be spent on impulse, would make an immense difference to the livelihood of a farmer in an underdeveloped country.

As a further point, concern about gaps between developed and underdeveloped countries is restricted mainly to academics, intellectuals, and some Third World governments who have a high degree of contact with the rich. Very few peasants, workers, or business persons in Africa, Asia or Latin America care much about gaps. The major objective of most Third World people is to increase their own standard of living.

Migration

> ### INCOME DISTRIBUTION IN THE UNITED STATES
>
> The United States Census Bureau conducts an annual survey of 47,000 representative households to determine how much income they received in the previous year. It considers the survey more reliable than the full-scale decennial census. Although the annual survey is the basis for much that is written about U.S. income distribution, it does contain many biases. In particular, data for upper income groups are inaccurate for at least two reasons: (1) the rich are reticent to disclose their incomes; and (2) the Census Bureau assumes that no one earns more than $99,999.
>
> Some of the results of the March 1976 survey and earlier years are shown in the table. The most significant points to be derived from the table are: (1) the remarkable stability of income distribution; (2) the richest fifth receive over 40 percent of all income; and (3) the poorest fifth receive less than one-tenth as much as the most affluent group.
>
> Percentage share of total income received by each fifth of all families and unrelated individuals, 1950–1975
>
> | Group | 1950 | 1960 | 1970 | 1975 |
> |---|---|---|---|---|
> | Richest Fifth | 44.9 | 44.0 | 44.1 | 44.5 |
> | Fourth Fifth | 24.1 | 24.7 | 24.7 | 29.9 |
> | Middle Fifth | 17.3 | 17.6 | 17.2 | 16.7 |
> | Second Fifth | 10.6 | 10.6 | 10.3 | 10.3 |
> | Poorest Fifth | 3.1 | 3.2 | 3.6 | 3.6 |
>
> Note: In 1975 the poorest fifth included families and unrelated individuals earning less than $4,500. The second fifth reached up to $8,700, the middle fifth to $13,500, and the fourth fifth to $19,800.
>
> SOURCE: *U.S. Census Bureau Report P-60, 1977, No. 105, p. 57.*

Migration Process

Migratory Selection The migratory process is selective: some elements of the population are more migratory than others. Major population characteristics influencing migration are age, sex, marital status, occupation, and educational attainment. As a generalization, young people, unmarried persons, and low-skill workers are the most mobile in the United States.

Causes of Migration The causes of migration are sometimes described by a simple *"push-pull" model*. According to this model, regions or countries of emigration exert a "push" and areas of immigration a "pull." For example, "push" factors, such as population pressure, shortage of land, and lack of employment opportunities in rural areas are commonly advanced as the main reasons for migration to cities in underdeveloped countries. "Pull" factors, such as the attraction of "bright lights," draw migrants toward the city for economic and personal reasons such as improved living conditions and life chances.

Terry McGee argued that the "push-pull" hypothesis is not an adequate explanation for the process of rural-to-urban migration. In the Third World context, he said that it is "a condition of society which is responsible for increased mobility—increased educational facilities and improved communications make the rural dweller far more aware of the urban environment" (1971:116).

Barriers to Migration. While political restrictions and characteristics of potential migrants may prevent migration, the most important barrier is distance. In general terms, the propensity to migrate between region i and region j is a direct

---

RAVENSTEIN AND THE "LAWS" OF MIGRATION

In the late nineteenth century, E. G. Ravenstein discussed the "Laws of Migration." These "laws" or generalizations are

1. *Migration and distance:*
   "The great body of our migrants only proceed a short distance" and "migrants enumerated in a certain center of absorption will ... grow less [as distance from the center increases]" (1885:198–9).

   "Migrants proceeding long distances generally go by preference to one of the great centers of commerce and industry" (1885:199).

2. *Migration by stages:*
   "The inhabitants of the country immediately surrounding a town of rapid growth flock into it; the gaps thus left in the rural population are filled up by migrants from more remote districts, until the attractive force of one of our rapidly growing cities makes its influence felt, step by step, to the most remote corner of the kingdom" (1885:199).

   "The process of dispersion is the inverse of that of absorption, and exhibits similar features" (1885:199).

3. *Stream and counterstream:*
   "Each main [stream] of migration produces a compensating [counterstream]" (1885:199).

4. *Urban-rural differences in propensity to migrate:*
   "The natives of towns are less migratory than those of the rural parts of the country" (1885:199).

5. *Predominance of females among short-distance migrants:*
   "Females appear to predominate among short-journey migrants" (1889:288).

Ravenstein's "laws of migration" have been often cited and sometimes challenged by scholars, but in nearly 100 years few additional generalizations on the migration process have been advanced.

Migration

function of their populations and an inverse function of the distance separating them. Mathematically the relationship is given by the following expression:

$$M_{ij} = \frac{P_i P_j}{d_{ij}}$$

where M_{ij} = migrants going between region i and region j.

P_i, P_j = size of population in region i and region j.

d = distance separating regions i and j.

The formula is called a "gravity model," since its origins are found in Newtonian physics. In practice it is customary to modify the model to fit empirical data. For example, we may need to consider intervening employment opportunities between place of origin and destination.

Consequences of Migration Beyond varied beneficial and harmful social and economic consequences, the effects of migration are demographic. Migration from region A to region B causes the population of B to increase and of A to fall. But because of migratory selection, the effects are more complicated. If migrants are young adults, their departure will increase the average age, raise the death rate, and lower the birth rate in region A. In the region of reception, B, the exact opposite will be true. Thus A's loss and B's gain would be accentuated in the short run. The long run effects of migration are much more complex.

Patterns of Migration

Given the great importance of national boundaries and the availability of data on a national scale, geographers consider migration as either external (international) or internal (within a nation). They subdivide external migration into inter- and intra-continental, and internal migrations into inter-regional, rural-urban, and inter-metropolitan. International migrations, so important in the past, are now far exceeded by internal population movements, expecially to and between cities.

Intercontinental Migration The trans-oceanic exodus of Europeans and the Atlantic slave trade are spectacular examples of intercontinental migration. In the five centuries before the economic depression of the 1930s, these population movements contributed strongly to a redistribution of the world's population.

Between 1451 and 1870, about nine million slaves were hauled by Europeans into the sparsely inhabited Americas. The importance of the so called "triangular trade" between Europe, Africa, and the Americas can hardly be exaggerated, especially for British economic development. Africans were purchased with British manufactured goods. They were transported to plantations where they undertook production of sugar, cotton, indigo, molasses, and other tropical products. The processing of these products created new British industries. Plantation owners and slaves provided a new market for British manufacturers. The profits obtained helped further to finance Britain's industrial revolution.

The Atlantic slave trade, however, was dwarfed by the voluntary intercontinental migration of Europeans. Mass emigration began slowly in the 1820s and peaked on the eve of the First World War, when the annual flow reached 1.5 million. At first, sources of flow were from densely-populated Northwestern Europe, and later from poor and oppressed parts of Southern and Eastern Europe. Between 1840–1930 at least 50 million Europeans emigrated. The main destination was North America, but the wave of migration spilled over into Australia and New Zealand, Latin America, Asia, and Southern Africa. These new lands were important for Europe's economic development. They offered outlets for population pressure and provided new sources of foodstuffs and raw materials, markets for manufactured goods, and openings for capital investment.

Since the Second World War, the pattern of intercontinental migration has changed. Instead of heavy migatory flow from Europe to the New World, the tide of migrants is now overwhelmingly from underdeveloped to developed countries. Reverse migration into industrial Europe and continued migration to North America is caused partly by widening technological and economic inequality, and by rapid rates of population increase in the underdeveloped world. Emigration to the developed world has adverse effects on underdeveloped countries, since many of the migrants are among the most skilled and educated members of the population. Between 1961 and 1970, 53,616 scientists, engineers and physicians from underdeveloped countries took residence in the United States alone. In 1970, the estimated income transferred through the "brain drain" to the United States amounted to roughly $3.7 billion. The same year, the United States total official development assistance to underdeveloped countries amounted to $3.1 billion. In this international transfer India was one of the biggest donor countries and the U.S. the biggest recipient country (UNCTAD Study TD/B/AC 11/25).

Intracontinental Migration An important aspect of contemporary intracontinental migration is *labor migration*. In recent years the most prosperous industrial countries of Europe (and North America) have attracted workers from the agrarian periphery. France and Germany are the main receiving countries of intracontinental European labor migration. France attracts workers especially from Spain, Italy and North Africa, and Germany draws a large influx of workers from Italy, Greece, and Turkey. Migrant workers from southern Europe usually have low skills and perform jobs unacceptable to native workers. Most migrants are young males and they leave their families at home for an initial period and send money to support them. Eventually, a high proportion of migrant workers (75 percent of Greek migrant workers during the 1960s) decide to settle permanently in the European core area and bring their families to join them.

The system of extra-territorial migrant labor also exists in the underdeveloped world, most notably in Africa. African laborers move great distances to work on mines and plantations, usually on contract for a stated period. Conservative estimates place five million people on the move as migrant laborers each year in Africa south of the Sahara. In West Africa, the direction of labor migration is from the interior to coastal cities and export agricultural areas. In East Africa, agricultural estates, especially in Kenya, attract extra-territorial labor. In Southern Africa, migrants focus on the mining-urban-industrial zone that extends from Southern Zaire in the north, through Zambia's Copperbelt and Rhodesia's Great Dyke, to South Africa's Witwatersrand in the South.

Migration

Workers bring baskets of freshly picked cotton to a collection point on the plot of a tenant farmer in the Sudan's Gezira plains, between the White and the Blue Nile Rivers. Each year, several hundred thousand migrant workers find employment on holdings in the area during the picking season. SOURCE: *United Nations.*

Interregional Migration Colonizing migration and population drift are two types of interregional migration. Examples of colonizing migration include the spontaneous trek westward in nineteenth century America and planned eastward movement in the Soviet Union after 1925. In 1926, Russia beyond the Urals contained a population of 27 million. Today there are some 60 million people east of the Urals. Russian colonization stimulated economic development of Siberia and the Soviet Far East, and it strongly affected ethnic composition.

General drifts of population occur in almost every country, and they tend to accentuate the unevenness of population distribution. Since World War I there has been a drift of black Americans from the rural South to the cities of the nation's industrial heartland. During the 1960s in the United States, there was net out-migration from the center of the country to both coasts and a slow shift of population to the "Sun Belt" (Figure 2.14). States which gained migrants generally had two or more of the following factors working favorably for them: climatic attractiveness, recent urban growth, accessibility to markets, and momentum from an initial advantage of industrial employment.

Rural-Urban Migration The most important type of internal migration is rural-urban migration, usually in response to economic motives. The relocation of farm workers to industrial urban centers was a major characteristic of developed countries during the nineteenth century. Since the Second World War, migration to large urban centers has been a striking feature of nearly all underdeveloped coun-

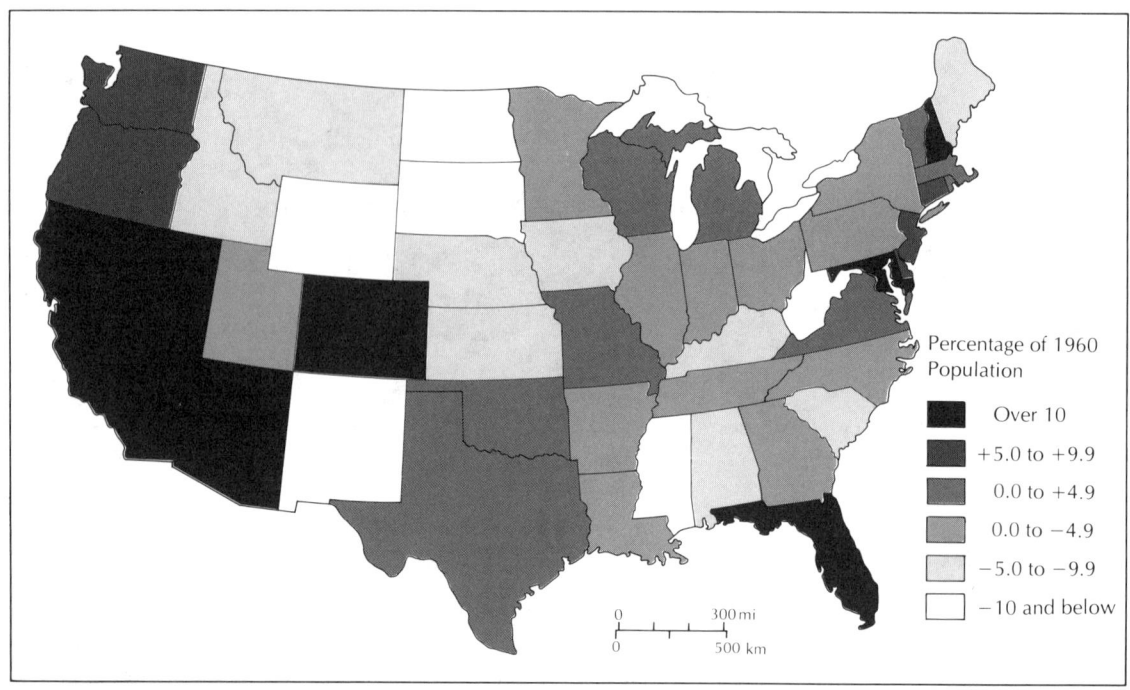

FIGURE 2.14 United States: net migration by states, 1960–1970.
SOURCE: *County and City Data Book,* 1972.

TABLE 2.9 Estimates of migrants as a percent of recent population increases

City	Period	Total Population Increase (Thousands)	Migrants as a Percentage of Total Population Increase
Abidjan	1955–63	129	76
Djarkata	1961–68	1,528	59
Bombay	1951–61	1,207	52
Lagos	1952–62	393	75
Nairobi	1961–69	162	50
São Paulo	1960–67	2,543	68
Seoul	1955–65	1,697	63

SOURCE: International Bank for Reconstruction and Development, *Urbanization-Sector Working Paper,* 1972.

tries. Burgeoning capital cities, in particular, have functioned as magnets attracting migrants in search of the "good life" and employment (Table 2.9).

Intermetropolitan Migration In highly urbanized developed countries like the United States, rural-urban migrations are being replaced by inter-urban migrations. Job mobility and ease of transportation are major determinants of inter-city migration.

Population Growth

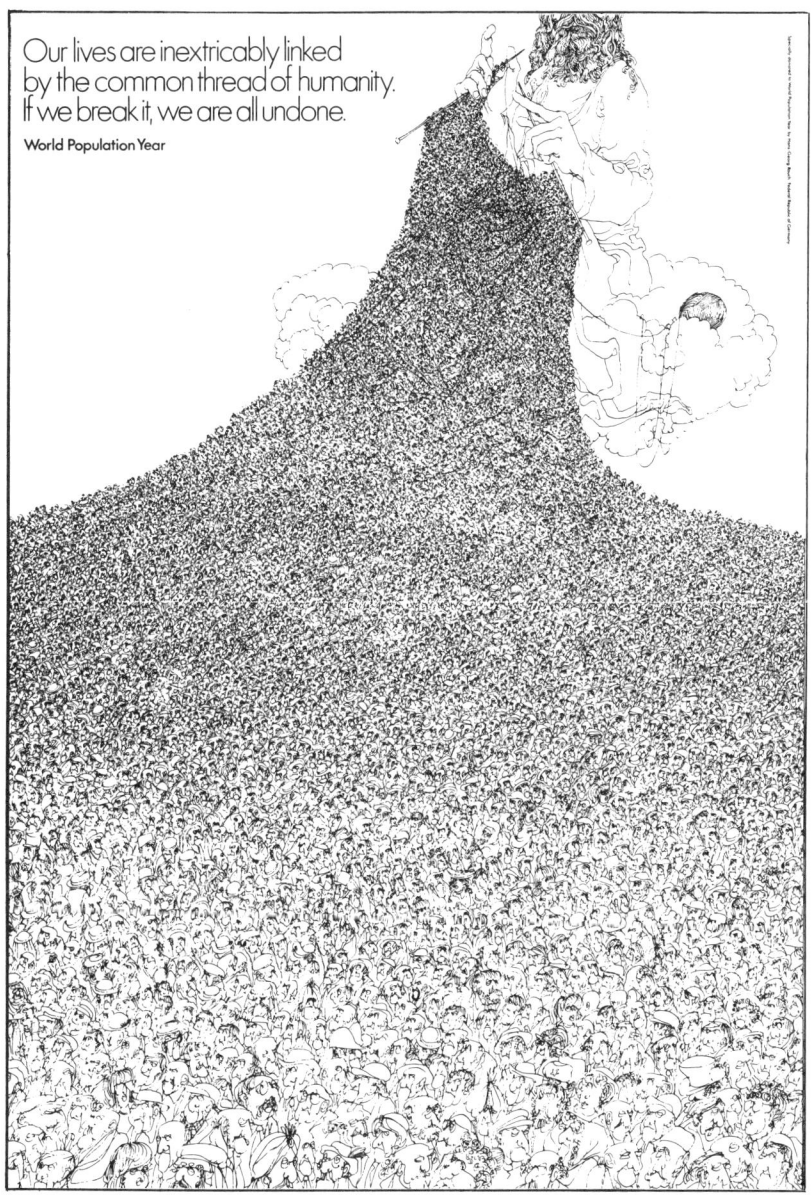

One of several posters prepared to advertise World Population Year in 1974. SOURCE: *United Nations*.

The principal force affecting world population distribution today is *natural increase,* the excess of births over deaths. Population is increasing at a rapid rate. Every three years the earth has an additional population the size of the United States. The major impetus to world population growth comes from underdeveloped countries where

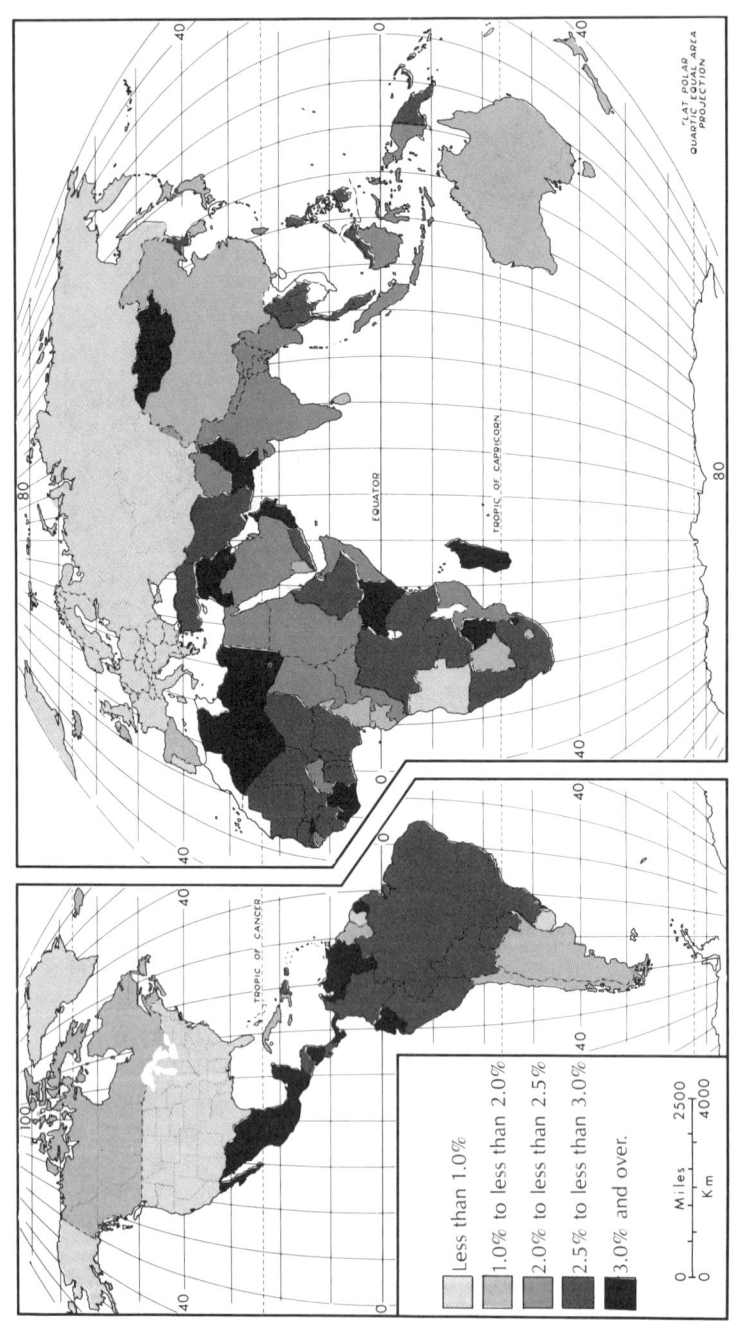

FIGURE 2.15 Average annual population growth rates, 1970–75.
SOURCE: *World Bank Atlas*, The World Bank, Washington D.C., 1977.

Population Growth

nearly 75 percent of the world's population lives (Figure 2.15). By proclaiming 1974 World Population Year, the United Nations expressed concern about the human consequences of continued geometric rates of growth. This concern originated primarily in an elite who have an interest in stabilizing a resource system that is under severe stress.

Rates of Growth

The current rapid rate of world population growth is a recent phenomenon. It took from the emergence of humankind until 1850 for population to reach one billion (Figure 2.16). The second billion came along in 80 years (1850–1930), the third in 30 years (1931–1960), and the fourth in only 16 years (1960–1976). If present trends continue, the fifth billion will be added in only a decade.

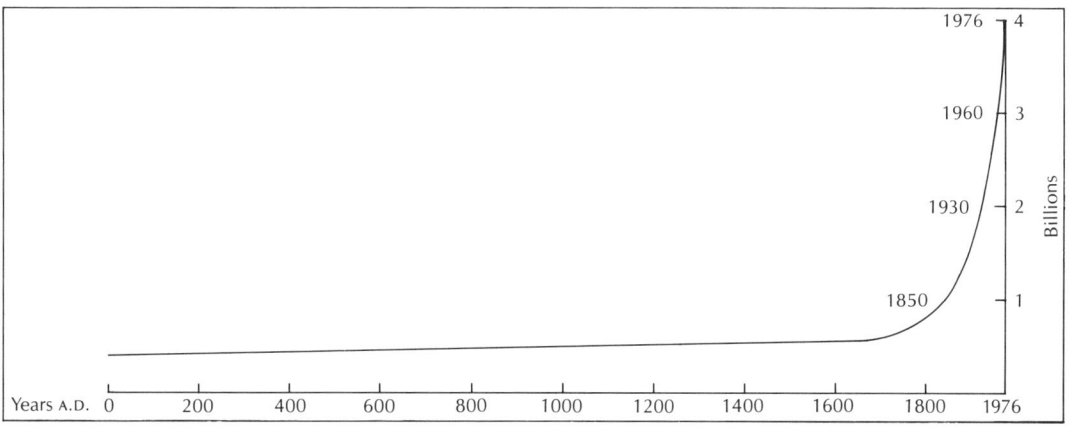

FIGURE 2.16 Arithmetic growth curve for world population from A.D. 1 to the present. SOURCE: *Population Bulletin*, 18, No. 1, 1962. The Population Reference Bureau, Inc., Washington D.C.

The graph in Figure 2.16 is plotted on an arithmetic scale, and is somewhat misleading. If the graph were to originate when people first inhabited the earth, say two million years ago, then it would be over 50 meters long. Most of the graph would be flat, and only the last seven centimeters would show the *population explosion* of the last 300 years.

If, instead of an arithmetic scale, human numbers are plotted on a log-log scale, which describes rates of population change, population growth is seen as occurring in three surges rather than one (Figure 2.17). Deevey (1960) argued that these surges related to revolutions which increased the earth's capacity to support large numbers of additional people. These revolutions are the toolmaking or cultural revolution, the agricultural or neolithic revolution, and the scientific-industrial revolution.

We can draw quite different conclusions from a study of Figures 2.16 and 2.17. Figure 2.16 suggests continued rapid increases in population numbers. By

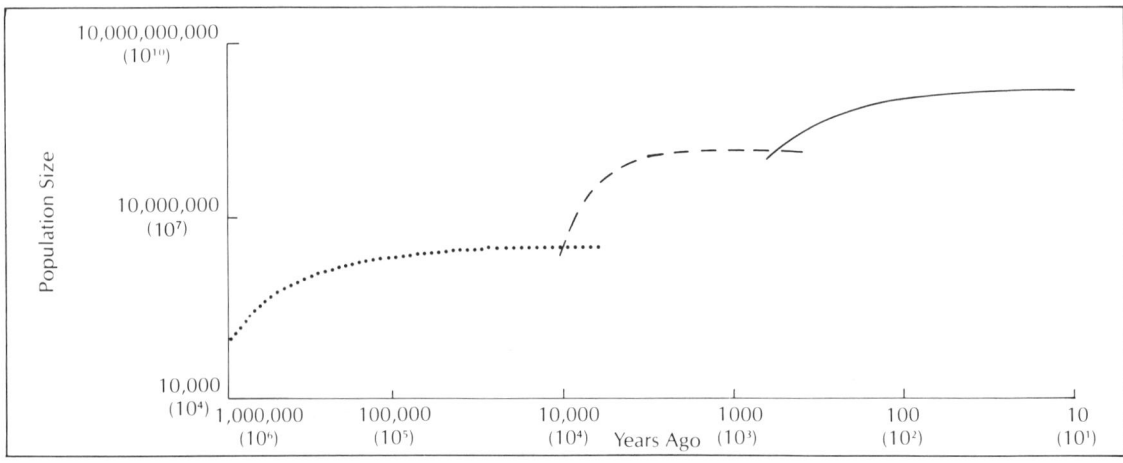

FIGURE 2.17 Logarithmic growth curve for world population from 1,000,000 years ago. SOURCE: Edward S. Deevey, Jr., 1960, "The Human Population," *Scientific American*, September, p. 52.

contrast, Figure 2.17 suggests that population tapers off after each revolution, and therefore, implies an eventual slowing down of current population growth rates.

To measure ways populations change size we need some simple indices. The crude *birth rate* is the number of babies born per thousand people per year and the crude *death rate* is the number of deaths per thousand people per year. For example, the United States' birth rate in 1970 was 18.2, and the death rate was 9.4. During that year, the growth rate was 18.2 minus 9.4 or 8.8 per thousand. This is a percent rate of natural increase of 0.88.

Population grows at an exponential rate, just like money earning compound interest in the bank. At 0.88 percent annual increase, the doubling time for the United States' population is 87 years. As growth rates increase, doubling times decrease sharply. At 2 percent, the rate of world increase, doubling time is 35 years. The rate of growth in Mexico, Venezuela, and Colombia is 3.4 percent, and the doubling time is 21 years. Kuwait's annual rate of population growth is 8.2 percent. The doubling rate in this small Middle Eastern country is an incredible nine years. Table 2.10 illustrates the relationship between percent annual increase and the doubling time. In general, it is possible to approximate the doubling time for a population by dividing the constant annual growth rate into the number 70.

TABLE 2.10 Annual percent increase and the doubling time

Annual Percent Increase	Doubling Time (Years)
0.5	139
0.8	87
1.0	70
2.0	35
3.0	23
4.0	17

The poor Andean Indian woman in the photograph is breaking up the soil in the field before planting potatoes. Latin America has the fastest growing population in the world. Would a slower increase in the number of people result in better living conditions for the masses in Latin America or in the Third World as a whole? SOURCE: *FAO*.

Malthus' Theory of Population

Much attention has been paid to problems of population growth, and various theories have been advanced. In Western social science, the most frequently discussed theory is that of Thomas R. Malthus, who pulished his first *Essay on the Principle of Population,* in 1798. He asserted that population, when unchecked, increases in a geometric ratio (2, 4, 8, 16), but subsistence increases only in an arithmetic ratio (2, 4, 6, 8). On the basis of this proposition, he concluded that for a population living in a specific region and drawing food supplies therefrom, the *law of diminishing returns* eventually reduces productivity per head. In classical economics this principle is regarded as *absolute* and states that additional applications of labor and capital to a given area of land will, in general, increase production, but not in proportion to the increased application of labor and capital. Diminishing per capita production which is bad for the capitalist continues until a new equilibrium is established. Excess population is removed by what Malthus termed the positive checks of disease, famine, and war. Later he admitted there is an escape from the deadly equilibrium: moral restraint before and moderation during marriage.

Malthus' *Essay* had a social purpose. It supported the interests of landlords and industrialists and rejected recommendations to help lower classes escape the positive checks. Malthus argued that aiding the poor results in a reduction in the living standards of all members of society, and a decline in the incentive to work. He also argued that by providing welfare to "a part of society that cannot be considered as the most valuable part diminishes the shares that would otherwise belong to more

EXPONENTIAL GROWTH AND GROWTH OF WORLD POPULATION

A simple example of exponential growth is the case of the benevolent employer, who promises to double a worker's pay each day for a month (30 days). A worker's wage is one cent for the first day. How much will the employer pay a worker on day 30? The employer will pay a worker two cents for the second day, four cents for the third day, over $1 for the seventh day, over $300 for the fourteenth day, and over $10 million for the last day of the month. Clearly, exponential growth is a very dynamic process, as the graph of world population increase illustrates.

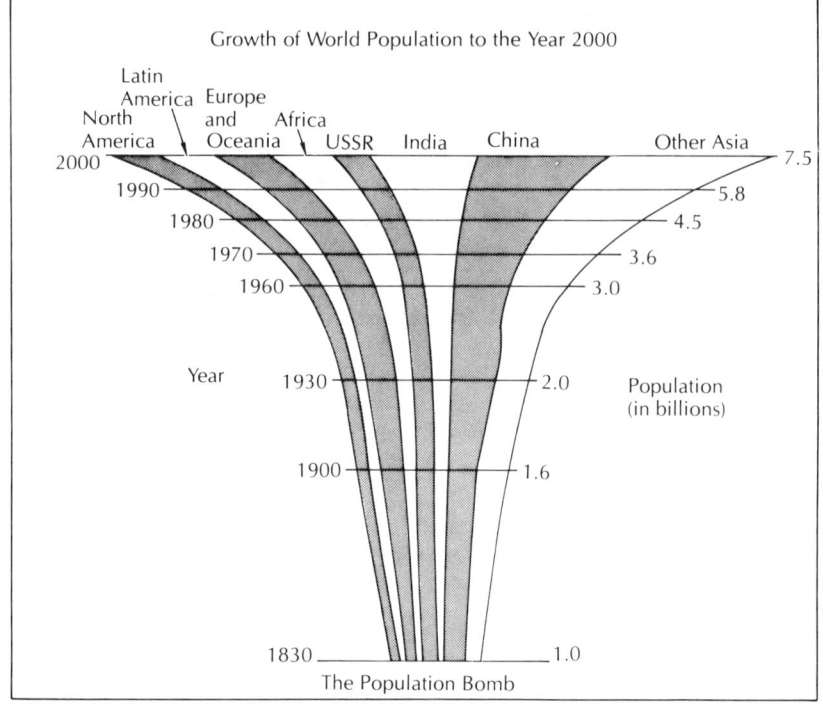

SOURCE: U.S. Department of State.

industrious and worthy members, and thus forces more to become dependent" (1970:97).

From this Malthus went on to say:

> Hard as it may appear in individual instances, dependent poverty ought to be held disgraceful. Such a stimulus seems to be absolutely necessary to promote the happiness of the great mass of mankind, and every general attempt to weaken this stimulus, however benevolent its apparent intention will always defeat its own purpose . . . I feel no doubt whatever that the parish laws of England have contributed to raise the price of provisions

THOMAS ROBERT MALTHUS (1766–1834)

The eighteenth century had been an age of very great optimism in Western Europe. Intellectuals predicted the end of human want and suffering. They believed a large population was a basis of national strength. By the end of the eighteenth century a reaction occurred. It was a period of high food prices, of human misery brought on by the agricultural and industrial revolutions. What was the solution to problems of poverty in town and country?

The solution was provided by Malthus. He was an English country gentleman of independent means. He was educated at Cambridge, where he read mathematics, and graduated with first class honors. After graduation he took Holy Orders, and in 1796 he became a curate of a parish church. In 1804 he accepted a position as professor of history and political economy at the East India Company's College at Haileybury, where he remained until his death.

Malthus traced the causes of poverty not to the revolutionary changes industrial urbanization had brought, but to large impersonal forces over which governments had little or no control. The problem of the poor was moral. He said "food is necessary to the existence of man" and that "the passion between the sexes is necessary and will remain nearly in its present state." These facts led to the principle that "the power of population is infinitely greater than the power in the earth to produce subsistence for man." He argued that an increase in population inevitably brought an increase in poverty, and that the balance of nature was maintained by national disasters.

Thomas Robert Malthus. SOURCE: *The Bettmann Archive, Inc.*

Malthus' principle of population was a dismal theory for the poor, but a great doctrine for the wealthy, because it gave them the best of reasons for doing nothing about a serious problem. Malthus insisted that the causes of poverty were not rooted in the structure of society or in the distribution of income. The poor were responsible for their own fate. All they had to do to improve their condition was to practice moral restraint. Malthus, a deeply religious man, considered artificial birth control theologically unacceptable.

Malthus theory of population was a major building block of classical economics. It pointed out a key relationship for improving human welfare under capitalism. If living standards were to be improved, production had to increase faster than population. By intensifying and extending the field of capitalism in the nineteenth century, Europe and North America succeeded in achieving that relationship.

FOOD IN A WINDOW BOX

If there were no principle of diminishing returns, then, according to classical economic theory, enough food for the world's population could be grown in a window box. To illustrate how this can be done, suppose that the size of the window box is fixed in amount and that labor, seeds, and fertilizer are variable in amount. A unit of each variable input to the soil yields five kilograms of food. A second application of the variable input brings in another five kilograms. By the tenth application, the window box is producing at least fifty kilograms. And, so it goes on. Thus, under conditions of constant or increasing returns the world's food supply could be grown in a window box. But classical economists argue that diminishing returns operate in the real world: variable inputs (machines and workers) become progressively less efficient or profitable and fixed resources become more and more crowded.

---

and to lower the real price of labour. They have therefore contributed to impoverish that class of people whose only possession is their labour. It is also difficult to suppose that they have not powerfully contributed to generate that carelessness and want of frugality observable among the poor, so contrary to the disposition to be remarked among petty tradesmen and small farmers. The labouring poor, to use a vulgar expression, seem always to live from hand to mouth. Their present wants employ their whole attention, and they seldom think of the future. Even when they have an opportunity of saving, they seldom exercise it, but all that is beyond their present necessities goes, generally speaking, to the ale-house. The poor laws of England may therefore be said to diminish both the power and the will to save among the common people, and thus to weaken one of the strongest incentives to sobriety and industry, and consequently to happiness (1970:98).

Thus, according to Malthus, the best thing to do about misery and poverty among the masses is absolutely nothing. By contrast to the rich, who practice prudent sexual habits out of fear of a decline in their station of life, the poor breed like rabbits when given half a chance. The provision of a system of welfare is all that would be needed for the poor to breed imprudently.

Marx and the Population-Resources Problem

Malthus' principle of population was endorsed by Ricardo, but criticized by Marx. Marx argued that the works of Malthus and Ricardo were political tracts that defended the interests of landlords and industrial entrepreneurs.

According to David Harvey,

> Marx does not talk about a population problem but a poverty and human exploitation problem. He replaces Malthus' concept of over-population by the concept of a relative surplus population. He replaces the inevitability of the "pressure of population on the means of subsistence" (accepted by both Malthus and Ricardo) by an historically specific and necessary pressure of labor supply on the means of employment produced internally within the capitalist mode of production. Marx's distinctive method permitted this reformulation of the population-resources problem, and put him in a position from which he could envisage a transformation of society that would eliminate poverty and misery rather than accept its inevitability (1974:269).

Harvey (1974) applied a Marxist orientation to the population-resources problem. First, he defined the concepts of "subsistence," "resources" and "scarcity" in Marxist terms. *Subsistence* is relative, not absolute. It is defined internally to a mode of production and changes over time. *Resources* are technical and cultural appraisals of nature, defined at a particular stage of development. *Scarcity* is social and cultural in origin, and not something inherent in nature. In the Western world, the *social organization of scarcity* results from a market economy which is based on different types of *classes* who employ *private property* concepts to exclude other classes from obtaining *equal access* to *wealth* in general. Using these definitions, Harvey proceeded to analyze a simple sentence:

> "Overpopulation arises because of the scarcity of resources available for meeting the subsistence needs of the mass of the population." If we substitute our definitions into this sentence we get: "There are too many people in the world because the particular ends we have in view (together with the form of social organization we have) and the materials available in nature, that we have the will and the way to use, are not sufficient to provide us with those things to which we are accustomed." Out of such a sentence all kinds of possibilities can be extracted:
>
> (1) we can change the ends we have in mind and alter the social organization of scarcity;
>
> (2) we can change our technical and cultural appraisals of nature;
>
> (3) we can change our views concerning the things to which we are accustomed;
>
> (4) we can seek to alter our numbers.
>
> A real concern with environmental issues demands that all of these options be examined in relation to each other. To say that there are too many people in the world amounts to saying that we have not the imagination, will, or ability to do anything about propositions (1), (2), and (3). In fact (1) is very difficult to do anything about because it involves the

replacement of the market exchange system as a working mode of economic integration; proposition (2) has always been the great hope for resolving our difficulties; and we have never thought too coherently about (3) particularly as it relates to the maintenance of an effective demand in capitalist economies (nobody appears to have calculated what the effects of much reduced personal consumption will have on capital accumulation and employment). I will risk the generalization that nothing of consequence can be done about (1) and (3) without dismantling and replacing the capitalist market exchange economy. If we are reluctant to contemplate such an alternative and if (2) is not performing its function too well, then we have to go to (4). Much of the debate in the western world focusses on (4), but in a society in which all four options can be integrated with each other, it must appear facile to discuss environmental problems in terms of naturally arising scarcities or overpopulation. The trouble with focusing exclusively on the control of population numbers is that it has certain political implications. Ideas about environment, population, and resources are not neutral. They are political in origin and have political effects. Historically it is depressing to look at the use made of the kind of sentence we have just analyzed. Once connotations of absolute limits come to surround the concepts of resource, scarcity, and subsistence, then an absolute limit is set for population. And what are the political implications (given these connotations) of saying there is "overpopulation" or a "scarcity of resources"? The meaning can all too quickly be established. Somebody, somewhere, is redundant, and there is not enough to go round (1974:272-273).

The Demographic Transition

Most Western theorists do not adopt Marx's conception of the population-resources relationship. They tend to agree with Malthus' assessment of the trends of population increase and food production, and hope that the poor countries can reduce their fertility rates. This hope is expressed in the theory of the *demographic transition* which is an idealized sequence of changes that took place in European demographic patterns during the last 200 years. According to this theory, countries are supposed to pass through four distinct phases as they undergo economic development (see Figure 2.18 and box).

High Stationary Phase Population grows slowly, if at all. It is kept relatively stable by a combination of high birth rates and high fluctuating death rates. Variable death rates are caused by the effects of epidemics and variations in food supplies. This phase characterized Europe before the Industrial Revolution and describes some contemporary ethnic groups in Africa, Asia, and Latin America.

Early Expanding Phase Death rates fall and birth rates remain high. The result is a "population explosion." Reductions in mortality are caused by improvements in nutrition, sanitation, public health, and medicine. The phase began in Europe and North America in the late eighteenth and early nineteenth century. Before the start of the transition, average life expectancy was only 35 years, but by 1970 it was 70 years or more in most advanced industrial nations. In the underdeveloped world the transition began later, often in the twentieth century. At present, most underdeveloped countries are in stages one and two of the demographic transition.

Population Growth

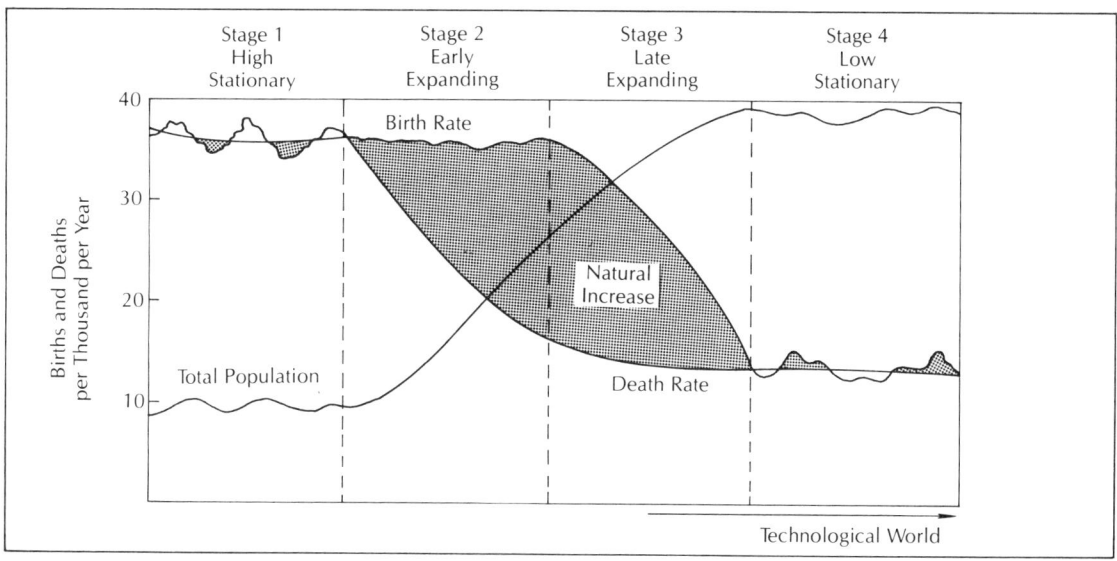

FIGURE 2.18 The demographic transition in idealized form. SOURCE: Peter Haggett, 1972, *Geography: A Modern Synthesis*. New York: Harper and Row, p. 174, Fig. 7–10.

TRANSITION THEORY AND DEVELOPED COUNTRIES

Transition theory is not a theory in the strict sense of the word. It provides a broad, macro-historical interpretation of demographic, social and economic events that took place in Europe, but it does not contain a specifiable and measurable mechanism of "causation" or a definite time scale.

European data show that a high level of economic development eventually established preconditions for a decline in fertility within marriage. Preconditions for declining fertility include an ability of individual couples: (1) to balance the pros and cons of having a child; (2) to perceive fertility decline as advantageous; and (3) to accept and use safe family planning techniques.

Transition theory, however, does not pinpoint threshold levels of economic development necessary for these preconditions to take hold. It fails to predict precisely the onset and pace of fertility decline. Moreover, it is unable to explain how fertility decline occurred in areas of slight economic development such as the highlands of Scotland or the Central Massif of France (Teitelbaum: 1975, 422).

Late Expanding Phase Birth rates decline. Population expansion slows down. In urban-industrial society, the changing status of women, delayed marriages, economic disadvantages of children, spread and acceptance of knowledge of birth control, and rising expectations depress the birth rate. In most of the contemporary underdeveloped world, where the process of industrialization is not advanced, declining mortality rates are not accompanied, as yet, by falling birth rates.

Low Stationary Phase Population increases slowly or is stable (zero population growth). Mortality and fertility rates are low. Death rates are relatively constant, but birth rates may vary. The demogrpahic transition from high to low fertility is complete. Countries of Western Europe, North America, and Oceania are entering the terminal phase of the demographic transition.

The demographic transition appears to be following a different course in underdeveloped countries than it took in the United States and Europe. Present

---

TRANSITION THEORY AND UNDERDEVELOPED COUNTRIES

Researchers now make only modest claims for transition theory as an explanation of demographic events in nineteenth-century Europe. The explanatory and predictive power of the theory is subject to additional questions when applied to the socio-economic and demographic circumstances of contemporary Africa, Asia, and Latin America.

The proposition that a high level of economic development will eventually lead to high reductions in fertility offers underdeveloped countries advice of doubtful validity. In particular, transition theory fails to answer two questions of policy significance:

1. Sufficiency: Will the moderate levels of [economic] development to which many developing countries can realistically aspire in the medium-term future be sufficient to establish the preconditions for "natural" fertility decline?
2. Timeliness: If such declines do occur, will they occur soon enough and at a pace rapid enough to compensate for the sharply increased pace of mortality decline and higher initial fertility levels of these countries as compared with transitional Europe? (Teitelbaum:1975, 424).

---

population increases are much faster than they were in nineteenth century America and Europe. Prior to the Second World War, underdeveloped countries had high birth rates, but their population increases were checked by comparable death rates. Since then, birth rates have continued high, but death rates have plunged toward the low levels of developed countries (Table 2.11). Mortality dropped precipitously because of the penetration of Western medical technology and health measures. It probably will continue to fall in the future.

Population Growth and Underdeveloped Countries

Rapid demographic growth (and a highly dependent population structure) can be a stumbling block to economic progress in underdeveloped countries, especially in

TABLE 2.11 Birth rates and death rates for developed and underdeveloped regions

Region	Birth Rate (Per 1000 Population per Year)	Death Rate (Per 1000 Population per Year)	Annual Rate of Natural Increase (Percent)
World	33	13	2.0
Developed Countries	17	9	0.8
Underdeveloped Countries	39	14	2.5

SOURCE: *United Nations Demographic Yearbook,* 1973.

the crowded lands of Asia. Growing populations can aggravate or create problems of raising education and income standards, foreign debt payments, unfavorable trade balances, industrialization, employment, food distribution, and agricultural productivity.

According to the medium variant of the United Nations demographic statistics, the world's population by the year 2000 will be 6.5 billion (Figure 2.19). A little more than 22 percent, or 1.5 billion will live in developed regions, and 5 billion in the rest of the world. Since the bulk of the forecast population increase will take place in the underdeveloped world, the question often raised is: What can be done about the population "problem" as it affects underdeveloped countries? Any answer to this question has political implications.

A Solution? Three Views

Conservatives, who are ideologically committed to the preservation of the capitalist order, say the way to cure the world's population "problem" is to do nothing to eliminate poverty, hunger, and disease.

A more "respectable" approach to the population "problem" is advocated by liberals, who also want to preserve the existing world order. They argue that methods to effect a decline in levels of fertility must be imposed on peoples of the Third World. A few years ago they believed that the only way to stabilize or reduce population size was through birth control. They warned that countries must slow down the birth rate before the welfare of much of the world's population can be significantly improved. Today they point to evidence that indicates that policies that improve the welfare of the entire population of a country are the ones with the greatest effect on controlling population growth. This evidence shows that strategies combining economic growth, greater economic and social justice (giving people effective land reform and more income), and access to birth control programs appear to bring about a much greater reduction in fertility than can any one of these factors alone (Figure 2.20). In countries which have experienced more equal distribution of income, such as Taiwan, South Korea, Argentina, Sri Lanka and Malaysia, birth rates dropped over the past two decades. By contrast, in countries such as Mexico, Venezuela, Brazil and the Philippines where very unequal income distributions have continued, birth rates remained high.

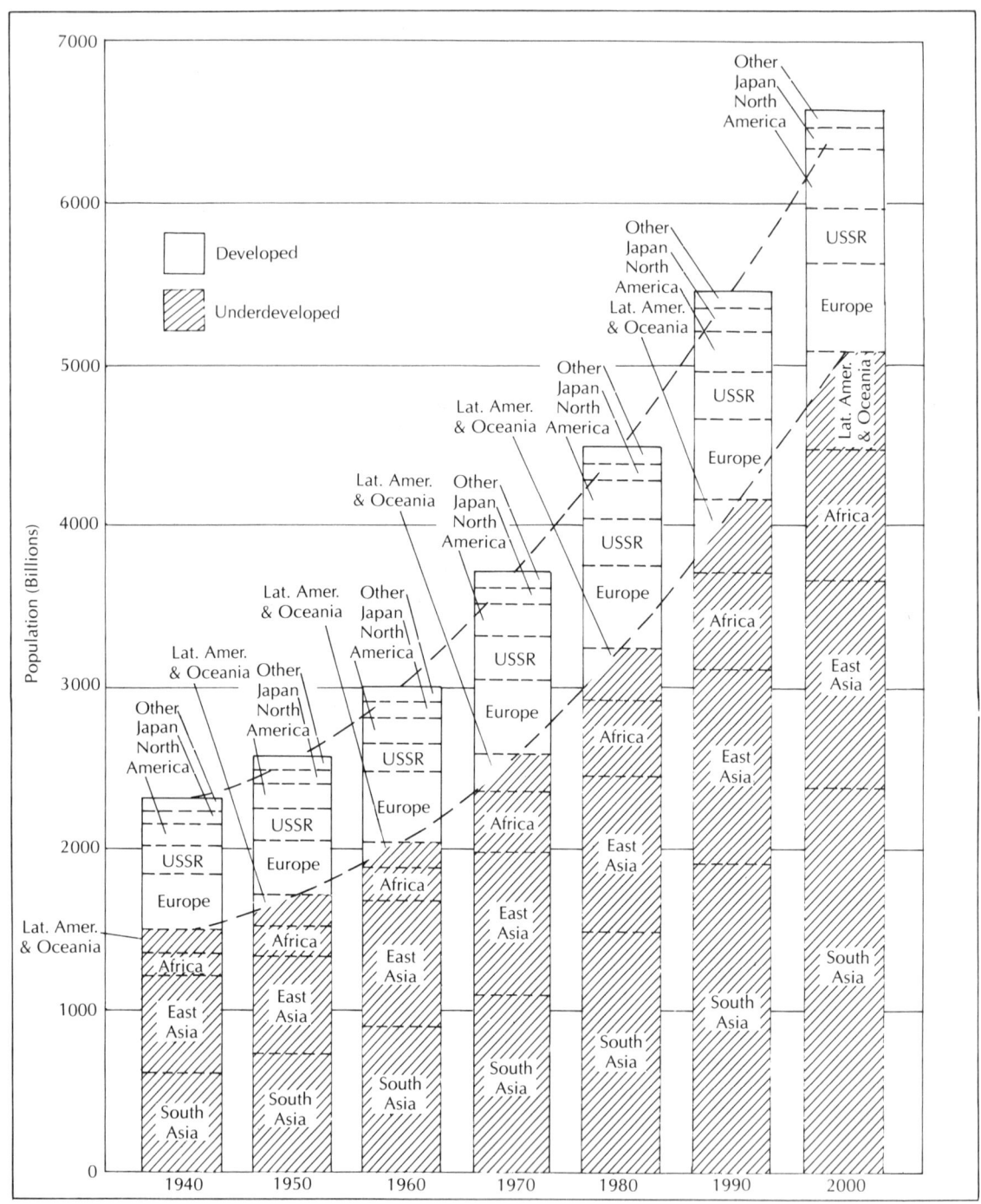

FIGURE 2.19 World population by regions, 1940–2000. SOURCE: World Bank Group, *Trends in Developing Countries*. Washington D.C.: International Bank for Reconstruction and Development, 1971.

> **CONTROLLING POPULATION**
>
> Various solutions to the population "problem" have been proposed. Here are three divergent suggestions:
>
> 1. *The Conservative View.* For biologist Garrett Hardin (1974), the solution to the population problem is lifeboat ethics. "Metaphorically, each rich nation can be seen as a lifeboat full of comparatively rich people. In the ocean outside each lifeboat swim the poor of the world, who would like to get in . . . What should the lifeboat passengers do?" (1974:18). He argued against the rich helping the poor. If the poor in their teeming billions breed like rabbits, they should die like rabbits. Everyone will be ruined if we help "our poor brothers." In Hardin's view, complete justice is complete catastrophe.
>
> 2. *The Liberal View.* Lord Ritchie-Calder (1974), a United Nations adviser, considered the deliberate discrimination of the rich against the poor morally abhorrent. He argued that poor people must be exposed to family planning. The poor must have the "means to practice 'responsible parenthood.' The means must be reliable, cheap, simple to use, not irreversible (sterilization, like abortion, is a last resort) and psychologically acceptable" (1974:2).
>
> 3. *The Radical View.* Novelist and surgeon Han Suyin (1974) wrote that family planning, especially when it is imposed on poor people from outside, is not a solution to the population problem. She cited the failure of the family planning program in India. "It has been a failure because the material conditions were not there, because the socio-economic problems of exploitation have not been dealt with" (1964:5).
>
> At best, Hardin's suggestion may be viewed as a response to Suyin's demand for equity and justice. Ritchie-Calder's suggestion epitomizes the Western stereotypical view of what underdeveloped countries must do to escape the ghost of Malthus.

Radicals charge that conservatives and liberals do not identify the underlying reasons for the population "problem." They argue that runaway rates of population growth were brought about largely by the penetration of the capitalist economic system into indigenous societies. They insist that the population "problem" cannot be solved until policies of imperialism and neo-imperialism have been dealt with. For example, they ask, How can the population "problem" be solved when much of the world's farming land is utilized below capacity or is not in cultivation at all? A study of Guatemala's 1960 census revealed that

> twenty per cent of the *fincas* (farms) occupied ninety per cent of the farm area. Twenty-two of the largest *fincas* covered 13.4 per cent of the total area, and belonged to three owners. The United Fruit Company, which owned 650,000 acres, was the largest *latifundista;* only eight per cent of its land was cultivated. Whereas the *minifundia* were 100 per cent cultivated, only 5.7 per cent of the large properties were cultivated . . .

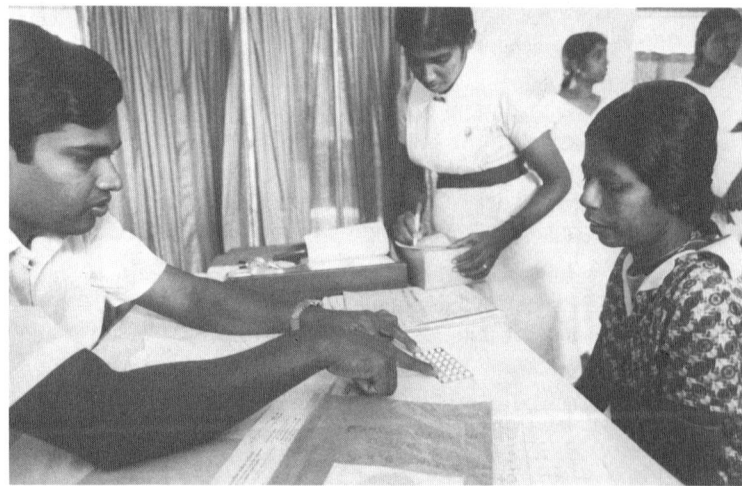

Family planning (A) Family Planning Clinic at Kampala, Uganda, where advice is given on the use of contraceptives. SOURCE: *World Health Organization;* (B) At the General Hospital of Colombo, Sri Lanka, advice on contraceptive pills is given to a woman who comes for the first time. SOURCE: *World Health Organization Photo* by J. Mohr.

> The *latifundistas* have no reason for increasing production. The fact that hundreds of millions in the world are going hungry is not reason enough for them. Just as their political monopoly is a source of enrichment, so their monopoly of land and other productive resources is a source of growing power (Hensman, 1975: 133-134).

People in Guatemala and in most other parts of the Third World are going hungry for lack of justice. According to the world land census conducted by the FAO in 1960, "*2.5 percent of land owners with holdings of more than 100 hectares control*

Population Growth

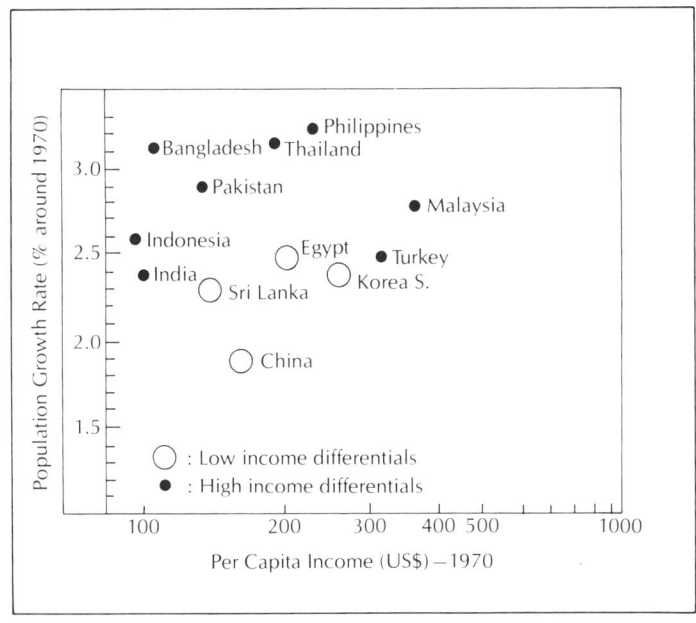

FIGURE 2.20 Population and equality.
SOURCE: *Development Forum*, 1977, Vol. 5, No. 1; p. 5.

nearly three quarters of all the land in the world—with the top 0.23 percent controlling over half" (George, 1977:35).

After internal self-transformation, radicals point out that dealing with the population "problem" may still be a difficult task, but much becomes possible. For example, when Mao Tse-tung came to power in China in 1948, he sought to transform the country's population problem "into a solution through the mobilization of labor power to create resources where there had been none before. The resultant transformation of the Chinese earth . . . has eliminated famine, raised living standards, and effectively eliminated hunger and material misery" (Harvey, 1974:274).

Radicals, therefore, suggest that hunger and rapid population growth reflect the failure of the world's existing political and economic system. They also explain why poor people who live outside of planned societies *must* have large families (Mamdani, 1973; and George, 1977).

According to Susan George:

> Another baby for a poor family means an extra mouth to feed—a very marginal difference. But by the time that child is about four or five years old, it will make important contributions to the whole family—fetching water from the distant well, taking meals to father and brothers in the field, feeding animals. Later the child will help with more complicated tasks which would all devolve upon the mother of the household if she could not count on her children. Women may have to suffer the biological servitude of pregnancies, but at least they can be spared . . . the much longer and far more burdensome servitude of carrying out all the household and many of the farming tasks without even simple conveniences like running water and without any help whatsoever. Most

Third World mothers have only a 50/50 chance of seeing their children live beyond the age of five. Once we realize that children are an economic *necessity* for the poor, then we can understand that poor families will have to plan their births every bit as carefully as couples in Westchester or West Harrow—and allow for the predictable mortality rate (1977:37).

The essential point we note from this discussion of the population "problem" is that it is not possible to deal with the subject matter in a neutral way. Conservatives, liberals, and radicals express ideological positions that lead to different conclusions.

Summary

Since the organization of the world's economic system is dependent upon people, it is necessary to study population distribution, qualities, and dynamics. In this chapter, we first considered the variable *distribution* of population over the earth. The uneven distribution stems in part from different combinations of national and human-made resources. Any attempt to understand the spatial distribution of population in an area, however, requires detailed study of historical, social, economic, geographical, and demographic processes that created the pattern.

Second, we enumerated *population qualities*—demographic traits, age composition, cultural attributes, labor, and income. The characteristics of a population are the work of people, and they differ from region to region. Some of the greatest distinctions are between developed and underdeveloped countries.

Third, we concerned ourselves with *population change*. We identified and considered the components of population change: *migration* and *differential growth rates*. Finally, we paid special attention to the population "problem." Is "*overpopulation*" the primary obstacle to economic development in Third World countries? Many Western conservative and liberal experts assert as much (see Gray and Tongri: 1970). Radicals agree that too many people is a problem in many underdeveloped countries, but they remind us that overpopulation is always *relative* to growth of output. They argue that output is rising slowly, and in some cases not at all, because the problem of national and international exploitation has not been solved.

DISCUSSION QUESTIONS

1. Explain why population distributions can be explained only in terms of the past.
2. Compare and contrast patterns of urbanization in developed and underdeveloped countries.

3. Analyze the significance of (a) sex ratios, and (b) participation rates of the labor force, in studies of population structure.
4. Discuss: The population crisis must be confronted in the broader context of the development crisis of underdeveloped countries.
5. Describe and evaluate Malthus' contribution to an appreciaton of the population—food supply relationship.
6. Discuss: Overpopulation arises because of the scarcity of resources available for meeting the subsistence needs of the mass of the population.
7. Is the story of human population growth primarily a story of changes in death rate? Explain.
8. Describe the changing pattern of labor force structure in the United States over the past 200 years.
9. Describe patterns of interregional migration in the United States in the decade of the 1960s.
10. Do you agree that a cure of the population problem lies in the industrialization process?
11. Describe with examples the phases of the demographic transition.

SUGGESTED READINGS

Basic Concepts of Population Geography

Clarke, J. I., *Population Geography*. Elmsford, New York: Pergamon, 1966.

Demko, G. I., H. M. Rose, and G. A. Schnell, eds., *Population Geography: A Reader*. New York: McGraw-Hill Book Company, 1970.

Zelinsky, W., *Prologue to Population Geography*. Englewood Cliffs, New Jersey: Prentice-Hall, 1966.

Population Growth and Surveys of Population Trends

Cipolla, C. M., *The Economic History of World Population*. Harmondsworth, England: Penguin Books, 1970.

Coale, A. J., "The History of the Human Population," *Scientific American*, September 1974, pp. 40–51.

Commoner, B., "How Poverty Breeds Overpopulation," *Ramparts*, August/September (1975), pp. 21–25, 58–59.

Ehrlich, P. R., and A. H. Ehrlich, *Population, Resources, Environment: Issues in Human Ecology*. San Francisco: W. H. Freeman and Company, 1970.

Freedman, R., and B. Berelson, "The Human Population," *Scientific American*, September 1974, pp. 30–39.

Harvey, D., "Population, Resources, and the Ideology of Science," *Economic Geography*, **50** (1974): 256–277.

Johnson, S. (ed.), *The Population Problem*. New York: John Wiley and Sons, Inc., 1973.

Mamdani, M., *The Myth of Population Control*. New York: Monthly Review Press, 1973.

Peccei, A., "Controlling the Population Will Be the Rule," *Development Forum*, **2** (1974): 4.

Teitelbaum, M. S., "Relevance of Demographic Transition Theory for Developing Countries," *Science*, **188** (1975): 420–425.

3

RESOURCES

KEY TERMS

- carrying capacity
- cowboy life-style
- depletion curves
- ecosystem
- entropy
- green revolution
- intermediate technology
- logistic curve
- malnutrition
- maximum sustainable yield
- minerals
- net energy
- non-recurring input
- nonrenewable resource
- optimum population
- overpopulation
- population crash
- pollutants
- recurring input
- recycle
- renewable resource
- reserve
- resource
- second law of thermodynamics
- spaceship life-style
- steady-state
- undernutrition

3

Natural resources are needed for economic activity. In particular, energy is required to convert raw materials into finished products. Supplies of resources currently regarded as essential for the continued growth of developed countries, however, are dwindling. At the same time, economic activities are spoiling the environment. How did developed countries get into this situation? What can they do to solve current resource and environmental "crises"?

Marxists argue that the Western world got into trouble under the capitalist law of accumulation. The mindless exploitation of nature under capitalism pushes society to the limits of its resource base. Although technological change may roll back resource limitations, capitalist accumulation soon reaches these new limits (Harvey, 1974:266).

Non-Marxists may be divided into resource optimists and resource pessimists. Resource optimists believe that capitalist accumulation can continue indefinitely, because there "are no substantial limits in sight either in raw materials or in energy that the price structure, product substitution, anticipated gains in technology and pollution control cannot be expected to solve" (Notestein, 1970:20). Resource pessimists question how much future growth is possible. They argue that indefinite growth in a finite world is impossible. "Present reserves of all but a few metals will be exhausted within 50 years, if consumption rates continue to grow as they are" and, "if current trends are allowed to persist . . . the breakdown of society and the irreversible disruption of the life support systems on this planet are inevitable" (Goldsmith, 1973:14).

Until the Arab oil embargo and escalation of petroleum prices in 1973, most Americans dismissed utterances of resource pessimists as doomsday prophesies. Among other things, the energy "crisis" has made Americans aware of the fact that resources are scarce. But at the same time they wonder whether these scarcities are arising naturally or whether they are being socially created. Some Americans are feeling poorer than they used to be, and they wonder what the future may bring. Clearly the capitalist system will ensure that the majority of Americans will not starve, although the United Nations has forecast significant malnutrition for 75 percent of Asia's population by 1985. And there is little danger that material standards of American life will decline sharply in the immediate future. Nonetheless,

Objectives

Americans cannot ignore mounting evidence of resource and ecological problems that exist on a world-wide scale.

We can see several options for attacking resource and environmental problems. For example, we can reduce the number of people on the planet. We can conclude that a stationary state is inevitable sooner or later and substitute non-growth for industrial growth. We can end the present conflict between the system of nature and the capitalist mode of production. This solution would involve transforming our present "cowboy" life-style, which is based on a goal of ever increasing growth, to a "spaceship" life-style which is designed for balance and permanence. A "spaceship" life-style would include: an equitable and modest use of resources, a production system which is in balance with the environment, and small-scale technology. The aim of a "spaceship" earth economy is maximum human well-being with a minimum of material consumption. Growth occurs, but only that which truly benefits the population at large. It remains uncertain as to whether Americans are prepared to dismantle their existing system of production, and to accept a life-style that seeks satisfaction more in quality and equality than in quantity and inequality. It also remains to be seen whether Americans who have been programmed for maximum consumption via advertising and their value system can readily change life-styles, i.e., can Americans change from "cowboys" to "space-men"?

This chapter provides a general overview of resource problems and discusses "cowboy" versus "spaceship" philosophies of resource use. It is divided into five parts: first, population-natural resource relationships; second, resource types; third, renewable food resources; fourth, nonrenewable mineral resources; and finally, energy resources.

OBJECTIVES

By the end of this chapter you should be able:

1. To discuss relationships among population, resources, technology, and living standards.
2. To distinguish resources from reserves, and renewable resources from nonrenewable resources.
3. To assess world food problems and proposals to increase the food supply.
4. To describe the implications of the second law of thermodynamics.
5. To discuss estimated time spans for depletion of mineral and metal resources.
6. To discuss the causes and consequences of the energy "crisis."
7. To describe and discuss differences between "cowboy" and "spaceship" life-styles.

Resources and Population

The earth and its resources are finite. The need to limit population growth, as we saw in Chapter 2, is perceived much more clearly than is the need to limit economic growth with its increasingly massive use of resources. Programs supported by most governments presuppose a maximum growth economy which assumes a world which can tolerate rampant waste, unlimited pollution, and indestructible ecosystems.

The earth is our only suitable habitat. SOURCE: *NASA/U.S. Geological Survey EROS Data Center, Sioux Falls, South Dakota.*

The United States, in particular, has suffered from a limitless view of resources. But its affluent way of life is threatened in a world economy under great stress. The urban-industrial system is liquidating the resources on which it was built. The situation is aggravated by other nations which aspire to affluence through American-style urban industrialization. To bring the world's population to existing American levels of consumption has been likened to giving everyone a trans-Atlantic voyage on the Titanic. According to one calculation, the world's life-support system can only support about 500 million people at the United Sates level of affluence, which itself is very unevenly distributed by class and region (Miller, 1975).

Resources and Population

Carrying Capacity and Overpopulation

Each day "Spaceship Earth" is adding 200,000 additional people. They must be fed, clothed, and housed. This would be no problem if they had access to adequate resources. Unfortunately, this is not the case: one-half of the world's population is already either hungry or malnourished.

If present trends of population growth and patterns of consumption continue, then "Spaceship Earth" could eventually be brought into a *steady state* known as *carrying capacity*. The *carrying capacity is the population that can be supported by available resources*. When population exceeds an adequate supply of

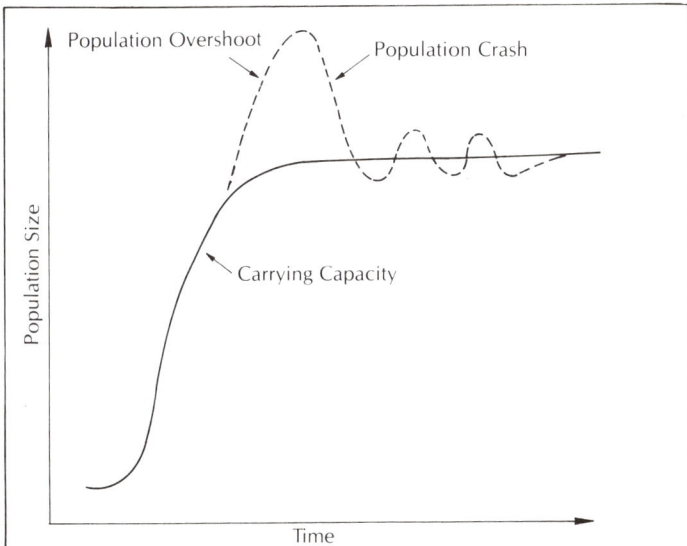

FIGURE 3.1 Population crash.

resources for maintaining life, a *population crash* occurs (Figure 3.1). A population crash may be a result of overpopulation relative to the food supply, which has been described as Malthusian overpopulation, or a result of overpopulation relative to the rate of consumption of energy and resources and to the resulting increase in pollution (neo-Malthusian overpopulation).

Before a population crash occurs, several options are available to solve population-resource problems. As noted in Chapter 1, we could seek to alter the social organization of scarcity, change our consumption patterns and tastes, change our technologies, or alter our numbers. In the Western world, emphasis is on controlling population or on improving technologies.

Some would have us believe that modern technology can solve all problems. It increases agricultural yields, and produces more electric power. In the last 200 years, technological improvements have raised the earth's carrying capacity; future technical innovations will raise carrying capacity still further. Modern technologies use fewer resources and produce fewer wastes per unit of product than old ones, and they will even solve pollution problems.

> **NEO-MALTHUSIAN OVERPOPULATION**
>
> Some neo-Malthusians are optimistic about the population-resource relation and suggest, like Ricardo, that the inevitable stationary state is a long way off (Cole et al, 1973). Others are highly pessimistic and believe that the stationary state is close at hand (Meadows et al, 1972). Pessimists usually insist that the United States is the most overpopulated country in the world. They argue that each American consumes about seven times the amount of the average world citizen. Each American has roughly 50 times the negative impact on the world's life-support systems as the average citizen of India. In terms of ecosystem destruction, adding 75 million more Americans is the equivalent of adding 3.7 billion Indians to the world population.
>
> Whether neo-Malthusians are optimists or pessimists, they all suggest that society will eventually enter a stationary state. This conclusion is highly restrictive. It assumes that "human inventiveness and creativity apply only in the sphere of technology" and neglects the fact that "human beings can and do create social structures as well as machines" (Harvey, 1974:271).

According to Ernest Schumacher (1973), however, no technological solution to problems of overpopulation is possible. Technologies will be unable to bring forth the resources necessary for human existence. Humankind must reckon with the *second law of thermodynamics* (see box). The law tells us that the amount of energy in the world is fixed, but the amount of work that can be derived from that energy is irreversibly diminished. Gasoline, for example, is a source of energy, but once it is burnt in the engine of an automobile its value as a source of useful energy is gone forever.

Modern physicists, some engineers, and NASA would argue strongly and persuasively that Schumacher presents too narrow a view. They would indicate, for example, that American spaceships use energy from an environment that is larger than the ship itself.

> **THE LAWS OF THERMODYNAMICS**
>
> There are two laws of thermodynamics. The first law of thermodynamics states that the total amount of energy in the universe remains constant. In other words, energy can neither be created nor destroyed. The second law of thermodynamics insists that the overall tendency in all processes is away from concentration and away from high temperature. Thus when energy is used it becomes less and less usable. The degradation of high-grade energy produces heat, but at relatively low and useless temperatures. Unfortunately, the production of this low-grade heat may make the earth uncomfortably warm before the depletion of high-grade energy resources.

Optimum Population and the Quality of Life

The best of all possible worlds would be one with an optimum population that permits improvements in human well-being. But "optimum" is a qualitative adjective. "Optimum" differs from country to country. The optimum population for an isolated resource-rich country consuming a large quantity of resources is lower than that for an isolated resource-poor country.

In simple terms, human well-being is a function of the relationship between population and the ability to make efficient use of resources. If we assume fixed resources and population growth in a given country, then average well-being diminishes as resources are consumed. In reality, the situation is much more complex. Other factors are involved: some make the situation better, and others make it worse. A useful, but still crude, model of human well-being is as follows:

$$\text{Human Well-being} = \frac{\text{Resources} \times \text{Improved Extraction} \times \text{Recycling} \times \text{Resource Substitution} \times \text{Imports}}{\text{Population} \times \text{Population Density} \times \text{Per capita Consumption} \times \text{Harmful Technology}}$$

Although this equation ignores such fundamental factors as the social organization of scarcity, it does reveal some of the complexities of the world's resource situation. Improved extraction techniques, recycling, and finding substitutes for resources decrease the rate of resource depletion, but increasing the per capita rate of consumption and harmful technology can accelerate resource depletion and increase pollution.

Types of Resources and Their Limits

Resources are customarily classified as human or natural. Humankind, not nature, is the most important resource. All economic development comes out of human labor and skills, but in order to produce goods and services, we need to obtain natural resources from the earth. What are natural resources and what are their limits?

Resources and Reserves

Broadly defined, the term *"resource"* refers to the supply of anything that is regarded as useful to humans. It is a technical and cultural concept, a term of appraisal. This concept of a resource, however, is unsatisfactory in market economies where commodities have little utility unless they can be obtained at a profit. The U.S. Geological Survey and the U.S. Bureau of Mines define resources pragmatically: *Resources are naturally occurring substances that are profitable and potentially feasible to extract under prevailing conditions.*

Resources are not *reserves* (Figure 3.2). *A reserve is a portion of the total resource which is identified and from which usable materials can be economically and legally extracted at the time of the evaluation.* Resources include identified reserves plus other identified or undiscovered material components of the environment. A financial analogy clarifies the distinction between reserves and resources. Reserves are liquid assets like money in a checking account, and resources are frozen assets or future income that cannot be used to pay this month's car payments.

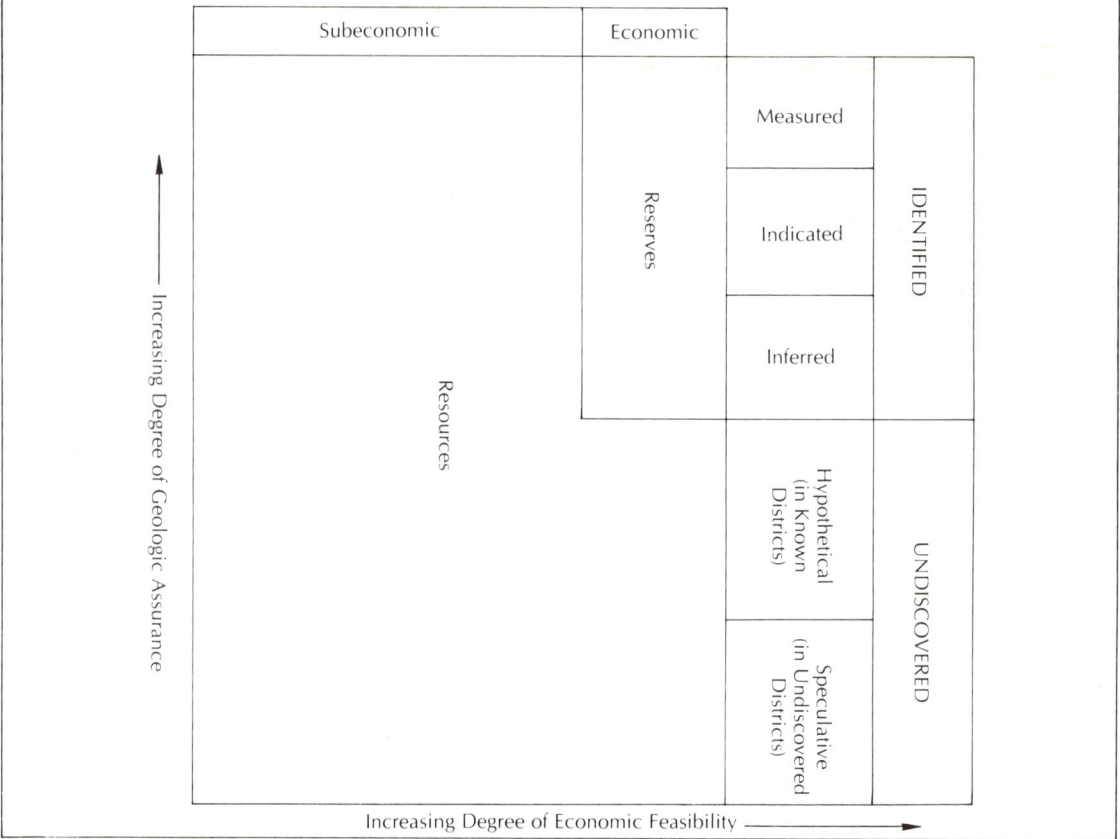

FIGURE 3.2 Classification of mineral resources. SOURCE: "Principles of the Mineral Resource Classification System of the U.S. Bureau of Mines and U.S. Geological Survey," *Geological Survey Bulletin* 1450-A (1976), pp. A2–A3.

Renewable and Nonrenewable Resources

The distinction between nonrenewable and renewable resources is vital. Nonrenewable or fund resources such as fossil fuels and metals cannot be used without depletion. They are fixed in amount and usually form very slowly. They are not necessarily destroyed by production, however. For example, iron ore deposits are depleted by mining, but this does not mean the world is less rich in steel. The steel from discarded automobiles can be recycled. Recycling possibilities set the limits on the sustainable use of a nonrenewable resource. At present, these limits are very low in relation to current mineral extraction.

Types of Resources and Their Limits

Renewable or flow resources are capable of yielding output indefinitely without impairing productivity. Renewable resources include soil, vegetation, air, and water. Renewal is not automatic, however. Renewable resources can be depleted; they can be permanently reduced by heavy use or misuse. Productive fishing grounds can be destroyed by exploitation. Fertile top soil, destroyed by erosion, can be difficult to restore and impossible to replace. The future of agricultural land is guaranteed only when production does not exceed its *maximum sustainable yield.*

The misuse of resources can be described in terms of the "tragedy of the commons." By this we mean the way public resources are misused by each of us. We appear to be unwilling to use a minimum share of a resource. People who fish are likely to take as many game fish as possible out of a lake if there is no rule of capture. They reason that if they do not catch them, then others will. Similarly, dumping waste and pollutants on public waters and land or into the air is the cheapest way to dispose of worthless products. Unless forced by law, we seem unwilling to dispose of these materials by more expensive means.

Limits of Natural Resources

We can illuminate resource limitations placed upon growth with two simple models: one, for a renewable resource, the other, for a nonrenewable resource.

Renewable Resource Let us assume (1) that a renewable resource such as land produces a single consumer good, food; (2) that population and maximum sustainable yield per hectare (about 2.5 acres) are fixed; and (3) that cultivated land and food production grow exponentially. Eventually no more land can be cleared for cultivation without spoiling the environment, and the economy reaches point C in Figure 3.3. The best strategy is to stop growth at C and sustain maximum sustainable yield thereafter, but it is difficult to accomplish in practice. The physical limits are often reached quickly. To illustrate, when production increases at a modest annual rate of 4 percent per annum, the doubling time is only 19 years. Land soon becomes a scarce factor of production. Furthermore, farmers at C are accustomed to a higher standard of living, and they will hope to maintain the improvement. They clear additional land, overcrop existing land, and ruin the precious soil. In order to avoid

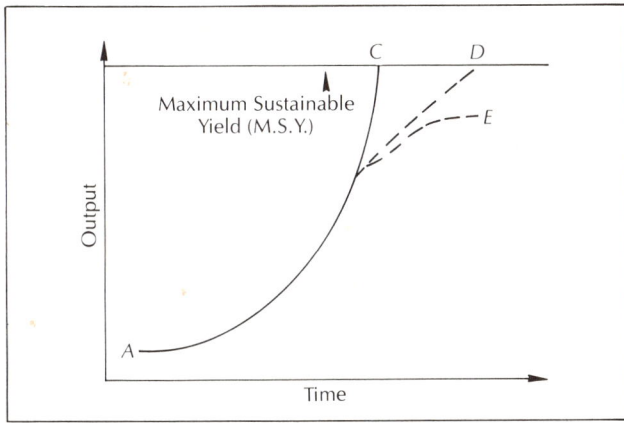

FIGURE 3.3 Limits to growth of a renewable resource. SOURCE: Richard Lecomber, 1975, *Economic Growth Versus Environment,* p. 38, Fig. 8. By permission of Macmillan, London and Basingstoke.

this outcome, a society must slow growth at say, *B*, and follow path *ABD* or, more cautiously, path *ABE*.

Nonrenewable Resource Let our nonrenewable resource be a fossil fuel, say coal, and let us assume, as before, that population and resource productivity are fixed. Coal supplies are soon exhausted (Figure 3.4). At 3 percent annual growth in mining activity the depletion time for a 250 years' supply of coal is 80 years (Curve *A*). Even if coal supplies are doubled, the depletion time is postponed only 25 years (Curve *B*).

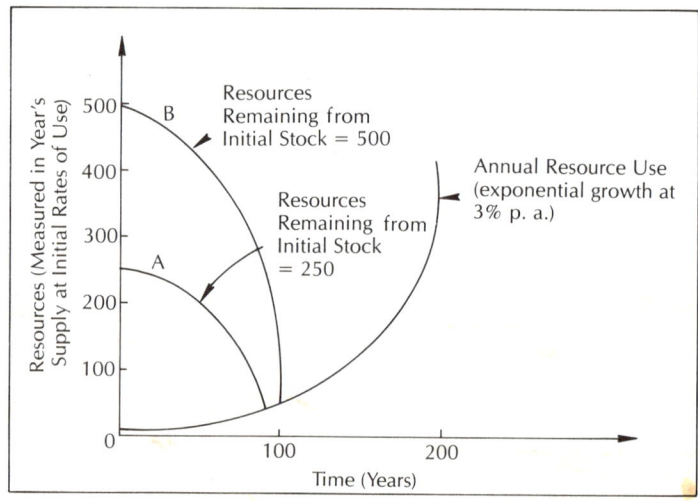

FIGURE 3.4 Limits to growth of a nonrenewable resource. SOURCE: Richard Lecomber, 1975, *Economic Growth Versus Environment*, p. 39, Fig. 9. By permission of Macmillan, London and Basingstoke.

The two models demonstrate that resources, both renewable and nonrenewable, are exhaustible. However, the models project resource depletion on the basis of unrealistic assumptions. We assumed, for example, that resource productivity is constant. Yet we know that resource productivity can be expanded by technical progress or by substitution of other resources.

Food Resources

Food is the most important resource. Given rapid population growth in the next few decades, worldwide need for this resource will increase several times. Food production is projected to double between 1970 and the year 2000. Yet the world food supply is already low. World food stockpiles for emergency relief are declining rapidly. Expressed as days of world grain consumption they have declined from 105 days in 1961 to about 31 days in 1976. Forty-three "food priority countries" in the underdeveloped world have large grain deficits. In the last three decades some food exporting countries, especially in Latin America and Eastern Europe, have become food importers. North America and Australia are the only major food exporting regions. North America, for example, is the producer of more than two-thirds of the world's cereal exports. Poor countries around the world are dependent on these exports. Harvest failures in North America caused by any number of factors such as

Food Resources

adverse weather conditions—the major factor affecting crops everywhere—could kill millions of hungry people.

Children, in the less serious stages of malnutrition, sit on the bare earth in the improvised kitchen in the courtyard of the Niger Clinic in Port Harcourt, Nigeria. They are fed with a mixture of stockfish and beans. SOURCE: *UNICEF*/Poul Larsen.

According to one estimate, two and one-half billion people suffer from *undernutrition* (lack of calories) and *malnutrition* (lack of protein, vitamins, and essential nutrients). They are concentrated in underdeveloped countries (Figure 3.5). Because of the large number of people affected, the most critical gap between food need and food supply is in South Asia.

Food Problems

At least five food problems occur: food quantity, food quality, food distribution, poverty, and harmful effects of modern agriculture. Let us survey each of these problems briefly.

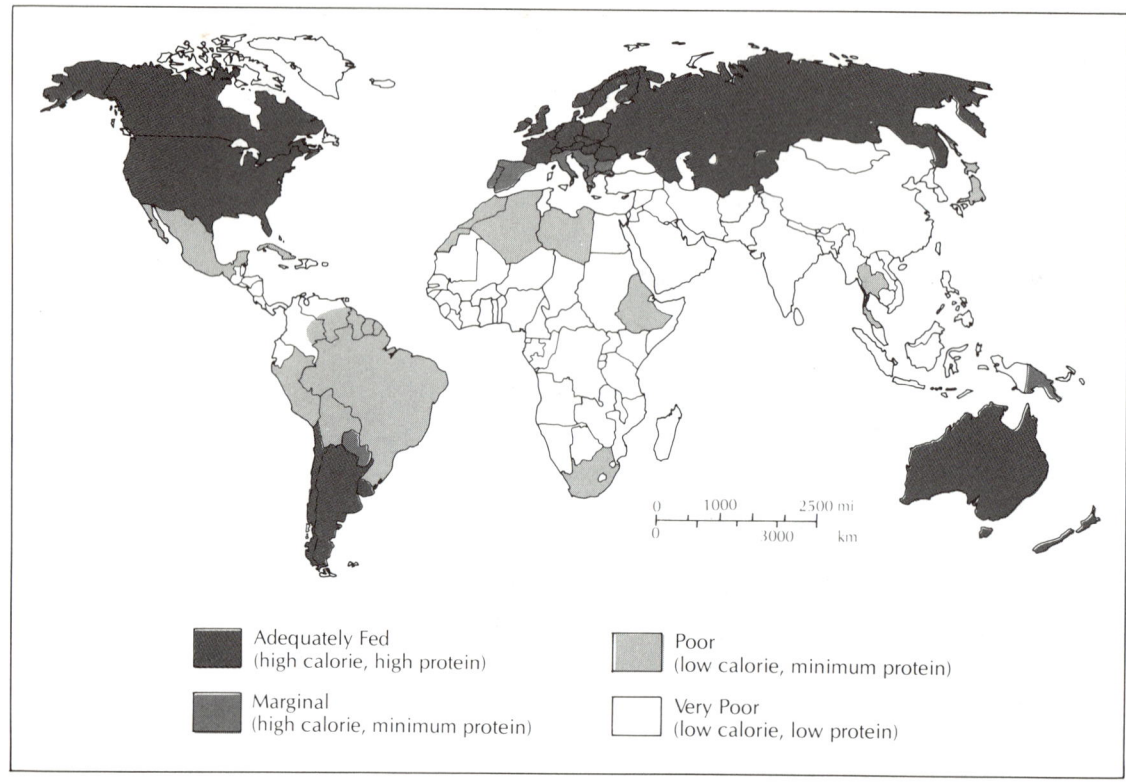

FIGURE 3.5 Geography of hunger and malnutrition. SOURCE: U.N. Food and Agricultural Organization, 1965.

Food Quantity By food quantity we mean providing people with enough calories, and not whether adequate protein and other nutrients are available. Food production in 1975 was sufficient to feed the world's population adequately. Unfortunately it was not distributed equitably.

The world is feeding more people than ever before, but there are more hungry people than at any previous time. Estimates of the number of people eating less than the number of calories needed to maintain ordinary physical activity in 1976 ran from 0.46 billion to 1.03 billion. Food production increased in developed and underdeveloped countries at similar rates from 1961 to 1975. Yet it appears that the increase was cancelled in the underdeveloped world where rapid population growth reduced per capita food production (Figure 3.6). These data of developed and underdeveloped market economies conceal differences between countries and between regions within countries. To gain an accurate picture it is necessary to look at individual countries separately (see box).

Total production figures are a crude indicator of the food situation in the underdeveloped world. For instance, a big difference exists between production and availability for human consumption. In some areas there are substantial losses to

Food Resources

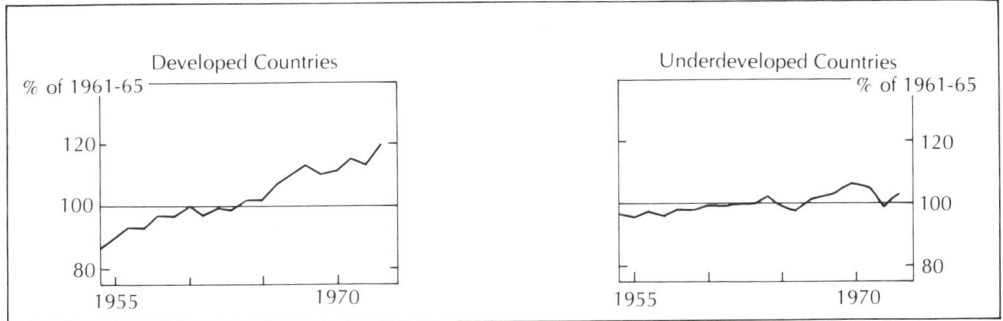

FIGURE 3.6 Food production per capita, developed and underdeveloped countries. SOURCE: *The World Food Situation and Prospects to 1985*. Washington, D.C.: Economic Research Service, U.S. Dept. of Agriculture, Foreign Agricultural Economic Report, No. 98, 1974, p. 15.

FOOD PRODUCTION IN CHINA

Composite statistics hide more than they reveal. They hide, for example, the ability of Chinese farmers to produce enough food for over 800 million people. China possesses less agricultural land than the United States, but it is able to feed a population about four times as great. In China, there are 0.13 hectares of crop land per person compared to 0.16 in Bangladesh, 0.30 in India, and 0.40 in Pakistan which are three chronically underfed countries. Key factors in China's impressive achievement are the *structure* or distribution of landholdings, expansion and intensification of traditional agricultural practices, water control techniques, and utilization of human and animal wastes and of crop residues that permit as many as 12 crops to be grown annually on some plots of land. (Sprague: 1975, 549-555).

---

insects, pests, and spoilage before food reaches the market. Nonetheless, food production figures do tell us that the underdeveloped world is somehow losing the capacity to feed itself. Many Westerners believe that Third World hunger is caused by population pressure and/or a lack of technical skills rather than by the failure of a social and economic system.

Food Quality People are malnourished when they do not consume enough essential nutrients, especially protein. For more than 50 percent of the world's population the protein content of the average diet is about two-thirds of the daily need. Poor people are forced to live on a starchy diet of grain rather than animal protein. When food is in short supply, sustenance depends on a short *food chain*.

A Liberian woman cooking rice. Rice thrives in the wetter tropics, and is usually planted in natural or irrigated swamps. It is estimated that rice is the staple food for more than half of the world's population. Rice and other grains supply energy for people, and some protein. But to be healthy, people must supplement grains with foods such as fruits, nuts, vegetables, dairy products, fish, and meat. SOURCE: *FAO*.

A food chain starts with green plants, which capture solar energy through the process of photosynthesis. At the second and third levels are primary consumers (plant eaters) and secondary consumers (meat eaters) respectively. People are primary consumers when they eat grain and secondary consumers when they eat meat.

According to the second law of thermodynamics, usable energy is lost at each stage of the food chain; 80 to 90 percent of the energy stored at one level is unavailable at the next highest level. Since the amount of energy entering the food chain is fixed by photosynthesis, there is more energy available at successively lower levels of the food chain. Consequently, more people can be supported on a diet of grain and starchy vegetables than on luxury foods such as meat, poultry, fish, and eggs.

Human nutrition requirements cannot be met by eating only plants that contain lots of calories, but few proteins, vitamins, and minerals. To keep healthy, people need an average of 60 grams of protein a day. Protein needs can be met with cheaper foods than meat. Grains can be supplemented by fruits, nuts, vegetables, and dairy products. Without proper nutrition, especially in the early years of life, people contract deficiency diseases. Their effects include physical and mental retardation, susceptibility to infections, and eventual death.

Food Resources

Food Distribution   By food distribution we mean the transport, storage, and marketing of agricultural commodities. Problems of food distribution are particularly serious in underdeveloped countries. Supplies of seed and fertilizer do not always flow smoothly or in accord with needs of the farm calendar. Marketing and storage facilities in many places are not adequate to meet substantial crop movement. The result is frequent loss to farmers through spoilage and market gluts.

Much more is known about how export crops move within colonial transportation networks and through port cities than is known about the marketing of food products for consumption in underdeveloped countries. The task of improving domestic food distribution systems has been neglected. A most important reason for this neglect is that government leaders, many of whom are military officers and lawyers, know relatively little about agriculture and food distribution.

Unequal Purchasing Power   A feature of the world's political economy is the concentration of purchasing power in developed countries. The advantage held by rich countries of the world in the trade of agricultural commodities is illustrated by the pattern of protein flow. In 1968 developed countries exported about 2.5 million metric tons of low grade grain protein to underdeveloped countries, and the latter delivered to developed countries about 3.5 million metric tons of high quality protein in the form of shrimp, fish meal, presscake of oilseed, and soybeans. This exchange resulted in a net loss of one million metric tons of protein for underdeveloped countries. Underdeveloped countries supply developed countries with protein because poor people have little money to purchase high grade protein food on the market. Europeans and Americans can pay more for this protein.

Harmful Effects of Modern Agriculture   To increase food quantity and to improve food quality, modern industrial agriculture supplements an abundant source of low entropy, solar energy, with a less abundant source of low entropy, the earth's endowment of fossil fuels. Entropy is a measure of disorder or energy not available for useful work. Fossil fuel powered technologies, which include mechanization, irrigation, chemical fertilizers, and pesticides and herbicides, increase disorder or entropy in the environment as required by the second law of thermodynamics. They deplete the earth's low entropy resources, and they pollute water, air, and land.

Pollutants are biological or chemical substances released into the environment in amounts known to be dangerous to desirable living organisms. Many pesticides, for example, are known to be serious pollutants. The use of chlorinated hydrocarbons, such as DDT, has damaged food chains, and their continued release into the environment may cause ecological catastrophe.

Although we do not know all the environmental effects of modern agriculture, we do know that it cannot succeed in feeding world population in the long run because there are insufficient supplies of world energy. Industrial agriculture requires five to ten calories of energy input to get one calorie of food; traditional agriculture requires one calorie of input to obtain five to fifty in food. In other words, modern agriculture requires twenty-five times more energy (see box).

ENERGY SUBSIDIES FOR VARIOUS FOODS

American agriculture is increasingly energy intensive. Consideration of this diagram should lead us to question the desirability of exporting the system of food production and the eating habits of the United States. It should also lead us to question whether United States agriculture itself can sustain its energy intensive ways.

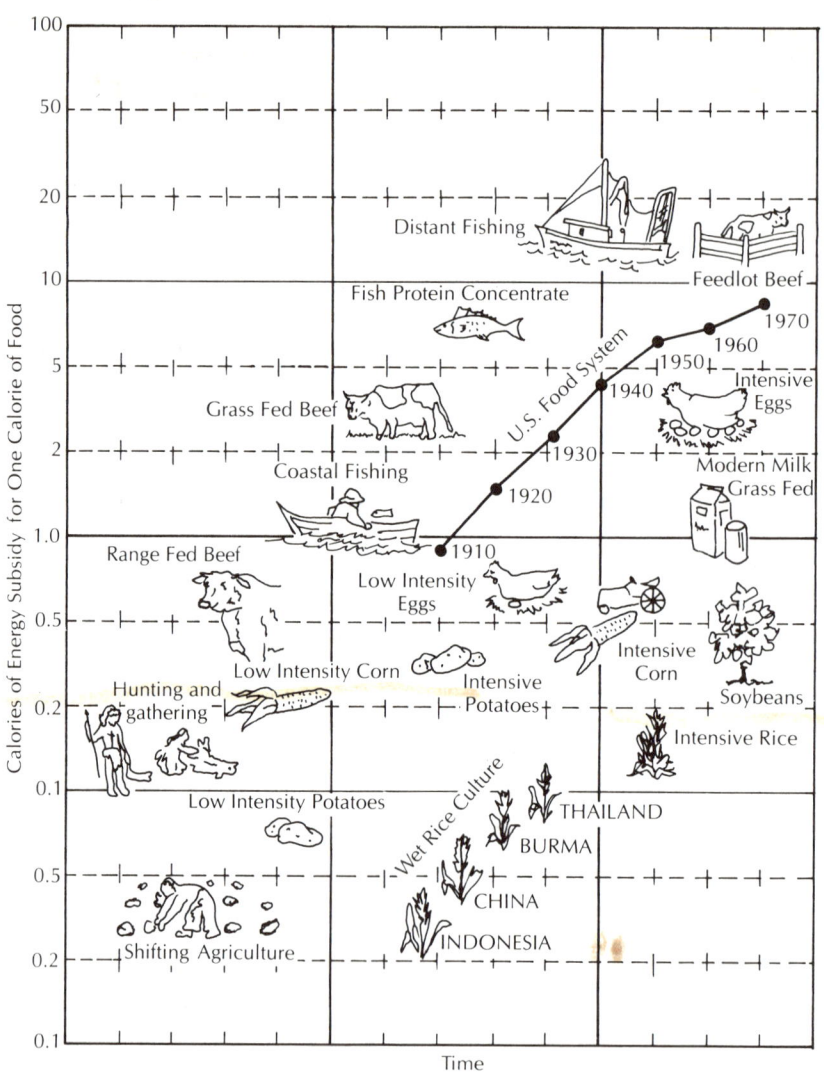

SOURCE: From *Energy: Sources, Use, and Role in Human Affairs* by Carol E. Steinhart and John S. Steinhart. © 1974 by Wadsworth Publishing Co., Inc., Belmont, CA 94002. Reprinted by permission of the publisher, Duxbury Press.

Food Resources

Proposals to Increase Food Production

Hunger is usually defined as a problem of inadequate production. Therefore, many proposals have been suggested for expanding food supply. These include expanding the amount of land under cultivation, increasing yields per unit of land, catching more fish, and developing synthetic foods. Let us examine these proposals in some detail.

Expanding the Cultivated Area The amount of potentially arable land in the world has been estimated at about twice the cultivated area. Vast reserves are theoretically available in Africa, South America, and Australia, and to a lesser degree in North America and the Soviet Union (Figure 3.7 and Table 3.1). Land that can be cultivated at a reasonable cost and with present technology is easier to find in temperate areas than in the tropics where fragile soils and aridity are limiting factors.

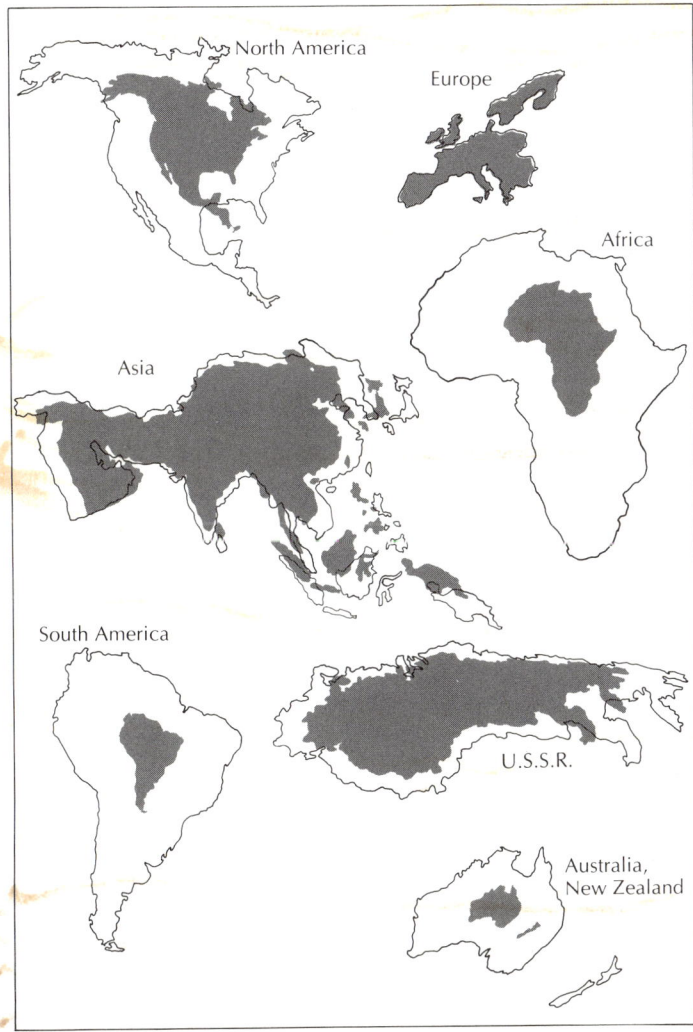

FIGURE 3.7 Continents sized in proportion to the area of their potentially arable land. The silhoutte map within each outline shows how much of that potentially arable land was being cultivated as of the mid-1960s. SOURCE: From "The Development of Agriculture in Developing Countries," by W. David Hopper, *Scientific American,* Vol. 235, Sept., p. 199. Copyright © 1976 by Scientific American, Inc. All rights reserved.

TABLE 3.1 Percentage of potentially arable land under cultivation (mid-1960s)

Region	Percentage of Arable Land Now Cultivated	Limitation
Europe	88	
Asia	83	
USSR	64	
North America	51	
Africa	22	Desert and Tropical Soils
South America	11	Tropical Soils
Australia and New Zealand	10	Lack of Water

Note: In underdeveloped countries much tillable land is kept out of production by large landowners and corporations.

Sixty percent of the world's potentially arable land lies within the tropics, especially in the rain forests of the Congo and Amazon basins. Chances for large expansion of agriculture in these rain forests are limited. Soils beneath the rich vegetation canopies are not very good for growing food. Once the trees are cleared, the soils are vulnerable to rain, and they soon lose their fertility. Furthermore, these soils have a high iron content and are baked by the sun into a material called laterite that has the texture of concrete.

Most of the remaining land reserves are found in areas of excessive dryness. This land must be irrigated if it is to become productive, but irrigation projects are expensive. The United Nations estimates that irrigation costs run an average of $1000 dollars per hectare, which may be a prohibitive price in many underdeveloped countries where farmers generally make well under $100 dollars a year.

Significant increases of the cultivated land area are possible in the United States, but some of the most productive farmland is being converted to other uses. Each year one-half million hectares become part of the urbanized landscape. California, the nation's foremost agricultural state, loses 120 hectares of agricultural land each day.

Raising the Productivity of Existing Farmland The quickest way of increasing the food supply is to raise yields per hectare. During the twentieth century, developed countries have achieved remarkable increases in agricultural yields through widespread adoption of new technologies.

Corn yields in the United States illustrate the use of new technologies. Yields increased dramatically after the Second World War with the use of hybrid varieties, mineral fertilizers, and herbicides (Figure 3.8). Data for the 1970s indicate that the rate of increase in corn yields is slowing down.

Crop yield increases are primarily dependent upon fertilizer-sensitive hybrid improvements. A hybrid, which is sometimes called a high-yielding variety (HVA for short), or more precisely a high-*potential* variety, is a *non-recurring source of productivity*. Under ideal conditions it results in rapid increases in output until fully adopted, after which further increases in yields are limited. By contrast, a recurring source of productivity increase such as fertilizer provides increases in output, even

Food Resources

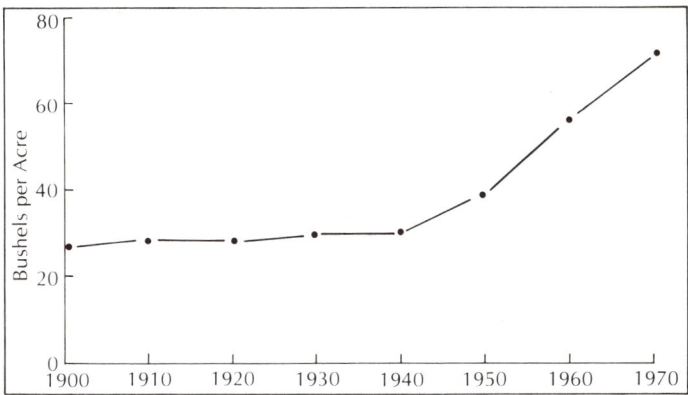

FIGURE 3.8 Corn yields in the United States, 1900–1970. SOURCE: U.S. Department of Agriculture.

when fully adopted, through more intensive application. Eventually it may not be possible to improve hybrid varieties of corn, and yields will increase at a decreasing rate or cease altogether despite additional applications of fertilizer. We can show this yield trend schematically by means of a "S-shaped curve" or a "logistic curve" of growth (Figure 3.9).

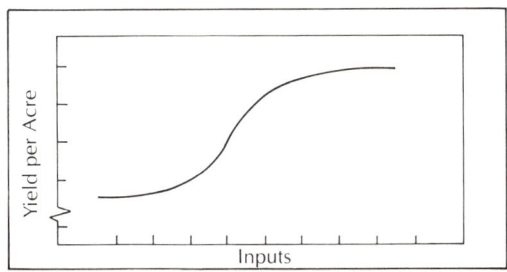

FIGURE 3.9 S-shaped yield curve (schematic representation).

The approach for increasing land productivity in developed countries has been proposed for underdeveloped countries. This Western technology-package approach to farming in the underdeveloped world is known as the *Green Revolution*. The term *Green Revolution* means breeding plants that will produce more edible grains, and that can be adapted to a wide range of environments. The "Green Revolution" began in 1943 when four American scientists financed by the Rockefeller Foundation went to Mexico. On mainly large farms in the Sonora District the scientists introduced new wheat and maize seeds, and soon crop yields began to increase. Following this triumph, the Rockefeller Foundation teamed up with the Ford Foundation to introduce "miracle" rice to selected parts of Asia such as the Philippines.

"Green Revolution" is a major scientific achievement, but it is not a panacea. It depends on new seeds, fertilizers, pesticides and herbicides produced and controlled by multinational corporations such as Fisons, Imperial Chemical Industries and Standard Oil. It depends on large-scale, one-crop farming which is ecologically unstable because of its susceptibility to pestilence. It depends on controlled water supplies which have been instrumental in increasing the incidence of human diseases such as malaria and schistosomiasis. It is restricted primarily to

The Green Revolution: high-yielding rice grown on terraces at Banaue, Philippines. SOURCE: *World Bank Photo* by Edwin G. Huffman.

wheat, rice, and corn which are starchy, low-grade-protein foods. It is confined to a few selected areas of Asia and Central America with adequate water supplies.

Even in areas where the "Green Revolution" has been technologically successful, it has not benefited large numbers of hungry people who need to buy the newly produced food. In the Punjab, India, for example, it has benefited mainly the farmers who were already wealthy enough to adopt complex integrated technical inputs. A higher return on capital invested in such inputs is realized by mechanizing farm operations and by purchasing more land. Some effects of labor-displacing machinery and the purchase of additional land by rich farmers include agricultural unemployment, increased landlessness, rural-urban migration, and increased malnutrition for the unemployed who are unable to purchase food produced by the "Green Revolution."

Where does the food produced by the "Green Revolution" go? In Pakistan hybrid maize is processed into corn sweetener for soft drinks for the urban middle and upper income groups. By 1973, two thirds of the "Green Revolution" rice in Colombia was going to feedlots and breweries. In the late 1960s, Mexico, despite the malnutrition of 80 percent of its rural population, began to export its "Green Revolution" wheat. In Central America fruits and vegetables for export to the United States are shut out from an oversupplied market or fail to meet U.S. "quality"

Food Resources

> **PESTICIDES AND INSECTS**
>
> D. Zwerdling (1977) reported that pesticides are creating monsters out of previously harmless insects, and concluded that America's "green revolution" is backfiring. Under the subtitle "Amber Waves of Grain" he said:
>
> > Before World War II, farms in the corn belt flourished with a rich diversity of crops and livestock. Farmers planted different crops every year, rotating them, so insects attracted to one crop would disappear with the next. They enriched the land with manure from their livestock; chemical fertilizer was unnecessary.
> >
> > But then, in 1945, DDT and the herbicide 2 4-D hit the market and, like the atomic bomb that exploded over Hiroshima that same year, the chemicals changed the political and economic future of the nation. With pesticides, farmers planted vast acreages of a single, highly profitable crop, controlling insects and other pest infestation with the spectacular new chemicals.
> >
> > Dependence on pesticides has created a whole new complex of insects now plaguing crops, insects that were scarcely a problem before the pesticides were begun. Western beef cutworms, once limited mainly to Nebraska, have become an "unexpected problem," according to the National Academy of Sciences (NAS), for farmers in the corn belt. Farmers are reporting damage caused by seed-corn beetles "with increasing frequency," says the NAS, apparently "due to the development of resistance" to insecticides. While the overall use of pesticides on crops has increased 12 times since WWII to more than 600 million pounds per year, the losses due to insects on corn alone have more than tripled (Zwerdling, 1977: 35-36).

standards. Since the local people are too poor to buy anything, 65 percent of production is fed to livestock (which, in turn, are exported) or dumped (Lappé and Collins, 1976:2).

The "Green Revolution" is not winning its battle against hunger because its focus is on food production. The world food problem is not so much one of food production, but of food demand in the economic sense. Unfortunately, the "Green Revolution" does not increase the ability of the poor to buy food; it reduces it.

We have portrayed the "Green Revolution" as a poisoned gift. It has helped to create a landscape of larger and larger commercial farms alongside fewer and smaller peasant plots. But given a different *structure of landholdings* and the use of appropriately *intermediate technology,* the "Green Revolution" could help underdeveloped countries along the road towards agricultural self-sufficiency and the elimination of hunger. *Intermediate technology* is a term coined by British economist Ernest Schumacher to mean low-cost small-scale technologies "intermediate" between "primitive" stick-farming methods and complex Western agro-industrial technical packages.

Catching More Fish and Developing Synthetic Foods Fish catches have tripled since the Second World War, but this source of food provides less than 1 percent of the world's total. Conventional seafoods cannot be counted on to contribute significantly to world food needs. Increased fish catches of the 1950s and 1960s have not been maintained in the 1970s because of overexploitation and pollution of fishing grounds.

From time to time we read of new food technologies that will multiply the world's food supply. New methods will replace traditional food chains with an artificial chain that produces synthetic foods. Given present knowledge, large scale manufacture of synthetic foods is not feasible. Moreover, novel foods must be purchased before they can be eaten. Poor, hungry people do not have the money to buy novel foods. They must rely on increased production of traditional foods.

A Solution to the World Food Supply Situation

It is a widely shared belief that people are hungry because of insufficient food production. We learn of new breakthroughs—protein from petroleum, harvests of kelp, extracts from alfalfa—to expand the food supply. We are told that strains on the food producing capacity of the Earth would be lessened if the affluent one-third of humankind did not consume two-thirds of the world's total food supply. We are reminded that Americans eat about 75 percent of the world's meat, and that we should eat "one less hamburger a week" in order to increase the food supply for the hungry.

Thus, many see the production of more food as necessary to solve the world food "crisis." But food production is increasing and yet there are more hungry people than ever before. Since there is more food than ever before,

> we are left with two possible conclusions: (1) Either the production focus is correct, but soaring numbers of people simply overrun even these dramatic production gains; (2) or the diagnosis is incorrect—scarcity is not the cause of hunger, and production increases, no matter how great, can never solve the problem.
>
> The simple facts of world grain production make it clear that the over-population/scarcity diagnosis is actually incorrect. Present world grain production could more than adequately feed every person on earth. Even during the "scarcity" years, 1972 to 1973, there was nine percent more grain per person than in an "ample" year like 1960. Inadequate production is clearly not the problem.
>
> In fact, as ironic as it may sound, a narrow focus on increased production has actually compounded the problem of hunger. Because it goes against the popular wisdom, we found ourselves wanting to verify and re-verify this conclusion in our research at the Institute for Food and Development Policy.
>
> What have we found? The production focus quickly becomes synonymous with "modernizing" agriculture—the drive to supply the "progressive" farmer with imported technology: fertilizer, irrigation, pesticides, and machinery. The green revolution seeds only reinforce this definition of development because their higher yields depend heavily on these inputs. Agricultural progress is thus transformed into a narrow technical problem instead of the sweeping social task of releasing vast, untapped human resources (Lappé and Collins, 1976:2).
>
> In the underdeveloped world the limiting factor in feeding large numbers of people is not a lack of land or farming methods nor a lack of ability or interest among millions and millions of small farmers. The bottleneck is with politicians and

Food Resources

> **ALTERNATIVES FOR SOLVING THE WORLD FOOD PROBLEM**
>
> Following are two arguments for dealing with world hunger and malnutrition:
>
> 1. *Triage.* W. and P. Paddock's book, *Time of Famines,* argued for triage as an inevitable and acceptable solution to the world food problem. Triage is a variant of "lifeboat ethics," the notion popularized by Garrett Hardin.
>
>> 'Triage' is a term used in military medicine. It is defined as the assigning of priority of treatment to the wounded brought to a battlefield hospital in a time of mass casualties and limited medical facilities. The wounded are divided on the basis of three classifications: (1) Those so seriously wounded they cannot survive regardless of the treatment given them; call these the 'can't-be-saved.' (2) Those who can survive without treatment regardless of the pain they may be suffering; call these the 'walking wounded.' (3) Those who can be saved by immediate medical care (Paddock and Paddock, 1976:206).
>
> Applying this thesis to the food problem, Paddock and Paddock said that limited stocks of American foods should not be available to nations that form the "can't-be-saved" group. Food would not be needed for the "walking wounded" nations because they have the necessary agricultural resources or foreign exchange to obtain the food they require. Only nations that can be saved would be recipients of American food. According to Paddock and Paddock, compassion is a luxury no longer affordable in this era of scarcity. We must learn to let people die for the survival of the human race.
>
> 2. *Transforming the World Economic System.* F. M. Lappé and J. Collins in *Food First* explained that the cause of hunger is not too many people, not scarcity of arable land, not lack of technology, and not overconsumption by greedy Americans. For Lappé and Collins no country, not even a Bangladesh, is a "basket case." Every country has the capacity to feed itself. The real food problem is the inequality generated by the world's political economy. Social justice is a priority.
>
>> There is no other road to food security—for others or for us. Americans are made to believe that if justice becomes a priority, production will be sacrificed. We have found the opposite to be true. It is the land monopolizers, both the traditional bonded elites and corporate agribusiness, that have proved themselves to be the most inefficient, unreliable, and destructive users of food resources. The only guarantee of long-term productivity and food security is for people to take control of food resources here and in other countries (Lappé and Collins, 1977:8-9).

vested interests—professionals and the wealthy—who benefit from the way things are. These people influence the access to knowledge and the availability of credit to farmers, the profitability of growing enough to sell a surplus, and the efficiency of marketing and distributing food on a broad scale. Politicians must have the will to develop agriculture and make resources available for domestic consumption, if the hungry are to be fed.

Contrary to popular opinion, small, carefully farmed plots are more productive per hectare than large estates and use fewer costly inputs (Figure 3.10).

Yet despite considerable evidence from around the world, Third World government production programs pass over small farmers. They rationalize that working with bigger production units is a faster road to increased productivity.

> **PLENTY OF FARMING LAND IN UNDERDEVELOPED COUNTRIES**
>
> Underdeveloped countries are not in danger of running out of land for growing foodstuffs. Much good farming land is left uncultivated. Corporations keep large tracts of land out of agriculture for their mining operations in Malaya. Land holders who control large amounts of land in Africa and Latin America leave land unplanted. An example is Colombia. Keith Griffin reported in *Land Concentration and Rural Poverty* that small farmers owning up to six hectares cultivate 66 percent of their land whereas the largest farmers controlling 70 percent of the agricultural land cultivate only 6 percent of their land. Large amounts of land in underdeveloped countries grow luxury crops for export rather than food crops for local people. The World Bank reported that in Mali, "peanut exports to France increased notably during the years of drought while production of food for domestic consumption declined by 1974 to one quarter of what it had been in 1967" (Lappé and Collins, 1977:15).

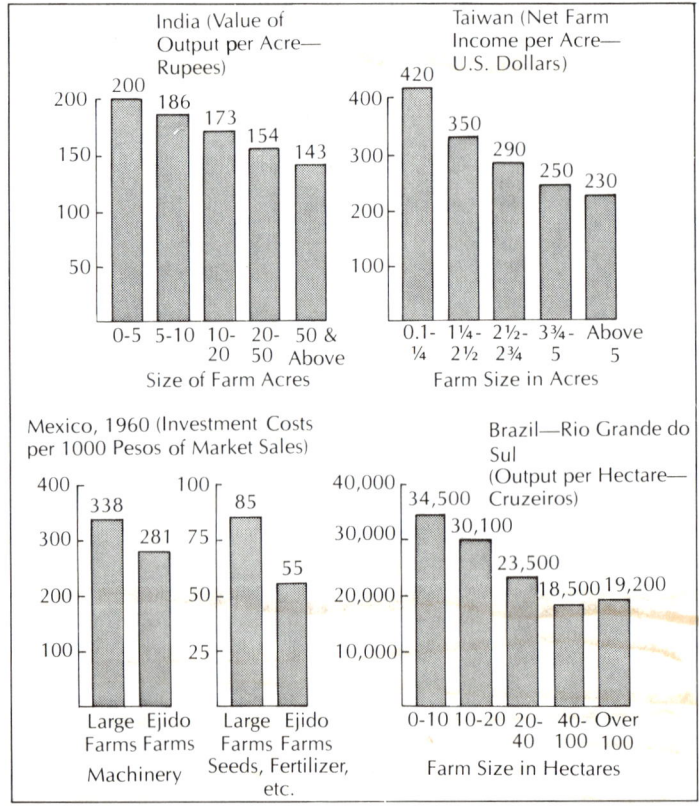

FIGURE 3.10 Small farm efficiency: India, Taiwan, Mexico, Brazil. SOURCES: Raymond P. Cristensen, 1968, *Taiwan's Agricultural Development: Its Relevance for Developing Countries Today*. Washington, D.C.: Economic Research Service, U.S. Dept. of Agriculture, p. 41; Lester Schmid, *Relation of Size of Farm to Productivity*. Madison, Wisc.: Land Tenure Center, University of Wisconsin; Folke Dovring, 1970, *Land Reform in Mexico*. Washington, D.C.: AID, Spring Review of Land Reform, p. 52.

Nonrenewable Mineral Resources

Although we can raise world food output, we cannot raise the supply of nonrenewable mineral resources. Minerals are elements, chemical compounds, or rocks that are concentrated either in the crust of the earth or in the oceans. Our discussion of minerals centers on metallic elements. However, note that with the exception of iron, non-metallic elements, such as carbon, sodium, nitrogen, oxygen, sulfur, potassium, and calcium, are consumed at much greater rates than elements used for their metallic properties.

On a per capita basis, Americans use more minerals than any other people. They consume about one-third of the world's minerals to supply less than 6 percent of the world's population. If the entire world population were to use metals at the same rate as the United States did in 1970, world production of iron would need to increase 75 times, that of copper 100 times, and that of tin 250 times.

Depletion Curves and Depletion Rate Estimates

By "depletion" we mean the time it takes to consume a major proportion of a resource, typically 80 percent. We do not speak about completely running out of a mineral, since it is too expensive to exploit marginal deposits because of either low quality or inaccessibility.

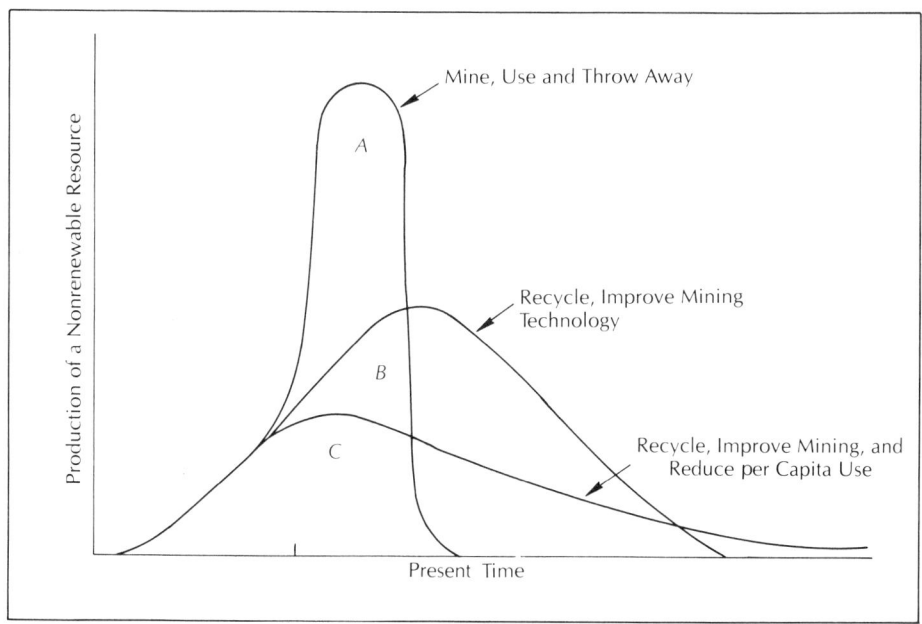

FIGURE 3.11 Depletion curves for a nonrenewable resource; after M. K. Hubbert, 1962, *Energy Resources: A Report to the Committee on Natural Resources*. Washington, D.C.: National Academy of Sciences, Publications 1000-D.

To project the lifetime of a nonrenewable resource we construct *depletion curves* (Figure 3.11). Curve A assumes that we continue our present practice of mining, using, and discarding a resource. Curve B assumes improved mining techniques and recycling. Curve C assumes improved mining techniques and recycling, but also reduced demand. Obviously a substitute resource would negate curves A, B, and C.

Projected Reserves of Key Metals

Our knowledge of world metal reserves is summarized in Table 3.2. It shows the number of years sixteen metals of vital importance to industrial societies will last under three sets of assumptions: (1) the number of years reserves will last with consumption growing at current rates (Column 2); (2) the number of years reserves will last with consumption continuing to grow exponentially (Column 3); and (3) the number of years the reserves could meet growing consumption if they increased five

TABLE 3.2 Projected world reserves of selected metals

Resource	Static Index (Years)*	Exponential Index (Years)†	Exponential Index Calculated Using 5 Times Known Reserves‡ (Years)	U.S. Consumption as Percentage of World Total
Aluminum	100	31	55	42
Chromium	420	95	154	19
Cobalt	110	60	148	32
Copper	36	21	48	33
Gold	11	9	29	26
Iron	240	93	173	28
Lead	26	21	64	25
Manganese	97	46	94	14
Mercury	13	13	41	24
Molybdenum	79	34	65	40
Nickel	150	53	96	38
Platinum	130	47	85	31
Silver	16	13	42	26
Tin	17	15	61	24
Tungsten	40	28	72	22
Zinc	23	18	50	26

NOTES: *Static Index refers to the number of years reserves will last to 80 percent depletion with consumption growing at current rates.
†Exponential Index refers to the number of years reserves will last to 80 percent depletion with consumption increasing at 2.5 percent per annum.
‡Exponential Index refers to the number of years a fivefold increase in known reserves will last to 80 percent depletion with consumption increasing at 2.5 percent per annum.

SOURCE: U.S. Bureau of Mines, 1970.

Nonrenewable Mineral Resources

times (Column 4). Data in Columns 3 and 4 are much more realistic than those in Column 2, and they show that most of the key metals will be exhausted within 100 years, and some will be depleted within a decade or two. The last column of Table 3.2 shows "U.S. Consumption as Percentage of World Trade." In only a few of these commodities is domestic production sufficient to cover consumption.

The United States appears to be running short of domestic resources that made its urban industrialization possible. By comparison to the Soviet Union, we are heavily dependent on foreign sources of key metals (Table 3.3). In the next 30 years, we will become increasingly dependent on imports. Some indication of the growth of United States mineral dependence can be seen in Table 3.4. In 1950 we were

TABLE 3.3 Comparison of self-sufficiency in major industrial raw materials for the United States and the Soviet Union, 1970

Resource	Self-Sufficient United States	Self-Sufficient Soviet Union	Resource	Self-Sufficient United States	Self-Sufficient Soviet Union
Aluminum			Mercury		
Chromium		+	Molybdenum	+	+
Cobalt		+	Nickel		+
Copper		+	Platinum		+
Gold	+	+	Silver	+	+
Iron		+	Tin		
Lead		+	Tungsten	+	
Manganese		+	Zinc		

SOURCE: Adapted from *Living in the Environment: Concepts, Problems and Alternatives* by G. Tyler Miller, Jr. Table 12.1. © 1975 by Wadsworth Publishing Company, Inc., Belmont, California 94002. Reprinted by permission of the publisher.

TABLE 3.4 Rapid growth of import dependence by the United States for twelve raw materials

Resource	Percent Imports 1950	1970	1985	2000	Major Sources of World Reserves in 2000
Chromium	99	100	100	100	U.S.S.R., South Africa, Turkey
Tin	77	100	100	100	Malaysia, Bolivia, Thailand
Manganese	85	95	100	100	U.S.S.R., South Africa, Brazil, Gabon
Nickel	94	90	88	89	Canada, New Caledonia, U.S.S.R., Cuba
Aluminum	40	85	96	98	Jamaica, Surinam, Australia
Zinc	38	59	72	84	Canada, Mexico
Lead	39	57	62	67	Australia, U.S.S.R., Canada, Mexico, Peru
Tungsten	40	40	65	93	China, Canada, Peru
Iron Ore	8	30	55	67	Brazil, U.S.S.R., India, Canada, Venezuela
Potassium	14	42	47	61	Canada, Germany
Copper	31	39	45	75	Chile, U.S.S.R., India, Canada, Zambia, Zaire
Sulfur	2	0	28	52	Canada, Mexico

SOURCE: Adapted from *Living in the Environment: Concepts, Problems, and Alternatives* by G. Tyler Miller, Jr. Table 12.2. © 1975 by Wadsworth Publishing Company, Inc., Belmont, California 94002. Reprinted by permission of the publisher.

dependent (more than 50 percent) on imports for only four out of 16 materials listed. By the year 2000 we are projected to import more than 50 percent of all these vital elements.

Metals projected as future needs by the United States are unevenly distributed around the world. Many of them are located in the Soviet Union and Canada, and in the underdeveloped countries of Africa, Asia, and Latin America (Table 3.4). Whether these critical substances will be available to the United States may depend less on scarcity and more on international politics and tensions.

Is our technological society gravely threatened by the degree to which domestic supplies must be supplemented by importing them from other nations? Just because a particular material must be imported does not mean that it does not exist in quantities that could be mined domestically. We have merely scratched the solid crust of the earth for the materials we need. Given an economical source of ultraterrestrial energy (solar radiation) and ever more ingenious methods of extraction, who can say how much of our mineral needs could eventually be obtained domestically? The environmental cost of "moving mountains" to win these commodites would be another matter, however.

Ocean Mineral Resources and Recycling

Affluent countries are unlikely to be defeated easily by a looming mineral shortage. In the next thirty years, they will devote attention to programs for discovering new deposits, developing substitutes, and improving mining technology. They will be forced to win more resources from the sea and to *recycle* and reuse more resources. Are the oceans and recycling the answer to our mineral problems?

Minerals from the Sea   Vast mineral resources exist in sea water and on the bottom of oceans. With existing technology only a few minerals (magnesium, table salt) are abundant enough to be extracted from sea water profitably. The deep-ocean floor is unlikely to solve mineral shortages. The only known minerals on ocean floors are manganese oxide nodules, which contain about 24 percent magnesium, 14 percent iron, and small amounts of copper, nickel, and cobalt. Although manganese mining is feasible and potentially profitable, political considerations are postponing actual mining operations. Developed countries are fighting among themselves over who should be allowed to exploit seabed wealth. Leaders of underdeveloped countries are opposed to exploitation of these resources by developed countries. They maintain that deep ocean resources belong to all humankind, and should be divided equitably.

Recycling of Resources   Every year in the United States huge quantities of household and industrial waste are disposed of at sanitary landfill sites and open dumps. These materials are sometimes called "urban ores," because they can be recovered and used again to provide energy or new products. For years, the United States has been recycling scarce and highly valuable metals (Figure 3.12). But large amounts of scrap metals are still being wasted. Although we could recover a much greater proportion of scrap with improved technology and economic incentives,

Nonrenewable Mineral Resources

recycling is not going to solve our present environmental problems. Reclaiming and recycling still depends on one resource that cannot be recycled—energy.

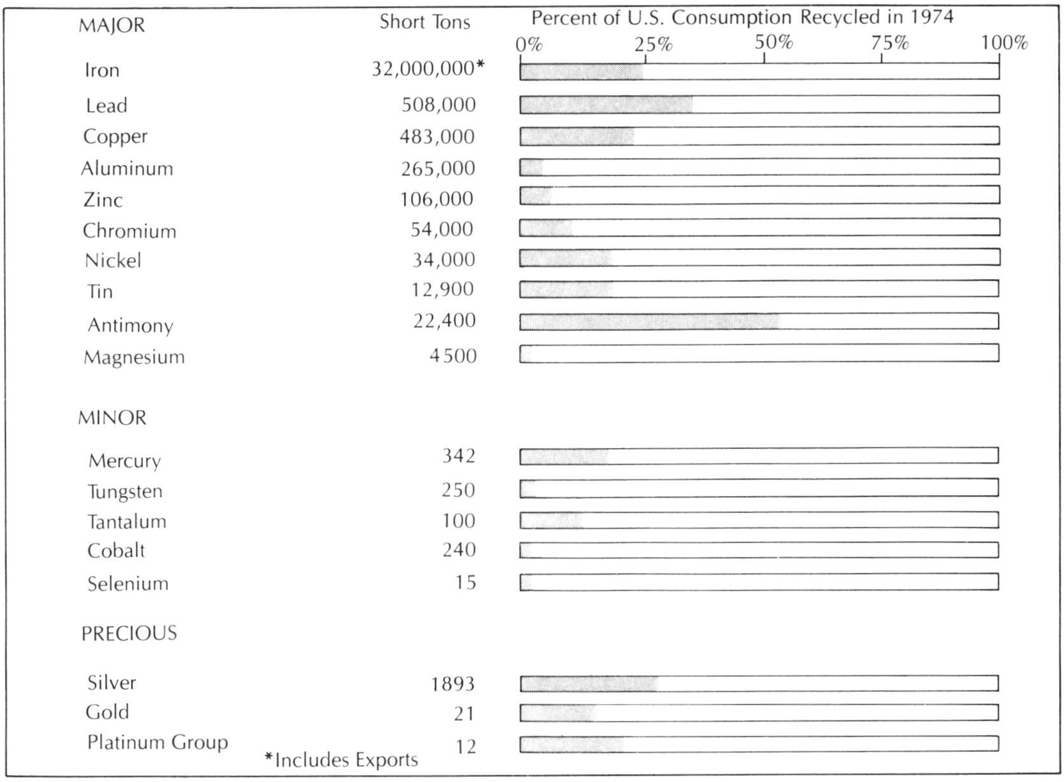

MAJOR	Short Tons	Percent of U.S. Consumption Recycled in 1974
Iron	32,000,000*	~25%
Lead	508,000	~30%
Copper	483,000	~20%
Aluminum	265,000	~5%
Zinc	106,000	~5%
Chromium	54,000	~10%
Nickel	34,000	~15%
Tin	12,900	~15%
Antimony	22,400	~60%
Magnesium	4500	~3%
MINOR		
Mercury	342	~15%
Tungsten	250	~10%
Tantalum	100	~5%
Cobalt	240	~30%
Selenium	15	~5%
PRECIOUS		
Silver	1893	~50%
Gold	21	~30%
Platinum Group	12	~30%

*Includes Exports

FIGURE 3.12 Old scrap reclaimed in the United States, 1974. SOURCE: U.S. Bureau of Mines, 1975.
Note: Although there is more interest in recycling scrap metals, technological and market constraints hamper recycled scrap from playing an important role in supplying U.S. material needs.

Environmental Impact of Mineral Extraction

Mineral extraction has a varied impact on the environment, depending on: mining procedures, local hydrologic conditions, and size of operation. Environmental impact also depends on the stage of development of the mineral: exploration activities usually have a smaller impact than mining and processing mineral resources.

Minimizing the environmental impact of mineral extraction is in everyone's best interest, but the task is difficult since demand for minerals continues to grow, and ever-poorer grades of ore are mined. For example, in 1900 the average grade of copper ore mined was 4 percent copper. By 1973 ores containing as little as 0.53 percent copper were mined. Today more and more rock has to be excavated, crushed, and processed to extract the copper we need. As a consequence there are immense copper-mining pits in Montana, Utah, and Arizona. Some of the excavations cover an area of several square kilometers to a depth of nearly a kilometer.

The Bingham Canyon copper mine, Utah. It is one of the largest excavations in the world, reaching a depth of nearly a kilometer. SOURCE: *Kennecott Copper Corporation* photograph by Don Green.

Open-pit mines and quarries amount to less than one-half of one percent of the total area of the United States. In general, their impact on the environment has been local. But so long as our future remains technological and materialistic, the demand for minerals is going to increase. Lower and lower quality minerals will have to be used, and even with good engineering, environmental degradation will extend far beyond excavation and surface plant areas.

Energy

During the winter of 1976/77 most Americans came face to face with the energy "crisis." A combination of below normal temperatures and a shortage of natural gas was devastating. Thousands of factories were cut back to "plant protection" levels and had to shut down, and over three million workers were laid off. Americans began to appreciate that the energy "crisis" was not just one problem along with many others. They learned first hand that when energy fails, everything fails in an urban industrial economy.

The Energy "Crisis"

The energy "crisis" is our central resource problem. It began when the gap between demand for energy and domestic production started to widen in the 1960s. From

ENERGY

(A) Mammoth tankers bring oilfields "closer" to Western refineries. They reduce transportation costs by hauling large quantities of crude (over two-and-a-quarter million barrels) from the Middle East to deep water transshipment terminals in Europe and North America. SOURCE: *Gulf Oil Corporation*, (B) From the transshipment terminals oil is transported to refineries in conventional vessels. SOURCE: *Exxon Corporation*.

1950 to 1973, United States energy consumption increased at an annual growth rate of 3.5 percent, while domestic production increased at under 3 percent. To make up the difference between domestic energy production and consumption, the United States has become increasingly dependent on foreign fuel supplies. Imported oil as a proportion of total United States demand, for example, increased from 11 percent in 1967 to 50 percent in 1977. The widening gap between domestic energy production and consumption, and the greater gap within the petroleum sector are shown in Figure 3.13.

Energy Consumption Today the United States consumes a third of the world's energy with only 6 percent of its population. By contrast, underdeveloped countries consume only 20 percent of the world's energy and they have 75 percent of the population (see box). The striking relation between energy consumption and income per capita for selected countries is shown in Figure 3.14. Study of Figures 3.15–3.17 and Table 3.5 showing changing world energy production, flows, and consumption, reinforces the image of the developed world as an all-consuming energy sink. Underdeveloped countries receive a meager energy ration, which is well below levels consistent even with moderate rates of economic growth. They do not have the money to buy a better energy ration.

In the United States, industry is the most energy-hungry sector of the economy, generating about 50 percent of the total demand. Transport creates an

TABLE 3.5 World energy: production, trade and composition

World and Region	Year	Production/Trade Total Production + Import/Export Million Metric Tons (Coal Equivalent)			Consumption per Capita Metric Tons
World					
	1955	3298	−	15*	1.29
	1960	4311	−	27	1.41
	1965	5324	−	38	1.59
	1970	7000	−	74	1.89
	1974	8621	−	668	2.05
Anglo-America					
	1955	1320	+	57	6.37
	1960	1441	+	118	7.80
	1965	1767	+	151	9.06
	1970	2260	+	184	10.94
	1974	2388	+	267	11.32
Western Europe					
	1955	571	+	184	2.52
	1960	563	+	284	2.57
	1965	574	+	527	3.05
	1970	557	+	853	3.78
	1974	625	+	914	4.28
Oceania					
	1955	25	+	14	2.86
	1960	31	+	15	2.95
	1965	42	+	20	3.63
	1970	71	+	11	4.03
	1974	109	−	15	4.54
Gulf-Caribbean					
	1955	190	−	136	n.d.
	1960	263	−	180	0.89
	1965	317	−	222	0.99
	1970	357	−	217	1.12
	1974	361	−	188	1.25
Southern America					
	1955	19	+	29	0.56
	1960	34	+	28	0.51
	1965	49	+	28	0.58
	1970	70	+	36	0.71
	1974	103	+	44	0.84
Middle East					
	1955	216	−	182	n.d.
	1960	351	−	301	0.26
	1965	555	−	497	0.35
	1970	942	−	856	0.78
	1974	1668	−	1548	1.03

TABLE 3.5 (continued)

World and Region	Year	Production/Trade Total Production + Import/Export Million Metric Tons (Coal Equivalent)			Consumption per Capita Metric Tons
South and East Asia					
	1955	121	+	25	0.22
	1960	165	+	55	0.24
	1965	199	+	146	0.32
	1970	242	+	354	0.48
	1974	310	+	367	0.67
Africa					
	1955	38	+	16	0.26
	1960	58	+	7	0.31
	1965	197	−	101	0.32
	1970	450	−	337	0.31
	1974	483	−	343	0.40
Centrally planned economies†					
	1955	798	−	21	0.85
	1960	1406	−	53	1.28
	1965	1623	−	90	1.45
	1970	2051	−	102	1.69
	1974	2576	−	167	1.99

*The negative figures in column three for world totals refer to energy in transit.
†Eastern Europe, China (except Taiwan), North Korea, North Vietnam and U.S.S.R.

NOTE: *Production data* are a summation of all major inanimate fuel and energy sources. These include coal, lignite, crude petroleum, natural gas, and hydro and nuclear electricity; where peat used as fuel is important, it is included with coal and lignite. *Consumption data* are based on the apparent consumption of coal, lignite, petroleum products, natural gas and hydro and nuclear electricity. Coke, manufactured gas, and electricity internationally traded are considered to have been consumed by the importing country. Comparison between coal and other sources of energy is based on a conversion to equivalent metric tons of high grade bituminous coal. The first column refers to a region's production, the second column refers to the region's import/export balance. A positive figure means that the region imports so much, in addition to its own production. A negative figure means that the region exports that amount of its production to other parts of the world.

SOURCE: United Nations *Statistical Yearbook*, New York, 1955, 1956, 1960, 1961, 1965, 1966, 1970, 1971, 1975.

additional 25 percent demand, and residential and commercial users demand a little over 25 percent.

Gross United States energy demand increased at about 4 percent a year in the 1960s, but varied by end use (Table 3.6). Commercial energy demands increased fastest, at a rate of 5.4 percent per year, and reflected the growth in the size, number, and importance of services such as offices, shopping centers and schools. Residential demand was stimulated by population growth and rising affluence. The growth of household energy consumption was led by air conditioners, clothes dryers, refrigerators, lighting, and television. Growth of transportation energy use came mainly from automobiles; they carried 95 percent and 85 percent of urban and

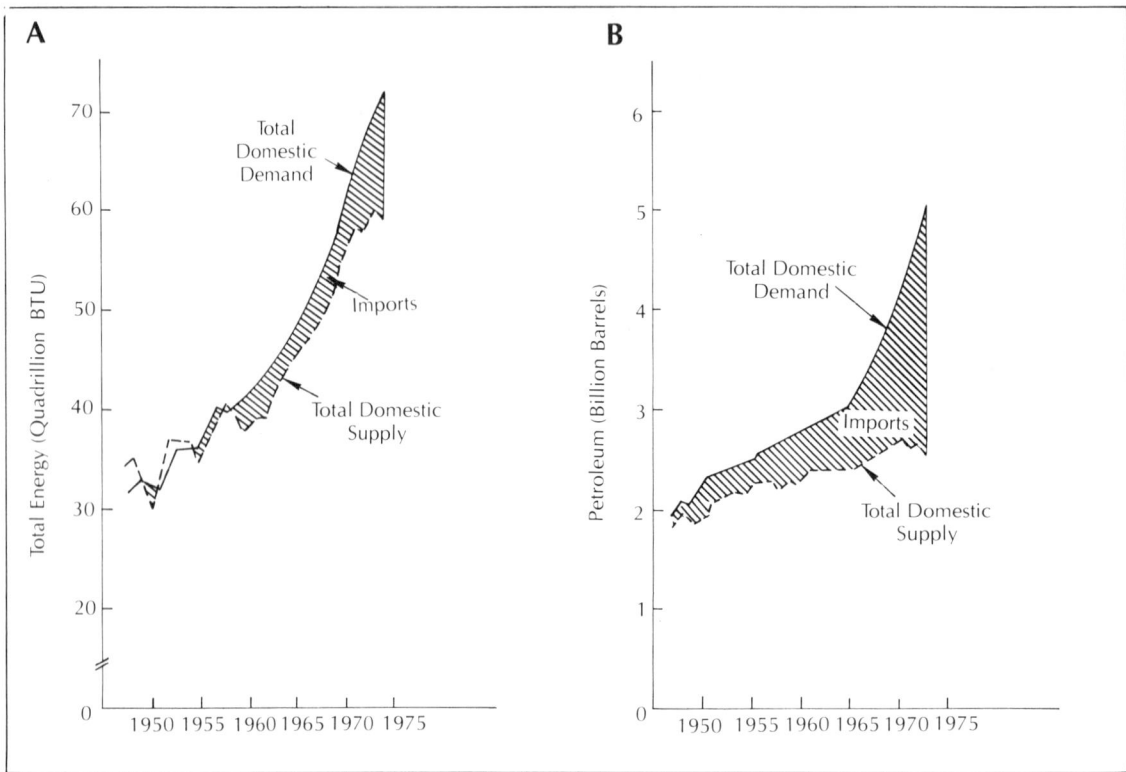

FIGURE 3.13 The widening gap between (A) U.S. energy production and consumption, 1947–1973, and (B) U.S. petroleum production and consumption, 1947–1973. SOURCE: U.S. Bureau of Mines.

interurban passenger traffic, respectively. Increasingly industrial energy use lagged behind other sectors. Most of the growth in industrial energy demand came from six groups: food processing, paper, chemical, petroleum refining, stone, clay, and glass products, and primary metals especially aluminum and steel.

Energy Supply Prior to the fuel supply scare of 1970, the United States energy position seemed so comfortable that most people believed that the abundance of cheap energy sources was a permanent and irreversible state. The nation had become accustomed to a joyride of fossil fuel energy. Between 1880 and the present, we switched from wood to coal, and then from coal to oil and natural gas, which supply about 77 percent of our energy requirements (Figure 3.18).

Between 1950 and 1970, domestic petroleum was plentiful. The arguments of doomsday prophets, who pointed to severe energy shortages in the foreseeable future, were derided or ignored. There was no economic indication that we would be unable to purchase as much energy as we required. During the 1960s, the price of energy was a bargain relative to the price of most other items. Besides low prices, energy consumption was stimulated by: (1) promotional advertising by corporations that encouraged the use of energy consuming goods such as color

Energy

THE FIREWOOD CRISIS

In the underdeveloped world the real energy crisis is the firewood crisis. Most families still rely on firewood as their chief source of energy for cooking and heating. However, their quest for firewood consumes more and more time. For example, the amount of time spent gathering firewood in the once-forested Himalayan foothills has increased from a few hours to a day's labor. What is the solution to the fuel crisis in underdeveloped countries? Is it replanting? Or is it importing expensive oil and gas?

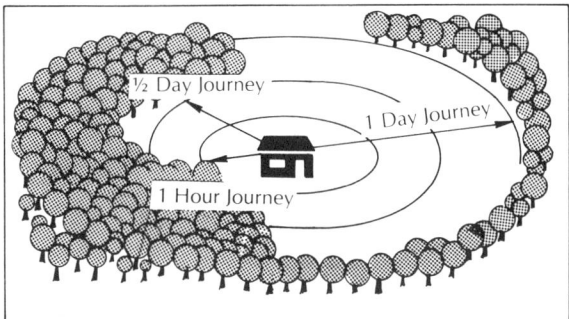

Firewood—the increasing trek for family fuel. SOURCE: *Development Forum*, 1978, **6** (No.1); p. 6.

TABLE 3.6 Total fuel energy consumption in the United States by end use

End Use	Consumption (Trillions of Btu) 1960	1968	Annual Rate of Growth (Percent)	Percent of National Total 1960	1968
Residential	7,968	11,616	4.8	18.6	19.2
Commercial	5,742	8,766	5.4	13.2	14.4
Industrial	18,340	24,960	3.9	42.7	41.2
Transportation	11,014	15,184	4.3	25.5	25.2
National Total	43,064	60,526	4.3	100.0	100.0

NOTE: Electric utility consumption has been allocated to each end use.
SOURCE: Stanford Research Institute, *Patterns of Energy Consumption in the United States*, prepared for the Office of Science and Technology, Executive Office of the President, 1972.

televisions, air conditioners, and automobiles; (2) interstate highway construction that brought a rapid increase in intercity, high-speed auto travel; (3) growth in suburbia that resulted in the soaring use of gasoline for commuters and other energy

A firewood market in the old town of Harar, Ethiopia. In many underdeveloped countries the real fuel "crisis" is the shortage of firewood for cooking and heating. SOURCE: *World Bank Photo* by Kay Muldoon.

for single-family homes; and (4) investment tax incentives and rising wage rates that encouraged industry to expand with energy-intensive capital equipment.

The era of energy abundance ended in 1970. American domestic energy sources diminished and energy demands continued to rise. The Arab oil embargo in October, 1973, resulted in energy shortages visible to motorists who waited in long lines to get gasoline. The Organization of Petroleum Exporting Countries (OPEC), with assistance from multinational oil corporations, proved that they could administer an embargo and make a 400 percent hike in the price of oil stick. The cold winter of 1977 brought with it a natural gas and oil crisis that triggered fears of even greater shortages, higher energy prices, and a new round of inflation in the future. Americans, born into a vision of abundance, realized that lavishness in the use of resources is a luxury of the past.

Energy Policy   According to some experts, the energy "crisis" occurred in the United States because a national energy policy was not a high priority item in government until recently, in contrast to Western Europe where effective national

ENERGY

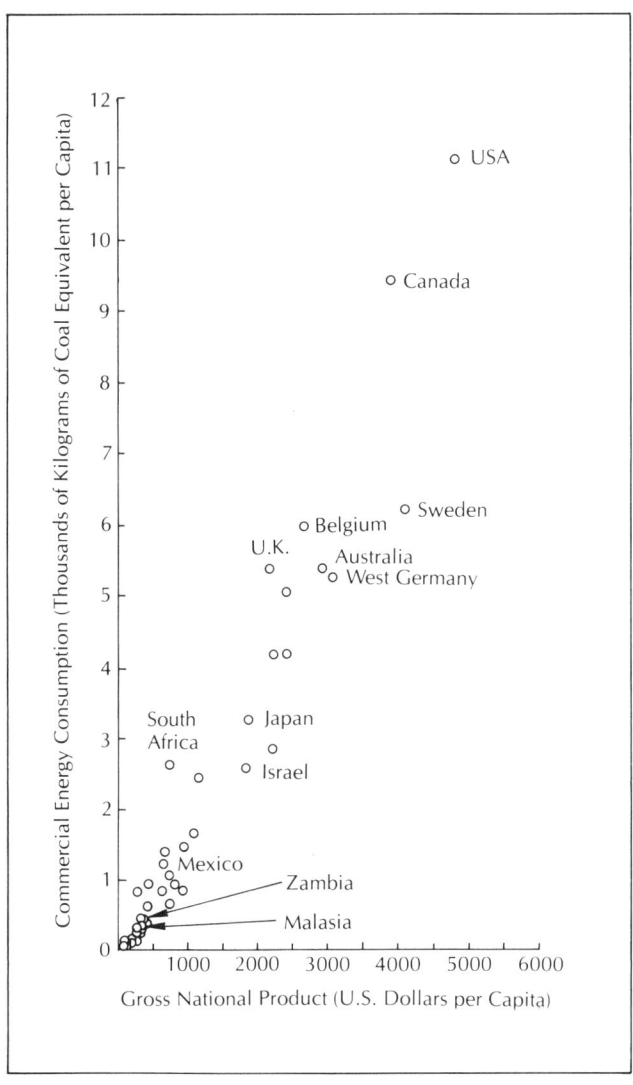

FIGURE 3.14 Relationship between energy consumption and gross national product. SOURCE: *U.N. Statistical Yearbook,* 1974.

energy policies exist. Since the Arab oil embargo, the United States has begun to form a national energy policy and has enacted a major piece of legislation, the Energy Policy and Conservation Act of 1975. An important goal of this law is to reduce energy demand through conservation.

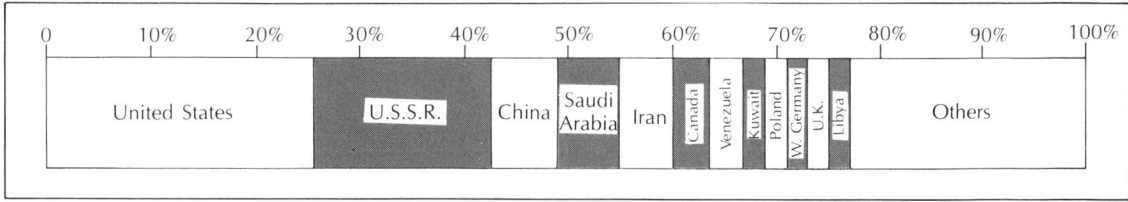

FIGURE 3.15 World energy production, 1975. SOURCE: United Nations.

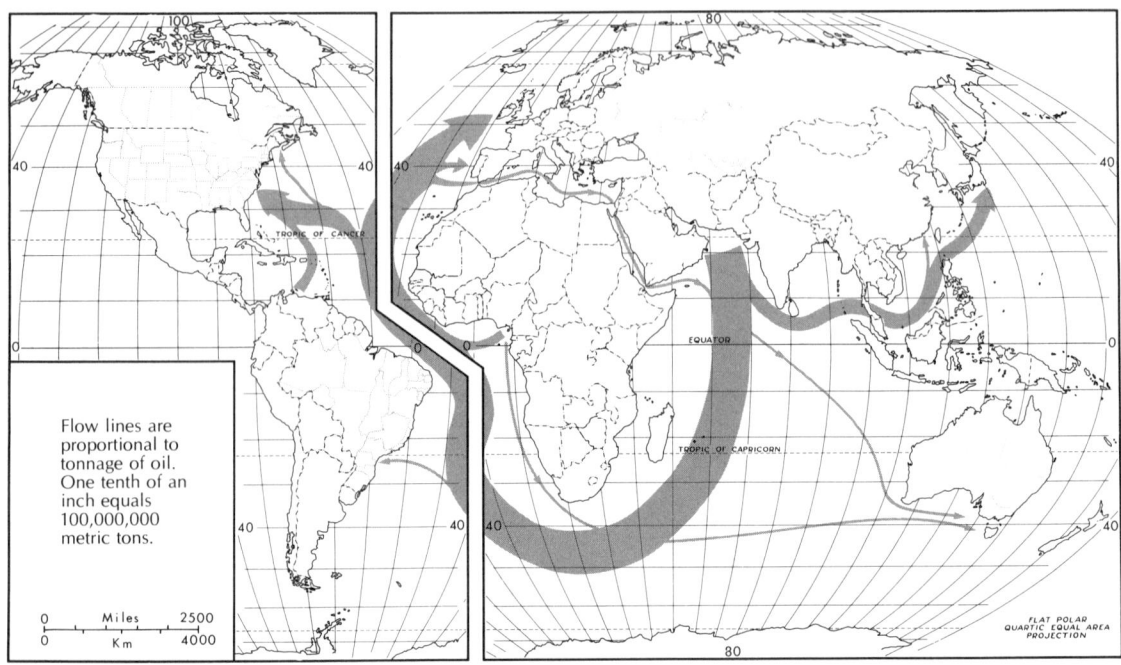

FIGURE 3.16 Movement of petroleum, 1975. SOURCE: United Nations.

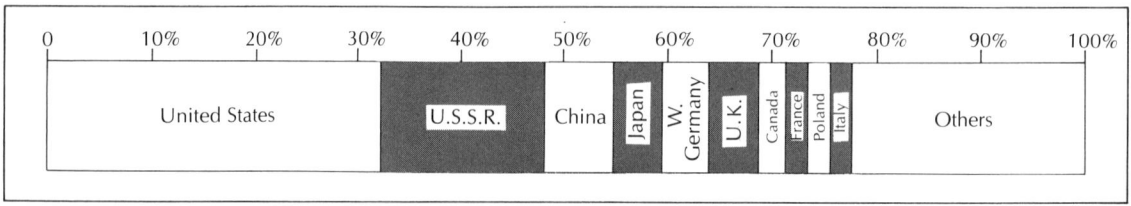

FIGURE 3.17 World energy consumption, 1975. SOURCE: United Nations.

To resolve the energy problem, experts argue that the United States must develop a firm energy policy which requires several objectives, such as assuring a reliable and flexible supply; achieving the lowest cost to society for energy; avoiding economic and regional inequities; and maximizing environmental quality. In addition, recurrent "crises" can only be prevented if the United States takes full account of world energy considerations. Energy is a world wide problem which cannot be solved by groups of nations confronting each other. Sharing energy is essential to protect the interests of all producers and consumers.

Is There an Energy "Crisis"? Radicals believe that the American economy has plenty of energy reserves for the next few decades. In the short run, the problem is what companies are willing to produce. In the long run, shortages will recur if the present economic system prevails.

Energy

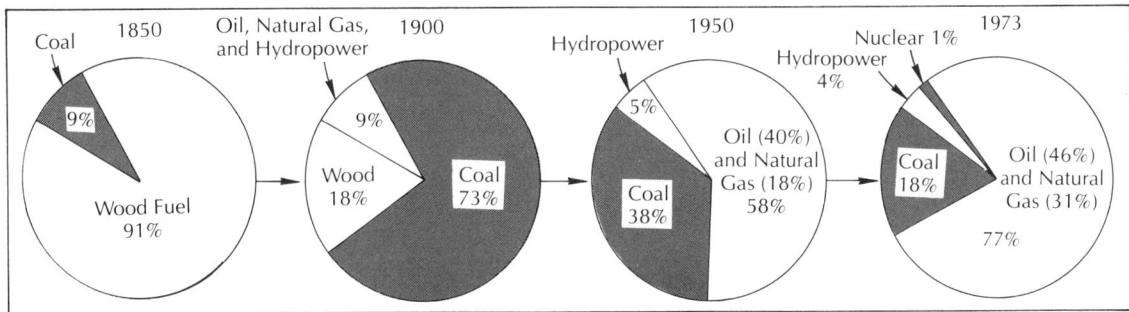

FIGURE 3.18 Changing patterns in energy consumption in the United States. SOURCE: U.S. Bureau of Mines.

Oil exploration in the United States and around the world was stimulated by a dramatic increase in the price of oil in the 1973–1974 energy "crisis." Successful oil exploration may provide a glut for a few years, or buy time to find an alternative energy source. SOURCE: *Standard Oil Company (Indiana) and Amoco Subsidiaries.*

Who do radicals blame for today's energy "crisis"? They blame the big oil companies and electric companies which restrict production because they are *monopolies* and *oligopolies*. Monopoly and oligopoly essentially mean restricted production, more advertising, and higher profits. There is no doubt that the oil companies have been obtaining fatter and fatter profits in the 1970s. According to Ackerman and MacEwan (1974) the profits of the nine largest companies rose by 45 percent in the first nine months of 1973.

Who has suffered from the energy "crisis"? Most consumers, especially those on fixed incomes, many small businesses, and even the independent oil companies have been hurt. What is a reasonable solution to the energy "crisis"? For radicals, it is a democratically controlled energy industry, which would not only expand production, but also reduce profit margins and sponsor basic research into energy options.

Adequacy of Fossil Fuels

United States energy demands are expected to increase about three times faster than population in the next few decades. What resources will be available to meet those demands? Let us examine the availability of different energy sources. Consider first the adequacy of fossil fuels.

Oil and Natural Gas How long can we expect supplies of oil and natural gas to last? Several answers to this question are possible depending on the accuracy of estimated reserves, the likelihood of finding new accumulations, and rates of usage. Based on present information, available supplies of oil and gas will be exhausted as major energy sources between 1990 and 2015 in the United States. Even these estimates may be optimistic; they are based on total resource reserves, not *net energy*. By net energy we mean total energy available minus energy used for discovering, concentrating, and marketing fuels.

Oil Shales Large accumulations of oil-bearing shale are known. The largest deposit in the United States underlies public land in Colorado, Utah, and Wyoming. It is estimated that these states are capable of yielding up to three trillion barrels of oil, or three times known world reserves. Unfortunately, it takes almost as much energy to extract oil from shale as the shale oil produces, with today's technology. If this assessment is correct, shale oil will not become a source of readily available net energy in the near future. Furthermore, oil shale development raises environmental problems. With surface or conventional underground mining, for example, it is difficult to dispose of huge quantities of spent shale and to revegetate the soil.

Coal Coal is the most abundant fossil fuel, and the United States contains nearly 20 percent of the world's reserves (Table 3.7). It constitutes 80 percent of America's fossil fuel resources, yet supplies only 19 percent of our energy consumption. If this share does not increase, the projected life of coal is 200 to 400

TABLE 3.7 World coal reserves, major countries, 1966

Nation	Percent of World Total
USSR	56.4
USA	19.5
Asia (mainly China)	8.9
Canada	7.9

SOURCE: Paul Averitt, 1969, *Coal Resources of the United States–January 1, 1967*. United States Government Printing Office, U.S. Geological Survey Bulletin 1275.

years. If this share increases, and more than one half of the net energy is lost in mining, shipping, or by converting to more convenient forms of energy such as electricity, gas, and synthetic oil, the projected life is sharply reduced. Scientists say coal gasification and liquefaction could deplete United States supplies within 50 years.

The United States government considers coal a temporary solution to diminishing liquid and gaseous fuels. It wants to increase coal production as the cornerstone of a national energy policy—from 665 million tons in 1976 to around one billion tons by 1985. But there are so many problems to overcome, ranging from mine-safety and labor strife to air pollution and land reclamation, we find it hard to see how this goal can be met.

Coal is plagued by environmental problems. It produces the most air pollution from sulfur oxides. Sulfur-dioxide scrubbers have to be installed on smokestacks of utilities and factories before plentiful high-sulfur Eastern and Midwestern coals can be burned cleanly. Surface mining, which accounts for more than one-half of current production, denudes large areas, creates soil erosion, pollutes streams, and destroys wildlife habitats. Strip-mined land is restorable in level areas of the Midwest, but is difficult to restore in hilly Appalachia, and even more difficult in the arid climate of Montana, Wyoming, New Mexico, Arizona, and the Dakotas, which contain large reserves of low sulfur coal. Soils in the West are thin, and revegetation is difficult because water to establish new vegetation is scarce. Moreover, water scarcity limits the development of Western coal conversion industries. Processes such as coal gasification, liquefying coal, and generating power require huge quantities of water.

The United States is caught in an environmental-energy dilemma. Increased coal consumption is not now compatible with either the Clean Air Act of 1970 or strict land reclamation. We wonder whether mounting pressure to increase coal consumption will result in a relaxation of existing environmental laws and standards.

Energy Options

The age of cheap fossil fuels is over. We are told by corporations and the government that the current energy "crisis" in the United States will require time and effort to overcome. We are also told that we must conserve energy and find alternatives to fossil fuels, especially alternatives that will not rape the environment.

Conservation According to utility companies and the government, the only way to reduce the gap between domestic production and consumption in the short run is for consumers to restrict consumption. Energy conservation stretches finite fuel resources and reduces environmental stress. Conservation can substitute for expensive, environmentally less desirable supply options, and help to buy time for the development of other more acceptable sources of energy.

Many people believe that energy conservation means a slow growth economy. Evidence indicates that energy growth and economic growth are not inextricably linked. In the United States, from the early 1870s to 1950, gross national

FIGURE 3.19 Energy consumption per unit of gross national production. SOURCE: U.S Bureau of Economic Analysis and U.S. Bureau of Mines.

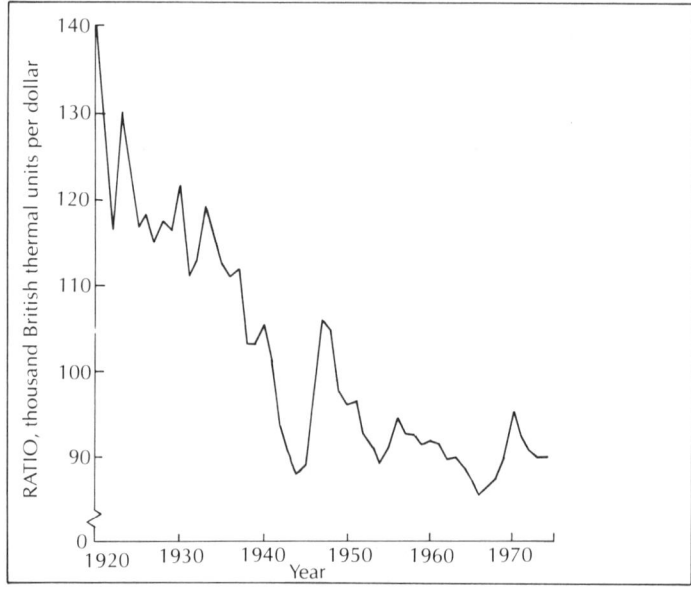

product per capita increased sixfold, whereas energy use per capita slightly more than doubled. As indicated in Figure 3.19, *energy efficiency,* the ratio of useful energy output to total energy input, increased substantially between 1921 and 1975.

At least two approaches to energy conservation have been suggested by the government and energy companies. One approach is to increase energy efficiency. Consumers can add insulation and storm windows to their homes; they can drive more slowly, use smaller automobiles, and ride buses. Power plants can transmit "waste heat" to nearby plants. At best, utilities convert 27 percent of fuel energy into electricity. The rest escapes as heat in the form of warm air and gases. Consumers can lower thermostats, switch to lower wattage light bulbs, and take showers instead of baths. Industry could rely on less energy and more labor. The other approach is less attractive to most Americans: compulsory allocation and rationing. If consumers are not willing to alter their styles of life voluntarily in order to save energy, then compulsory methods can be introduced to make sure that everyone shares the burden equally.

Alternative Energy Options The United States may be running out of fossil fuels, but it is in no danger of running out of energy. One hotly debated alternative is nuclear energy (Fig. 3.20). Nuclear energy generates less than 6 percent of America's total electric supply, but it is becoming a more important source. The United States Atomic Energy Commission has recommended that this proportion rise to 60 percent by the year 2000. Proponents of atomic energy argue that it is the safest, cheapest, and cleanest of available alternatives to meet projected energy growth. On the other hand, opponents question the desirability of nuclear power, because it may impose severe environmental penalties (Table 3.8). The possibility of fall-out of deadly radioactive materials is a major concern. An accidental release of only 1 percent of the radioactivity at the fuel processing plant in South Carolina, for example, would probably require the evacuation of the entire East Coast. The wisdom of a commitment to nuclear power depends ultimately on the ability of technology and institutions to manage a very hazardous enterprise. There is little agreement as to whether human institutions are capable of managing nuclear energy wisely. But so long as the United States' economic system is hooked on increased energy consumption it seems inevitable that nuclear power will be required to help meet the demand. Only if there were a long term commitment to the development of other energy sources could a curtailment of nuclear power growth be taken seriously.

FIGURE 3.20 Nuclear power reactors in the United States, 1974. Note that many nuclear power reactors are located near large population clusters. SOURCE: Office of Industry Relations, The Nuclear Industry, 1974.

Geothermal power development holds promise for the future, especially in the western United States, where natural heat flow from the earth's core is relatively high. Electricity produced from geothermal power will never exceed a few percent of the total power generated in the United States, but it will be significant. Largely because of technical limitations, widespread geothermal power production is not now feasible. Production is limited to one easily exploited vapor-dominated system called The Geysers, north of San Francisco.

Another source of electrical power, and one that is virtually inexhaustible, is energy from rivers. Hydroelectric power plants provide about 15 percent of the total electricity produced in the United States. Although this proportion is likely to be reduced to about 10 percent by the year 2000, it will remain an important source of power in regions of the country such as the Pacific Northwest. Future development of hydro-electric power is limited because many of the best sites are

TABLE 3.8 Comparison of environmental effects of coal, oil, gas and uranium electrical power generation

Energy Source	Effects on Land	Effects on Water	Effects on Air	Biological Effects	Supply
Coal	Disturbed land; large amount of solid waste	Acid mine drainage; increased water temperature	Sulfur oxides; nitrogen oxides; particulates; some radio-active gases	Respiratory problems from air pollutants	Large reserves
Oil	Wastes in the form of brine; pipeline construction	Oil spills; increased water temperature	Nitrogen oxides; carbon monoxide; hydrocarbons	Respiratory problems from air pollutants	Limited reserves
Gas	Pipeline construction	Increased water temperature	Some oxides of nitrogen	Few known effects	Extremely limited domestic reserves
Uranium	Disposal of radioactive waste	Increased water temperature; some radioactive liquids	Some radioactive gases	None detectable in normal operation	Large reserves if breeder reactors are developed

SOURCE: Pennsylvania Department of Education, 1973, *The Environmental Impact of Electrical Power Generation: Nuclear and Fossil.*

Energy

Alternative energy options: (A) nuclear energy (SOURCE: *United States Department of Energy*); (B) geothermal energy (SOURCE: Photo courtesy of *Pacific Gas and Electric Company*); (C) hydroelectric power (SOURCE: *Tennessee Valley Authority*); (D) solar energy (SOURCE: *Westinghouse Electric Corporation*); and (E) wind energy (SOURCE: Eric Schwab for *World Health Organization*).

already used. Furthermore, many rivers are being protected from development by legislation.

Like river power, tidal and wind energy are inexhaustible. Electricity produced from tidal power is expected to increase in the future, but it will never have more than local significance. It depends on major differences between high and low tides, and, because of this, it can supply only a fraction of the potential of river power. Windpower has the disadvantage of low concentration, and in most places, unpredictable strength. It should not, however, be dismissed as of little value; the potential of windpower should be investigated.

Enormous amounts of energy with negligible environmental effects are potentially available from the sun. This desirable energy alternative has caught the public's eye through publicity of the few solar homes and buildings built in the United States. The sun's energy is gathered in rooftop collectors to provide most of the energy for heating and cooling. Large-scale utilization of solar radiation, however, poses technical difficulties, particularly that of low concentration of the energy. The energy of the direct rays of the sun at sea-level has been estimated at slightly more than one horse-power per square meter. So far, technology has been able to convert only 10 percent of this energy into electricity. If research programs are successful, solar energy could provide a large fraction of our power needs within a few decades. It is hoped that by the year 2020, solar energy could provide between 15 and 30 percent of the total United States energy demand.

Solar, geothermal, wind, and other alternatives to nuclear power and fossil fuels have received relatively little funding in the United States. It is a short-sighted policy to restrict future energy options. Emphasis on oil, coal, and nuclear power could lead to energy, environmental, and human catastrophes. It is essential to explore a wide range of energy ideas so that we may have available the best combination of options 20, 40, or 100 years from now in terms of both net energy and environmental impact.

From a Cowboy to a Spaceship Life-style

Energy availability will not place a limit on economic growth; plenty of energy options exist. The ultimate limit to the use of energy will be determined by the amount of contamination the environment can absorb.

In countless ways, energy improves the quality of our lives, but it also pollutes. As the rate of energy consumption increases, the amount of waste and heat

---

VIEWS ON POLLUTION

Pollution, like planned obsolescence, and lack of conservation, is a form of economic waste. Conservatives argue that non-pollution of land, air, and water could be given a price and bought and sold in the market, thus automatically solving the problem. Liberals insist that the capitalist state must pass and enforce laws to prevent pollution by private enterprise. Radicals charge that both conservatives and liberals fail to appreciate that the "right to pollute" is imbedded in our present economic system. Managers have their attention focused on profit targets and production schedules, and naturally oppose legal controls. For radicals, an end to waste and pollution is possible only within a democratic socialist society.

Energy 137

Paris, France. Waste products of all kinds are discharged into the rivers, causing pollution dangerous for aquatic life and for people. Detergents are among the most common forms of pollution, easily recognized by a thick white foam. SOURCE: F. Bibal for *UNESCO*.

discharged into the environment also increases. Industrial wastes, sewage, and detergents flow into lakes and rivers. Waste gases and solid particles in the atmosphere reduce visibility, damage buildings, clothes and crops, and endanger human health. Energy consumption in the United States, as in other technological societies, is now producing a volume of solid wastes and gases that cannot be dissipated by natural processes.

Pollution is one of the costs generated by an economic system based on a goal of ever increasing growth, which we will call a "cowboy" life-style. A "cowboy" life-style distorts the environment and robs the earth of its resources for more and more electric hair dryers and air conditioners. "Growthmania" is a road to nowhere. It is easy to see why. If an economy grows at a 5 percent annual growth rate, it would by the year 2100 reach a level 50,000 percent higher than the present level. Problems of acquiring, processing, and disposing of materials stagger the imagination. If the human species is to survive, we must change our "cowboy" economy into a "spaceship" economy (Table 3.9). "Spaceship" economics explicitly recognizes the Earth's finiteness. It assumes that resources are exhaustible, that they must be recycled, and that input rates must be reduced to levels that do not irreversibly damage the world's life-support systems. A spaceship economy would not mean zero growth. Growth will occur; undesirable material and industrial growth will be controlled, while desirable low-energy, high-labor growth will be encouraged.

Humankind is confronted with two choices: one, that of continuing along the present path of economic growth, the other, that of starting along the path of a "spaceship" economy. The first choice involves a short-run philosophy of

TABLE 3.9 Comparison of cowboy and spaceship life-styles

Cowboy Lifestyle	Spaceship Lifestyle
Essentially infinite resources and energy.	Finite resources and infinite energy (if fusion or solar energy can be developed).
Linear flow of matter and energy.	Linear flow of energy but recycling of matter.
Increase flow rates of matter and energy and output (maximize throughput).	Stabilize flow rates of matter and energy by deliberately reducing throughput—a steady-state system with balanced inputs and outputs well below the limits of the system.
Goals of efficiency, quantity, simplification, and cultural and physical homogeneity to attain short term stability	Goals of quality and deliberate preservation of cultural and physical diversity to attain long term stability at the expense of some efficiency.
Output control of pollution (consequences of second law of thermodynamics can be avoided or minimized by cleaning up output).	Input and output control (consequences of the second law of thermodynamics can be decreased in the long run by decreasing input and flow rates along with controlling output).
Continued growth provides capital for output control and redistribution of wealth (trickle down theory).	If growth continues, capital must be increasingly devoted to maintenance and repairs, thus decreasing life quality and preventing redistribution of wealth.
Free enterprise, a competitive market system, or a centralized control economy that can respond to undesirable side effects.	Market responds only if we find ways to include quality of life indicators into the price of goods and services.
Short term view and planning.	Long term view and planning.
Local and national outlook.	Global outlook.

NOTE: The table suggests that we can transform our "cowboy" lifestyle to a "spaceship" lifestyle without restructuring our economic system. Can we become "spacemen" and, at the same time, maintain our existing market system?

SOURCE: Adapted from *Living in the Environment: Concepts, Problems, and Alternatives* by G. Tyler Miller, Jr. © 1975 by Wadsworth Publishing Company, Inc., Belmont, California 94002. Reprinted by permission of the publisher.

resource use; a temporary life-style of abundant red meat, two or more cars per family, and a plentitude of energy-extravagent home appliances; and uneven and unequal distribution of quality of life. This choice will compound all our present resource and environmental crises.

Summary

Smokestacks, such as these in the Saar industrial region of the Federal Republic of Germany, contribute to the creation of serious problems through pollution of air and water, damage to agricultural lands, and destruction of scenery. Combustion of fossil fuels has increased the amount of atmospheric carbon dioxide by 10 percent over the last 100 years. SOURCE: *United Nations.*

The second choice entails restructuring our economic system and rethinking old assumptions and old emphases about economic growth. If adopted, it will lead to a beginning, not to an end. Can we respond to a permanent requirement for lowered material expectations? Can we be satisfied with a future that seeks more in quality and equality than in quantity and inequality? If we can become proud of saving and conserving as our grandparents did, rather than of spending and discarding, then current "crises" in energy, minerals, water, and food may be lessons in disguise.

Summary

This chapter began by restating the resources-population relation. It is possible to solve resource problems by (1) altering the social organization of scarcity, (2) changing consumption patterns, (3) changing technology, and (4) altering population numbers. In the Western world much of the emphasis is on (3) and (4).

Following a review of renewable and nonrenewable resources, we turned to the question of food resources. Let us repeat that the food "crisis" is essentially a result of the *social organization of scarcity.* There *is* more food being produced by *capital-centered* methods, but there are also *more* hungry people. Why? Agriculture is being *transformed.* Once the livelihood for millions and millions of small farmers in the Third World, agriculture is being turned into a profit base for traditional landed elites, military officers, city-based speculators, and foreign corporations (Lappé and Collins: 1976). In the course of this transformation, the hungry are being forced out of the production process. According to Lappé and Collins, the only guarantee of "long-term food security is for people to take control of food resources" (1977:9).

We looked at mineral resources and discussed the energy "crisis." Do you think that current energy shortages are caused by the capitalist law of accumulation and by big energy companies? The chapter ended by indicating that the quality of economic growth (with a minimum of waste and pollution) is more important than the *quantity* of growth.

DISCUSSION QUESTIONS

1. Write an essay on population–natural resource relationships.
2. Is the United States the most overpopulated country in the world? Why or why not?
3. Explain why most people in the world do not eat very much meat.
4. Give arguments for and against the "Green Revolution."
5. Explain why food production is increasing and yet there are more hungry people than ever before.
6. Discuss: Modern agricultural technologies are narrow-minded and out of step with natural cycles.
7. Discuss: Technology will help solve world environmental problems.
8. Is there an energy "crisis"?
9. Explain why a lasting solution to the resource "crisis" can only be effected within a world framework.
10. "Growthmania" is a road to nowhere. Discuss.
11. What is a "cowboy" economy? Compare it with a "spaceship" economy.

SUGGESTED READINGS

Population-Resource Relations

Callahan, D., ed., *The American Population Debate*. Garden City: Doubleday and Co., Inc., 1971.

Commoner, B., *The Closing Circle: Nature, Man and Technology*. New York: Knopf, 1971.

Suggested Readings

Ehrlich, P. R., and A. H. Ehrlich, *Population, Resources and Environment: Issues in Human Ecology.* San Francisco: W. H. Freeman and Company, 1970.

Harvey, D., "Population, Resources, and the Ideology of Science," *Economic Geography,* **50** (1974): 256–277.

Growth and Environment

Lecomber, R., *Economic Growth Versus Environment.* New York: John Wiley & Sons, 1975.

Meadows, D., et. al., *The Limits to Growth.* New York: The New American Library, 1972.

Mesarovic, M., and Edward Pestal, *Mankind at the Turning Point.* New York: Signet, 1976.

Mishan, E. J., *Technology and Growth: The Price We Pay.* New York: Praeger, 1969.

Ridker, R. G., "To Grow or Not to Grow: That's Not the Relevant Question," *Science,* **182** (1973): 1315–1318.

Schumacher, E. F., *Small is Beautiful.* London: Blond and Briggs, Ltd., 1973.

Food, Mineral, and Energy Problems

Allaby, M., *The World Food Problem. Can We Solve It?* London: Tom Stacey, Ltd., 1972.

Brobst, D. A., W. P. Pratt, and V. E. McKelvey, *Summary of United States Mineral Resources.* U.S. Geological Circular **682,** 1973.

Brown, L. R., and G. W. Finsterbusch, *Man and His Environment: Food.* New York: Harper and Row, 1972.

Cook, E., *Energy: The Ultimate Resource.* Washington, D.C.: Association of American Geographers Commission on College Geography, Resource Paper No. 77-4, 1977.

Clarkson, W., *Energy for Survival: The Alternative to Extinction.* New York: Anchor/Doubleday, 1974.

Fagan, J. J., *The Earth Environment.* Englewood Cliffs, New Jersey: Prentice-Hall, 1974.

George, S., *How the Other Half Dies—The Real Reasons for World Hunger.* Montclair, New Jersey: Allanheld, Osmun and Co. Publishers Inc., 1977.

Knight, C. G., and R. P. Wilcox, *Triumph or Triage? The World Food Problem in Geographical Perspective.* Washington, D.C.: Association of American Geographers, Commission on College Geography, Resource Paper No. 75-3, 1976.

Lappé, F. M., and J. Collins, *Food First. Beyond the Myth of Scarcity.* Boston: Houghton Mifflin Company, 1977.

Odun, H. T., *Environment, Power and Society.* New York: John Wiley & Sons, 1971.

U.S. Geological Survey, *Mineral Resource Perspectives 1975.* U.S. Geological Survey Professional Paper 940, 1975.

4

Agriculture and Rural Land Use

KEY TERMS

- agribusiness
- agriculture
- average product
- capital-intensive
- cultural preferences
- domestication hearths
- economic rent
- environmental perception
- extensive margin
- highest and best use
- intensive margin
- isolated state
- labor-intensive
- marginal product
- optimizer
- permanent cultivation
- plantation
- relative location
- rent gradient
- shifting cultivation
- site characteristics
- space-cost curve
- spatial margins to profitability
- stages of production
- systems of production
- total product

4

Farming is the most pervasive of all economic activities. In underdeveloped countries, as much as two-thirds of the population are directly engaged in food production. In most developed countries, however, less than one-quarter of the population is now required for the production of food. Agricultural and industrial revolutions in the last 200 years released people for other pursuits.

In the United States, the proportion of the labor force in agriculture was 27 percent at the end of World War I, but only 4 percent in 1970. This decline is associated with a flight to the cities. In many instances, small farmers have been pushed from the land by unstable and low farm prices and the invasion of agribusiness. During the last 40 years, the number of farms in America has decreased from 6.8 million to 2.8 million. Most of the farms left in the United States are still family operated, but they produce very little compared to a few huge "corporate farmers." About 4 percent of America's farms produce half of all the food that feeds the farming and non-farming population, and provides millions of tons for export as well (George, 1977:3).

Around the world, the type and intensity of farm production varies enormously. Major variables producing diversity are site characteristics such as climate and soil type, cultural traits of farmers and consumers, systems of production such as capitalism or communism and relative location or situation.

Economic geographers try to explain the location of distinctive agricultural types by an agricultural location model formulated by Thünen, a nineteenth century German landowner. In his study, *The Isolated State,* Thünen showed that *transport to market* is the primary force determining rural land use patterns. Although his model was developed for a landlord/peasant system of agriculture, it provides insights into present land use patterns in many parts of the world.

We begin this chapter with a discussion of the diffusion of agriculture and the impact of food production on the land. That section is followed by an examination of the basic factors that influence agricultural patterns. The last two sections deal with Thünen's model of agricultural location. They describe the origin, content, and usefulness of his model and compare his theoretical principles against real world examples at different geographical scales.

OBJECTIVES

By the end of this chapter you should be able:

1. To describe the origin and diffusion of agriculture.
2. To discuss the effects of agricultural practices on the land.
3. To identify and discuss variables that help to control patterns of agricultural land use.
4. To define the concepts of *diminishing returns* and *economic rent*.
5. To discuss the relationship between location, rent, and transport costs.
6. To discuss the relationship between the intensity of agriculture and distance from the market.
7. To discuss a farmer's choice of crops at varying distances from the market.
8. To discuss how changes in market prices, production, and transport costs alter the distribution of agricultural activities.
9. To know the socio-economic conditions under which the Thünen model was developed.
10. To explain the usefulness of Thünen's model.

Transforming Nature: Agriculture

The course toward complex urban-industrial life is marked by the rise of farms at the expense of the wilderness, and by the rise of cities at the expense of the countryside. *Agriculture* was the first humanized land use capable of significantly modifying the natural environment. Before agriculture, landscapes evolved under the laws of nature.

The Emergence of Agriculture

When humans discovered agriculture, they learned how to trap solar energy to produce food and fiber plants by using the basic components of soil, moisture, and the atmosphere. They learned how to tame and control the breeding of animals. Domestication of plants and animals was a halting, slow process, not a sudden event. Raising crops and animals probably emerged as an extension of food gathering activities of preagricultural hunters and gatherers, and as a response to a slow sustained increase in population pressure.

Scholars have been unable to say exactly where and when the shift from food collection to food production took place. However, many archeologists, who have studied the origins of agriculture, suspect that farming began in the Fertile

Crescent of the Middle East nearly 10,000 years ago (Figure 4.1). This was a well-watered area extending from the highlands of the eastern Mediterranean through the foothills of the Tauras and Zagros Mountains. Archeological finds also show that independent farming patterns began early in parts of Central America and Southeast Asia.

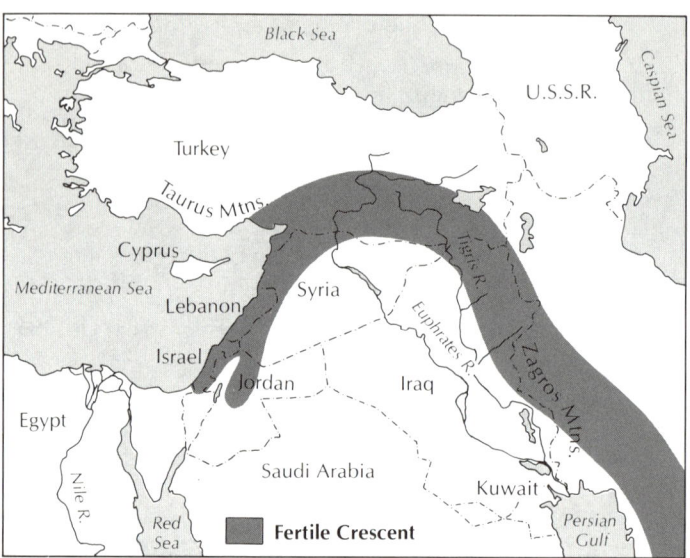

FIGURE 4.1 The Fertile Crescent.

Although the precise origin and location of agriculture is uncertain, the impact of agriculture is incontestable. A reliable food supply released people from food gathering. Craft industries developed, and specialized goods, pottery and cloth for example, were exchanged and traded. Forces that scattered population weakened, while forces that concentrated population strengthened. Agriculture permitted population to agglomerate in villages and towns and to reach densities many times higher than those found in preagricultural communities.

Agricultural methods that emerged during the first agricultural revolution persisted with only slight modification until the Middle Ages in Western Europe. The most important innovations associated with the second agricultural revolution were (1) the heavy plow; (2) the use of horses instead of oxen for plowing; and (3) the development of a three-course system. These advances increased agricultural production to feed a growing population, helped intensify human concentration in thousands of villages and towns, generated more commerce, and changed patterns of environmental exploitation. The forested lowlands of Western Europe, for example, were gradually cleared when the heavy plow was invented. Heavy lowland soils could not be cultivated with the old Mediterranean scratch plow.

Medieval farming methods prevailed in Western Europe until a third agricultural revolution occurred in the eighteenth and nineteenth centuries. Agriculture became commercialized. Open fields were enclosed by fences, hedges, and walls. Crop rotation replaced the medieval practice of fallowing fields. Seeds and breeding stock improved. New agricultural areas were opened up in the Americas.

Machinery took over agricultural jobs. A worldwide network of agricultural production, exchange, and consumption replaced localized patterns.

Since 1920, there has been a fourth agricultural revolution in the developed world. Some of the most far reaching changes include: the use of an array of synthetic fertilizers, herbicides, and pesticides; the switch from animal to fossil fuel power; the shift from pasture and open ranges to feedlots, where hundreds, even thousands, of animals are concentrated; the development of high yielding crops, livestock, and poultry; the gradual change from small diversified farms to large, specialized production units; and the establishment of large storage facilities and elaborate processing and marketing of foods. These inputs have created an extremely complex, integrated system of farming, whose long-range effects are imperfectly understood. The new agriculture is a far cry from simpler farming systems that prevailed a generation or two ago. This new approach to increasing food production is the one that the United States is trying to export to the rest of the world.

The Diffusion of Agriculture

We can identify at least ten major plant and animal *domestication hearths* (Table 4.1 and Figure 4.2). The dispersal of agriculture from these centers was a slow process. For example, archeologists, using radio-carbon dating, have calculated that it took from 6000 BC until 3000 BC for a form of shifting cultivation to spread along the Danube and Rhine corridors. Another 1000 years elapsed before agriculture reached southern England.

By 1500 AD, on the eve of European overseas expansion, agriculture had spread widely throughout the Old World and much of the New World (Figure 4.3). In Europe, the Middle East and North Africa, Central Asia, China and India, cereal farming and horticulture were common features of rural economy. Non-agricultural areas of the Old World were restricted to the Arctic fringe of Europe and Asia, where growing seasons are too short for agriculture, and to parts of southern and central Africa. Agriculture had not spread beyond the Eastern Indian Islands into Australia.

In the New World, the cultivation of maize, beans, and squash had spread, by the time of the first European voyages across the Atlantic, throughout Central America and the humid environment of the eastern half of North America as far north as the Great Lakes. In South America, only parts of the Amazon Basin, the uplands of northeastern Brazil, and the dry temperate south did not have an agricultural economy.

These patterns of agriculture persisted until the era of European overseas settlements. From the Age of Discovery to the middle of the seventeenth century, Europeans did not attempt to establish large overseas settlements. Eventually European settlement assumed two forms: "farm-family" colonies in the middle latitudes of North America, Australia, New Zealand, and South Africa, and "plantation" colonies in the tropical regions of Africa, Asia, and Latin America. These two types of agricultural settlement differed considerably. Farm colonization in the New World, for example, depended on a large influx of European settlers, whose agricultural products were initially for a local rather than an export market. European settlers

TABLE 4.1 Probable areas of origin of selected crops and domesticated animals

Area	Crops	Animals
Fertile Crescent	barley, cabbage, date, fig, grapes, oats, olive, onion, pea, rye, turnip, rutabaga, wheat	camel, cattle, dog, goat, pig, pigeon
Central Asia	almond, apple, carrot, cherry, flax, hemp, lentil, melon, pea, pear, turnip, walnut	camel, cattle, chicken, dog, horse?, reindeer, sheep, yak
North China	apricot, cabbage, millet, mulberry, peach, plum, radish, rice, sorghum, soybean, tea	chicken?, dog, horse, pig?, silkworm
Southeast Asia	bamboo, banana, black pepper, citrus, egg plant, mango, sugar cane, taro, tea, yam	cat?, cattle, chicken, dog, duck, goose, pig, water buffalo
Ethiopia	coffee	
Nile Valley	cotton, cucumber, lentil, millet, melon, pea, sesame, sorghum	cat, dog, donkey
West Africa	kola, rice, watermelon	
Central America	avocado, beans, cocoa, corn, cotton, potato, pumpkin, red pepper, squash, sunflower, tobacco, tomato	dog, turkey
Northern Andes	beans, potato, pumpkin, squash, strawberry	alpaca, guanaco, guinea pig, llama, vicuna
Eastern South America	beans, cassava, cocoa, peanut, pineapple, potato, sunflower, squash, sweet potato	dog, duck

NOTE: Question marks indicate uncertainty as to area or areas of origin. Occurrence of crops and animals in more than one area points to the likelihood of independent invention.

SOURCE: Marvin W. Mikesell, *Patterns and Imprints of Mankind*, from The International Atlas. (Chicago: Rand McNally, 1969), p. xxx. Encyclopaedia Brittanica, *Macropaedia*, Vol. 5, "Domestication, Plant and Animal." New York, 1974, pp. 936–942.

brought to the New World some of the characteristic cropping patterns and farming techniques found in their original home areas. Plantation colonization did not require substantial European settlement. *Plantations* are large-scale agricultural enterprises devoted to the specialized production of foodstuffs such as spices, tea, cacao, coffee, and sugar cane, and industrial raw materials such as cotton, sisal, jute, and hemp. These crops were selected for their market value in international trade,

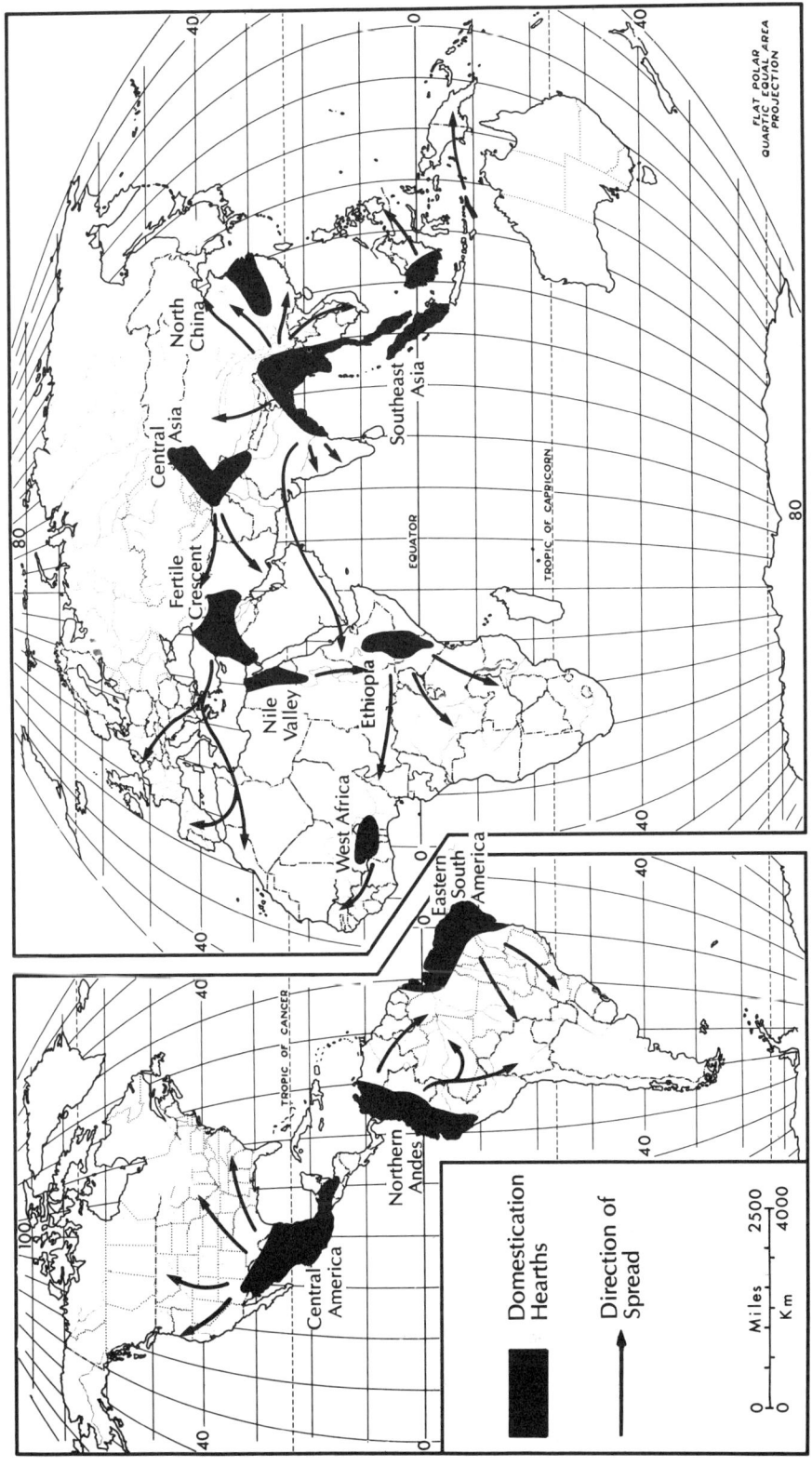

FIGURE 4.2 Origins of domesticated plants and animals. SOURCE: Peter Haggett, 1972, *Geography: A Modern Synthesis*. New York: Harper and Row, p. 302, Fig. 13-3.

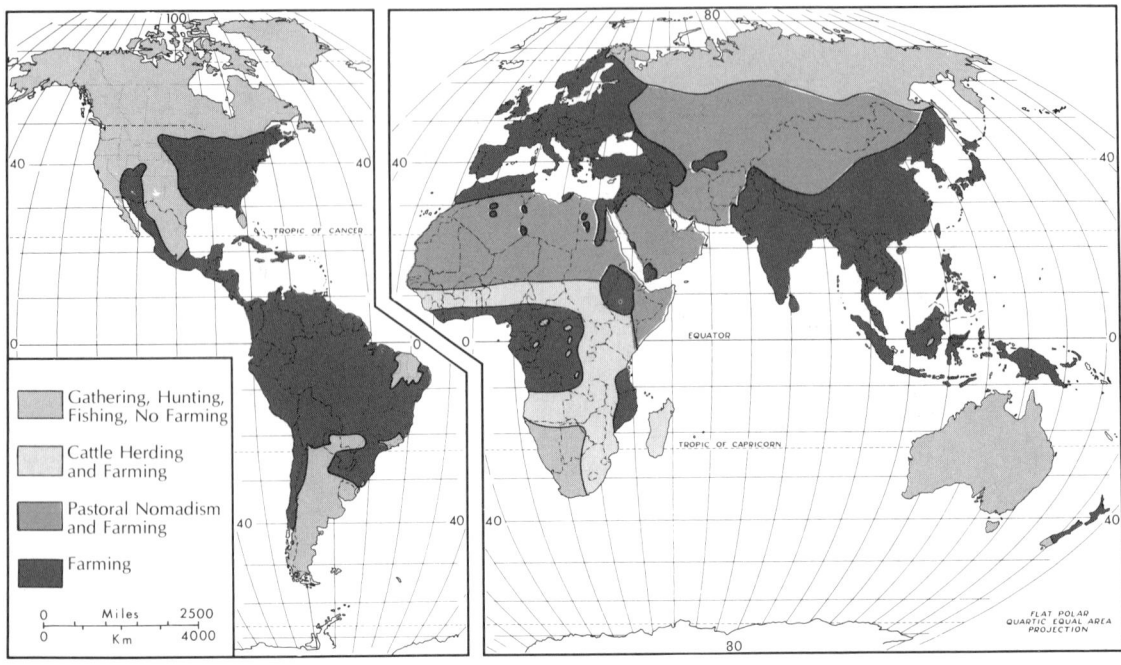

FIGURE 4.3 World patterns of land use, AD 1500.

Plucking tender leaves and buds on a tea plantation in Kenya. The woman tea-picker is paid according to the number of baskets she can fill and deliver to the nearby tea-packing house. Much of the tea grown in East Africa is exported, but some is re-imported after being blended and packaged. SOURCE: *Brooke Bond Oxo Ltd.*

and they were grown near the sea coast to facilitate shipping to Europe. The development of plantations sometimes involved taking land from local food crops; sometimes, by irrigation or by clearing of forest, new land was brought into cultivation. Europeans managed plantations; they did no manual labor. The plantation system relied on "cheap" indigenous labor. Very little machinery was used. Instead of substituting machinery for labor when local supplies of labor were exhausted, they went farther afield for additional supplies of labor. This practice was especially convenient because the world demand for tropical products expanded irregularly. During periods of increased demand, production could be stepped up by importing additional laborers. This obviated the need for installing machinery during booms, and minimized the financial problems of idle capital during slumps.

The effect of 500 years of European expansion was to reorganize rural land use worldwide. Large parts of the world remain empty, but an artificial landscape has spread across the habitable world. Hunters and gatherers have virtually disappeared. Pastoral nomads have declined substantially. Commercial agricultural systems are features of developed and underdeveloped countries. Subsistence farming still prevails, but only in areas where impoverished farmers, especially in underdeveloped countries, barely gain a living from tiny plots of land. Few completely self-sufficient farms exist; most farmers, even in remote areas of Africa, exchange some specialized products at local markets.

Human Impact on the Land

The impact of humans on the land has been cumulative with time. Our impact on the land may seem small in comparison to the erosion power of streams, but it is not insignificant. In capsule form, let's consider the impact agricultural practices may have on the land.

Hunters and gatherers hardly disturb the environment although they have exterminated some animal species. But farmers must displace vegetation to grow their crops and to tend their livestock. They are vegetation managers; they upset an "equilibrium" established by nature, and substitute one of their own. If farmers know a great deal about the environment wherein they live, the agricultural system may last indefinitely and remain productive. If farmers do not understand climate-soil-plant relationships, the environmental base may deteriorate.

As agriculture intensifies, environmental alteration increases. Boserup (1965) has proposed a simple five-stage model of agricultural systems based on the idea of frequency of use of land (Table 4.2). Stage 1, forest-fallow cultivation, involves cultivation for 1-3 years followed by 20–25 years fallow. In Stage 2, bush-fallow cultivation, the land is cultivated for 2–8 years, followed by 6–10 years fallow. In Stage 3, short-fallow cultivation, the land is fallow for only 1–2 years. In Stages 4 and 5, annual cropping and multi-cropping, fallow periods are either very short (a few months) or non-existent. Boserup argued that the transition from one form of agriculture to another was accompanied by increasing population density, improved tools, increasing integration of livestock with agriculture, improved trans-

TABLE 4.2 Agricultural intensification

Dimensions of Change	Stages				
	Forest Fallow	Bush Fallow	Short Fallow	Annual Cropping	Multicropping
Population Density Fallow: Cropland Ratio	Very low 10+	Low 4–10	Moderate 2–3	High Annual	Very High 2–3 Year
Tools	Fire, ax, digging stick, hoe	Fire, ax, hoe	Hoe, plow, fire, draft animals	Plow draft animals, hoe [Irrigation, tractors, chemicals may occur]	→
Livestock	Incidental	Possible manuring on some fields	Stock for plow and manure	Increasing provision of fodder; Increasing conflict between grazing and cultivation rights	→
Settlements	Unstable, dispersed	Stable, larger	Permanent settlement	Permanent settlements	→
Transportation	Paths, trails	Evolution of road network		Increasing link to urban system	Urban-focused road network

Social Infrastructure	Little formalization	Increasing complexity →		Social organizations, health, water, other services	Greater elaboration
Land Tenure	General use right without permanent interest	Increasing tenacity of tenure; Persistent rights to cultivation land →		Individual tenure	Permanent ownership possible, fragmental, landlord/tenant
Labor Specialization (Except by Sex, Age)	Little division of labor	Some division of labor crafts	Some non-agricultural fulltime craftsmen		Greater specialization; increasing labor inputs; emergence of wage labor →
Output to Labor	Very high	Moderate	Low		Moderate to high (industrial economies) Low (traditional, Oriental economies)
Output to All Land	Very low	Low	Moderate	High	Very high

SOURCE: C. Gregory Knight, "Prospects for Peasant Agriculture" in (ed.) C. Gregory Knight and James L. Newman, *Contemporary Africa, Geography and Change*. Englewood Cliffs, New Jersey: Prentice-Hall (1976), pp. 206–207, Table 13.2. Copyright © 1965 by George Allen & Unwin Ltd. Adapted with permission, from Esther Boserup's *The Conditions of Agricultural Growth* (New York: Aldine Publishing Company.)

portation, more complex social infrastructure, more permanent settlement and land tenure, and greater labor specialization (see box).

Forest-fallow or *shifting cultivation* survives in remote areas of the humid tropics, which have low potential environmental productivity and low population pressure. This form of agriculture leaves a good deal of original vegetation in place. Farmers make small discontinuous clearings in forests. They girdle some trees and cut down others, burn the debris, and prepare the soil by digging holes in a pattern of points for a variety of crops. Since no fertilizer is used, soil nutrients are quickly exhausted. Thus every few years, farmers abandon their plots, but rarely move their residences, and establish new gardens. Except on steep slopes, where soil erosion can be serious, this method of agriculture is benign to the land. It allows previous plots to regenerate natural growth.

By contrast, land is totally transformed under *permanent cultivation* (annual cropping and multicropping), which usually occurs in areas of high potential environmental productivity and high population pressure. Permanent agriculture need not impair the beauty and health of the land. Soils of the Paris Basin have been intensively cultivated for hundreds of years, yet they remain highly productive. In many parts of the Orient, carefully terraced hillsides have maintained the productivity of valuable soil resources for thousands of years. These agricultural landscapes do not mar nature.

Today modern farming conditions pose the main danger to land. They depend heavily on large machines and chemicals. Clean tillage on large fields, one-crop farming, and the breaking of soil structure by huge machines are a few

Ultimate mechanization: harvesting corn in Iowa. SOURCE: *Deere and Company.*

BOSERUP'S MODEL OF AGRICULTURE

Ester Boserup in *The Conditions of Agricultural Growth* challenged the Malthusian idea that population, if not checked, increases geometrically while food production increases only arithmetically. Her thesis was that *food production is highly responsive to human innovation and effort;* and she believed that the slow sustained pressure of population on resources teaches people the homely virtue of labor, and gives them the stimulation to innovate and effect agricultural improvements, thereby increasing productivity.

Her model of agriculture presents a continuum of forms (forest fallow, bush fallow, short or rotation fallow, annual cropping, and multicropping) that are based on the idea of frequency of use of land. For each of these types she discussed tools and techniques, relationships with livestock and grazing land, labor input, capital input, marginal return, land tenure, and social/political characteristics which are appropriate to each stage of agriculture.

A point central to her thesis is that the vegetation which characteristically returns at the end of a fallow cycle is best managed by a particular set of tools. For example, the digging stick, ax, and fire are the best (that is, labor minimizing) tools to use in preparing a regrowth forest for cultivation. As the fallow cycle is shortened, forest is replaced by bush, shrubs and grass; and a hoe replaces the digging stick as the best tool. A still shorter fallow leaves a grass turf to be prepared in reopening a field, and the plow becomes a more effective tool than the digging stick, ax, or hoe, although the hoe and various mounding techniques may be found in areas which lack draft animals.

The essence of Boserup's model is that the engine which drives agricultural growth is population pressure, and the fuel the engine runs on is human labor. A small, non-growing population is unlikely to go beyond the stage of primitive agriculture to a higher level of technique and cultural development, whereas a growing population will be faced with the need to improve the land and perform other investments in agriculture.

Some of the inadequacies of Boserup's model have been noted. First, the model, which sets up a continuum from forest to continuously cropped land, does not pay sufficient attention to other vegetational forms, particularly to tropical savannas and grasslands. Second, the model does not take adequate account of spatial aspects, marketing, cash attributes of economies, and the process of underdevelopment in Third World countries. According to B. Datoo, a "fundamental inadequacy of Boserup's theory . . . is that she considers the development of a cash economy and market exchange, just as she regards the evolution of social differentiation and political institutions, always as *consequences* of changes in agricultural systems and never as *determinants* of the changes themselves" (1976:8). In other words a colonial government's requirement that farmers grow an export crop (cotton, coffee, groundnuts) may have caused increased population pressure. There is an inherent difficulty in sorting out cause from effect, of knowing whether increased population pressure is cause or consequence of agricultural development (SOURCE: de Souza and Porter, 1978:20–23).

factors that harm the soil. Duststorms of the 1930s and 1970s in the Great Plains of the United States are an example of how nature and industrial agriculture may combine to destroy the health of a steppe landscape, and transform it into a desert.

Whether farmers achieve a harmonious relationship with nature does not depend necessarily on their technologies or their political philosophies. Farmers with simple tools and techniques may destroy the long-run food producing capacity of the land. Mechanized agriculture in both capitalist countries, like the United States, or socialist countries, like the Soviet Union, may despoil the environment.

Agriculture threatens ecological balances when we believe we have emancipated ourselves from dependence on nature. In our present economic system we want to maximize profits in the short-run. We want to make land use more efficient and land more productive. We regard mechanized farming as just another industry. But agriculture is fundamentally different from industry. Land is more than a factor of production. It is finite and spatially fixed and ecologically fragile. If we desecrate the land, human life cannot continue. In his book *Small is Beautiful*, Ernest Schumacher pointed out three important goals of rural land use: health, beauty, and permanence. If these are not the objectives of rural land use, how can we produce, on a long-term basis, the foods that sustain us?

Factors Affecting Rural Land Use

Variations in rural land use developed as agriculture spread throughout the world. To highlight these variations, we frequently use the concept of the "region." Geographers divide the world into parts to simplify description and for ease in comparing different areas. Thus we speak casually of, say, the winter wheat region, the corn belt, and the cotton belt. We map world agriculture into distinctive types and devote much time to the details of each system of farming (Figure 4.4).

The most important feature about a map of world agricultural regions, however, is not the number of farming types, but the similarity of land use decisions farmers make within them. Why do farmers make the same land use decisions as their neighbors? For example, why does a farmer on the slopes of Kilimanjaro decide to plant the same combination of coffee and bananas as his neighbors? The land use pattern on Kilimanjaro as elsewhere reflects a host of factors. Geographers identify at least four groups of variables that determine rural land use: site characteristics; cultural preferences and perception; systems of production; and relative location. Let us look briefly at these factors, but then consider, in more detail, the question of relative location.

Site Characteristics

Variations in rural land use depend, in part, on *site characteristics,* which make up the inherent qualities of a given location. Site attributes include the nature of land ownership, size of enterprise, population density of an area, and environmental influences such as soil fertility, altitude, drainage, and climate.

Factors Affecting Rural Land Use

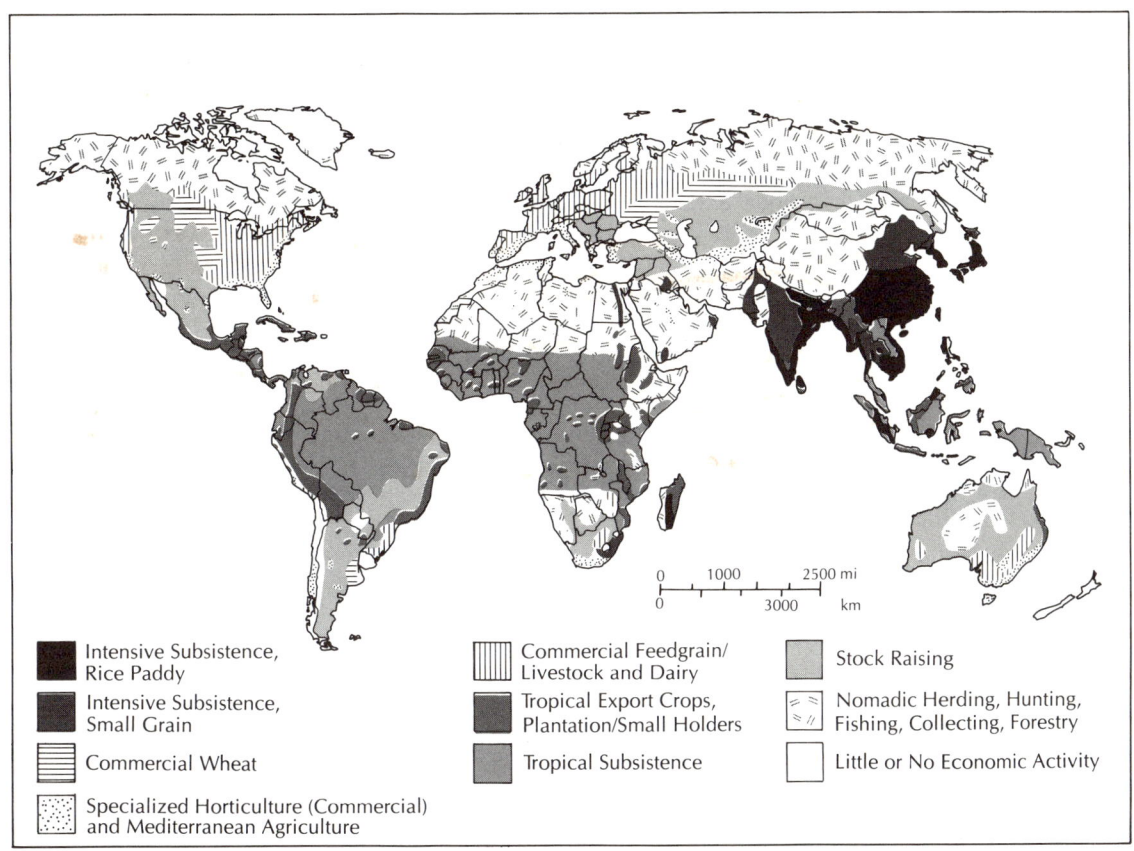

FIGURE 4.4 World agriculture. SOURCE: John F. Kolars and John D. Nystuen, 1974, *Human Geography: Spatial Design in World Society.* New York: McGraw-Hill, p. 226, Fig. 11-1.

Consider the climatic milieux in which crops grow as an example of site characteristics. Plants require particular combinations of temperature and moisture conditions. The range for a hypothetical crop is given in Figure 4.5. Increasing rainfall is plotted on the horizontal axis and increasing temperature on the vertical. Absolute physical limits of the crop are too wet, too dry, too cold, and too hot. Absolute climatic limits are large for some crops, such as maize and wheat, and restricted for others, such as pineapples, bananas, and certain wine grapes. A series of isopleths (see box) connecting points of equal dollar yield per hectare, mark optimum conditions. The optimum and limits schema emphasize that a particular combination of temperature and moisture conditions characterize every site.

Cultural Preferences and Perception of Environment

Different *cultures* have different food *preferences* and *prejudices*. Some cultural groups would rather starve than eat foods subject to taboos. Many Africans avoid

ISOPLETHS

An *isopleth is a line connecting points of equal value* and is an important cartographic tool used by geographers. "Isopleth" is a generic term, but there are many specially named isopleths. A contour line, for example, is a line connecting points of equal elevation. The *isobars* on a weather map connect points of equal barometric pressure. *Isohyets* on a map connect points of equal rainfall. We usually make a specific term by combining the prefix "iso" ("equal") with another descriptive word. "Iso-cost" and "iso-rent" are examples. This concept plays an important role in this book, so you should consider its definition carefully. There are two important properties of isopleths which you should keep in mind: (1) isopleths of different values can *never* cross, and (2) the distance between isopleths indicates the rate of change across space in the variable being mapped. When isopleths are close together, the rate of change is rapid, and vice versa. The accompanying figure is a map of iso-rent lines. Rent ($) falls very rapidly (per kilometer) to the right, but very slowly to the left.

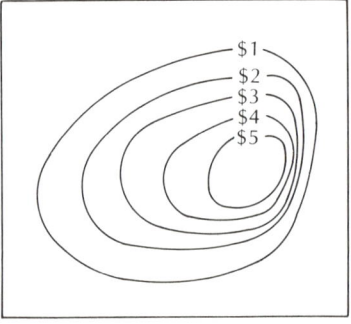

protein-rich chickens and their eggs. Despite the many livestock in South Asia, many Indian Moslems and Hindus eat no pork and beef, respectively. A preference for particular kinds of food exerts a powerful influence on the type of agricultural land use within an area. In the United States, for example, a preference for meat leads farmers to put a greater proportion of their land in forage crops than do European farmers, who grow more food crops.

People interpret the environment through different cultural lenses. Their agricultural experiences in one area influence their *perceptions of environmental conditions* in other areas. Consider the settlement of North America. Many early migrants were Anglo-Saxons and were used to moist conditions and a tree-covered landscape. Farmers equated trees with fertility. New England met their expectations of a fertile farming area. When subsequent waves of migrants edged onto the prairies and the Great Plains to the west of the Mississippi, they encountered a treeless grass-covered area. They viewed land without trees with suspicion. The richness of grassland soils was underestimated. The area was commonly referred to as the "Great American Desert." W. H. Emory, United States Commissioner of the United

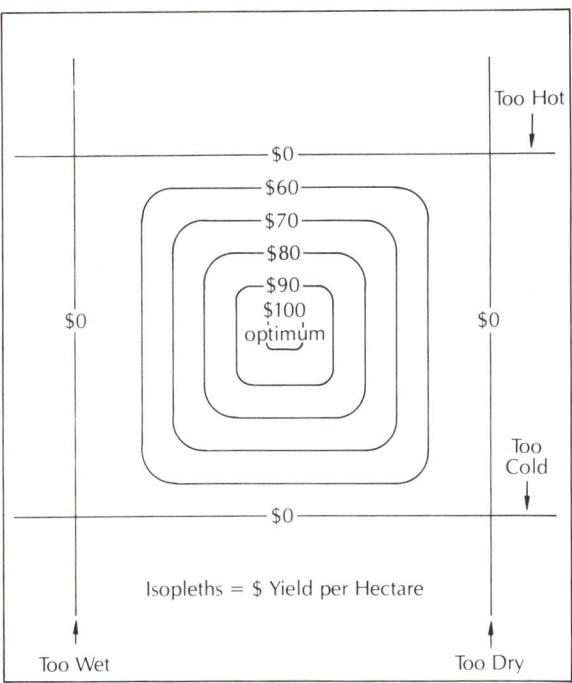

FIGURE 4.5 Optimal and marginal fertility ranges. SOURCE: Harold H. McCarty, James B. Lindberg, *A Preface to Economic Geography,* © 1966, p. 61. Reprinted by permission of Prentice-Hall, Inc., Englewood Cliffs, New Jersey.

Settlers pose in front of their sod home in Nebraska in 1887. In the late nineteenth century, agriculture meant a livelihood for half the American population. SOURCE: *United States Department of Agriculture.*

States and Mexico Boundary Commission, wrote that the Great Plains west of the one hundredth meridian are "wholly unsusceptible of sustaining an agricultural population, until you reach sufficiently far south to encounter the rains of the tropics . . . or westward until you reach the last slope of the Pacific." Late nineteenth century migrants from the steppe lands of Eastern Europe interpreted the "naked" lands of the West quite differently. They helped to change the perception of the areas from the "Great American Desert" to the "Great American Breadbasket." Certainly factors other than the way immigrants perceived the environment influenced agricultural settlement in the Great Plains. For example, the mold-board plow and barbed wire fencing were required for "mastery" of the environment.

Systems of Production

Systems of agricultural production set their imprint on rural land use. Like manufacturing, agriculture is carried out under three systems of production—peasant, capitalist, and socialist (Table 4.3). The major distinction among these systems is the labor commitment of the enterprise. In the peasant system, production comes from small units worked entirely, or almost entirely, by family labor. In the capitalist system, family farming is still widespread; but, as in the socialist system, labor is a commodity to be hired and dismissed by the enterprise according to changes in the scale of organization, degree of mechanization, and the level of market demand for products.

TABLE 4.3 Systems of production

The Enterprise	Peasant	Capitalist	Socialist
Labor Commitment of the Enterprise	Total	Non-total	Non-total
Institutional Basis	Family	Family Joint Stock	Combine
Control and Direction	Family	Family-Managerial	Managerial
Means of Distribution	Barter-Market	Market	Prescription-Market
Media of Distribution	Kind-Money	Money	Money
Mechanization	Possible	Usual	Usual
Regulator	Labor Supply	Market	State

SOURCE: Adapted from S. H. Franklin, "Systems of Production: Systems of Appropriation," *Pacific Viewpoint,* **6** (1965), Table 1, p. 149.

Peasant Mode of Production Peasant agriculture is associated with underdeveloped countries, and it is *labor-intensive* (labor-centered). Farmers are small-scale producers who buy little mechanized equipment or chemicals. Food is produced for sale, but it is produced mainly to satisfy a family's immediate needs. To obtain the output required, peasant farmers are frequently willing to raise inputs of labor to very high levels, especially in crowded areas where land is short.

Peasant agriculture is not resistant to change. It is sometimes assumed that peasant farmers lack the motivation for adopting new ideas and techniques. They may lack capital, outside information, and scientific methodology for raising

Factors Affecting Rural Land Use

A   B

Labor-centered and capital-centered agriculture: (A) harvesting wheat by hand in Pakistan. SOURCE: *World Bank Photo* by Tomas Sennett; and (B) harvesting wheat by combine in the United States (SOURCE: *United States Department of Agriculture*).

agricultural productivity. They may find themselves with a land or marketing system that holds down the scale of their operations. Given proposals for change that will work in the environment wherein they live, peasant farmers in underdeveloped countries are as willing to implement new ideas as their American counterparts.

Capitalist Mode of Production United States agriculture may be viewed as a stereotype of advanced commercial agriculture. Modern American farming is quick to respond to new developments, such as new production techniques. Consequently, farmers with sizable investments of money, materials, and energy can bring about drastic changes in patterns of land use. For example, farmers between the 10 and 20 inch isohyet in the Western United States have converted large areas of grazing land to forage and grass production with the use of center-pivot

> **AGRIBUSINESS AND THE SMALL AMERICAN FARMER**
>
> The dominant trend in American agriculture has been for production to exceed demand, thus ensuring a relatively cheap food supply and low incomes for small farmers. In the past three decades small farmers have left the land in record numbers and the average size of farms has increased, especially with the emergence of agribusiness which has come to dominate the food industry. The United States Chamber of Commerce has defined agribusiness as "commercial farms, input industries . . . and marketing and processing firms which contribute to the total food sector."
>
> The extent of the invasion of agribusiness into direct agricultural production is still modest. Corporate farming is restricted to certain types of crops and regions. It is significant in the production of fruits, vegetables, feed cattle, turkeys, chickens and eggs where the return on investment is high. It is prevalent in western and southern states like California and Florida that have had a long history of large landholdings.
>
> Much more important than the role of agribusiness in production is the relationship of corporations to small farmers. Small farmers are increasingly dependent on corporations for information, expertise, credit, machinery, fertilizer, pesticides, and fuels. This tendency has contributed to the contemporary demise of small-town merchants.
>
> The revolution in American agriculture has raised productivity—at a cost. Critics charge that the new agriculture is producing crops for machines, not for consumers, and that corporations who can adjust to wild fluctuations in farm prices are driving small farmers out of business. The United States Department of Agriculture is not trying to reverse the trend toward increasing concentration in agriculture. Indeed, the USDA's Director of Agricultural Economics, speculating on the future of American agriculture, has predicted a "highly coordinated industry of large farms very likely . . . operating in much the same fashion as non-farm manufacturing industries" (*Feedstuffs*, August 16, 1976, p. 10).

irrigation systems. Other farmers grow sugar beets and potatoes in Western oases because of federally subsidized water projects.

American farmers are more vulnerable to catastrophic events than their peasant counterparts. Peasant farmers can provide, for the most part, their families with food, clothing, and shelter. Most American farmers are completely tied to an elaborate marketing system. If their communication lines with the wider space-economy were cut, they would quickly run out of essential things: fuel, spare-parts, fertilizers and seeds, and storebought food and clothing.

At the frontier of American agriculture is *agribusiness*. The word "agribusiness" was coined by Harvard Business School Professor Ray Goldberg in the early 1960s, and it is associated with the trend on the part of giant food companies such as Ralston Purina, General Mills, General Foods, Hunt Foods, and United Brands to control the whole food chain from "seedling to supermarket." The concept to describe the control by food companies of production, processing, and marketing

Factors Affecting Rural Land Use

Corporate farming: cattle on a huge feedlot, Greeley, Colorado.
SOURCE: *Monfort of Colorado, Inc.*

A

B

Center-pivot irrigation: (A) oblique aerial view of a center-pivot irrigation system in Colorado; and (B) ground-level view of a center-pivot irrigation system in Oregon. The development of the center-pivot system some twenty-five years ago has enabled farmers to irrigate large tracts of land automatically. As a result of low cost government loans and low water rates, thousands of circular fields now dot the western United States. Most center-pivot systems are supplied by deep wells. In many areas, for instance the Texas Panhandle, there is the problem of the depletion of underground water reservoirs. Moreover, center-pivot systems are energy intensive. It is reckoned that 43 percent of the energy devoted to agriculture in Nebraska goes to pumping water for irrigation.
SOURCE: *USDA, Soil Conservation Service.*

is *vertical integration*. In recent years the promise of high profits and a favorable tax structure has attracted non-food companies to move into food production. These include tractor firms, fertilizer and pesticide manufacturers, oil companies, and aircraft companies.

At the farm level, agribusiness is *capital-intensive*, energy-intensive, and has very high per capita productivity, which results in rural depopulation. Examples of modern food production farms include fiber production, fruit and vegetable growing and processing operations, poultry ranches, egg factories, and beef feedlots. These low-risk activities are so congenial to "superfarmers" that in "recent years corporations have accounted for the production of about 90 percent of California's melons, two-thirds of its lettuce, 40 percent of its cotton, and one-third of the sugar beets, carrots, and potatoes" (Parsons, 1977: 355). Cattle fattening in feedlots is also highly concentrated: "1 percent of U.S. feedlots now raise 60 percent of the beef cattle" (George, 1977:5).

American corporate farming is also extending overseas to become a world wide food system model. Family farming is still dominant in Western Europe, but beef feedlots are found in the Italian Piedmont. Poultry-raising operations in Argentina, Pakistan, Thailand, and Taiwan are like those in Alabama. Enterprises such as United Brands, Del Monte, Unilever and Brooke Bond Oxo are diverting more and more food production in underdeveloped countries toward consumers in developed countries. "Central America," for example, "has increased its beef exports to the U.S. fivefold in ten years" (George, 1977:19).

Agribusiness means different things to different people. To corporate farmers agribusiness means a profitable return to stockholders. To critics, agribusiness means gains to profit-conscious executives headquartered in large cities, but losses to most people in developed and underdeveloped countries. In developed countries, for example, megafarming operations are harmful to small farmers who are driven out of business. They are harmful to consumers because the free market does not exist in an industry controlled by large firms. They are harmful to workers who "get in the way of corporate 'rationalization of production' or the 'free flow of capital'" (George, 1977:141). According to Susan George:

> It is not "rational," for instance, to produce pineapple in Hawaii if cannery workers are going to make unreasonable demands—like being paid half as much as workers in other U.S. industries. So Del Monte and Dole have shifted part of their pineapple growing to the Philippines and to Thailand where a worker gets $1.20 a day for eight hours work. This does not mean that the price of a can of pineapple goes down (1977:141).

Socialist Mode of Production One form of the socialist system of agriculture is found in the Soviet Union. The capitalist and socialist modes of production may be contrasted as follows: capitalist production is based on the theory of marginal productivity, in which there is private ownership of the means of production and competition among owners for surplus product (profits); socialist production is based on the labor theory of value, in which the State, representing the peasants and workers, distributes collective wealth according to need, rather than according to ownership of land, factories, or stores.

Factors Affecting Rural Land Use

Before the Bolshevik Revolution, agricultural land in the Soviet Union consisted of a mixture of small peasant holdings and estates of the rich. Subsequently, the Communists organized the land into *Sovkhozes* and *Kolkhozes*. Sovkhozes, established initially on confiscated estates, are factory farms; they are very large (average size is 20,000 hectares) single-purpose units managed by workers, but controlled by the state.

The Kolkhoz represented a temporary solution to problems facing leaders of the Soviet Union when they assumed power. It was a response to the poorly organized peasant holdings and villages inherited from the Bolsheviks. A Kolkhoz is a collective farm, the principal element of which is a peasant family. Each Kolkhoz family lives in a cottage, retains some land to cultivate for itself, and works full time on large tracts of surrounding state-owned land. Cultivators own the tools of production, and share the proceeds of the harvest equally. Decisions on the running of Kolkhozes are made not by the villagers, but by the agricultural management of the Communist Party. Although cultivated land in the Soviet Union is now evenly divided between Kolkhozes and Sovkhozes, it is intended eventually to convert Kolkhozes into state farms on which cultivators will not be peasants, but workers who will be treated like their industrial counterparts.

Compared with the miraculous transformation of the Chinese earth, the organization of socialist agriculture in the Soviet Union has not been strikingly successful. Soviet agricultural achievements have also been less impressive than their accomplishments in industry. Between 1930 and 1970 agricultural production increased by only 70 to 80 percent, whereas industrial output increased more than tenfold. According to Rhoads Murphy, a major reason "agriculture has failed to match the gains of manufacturing and faced recurrent crises over food production has been the difficulty of changing archaic systems of land use in an immense country of nearly 260 million people. It has been much easier to change industrial techniques because there was less resistance to change, and fewer individuals, groups or traditional regional structures were involved" (1978:172).

The Soviet Union has attempted to increase agricultural production first, by opening up new, but mainly marginal, lands on the cold and dry fringes; second, by improving farming methods (e.g. irrigation) and crops (e.g. drought resistant varieties); and third, by mechanizing, especially its wheat and other grain lands. None of these three methods has been totally successful. Aside from poor climate and soils, Murphy attributed the poor Soviet performance to a relatively low level of agricultural investment in the past, and to a lack of incentive among farm workers to increase their output on collective and state farms.

In the last few years, the Soviet government has increased levels of investment in agriculture, and increased incentives for collective and state farm workers, providing additional benefits for higher output. Despite the necessity for grain imports in the 1970s, due mainly to late frosts and droughts, Soviet agricultural production is beginning to keep pace with population increase, which has begun to slow down.

In general, we can argue the following about peasant, American, and Soviet agriculture. The peasant system of production is the most efficient from the standpoint of value of output per hectare. American agribusiness is the most productive, but it uses costly inputs. Soviet agriculture is less efficient than peasant agriculture, and less productive than American agriculture.

Relative Location

Despite the growing importance of public companies and corporations, world farming is still for the most part a family business. An important factor that shapes individual farmers' land use decisions is *relative location* or situation of a place in terms of its access to other places. Worldwide, the relative importance of situational components in agriculture increased as market exchange economies grew and developed. At one time, before commercial agriculture, a farmer's site, links with soil, sun, rain, and crops were overwhelmingly important to livelihood. Today site relations have not ceased to be important. Farmers are still dependent on the weather. But site relations have weakened as farmers have been drawn increasingly into situational relationships as communication lines between farm and market link them even more strongly to a wider spatial economy (de Souza and Porter, 1974:69).

Thünen's Model

Relative location is a determinant of agricultural land use both at the local level and in the world. The importance of relative location in rural land use was first discussed by Johann Heinrich von Thünen, a north German estate owner interested in economic theory and local agricultural conditions (see box). From his experience as an estate manager, he observed that identical plots of land (sites) would be used for different uses depending on their accessibility to market (situation). In 1826 he published a book, *The Isolated State,* with the aim of finding the laws which govern the interaction of agricultural prices, distance, and land use as landlords seek to maximize their income. Our interest in Thünen's work lies not in the landlord/peasant system under which his model was developed, but in his method of analysis, and in his emphasis on the role of geographical location.

The Law of Diminishing Returns and the Concept of Rent

We preface a review of Thünen's model of agricultural land use with a brief discussion of two classical economic concepts: the law of diminishing returns and the concept of economic rent.

The Law of Diminishing Returns An important aspect of Thünen's model has to do with limitations in the intensity of land use, which is referred to as the law of diminishing returns. This classical or conservative law considers short-run possibilities of combining inputs of land, labor, and capital. It considers the state of technical knowledge as given, and that there are no fundamental cost-reducing production changes. The principle states: As successive units of a *variable input* (say

Thünen's Model

> **JOHANN HEINRICH VON THÜNEN (1783-1850)**
>
> Thünen is credited with the first economic model of spatial organization. Born on the North Sea Coast in East Friesland in northwest Germany, he had a university education in economics, and in 1810 he purchased a large estate at Tellow, southeast of Rostock. He devoted his life to increasing agricultural production in Mecklenburg through the application of English agricultural principles, mathematical analysis, and experimentation. The basic framework for *Der Isolierte Staat (The Isolated State)* came from meticulous records of his management of Tellow. The first draft was written in 1818–19 and *The Isolated State* was published in 1826.
>
>
>
> SOURCE: *The Bettmann Archive, Inc.*

labor) are applied to a *fixed input* (say land), *total product* (output) passes through three stages. First total product increases at an increasing rate; second it increases at a declining rate; and, third, it declines.

    Figure 4.6 and Table 4.4 give a standard example of how the principle of diminishing returns works. Assume one fixed input, land, and one variable input, labor. *Average productivity* (AP) of labor is the total product (TP) divided by the number of labor units. *Marginal productivity* of labor (MP) is the addition to total output attributable to the last labor input employed. Throughout stage 1 marginal

Agriculture and Rural Land Use

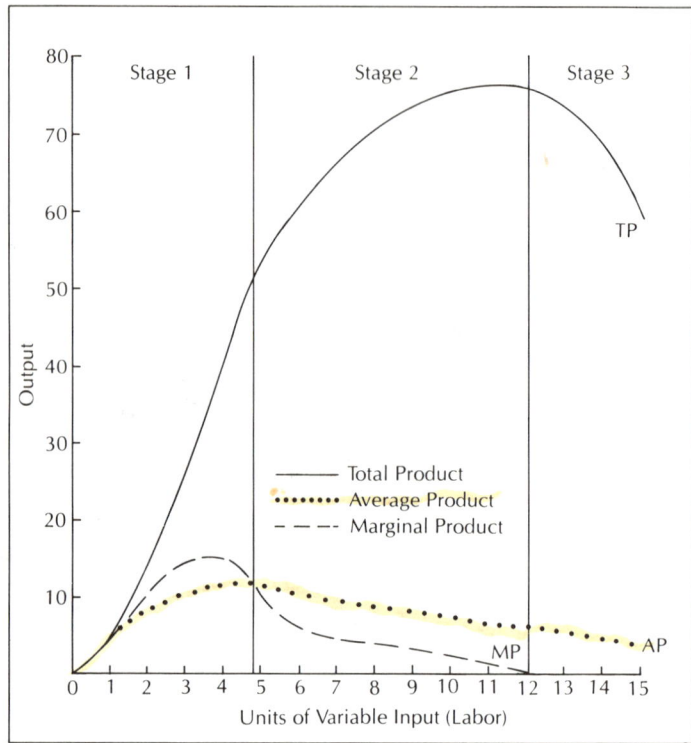

FIGURE 4.6 The stages of production.

TABLE 4.4 An illustration of the law of diminishing returns

Variable Input	Total Product	Average Product	Marginal Product	Stages of Production
0	0	0.00	0	
1	5	5.00	5	
2	16	8.00	11	I
3	30	10.00	14	
4	45	11.25	15	
5	55	11.00	10	
6	61	10.16	6	
7	66	9.42	5	
8	70	8.75	4	II
9	73	8.11	3	
10	75	7.50	2	
11	76	6.91	1	
12	76	6.33	0	
13	73	5.61	−3	
14	69	4.93	−4	III
15	60	4.00	−9	

Thünen's Model

product exceeds average product. The intersection of the marginal product curve marks the end of stage 1 and the beginning of stage 2. During stage 2 the marginal product curve declines until it finally becomes zero. This marks the end of stage 2 and the beginning of stage 3.

Knowledge of total, average, and marginal productivity establishes some general boundaries for rational or profitable zones of agricultural production in market exchange economies. If farmers are trying to obtain a maximum return for their investments, they will never operate in stage 1. The level of intensity is too low, that is the amount of the variable input (labor) per unit land area is too small. Land is used too extensively. Farmers would want to take advantage of increasing returns to scale and add more variable inputs to intensify their operations. The boundary between stage 1 and stage 2 is termed the *extensive margin* of cultivation.

If farmers are trying to maximize their returns, they will never operate in stage 3. This is evident: no rational farmer will operate in the range in which additional units of labor decrease total production, causing negative product values. The boundary between stage 3 and stage 2 is known as the *intensive margin* of cultivation. This leaves stage 2 as the zone of "feasible" production. In the real world, many enterprises—particularly large ones—do operate in stage 3 because of lack of true economic competition, federal regulations, and subsidies.

Radicals have criticized the classical law of diminishing returns. Given the assumption of profit maximization, they claim the law is tautological because the conclusions are concealed in the definitions. Farmers, for example, hire workers as long as they produce a surplus above their wages. When the additional profit falls to zero (*i.e.,* when the marginal product of the last unit of labor added equals zero) then farmers stop adding workers. Radicals admit that the law shows farmers how to manipulate labor and capital to maximize profits, but argue that in a capitalist society, it operates to the disadvantage of workers.

Economic Rent The concept of *economic rent* is central to Thünen's discussion of agricultural land use. Economic rent provides a means whereby competition for the use of land is resolved to produce patterns of land use. It is not the same concept as contract rent—the amount paid by a tenant for the right to occupy and use a certain property. *Economic rent is a relative measure of the advantage one parcel of land has over another.* According to classical theory, differential economic rents arise because of production cost factors such as the productivity of different parcels of land, and transport costs to a market.

At the beginning of the nineteenth century, David Ricardo presented the idea of rent variations due to the productivity of "physical factors." He defined rent as a payment for "the use of the original and indestructible powers of the soil." He said land was an inexhaustible and non-reproducible agent, unalterably fixed in supply, and homogeneous in quality except for differences in fertility and location. Ricardo focused his attention on fertility. He noted that when land differs in fertility, the scarcity of land of a particular fertility gives rise to different rents. He pointed out that the most fertile land is always put to use first, and that less favored land is put to use as demand for agricultural products increases, because the total returns to input factors on the more fertile land is greater than on a similar area of land near the extensive margin.

We can generalize Ricardo's idea of rent variations in a productivity schema for a spatially restricted area (Figure 4.7). The isopleths are based on cost, not yield per hectare. Outward from a particular crop's optimum physical conditions, costs per hectare increase. A cross-section is drawn along the line A-A^1 (side view of Figure 4.7). The cross-section is a *space-cost curve* and graphs change in cost across the area. Let a price of $80 cover costs per hectare. In this imaginary case, limits of production are determined by the intersection of the price line and the space-cost curve. No production occurs outside the $80 isoline, but rent increases toward the optimum.

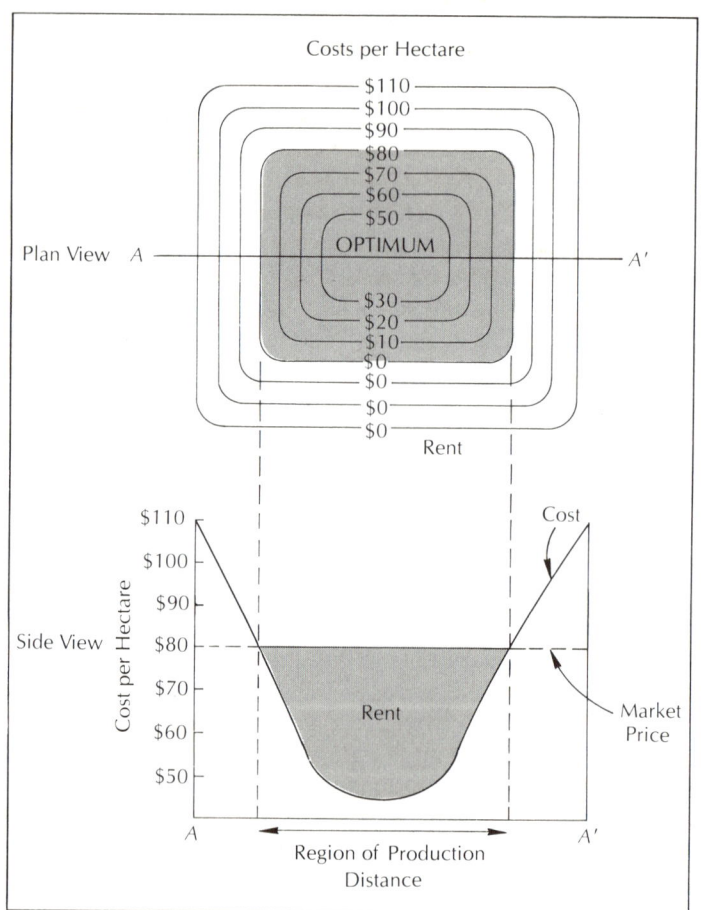

FIGURE 4.7 Optimal and marginal limits: the space-cost curve.

What happens if the market price for a crop rises to $100 because of increasing demand (Figure 4.8)? The *spatial margins to profitability* spread outward. Previously sub-marginal land is brought into cultivation, and higher rent land is used more intensively. Similarly, if the market price falls to $60, spatial margins to profitability retreat. Lower quality land is abandoned and superior quality land is used less intensively.

An alternative view of economic rent was provided by Thünen. Holding land quality constant, he showed rents decline with distance from the market center.

Thünen's Model

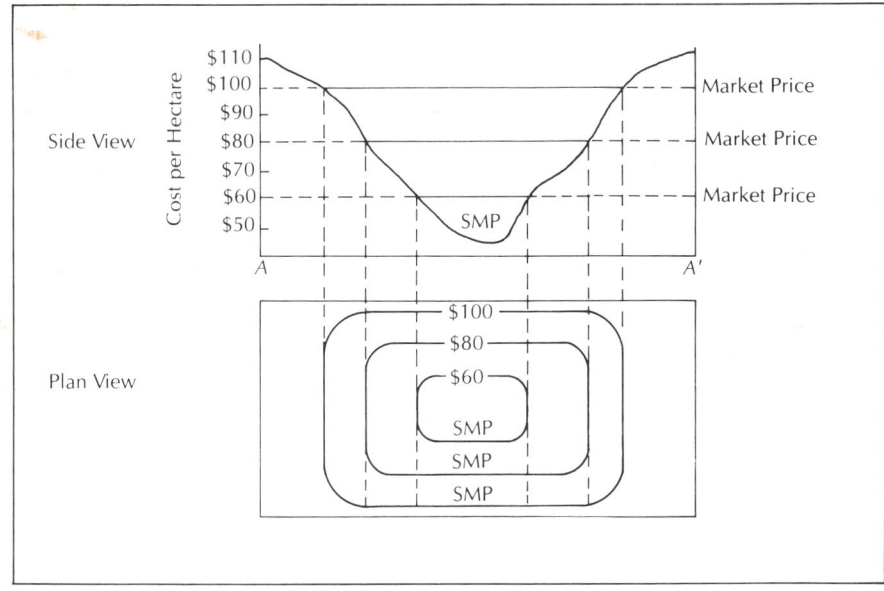

FIGURE 4.8 Spatial margins to profitability.

He demonstrated (1) that rent reflects differences in costs of production and transportation at various locations; (2) that a location near the market place is the most productive; and (3) that net profits fall to zero at the margin of cultivation. Geographers often use the term "location rent," as opposed to "economic rent," to express the idea that rents decline with distance from the market place.

The Isolated State

In order to find the most profitable way to use his land, Thünen developed a static abstract model. (The objective of abstract models is to simplify the real world in order to understand some of its characteristics.) Thünen appreciated the significance of abstract models, and in *The Isolated State* he asked the reader:

> ... not to be deterred by the initial assumptions which deviate from reality and not to consider them as arbitrary and without purpose. On the contrary, these assumptions are necessary in order to clearly understand the effect which a given variable has. In actual life we have only a vague idea of the effect and operation of any single variable because it appears always in conflict with other variables operating at the same time. This procedure has thrown light on so many problems in my life and seems to me to be so generally applicable that I consider it the most important feature of my work.

Features of the Isolated State Thünen began his analysis of agricultural land use by stating his assumptions. He envisioned a very large town at the center of a circular state consisting of a homogeneous plain. Throughout the plain the soil was of uniform fertility. Far from the town, the plain turned into an uncultivated wilderness, which cut off all communication between the state and the outside world. The central town and the countryside were interdependent. The town supplied the rural areas with manufactured goods, and in turn obtained its provisions from the surrounding countryside. All agricultural labor costs were uniform. Independent producers moved their agricultural produce to market by horse-drawn wagons along the most direct route. Prices for agricultural commodities were stable and fixed at the market place. Farmers could not alter the price of crops through individual or collective action. Farmers were optimizers. They had perfect knowledge of all possible outcomes of a given action, and they responded solely to maximize their profits. Finally, Thünen assumed a steady-state economy without government or social classes. With all these constraints, he introduced one variable: transportation to the central town, its costs increasing at a rate proportional to distance.

Thünen's ideal construct is unrepresentative of actual conditions either in the early nineteenth century or in the late twentieth century. Indeed Thünen regarded the Isolated State as an Ideal State, the ultimate stage in the development of "bourgeois" society. He said the Ideal State is a goal humankind should attempt to attain. When it is achieved, no further change occurs. People live in a harmonious society free of exploitation. For Thünen the Ideal State is a world without chaos, a utopian state.

The Problem After stating his assumptions, Thünen posed the problem which he wanted to investigate.

> The problem we want to solve is this: what pattern of cultivation will take shape in these conditions?; and how will the farming system of the various districts be affected by their distance from the town? We assume throughout that farming is conducted absolutely rationally.
>
> It is on the whole obvious that near the town will be grown those products which are heavy or bulky in relation to their value and which are consequently so expensive to transport that the remoter districts are unable to supply them. Here also we find the highly perishable products, which must be used very quickly. With increasing distance from the town, the land will progressively be given up to products cheap to transport in relation to their value. For this reason above, fairly sharply differentiated concentric rings or belts will form around the town, each with its own particular staple product.
>
> From ring to ring the staple product, and with it the entire farming system, will change; and in the various rings we shall find completely different farming systems.

Thus Thünen suggested that in a landscape free from all extraneous disturbances, locational differences are sufficient to produce a varied pattern of land use. After he observed the role of transport costs, Thünen relaxed his rigid assumptions, and introduced other variables to see how they modified his ideal pattern of land use.

Location Rent for a Single Crop at the Same Intensity To illustrate Thünen's concept of differential rent, let us take an example of an isolated state producing one commodity, say wheat, grown at a single intensity (see box). All wheat produced is sold at the central market, which sets a price of $100 per hectare per year (Figure 4.9). It costs every farmer in the state $40 to produce a hectare of wheat. The gross profit a farmer receives is market price, $100, minus production costs, $40, or

Thünen's Model

> **LOCATION RENT**
>
> Location rent for any crop may be calculated by the following formula (Dunn, 1954:7):
>
> $$R = E(p - a) - Efk$$
>
> where:
>
> R = location rent per unit of land
> E = output per unit of land
> k = distance to market
> p = market price per unit of output
> a = production cost per unit of land (including labor)
> f = transport rate per unit of distance per unit of output
>
> Thus if we assume a wheat farmer located 20 kilometers from market obtains a yield of 1000 metric tons/km², has production expenses of $50/ton/km² to transport grain to market, and receives a market price of $100/ton at the central market, then the location rent accruing to a km² of the farmer's land can be calculated as follows:
>
> $$R = 1000\ (\$100 - \$50) - 1000\ (\$1 \times 20)$$
> $$= \$50{,}000 - 20{,}000$$
> $$= \$30{,}000$$
>
> At 50 kilometers from the market the location rent per km² of land in wheat is $0. Obviously beyond 50 kilometers from the market, no rational farmer in a competitive market economy would grow wheat.

$60 per hectare. Farmers located adjacent to the market place pay no transport costs, and, therefore, their net profits are $60 per hectare. Most farmers, however, are located at a distance from the market place, and they have to transport wheat to market. Let us assume transport costs are $5 per kilometer for each hectare of wheat. A farmer located one kilometer from the market receives a net profit equal to market price ($100) minus the cost of production ($40) and the cost of transporting wheat to market ($5 × 1) or $55. Net profit per hectare decreases as the distance to the market increases. At six kilometers from the market a farmer earns a net profit of $30, and at 12 kilometers, the extensive margin of cultivation, net profits per hectare are zero.

Farmers near the central market pay lower transport costs than those at the margin of production. Their net profits are greater and the difference is known as economic rent. Farmers recognize this condition, and they know that it is in their best interest to bid up the amount they will pay for agricultural land closer to the market. Bidding continues until bid-rent equals location rent. At that price, farmers recover production and transport costs, and land owners receive location rents as payments for their land. Competitive bidding for desirable locations cancels income dif-

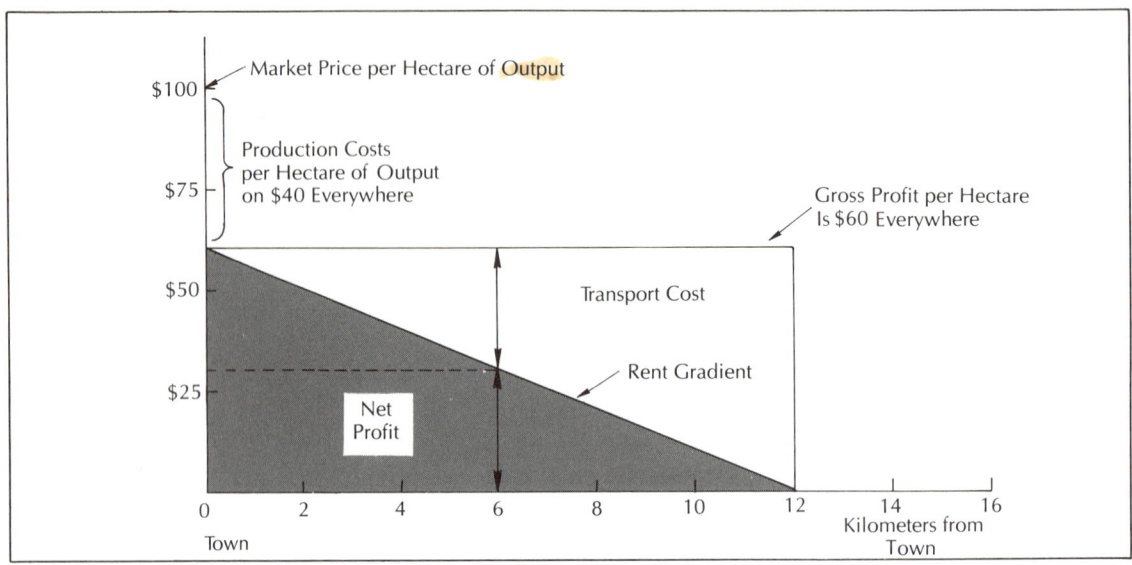

FIGURE 4.9 Net income from wheat production decreases with increasing distance from the market.

ferentials attributable to accessibility. The bid rent produces a spatial equilibrium situation. It declines just enough from market to cover additional transport costs, and farmers are indifferent as to their distance from market.

We can redraw Figure 4.9 more simply by including production costs in a single expression with the market price. This is illustrated in Figure 4.10A, which shows a rent gradient sloping downward with increasing distance from the central market. When the *rent gradient* is located around the market town it becomes a rent cone, the base of which indicates the extensive margin of cultivation for a single crop grown at a single intensity (Figure 4.10B).

Location Rent for a Single Crop at Different Intensity Levels Thünen argued that land located close to the central market is high-priced, because it has a transport advantage over more distant locations. High-priced land provides farmers with an incentive to increase output per hectare by increasing inputs of capital and labor. As we know, additional variable inputs eventually result in diminishing marginal product. Farmers add variable inputs as long as each extra unit pays for the transport of the marginal yield to market. When transport costs are lower, farmers can proceed farther along the marginal product curve. This results in higher intensities of land use toward the market.

Let us suppose a single crop, wheat, is grown at two intensity levels reflecting different systems of production (Figure 4.11). The more intensive farming system has a steeper rent curve, and is profitable up to 36 kilometers from the market. The less intensive system occurs from 36 kilometers to the limits of wheat farming at 70 kilometers. As Figure 4.11 shows, the margin of transference between the two systems of wheat farming occurs at the intersection of the bid-rent curves. The

Thünen's Model

BID RENT CURVE

A bid rent curve is a line that represents the trade off of rent levels with transport costs. The rate of decline of a bid rent curve may be solved with a linear equation that takes the form:

$$Y = a - bX$$

where:

Y = market price per unit of output
X = distance to market
a and b = *parameters* of the equation.

The parameter a is called the "Y-intercept" or "origin" because it determines where the line will intercept the Y-axis. At this point, $X = 0$ so that $Y = a$. The b parameter is called the "slope" and measures the change in Y with each unit change in X. The accompanying figure graphs the equations $Y = 10 - 1X$ and $Y = 10 - 3X$. Both equations have the same Y-intercept (*a*), but different slopes (*b's*). Y declines by 1 unit (per unit change in X) in the first equation and by 3 units in the second.

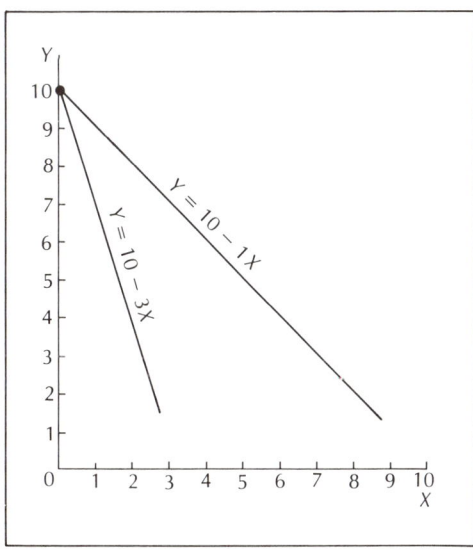

separation between more intensive and less intensive systems illustrates the principle of highest and best use of land. According to this principle, land is allocated to the use that earns the highest location rent for its owners, but not necessarily for their agricultural workers.

Location Rent Gradients for Competing Crops Thünen produced a crop model showing a farmer's choice of land uses. Patterns of agricultural land use

FIGURE 4.10 From (A) rent gradient to (B) rent cone.

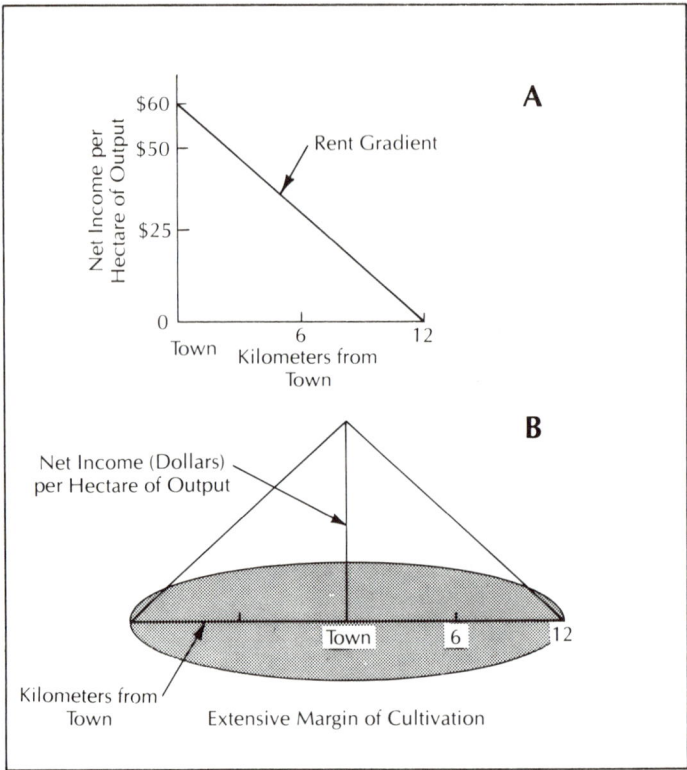

FIGURE 4.11 Rent gradient for a single crop grown at different intensities.

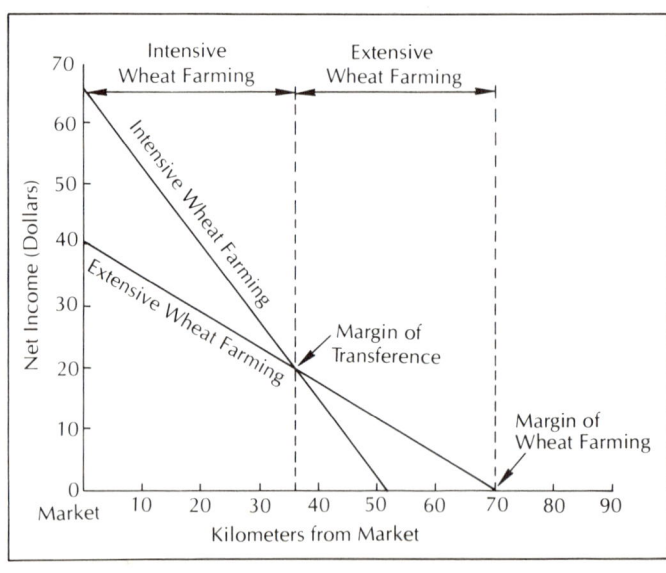

form according to the principle of highest and best use as measured by the location rent at each distance from the market. Crops compete with one another for locations that reduce transport costs. At any given distance from the market, the crop which can pay the highest location rent is chosen, and agricultural land use forms zones of homogeneous activity around the market.

Thünen's Model

Thünen's crop model can be illustrated for an isolated state in which farmers have three land use choices: vegetables, dairying, and beef production. Farmers close to the market could profitably carry on any one of the three activities. But which activity should they choose if they want to maximize their income? The graph in Figure 4.12 shows that vegetable production, which is very sensitive to displacement away from the market, has the highest rent paying ability. All farmers seeking to maximize their incomes make the same decision: they grow vegetables between zero and 10 kilometers from market. Dairying is the land use choice between 10 and 25 kilometers. Beef production, the activity least sensitive to distance displacement, is the choice between 25 and 50 kilometers from the market. Beyond 50 kilometers no commercial land use is feasible.

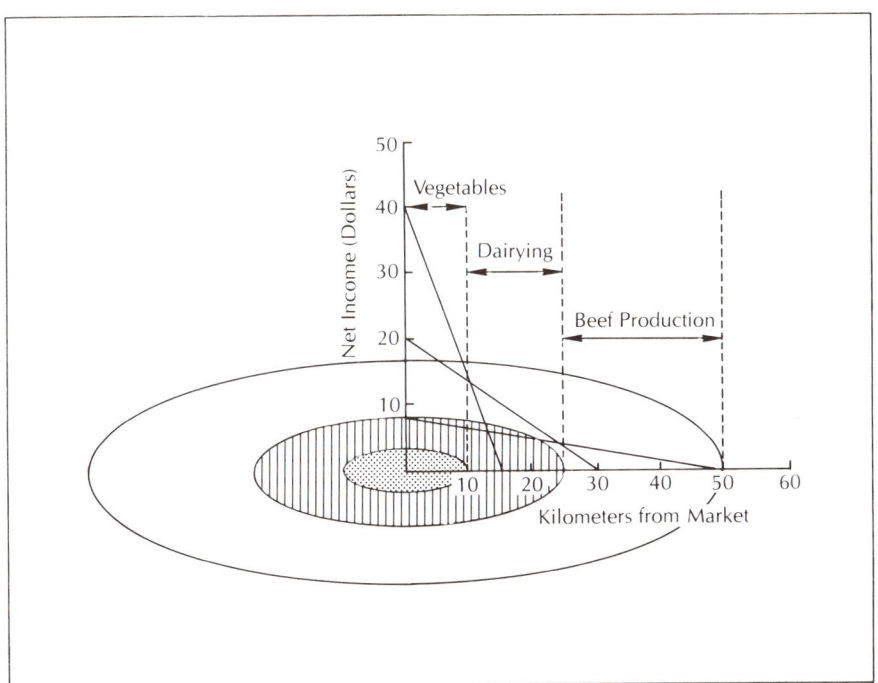

FIGURE 4.12 Location rent gradients for competing crops.

Thünen's Original Crop System Under the highly abstract conditions of the Isolated State, Thünen described six farming systems arranged in a series of concentric circles around the central city (Figure 4.13 and Table 4.5). The innermost zones produced perishable products (fluid milk and fresh vegetables), and heavy, bulky commodities in proportion to their value (wood fuel and lumber). On land most distant from the market, where transport costs were highest, there would be only animal husbandry requiring little investment, but large amounts of space (livestock ranching). Between these inner and outer rings, agriculture consisted of intensive and extensive arable farming.

On first thought it seems odd that Thünen put a forestry zone close to the market. This arrangement does not seem to accord with our image of reality. But timber and fuel were in great demand in early nineteenth century Germany. Con-

TABLE 4.5 Land-use zones in Thünen's Isolated State

Zone	Area Percent of State Area	Relative Distance from Central City	Land-Use Type	Major Marketed Product	Production System
0	<0.1	–0.1	Urban-industrial	Manufactured goods	Urban trade center of state; near iron and coal mines
1	1	0.1–0.5	Intensive agricultural	Milk; vegetables	Intensive dairying and trucking; heavy manuring; no fallow
2	3	0.6–3.5	Forest	Firewood	Sustained-yield forestry
3a	3	3.6–4.6		Rye; potatoes	6-year intensive crop rotation; rye (2), potatoes (1), clover (1), barley (1), vetch (1); no fallow; cattle stallfed in winter
3b	30	4.7–33	Extensive agriculture	Rye; animal products	7-year rotation system; field grass with an emphasis on dairy products; pasture (3), rye (1), barley (1), oats (1), fallow (1)
3c	25	34–44		Rye; animal products	3-course system; rye, etc. (1), pasture (1), fallow (1)
4	38	45–100	Ranching	Animal products	Mainly extensive stock-raising; some rye for on-farm consumption
5	—	Beyond 100	Waste	None	None

SOURCE: P. Haggett, 1965, *Locational Analysis in Human Geography*, p. 165, Table 6.4. New York: St. Martin's Press, Inc., Macmillan & Co. Ltd.

Thünen's Model

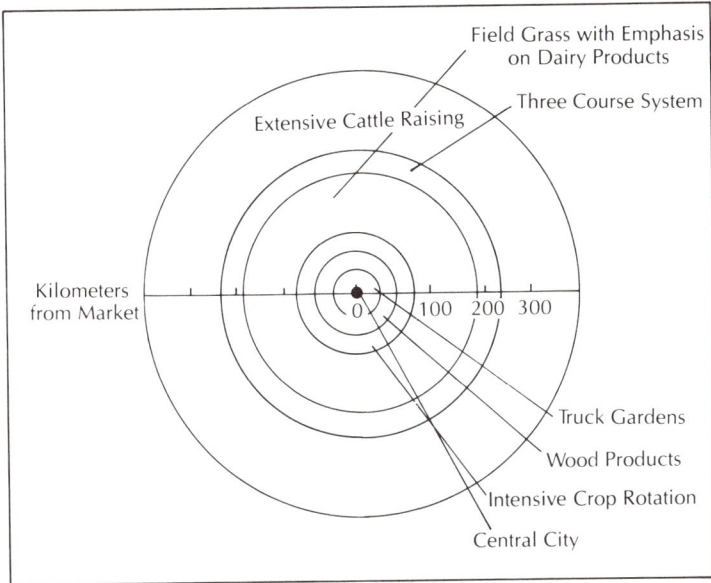

FIGURE 4.13 Land use zones in Thünen's isolated state.

sumers were not willing to pay high prices for items which were expensive to haul over long distances. The fact that patterns of agricultural land use in developed parts of the world in the twentieth century differ from those of the early nineteenth century does not undermine Thünen's method of analysis.

Modified Patterns of Agricultural Land Use Thünen was acutely aware that many complicating factors—physical, technical, cultural, historical, and political—would modify the concentric pattern of agricultural land use. He relaxed some of his initial assumptions to approximate actual conditions more closely.

For example, he relaxed his transport assumption, and considered the distorting effects of navigable waterways (Figure 4.14). Agricultural commodities could be transported over land by the shortest route to navigable water, and then moved by less expensive barge or boat to the marketplace. Each zone of production was distorted along the axis of the river. The innermost zone changed least in shape, because water transport was no faster than wagon transport. Water transportation was of little benefit to "truck" farmers for whom the important variable was time.

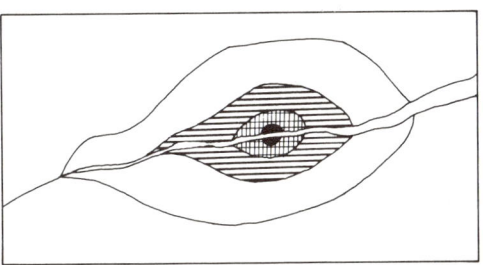

FIGURE 4.14 Transportation effects.

He removed the assumption of a single market town, and considered the effects of a second market center, which had a small trade area producing commodities of the Zone 1 type (Figure 4.15). He acknowledged but did not elaborate on the effects of several competing centers and a system of radiating highways. We can presume, however, that the tributary areas of competing centers would have a variety of crop zones enveloped by those of the principal market town, and that a system of radiating highways would produce a "starfish" pattern (Figure 4.16).

FIGURE 4.15 Effects of a subsidiary market.

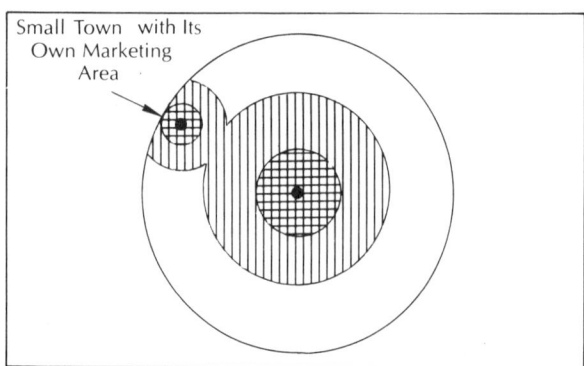

FIGURE 4.16 Effects of several competing centers and arterial road system. SOURCE: Edgar C. Conkling and Maurice Yeates, 1976, *Man's Economic Environment*. New York: McGraw-Hill, p. 24, Fig. 2-7.

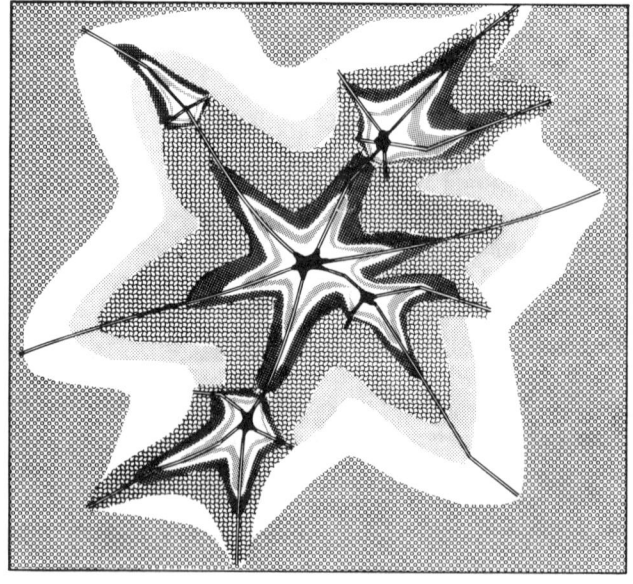

He dropped the assumption of uniform physical conditions and labor costs, and raised the question of variable production costs. He contemplated the effects of differing soil fertility, climate, topography and labor. He discovered that land uses vary considerably when one part of a region has a production cost advantage over another part. Zones of land use spread out in an area having some production cost advantage, and contract or even disappear in an area having a production cost disadvantage (Figure 4.17).

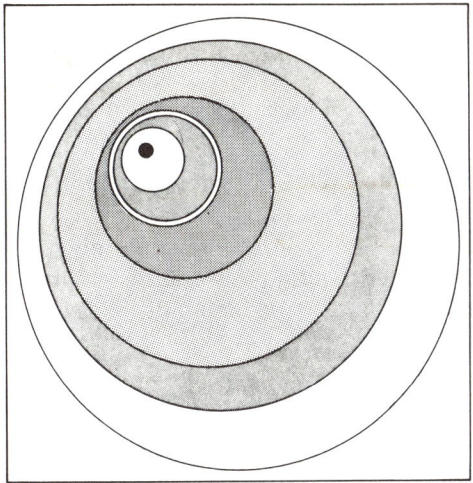

FIGURE 4.17 Effects of variable production costs.

Thünen considered other complicating factors such as the effects of foreign trade, taxes and subsidies. He found that the role of distance on agricultural land use was much the same at the scale of the farm as at the scale of the nation. He noted a tendency for intensive, high-value production to occur near farmsteads and land uses needing less intensive care to occur in more remote fields.

Evaluation of Thünen's Model

Thünen presented a *normative model* of agricultural land use. Among the conclusions we can derive from his model are:

1. that there is an inverse relationship between location rent and transport costs;
2. that there is a limit to commercial farming on a homogeneous plain with an isolated market town at its center;
3. that land values and intensity of land use increase toward the market; and
4. that crop types compete with one another and are ordered according to the principle of the highest and best use.

Thünen's most important contribution to studies of spatial organization in market exchange societies was the use of the principle of *highest and best use* and the concept of *location rent*. These two notions identify three major aspects of land use patterns: circular bands or circles of land use around points of greatest accessibility; axes of land use development along major transport arteries; and multiple nuclei with the emergence of additional satellite centers.

We have noted some limitations of Thünen's model:

1. His model does not succeed in describing the spatial structure of an economic system. It oversimplifies the relationship between town and country. Although he introduced multiple markets, his analysis concentrated on

various types of agriculture within a single market area having a large town at its center. He ignored the fact that agriculture tends to stimulate the growth of small *weight-losing* processing centers (e.g. sugar mills and distilleries), and that these industrial centers are connected to other larger centers. "Weight-losing" industries have large weight losses in processing.

2. His model assumes that differences in land rents have their origin solely in differences in costs of production. It does not pay attention to the existence of monopoly and absolute rents. Landowners receive monopoly rents (rents from excess profits due to monopoly prices), and they exact absolute rents, positive returns on all land in use including that at the margin of cultivation.

3. His model is static and deterministic. It represents a land use system at one point in time, and therefore cannot predict changing patterns of rural land use. Furthermore, it assumes that any change in technology, demand, or transport cost brings instantaneous adjustments in land use patterns.

4. His model does not consider the ways in which costs of production are affected by economies of scale. Economies of scale around a large market may substantially lower production costs relative to a small market.

5. His model assumes constant, not variable, transport costs. This, however, was an appropriate assumption under transport conditions in early nineteenth century Germany.

6. His model assumes that a farmer is *homo economicus* or Economic Person, who has perfect information and uses it with complete rationality to maximize profits. Clearly it is unrealistic to assume that farmers are *optimizers*; they make sub-optimal decisions because they have less than perfect information; and they depend on uncertain weather and economic conditions.

7. His model assumes competitive agricultural markets. But over the past few decades the agricultural industry especially in the United States has become controlled increasingly by giant corporations. "Super-farmers" are as profit-oriented as small farmers, but they are price-makers not price-takers, and can, therefore, operate successfully beyond the zone of "feasible" production.

Despite these and other limitations, Thünen's model remains valuable. It provides insights into patterns of rural land use, and it can be used as a norm against which actual land use patterns can be compared.

Evidence in Support of Thünen's Model

The purpose of this section is to compare Thünen's model against real world examples. Does the intensity of agricultural land use and the value of land increase toward the market as predicted? We answer this question by examining agricultural locations at local, regional, national and international scales.

Agricultural Locations at Local Scales

M. D. I. Chisholm (1968) described several European studies that illustrate distance-related adjustments in land use at the scale of the farm and village. He cited three studies of Finnish farms that measure the effect of distance on the level of net production per hectare. Farmers walk to and from their fields and use draught animals for plowing and transporting goods. Table 4.6 shows that net output (the

TABLE 4.6 Finland: relation of production per hectare and distance to farm plots (0–0.1 km equals 100)

Distance in Kms	Wiiala Gross Output	Wiiala Net Output	Virri Gross Output	Virri Net Output	Suomela Net Output
0–0.1	100	100	100	100	100
0.5	92	78	89	67	83
1.0	84	56	80	50	68
1.5	77	34	73	40	56
2.0	69	13	67	33	46
3.0	—	—	57	25	32
4.0	—	—	50	20	—
5.0	—	—	44	17	—

SOURCE: M. Chisholm, *Rural Settlement and Land Use*. London: Hutchinson Publishing Group Ltd., 1968; p. 50. Table 2.

yield per hectare minus production and transport costs) at the center of each study area represented 100 percent of the possible rent to be obtained from the use of any parcel of land. In every case, net profits as a percentage of the profit earned on the central hectare declined as distance to farm plots increased. Results from the Finnish studies are not unexpected; independent farmers find it worthwhile to increase inputs of labor on land near their farmsteads. A Dutch study revealed that the number of person-hours spent on land near farmsteads was much higher than on remote plots (Table 4.7). Arable plots, for example, at a 0.5 kilometer distance received 400 person-hours per annum per hectare. At 2.0 kilometers the level of labor input dropped to 300 person-hours, and at 5 kilometers it had declined to 150 person-hours.

TABLE 4.7 Netherlands: person-hours per annum per hectare actually worked on plots of over 15 hectares

Distance from Farmstead in Kms	Greenland Plots	Arable Plots
0.5	220	400
1.0	210	360
2.0	180	300
3.0	160	240
4.0	130	190
5.0	110	150

SOURCE: M. Chisholm, *Rural Settlement and Land Use*. London: Hutchinson Publishing Group Ltd., 1968, p. 53, Table 2.

Farmers may adjust to the relative friction of distance by substituting less demanding products at greater distances from the settlement. Chisholm provided evidence of this type of adjustment in a study of the land use pattern around the Sicilian settlement of Canicatti, an agri-town of 30,000 located some 18 kilometers from the nearest settlement of similar size. Townspeople are engaged in a variety of agricultural activities. Vegetable gardens, citrus orchards, vineyards, olive groves, almond, hazel and pistacchio trees, dry grain farming, pasture, and coppice wood surround the community. Table 4.8 shows that vines, olives and arable-with-trees diminish in importance as the distance from Canicatti increases. Four kilometers is the critical distance separating grain fields from olives and vines. The right hand column of Table 4.8 indicates the nature of the land-use sorting process. It gives the average number of person-days per hectare in each distance zone. Labor expenditure is 52 person-days in the first zone, but only 39 person-days in the eighth zone.

Zoning also characterizes land use patterns at the local scale in the underdeveloped world. P. M. Blaikie (1971) observed that small farmers in north India adjust land use to distance from their villages in order to reduce the total amount of work to be completed. Horvath (1969) discussed land use banding around Addis Ababa, Ethiopia. Prothero (1957) described zoning around villages in northern Nigeria. He distinguished four zones. The first is an inner garden zone which is heavily fertilized and continuously planted with a variety of food crops. A second zone, which occurs between 0.8 and 1.2 kilometers, also is planted continuously with guinea corn, cotton, tobacco, and groundnuts. A third zone extending to 1.6 kilometers is under rotation farming, and a fourth zone is in heavy bush, but with a few isolated clearings, each reproducing the three-zone sequence of the main villages.

Agricultural Locations at Regional Scales

We have seen that orderly patterns of agricultural production occur at the local level in many places. Does the Thünen model work at other scales? Let us move up the scale from the local to the regional level, and take as our example the famous Whisky Rebellion of western Pennsylvania farmers in 1794.

In the late eighteenth century the urban markets of New York, Philadelphia, and Baltimore were supplied with products by inland farmers. Close to the national market were dairy farms, market gardens, and woodlots supplying fuel and lumber for construction. Beyond the woodlots were grain and meat-producing areas. Still further from the eastern seaboard, frontier farmers could profit only by raising grain and converting it to whiskey. Whisky, which has a high value per unit of weight, was easy to transport. A few kegs were lashed onto the backs of mules and moved to market at low kilometer costs. These land use patterns are illustrated in terms of Thünen's model in Figure 4.18A.

Until 1794 everything went smoothly for western Pennsylvania whisky producers. In that year President Washington and the new Congress levied a special tax on inland whisky, which was competing with imported rum. The tax reduced the net profit zone for whisky. Figure 4.18B shows that the zone of profitable farm production shrank eastward. Frontier farmers lost their source of income and rose up

TABLE 4.8 Canicatti, Sicily: percentage of land area in various uses and annual labor requirements per hectare in person-days

Distance in kms from Canicatti	Urban	Irrigated arable and vegetables	Citrus fruits	Vines	Arable with trees	Olive	Trees*	Arable, unirrigated	Pasture and productive waste†	Coppice wood	Average number of person-days per hectare in each distance zone
0–1	44.7	—	—	15.8	—	—	19.7	19.7	—	—	52
1–2	—	—	—	18.0	16.7	8.4	41.0	15.9	—	—	50
2–3	—	—	2.5	2.3	21.8	14.4	35.4	23.6	—	—	46
3–4	—	—	2.1	13.3	18.7	0.6	47.2	18.1	—	—	50
4–5	—	—	—	5.1	19.2	2.4	28.4	43.4	1.4	—	42
5–6	—	1.0	—	6.3	4.7	1.6	17.6	64.1	4.7	—	41
6–7	1.3	0.7	—	3.3	6.7	—	18.3	68.7	0.9	—	40
7–8	—	—	—	4.0	7.7	—	23.6	62.4	0.8	1.6	39
Total	1.0	0.3	0.4	6.1	11.1	2.2	26.3	50.8	1.4	0.4	—
Average number of person-days per hectare	300	300	150	90	50	45	40	35	5	5	42

*Mainly almond, hazel, carob and pistacchio.
†Sometimes sown.

SOURCE: M. Chisholm, *Rural Settlement and Land Use*, London: Hutchinson Publishing Group Ltd., 1968, p. 57, Table 6.

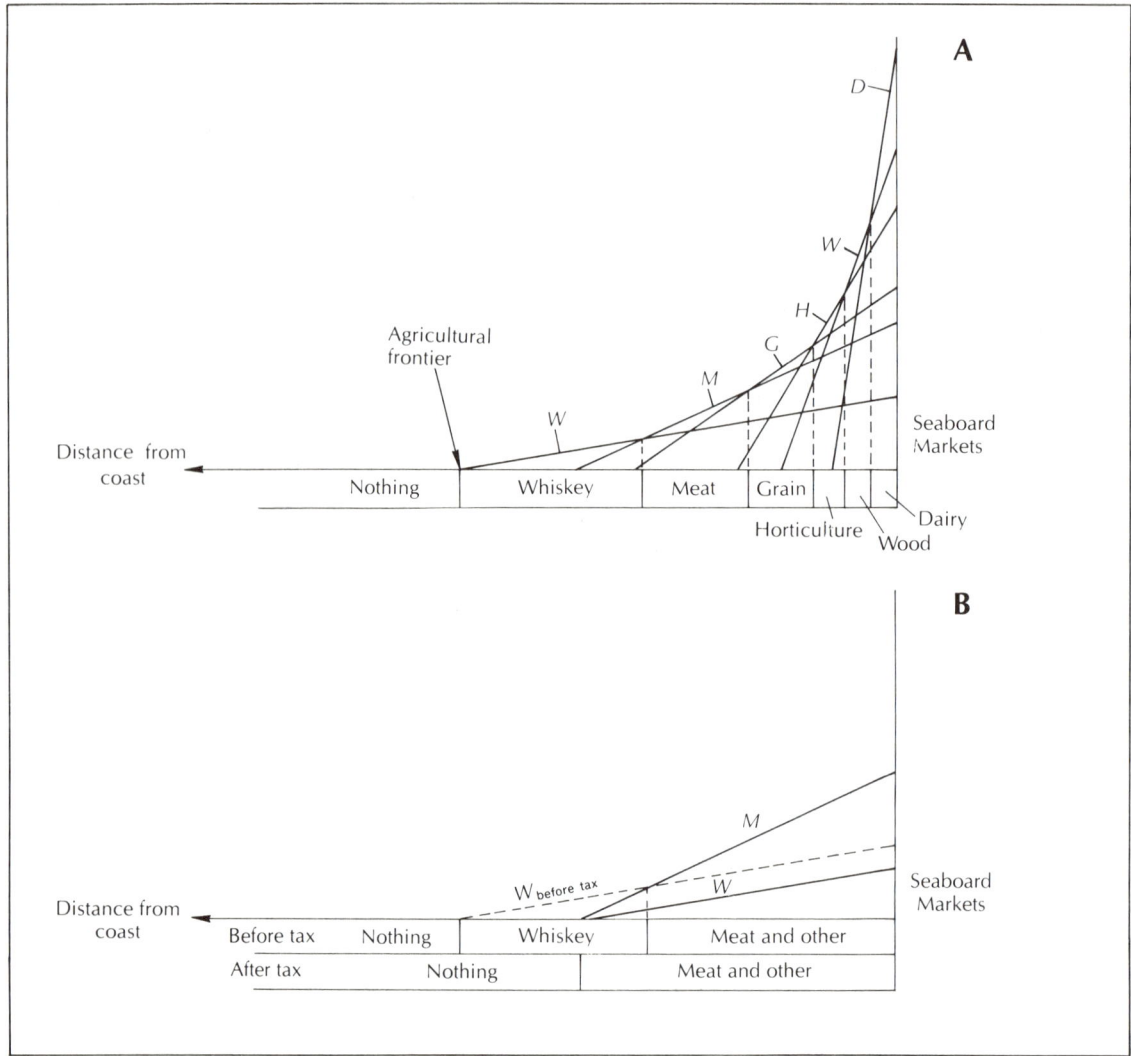

FIGURE 4.18 Circumstances leading to the Whiskey Rebellion. SOURCE: Abler, Adams, Gould, *Spatial Organization: The Geographer's View of the World,* © 1971, p. 352. Reprinted by permission of Prentice-Hall Inc., Englewood Cliffs, New Jersey.

in rebellion. Federal troops were called in to restore order. Happily, the discriminating tax was not permanent; it was repealed during Jefferson's administration.

Agricultural Locations at National and International Scales

The final shift in scale brings us to national and international levels. Let us take agricultural production in the United States as our example for the national scale. We will proceed from abstraction to reality. Figure 4.19A is a map of hypothetical land

Evidence in Support of Thünen's Model

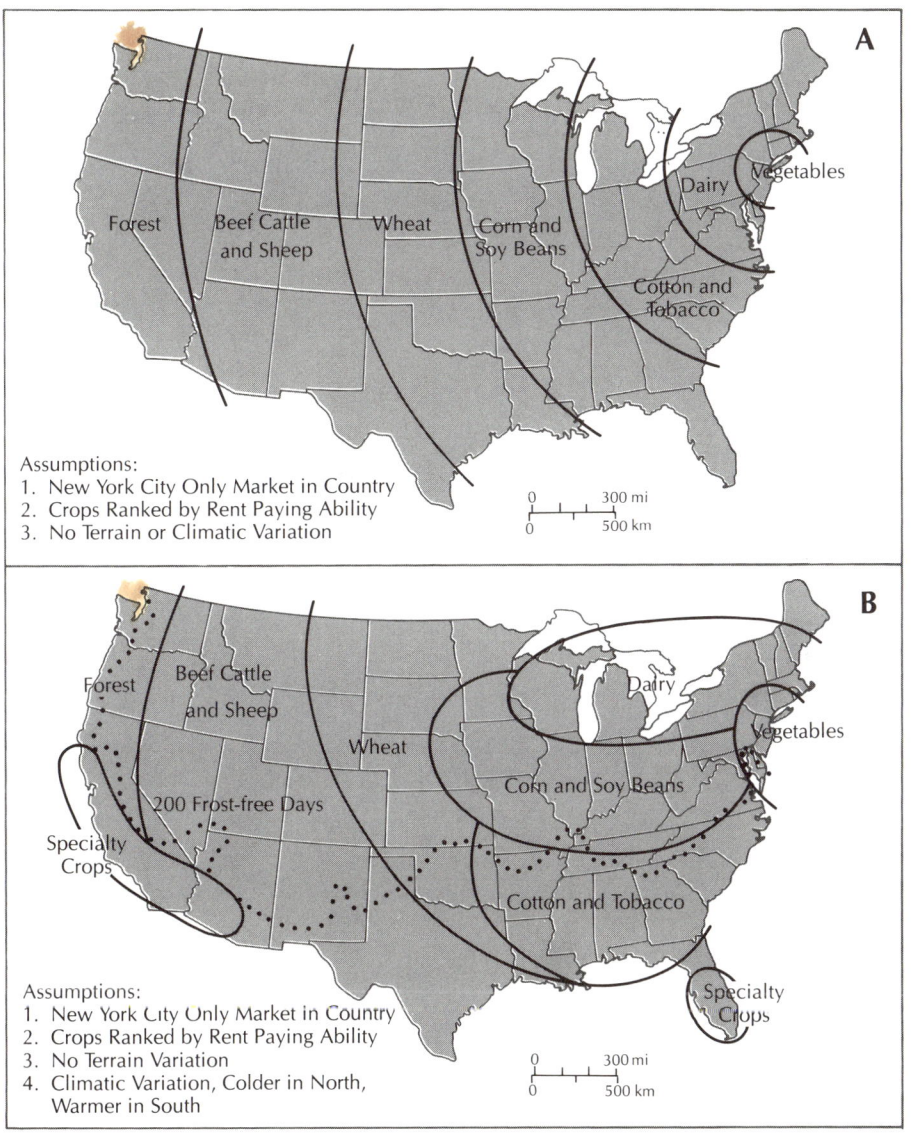

FIGURE 4.19 Theoretical land use rings in the United States. SOURCE: John F. Kolars and John D. Nystuen, 1974, *Human Geography: Spatial Design in World Society*. New York: McGraw-Hill, p. 258, Fig. 12-12.

use rings. It assumes that the United States is a homogeneous plain, that New York City is the only national market, that transport costs are uniform in all directions from New York City, and that crops are ranked by rent paying ability. Reality does not conform to these land use zones. The addition of other assumptions such as the adoption of a north-south temperature gradient would result in a more complex and realistic pattern, as in Figure 4.19B.

188 Agriculture and Rural Land Use

Let us now look at two maps which depict the actual pattern of agricultural production in the United States. Figure 4.20 shows the average value per hectare in dollars for all types of agriculture excluding livestock and poultry. Letters indicate for each state the two leading crops in order of their importance. Viewed in

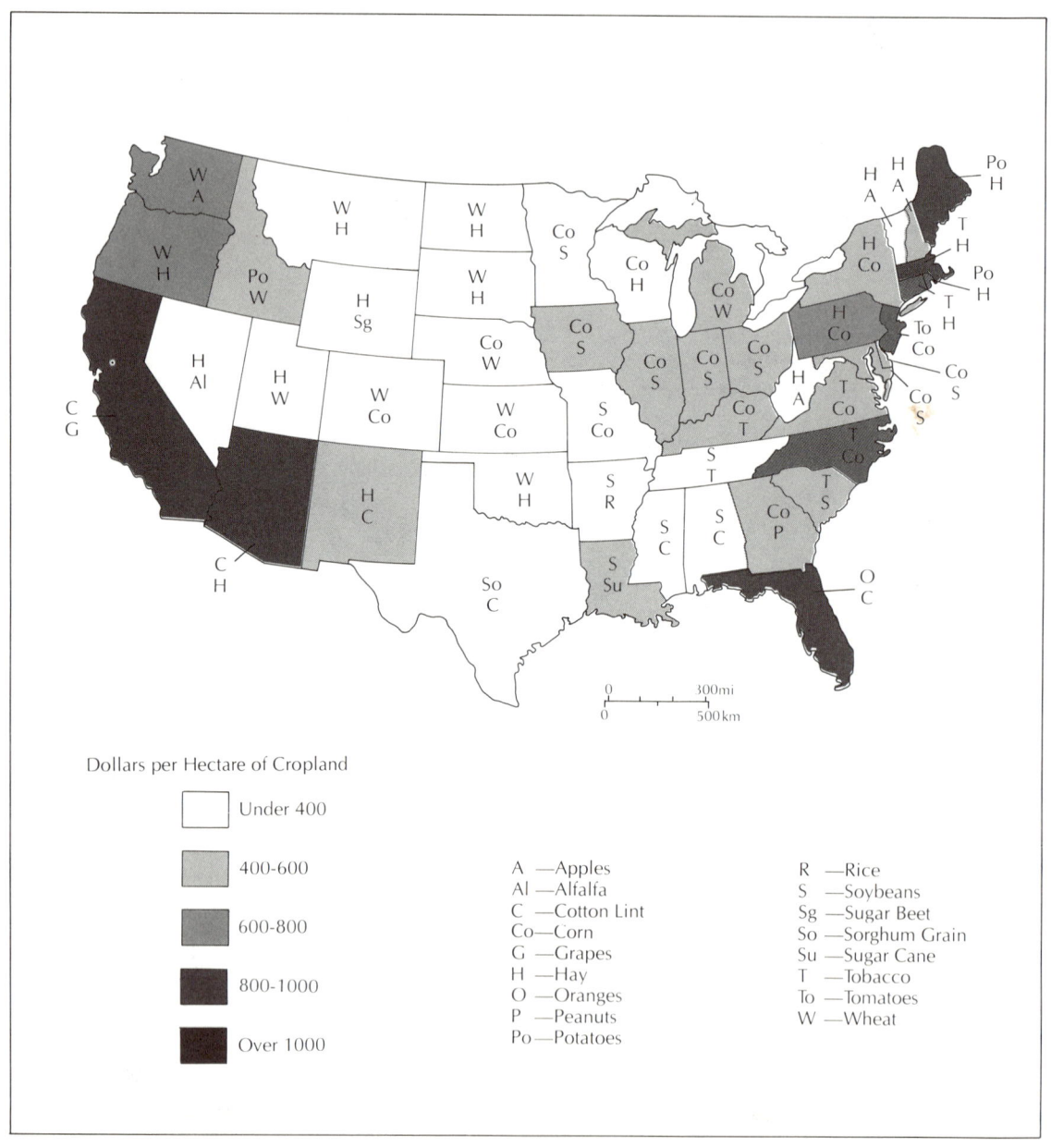

FIGURE 4.20 Average value (dollars) per hectare of cropland.
SOURCE: *Statistical Abstract of the United States,* 1976.

Evidence in Support of Thünen's Model

general terms, farm values decline irregularly with distance from the national market, which is that portion of Megalopolis between Massachusetts and New Jersey. Some interesting anomalies occur, however. Maine's values seem too high compared with expected values, but potatoes, hay and apples raise land rents. Tobacco plays an important part in raising the average value of land in North Carolina. Idaho, Washington, Oregon, California and Arizona have much higher values than surrounding western states. Large areas of dry land in these states have been reclaimed through huge federal investments in irrigation projects. Wheat, potatoes, hay, and apples raise returns in the Pacific Northwest. California and Arizona produce cotton, and they are major truck farming states. These two states have mild winters, and with the help of irrigation they produce large crops of fruits and vegetables. Truck farming is made possible by modern processing techniques and fast, cheap transportation. Florida has the highest value of cropland in the nation. It is second to California as a truck farming state and has a similar set of climatic advantages.

A

B

(A) A dairy farm in Wisconsin. Dairying is the prevalent form of agriculture across much of the northern half of the northeastern United States. The belt stretches from Maine to Minnesota. Dairying developed in response to environmental and cultural conditions and concentrates mainly on milk products (butter, cheese, powdered milk) for the national market (SOURCE: *University of Wisconsin—Extension*). (B) Near major cities, however, transportation costs favor the production of fluid (fresh) milk for local urban markets and milksheds of fluid milk production surrounded by other types of dairying are evident. Can you think of other types of intensive agriculture which form around most American cities? (SOURCE: *Clover Leaf Creamery Company*).

Figure 4.21 illustrates the major agricultural regions of the United States. Note the similarity between Figure 4.21 and our hypothetical maps in Figure 4.19. (A major difference is corn, which is forced northward by two special crops, cotton and tobacco.)

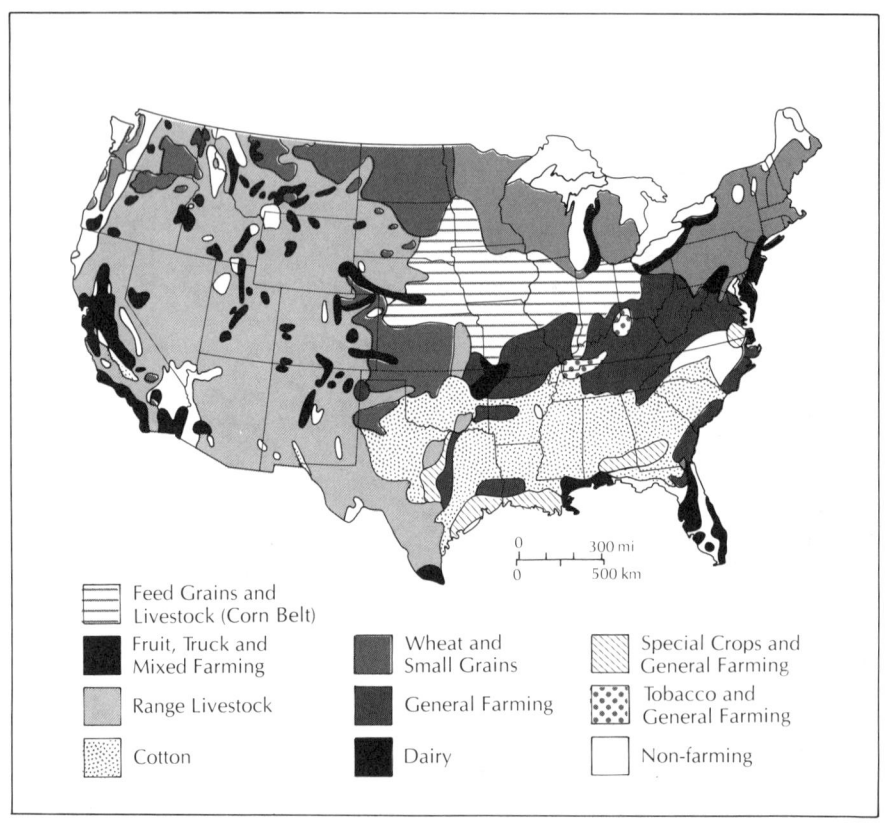

FIGURE 4.21 Major agricultural regions of the United States. SOURCE: John F. Kolars, and John D. Nystuen, 1974, *Human Geography: Spatial Design in World Society.* New York: McGraw-Hill, p. 261, Fig. 12-15.

Maps of agricultural production in Europe also support Thünen's model. Consider wheat as an example of a crop whose yield decreases with distance from the market (Figure 4.22). Although the ideal climate for growing wheat is the Mediterranean region, yields are much higher further north, not far from the climatic limits of where the crop may be grown. Wheat production is most intense in the area centered on the Low Countries, Denmark, north Germany, and southeast England. Northwestern Europe is an immense urban-industrial complex and a major center of consumption and marketing facilities.

Finally, we can see the world as a set of Thünen rings. At this scale, the world is the Isolated State and Europe-North America is the "Thünian-town." Figure 4.23 is a map projection centered on Europe showing the average calorie yield for

Summary

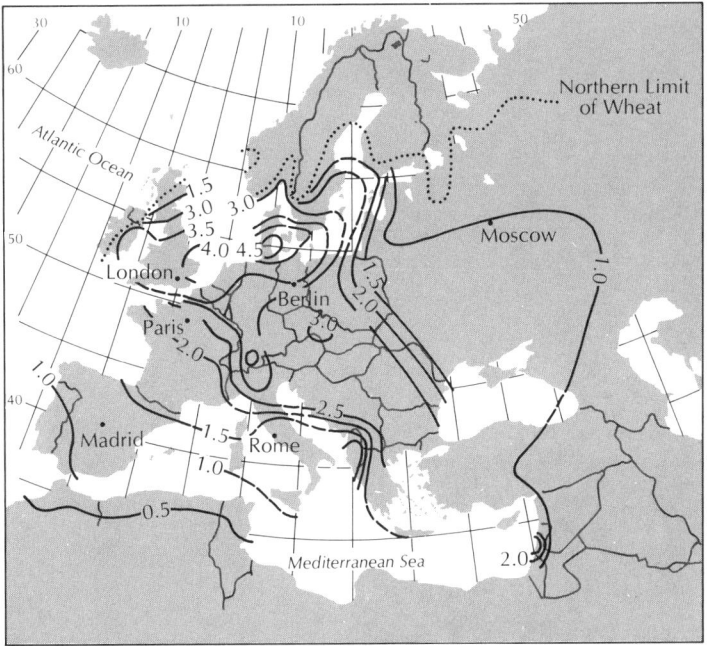

FIGURE 4.22 Yields of wheat in metric tons per hectare. SOURCE: John F. Kolars and John D. Nystuen, 1974, *Human Geography: Spatial Design in World Society.* New York: McGraw-Hill, p. 264, Fig. 12-17.

small grains (wheat, rice, barley, rye, oats, maize) and potatoes. The general pattern is one of low average calorie yields in the underdeveloped world, and intensive agricultural production in the core region near the Atlantic Ocean. Beyond the core area of world urban industrial development, there are a few outlying areas of high yields such as Japan and Argentina.

Summary

In this chapter we first reviewed agricultural origins and dispersals and the impact of food production on the land, and then concentrated on basic factors that influence agricultural patterns (site characteristics, cultural preferences and perceptions, systems of production, and relative location). Despite the fact that some geographers would argue that agricultural land use patterns are more a consequence of *site characteristics* than *relative location,* we chose to emphasize the latter.

This emphasis gave us an opportunity to introduce the first location model, which was developed by Thünen. His model was developed for a *feudal* system of agriculture, in which landlords lived off the labor of peasants who farmed their fields. Our interest in Thünen's model was not in the landlord/peasant system, but in his method of analysis, and in his emphasis on the role of geographical location. We considered the content of the Thünen model, and then applied it to

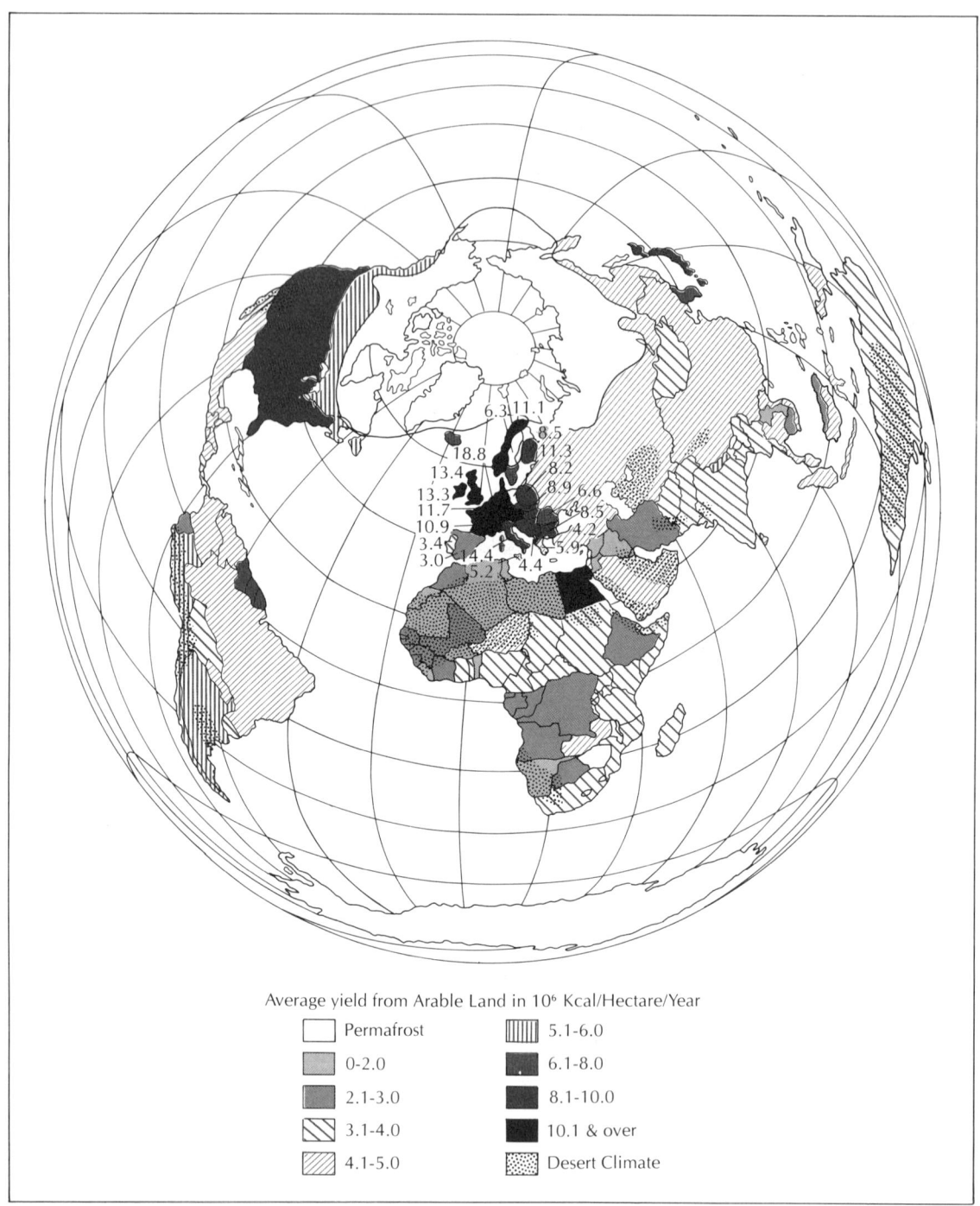

FIGURE 4.23 Average caloric yield from arable land as measured by yields from small grains and potatoes. SOURCE: John F. Kolars and John D. Nystuen, 1974, *Human Geography: Spatial Design in World Society*. New York: McGraw-Hill, p. 266, Fig. 12-18.

every scale of agricultural landuse. One of the key concepts of the Thünen model is *economic rent*, which leads one to believe that differences in land rents always owe their origin to differences in the cost of production. Remember, however, that in the capitalist world today landowners may receive *monopoly rents* and exact *absolute rents* (Barnbrock, 1974). Note also that Thünen's economic ideal of a competitive, beautiful, well-ordered, just world does not exist in the United States today. Although a large share of agricultural output still originates from small producers, the agricultural industry has been increasingly coming under the control of giant corporations (*agribusiness*) that fail to resemble the small relatively powerless producer pictured in the model.

DISCUSSION QUESTIONS

1. Agriculture is just another industry. Do you agree?
2. Write an essay on the emergence and diffusion of agriculture.
3. Distinguish between socialist and capitalist modes of agricultural production.
4. Distinguish between site and situation in determining crop types.
5. Using examples from North America and Europe, show how government policies have influenced patterns of agricultural activities.
6. Explain why the American wheat belt shifted westward from Pennsylvania through the Midwest to its present location in the Great Plains.
7. What does the Thünen model tell us about the intrinsic value of land close to the market? What underlying assumptions lead the model to this conclusion?
8. Explain why Thünen put forestry as the land use occupying the zone second from the central market.
9. Thünen regarded the use of a simpler-than-reality model as his most important scientific achievement. Why?
10. Compare and contrast Ricardo's and Thünen's arguments regarding the nature of economic rent.
11. Discuss: Differential rent is an inadequate land rent in twentieth century North America.

SUGGESTED READINGS

Emergence of Food Production

Isaac, E., *Geography of Domestication*. Englewood Cliffs, N.J.: Prentice-Hall, 1970.

Leonard, J. N., *The First Farmers*. New York: Time-Life, 1973.

Sauer, C. O., *Agricultural Origins and Dispersals*. New York: American Geographical Society, 1952.

Human Impact on the Land

Thomas, W. L., Jr., (ed), *Man's Role in Changing the Face of the Earth*. Chicago: University of Chicago Press, 1956.

Agricultural Systems

George, S., *How the Other Half Dies*. Montclair, New Jersey: Allanheld, Osmun and Co., 1977: Chapter 7.

Gregor, H. F., *Geography of Agriculture: Themes in Research*. Englewood Cliffs, N.J.: Prentice-Hall, 1970.

Whittlesey, D., "Major Agricultural Regions of the Earth," *Annals* of the Association of American Geographers, **26** (1936): 199–240.

Thünen's Model

Barnbrock, J., "Prologomenon to a Methodological Debate on Location Theory: The Case of von Thünen," *Antipode,* **6** (1974): 59–66.

Chisholm M. D. I, "Agricultural Production, Location, and Rent," *Oxford Economic Papers,* **13** (1961): 342–359.

Chisholm M. D. I, *Rural Settlement and Land Use*. London: Hutchinson, 1966.

Found, W. C., *A Theoretical Approach to Rural Land Use Patterns*. Toronto: MacMillan of Canada, 1971.

Hall, P. G., (ed.), *Von Thünen's Isolated State*. London: Pergamon Press, 1966.

Harvey, D., "Theoretical Concepts and the Analysis of Agricultural Land Use Patterns in Geography," *Annals* of the Association of American Geographers, **56** (1966): 361–374.

Applications of the Thünen Model

Blaikie, P. M., "Spatial Organization of Agriculture in Some North Indian Villages: Part 1," *Transactions* of the Institute of British Geographers, **53** (1971): 1–40.

Harvey, D., "Locational Changes in the Kentish Hop Industry and the Analysis of Land Use Patterns," *Transactions* of the Institute of British Geographers, **33** (1963): 123–44.

Horvath, R. J., "Von Thünen's Isolated State and the Area Around Addis Ababa, Ethiopia," *Annals* of the Association of American Geographers, **59** (1969): 308–323.

Muller, P., "Trend Surface of American Agricultural Patterns: A Macro-Thünen Analysis," *Economic Geography,* **45** (1973): 228–42.

Peet, J. R., "The Spatial Expansion of Commercial Agriculture in the Nineteenth Century: A von Thünen Interpretation," *Economic Geography,* **45** (1969): 283–301.

Sinclair, R., "Von Thünen and Urban Sprawl," *Annals* of the Association of American Geographers, **57** (1967): 72–87.

Cities and Urban Land Use

KEY TERMS

- average total costs
- ceiling rent
- central business district
- central city
- competitive bidding process
- concentric zone model
- egalitarian societies
- filtering process
- fixed costs
- generative cities
- ghettos
- invasion and succession
- market exchange
- megalopolis
- minicity
- multiple-nuclei model
- private land use decision process
- polarized metropolis
- production function
- profit-maximizing firms
- pure competition
- rank societies
- reciprocity
- redistribution
- scale economies
- sector model
- social surplus
- spread city
- stratified societies
- suburb
- transport costs
- variable costs
- zoning

5

According to archaeologists, the earliest cities emerged in the Fertile Crescent between 3000 and 2500 B.C. Recent evidence suggests that the growth of these cities was more closely related to their role as ritual centers than market centers. By the time urban life reached the eastern Mediterranean, however, cities and marketing systems were highly interrelated.

In Roman times, cities diffused from the Mediterranean to northwest Europe. Although many centers collapsed with the fall of the Roman Empire, some European cities survived to become major centers of trade in the Medieval period. From 1500 A.D., European urban hierarchies spread out to dominate the world.

The manifestations of the urban process varied from place to place. Since we cannot hope to describe all of them in one chapter, we choose instead to concentrate attention on the North American city.

Cities reflect the social systems in which they exist; North American urban growth has taken place within the context of free enterprise capitalism. This tradition of privatism has been called

> the most important element of [American] culture for understanding the development of cities. [It] has meant that the cities of the United States depended for their wages, employment, and general prosperity upon the aggregate successes and failures of thousands of individual enterprises, not upon community action. It has also meant that the physical forms of American cities, their lots, houses, factories and streets have been the outcome of a real estate market of profit-seeking builders, land speculators, and large investors. Finally, the tradition of privatism has meant that the local politics of American cities have depended for their actors, and for a good deal of their subject matter, on the changing focus of men's private economic activities (Warner, 1968:4).

In addition to the relative absence of public intervention, the United States urban experience has been dominated by rapid economic and technological changes. These changes produced concentrated industrial cities of the nineteenth century, and decentralized metropoli and gigantic urban regions of the twentieth century.

The compact industrial city developed to lower transport and communication costs for entrepreneurs who needed to interact with one another. Hence most commercial and industrial enterprises were concentrated in and around the *central business district* (CBD), the most accessible part of the city. The entrepreneurs, the owners of capital, chose to live on the outskirts of cities. Meanwhile, workers, who had less income to spend on travel to work, were forced to live adjacent to the central business district at high densities. Their living conditions were deplorable and health conditions were terrible.

During the twentieth century, increasing affluence and the technologies of mass transportation, the automobile, truck, and modern communications led to urban decentralization. Two notable features of the spreading out of the American city have been the middle class move to the suburbs in search of the "good life" and more recently for employment in commerce and industry. This twentieth century urban transformation was forecast by H. G. Wells (1902), who, like many of his educated contemporaries, regarded suburbanization as a solution for the urban ills of the nineteenth century city. Wells wrote that

> [T]hese coming cities will not be, in the old sense, cities at all, they will present a new and entirely different phase of human distribution. [The] social history of the middle and later third of the nineteenth century . . . all over the civilized world is the history of a gigantic rush of population into the magic radius of—for most people—four miles, to suffer there physical and moral disaster less acute but, finally, far more appalling than any famine—that ever swept the world . . . But . . . these great cities are no permanent maelstroms. [N]ew forces, at present so potentially centripetal in their influence, bring with them, nevertheless, the distinct promise of a centrifugal application that may finally be equal to the complete reduction of all our present congestions. The limit of the pre-railway city was the limit of man and horse. But already that limit has been exceeded, and each day brings us nearer to the time when it will be thrust outward in every direction with an effect of enormous relief. So far the only addition to the foot and horse . . . are the suburban railways . . . The star-shaped contour of the modern great city, thrusting out . . . knotted arms of which every knot marks a station, testify . . . to the relief of pressure thus afforded.
>
> We are . . . in the early phase of a great development of centrifugal possibilities . . . [A] city of pedestrians is inexorably limited by a radius of about four miles . . . a horse-using city may grow out to seven or eight . . . [I]s it too much . . . to expect that the available areas for even the common daily toilers of the great city of year 2000 . . . will have a radius of over one hundred miles?
>
> What will be the forces acting upon the prosperous household . . . ? [T]he passion for nature . . . the allied charm of cultivation . . . [and] that craving . . . for a little private *imperium* [are] the chief centrifugal inducements.
>
> [T]he city will diffuse itself until it has taken up considerable areas and many of the characteristics of what is now country . . . [T]he country will take itself many of the qualities of the city. The old antithesis will . . . cease, the boundary lines will altogether disappear.
>
> '[T]own' and 'city' will be, in truth, terms as obsolete as 'mail coach' . . . We may call . . . these coming town provinces 'urban regions.'

This chapter is divided into five parts. We consider, first, the types of society and associated modes of economic exchange that produce cities. We then turn to a discussion of the economic reasons for cities in competitive market societies. The last three sections consider urban land use. In them we examine classical urban location theory, spatial models of urban land use, and patterns and problems of the contemporary city.

OBJECTIVES

By the end of this chapter you should be able:

1. To recognize the main types of society and associated forms of economic exchange.
2. To show how scale economies and transport costs influence city building.
3. To describe how firms and households in the private land market select urban sites.
4. To define the terms: concentric zone model, sector model, and multi-nuclei model.
5. To discuss the consequences of the filtering process and the process of invasion and succession.
6. To discuss the differences between the contemporary spread city and the historic compact city.
7. To give reasons for the suburbanization of the American city.
8. To show how surplus value is appropriated and allocated to the advantage of wealthy people in United States urban areas.

Cities and Societies

Human beings established cities. The city represents our greatest impact on the land. It is a tangible expression of religious, political, economic, and social forces, in the form of a physical structure that houses a host of activities in close proximity to one another.

Cities are products of particular types of society in which they develop. A society is a group of people sharing a self-sufficient system of action that exists longer than the life span of an individual. To maintain conditions of self-sufficiency, human groups must have forms of social organization capable of producing and distributing goods and services.

We can identify three main types of society, with associated forms of economic exchange. These types, in order of increasing complexity, are as follows:

1. egalitarian, characterized by reciprocity;
2. rank, characterized by redistribution; and
3. stratified, characterized by market exchange.

Cities and Societies

The following review examines these basic forms of society and economic integration in more detail. The concepts discussed will help us to interpret our kaleidoscopic urban world.

Basic Forms of Society

An *egalitarian society* has "as many positions of prestige in any given age-sex grade as there are persons capable of filling them . . . " (Fried, 1967:33). It is forged through voluntary cooperative behavior, and, therefore, its economy is dominated by reciprocity. *Reciprocal* forms of interaction may take the form of the mutually beneficial exchange of goods and services or the movement of materials from those better-off to those worse-off. Large settlements are unlikely to evolve in egalitarian societies because they are unable to extract, appropriate, and redistribute a socially derived surplus product. A *social surplus product is that part of the annual product of any society which is neither consumed by the direct producers nor used for the reproduction of the stock of the means of production available at the start of the year.* In a class divided society, the social surplus product is appropriated by the ruling group.

    A *rank society is "one in which positions of valued status are somehow limited so that not all of those of sufficient talent to occupy such statuses actually achieve them"* (Fried, 1967:117). *Redistribution* may be sustained cooperatively or through the use of force or coercion. This more complex form of economic exchange can produce large settlements.

    A *stratified society is "one in which members of the same sex and equivalent age status do not have equal access to the basic resources that sustain life"* (Fried, 1967:186). Like other societies, it exists to mediate natural resource scarcities. Stratified societies adapt to scarcity through *market exchange.* A market exchange economy is a system that establishes market prices; the prices are the mechanism for connecting economic activity among a large number of individuals and for controlling a large number of decentralized decisions. Market exchange facilitates division of labor, specialization of production, and technological and organizational advances. It produces wealth for society out of scarcity, but at the cost of increasing scarcity for some (the poor) and easing it for others (the rich). Socially created scarcities cannot be eliminated in market-exchange economies. Contemporary Western cities exist in stratified societies. They generate large economic surpluses by directing their accumulated surpluses into productive uses such as investment in industry, research, and education.

    Growth promoting cities are classified as *generative,* not *parasitic.* Parasitic cities are vulnerable. Rather than investment in industry, they use their economic surpluses for dramatic, symbolic, and non-productive urban consumption such as grandiose buildings. Many cities of the underdeveloped world are *parasitic,* acting as curbs to economic growth. Cities represent both kinds to different degrees.

Transformation of Market Exchange

Modes of economic exchange may be organized in different ways. To illustrate, consider the changing nature of market exchange in the modern history of Western cities.

Prior to 1776, cities were usually extensions of the personalities of those who governed them. Venice was the city of the Doges and Florence was the city of the Medicis. With the industrial revolution, cities ceased to be reflections of individuals or dynastic personalities; they became instruments and results of industrial growth.

A

B

C

The merchant city. (A) Venice, Italy: the greatest and best preserved of the merchant cities. The northern counterpart to Venice during the mercantile period was Bruges in Belgium, which was a member of the Hanseatic League. SOURCE: Courtesy of the *Italian Government Travel Office*. (B) Lubeck, Germany: A Hanse town. SOURCE: *R. Janke.* (C) Innsbruck, Austria, a city located north of the strategic Brenner Pass that linked German and Italian merchant cities.

Cities and Societies

In the early stages of the industrial revolution, market economies were organized along individualistic lines. There was an absence of monopoly and a good deal of freedom from government involvement. Cities registered high rates of industrial innovation, and huge increases in productive power. Their standards of achievement were those of industry and technology. If these prospered, then the city was considered to be good. The "best" city was the one that was busiest, grew most quickly, and recorded the largest increases in bank clearings. However, manufacturing cities were ugly creations and horrifying environments for the laboring poor. It is sufficient to comment that no industrial city attracts tourists in search of urban beauty. Tourists over-run poor preindustrial cities like Toledo, Spain, and avoid rich industrial cities like Toledo, Ohio!

The industrial city: Belfast, Northern Ireland.

The market mode of economic integration took on a different appearance toward the end of the nineteenth century. The economy drifted from individual capitalism to monopoly capitalism. Large industrial and financial corporations emerged and diminished the community of competition. They have had a pervasive influence on the twentieth century Western city.

The geography of modern Western cities has been affected by the necessity of corporate enterprises (1) to find ways to absorb their rapidly accumulating surpluses, and (2) to increase demand for their products and services. Corporations like to dispose of some of their surpluses through urban renewal projects. Funds are sometimes used to replace low income housing areas with luxury office and apartment complexes. Corporations also find the national economy a place to exploit need creation, a process whereby luxuries are transformed into needs. This process operates not only through daily appeal to customer tastes, but also as a consequence of urban spatial organization itself. For example, low density metropoli, such as Los Angeles and Minneapolis-St. Paul, make a car, or two cars, a necessity. They literally force residents to drive cars produced by the auto industry.

Relative Importance of Different Modes of Exchange

All three modes of economic exchange (reciprocity, redistribution, and market exchange) operate in most cities, but the emphases differ over time. Cities of medieval Europe reflected the dominant influence of redistribution, but market exchange also operated. In general, cities in the zone between the North Sea and Italy were more supportive of the market than those on the margin of this region. In this commercial area, the old feudal ordering of society was declining and merchants became socially and politically more influential. Where commerce was permitted to operate freely, as in Venice and Florence, the market place became a notable feature of city structure. Yet the disposal of accumulative wealth through the construction of massive cathedrals, public buildings, and universities emphasized the domination of symbolic and social values over economic values.

From the late medieval period onward, the importance of market exchange increased. Large commercial cities like London, Amsterdam, and Antwerp boasted the triumph of the market over redistribution. By the nineteenth century, market exchange dominated life in Western Europe.

In North America, where medieval forms did not exist, the nineteenth century city was an expression of economic forces. The force of the American city was not the nominal government; it was the dominant economic institutions, usually industrial establishments. Nonetheless, city government did play a redistributive role that grew more important as the industrial revolution proceeded. Urban bureaucracies collected taxes and provided a range of public services. Although much less prominent than the other modes of integration, reciprocity was found at every level of society, especially in working class neighborhoods, where it provided residents with a degree of social solidarity and security.

In the contemporary Western city, reciprocity has a very abridged role to play. Market exchange dominates life, but it is challenged by redistribution. Redistribution is far more important than it was in the nineteenth century because of the growth of two powerful institutional forms: big business and big government, that contain within themselves elements of the rank society such as the rank and status of employees. Corporate and government bureaucracies have become major agents of redistribution in urban areas. Government, for example, collects resources and redistributes them in the form of public services, welfare programs, public projects, and subsidies.

Process of City Building

What general forces help to concentrate economic activities in cities? One way to answer this question is to restrict attention to a purely competitive market situation and to regard city building as the result of two opposing vectors. These contrasting

Process of City Building

forces are *scale economies* and *transport costs*. What do the terms *scale economies* and *transport costs* mean, and how do they influence city building? To answer this question we must first survey the classical economic principles that relate to the production and cost behavior of the single firm.

Production and Cost Behavior of the Single Firm

Although Western market economies are oriented along monopolistic lines, a *pure competition* model provides one explanation for spatially concentrated production. It is a reasonably correct model for nineteenth century market economies which were so influential in city formation. The purely competitive market structure of industry consists of many small individual firms producing homogeneous products. In this situation firms are price-takers not price-makers; that is, they have so little power individually that they accept prices as given by market forces beyond their direct control. Decision makers make rational calculations in order to maximize their own profits. In other words, managements strive to obtain output levels that maximize differences between total revenues and total costs. (Figure 5.1.)

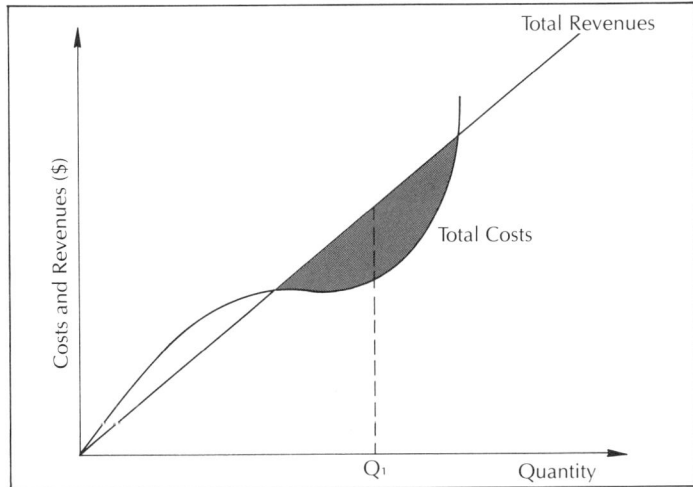

FIGURE 5.1 Output level for a profit-maximizing firm.

    Firms face short-run and long-run planning periods that economists explain in terms of the *production function*. The production function is a statement of the relationships between inputs (land, labor, and capital) used by a firm and the flow of output (goods and services) resulting from their use. Economists define long-run as a period long enough to permit a firm to vary the quantity of all the inputs in its production function, and short-run as a period short enough for at least one input to be fixed in amount and invariable. The firm's important long-run decision is to determine its future size, whether it should be smaller or larger than its present size. The firm's important short-term decision is to determine the most profitable rate of operation for the present plant size.

    Consider the short-run with a simplified production function consisting of two inputs—a fixed supply of capital and a variable supply of labor. What are the relevant short-run costs of production? Firms incur two types of costs: *fixed costs*, for example, capital, and *variable costs* such as labor. Fixed costs or "overhead" costs are expenditures firms must make in order to obtain the use of variable inputs. Fixed costs such as land and buildings do not vary as output varies. By contrast, variable costs change as output changes. As output rises, these costs rise; as output falls, these costs fall.

Managements of *profit-maximizing firms* are interested in their total costs—that is total fixed costs plus total variable costs. They are interested in a profit-maximizing rate of output at a price given by the market. One way to determine what firms should supply at each relevant price is to apply the law of diminishing returns. Cost implications of this law are shown in Table 5.1. Our hypothetical illustration assumes that the price for a given amount of a variable input (column 2) and a fixed input (column 3) is $1. Total costs for different levels of output (column 1) are given in the fourth column. At four units of output, for example, total costs are $33; that is $17 for the variable input plus $16 for the fixed input. Average total costs (column 5) are calculated by dividing total costs (column 4) by total output (column 1).

TABLE 5.1 Cost implications of the law of diminishing returns

Output (1)	Variable Input (2)	Fixed Input (3)	Total Costs (4)	Average Total Costs (5)
1	6	16	$22	$22.00
2	10	16	26	13.00
3	13	16	29	9.67
4	17	16	33	8.25
5	24	16	40	8.00
6	36	16	52	8.67
7	55	16	71	10.14

The average total cost curve is important to a firm because it fixes the most profitable rate of operation. It is usually U-shaped, indicating a level of output that is optimum in the sense of yielding least-cost output. In our hypothetical example, this is at point X (Figure 5.2). The cost per unit of output is $8 and 5 units of output are produced. Beyond 5 units, diminishing returns cause average costs to rise.

Scale Economies and Diseconomies of the Single Firm

Spatially concentrated production is closely associated with long-run costs of firms. Two sets of forces influence long-run costs of firms. First there are *internal scale economies* subject to direct management control. Managers may be able to take advantage of labor economies (more efficient labor specialization), technical economies (larger, more efficient machines), market economies, and managerial economies. Internal economies arise because many factors of production (inputs) are indivisible and can be used more efficiently at larger scales of output. Thus the

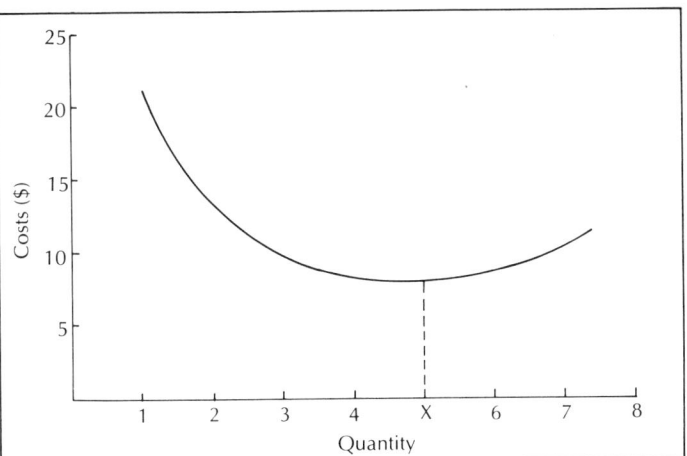

FIGURE 5.2 Average cost curve.

concept of internal economies to scale refers to cost-reducing changes that tend to lower average costs of firms as they grow in size (Figure 5.3A).

Second, there are *external economies,* which represent two forms of agglomeration: *localization* or *industry economies,* and *urbanization economies.* Localization economies refer to declining average costs for firms as the output of industries of which they are a part increases (Figure 5.3B). These economies stem from acquired benefits industries derive within restricted geographical areas, such as the development of a large labor pool with skills needed by the industry.

Urbanization economies refer to declining average costs of firms as cities increase their scales of activity (Figure 5.3C). Cost reductions, that tend to be greater in larger cities, stem largely from a technology that stimulates production on a scale that can only be achieved with firm specialization. Firm specialization occurs when plants perform only one or a few functions in the overall production process. It leads, as a result of transport costs, to geographical clustering which, in turn, promotes more geographical specialization and concentration. The garment industry of New York and London, and the metal trades of Ohio and the West Midlands are outstanding examples of geographical clustering of specialized firms.

Diseconomies of scale are also possible. Consider, for example, internal diseconomies. At first, firms experience cost-reducing internal economies, but eventually cost-increasing diseconomies set in (Figure 5.3D). Some hold that rising average costs occur after a certain scale of production is attained, because it is not possible to vary proportionately all inputs used in the production process. It is argued, for example, that management does not grow proportionately as firms expand. Thus managers are forced to spread themselves ever more thinly over wider and wider areas of decision making. Decreasing returns set in, and firms become less efficient.

We can also think of external diseconomies. Urbanization diseconomies, for example, are said to exist when a firm's average costs rise as the scale of activity within a city increases. Firms might experience higher costs in a larger city because of an increasing scale of activity within the city, such as growing scarcity of inputs like land, or because of problems of congestion, pollution, crime, and finance.

FIGURE 5.3 Scale economies and diseconomies: (A) internal economies; (B) localization economies; (C) urbanization economies; (D) internal economies and diseconomies.

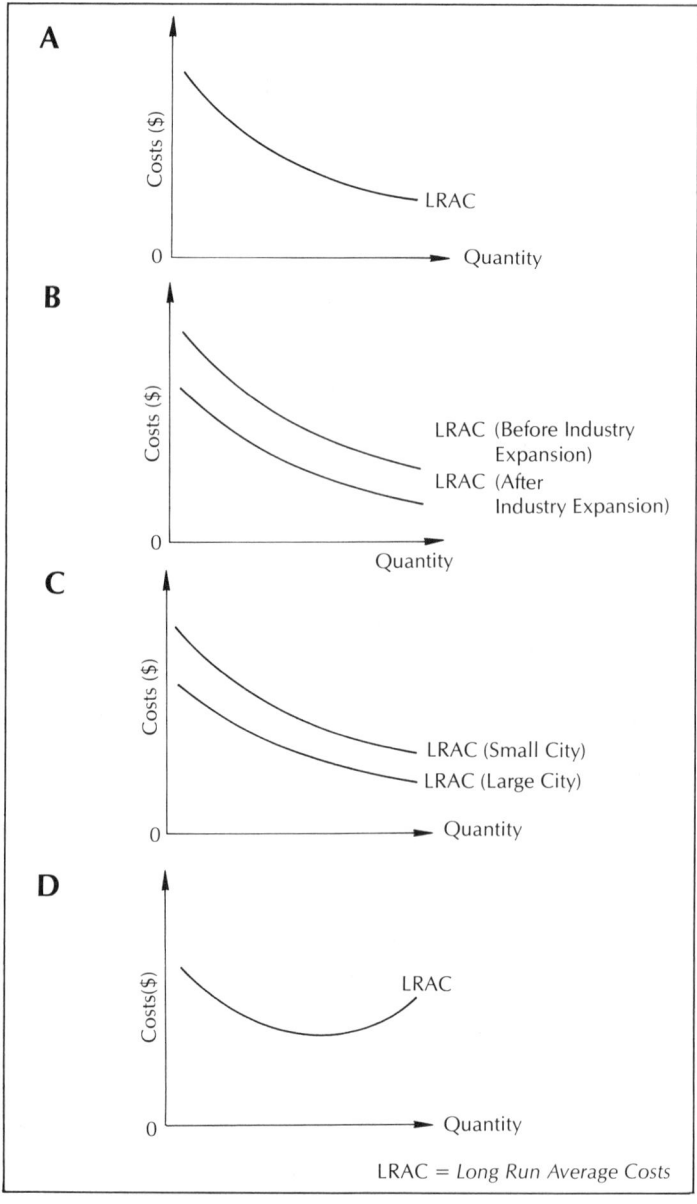

Transport Costs of the Single Firm

We would not need to worry about transport costs if resources were ubiquitous, if technical conditions of production were the same everywhere, and, of course, if movement were instantaneous and free. But resources are rarely ubiquitous, technical conditions of production are highly variable, and movement over geographical space always encounters resistance. Transport costs are the alternative output we give up when we commit inputs to the movement of people, goods, information and ideas over geographical space. They are the swimming pools and libraries that must be surrendered for roads and railways.

What effect does the cost of overcoming the friction of distance have on the location of economic activities? As transport costs are directly correlated with distance, profit-maximizing individuals choose sites that reduce geographical distances affecting their activities. Firms select sites close to their inputs, to other firms or consumers who buy their products. Workers decide to live near their place of employment. Accessibility pays off in the form of transport cost savings that concentrate firms and households. Moreover, incentives to concentrate activities are intensified by existing transport systems, which provide a high degree of access to only a limited number of geographical areas.

Economic Costs and City Building

Having looked at the concepts of scale economies and transport costs, we are finally in a position to see how they influence city building. First, consider an area in which people are dispersed geographically and a production technology in which economies of scale are absent. As firms grow in size, they experience only constant returns to scale; that is, their output increases proportionately as the amount of all inputs increases. Firms could, if they choose, locate in close proximity to one another, but such a choice would result in falling profits and rising costs. Geographically concentrated production would increase the distance and, hence, the cost of getting goods and services from producers to consumers. When scale economies are absent there is no incentive for profit-maximizing firms to concentrate production in space.

Now let us alter the situation. Suppose a new technology generates increasing returns to scale. If consumers remain dispersed geographically, concentrating production will again increase transport costs. But this time transport cost increases are more than offset by cost-reducing economies of scale. Profit-maximizing firms will choose city sites. When this happens, people who work in cities live in or very near cities. Firms selling goods and services to these firms and households also move into cities. In this way city building is cumulative; concentration demands more concentration because of the impact of transport costs.

Location of Land Uses Inside Cities

Preceding sections discussed reasons for the growth of cities with particular reference to market exchange societies. In the last three sections of this chapter we turn attention to the city as a discrete area whose spatial structure is to be analyzed. *Urban structure* refers to the geographical dimension of activities in cities. When we study urban spatial structure, we learn about the density of activities and land use arrangements.

In this section we ask: How do various land using activities come to be located where they are in cities? Classical urban location theory provides one answer to this question. This theory concerns the *private land use decision process*, and is based on Thünen's concept of location rent. Assumptions embodied in urban location rent are first, that the *central business district* (CBD) is the most economically productive location because of the concentration of transportation facilities; second, that rent falls to zero at the fringe of the city; third, that firms are competitive price-takers not price-makers; and finally, that cities exist in competitive market exchange economies without government and social classes. Although the concept of differential rent is a useful arranger of land uses, a word of warning is in order. The pursuit of the most profitable use of land in contemporary Western cities is inhibited by industrial monopoly, class division of society, racial discrimination, and public authority. Despite its deviations from the real world, many geographers and economists still use classical urban location theory to interpret and indicate problems of land use in cities.

The Competitive Bidding Process

Classical location theory states that activities locate in cities according to the outcome of the *competitive bidding process*. Those people who are willing and able to pay the highest price for a particular site win the competition, and put it to the economically highest and best use. Highest and best use, of course, can change over time as external market forces change. These forces include effective demand, public tastes and standards, and land use regulations.

Let us apply the bidding process to a simple example. Imagine a city located on a featureless plain in which there are two demanders of land, Jason and Sam. Figure 5.4 indicates the price bids of both Jason and Sam for sites that stretch from the CBD to the perimeter of the city. Jason is willing and able to pay more for some sites and Sam is willing and able to pay more for other sites. At site D_1, Jason is willing and able to pay $25 and Sam is willing and able to pay $20. On the other hand, Jason has no interest whatsoever in land at D_3, but Sam is willing to pay $15 for site D_3. If the bid rent curves for Jason and Sam actually represent their behavior in

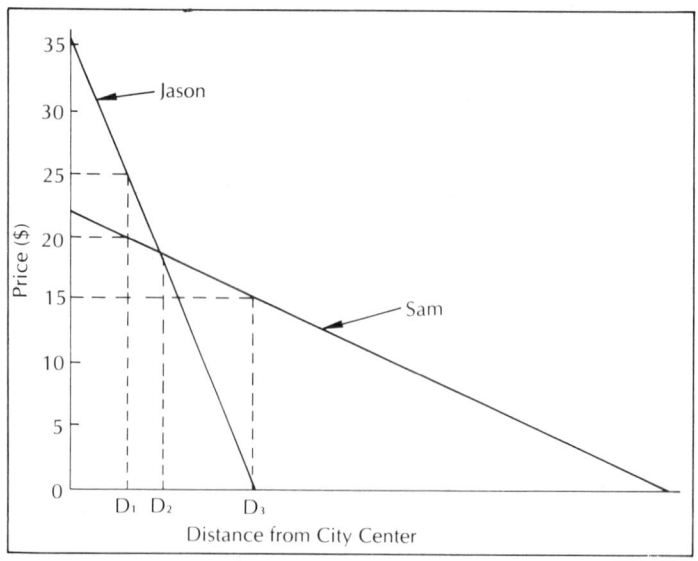

FIGURE 5.4 The bidding process.

the urban land market, then the outcome of the competitive bidding process would have Jason located between the CBD and D_2, and Sam beyond site D_2.

Our hypothetical example raises a fundamental question: Why do users bid for particular parcels of land? In some instances, a user will find inherent characteristics of the site valuable. For a residential user it may be a scenic vista; for a commercial user it may be well situated to potential customers. In other instances, site attributes such as natural hazards may detract from the value of a tract to all potential developers or bidders.

Although part of every tract's value depends on site characteristics, relative location is usually much more important. By relative location we mean a tract's situation in relation to other tracts. For particular activities some land parcels have more desirable locations than others because they have better accessibility. They save users transportation costs. For example, if accessibility to work is important to residential users, bid rent curves will show higher bids near places of employment.

Ceiling Rents

According to classical economic theory, the competition for the use of available locations results in the occupation of each site by the use able to derive the greatest utility or profit from it, and therefore able to pay the highest rent. The maximum rental that a particular user pays for a site is called the *ceiling rent*.

Consider a hilly tract of land, commanding excellent views, on the outskirts of a city. Ceiling rents for this parcel of land might be $90 for residential, $60 for retailing, and $50 for manufacturing. Clearly this tract of land is likely to be sold or leased for residential land use. But if the tract owner thinks the site is worth more than $90 the land will remain vacant.

Another tract of land is for sale a few kilometers away from the parcel put to residential use. It is relatively flat and is located adjacent to a major highway. Ceiling rents might be $30 for residential, $100 for retailing, and $70 for manufacturing. In this case the tract is sold or leased for retailing—say a shopping center.

The Residential Location Decision

Let us now see how households and firms select sites. For simplicity we will assume that users are concerned only with the relative location of a site in a single-centered city, *i.e.* a city with one center of employment—the CBD.

One important decision most people make when selecting a home is accessibility to where they work in the city. Their decision depends on the amount of money and time they can afford to expend on overcoming relative distance.

First, consider patterns of residential land use and the cost of commuting to work. A family's budget is divided between living costs, housing costs, and transport costs. Assume that people are either rich or poor. Poor families, who have little money to spend on commuting after living and housing expenses are deducted from income, have sharply negative bid rent curves (Figure 5.5A). They are forced to live close to places of work. The only way the inner-city poor can afford to live on high rent land is to consume less space. Rich families with plenty of money to spend on transportation have more locational freedom. They do not have to select sites near their places of employment. They can trade access to employment for spacious lots away from the center.

Now consider the impact of time costs on the residential location decision. Time spent commuting is time that could otherwise be devoted to earning income. In this case, distance is more critical for the rich than for the poor, because the rich make more money. Rich households have steep bid rent curves, and they live close to the city center (Figure 5.5B). Meanwhile the poor with shallow bid rent curves live further away. This land use pattern is characteristic of many Third World cities; the poor often live in peripheral squatter settlements and the rich live in opulent city residences.

Up to now a single mode of travel to work has been assumed. Conditions are more realistic if two modes of travel, walking and driving, are introduced with different assessments of the cost of travelling time for rich and poor households (Figure 5.5C). The steepest bid rent curve is for the rich walking to work, followed by the poor walking, the rich driving, and the poor driving.

(A) The poor live at high densities on high-priced land close to the downtown. (B) The affluent live in new subdivisions miles from downtown. SOURCE: *University of Wisconsin—Extension.*

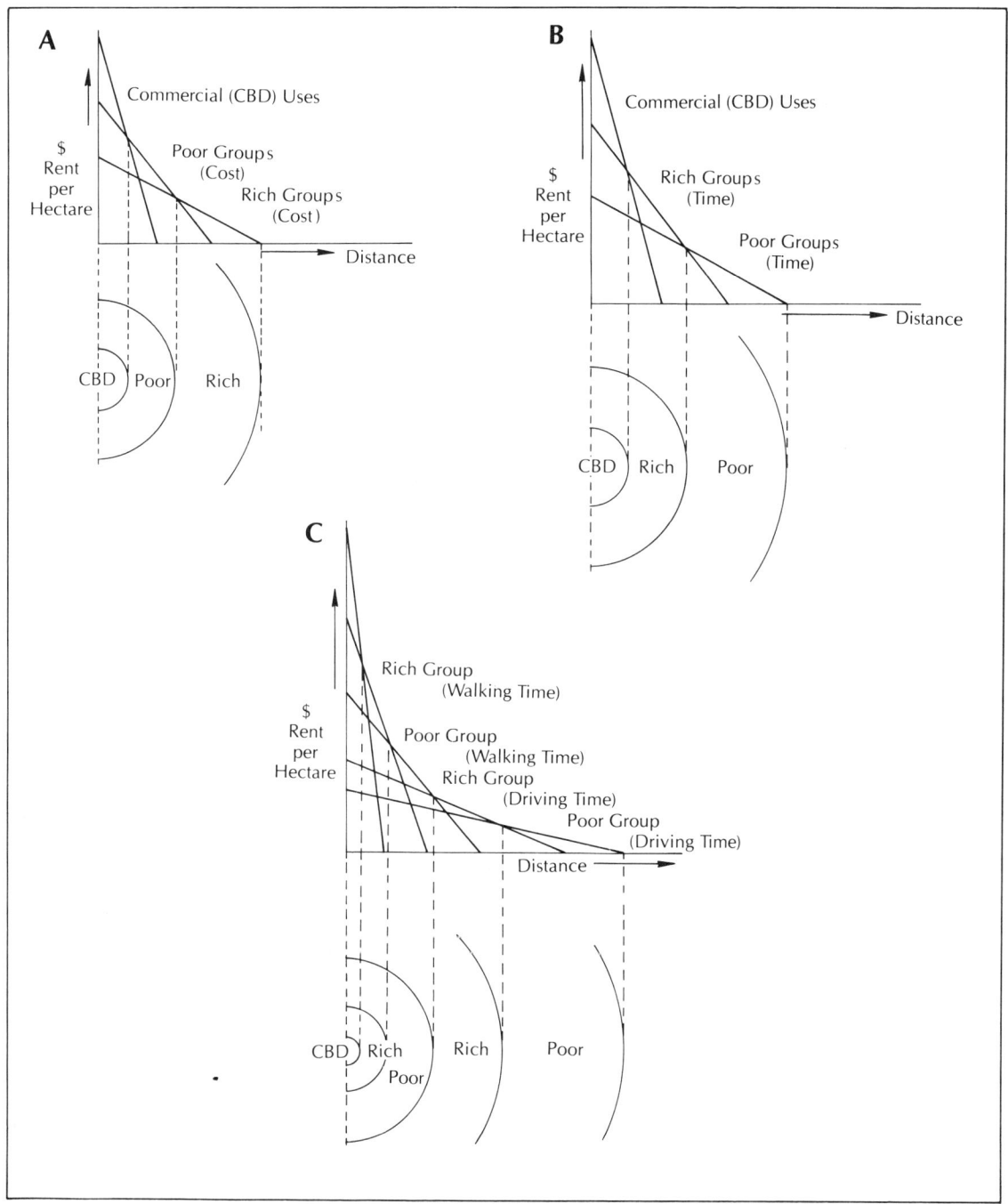

FIGURE 5.5 Land use patterns: (A) cost criterion; (B) time criterion; (C) travelling time criterion. SOURCE: From David Harvey, *Society, the City and the Space-Economy of Urbanism* (Washington, D.C.: Association of American Geographers, 1972), Resource Paper for College Geography Number 18, pp. 17, 18.

Although cost, time, and mode of travel to work have important influences on residential location, other dimensions to accessibility such as nearness to services must be considered. These and other factors influence bid prices. In every situation, however, the rich can always outbid the poor. Thus the results of the competitive bidding process for households are always relatively advantageous to the rich and always relatively disadvantageous to the poor in market exchange societies (see box).

> **PROFITS FROM THE SLUMS**
>
> What are the causes of the progressive rings of slum and suburb around the city centers? Why are slums located in the centers of cities? Why are not the poor and rich integrated in random patterns? Basically the answer is that the land nearest the city center can earn the highest rent per unit of land; this fact determines land use.
>
> Technically, the explanation is known as the von Thünen rent model. In 1826, von Thünen, a German land owner, explained the rings of agricultural land use around settlements. The land closer to the settlement shows greater agricultural profitability and therefore earns higher rents. As the settlement grows, the rings grow in proportion. The shifts of farm economies in Fitzgerald, from forestry through berry farming, were caused by the expansion of these successive rings through the neighborhood. Urbanization merely shifts the "crop" from agricultural to human. Rather than the agricultural products being more valuable as they are nearer the city, the human residents must be more valuable, must pay more rent per unit of land.
>
> Transport costs per unit of land are an important factor in the location of slums. A bus fare hike represents an added cost for the individual, and limits how far he can live from his work. Slow transportation systems, requiring long waits for buses, represents a real cost. If a man with an automobile can go from one point to another in a city in half an hour, while another who waits for one bus and then a transfer bus makes the same trip in an hour and a half, the bus rider has paid the price of an extra hour's worth of time. Even a dollar-an-hour worker is paying a bus fare of one dollar and thirty-five cents, not just the thirty-five cent fare. The effect of high transport costs is to lock the slum dweller in the slum, and tends to keep him from work: a "hidden" structural unemployment.
>
> Tragically, people fail to see the expansion of rings to be economically determined, not willfully caused by groups. The horror of this misconception is doubled: first, it causes wave after wave of "Founding Fathers" to hate wave after wave of "Invaders;" second, it diverts people from their only effective action, attack on the rent structures.
>
> To measure the flows of Detroit's rent money, we simply make a mathematical application of von Thünen's discoveries. The total rent per unit of land (e.g.— square mile or neighborhood) equals the number of individual renters in a neighborhood, times the difference between the average rent charged for an individual dwelling unit and the average cost of owning an individual unit (a cost that includes maintenance and taxes). In addition, it is necessary to subtract from the total rent the product of the number of renters per neighborhood times the

Location of Land Uses Inside Cities

round-trip transportation costs per month; because the more a neighborhood pays out for the inconvenience of the location, the less the neighborhood has available to pay out in rents. The daily transportation cost must be multiplied by thirty in order to convert this daily expense of commuting to a monthly cost comparable to monthly rental payments. The average geographic point of urban travel is downtown, though many trips do not originate or terminate there. "Downtown" is similar, as an average location of trip destination for householders, to "mass point," as an average location of mass in physics.

In functional form:

$$R = A(P - C) - 30\ ATD$$

where:

R = total rent per neighborhood
A = number of renters per neighborhood
P = per household unit rent
C = per household unit ownership cost
T = round-trip transport cost per unit of distance
D = distance to downtown

Graphing the formula shows that the rent commanded is always highest downtown, where transportation costs approach zero. Naturally, the residential use commanding the highest rent per unit of land at a particular distance from downtown is the residential use that prevails at that distance. The distance from downtown where a dominant rent changes, say from upper middle class to rich, is the change-of-class distance from downtown. By swinging a radius of this distance about the center of a city, residential class rings roughly corresponding to rent rings can be mapped around the center of a city.

Paradoxically, slums command the highest rents per land unit. The wealthy cannot afford to live in the slums. They cannot afford the rent, for although as individuals they pay much higher rent, per acre of land they pay much lower. Similarly, though the affluent may travel by expensive chauffeur, they cannot afford the collective transportation costs that slum dwellers pay per unit of impacted slum land. The rent per individual and transportation costs per individual is lower in the slums than elsewhere in the city. Slum dwellers, with their low incomes, are compelled to live there. Because of the number of people crammed into the hovels, the rent *per acre* is highest while *per individual* the rent is the lowest.

The irony of the slums is acrid. Considering the rent structure, sophisticated property owners welcome the slums since the slums are a financial "blessing" to those who own them. Homeowners detest slums because slums ruin the homes. Thus, home ownership and property ownership are at war. It is a bitter, bitter truth that the monetarily most profitable land is humanly the most bankrupt. "High profits" mean "low life." This contradiction has produced a multi-billion dollar racket in America called "income property investment." Contrary to incessant propaganda that the slums suck money from the rest of the city, the truth is precisely the opposite! Living elsewhere and paying taxes elsewhere, slum-owners earn their incomes from the slums.

The equation of the von Thünen rent model yields some interesting "guesstimates" as to the magnitude of the economics involved. Assuming that a posh

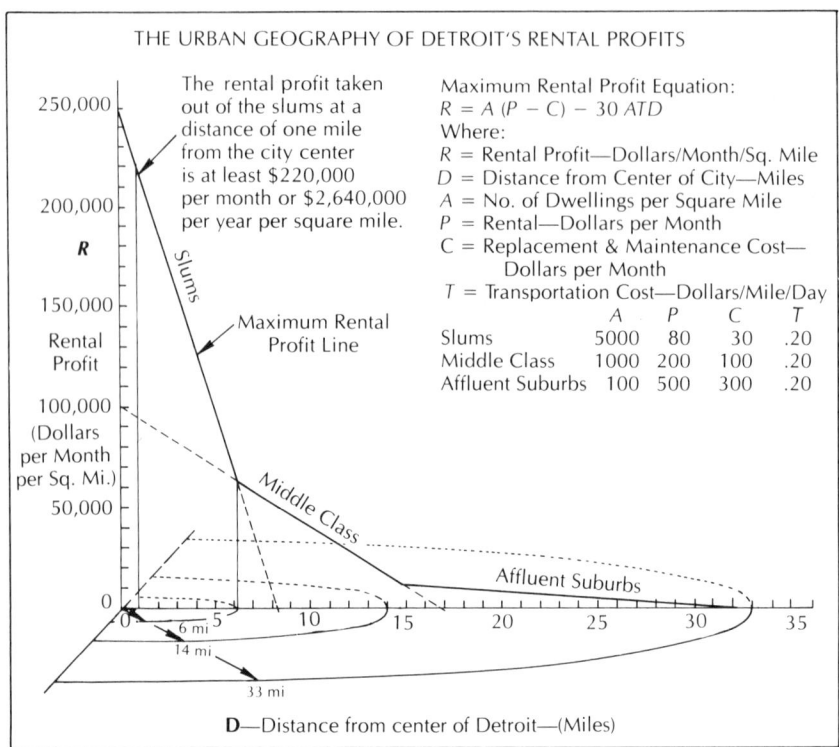

The urban geography of Detroit's rental profits.

suburban square mile contains one hundred family units (a high estimate), charges an average rent per family of five hundred dollars per month with an overhead of three hundred dollars per month, demands a round-trip travel cost of twenty cents per mile, and lies fifteen miles from the city's center, what would be the per square mile rent in a thirty day month in this suburb?

$$R = 100 (500 - 300) - 100 (.20) 15 (30)$$
$$R = 20,000 - 9,000$$
$$R = 11,000$$

If the homes are fully paid for, this one square mile of affluent suburb yields $11,000 of paper rent per month or $132,000 per year. More likely the homeowners have whopping mortgages but the owners of the mortgages, the bank executives and so forth, all live in such neighborhoods so the money stays in the community though it might shift from one household to another within the community.

Turning to the slums, assume that a square mile contains 5,000 family units (a low estimate), with an average rent per family of eighty dollars per month, an overhead of thirty dollars per month, and a round-trip travel cost of twenty cents per mile. What would then be the rent in this slum in a thirty day month, if it were two miles from the city's center?

$$R = 5,000 (80 - 30) - 5,000 (.20) 2 (30)$$
$$R = 250,000 - 60,000$$
$$R = 190,000$$

Location of Land Uses Inside Cities

> That is, a square mile of slum at a two mile distance from downtown yields $190,000 per month. The money being pumped out from the slums to the slum lords of the suburbs is $2,311,345 per square mile a year.
>
> The slumowner's deal is fattened still further through the American tax system. Since property taxes are based on the attractiveness of the property rather than profitability per unit of land, taxes drop as slum blight increases. Contrary to popular thought, the shrunken tax base of the slum is a very agreeable fact to the rich slumowner (who, as we said, lives in the suburbs). Essentially, the lower the taxes, the more money for slum profits. The shrinking of the taxes on slums deprives the city, not the suburbs, of tax money. Costs of maintaining and cleaning the buildings and controlling the rats are also notoriously low in slums.
>
> SOURCE: William Burge, 1971, *Fitzgerald: The Geography of a Revolution.* Cambridge, Massachusetts: Schenkman Publishing Company, Inc. pp. 132–133.

Site Demands of Firms

Firms also compete for urban space, but they make locational decisions on a different basis from households because of the nature of their activities. Given a rational market exchange economy, firms want to maximize profits and households want to maximize satisfactions. If intra-urban accessibility is important to sales, then firms should be willing to make high bids for locations that are central to all potential customers. Movement away from the more productive locations in the urban area should increase costs to customers and therefore reduce sales, thereby decreasing revenues, and, hence, producing lower profits. To *non-basic* firms this is true, but to *basic firms* it is not. Basic firms export what they produce to surrounding areas and other cities, and non-basic firms sell to city residents and businesses.

> **THE ECONOMIC BASE OF CITIES**
>
> *Economic base* is a concept that assigns exports the critical role in the growth of an urban economy. Activities that are net exporters of goods and services are known as *basic* industries. That is, they produce and export more of a good or service than is consumed or purchased locally. Basic industries may be manufacturing, wholesaling, retailing, educational services, health services, or financial services. It all depends on what a city exports.
>
> Basic industry is generally measured in terms of its employment, although payroll or sales can also be used. An industry is said to be basic if local employment in that industry is a higher percentage of total local employment than national employment in that industry is of total national employment. This is expressed as the industry's *location quotient*:
>
> $$LQ = \frac{LE_i}{LE_t} \div \frac{NE_i}{NE_t}$$
>
> A basic industry has a location quotient of more than 1. Its symbol is E_b.

Cities also require *non-basic* activities. Products and services of non-basic industry are consumed locally. Non-basic activities are import oriented; they depend on money brought into the community by the basic sector of the economy. Their symbol is E_s.

Economic base analysis is regarded as a major technique for analyzing the structure and trends in an urban economy. This kind of analysis assumes that urban employment growth is a consequence of changes in exports. Structural relationships within a city are found by:

$$E_t = E_b + E_s \text{ (Total employment equals basic employment plus non-basic employment.)}$$

$$E_t = E_b \times \frac{E_t}{E_b}$$

To forecast changes in total employment it is necessary to use an *urban multiplier* that gives the constant proportion between a city's total employment and basic employment. It is found by:

$$K_e = \frac{E_t}{E_b}$$

The formula to forecast total employment in a city is expressed as:

$$E_t = E_b \times K_e$$

Let us illustrate economic base analysis with a simple example. A city has a total employment of 48,000 and basic employment of 20,000. It is announced that a new firm will employ 3000 more basic workers in the next three years. What will be the probable impact on total urban employment? The first step is to find the urban employment multiplier:

$$K = \frac{E_t}{E_b} = \frac{48,000}{20,000} = 2.40$$

Now we are in a position to forecast total employment after three years:

$$E_b = 3,000$$
$$E_t = E_b \times K_e = 3000 \times 2.40 = 7,200$$
$$E_t \text{ after 3 years} = 48,000 + 7,200 = 55,200$$

Although economic base analysis provides a simple and widely understood technique for studying and predicting urban growth, it has shortcomings. It assumes that basic employment is the only cause of growth, and needs constant ratios over the period of analysis. Evidence shows, however, that ratios are volatile during periods of urban expansion. Economic base analysis also requires careful identification of what basic industry and employment are locally. But the most serious objection to economic base analysis is that the city is viewed as a local economy that balances imports from the "rest of the world" against exports. This notion suggests that there is a reciprocal relation between a city and its surrounding economy, and there is not such a relationship established by the data used.

Revenues of non-basic firms decline as they move away from downtowns or from other central locations. Department stores, for example, have high revenue requirements for profitable scales of operation. Traditionally, these firms required access to all parts of a city. They were willing to pay high rents for downtown sites where intra-urban transport lines converge. Many non-basic firms, such as grocery stores and beauty parlors, have much lower revenue requirements. Their revenue conditions allow smaller geographical scales of operation in the city.

Location within the city has little impact on the revenues of basic firms, but more impact on some of their costs. Firms requiring large amounts of space might purchase sites at marginal locations where land costs are lower. Those drawing labor from residential areas throughout the city might be willing to pay high rents for central locations. Movement away from central locations could result in higher wage bills. To attract necessary labor, firms might be forced to increase wages to compensate for higher journey-to-work costs.

Market Outcomes

We have looked separately at locational decisions of households and firms as they deal with distance frictions. Now let us fashion a model analogous to Thünen's crop model, that shows how a multitude of individual decisions combine to produce a pattern of urban land use in which rents are maximized and all activities are optimally located.

Consider three land use categories: manufacturing, commercial, and residential. Figure 5.6A shows distinctive bid-rent curves for the three types of land use in our hypothetical single-centered city. Commercial activities that require the most productive central sites have steeply sloping rent gradients. Industries have shallower bid rent curves. They cannot afford to pay the high costs of a central location. Residences have gently angled bid rent curves and are relegated to the outer ring where land prices are lower. We can complicate matters by considering a land rent profile in a multicentered city (Figure 5.6B). Apart from secondary peaks, perhaps at intersections of main traffic routes, the rent gradient still shows price bids declining outwards from the CBD.

Spatial Models of Urban Land Use

Thus far our discussion of city structure has been static. In this section we will describe and assess three models proposed at different times to depict spatial patterns of land utilization in competitive market societies. The first is the concentric model of Ernest Burgess (1925), the second is the sector model of Homer Hoyt (1939), and the third is the multiple-nuclei model of Chauncy Harris and Edward Ullman (1945).

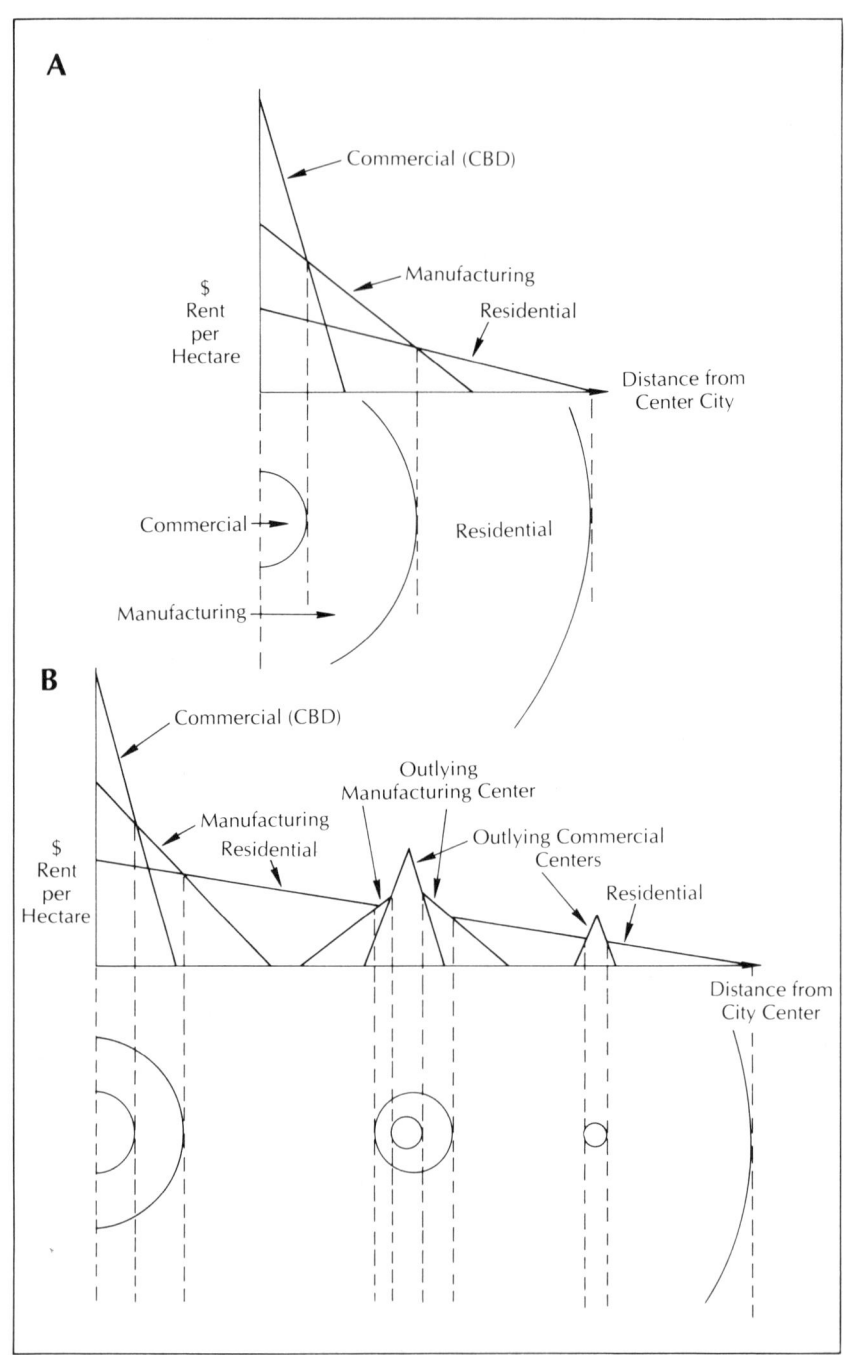

FIGURE 5.6 Multiple land use patterns: (A) single-centered city; (B) multi-centered city.

Spatial Models of Urban Land Use

The Concentric Zone Model

The *concentric zone model* is associated with Ernest Burgess and the Chicago school of sociologists of the 1920s. It was designed to have some generality within North American cities and to describe urban structure in the 1920s and 1930s. The model assumes that accessibility and land values decline with equal regularity in all directions from a common central point. Burgess suggested a sequence of five zones from center to periphery (Figure 5.7). The characteristics of these zones are as follows:

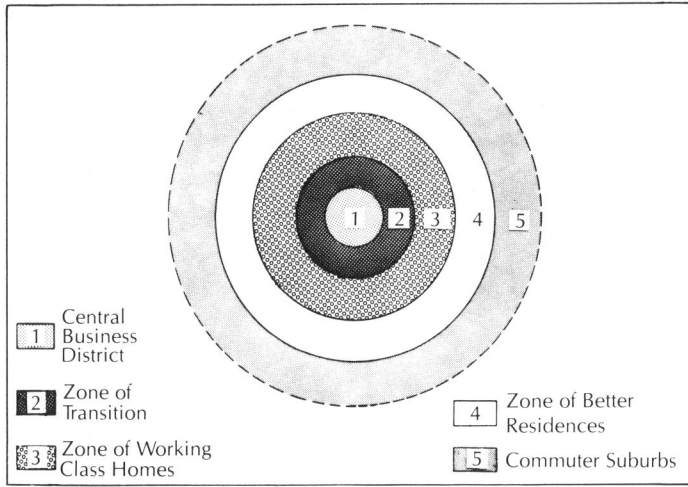

FIGURE 5.7 Burgess' concentric model of urban structure.

1. The Central Business District This zone is considered to be the focus of commercial, social, civic life, and of transportation. It contains department stores, specialty shops, office buildings, banks, organization headquarters, law courts, hotels, theaters, and museums. Encircling the downtown retail district is a mixture of wholesaling, light manufacturing, truck and retail depots.

2. The Zone of Transition This area is a zone of residential deterioration. Older private homes are subdivided into rooming houses and mansions are taken over for offices and light manufacturing (functional change). Abandoned dwellings are torn down to provide space for urban renewal (morphological change). According to Ernest Burgess, this zone contains "slums" with their areas of diseases, poverty, illiteracy, unemployment, and their underworlds of vice. In many American cities, the zone of transition is inhabited by recent immigrants, and it is said to be home to unstable social groups.

3. The Zone of Working Class Homes This ring is characterized by decreasing residential density and increasing quality and cost of homes. It is in-

San Francisco's central business district. SOURCE: *The Trane Company*.

habited by blue collar workers who have "escaped" the zone of residential deterioration, but who need to live close to work. It is regarded as an area of second generation immigrants who have had enough time to save money to buy their own homes.

4. The Zone of Better Residences Still further from the CBD, working class residences give way to newer more spacious single-family dwellings and high-class apartment buildings occupied by middle-class families.

5. The Commuter Suburbs Beyond the zone of better residences is a broad commuter area. It is an incompletely built up area containing small satellite towns and middle and upper class residences along rail lines and major highways.

The Burgess model suggests that as cities grow, resistances are encountered. Characteristic land uses of one zone exert pressure on the future land uses of the next outer zone. This process is called *invasion* and the result is a *succession* of land uses in each zone over time. Residents of one zone try to improve their situation by moving outward into better housing units. New housing constructed at the edge of the city triggers a complex chain of moves. Dwellings vacated by the outmigration of middle and higher income families are filled by lower income families moving from the next inner zone. At the end of the chain, the working poor move out of the zone of transition, leaving behind the least fortunate families and abandoned housing units. The result is an inner city "slum." This *filtering process*, which exerts downward pressure on rents and prices of existing housing, enables lower income families to obtain better housing. The major reason the filtering process occurs is that low

Spatial Models of Urban Land Use

income housing is inelastic (a new demand generates a slow response by the housing industry) whereas high income housing is generally elastic (a new demand generates a quick response).

The Sector Model

The *sector model* was formulated by Homer Hoyt. Hoyt's model takes account of differences in accessibility and, therefore, in land values along transport lines radiating outward from the city center. Hoyt developed his model from an analysis of housing rental data for 142 North American cities in the 1930s. He demonstrated that residential land uses grow outward from the CBD within wedge-shaped areas along radial transport routes (Figure 5.8). Hoyt's model assumes that rentals grade downward in all directions from the most valuable sectors.

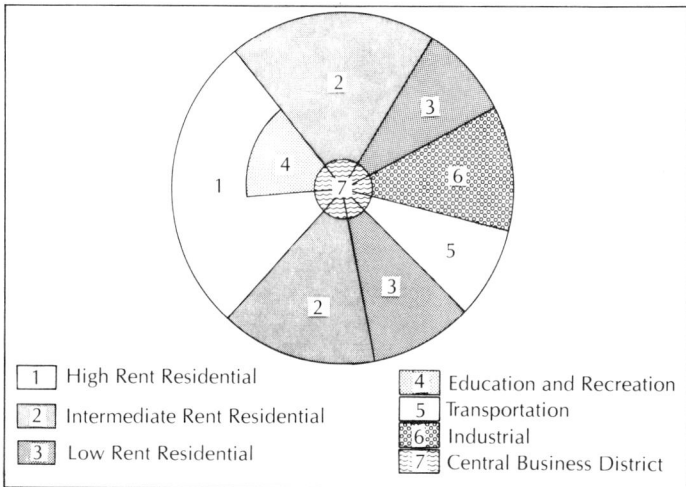

FIGURE 5.8 Hoyt's sector model of urban structure.

Hoyt paid particular attention to the growth of fashionable residential areas, and proposed a sector model of neighborhood change. He noted that "high rent neighborhoods of the city do not skip about at random in the process of movement—they follow a definite path in one or more sectors of the city" (Hoyt, 1939:144). He drew diagrams to show the expansion of fashionable residential areas in six North American cities (Figure 5.9). He explained that high-rent sectors originate near the center of cities where higher income groups work and farthest from manufacturing and warehousing areas where lower income groups work. They spread along lines of travel towards amenity land, homes of local community leaders, and existing trading centers. Hoyt pointed out that the direction and growth of high-class residential areas could be changed at any time by real estate developers.

Although Hoyt was concerned primarily with shifts in the location of residential areas, the sector model is applicable to many patterns of land use. Industrial establishments, for example, commonly concentrate along waterfronts,

FIGURE 5.9 The changing pattern of high-rent areas in six American cities, 1900–1936. SOURCE: H. Hoyt, 1939, *The Structure and Growth of Residential Neighborhoods in American Cities.* Washington D.C.: Federal Housing Administration, p. 115, Fig. 3-1.

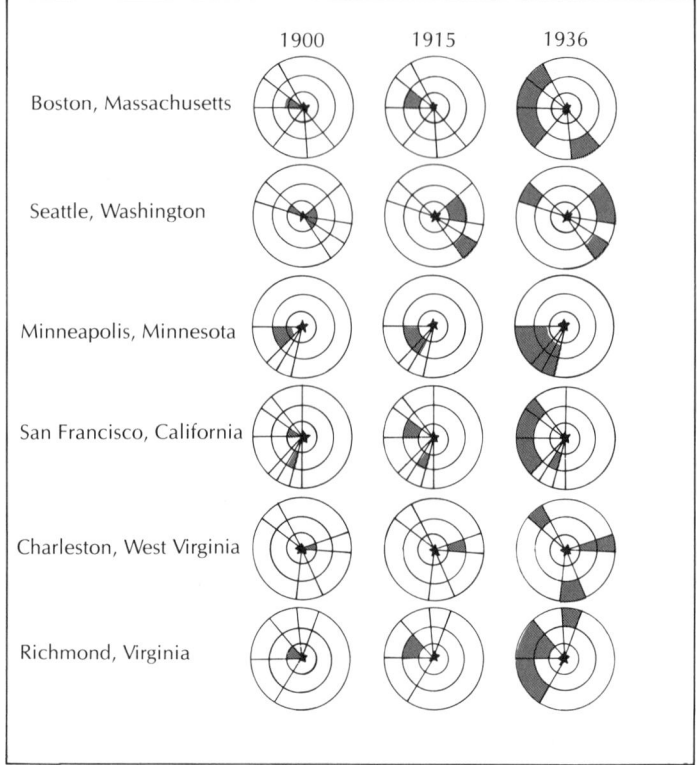

railroads, and expressways. In earlier times, when streetcars and buses were principal forms of transportation, thoroughfares leading from the CBD were lined on both sides with commercial development, especially shops.

The Multiple-Nuclei Model

The concentric and sector models describe single-centered cities. Most modern cities have *multiple-nuclei:* the downtown and a band of satellite centers on the periphery. In 1945, Chauncy Harris and Edward Ullman described a model city that develops zones of land use around discrete centers (Figure 5.10). The number and location of nuclei depend on the size of the city, and its overall structure and peculiarities of historical evolution. For American cities, Chauncy Harris and Edward Ullman identified five areas:

1. the central business district
2. a wholesaling and light manufacturing area near inter-urban transport facilities
3. a heavy industrial district near the present or past edge of the city
4. residential districts
5. outlying dormitory suburbs

Spatial Models of Urban Land Use

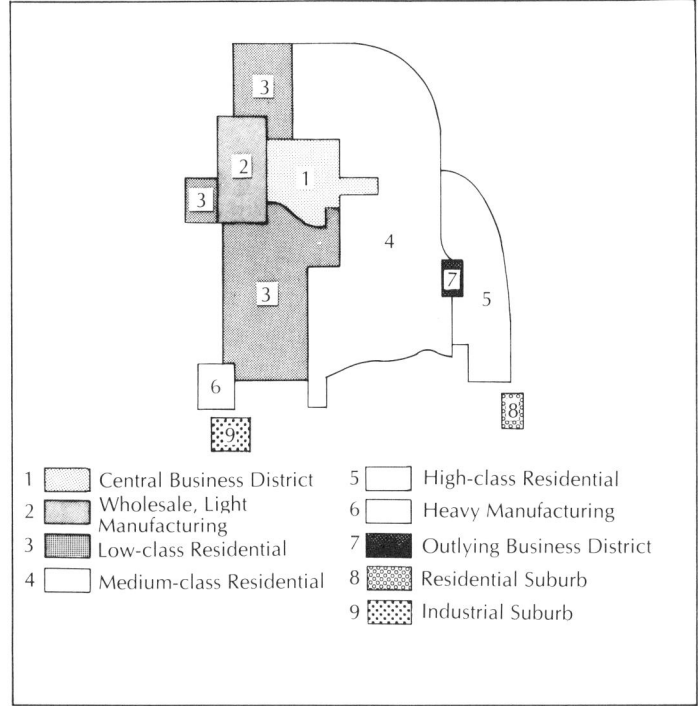

FIGURE 5.10 The Harris-Ullman model of urban structure.

Discrete nuclei and differentiated districts are said to arise because of the specialized requirements of some activities, the tendency of certain activities to group together because they profit from cohesion, the repulsion of some activities by others, and the differential rent paying ability, forcing activities to concentrate in separate districts within the city. These nuclei act as growth generators and often predictable patterns of land use develop in concentric fashion about them.

Evaluation of Land Use Models

The models of urban land use we have discussed are not mutually exclusive. Each model describes an aspect of urban structure. The Burgess model views the city as a series of annular rings, the Hoyt model as pie wedges, and the Harris and Ullman model as multi-centered. Elements of all three models can be recognized in many American cities, especially conurbations.

The classical models assumed a private land use decision process. Thus they fitted earlier periods of city growth in North America better than the present one. *Zoning ordinances,* for example, have invalidated the assumption of a private land market.

The classical models do not approximate the spatial structure of cities outside North America very closely. Public involvement in Western Europe, state control in Eastern Europe, and colonial administrations in the Third World have created distinctive patterns of urban land use.

> **ZONING**
>
> Most American cities have had zoning at least since World War II. Zoning can have a tremendous impact on the differential price of land. Land zoned residential, for example, has a value of zero to a commercial user. On the other hand, one may argue that different uses require such different sites in terms of site characteristics and relative location that zoning is unnecessary. The kind of location valuable for commercial development (e.g., a busy highway) would not be attractive for residential uses. Zoning may simply follow, rather than control, the general pattern of urban land use produced by market and other forces. Houston, Texas, for example, has no zoning and is not appreciably different in land use patterns from other American cities.

The classical models are historical statements depicting change through a process of invasion and succession. They focus on mechanistic change such as aging of structures (morphological change) and sequent occupance (functional change), but ignore the importance of behavioral factors influencing urban structure. They emphasize methodical processes of urban growth, but the real world varies considerably from this orderly picture. For example, the private land development process tends to skip over marginal tracts of land during the initial wave of building.

Finally, the classical models describe land use configurations but fail to explain that they are products of a particular form of an economic and political system. Ernest Burgess, for example, did not indicate that urban spatial organization has much to do with the need to produce and appropriate a surplus product. He regarded the city as an ecological unit and urban structure as a consequence of social solidarity. By comparison, Friedrich Engels, writing in the mid-nineteenth century, regarded the city as a producing center and urban spatial structure as a reflection of class relations. It is worth citing in full his graphic account of an English industrial town, which presents his interpretation of the concentric zoning phenomenon:

> Manchester contains, at its heart, a rather extended commercial district, perhaps half a mile long and about as broad, and consisting almost wholly of offices and warehouses. Nearly the whole district is abandoned by dwellers, and is lonely and deserted at night... The district is cut through by certain main thoroughfares upon which the vast traffic concentrates, and in which the ground level is lined with brilliant shops. In these streets the upper floors are occupied, here and there, and there is a good deal of life upon them until late at night. With the exception of this commercial district, all Manchester proper, all Salford and Hulme, . . . are all unmixed working people's quarters, stretching like a girdle, averaging a mile and a half in breadth, around the commercial district. Outside, beyond this girdle, lives the upper and middle bourgeoisie, the middle bourgeoisie in regularly laid out streets in the vicinity of working quarters . . . the upper bourgeoisie in remoter villas with gardens . . . or on the breezy heights . . . in free, wholesome country air, in fine, comfortable homes, passed every half or quarter hour by omnibuses going into the city. And the finest part of the arrangement is this, that the members of this money aristocracy can take the shortest road through the middle of all the labouring districts to their places of business, without ever seeing that they are in the midst of the grimy misery

that lurks to the right and left. For the thoroughfares leading from the Exchange in all directions out of the city are lined, on both sides, with an almost unbroken series of shops, and are so kept in the hands of the middle and lower bourgeoisie . . . [that] . . . they suffice to conceal from the eyes of the wealthy men and women of strong stomachs and weak nerves the misery and grime which form the complement of their wealth . . . I know very well that this hypocritical plan is more or less common to all great cities; I know, too, that the retail dealers are forced by the nature of their business to take possession of the great highways; I know that there are more good buildings than bad ones upon such streets everywhere, and that the value of land is greater near them than in remote districts; but at the same time I have never seen so systematic a shutting out of the working class from the thoroughfares, so tender a concealment of everything which might affront the eye and the nerves of the bourgeoisie, as in Manchester. And yet, in other respects, Manchester is less built according to a plan after official regulations, is more an outgrowth of accident, than any other city; and when I consider in this connection the eager assurances of the middle class, that the working class is doing famously, I cannot help feeling that the liberal manufacturers, the "Big Wigs" of Manchester, are not so innocent after all, in the matter of this sensitive method of construction (Engels, 1958:46–48).

Clearly the segregation patterns of a basically concentric type noted by Friedrich Engels in 1844 for a British industrial city is quite similar to the one discerned by Burgess in 1925 for a North American industrial city.

The Modern City: Spatial Patterns and Social Problems

The chief strength of the classical models is simplicity and the ability to explain and justify the interests of the wealthy. The classical models were developed with reference to the internal structure of the North American city for a particular point in time. They do not describe contemporary reality sufficiently. Changes in American society are producing a new form of city—the spread city.

The Spread City

Spread cities are contemporary American cities. They are the consequences of the urban process that transformed cities from tightly nucleated settlements into widely dispersed multi-nodal metropoli in less than two centuries. The spreading out of the American city is reflected in Tables 5.2, 5.3, and 5.4 which reveal decreasing residential and non-residential populations in central cities during the twentieth century. The 1970 census showed that for the first time suburban dwellers outnumbered central city inhabitants.

The essence of the spread city is captured in the following passage:

Vast arcs of economic activity have sprouted along newly-completed circumferential roadways, which are dotted with the physical monuments to the suburban success story. Regional shopping centers, office towers, and sprawling campus-style corporate headquarters represent the fullest flowering of the historic migration out of American cities. Huge numbers of Americans live, work, play, shop and dine within the physical confines of this freeway culture [as the suburbs emerge] as entities independent of the older central cities which they surround (Hughes, 1974:4).

TABLE 5.2 Central cities percentage of total SMSA population

Metropolis	1940	1950	1960	1970
New York	63.9	61.1	52.7	48.8
Los Angeles	57.2	53.5	46.8	45.1
Chicago	74.3	69.1	57.1	48.2
Philadelphia	60.4	56.4	46.1	40.4
Detroit	68.3	61.3	44.4	36.0
San Francisco	34.1	54.3	41.8	34.6
Washington	68.5	53.2	36.8	26.4
Boston	34.9	33.2	26.9	23.3
Pittsburgh	32.3	30.6	25.1	21.7
St. Louis	55.7	48.8	55.6	26.3
Baltimore	75.4	65.2	52.1	43.7
Cleveland	69.3	59.7	45.9	36.4
Houston	72.7	63.7	66.1	62.0
Minneapolis-St. Paul	80.6	72.3	53.7	41.0

SOURCE: U.S. Bureau of the Census

TABLE 5.3 Central cities percentage of manufacturing employment in selected SMSA's

Metropolis	1963	1972
New York	80.9	46.6
Los Angeles	36.1	36.0
Chicago	59.0	42.6
Philadelphia	49.5	40.7
Detroit	40.7	32.4
San Francisco	46.7	37.7
Washington	44.2	35.3
Boston	28.2	21.8
Pittsburgh	30.0	23.9
St. Louis	49.7	38.0
Baltimore	54.6	31.7
Cleveland	60.3	48.7
Houston	71.2	65.7
Minneapolis-St. Paul	67.3	54.7

SOURCE: U.S. Bureau of the Census

Figure 5.11A–D is an example of the spreading out of the American city. It shows the rapid pace of growth of the region around Detroit in the period 1900–1959. The map sequence uses percent of land in farms as an index of the extent to which non-agricultural uses have spread. The final map also shows the outer radius of daily commuting to Detroit in 1960.

Figure 5.12 reveals for 1960 the extent of areas within daily contact of central cities in the United States. Ninety percent of the United States population lived within commuting distance of some central city in that year.

The urban transformation continued in the 1960s. Geographer Jean Gottman recognized a new urban form of coalesced metropolitan areas on the northeastern seaboard which he defined as *Megalopolis* (Figure 5.13). This super-

The Modern City: Spatial Patterns and Social Problems

TABLE 5.4 Central cities percentage of retail sales in selected SMSA's

Metropolis	1963	1972
New York	67.1	N.A.
Los Angeles	41.3	40.0
Chicago	56.9	43.2
Philadelphia	43.4	33.3
Detroit	42.6	25.9
San Francisco	48.0	36.7
Washington	42.1	23.7
Boston	31.2	23.7
Pittsburgh	34.1	23.0
St. Louis	37.5	22.8
Baltimore	58.1	38.5
Cleveland	54.8	31.0
Houston	82.4	71.0
Minneapolis-St. Paul	61.5	37.1

SOURCE: U.S. Bureau of the Census

urban region stretches from Boston to Washington and includes a whole network of cities fused together by super-highways, tunnels, bridges and shuttle jets. Megalopolis is by no means the only super-city of its kind. Another is the loosely knit Lower Great Lakes Urban Region centered on Chicago, Detroit, Cleveland, and Pittsburgh.

By the year 2000, trend projections indicate that the United States will consist of four super-urban regions:

1. *BoWash* extending along the Atlantic Seaboard;
2. *ChiPitts* stretching from Chicago to Pittsburgh, and merging with BoWash via the "Mohawk Bridge" to form the Metropolitan Belt;
3. *SanSan,* a belt from San Francisco to San Diego; and
4. *JaMi,* a strip from Jacksonville to Miami.

These megalopolitan networks will be supplemented with about 22 other major urban regions each containing at least one million people (Figure 5.14 and Table 5.5). According to the findings of the Commission on Population Growth and the American Future (1972) five-sixths of the population will be concentrated on one-sixth of the Nation's land area.

Sources of Change

What causes the spreading out of the American city? A number of economic and non-economic factors are involved. Let us look at some of these factors with respect to locational decisions of firms and households.

Factors Affecting Locational Decisions of Households Outmigration of all but the lowest income families from central cities has been strongly associated

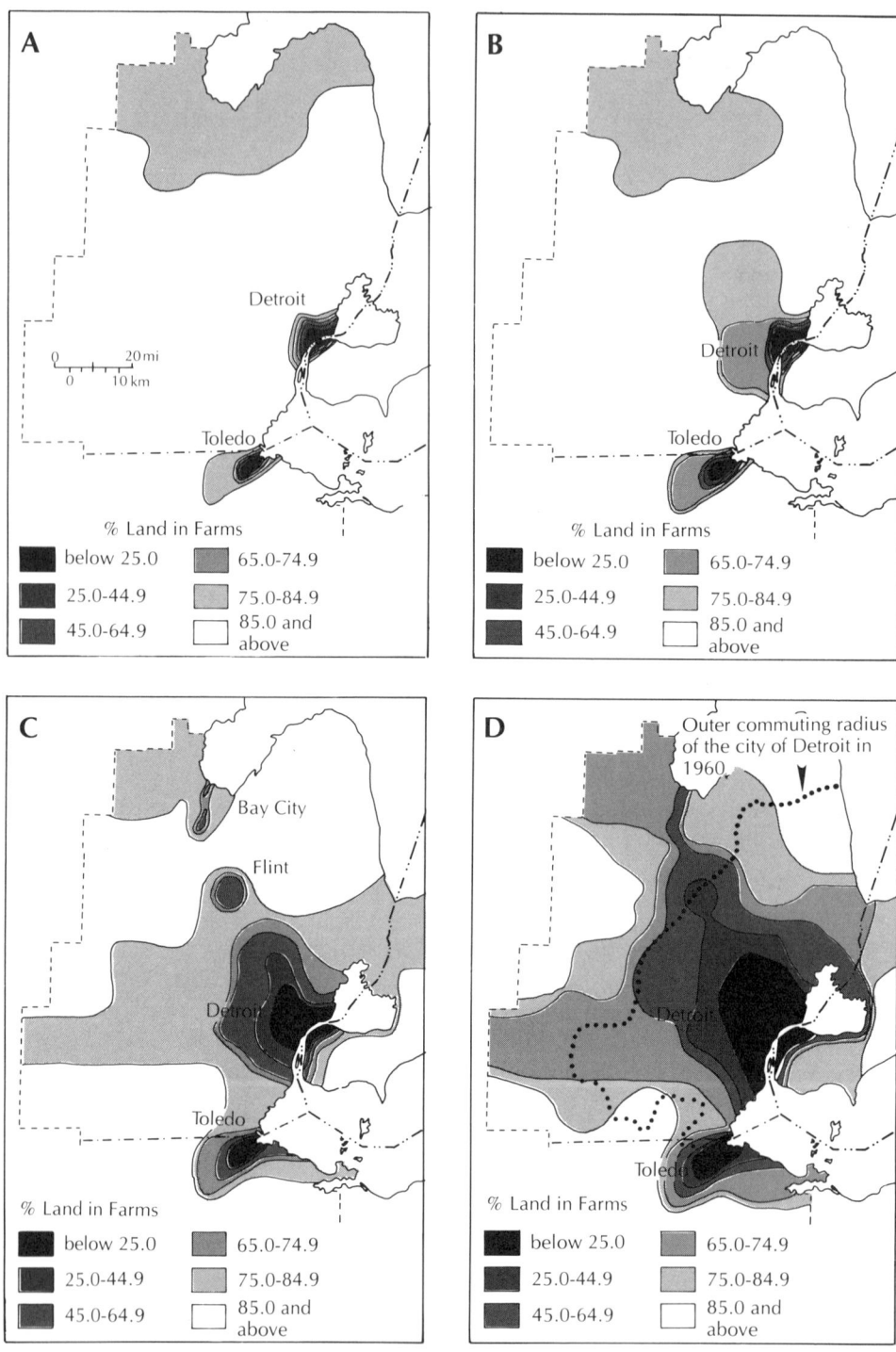

FIGURE 5.11 Urbanization in the Detroit region: (A) 1900; (B) 1920; (C) 1940; (D) 1959. SOURCE: B. J. L. Berry, 1973, *The Human Consequences of Urbanization–Divergent Paths in the Urban Experience of the Twentieth Century,* pp. 39, 40, 41, 42, Figs. 3, 4, 5, 6. By permission of Macmillan, London and Basingstoke.

The Modern City: Spatial Patterns and Social Problems

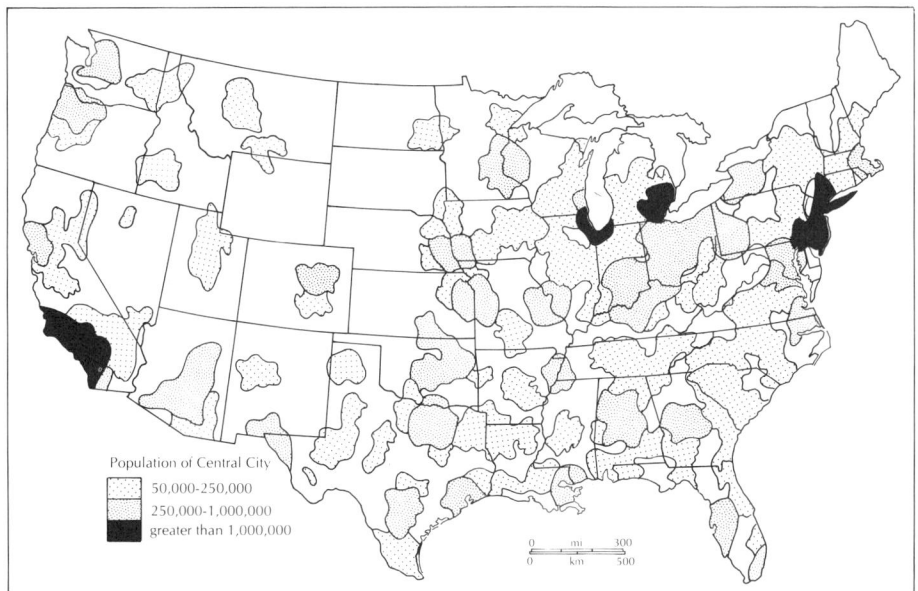

FIGURE 5.12 Extent of commuting fields in the United States in 1960. SOURCE: B. J. L. Berry, 1968, *Metropolitan Area Definition: A Reevaluation of Concept and Statistical Practice.* Washington, D.C.: Bureau of the Census, Working Paper No. 28.

FIGURE 5.13 Megalopolis as defined by Gottman.

with a succession of innovations in intra-urban passenger transportation. Figure 5.15 illustrates the relationship between transport improvements and the flight to the suburbs. Each revolution in transportation lowered travel cost and reduced the willingness of families to pay high rents for central locations. Since 1945, rates of

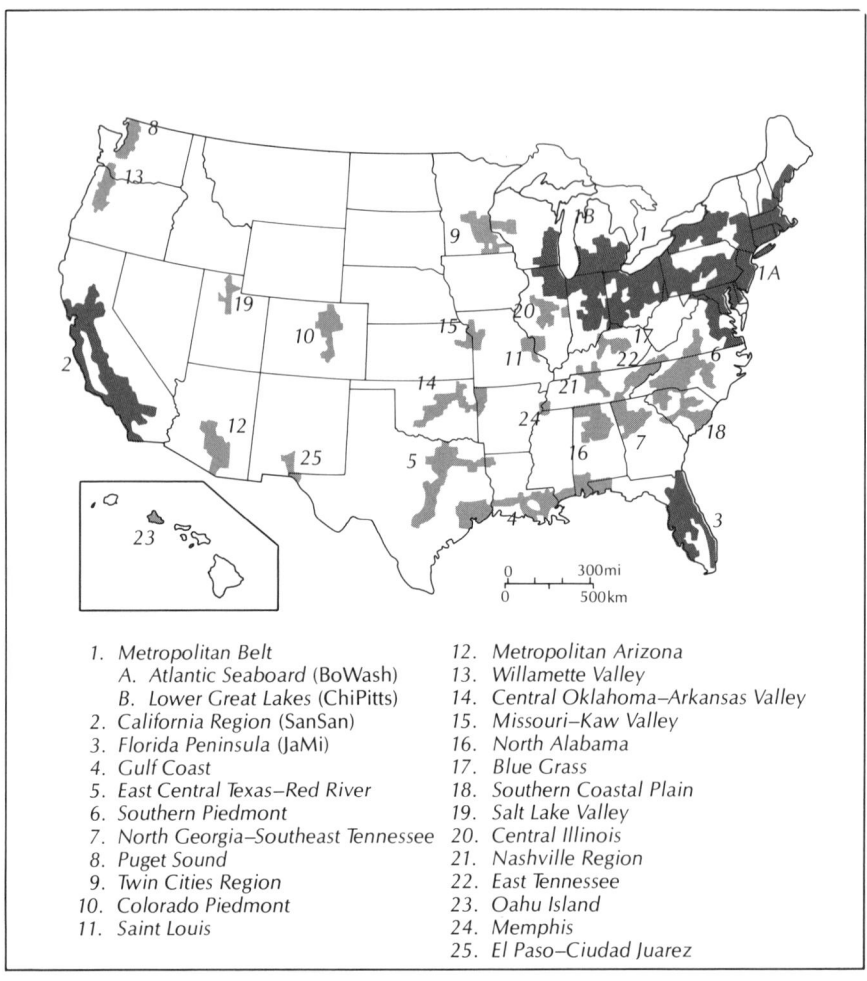

FIGURE 5.14 Projected growth of United States urban regions with a population of one million or more by the year 2000. The four super-urban regions are shown in a darker shade. SOURCE: J. P. Pickard, 1972, "U.S. Metropolitan Growth and Expansion, 1970–2000, with Population Projections" in *Population Growth and the American Future*. Washington D.C.: U.S. Government Printing Office, p. 143, Fig. 3.

suburban expansion have been very rapid indeed because of the desire for a single family home in the suburbs, the availability of low interest FHA and VA home loans, cheap transportation, and massive highway subsidies. The freeway-dominated auto era has removed virtually all restrictions on intra-urban population mobility, and residential land use has been feasible just about anywhere in the metropolitan area, especially since auto companies were buying up and closing down intra-urban street car lines across the country.

In the twentieth century, national real income gains have had an impact on the intrametropolitan distribution of population. Rising real incomes, attributable

TABLE 5.5 Urban regions of the United States, 2000

Urban Region	Land Area (Sq Km)	Number in Thousands	Density
Metropolitan Belt	467,089	132,013	283
Atlantic Seaboard	182,201	69,098	379
Lower Great Lakes	284,888	62,915	221
California Region	142,584	42,211	296
Florida Peninsula	57,553	15,453	268
Gulf Coast	77,108	10,750	140
East Central Texas–Red River	60,771	8,986	148
Southern Piedmont	64,744	6,714	104
Northern Georgia–Southeast Tennessee	31,467	4,668	149
Puget Sound	16,422	4,380	267
Twin Cities Region	42,057	4,355	104
Colorado Piedmont	29,353	3,890	133
St. Louis	13,598	3,578	257
Metropolitan Arizona	3,285	3,532	108
Willamette Valley	25,026	3,110	124
Central Oklahoma–Arkansas Valley	38,829	2,867	74
Missouri–Kaw Valley	14,689	2,497	170
North Alabama	33,845	2,328	69
Bluegrass	13,943	2,167	155
Southern Coastal Plain	20,262	1,891	93
Salt Lake Valley	12,242	1,744	142
Central Illinois	19,920	1,573	79
Nashville Region	17,353	1,401	81
East Tennessee	15,218	1,321	87
Oahu Island	1,537	1,290	841
Memphis	4,768	1,264	265
El Paso–Ciudad Juarez	8,964	825	92
Platte Valley	9,986	1,190	119
Las Vegas	11,941	1,175	98
East Iowa–Mississippi Valley	14,124	1,145	81
United States, total	500,805	268,318	206

SOURCE: Jerome P. Pickard, 1972, "U.S. Metropolitan Growth and Expansion, 1970–2000 with Population Projections" in *Population and the American Future*. Washington, D.C.: U.S. Government Printing Office, Table 16, p. 147. (Adapted.)

partly to technical changes (production and organizational developments) and partly to foreign extraction of surpluses have had the effect of "flattening out" bid rent curves. Families fortunate enough to have more money left over after deducting living expenses have been able to trade off accessibility for more space in the suburbs.

Population growth of cities has contributed to the urbanization of the suburbs. The manner in which population growth effects residential site selection may be explained in the context of the theory of the urban land market. The theory

FIGURE 5.15 Passenger transportation improvements and housing density. SOURCE: R. Abler et al., 1971, *Spatial Organization: The Geographer's View of the World.* Englewood Cliffs, N.J.: Prentice-Hall, p. 358, Fig. 10-16.

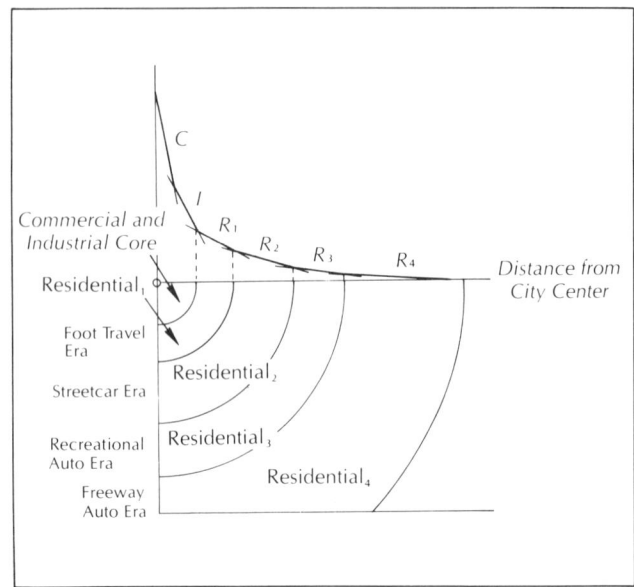

points out that inside a city, population growth results in higher housing costs because more people bid for the same amount of land. To escape higher housing costs, families might decide to select sites outside the existing city. Relocation might not bring lower overall consumption costs. Living on the periphery of the city increases commuting costs to the central city, and new housing on the periphery forces up land prices. According to urban location theory, what happens to city structure as population increases depends on what happens to housing costs and transport costs. If population growth is accompanied by an improving transport network that facilitates automobile travel, the consumption costs in the suburbs will decline relative to those in the central city, and both swift and massive suburban growth will occur. This supposition fits the American situation: population growth has reinforced outmigration brought about by the automobile.

Finally, fear of racial change accelerated the residential central city-suburban shift. Between 1940 and 1970 large numbers of southern blacks were displaced from mechanized farms and moved to northern cities. Black migration from the rural south to the urban north peaked in the late 1950s. As blacks "invaded" city neighborhoods, white middle class families experienced lower assessment of their properties, often spurred by "block busting" by real estate brokers. Meanwhile, they increased their valuations of suburban locations. The number of whites that moved to the suburbs in order to maintain social distance from the immigrant blacks of the inner city has not been documented, however.

In the late 1970s, there was reverse migration, middle class families moving from suburbs to central cities. The number of families involved is small, however. For every family moving back to inner cities, eight are moving out to the suburbs.

Factors Affecting Locational Decisions of Firms Suburbanization of retailing was a response to the residential flight to the suburbs, new merchandizing

The Modern City: Spatial Problems and Social Problems

techniques, and technical obsolescence of older retailing areas. The automobile provided customers with an attractive mode of transport to shopping places. Automobile use on shopping trips required adequate parking, but downtown facilities were scarce and expensive. Outmigration of families to suburbs reduced revenues and profits of downtown shops. A need to improve the parking situation and a need to increase profits impelled many retailers to the suburbs.

The decentralization trend began in the 1920s as stores began spreading out from the downtown along main thoroughfares. Yet it was not until the postwar years that retailers moved to the suburbs in any great numbers. First came the strip center or neighborhood center consisting of a small string of shops anchored usually by a supermarket. Then came the somewhat larger community center with a small department store or variety store as the principal tenant. The success of these early centers that catered to a limited trade area depended on a main road location, free parking, and also the competitive impacts of SUPER everything, DRIVE-IN everything, self-service stores, and discount stores.

Neighborhood and community shopping centers became vulnerable to more attractive regional shopping centers that appeared after 1955. The newest and biggest of these centers in distant suburbs have several floors, three or more department stores and scores of specialty shops. Surrounded by huge parking lots, these shopping complexes are usually enclosed, enabling customers to shop in climate controlled comfort. Unlike the neighborhood or community shopping center that evolved in response to the residential drift to the suburbs, the giant regional shopping centers of the 1970s are catalysts attracting a variety of activities to locate nearby.

Enclosed central court in a regional shopping center: Woodland Hills Mall, Tulsa, Oklahoma. SOURCE: *Dayton Hudson Properties.*

Decentralization of manufacturing began before the turn of the century. Technical advances, such as the development of continuous material flow systems, induced many manufacturers, especially those engaged in the large scale production of industrial goods, to spread outward along suburban rail corridors where land was relatively cheap and abundant. Nonetheless, most manufacturers, in spite of truck transportation, decided to remain in or near the central city until the 1960s when two technological breakthroughs were achieved.

> These post-1960 breakthroughs involved the completion of the intraurban expressway system and the long-delayed attainment of scale economies in local trucking operations. Completing the freeway network made it possible to assemble goods at any number of points equally accessible to the rest of the metropolis, and newly economical short distance trucking helped to neutralize the transportation cost differential between inner city and suburb. With the near equalization of these costs across much of the metropolis, intraurban goods movement via truck became as efficient as interregional freight transport. And by eliminating the locational pull of central city water and rail terminals, most of the remaining urbanization economies of downtown were quickly nullified (Muller, 1976:33).

In the freeway metropolis, the economic advantages of a central city location have disappeared. Consequently the spatial organization of manufacturing industry is responding increasingly to non-cost factors. Manufacturers are relatively free to select the most prestigious sites they can find in the outer city.

Office and service suburbanization began rather unpretentiously in the early postwar years. The suburban drift greatly accelerated in the 1960s, despite a brief downtown revival. Just as non-economic factors are influencing suburban industrial location so are they influencing the location of suburban office activity.

Suburban corporate headquarters: General Mills, Golden Valley, Minnesota. SOURCE: *General Mills*.

The Modern City: Spatial Patterns and Social Problems

Financial decision makers are attracted by the convenience, amenity, and prestige of a suburban address.

Initially, suburban business and commerce seemed to locate at virtually any convenient road intersection or site near the freeway network. Today suburban economic activities have a growing locational affinity for each other. Without doubt the focal point of the outer city is the giant shopping center. Super shopping-malls are catalysts for other commercial, industrial, recreational, and cultural facilities. The result is the emergence of miniature downtowns called *minicities* (Figure 5.16). These largely unplanned, loosely organized, multifunctional nodes are beginning to dominate the spatial organization of suburbia.

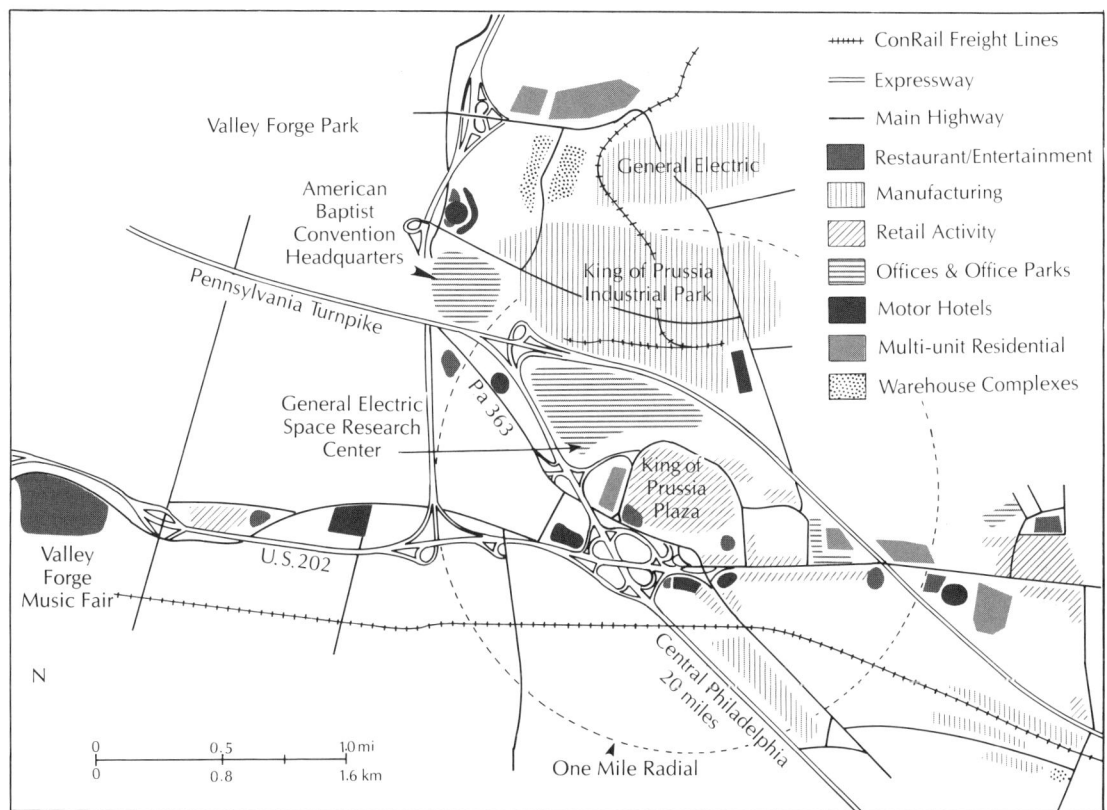

FIGURE 5.16 Internal economic geography of the suburban minicity: King of Prussia, Pennsylvania. SOURCE: Redrawn from Peter O. Muller, *The Outer City: Geographical Consequences of the Urbanization of the Suburbs* (Washington, D.C.: Association of American Geographers, 1975), Resource Papers for College Geography Number 75-2, Fig. 10. p. 41.

Polarization of Urban Areas

Before 1970 most middle class Americans appeared to be enthusiastic about the effects of the spread city on public welfare. The spread city provided an expanding context for economic life, more opportunities for employment, more goods and services, more manufacturing, and new kinds of entertainment. It blurred old distinctions between town and country, between farmers and city folk. It retained more open land than the older compact city and that was a plus for the new subdivision dweller.

Urban development in the 1970s. (A) Fragmented residential development on the fringe of a large city. Note dependence upon urban freeway. (B) New subdivision dwellers have fields outside their picture windows. What is the impact of this type of haphazard peri-urban development on surrounding farming land? SOURCE: *University of Wisconsin—Extension.*

With the advent of the ecological and energy crises of the 1970s, a distinct anti-spread city bias set in. Spread cities were deemed to be ugly sprawls, and wasteful of resources, especially land and energy. Public and scholarly attention turned to finding ways to solve problems of the spread city.

BANKRUPT CITIES

In contrast to the exploding slum-cities of the Third World, the main dilemma facing the richer nations is posed not by growth but by shrinkage. In the 1960s, it was blandly assumed that the diminishing city tax base was a purely American problem. But now the same applies throughout Europe, as not only individuals but whole industries, institutions, and social groups remove themselves to the suburbs and beyond.

Even where the inner city is not being actively colonized by minority, migrant or otherwise disadvantaged families, the wealthier are tending to flee, taking their tax-paying and job-creating resources with them. A vicious downward spiral is thus only too easily created: services decline, maintenance falls into arrears and the accelerating debt burden forces up rates and local taxes to levels where the remaining, usually much poorer, inhabitants are increasingly unwilling, or even unable, to pay. No longer is it possible to treat breakdowns in transport, garbage collection, education and housing as isolated "accidents" or the result of "mismanagement" which can be put right at leisure. Suddenly, in the last two or three years, these have coalesced into a whole matrix of intractable difficulties, and the monetary costs attached to them have soared.

Urban planners as eminent as Britain's Professor Peter Hall are now openly questioning whether the large city has a future as a mode of human organization. Faith in the "natural powers of metropolitan regeneraton," which was almost axiomatic a decade ago, has now largely evaporated. Attention has now switched . . . to easing what are seen as the inevitable pains of shrinkage and decline. Inner-city poverty, it is felt, can no longer be treated effectively *in situ,* and the patient must be moved, however carefully and gradually, to a more favorable ambiance.

Such pessimism—such readiness to treat great centres like distinguished geriatrics—is the product of cumulative failures in regenerative planning, leading to a sense that beyond these specifics of each city's most urgent problems, their size coupled with the complexity of their dilapidated infrastructures defy the possibilities of effective therapy. Despair is generated when New Yorkers blame the city's welfare burden . . . ; but Tokyo, which spends comparatively little on welfare and social services, is also broke. London's planners point ruefully to Victorian sewers and antiquated housing stock, but Hamburg—virtually rebuilt down to the foundation after World War II—is also in a situation where its prosperous workers cannot afford to buy a modest flat in the city centre.

[T]he cities' current troubles have been blamed on: oil-related inflation, increasing costs of maintaining outdated infrastructures, land speculation, and Parkinson's law of ever expanding local bureaucracies, which, in many cases, is beginning to look like Parkinson's disease. They are also directly related, in the great majority of cases, to rigid and outdated boundaries, which often take little account of the real mobility and work patterns of their "citizens."

This may indeed be one of the crucial factors, both in defining the problem and framing a solution. When a city is dying in the middle, like Detroit or East London, while its fringes both drain its prosperity and elude its tax net, one obvious ploy is to redraw the frontiers to reincorporate the scattered resources. This is by no means unknown. Both London and Moscow in recent years have drastically redefined their areas of municipal responsibility . . . No complete answer, of course, is to be found in this direction. Much of London's industry and office employment, for example, has moved not ten but 50 or 100 miles in the last few years . . .

. . . [M]ost major well-established cities now face a roughly similar situation. They have concentrated, often for decades, on relieving their space and welfare pressures by decanting population, either formally, as in Britain, to specially-planned "new towns" or, more haphazardly, to the surrounding districts. Offices were encouraged to move out at the same time that industry was imperceptibly dying. Opportunities to take advantage of falling population densities were largely missed, leaving substantial areas of urban blight. Land speculation contributed to unbalanced investment. Swiftly changing "fashions" in urban planning contributed to the inefficiency of transport services, and to the dehumanization of whole inner-city areas with the erection of high-rise housing estates.

Urban renewal in Liverpool, England, where high-rise housing estates replace nineteenth century terrace houses. SOURCE: *World Health Organization Photo by E. Spooner.*

. . . There should be a new emphasis on locating [new industries] in high-unemployment pockets; more flexible approaches to housing, emphasizing mixed tenure development and equity-sharing arrangements for poor families; and streamlining the unwieldy bureaucracies to enable them to adopt an interdepartmental approach.

In most cities, the proliferation of municipal bodies with overlapping powers—1,200 of them in New York—is often a greater impediment than finance to regenerative planning. Within the same authority, the interdepartmental fights for shares in the overall budget make long-range planning of transport, schools and housing facilities doubly vulnerable.

SOURCE: Peter Wilsher and Rosemary Righter, 1976, "Bankrupt Cities," *Development Forum*, Vol. IV, No. 5, pp. 1–2. (Note: Wilsher and Righter have a liberal ideology, believing that finely-tuned planning in advanced capitalist countries can solve urban problems.)

Solutions to urban land use problems such as *ghettos* can only come through a thorough understanding of the forces that created the spread city. Despite growing public intervention at state and local levels, American decentralized metropoli are primarily a consequence of the private land use decision process imbedded in supportive government policies and programs. They are an outcome of a market response to forces of societal change, particularly population and technical developments.

Let us look at one problem of the spread city: the deep-seated polarization between *central city* and *suburbs*. Increasingly, inner cities are home to the metropolitan disadvantaged and a few specialized services, and suburbs to the affluent and a wide range of functions. This pattern of spatial organization favors rich people who collect a disproportionate share of the surplus value with respect to the location of services and job opportunities.

Retail Stores Shop location is a reflection of the economic behavior of entrepreneurs. Their decisions, however, are usually subject to some public control through zoning. Decision makers select locations with a high demand potential. And since demand is income related, it is natural for entrepreneurs to choose affluent suburban areas first. Many large supermarkets, for example, are located in the suburbs, and sell their produce at lower prices than do inner city neighborhood stores. Evidence suggests that price and access variations to retail outlets contributed to the urban riots of the 1960s.

Medical Care Health care services provided by general practitioners, internists, and pediatricians are located mainly by private action. Since they are sensitive to demand potential, they tend to locate in affluent areas even though the need for medical care is likely to be higher in lower-income neighborhoods, where poorly equipped and low paid city hospitals take care of the needy.

Public Utilities Provision of water, electricity, sewage and sanitation, and transport services provide additional examples of the inequitable appropriation of the surplus. Take water as an example. In some metropolitan areas, water prices are not seasonally adjusted, yet the peak demand for water in summer comes mainly from suburban families, who use a great amount of water to sprinkle lawns and fill swimming pools. Inner city residents have neither yards to sprinkle nor pools to fill. When pricing systems for water fail to reflect seasonal demands, they effectively subsidize the already wealthy.

Noxious Attributes The value of a dwelling unit varies according to proximity to noxious attributes such as smoke, dust, noise and water pollution, and traffic congestion. The affluent who wield political clout usually manage to exclude noxious facilities from their neighborhoods. But these facilities must be put somewhere. Traditionally, facilities such as power stations have been located in inner city communities and in rural areas.

Employment Opportunities Private and public discrimination (e.g.: "redlining" by lending institutions, actions of realtors, screening devices adopted by subdivision developers) and exclusionary zoning practices give the poor, especially blacks, little option but to locate in inner city areas. Meanwhile, most new employment opportunities matched to the work skills of such people are in the suburbs that encourage desirable kinds of business and commerce. Thus the poor are faced with the problem of finding work in stagnating industrial areas of the inner city or commuting longer distances, with few public bus lines, to keep up with the dispersing job market. Although "reverse" commuting virtually doubled in the decade of the 1960s, barriers abound. These include transportation constraints such as increased time and money costs of the daily journey to work and inadequate public transport for non-car-owning groups; and communication constraints such as the lack of information concerning suburban job opportunities. Other serious obstacles to suburban employment include low work skills and biased hiring practices. In the face of these problems, many otherwise employable persons give up job hunting altogether, and contribute instead to the growing number of unemployed in inner city neighborhoods.

As we peer into the future, it appears that the poor will continue to live in inner city ghettos, experience still fewer employment opportunities, and bear an unequal share of the cost of generating the surplus product. A prime question is: How can we eliminate the *polarized* or dualistic metropolis? One way is to end racial discrimination and to eliminate the competitive bidding process for the use of land and introduce a socially controlled land market and a socially controlled housing market.

Summary

In this chapter, we emphasized that cities exist in societies that create the conditions necessary for the appropriation of the *surplus product*. These conditions are met in *stratified market exchange* societies. In the nineteenth century, stratified societies of Europe and North America experienced an urban-industrial transformation. During this period of widespread innovation, cities, especially large manufacturing ones, were ugly creations and horrifying environments for the poor. Denied access to the fruits of rapid economic growth, the workers bore the social costs of urban-industrialization. The early nineteenth century industrial city was characterized by a large number of small, relatively powerless enterprises. Toward the end of the nineteenth century, however, the market mode of economic integration took on a different appearance. There was a drift from *individual* to *monopoly* capitalism. As a result, control of the most important industries became more and more concentrated. Today large corporations have a pervasive influence on the Western city.

What general forces help to concentrate activities in cities? We answered this question with respect to the model of *pure competition* which approximated nineteenth century capitalism. It is important to remember that because of the growth of corporations and government involvement, a gap exists between the model and reality today.

Most of the chapter was devoted to a discussion of urban land use arrangements. To show how land using activities can be located where they are, we applied *classical urban location theory*. It assumes, among other things, that firms are *price-takers*. Despite the fact that we do not live in an age of economic liberalism, classical location theory is still widely used by geographers and economists. After describing and interpreting three spatial models of urban land use *(concentric, sector,* and *multiple-nuclei)*, we examined the spatial patterns and some of the problems of contemporary cities in North America.

DISCUSSION QUESTIONS

1. Why do cities evolve in stratified societies?
2. Describe changes in the form of market exchange during the last 200 years.
3. Analyze the significance of (a) scale economies; (b) transport costs in the growth of cities.
4. The urban population density gradient has been likened to a volcanic cone. Discuss the validity of this analogy.
5. Discuss: Transport is the maker and breaker of cities.
6. With the aid of a diagram show how the spread city differs from the compact city of the nineteenth century.
7. What factors account for the growing geographical disparity between housing and employment in the American metropolis?
8. Show with the aid of a diagram how the concentric zone city of Burgess is disturbed when roads of different quality are introduced.
9. How did Engels interpret the phenomenon of concentric zoning?
10. Compare and contrast urban site demands of basic and non-basic firms.
11. In the contemporary American city the poor are forced to bid for and live on high rent land. Why?
12. A cure for the dualistic housing market in the United States is a socialized housing market. Do you agree?

SUGGESTED READINGS

Cities and Societies

Harvey, D., *Society, the City and the Space-Economy of Urbanism*. Washington D.C.: Association of American Geographers Commission on College Geography, Resource Paper No. 18, 1972.

City Building

Evans, A., "The Pure Theory of City Size in an Industrial Economy," *Urban Studies,* **9** (1972): 49–77.

Stigler, G., "The Division of Labor Is Limited by the Extent of the Market," *Journal of Political Economy,* **59** (1951):371–385.

Ullman, E., "The Nature of Cities Reconsidered," *Papers and Proceedings of the Regional Science Association,* **9** (1962):7–23.

Location Theory and City Structure

Alonso, W., *Location and Land Use.* Cambridge, Mass.: Harvard University Press, 1964.

Muth, R., *Cities and Housing.* Chicago: University of Chicago Press, 1969.

Walker, R. A., "Urban Ground Rent: Building a New Conceptual Framework," *Antipode,* **6** (1974):50–58.

Classical Models of Urban Land Use

Harris, C. D. and E. L. Ullman, "The Nature of Cities," *Annals of the American Academy of Political and Social Sciences,* **242** (1945):7–17.

Hoyt, H., *The Structure and Growth of Residential Neighborhoods in American Cities.* Washington: Federal Housing Administration, 1939.

Park, R. E., E. W. Burgess, and R. D. McKenzie, *The City.* Chicago: University of Chicago Press, 1925.

Contemporary American City

Adams, J. S. (ed.), *Contemporary Metropolitan America: Twenty Geographical Vignettes.* Cambridge, Mass.: Ballinger Publishing Company, Association of American Geographers, Comparative Metropolitan Analysis Project, 1976.

Adams, J. S. (ed.), *Urban Policy-Making and Metropolitan Dynamics: A Comparative Geographical Analysis.* Cambridge, Mass.: Ballinger Publishing Company, Association of American Geographers, Comparative Metropolitan Analysis Project, 1976.

Breckenfield, G., "'Downtown' Has Fled to the Suburbs," *Fortune,* October 1972, 80–87, 156, 158, 162.

Gottmann, J., *Megalopolis.* Cambridge, Mass.: M.I.T. Press, 1964.

Masotti, L. H. and J. K. Hadden, (eds.), *The Urbanization of the Suburbs.* Beverly Hills: Sage Publications, Urban Affairs Annual Review, **7** (1973).

Muller, P. O., *The Outer City.* Washington, D.C., Association of American Geographers Commission on College Geography, Resource Paper No. 75-2, 1976.

Urban Land Use Problems

Harvey, D., *Social Justice and the City.* London: Edward Arnold, 1973.

Platt, R. H., *Land Use Control: Interface of Law and Geography.* Washington, D.C.: Association of American Geographers Commission on College Geography, Resource Paper No. 75-1, 1976.

Wolpert, J., Mumphrey, A., and J. Seley, *Metropolitan Neighborhoods: Participation and Conflict over Change.* Washington, D.C.: Association of American Geographers Commission on College Geography, Resource Paper No. 16, 1972.

Urban Hierarchies and Hinterland Trade

KEY TERMS

- administrative principle
- break-point model
- central function
- central place
- city-rich and city-poor sectors
- convenience good
- establishment
- functional region
- functional size
- functional unit
- hierarchy
- hierarchical marginal good
- law of retail gravitation
- linear market
- marketing principle
- mercantile model
- nearest neighbor analysis
- range of a good
- rank-size rule
- settlement-building function
- settlement-forming function
- settlement-serving function
- shopping good
- threshold
- trade area
- traffic principle

6

In Chapter 5, we concentrated on the internal city. Urban society, however, reveals itself not as one but many cities linked together in a system. The system takes the form of a hierarchical distribution of cities by size and function. Why do urban hierarchies exist? What determines the size and spacing of cities? Although there are many reasons for locational patterns of cities, one classical location theory, *central place theory*, provides insights into the urban hierarchy. Central place theory considers the locational pattern of market-oriented retail and service firms, and the hierarchy of urban places in so far as they are market centers.

Central places are settlements that trade advantageously with their hinterlands. They are places of greatest shopping convenience in terms of distance. The theory of central places describes the optimum pattern of these distribution points. It deduces a model arrangement of settlements that minimizes the distance consumers must travel for goods and services. It assumes that retailing and service firms search for sites which will maximize their revenues. Like any normative construct, central place theory can be used as a norm against which actual central place systems can be compared.

This chapter develops as follows. In it we first describe locational patterns of cities and methods used to define geographical areas organized by central places. We then turn to an examination of central place theory. The discussion begins with a simple one-dimensional hierarchy of central places and proceeds to elaborate two-dimensional hierarchies. Finally, we deal with evidence from reality, and emphasize local trade and urban hierarchies in North America.

OBJECTIVES

By the end of this chapter you should be able:

1. To describe the relationship between central places and their hinterlands.
2. To describe the law of retail gravitation.

Central Places and Their Hinterlands

3. To introduce the economic and locational principles necessary for understanding central place theory and its extensions.
4. To develop ideal sizes and shapes of hinterlands.
5. To show the hierarchical patterns produced by the interlocking of hinterlands.
6. To discuss the Christaller model and its modifications.
7. To present some empirical evidence of an organized central place system in the United States.
8. To define the rank-size rule.
9. To compare and contrast central place theory and the rank-size rule.

Central Places and Their Hinterlands

Locational Patterns of Cities

The concentration of population in cities is primarily the result of the spatial organization of secondary and tertiary activities. These economic activities can be conducted more profitably when they are clustered together rather than dispersed. Locational patterns of cities in market societies typically consist of three elements (Harris and Ullman, 1945): (1) A lined pattern of centers that perform break-of-bulk and related services organized in relation to communication routes. These centers grow along transport routes, and at the junction of different kinds of transport such as road and railway junctions and the head of sea, lake, or river navigation. Most of the major metropolitan centers of the United States had their origins as transport centers, examples being New York, Boston, and Chicago. (2) A clustered pattern of specialized-function centers. These centers tend to cluster around localized resources with mining and manufacturing as dominant occupations. Examples are cities of the Steel Belt Corridor—Pittsburgh, Youngstown, and Canton. Resort towns along the coasts of Florida and California are also settlements whose location is governed by physical resources. (3) A uniform pattern of centers that exchange goods and services with their hinterlands. Settlements that act as centers for the local exchange of goods and services are referred to as *central places.* Every city is a central place even though most cities do not depend exclusively on central place functions.

Central Places

No locational theory applies to all three components of a settlement pattern, but a great deal of research has been devoted to the arrangement and distribution of central places. The theory of central places is not a comprehensive theory, but a restricted theory for competitive market societies. It emphasizes that cities perform extensive services for their hinterlands (see box). Functions performed by central

Specialized-function center: Miami Beach, Florida. SOURCE: *U.S. Army Corps of Engineers.*

places include retailing and wholesaling services; banking, insurance and real estate services; recreational, leisure, medical, educational, religious, and cultural facilities; and urban government and administrative services.

CITIES AND TRADE

Cities are centers of trade. They trade with their hinterlands and other areas. Sales totally within the hinterland we shall call *settlement-forming* trade. A true central place is based exclusively on these functions and can never support a population that transcends its hinterland. The number of jobs and, therefore, population is a direct function of the demand generated in the hinterland. Most settlements have other functions that are not dependent upon hinterland size. A manufacturing plant that sells to a national market, a town that has a major state university or is a county seat, or a resort settlement that attracts people from the entire nation provide examples of jobs that are not directly dependent upon the local retail and service hinterland. Such activity is called *settlement-building* trade. Each settlement also does some business with itself, goods and services sold to the residents of the center. This business is called *settlement-serving* trade.

Hinterlands

Central places serve areas larger than themselves. These areas are called hinterlands, tributary areas, trade or market areas, or urban fields. A *trade area* theoretically may be continuous. Take, for example, the circulation of a city's newspaper. Most

Central Places and Their Hinterlands

papers are purchased by people who live in or near the city, but a few of them may be purchased by people living thousands of kilometers away. Figure 6.1 graphs this theoretical relationship. The curve gets infinitely close to the distance axis, but never reaches zero. For practical purposes, however, a city's trade area ends much closer to the origin. Geographers have often used a "median" or "line of indifference" boundary to delimit trade areas. The median boundary in newspaper circulation, for example, is the line between two cities along which 50 percent of the newspapers purchased are from one city and the remainder are from the competing city.

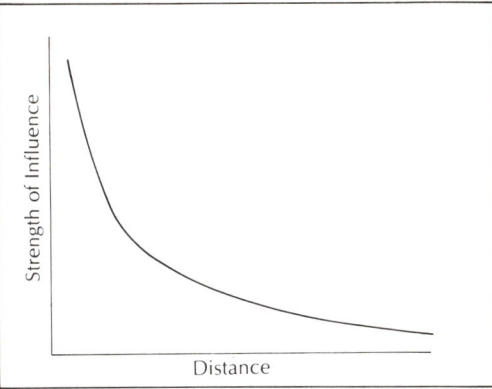

FIGURE 6.1 Cross section of an idealized trade area.

Figure 6.2 shows selected service areas of Mobile, Alabama. Isopleths are the 50 percent boundaries for each activity. The outermost lines depict the approximate boundary of Mobile's influence. From this map we could delimit the region over which the city exerts more or less total dominance.

The map of areas influenced by Mobile is the result of laborious fieldwork. To adopt the same method for a number of cities, particularly large cities,

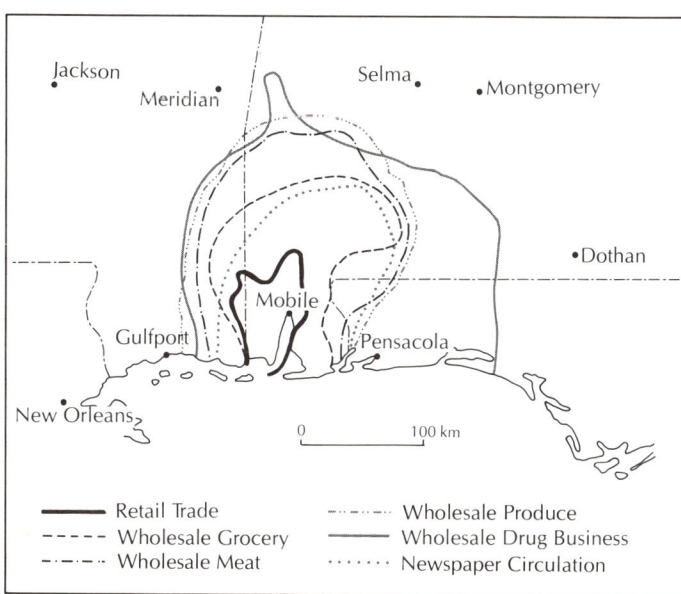

FIGURE 6.2 Service areas of Mobile, Alabama. SOURCE: E. L. Ullman, 1943, *Mobile: Industrial Seaport and Trade Center.* Chicago: University of Chicago Press.

would be a tedious undertaking. Consequently, it is the usual practice to select only one activity that is believed to be particularly expressive of a city's trade area. In the United States, metropolitan trade areas may be determined by the extent and intensity of long distance telephone calls, journeys to work, wholesale deliveries, and newspaper circulation. Figure 6.3 delimits metropolitan trade areas using newspaper circulation data. Newspapers are conceptually a good indicator of the social, economic, and cultural ties between a city and its tributary region. This is especially true for large metropolitan centers. People in the tributary area look to the regional newspaper for economic information such as sales and for cultural/social events (concerts, exhibits, etc.).

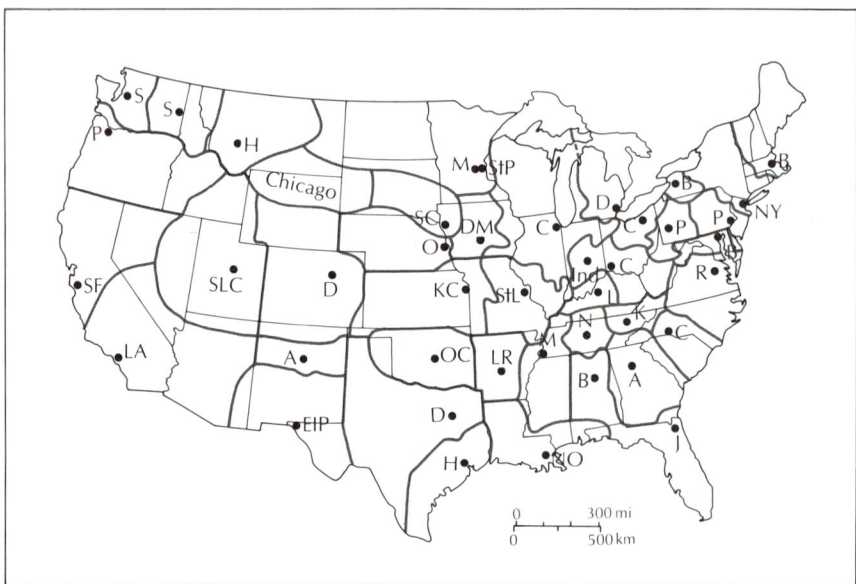

FIGURE 6.3 U.S. metropolitan trade areas based on newspaper circulation, 1933. SOURCE: R. E. Park and C. Newcomb, 1933, "Newspaper Circulation in Metropolitan Regions" in R. D. McKenzie, ed., *The Metropolitan Community*. New York: McGraw-Hill.

Areas that focus on central places through circulation networks are known as *functional* or *nodal* regions. Every city has its nodal region. The size and shape of this region depends on the size of the city, the influence or competition of neighboring dominant centers, and the ease of travel.

The Law of Retail Gravitation

Where satisfactory data are not readily available to determine urban trade areas, useful estimates can be obtained by applying a modification of W. J. Reilly's (1931)

Central Places and Their Hinterlands

law of retail gravitation. The "break point" between two cities may be estimated using the following formula:

$$D_j = \frac{d_{ij}}{1 + \sqrt{\frac{P_i}{P_j}}}$$

where
D_j = the distance from city j to the breaking point.
d_{ij} = the distance between the two cities i and j.
P_i = the population of the ith city.
P_j = the population of the jth city.

The breaking point obtained from the use of the formula is the boundary where the attraction of the two competing cities is equal.

Let us illustrate the *break-point model* with a simple example. City A and City B have populations of 20,000 and 80,000, respectively, and are 60 kilometers apart. According to the formula, the limit of the trading area of A in the direction of B is

$$\frac{60}{1 + \sqrt{\frac{80,000}{20,000}}} = \frac{60}{1 + 2} = 20 \text{ kilometers}$$

Therefore, according to the formula, the trading area of A would extend 20 kilometers toward B. This same analysis can be made in every direction from a particular city, resulting in a highly generalized trade area (Figure 6.4). An example of trade areas computed from the simple break-point formula is shown in Figure 6.5.

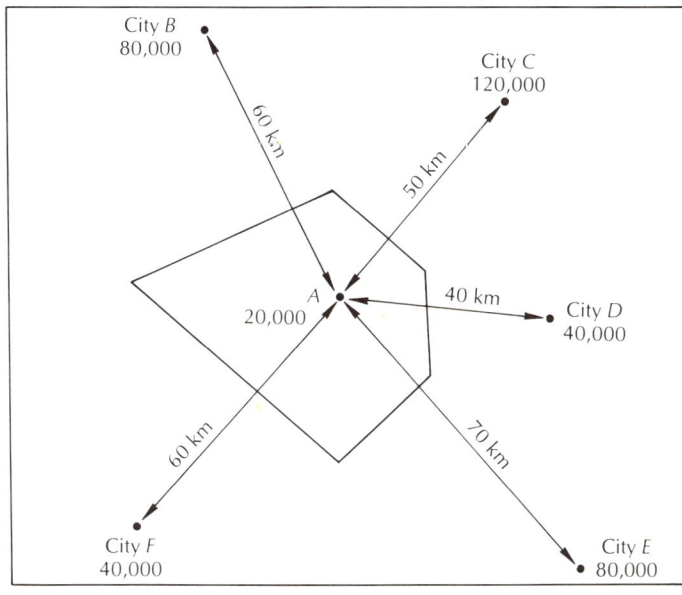

FIGURE 6.4 Hypothetical trade area based on the break-point model.

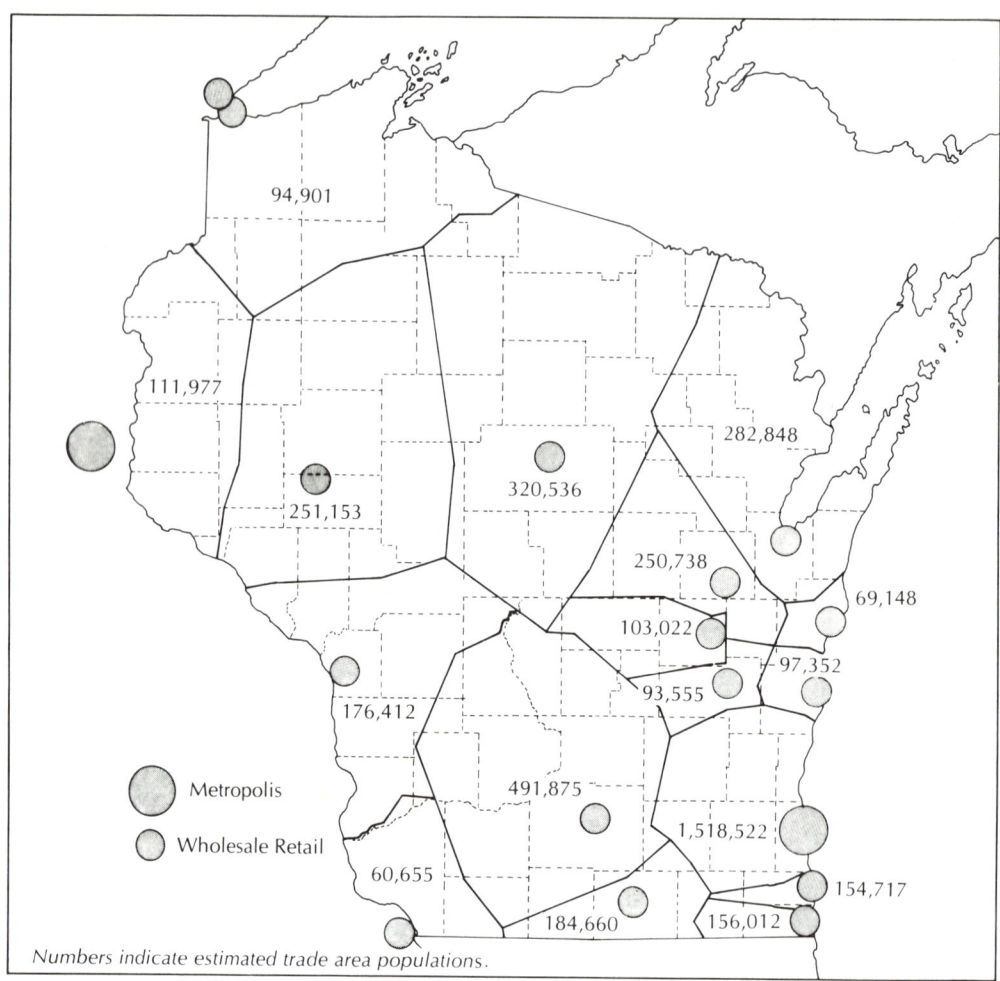

FIGURE 6.5 Wholesale trade areas in Wisconsin based on the break-point model.

Although the break-point model provides a short-cut technique for determining trade area boundaries, it has its problems. City populations are assumed to be homogeneous masses; that is, the formula does not take into account cultural, economic, and other differences among people. Multipurpose trips and variations in ease of transportation between places also are not considered.

More comprehensive break-point models try to take into account population and trade differences. They may describe the form of trade areas, but they do not help us to understand the process underlying the formation of these areas. Central place theory does, however, explain the process behind the formation of trade areas in market exchange societies, and we now turn to it.

An Elementary Central Place Model

Let us introduce central place theory with a simple normative model that assumes:

1. an isotropic surface
2. a given amount and uniform distribution of demand and population
3. equally easy transportation in all directions
4. settlements depending totally on hinterland trade
5. producers and consumers as optimizers
6. a steady state economy without government or social classes.

The model also assumes a *linear market* with consumers evenly spaced along a road that extends across the isolated plain (Figure 6.6). Given these severe constraints, we wish to investigate the number of central places required to meet consumer demand; the size of trade areas; and the most efficient spacing of central places.

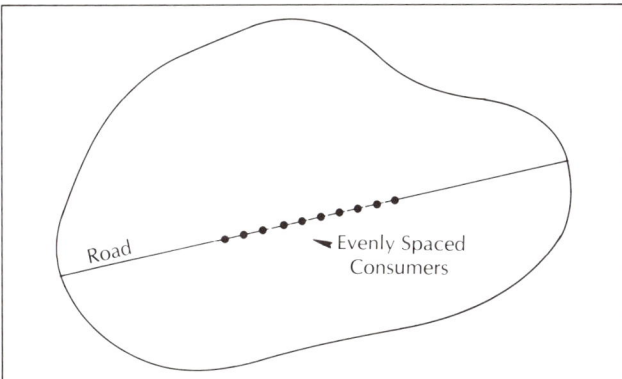

FIGURE 6.6 A linear market.

Threshold and Range

Threshold and *range* are key concepts in central place theory. For a firm to offer a good *(central function)* at a point along the road, it must sell enough to meet operating costs. *The minimum level of demand that will allow a firm to stay in business is called the threshold of a good.* But given the assumption of evenly distributed population and demand, we can also speak of the *minimum number of people* necessary to support a central function.

The range of a good is the distance people are willing to travel to obtain a good at the market place. Consider a good offered for sale at price P_1 (Figure 6.7A). A consumer living next door to the shop pays the store price. Another consumer living some distance from the store must pay the store price plus the cost of travel to the central place. Suppose bread is 50 cents a loaf and travel costs are 20 cents per kilometer. A consumer who lives five kilometers from the store and makes a trip to buy a loaf of bread pays $1.50 (Figure 6.6A). The theory of pure competition states that as the price of a good increases, the smaller the quantity demanded (Figure 6.7B). Thus if price increases with distance from a central place and demand declines with price, then demand should decline with distance and gradually reach zero. That point is the range of a good (Figure 6.7C). *The range of a good is the distance R in both directions from a distribution point on a linear market* (Figure 6.8).

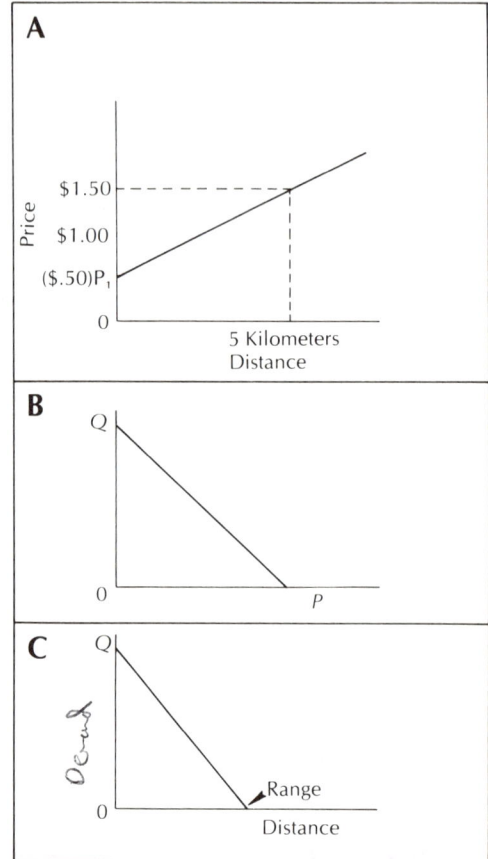

FIGURE 6.7 Price, demand, and the range of a good.

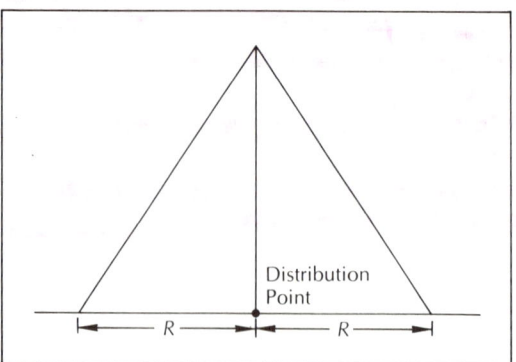

FIGURE 6.8 Range as distance.

An Elementary Central Place Model

Order of a Good

Different goods have different thresholds. Inexpensive, frequently purchased goods have low thresholds. Expensive, infrequently purchased goods have higher thresholds. Goods with low thresholds are called low-order goods. Goods with higher thresholds are called higher-order goods. Thus central functions can be ordered on the basis of their threshold size. The highest order good has the largest threshold and the lowest order good has the smallest threshold. Goods in Table 6.1 are ordered in this way. The highest order good has a threshold of 1,000 and the lowest order good has a threshold of 1.

TABLE 6.1 Goods (threshold size)

1000, 999, 998, 997, ..., 14, 13, 12, 11, 10, 9, 8, 7, 6, 5, 4, 3, 2, 1

Order of a Center

The order of a center is determined by the highest order good offered by the center. Low-order centers offer only low-order goods; high order centers offer high-order goods, but they also offer lower-order goods. In Table 6.1 a center that offers good 1,000 will offer all lower-order goods. If a center has a hinterland of 1,000 people (threshold of good 1,000), then it meets the threshold of goods 999, 998, ..., 2, 1. A center whose highest order good has a threshold of 25 can offer only goods with a threshold of 25 or lower.

Emergence of a Central Place Hierarchy

We can now derive a *hierarchy* of central places. Assume highest order places (*A*-level) offer all goods from 1,000 to 1 (Table 6.2). The market area of each *A*-level place must contain at least 1,000 people (threshold of the highest order good). If there are 10,000 consumers along our imaginary linear market, 10 *A*-level centers can be established. Two *A*-level centers and their market areas are shown in Figure 6.9. We have assumed a population density of 10 people per kilometer so that the

TABLE 6.2 Goods (threshold size)

		1000, 999, 998,	...,	502, 501, 500,	...,	252, 251, 250,	...,	3,	2,	1
CENTERS	A	X X X	X	X X X	X	X X X	X	X	X	X
	B			X X X	X	X X X	X	X	X	X
	C					X X X	X	X	X	X

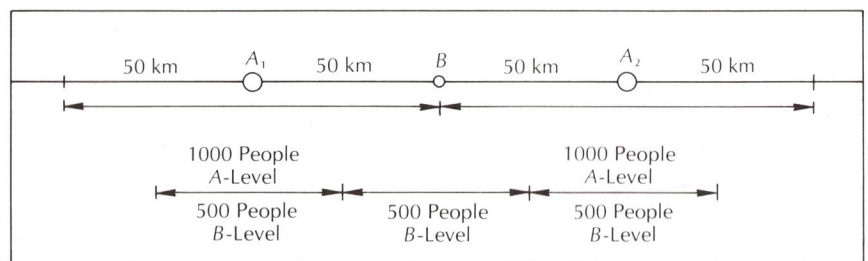

FIGURE 6.9 A $K=2$ hierarchy.

minimum market area of each A-level center is 100 kilometers (50 kilometers on either side of each A-level center). We assume that competition forces market areas to be as small as possible (100 kilometers = 1000 consumers). This minimizes the travel cost the most distance consumer from an A-level center must pay. A consumer on the dividing line between two A-level centers is indifferent, and will divide purchases equally between the two centers.

The good that defines the A-level of the hierarchy has a threshold of 1,000, but there is also a good with a threshold of A/2 or 500. The threshold market area for that good is 50 kilometers in length (25 kilometers on either side of a distribution point). A market area of 500 centered on A_1 and A_2 allows an additional 500 person market area centered on the midpoint between the two A-level centers. A central place locating there can offer all goods with a threshold of 500 or less. This is the B-level; and the good that defines the B-level has a threshold of 500 and is called a *hierarchical marginal good*. A hierarchical marginal good is the highest order good offered by a given level of the central place hierarchy.

What threshold size will define C-level centers? The threshold value will be B/2 (250) and C-level centers squeeze in midway between higher-order centers. If A-level centers are 100 kilometers apart, then C-level centers will be found every 25 kilometers along our imaginary road. Similarly the threshold size for D-level centers will be C/2 (125), and they will be found every 12.5 kilometers along the road.

This linear hierarchy follows the "rule of 2's": each successive level is defined by a function with a threshold one-half the size of the next highest hierarchical marginal good. The "rule of 2's" also applies to market area sizes and the spacing of centers. In central place theory, this type of hierarchy is known as a $K = 2$ hierarchy, because 2 is the constant parameter of the system. The letter K stands for the German word *Konstant*.

It is important to remember that our simple central place model generates a hierarchy wherein the number of required central places is minimized, the number of consumers served is maximized, and the aggregate distance consumers must travel for a given set of functions is also minimized. It shows that higher order centers have larger populations than lower order centers because they offer more functions and therefore more employment. Higher order centers also are more widely spaced, have larger market areas, and occur less frequently. In sum, our central place hierarchy may be regarded as a multiple system of nested centers and market areas. Lower order centers and their market areas nest under the market areas of higher order centers. Let us now consider more complex (two dimensional) hierarchies developed by Walter Christaller and others.

The Christaller Central Place Model

Foundations of central place theory were established in 1933 by Walter Christaller (see box). Christaller attempted to construct a deductive theory to explain the size, number, and distribution of clusters of urban trades and institutions. The inspiration for his ideas came from the work of economic location theorists such as Thünen and Weber.

> **WALTER CHRISTALLER (1893-1969)**
>
> Christaller was a German geographer. In the early 1930s he wrote his classic work, *The Central Places of Southern Germany,* which was his doctoral dissertation. He was regarded as a radical, and his ideas on the spatial structure of an economic system were accepted slowly in Western Europe and North America. In his later years he was awarded the gold medal from the King of Sweden, the highest geographical award that country can bestow, and the Association of American Geographers gave him their outstanding award, but *in absentia*. As a former member of the Communist party, he was refused a visa by the United States government.

Christaller argued that it was unnecessary to begin analysis of hierarchies of central places with a description of reality. He controlled complexities of the real world with simplifying assumptions which we have introduced. Unlike our linear market, the economic landscape considered by Christaller is two-dimensional.

To demonstrate hierarchical interrelations between central places in a competitive market society, Christaller constructed three geometric models. His central places are arranged according to marketing, transport, and administrative principles. According to Christaller, the three principles establish, each according to its own laws, the most efficient system of central places.

The Marketing Principle

The *marketing principle* assumes the largest provision of central-place goods and services from the minimum number of central places (Figure 6.10). Each *B*-level

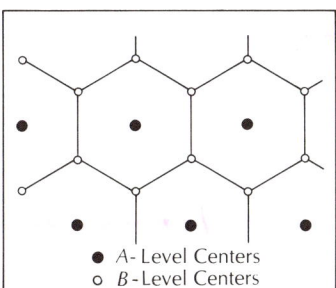

FIGURE 6.10 Location of centers: $K = 3$ hierarchy.

central place is located midway between three neighboring centers of the next highest order. Midway points are corners of hexagonal market areas of the next highest order. Each higher order place is surrounded by six places of the next lowest order.

REGULAR HEXAGONS

The best geometry of market areas across an isotropic plain is a regular hexagon. Although the circle is the optimum shape for individual market areas, circular market areas when packed together either leave some consumers unserved or they overlap. If people in overlap areas go to the nearest place, the result is a set of hexagonal market areas. Hexagons, the polygonal form closest to a circle in shape, "tile" space more efficiently than other geometric forms. They are the most efficient shape for minimizing distances between central places and their hinterlands.

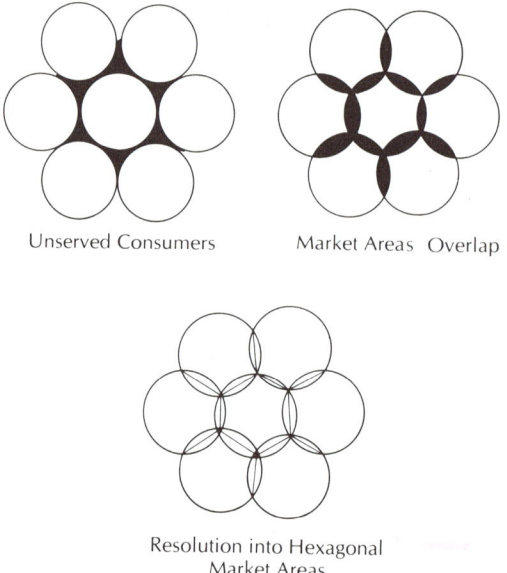

Unserved Consumers   Market Areas Overlap

Resolution into Hexagonal
Market Areas

Figure 6.11 illustrates the progression of central places and market areas for a three-level hierarchy. The market area of each A-level center passes through six lower order centers (B-level). A-level market areas are *three* times larger than B-level market areas. In Figure 6.11, each A-level market area includes all of the B-level market areas centered on an A-level center plus one-third of the six surrounding B-level market areas (1/3 of 6 = 2 + 1 = 3). Distances separating places at the same level of the hierarchy are the same. If lower order central places are located 1 unit apart, then rival higher order central places, dominating three times the area and

The Christaller Central Place Model

three times the population, are located $\sqrt{3}$ units apart or 1.732 units apart. This kind of arrangement of central places is a $K = 3$ network. The number of market areas at successively less specialized levels of the $K = 3$ hierarchy progresses by the "rule of 3's," that is, central places increase geometrically: 1, 3, 9, 27.

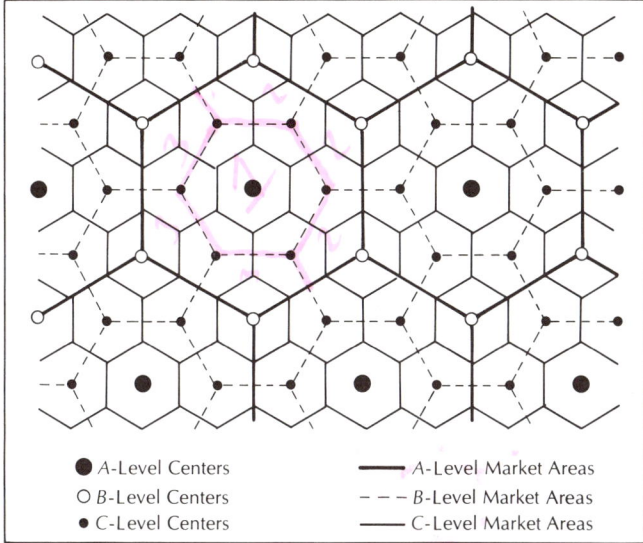

FIGURE 6.11 Market areas: $K = 3$ hierarchy.

Christaller argued that the system of central places developed on the basis of the range of a good is rational and efficient from an economic point of view. Yet he noted that the $K = 3$ model is imperfect because of distortions. Deviations under actual conditions are caused by historical circumstance, government interference, social stratification, income differences, and topographical variations.

The Traffic Principle

Figure 6.12A shows an optimum road network superimposed on a marketing hierarchy. Note that B-level centers do not lie on the A-level road network. More roads must be constructed if B-level centers are to be connected. Christaller rejected traffic routes in the marketing system, and asked: How can connectivity among places be *maximized* and network length *minimized*? He shifted B-level centers to a point *midway* between each pair of A-level centers, and found that this arrangement maximizes connectivity and minimizes network length (Figure 6.12B). This pattern of centers results in a $K = 4$ hierarchy. The B-level market areas are *one-fourth* the size of the A-level market areas. Each A-level market area dominates all of the B-level areas centered on it plus one-half of the surrounding six (equals 3) for a total of four.

The number of market areas at successively less specialized levels of the $K = 4$ hierarchy progresses by the "rule of 4's," that is, central places increase geometrically: 1, 4, 16, 64. Compared with the marketing principle, more centers at each level of the hierarchy are necessary if the entire landscape is to be adequately provided with central places for the distribution of goods and services. The advan-

FIGURE 6.12 The traffic principle: (A) optimum transportation net: maximum connectivity for A-level centers ($K = 3$); (B) a $K = 4$ hierarchy.

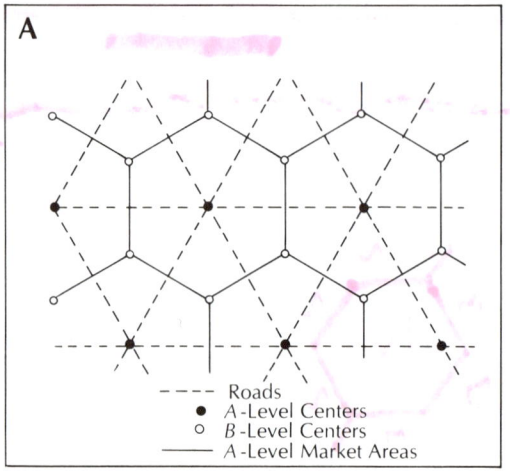

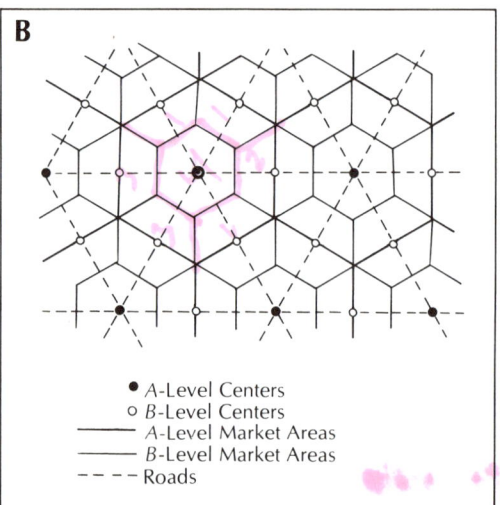

tage of a more efficient transport system for moving goods cheaply is counterbalanced by the additional distance consumers must travel to reach a center at a given level of the hierarchy.

The Administrative Principle

The *administrative principle* is based on political rather than economic considerations. It assumes a clear-cut separation of hinterlands, and is achieved when each central place entirely controls six dependent centers (Figure 6.13). Hinterlands nest according to a "rule of 7's" ($K = 7$). In the $K = 7$ hierarchy the progression of hinterlands is 1, 7, 49, 343. Hinterlands in the $K = 7$ hierarchy are larger than in either $K = 3$ or $K = 4$ systems, which means that consumers must travel even farther to reach a center of a given level in the system.

The Christaller Central Place Model

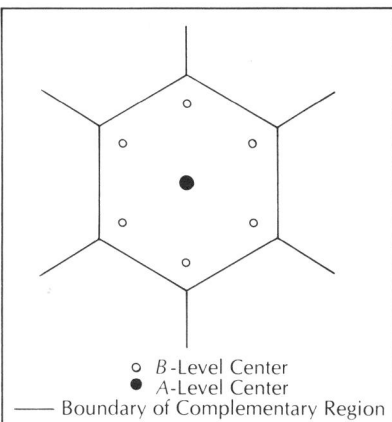

FIGURE 6.13 Two-level hierarchy of central places under the administrative principle.

Southern Germany

Christaller tested his central place model in Southern Germany, and the results are summarized in Table 6.3. Christaller claimed that figures computed for Southern Germany were also typical for most of Germany and Western Europe. The hierarchy of central places he examined has seven levels ranging from market hamlet (Markort) to regional capital city (Landeshaupstadt). Hinterland sizes and distances separating central places increase at successively higher levels of the hierarchy. Centers at each level of the hierarchy dominate three times the area (column 4) and three times the population (column 5). The distance between similar centers increases by $\sqrt{3}$ over the preceding smaller category (column 2). In the table, the smallest centers are located about 7 kilometers apart, because 4–5 kilometers, roughly a one hour

TABLE 6.3 The urban hierarchy in Southern Germany

	Towns		Tributary Areas	
Central Place (1)	**Distance Apart** (2)	**Population** (3)	**Size (Sq Km)** (4)	**Population** (5)
Market hamlet (Markort)	7	800	45	2,700
Township center (Amtsort)	12	1,500	135	8,100
County seat (Kreistadt)	21	3,500	400	24,000
District city (Bezirksstadt)	36	9,000	1,200	75,000
Small state capital (Gaustadt)	62	27,000	3,600	225,000
Provincial head city (Provinzhaupstadt)	108	90,000	10,800	675,000
Regional capital city (Laundeshaupstadt)	186	300,000	32,400	2,025,000

SOURCE: E. L. Ullman, 1940–1941, "A Theory of Location for Cities," *American Journal of Sociology,* Vol. 46, p. 857.

walking distance, corresponded to the market area for the smallest centers. Centers of the next order of specialization, township centers, are located 12 kilometers apart.

The actual distribution of cities, towns, and villages in Southern Germany is shown in Figure 6.14. Networks of central places nest within the market areas of Landeshaupstadts. The Landeshaupstadts are Munich, Frankfurt, Stuttgart, and Nuremburg together with the border cities of Strasbourg in France and Zurich in Switzerland.

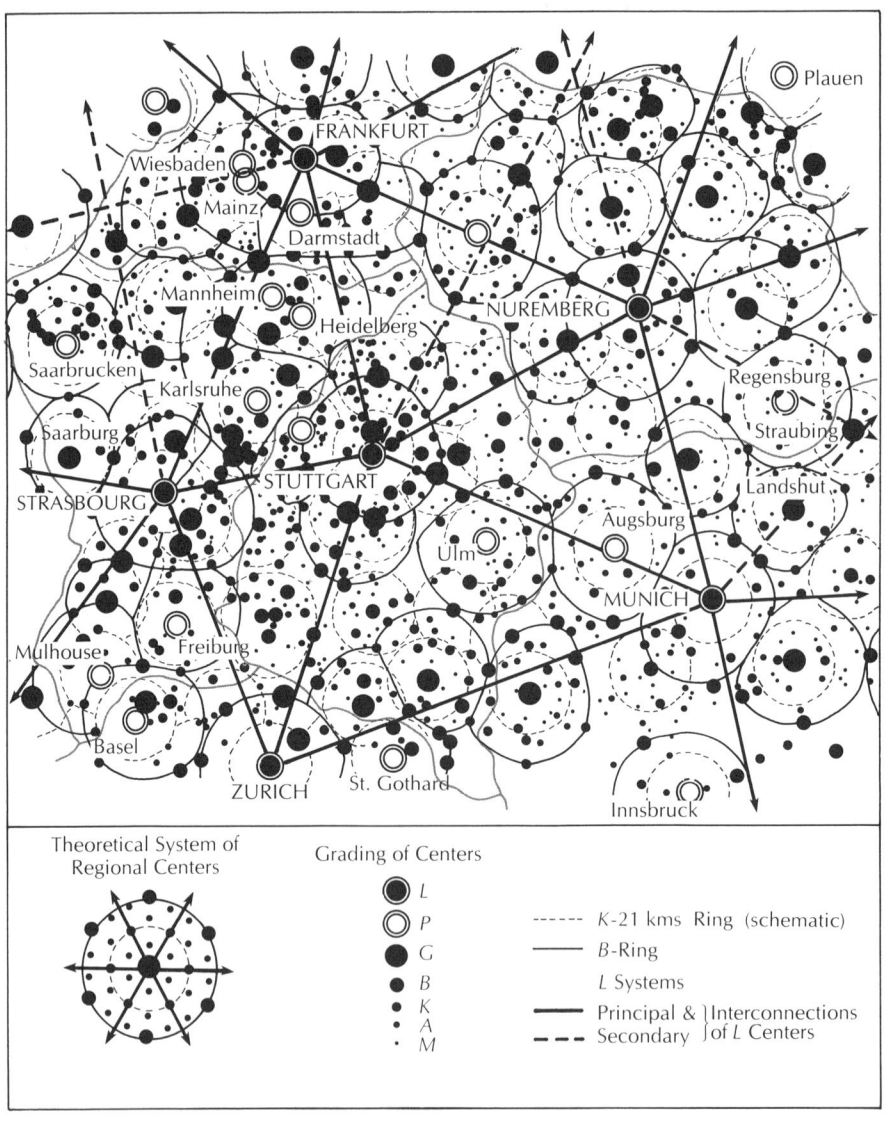

FIGURE 6.14 The distribution of central places in Southern Germany.
SOURCE: R. E. Dickinson, 1964, *City and Region*. London: Routledge and Kegan Paul, p. 75, Fig. 3.

Extensions of the Christaller Model

Central places in Christaller's test region: (A) Market hamlet (Markort) near Bamburg, Germany (SOURCE: R. Janke); and (B) Innsbruck, Austria, a provincial head city (Provinzhaupstadt).

Christaller found that the expected pattern was approached best in poor, thinly settled farm districts that were virtually self-contained. Thus, deviations from the rational pattern were not common in many parts of Southern Germany. Discrepancies were noted in other parts of Germany however. The theoretical ideal, for example, was not found in the highly industrialized Rhine-Ruhr.

Extensions of the Christaller Model

Lösch's Economic Landscapes

Following Christaller's original model, several scholars have attempted to modify and elaborate his ideas; one of the most interesting attempts is the scheme proposed by August Lösch, in *The Economics of Location*. His work on the nature of economic regions was based on classical economic theory of the firm. He also concluded that the hexagon is the most economical shape for economic areas. Lösch's main contribution, however, was to extend Christaller's fixed assumptions of the marketing, traffic, and administrative principles, which he regarded as interesting, but special limited cases.

Lösch produced a more comprehensive and flexible system of central places by changing the orientation and size of his hexagonal economic areas. He, like Christaller, began his analysis with the ideal region. He assumed an isotropic plain that contained only self-sufficient farms which produced uniform products.

Lösch's first step was to identify the three smallest market areas (Figure 6.15A). Let us suppose, Lösch said, that a farmer at A_1 produces a commodity in excess of immediate needs and sells the surplus at either farmstead A_2 or A_3. The result is a triangular market area. If A_1 increases output it may become a central place (B_1), and the farmer sells the output in a hexagon consisting of six triangles. The market area of B_1 would be expanded by invading the market areas of neighboring centers B_2 through B_7, either by rotating the hexagon around B_1 (Figure 6.15B) or by rotating and enlarging the hexagon so that it runs through open countryside without touching any settlement (Figure 6.15C).

The nest of the three smallest market area sizes all centered on the highest order central place is shown in Figure 6.16A. These market area sizes correspond to $K3$, 4, and 7 nets. Lösch said that these market areas are only the smallest in an infinite series. By rotating and enlarging hexagons again and again,

FIGURE 6.15 Lösch's basic market areas.

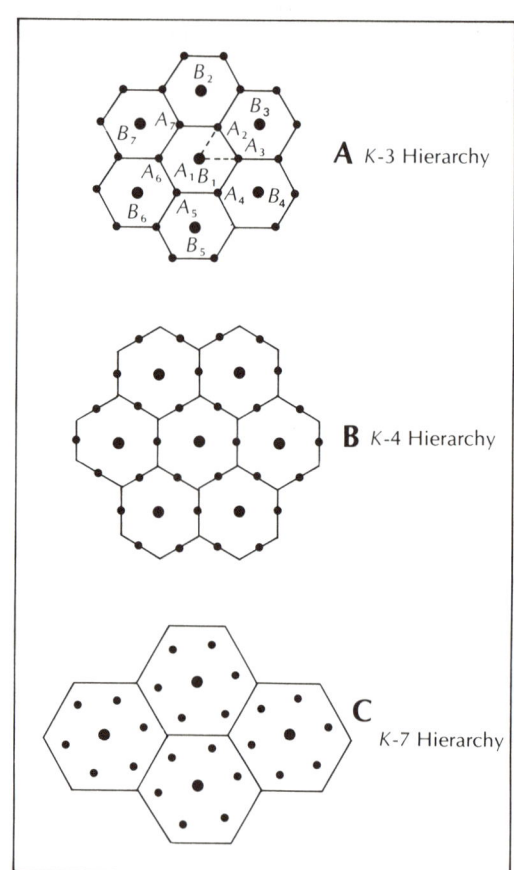

A K-3 Hierarchy

B K-4 Hierarchy

C K-7 Hierarchy

Extensions of the Christaller Model

successive market area sizes with K values of 9, 12, 13, 16, 19, 21, and 25 can be derived. Figure 6.16B illustrates the arrangement of all ten hexagonal nets rotated around the metropolis (A). Lösch argued that not all ten market area sizes are possible. Solutions that do not share markets, such as $K = 7$, 13, and 19, are very efficient. They are more likely to occur in practice than others, such as $K = 12$. Thus a Löschian landscape is made up of a discontinuous series of central place solutions, because of variations in the efficiencies of these solutions.

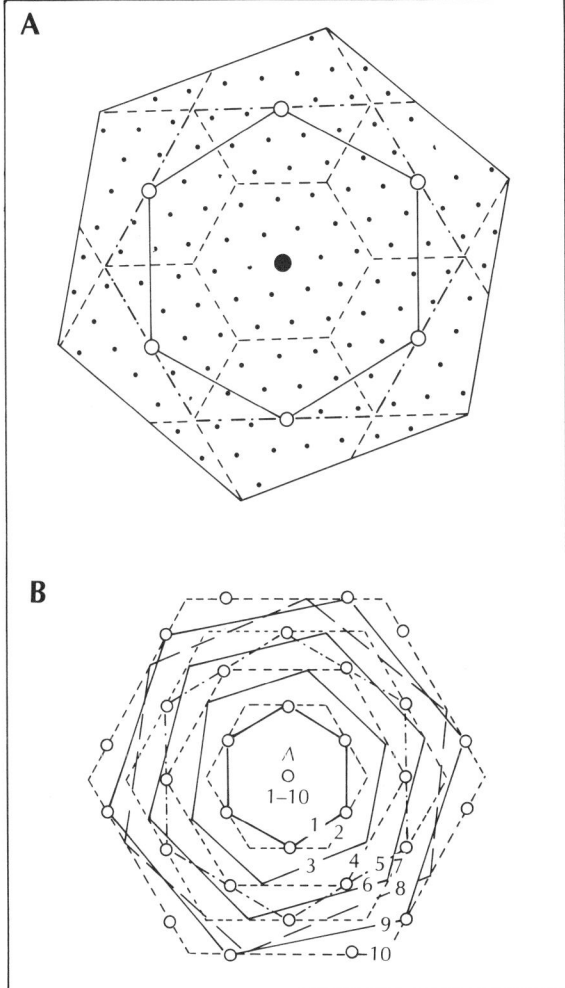

FIGURE 6.16 Lösch's market areas: (A) the nest of the three smallest market areas; (B) network of ten common-centered market areas.

City-Rich and City-Poor Sectors

By rotating all the possible hexagonal nets around the metropolis, Lösch obtained the maximum coincidence or agglomeration of production locations, the maximization of the amount of purchases made locally, and the minimization of total distance between production points. The result is shown in Figure 6.17A. The pattern consists of twelve alternating *city-rich* (or production-rich) and *city-poor* (or production-poor) *sectors*. The arrangement of linear clusters of central places conformed with what Lösch regarded as a major characteristic of human spatial organization: the *principle of least effort*. Lösch provided some evidence that sectors are approximated in the real world for the environs of Indianapolis and Toledo (Figure 6.17B and C).

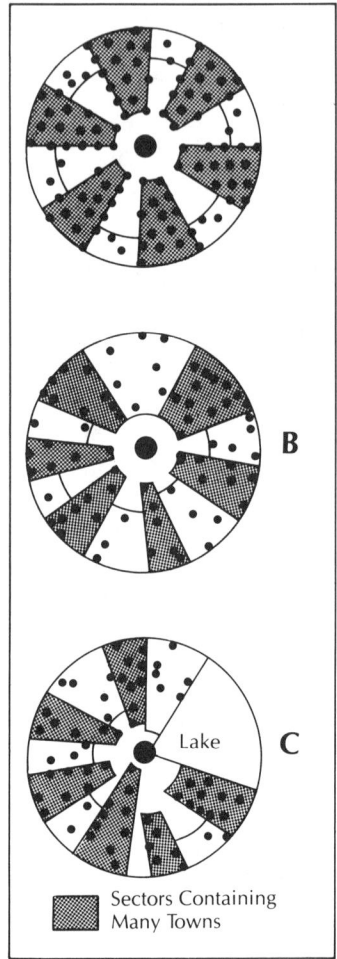

FIGURE 6.17 Lösch's economic landscapes. SOURCE: August Lösch, 1954, *The Economics of Location*. Stuttgart: Gustav Fischer Verlag, p. 125, Figs. 29, 30, 31.

Figure 6.18 represents the location and functions of central places in one 60° sector radiating from the metropolis (A). Only the metropolis produces all goods. The goods provided by the metropolis in ascending order of specialization are 1, 2, 3, 4, . . . 15, and they require market areas 1, 3, 4, 9, 12, 13, 16, 19, 21, and 25 times the size of the smallest hexagon. Every lowest order central place provides the lowest order good, designated by the number 1, but there is considerable variation in the incidence of functions provided by higher order centers. Reading along the transect from A to B, goods provided by central places beyond the metropolis are 1; 1, 3; 1, 2, 5; 1, 3, 8; 1, 11; 1, 2, 3, 5, 6, 15. This transect shows that as distance from the metropolis increases, the importance of larger centers increases.

Extensions of the Christaller Model

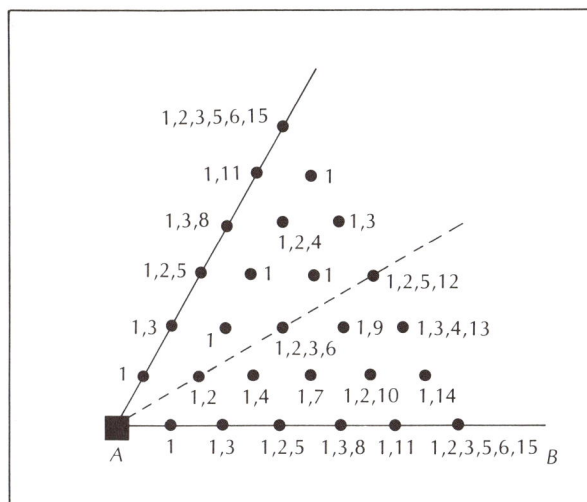

FIGURE 6.18 Size, spacing, and functional structure of central places in one 60° sector of Löschian economic landscape.

Economic Regions in Reality

Lösch considered limitations of theory when analyzing the actual economic landscape. In the theoretical model, he postulated three types of economic regions: market areas, regional networks, and regional systems. These three regional types are increasingly complicated, self-sufficient, and most important, increasingly rare in the real world.

Lösch noted that when the assumption of an isotropic plain is relaxed and the supposition of a uniform product is dropped, single product market areas overlap and are irregular in size and shape. Regional networks of markets are likely to occur in belts or zones. Lösch argued that regional systems differ most of all from the theoretical model. Discrepancies between theory and reality exist primarily because economic landscapes are the product of a historical process. Disturbed patterns of central places are sometimes the result of concentration and resource irregularities. In the real world one can expect neither an economically self-sufficient landscape, nor a metropolis that produces and supplies everything. The largest center in an economic region may not possess all the functions that the trade area demands. Consequently many goods are exchanged between economic regions. Within an economic region, several eccentrically located major cities may exist, especially in a highly industrialized area. Lösch concluded that the economic landscape is anything but simple; it may even appear chaotic.

Christaller and Lösch Compared

Christaller and Lösch agreed that the triangular pattern of settlement distribution and hexagonal shaped market areas represents the optimal spatial organization for a single good under the constraint of uniform population density on an unbounded plain. They agreed on three major concepts of central place theory: range, threshold, and hierarchy. However, they developed their economic landscapes from different starting points. *Christaller* built his hierarchy from the *highest order good downwards,* and *Lösch* built his from the *ubiquitous good upwards.* It appears that Christaller's procedure for deriving his system provides a framework for the analysis of an economic landscape founded in an area of sparse settlement, and that Lösch's method provides a better framework for the analysis of a landscape in a region of dense, long-established settlement undergoing rapid change. Furthermore, Christaller's system sheds light on the distribution of retailing and service activities especially for agricultural regions, whereas Lösch's system appears more relevant to an understanding of the distribution of market-oriented manufacturing activities.

The Löschian hierarchy of central places is quite different from that developed by Christaller. Christaller's formulation consists of a number of tiers in which all places at the same level of the hierarchy are the same size and have the same kinds of functions, and all places on a given hierarchical level contain all the goods of smaller central places. Lösch's formulation is less rigid. It consists of a more continuous distribution of central places. Cities of the same size do not necessarily perform the same functions, and larger cities, as in reality, do not take on all those found in smaller cities.

A major purpose of Christaller's analysis was to show that there are economic ways of developing rational arrangements of central places and that there are wasteful ways. He had a strong desire to put his theory to work. Lösch was not bent on trying to persuade planners to adopt his ideas. His main object was to explain the complexities of economic regions. He attempted to show the ideal relations between central places and their hinterlands. He did this by superimposing all possible hexagonal solutions in a regional system, which is a formulation quite different from Christaller's three separate hierarchical principles.

Formulations of Christaller and Lösch are based on classical economic theory. Their models emphasize that site selection of firms is a matter of finding a location at which profits are maximized. To look at firms in this way helps us to understand the location of some but not all firms. Classical central place theory helps us to understand the location of tertiary economic activities in market exchange societies.

Although classical central place theory provides many insights into the urban hierarchy, we can see several shortcomings. The classical models are static, descriptive equilibrium models. They ignore non-optimal consumer behavior. They lack historical perspective; that is, they do not consider the historical process of developing capitalism as the framework within which settlements become centers of dominance. Furthermore, they deal with closed local economic systems. Thus central place theory can deal only with relationships between producers and consumers within a region. It cannot deal with settlement patterns that have grown out of long-distance trading connections between regions. Finally, an assumption implicit in central place theory is "that space is uniform and objects and activities can be manipulated and freely located within it; differentiation by significance is of little importance and places are reduced to simple locations with their greatest quality being development potential" (Ralph, 1976:87). It, therefore, fails to treat places as centers of existential significance, and to consider their qualities of appearance. Low order places in Nebraska, for instance, are like low order places in Florida. In a capsule, central place theory lacks humanism and involves no sense of *place* at all.

Isard's Modifications

Walter Isard in *Location and Space Economy* criticized the equal-area pattern of hexagons used by Christaller and Lösch. Regular hexagons, he said, are unlikely to occur in practice because of urbanization economies. As we saw in Chapter 5, economies of urban concentration are savings in production costs obtained when activities agglomerate or cluster around a point.

Isard rejected Lösch's method of depicting the impact of urbanization economies. He objected to Lösch's system of nets of market areas because it assumes a uniform distribution of consuming population, and yet it permits different sizes of concentration of secondary and tertiary activities in six city-poor and six city-rich sectors, and along main transport lines. Isard argued that it was necessary to modify Lösch's hexagonal network so that it conforms to the underlying population pattern. As a consequence of the relatively high density of population at the central core or metropolis implied in the Löschian system, the size of hexagons needed to meet the threshold for a commodity is likely to be smaller at the core and larger toward the periphery.

Isard produced a diagram (Figure 6.19) which retains as many of Lösch's assumptions as possible, and illustrates a distorted hexagonal network of market areas decreasing in size toward the main core. The diagram also depicts a secondary core at which business activities and population are concentrated. Isard pointed out that it was extremely difficult to work with hexagonal forms, and as Figure 6.19 shows, "the hexagon loses much of its significance as a spatial form once agglomeration forces are admitted, and . . . inequalities in population distribution recognized" (1956:274). The hexagon is a pure concept for geographers much as perfect competition is a pure concept for economists. A framework free of hexagonal geometry provides a more realistic basis for understanding the forces that affect locations of production sites and retail stores.

Isard's locations of main traffic arteries are quite different from those in Lösch's system. Isard located major transport routes through the center of sectors, not along their boundaries. His arrangement of transport lines is logical. It illustrates the importance of urbanization economies and the effects of modern modes of transportation. In order to avoid complications, he did not locate a hierarchical array of satellite centers along transport lines. For examples of patterns of secondary and satellite centers, he referred readers to population and land use maps around major metropolitan areas.

Wholesaling and the Mercantile Model of Settlement

The argument that central place theory is a "special case" is presented by James Vance (1970). He said if parochialism is the rule, central place theory suffices as an

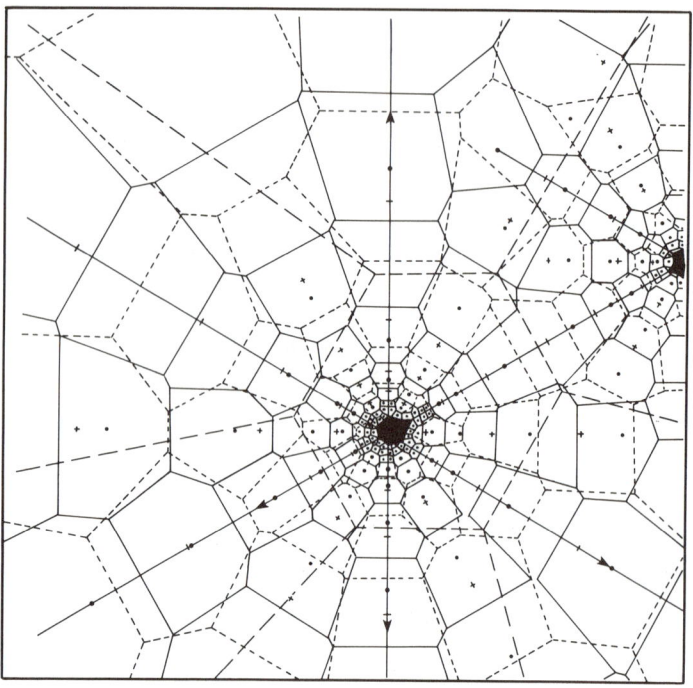

FIGURE 6.19 Isard's landscape modification. SOURCE: Reprinted from *Location and Space Economy* by Walter Isard, by permission of The MIT Press, Cambridge, Massachusetts.

explanation for the trading-settlement structure of an area. Central place theory deals with relationships between customers and sellers of goods and services *within* regions. It does not account for wholesale trade that links regions. Wholesaling which involves the sale of goods from one entrepreneur to another is conducted primarily *between* higher-order centers, and their locational patterns are influenced by external trade linkages. In addition, local settlement hierarchies are affected by the need for long-distance external ties.

Vance said external trade will occur if local self-sufficiency never existed or if it ceases to exist. Consider, for example, groups of people in different areas who produce surpluses of locally demanded goods. An ability to produce surpluses carries with it a desire to expand trade beyond the confines of a local area. Expansion occurs if outside consumers are informed about areas of abundance and areas of scarcity. They provide producers with markets and assure consumers access to products.

Wholesalers subject regions to external change and stimulate growth of wholesaling centers. For Vance wholesaling centers are "unravelling points" in the geography of trade. Wholesaling centers link production areas, mediate trade flows, and determine the metropolitan centers from which central place patterns develop to meet demands of consumers.

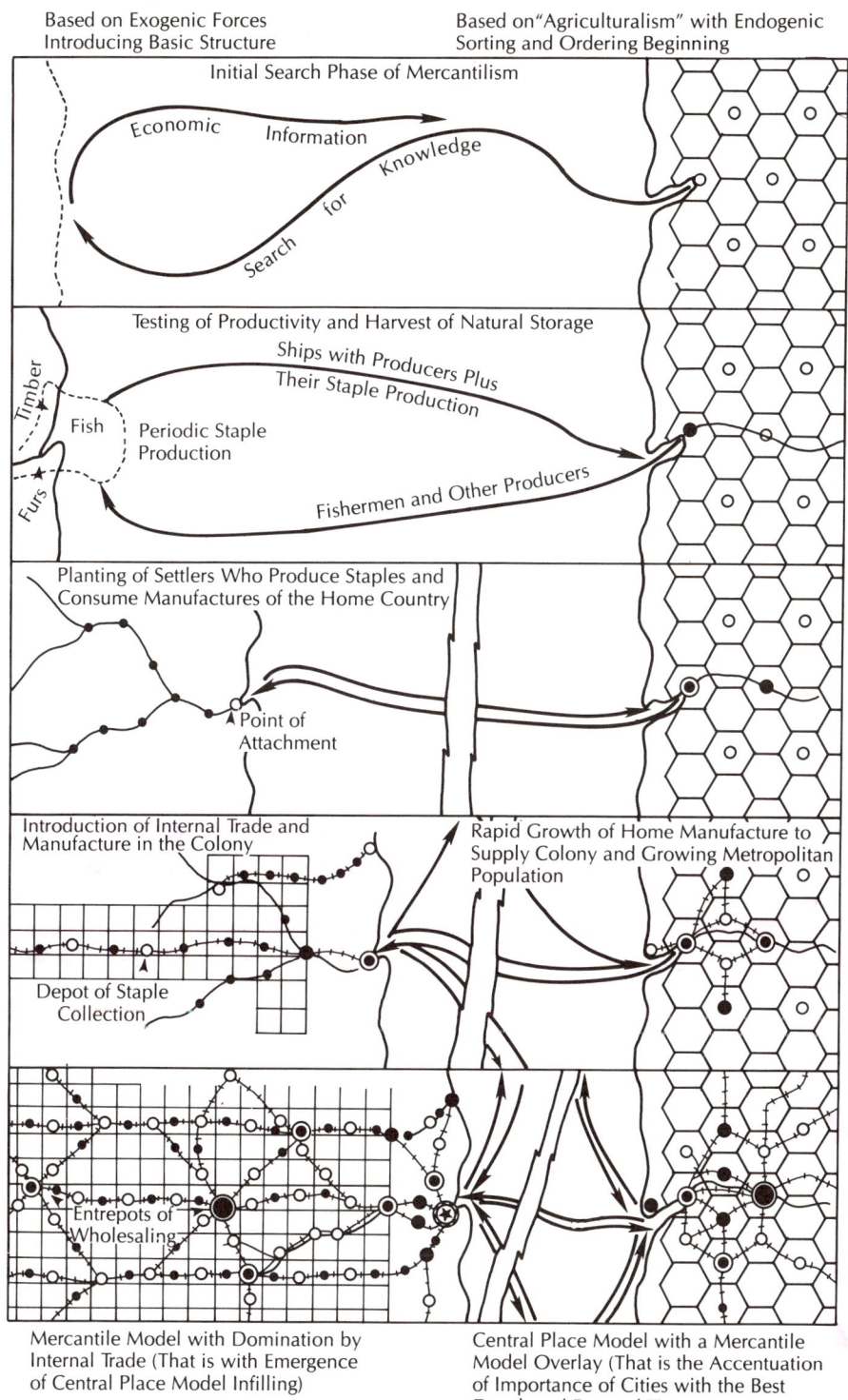

FIGURE 6.20 Urban evolution in the mercantile and central place models. Copyright J. E. Vance, Jr., from *The Merchant's World: The Geography of Wholesaling*. Englewood Cliffs: Prentice-Hall, 1970, p. 151, Fig. 18.

Vance showed that trading-settlement patterns do not grow entirely within the classical central place model. He doubted whether any region in North America was economically isolated enough to have begun in a closed local system. He preferred to view the history of settlement patterns in terms of local trading patterns (central place model) and long-distance trading connections (mercantile model). According to Vance, broad scale settlement of North America must be seen in the context of distant trade. Settlement and economic growth were introduced from the outside. Cities like Boston, Philadelphia, and Charleston were created before their hinterlands expanded.

Vance described the development of distant trade between Europe and North America, and the subsequent evolution of the American urban hierarchy. Figure 6.20 reveals the main contrasts between urban evolution in the *mercantile* and central-place model. Prior to settlement, Europeans sought knowledge to evaluate the economic potential of an area. After successfully testing the economic potential, mercantile centers were established. They linked European countries and their sources of raw materials. Mercantile centers grew as the size of the trading system increased, and eventually the central place model began to characterize settlement. Subsequently there was parallel growth of settlement in accordance with both central place and mercantile models.

Evidence in Support of Central Place Theory

The theory of central places has been criticized. Researchers have noted that theoretical networks of central places do not resemble real economic landscapes. But in the real world it is unreasonable to expect "ideal" hexagonal patterns of towns and cities. Central place theory is incomplete: many functions support cities. About one-half the support of American cities comes from non-tertiary activities, especially manufacturing. Central place theory should not be dismissed, however, just because pleasing hexagonal forms are not apparent in the real world. Richard Morrill (1970) asserted that the usefulness of central place theory depends on the way it answers the following questions:

1. Does the spatial organization of retailing and services reflect the level and distribution of purchasing power?
2. Do central place activities tend to be regularly spaced in areas with similar physical, cultural, and economic environments?
3. Do consumers try to reduce distances travelled to purchase goods and services?
4. Do consumers shop at a hierarchy of centers for different types of goods and services?

Many studies have dealt with these questions, which apply to tertiary activities within cities and to systems of cities. The object of this section is to explore evidence in support of the basic tenets of central place theory (see box).

Evidence in Support of Central Place Theory

CENTRAL PLACES AND UNDERDEVELOPED COUNTRIES

In one Chapter we cannot hope to describe all the empirical studies within the framework of central place theory (Berry and Pred, 1961). We limit ourselves to a few examples located in North America. It should be noted, however, that the concepts Christaller used to describe the settlement hierarchy in Germany can be applied not only to marketing systems in Europe and North America but also to marketing systems in underdeveloped countries. E. A. J. Johnson's book, *The Organization of Space in Developing Countries* provides an introduction to the role of central places in underdeveloped countries. A study by D. J. Grove and L. I. Huszar (1964) is a detailed analysis of the urban systems in Ghana and government policy objectives. Several works are devoted to periodic markets in underdeveloped countries (Stine, 1962; Skinner, 1964; Good, 1972; and Scott, 1972). An AID-USDA seminar publication, *The Marketing Challenge,* indicates the importance of indigenous markets for development and nation-building.

A four-day periodic market at Po in Upper Volta. SOURCE: James Pickerell for *International Development Association.*

Trade Centers of the Upper Midwest

Population Distribution The region coincides with the Ninth Federal Reserve District, which extends some 2500 kilometers along the Canadian border from Montana in the west to the Upper Peninsula of Michigan in the east. It includes the states of Montana, North Dakota, South Dakota and Minnesota, twenty-six counties of Northwestern Wisconsin, and fifteen counties of Michigan's Upper Peninsula. We might expect to find in this rather homogeneous region the regular pattern of hexagonal market areas suggested by Christaller. But the density of farm population varies considerably throughout the Upper Midwest (Figure 6.21). Rural population concentration is greatest in eastern Minnesota, and declines towards the west and northeastern Minnesota, northern Wisconsin, and the Upper Peninsula of Michigan. Areas of sparse population are agriculturally poor areas with short or dry growing seasons. A hexagonal lattice that conforms to the distribution of farm population in the Upper Midwest is shown in Figure 6.22. The size of cells is smaller in areas of high density of population, and larger in areas of sparse settlement, but the population of each cell is constant.

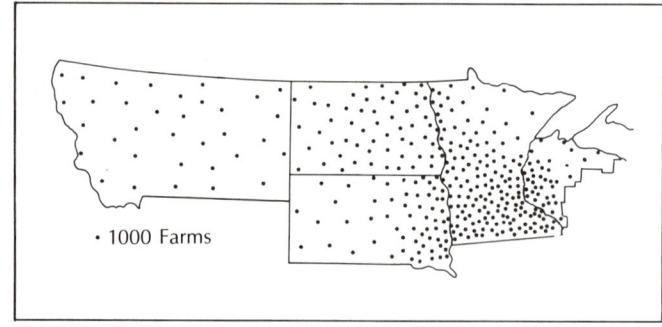

FIGURE 6.21 Distribution of farms in the Upper Midwest. SOURCE: John F. Kolars and John D. Nystuen, 1974, *Human Geography: Spatial Design in World Society*. New York: McGraw-Hill, p. 100, Fig. 5–10.

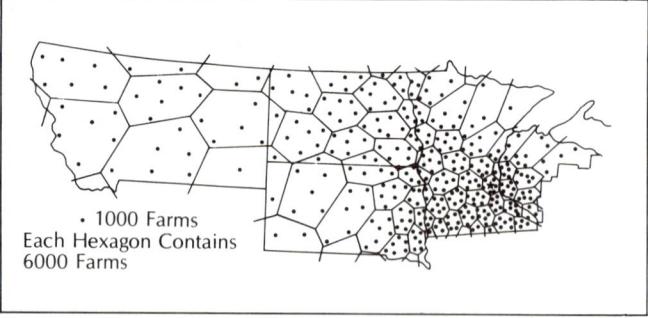

FIGURE 6.22 Hexagonal lattice conforming to the underlying rural population pattern in the Upper Midwest. SOURCE: John F. Kolars and John D. Nystuen, 1974, *Human Geography: Spatial Design in World Society*. New York: McGraw-Hill, p. 101, Fig. 5–11.

Hierarchy of Business Types John Borchert (1963) demonstrated that a hierarchy of central place functions exists in the Upper Midwest. He selected 46 functions, and determined those functions typical of various orders in the hierarchy of business types. Figure 6.23 shows these functions grouped into convenience, specialty, and wholesale categories. The diagram also shows eight types of central places. The bundle of central place goods and services characteristic of each type of trade center is as follows:

Evidence in Support of Central Place Theory

1. *Hamlets,* lowest order central places, have only gasoline service stations, and eating and drinking establishments.

2. *Minimum convenience and full convenience* centers provide everyday necessities. Minimum convenience centers have hamlet-level functions plus a bank, hardware store, drugstore, grocery, and two other convenience goods. Full convenience centers have all 10 convenience and hamlet-level functions plus stores concerned with laundry or dry-cleaning, clothing, jewelry, appliances or furniture, and up to three other functions.

3. *Partial shopping and complete shopping* centers offer specialty goods and services. Partial shopping centers have four to eight specialty functions and complete shopping centers have nine or more specialty functions plus all those business functions of lower-order places.

4. *Secondary whole-retail, primary wholesale-retail, and metropolitan wholesale-retail* centers are the highest order places. Wholesale centers have all the specialty, convenience and hamlet-level functions. Secondary wholesale-retail centers have 10–13 wholesale functions and over 50 wholesale establishments; primary wholesale-retail centers have all 14 wholesale activities and over 100 wholesale establishments; and metropolitan wholesale-retail centers have the complete range of wholesale functions and more than 500 wholesale establishments.

The frequency of trade center types in the Upper Midwest is shown in Table 6.4. As the hierarchical level increases, the number of trade centers decreases. The table also indicates a strong relationship between trade center class and population size classes.

Minneapolis-St. Paul is the largest trade center, and the only metropolitan wholesale-retail center in the region. Besides business functions listed in Figure 6.23, the Twin Cities provides other services for its massive trade area, such as

TABLE 6.4 Frequency and median size of trade center types in the Upper Midwest.

Type of Center	Number of Centers	Median Population (Thousands)
Wholesale-Retail Centers		
Metropolitan	1	1440.0
Primary	7	55.4
Secondary	10	32.2
Shopping Centers		
Complete	78	9.5
Partial	127	2.5
Convenience Centers		
Full	111	1.5
Minimum	379	0.8
Hamlets	1539	0.2

SOURCE: John R. Borchert, 1963, "The Urbanization of the Upper Midwest, 1930–1960," *Upper Midwest Economic Study,* Urban Report, No. 2, University of Minnesota, Minneapolis, Minn., p. 11, Table 2.

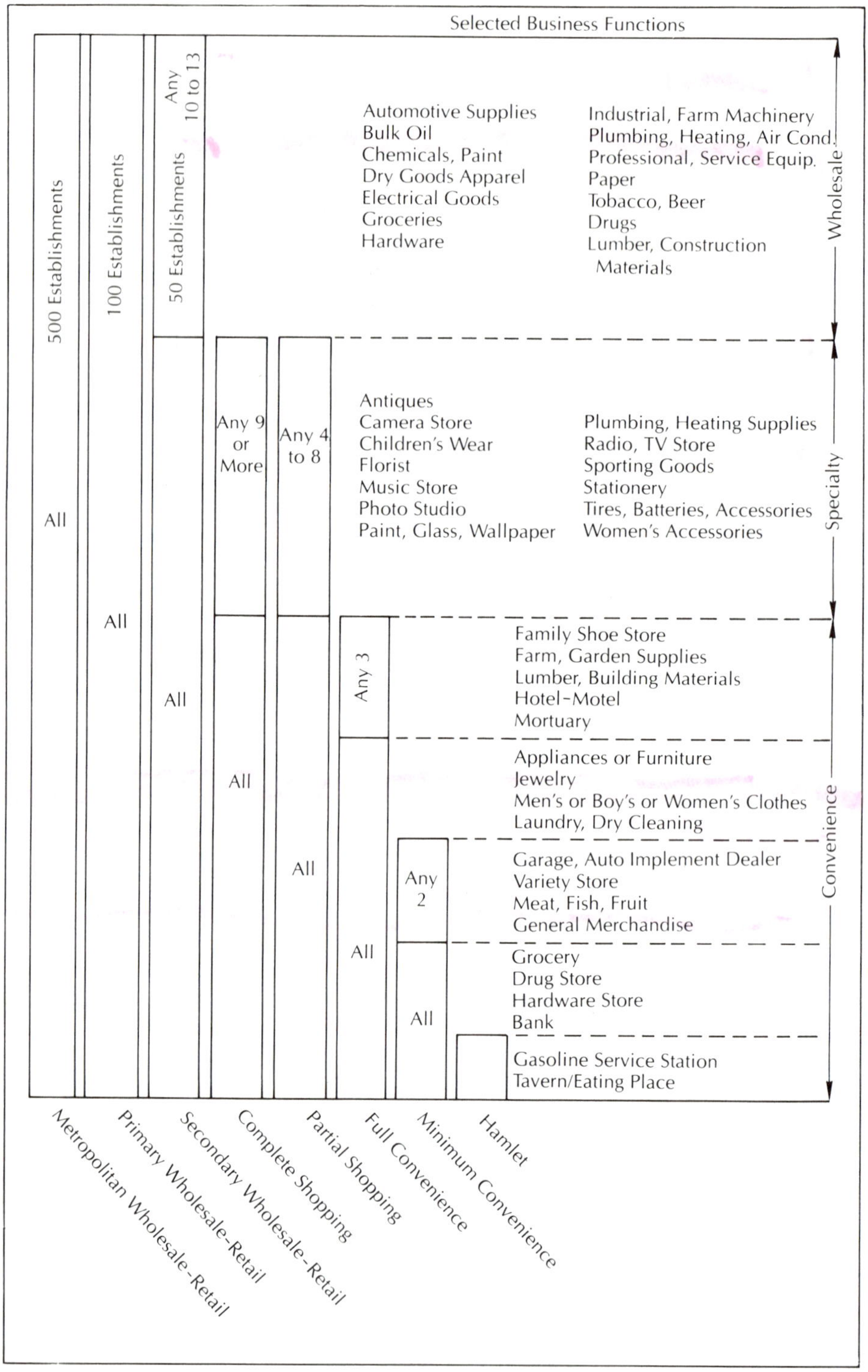

FIGURE 6.23 Trade center types in the Upper Midwest. SOURCE: John R. Borchert, 1963, "The Urbanization of the Upper Midwest 1930–1960," *Upper Midwest Economic Study,* Urban Report No. 2, University of Minnesota, Minneapolis, Minn., p. 12, Fig. 5.

Evidence in Support of Central Place Theory

Downtown Minneapolis. SOURCE: *Minneapolis Chamber of Commerce.*

regional head offices of insurance companies, specialized medical, educational, and administrative facilities. People living up to 1,600 kilometers away may never visit the Twin Cities. They obtain goods and services from lower-order trade centers. The highest level centers that many people living beyond the Twin Cities need to reach are primary and secondary wholesale-retail centers such as Eau Claire, Duluth, St. Cloud, Fargo-Moorhead and Billings. Nonetheless, the Twin Cities is the controlling center of the economy of the Upper Midwest. Trade area residents feel the influence of the metropolis through communications, banking, agricultural marketing, and retail-wholesale relationships.

Central Place Pattern The geographical distribution of trade centers in the Upper Midwest is mapped in Figure 6.24. The pattern conforms roughly to central place theory. Wholesale-retail centers are widely spaced and hamlets are the most numerous centers. Greater spacing of trade centers of all classes to the north and west is a striking feature of the map.

John Kolars and John Nystuen (1974) examined the correspondence between a five-level $K = 4$ hierarchy and the actual sequence of settlements along U.S. Highway 10 from Minneapolis-St. Paul to Spokane. They divided the highway from east to west into three parts: Humid Midwest (roughly Minneapolis-St. Paul to Fargo), Great Plains (Fargo to Billings), and Rocky Mountains (Billings to Spokane). They found that the $K = 4$ model underestimates the number of settlements along U.S. 10, especially across the Great Plains (Table 6.5).

There may well be too many trade centers in the Upper Midwest. The pattern of trade centers is a legacy of the pioneers. Most of the 2,500 cities and villages that dot the map of the Upper Midwest were established under conditions quite different from those that prevail today.

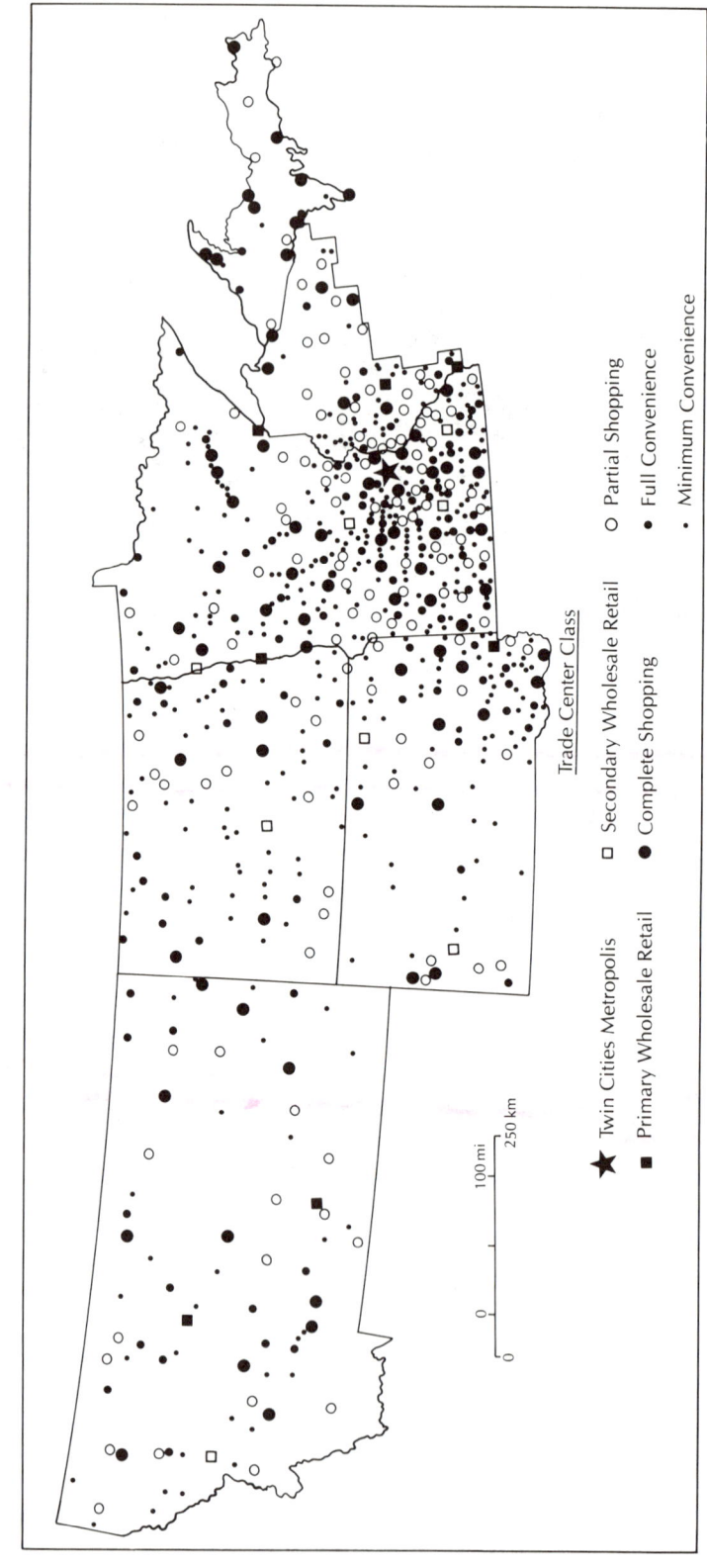

FIGURE 6.24 Distribution of trade centers in the Upper Midwest.
SOURCE: John R. Borchert, 1963, "The Urbanization of the Upper Midwest 1930–1960." *Upper Midwest Economic Study*, Urban Report No. 2, University of Minnesota, Minneapolis, Minn., pp. 13–14, Fig. 5.

Evidence in Support of Central Place Theory

Region	Expected	Recorded	% More Recorded Than Expected
Humid Midwest	8	13	162
Great Plains	9	23	255
Rocky Mountains	14	19	136

TABLE 6.5 Number of expected and observed trade centers along U.S. 10

SOURCE: John F. Kolars and John D. Nystuen, 1974, *Human Geography: Spatial Design in World Society.* New York. McGraw-Hill, p. 105, Table 5.3.

After railroads opened up the region in the late nineteenth century, immigrants established small farms, and low order central places developed to meet the needs of farm families. They were closely spaced in response to slow, difficult travel. In recent decades two changes have produced stress within the original framework of settlements: migration and transportation.

A street scene of a nineteenth century central place: Shakopee, Minnesota. SOURCE: *Minnesota Historical Society.*

Migration has had the greatest influence on the structure of trade centers. In the past half-century farm population has declined sharply as farms increased in size and farmland was abandoned. Farm population in this region declined by 300,000 between 1960 and 1970. The region experienced net out-migration between 1960 and 1970. In the Upper Midwest population progressively has shifted from farms and small trade centers into larger urban areas and from central cities into suburbs and countryside. Improvements in transportation after 1914, such as the widespread use of automobiles and paving of roads, enabled consumers to bypass smaller centers and patronize larger centers. Because of loss of farm population and changes in consumer mobility, small trade centers cannot compete with larger towns that offer a greater variety and quantity of services. Table 6.6 shows the main changes in the trade center hierarchy between 1930 and 1960: the decline or stagnation of the majority of small trade centers and the concentration of growth in a relatively small number of larger trade centers.

TABLE 6.6 Proportion of trade centers of the Upper Midwest in 1930–1960 growth rate classes

Trade Center Class	Number of Centers	Percent of Trade Centers in 1930–1960 (Growth Rate Classes)			
		Fast	Moderate	Slow	Decline
Wholesale-Retail					
Metropolitan	1	100	0	0	0
Primary	7	72	14	14	0
Secondary	10	80	10	0	10
Shopping					
Complete	79	62	26	4	8
Partial	126	54	26	9	11
Convenience					
Full	112	43	36	15	6
Minimum	379	28	30	23	19
Hamlet	1539	12	11	41	37

SOURCE: John R. Borchert, 1963, "The Urbanization of the Upper Midwest, 1930–1960," *Upper Midwest Economic Study,* Urban Report, No. 2. University of Minnesota, Minneapolis, Minn. p. 19, Table 3.

Dispersed Cities In the years to come, most of the population of the Upper Midwest will be concentrated in Minneapolis-St. Paul (metro cluster) and other low density metropoli (urban clusters). These urban clusters or dispersed cities are products of modern transportation and communication networks and are formed by linkages of complete and wholesale-retail centers (Figure 6.25). Although the metro cluster is unique in terms of population size and density, all of the urban clusters share the following important features:

1. Travel time the length of any link and any corridor is less than 60 minutes and 30 minutes respectively;
2. Each cluster contains multiple shopping and service centers, which are more complementary than competitive, serve essentially different trade areas within the cluster;
3. Each cluster contains large numbers of low-order retail and service centers;
4. Each cluster contains industrial and wholesale zones;
5. Each cluster has public higher education facilities;
6. Each cluster has public hospital facilities;
7. Each cluster has newspapers and broadcasting stations;

Evidence in Support of Central Place Theory

8. Each city within a cluster has a substantial degree of independence from all others, but there is much interdependence—travel in every direction for business, shopping, education, health care, social and recreational purposes.

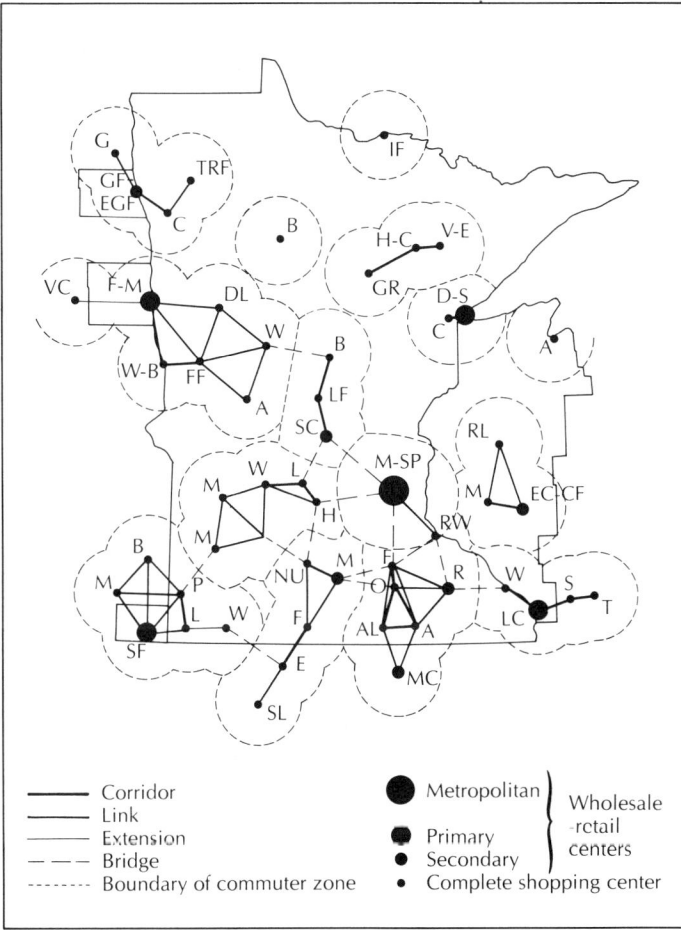

FIGURE 6.25 Dispersed cities. SOURCE: John R. Borchert and Donald D. Carroll, 1971, *Minnesota Settlement and Land Use 1985*. Center for Urban and Regional Affairs, University of Minnesota, Minneapolis, Minn., p. 14, Fig. 11.

High-Order Central Places Minneapolis-St. Paul is one of twenty-four high-order central places in the United States. John Borchert (1967) divided these important trade centers into three orders based on their size and functional complexity. The first-order center is New York City, which is the national metropolis providing the widest range of specialized activities. In addition to New York City, six second-order centers or regional metropoli exist: Boston, Philadelphia, Detroit, Chicago, San Francisco, and Los Angeles. Added to the seven second-order centers are 17 metropolitan centers to make a total of 24 high-order centers.

High-order central places and their trade areas are mapped in Figure 6.26A. The map shows great distortion in the distribution of high-order centers when they are mapped in absolute space. Most of the important centers are located in the industrial North East, and five of them are clustered along the East Coast. The spacing

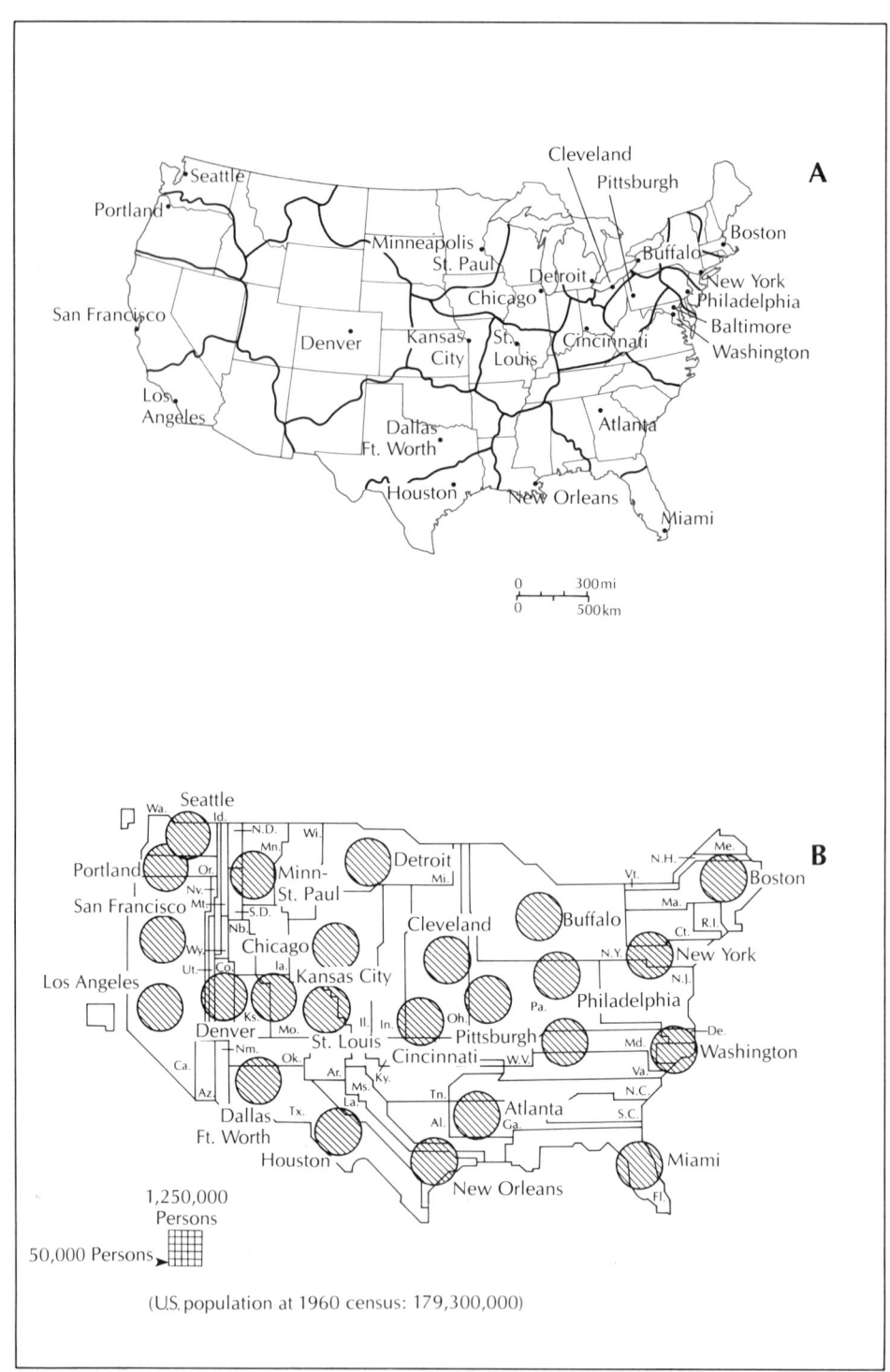

FIGURE 6.26 Higher-order trade centers and trade areas in the United States: (A) mapped in absolute space; (B) mapped in population space. SOURCE: Abler, R., J. S. Adams, and P. Gould, *Spatial Organization: The Geographer's View of the World*, © 1971, p. 377. Reprinted by permission of Prentice-Hall, Inc., Englewood Cliffs, New Jersey.

Evidence in Support of Central Place Theory

of centers fails to confirm central place expectations. However, when the cities are mapped in population space a much more regular pattern results (Figure 6.26B). The cartogram demonstrates an important point: the size and location of central places is adjusted to the distribution of people and purchasing power.

Rank-Size Rule

The hierarchical structure of trade centers is reflected not only in their functional complexity, but in their relative size. An urban size hierarchy is obtained when urban centers are ranked by population size. The most well known attempt to represent this hierarchy is the *rank-size rule,* an empirical finding popularized by G. K. Zipf (1949). In its simplest form, this rule states that if all urban settlements in an area are ranked in descending order of population size, the population of the rth city is $1/r$ the size of the largest city's population. Symbolically the rank-size rule may be expressed as:

$$P_r = \frac{P_1}{R}$$

where P_r = the population of the rth city
P_1 = the population of the largest city
R = the size rank of the rth city in the set

When plotted on double logarithmic graph paper this relationship produces a straight, downward-sloping line with a gradient of 45° (Figure 6.27). The hypothetical rank-size distribution describes an urban system containing a few large metropoli, a large number of medium size cities, and a still larger number of smaller towns.

Figure 6.28 shows the application of the rank-size rule to the United States. The size distribution conforms closely to the rank-size rule. When the rule is applied to individual cities we expect Los Angeles (the second ranking city) to have one-half of the population of the first ranking city, New York. In 1970, Los Angeles had a population of 8.35 million instead of 8.10 million as predicted by the rank size rule (Table 6.7). Chicago, the third ranking city, had a population of 6.71 million as against an expected 5.40 million, and Minneapolis-St. Paul, the twelfth ranking city, had a population of 1.70 million as against 1.35 million. Despite deviations for individual cities, the differences tend to cancel to produce a regular rank-size distribution.

Zipf argued that a rank-size distribution indicates a "balanced" system of cities. Yet there are situations where the population of the first or largest city is greater than would be expected from the rank-size distribution, and a condition of primacy exists (Figure 6.29).

Brian Berry (1961) tried to interpret city-size distributions through a comparative study of 37 countries. He found that thirteen countries had rank-size distributions, fifteen countries had primate distributions, and nine countries had intermediate distributions (Table 6.8). He suggested that there is no simple explanation for these different types of city-size distributions. Numerous forces that act randomly over a long period of time produce rank-size distributions, and a few powerful forces such as the impact of imperialism on underdeveloped countries

FIGURE 6.27 Rank-size rule: hypothetical size of the population of cities in relation to their ranking.

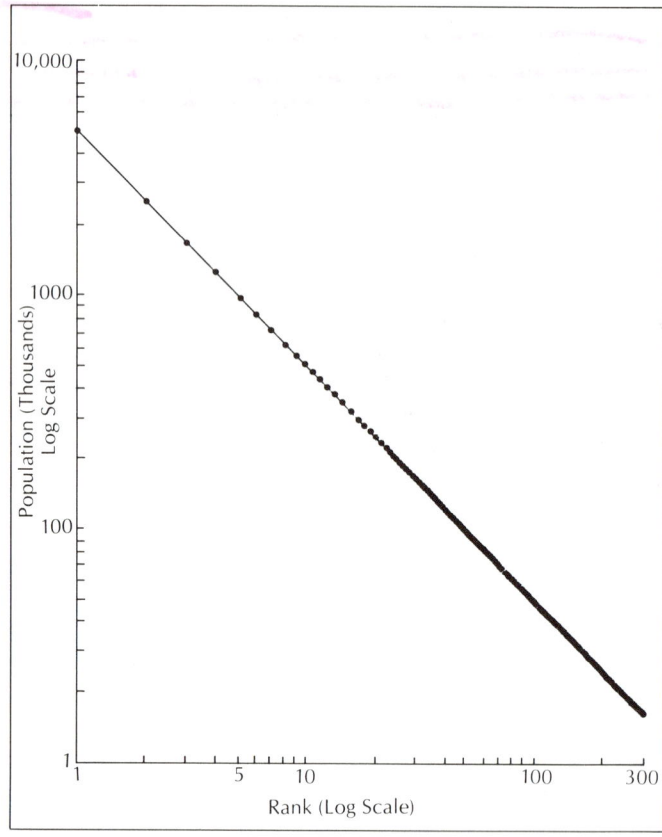

TABLE 6.7 Recorded and expected size of the top twelve urbanized areas in the United States, 1970

Urbanized Area	Recorded (Millions)	Expected (Millions)
New York–Northeastern N.J.	16.20	16.20
Los Angeles–Long Beach	8.35	8.10
Chicago–Northwestern Ind.	6.71	5.40
Philadelphia	4.02	4.05
Detroit	3.97	3.24
San Francisco–Oakland	2.98	2.36
Boston	2.65	2.31
Washington, D.C.	2.48	2.02
Cleveland	1.95	1.80
St. Louis	1.88	1.62
Pittsburgh	1.84	1.47
Minneapolis-St. Paul	1.70	1.35

SOURCE: *County and City Data Book,* 1972, U.S. Bureau of Census.

cause variations from the rank-size model. Berry concluded that as countries become politically, economically, and socially more complex, they tend to develop "normal" (straight line) rank-size distributions (Figure 6.30). His conclusion was

Evidence in Support of Central Place Theory

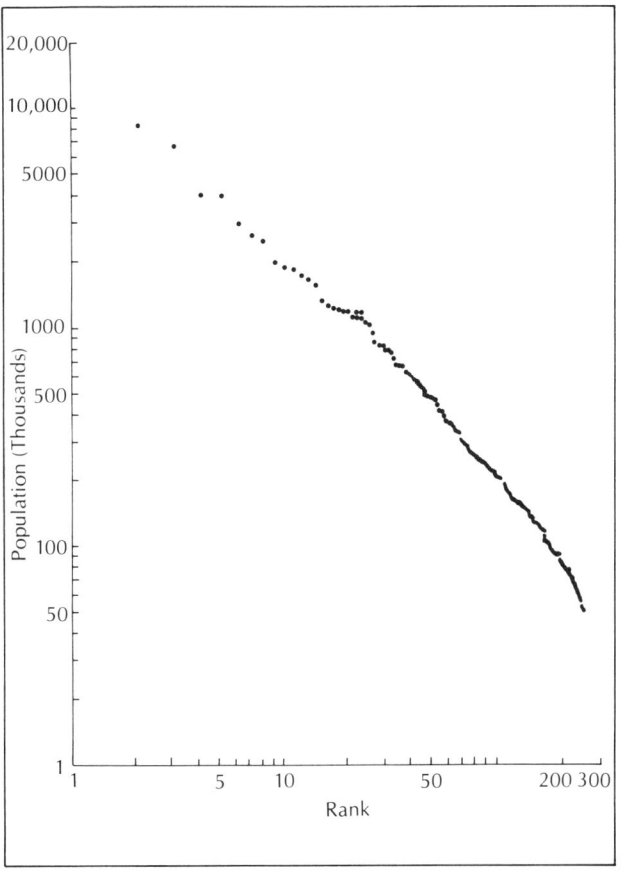

FIGURE 6.28 Rank size distribution of urbanized areas in the United States, 1970. SOURCE: *County and City Data Book,* 1972.

TABLE 6.8 City-size distributions in thirty-seven countries

Countries with Rank-Size Pattern	Countries with Primate Pattern	Countries with Intermediate Patterns
Belgium	Austria	Australia
Brazil	Ceylon	Canada
China	Denmark	Ecuador
El Salvador	Dominican Republic	England and Wales
Finland	Greece	Malaya
India	Guatemala	New Zealand
Italy	Japan	Nicaragua
Korea	Mexico	Norway
Poland	Netherlands	Pakistan
South Africa	Peru	
Switzerland	Portugal	
United States	Spain	
West Germany	Sweden	
	Thailand	
	Uruguay	

FIGURE 6.29 Primate distribution of city populations.

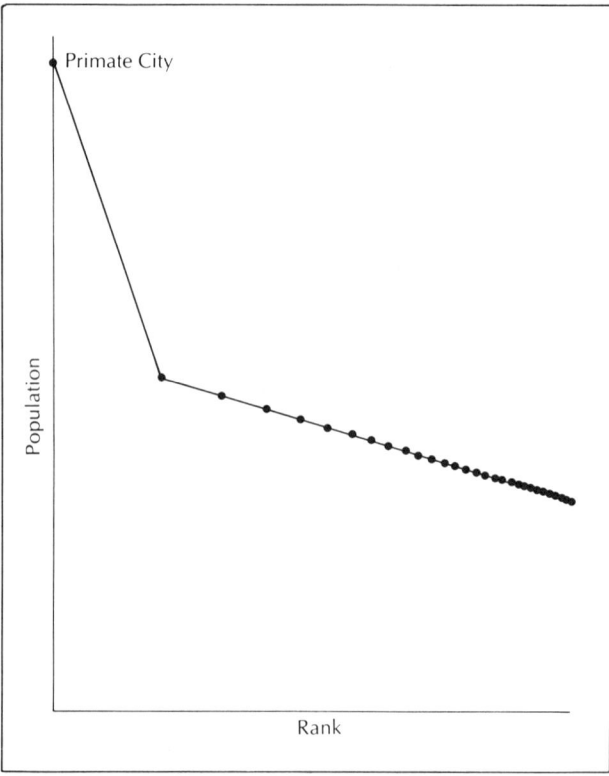

FIGURE 6.30 Idealized evolution of city size; distributions under increasing population size through three time periods.

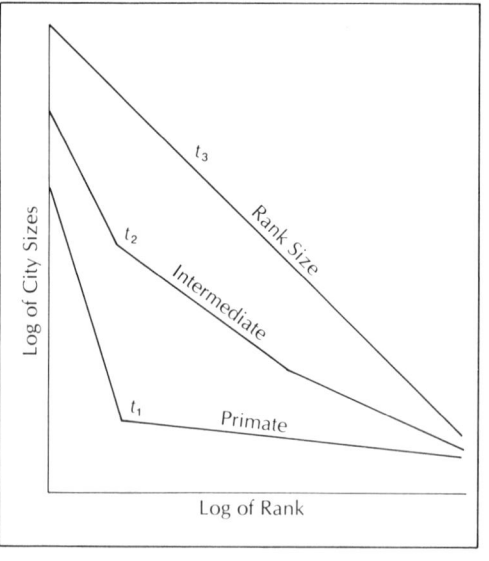

based on the work of H. A. Simon (1955), who postulated that a rank-size distribution is a limiting case for stochastic growth processes. Thus in the early phases of national development a simple primate pattern prevails, and is gradually transformed into a rank-size distribution which is the equilibrium or steady-state of an urban growth process (see box.).

Evidence in Support of Central Place Theory

RANK-SIZE DISTRIBUTION AND ECONOMIC DEVELOPMENT

Brian Berry (1961) found little relationship between rank-size distribution and economic development. Some underdeveloped countries have primate distributions. For example, Dar es Salaam, the largest city in Tanzania, has a population that is nearly five times larger than the second largest city, Tanga. Some underdeveloped countries have log-normal distributions. India, China, and Nigeria, all with a substantial history of urbanization, are examples.

The kind of primacy that is of great significance in underdeveloped countries is not necessarily of population, but of political and economic domination, and the concentration of communications and transactions. The table provides evidence of developmental primacy for Kenya.

What is the reason for developmental primacy? Growth is concentrated in the major cities because there is little incentive to decentralize urban activities. The markedly hierarchical, authoritarian nature of political and social organization prevents developmental impulses from filtering down the urban hierarchy, and diffusing its effects outwards within urban fields.

Measures of Developmental Primacy in Kenya

Variable	Nairobi (Percentage Share)
Total population	4
Urban population (over 5,000)	42
Televisions	78
Railway passengers	15
English newspapers	60
Swahili newspapers	27
Postal traffic	47
Telephone traffic	30
Telephones	55
Registered political societies	34
Manufacturing	42
African paid laborers	17
African wages	28

SOURCE: Adapted from E. W. Soja, *The Geography of Modernization in Kenya*. Syracuse, N.Y.: Syracuse University Press, 1968, p. 107, Table 24.

Rank-size refers to the stability of a whole system of cities. Individual cities in a system, however, may vary in importance over time. Between 1870 and 1950 New York City maintained its lead position, Los Angeles gained dramatically, and cities like New Haven and Savannah slipped in rank. Regular growth of the United States urban system has been accompanied by variations in the relative growth of individual cities.

To what extent is there a correspondence between central place theory and the rank-size rule? Some writers have argued they are incompatible (Vining, 1955 and Stewart, 1958). The central place hierarchy is based on the *functional size* of centers. Functional size is determined by the number and order of central functions offered by a place. Functional size is essentially tied to the role of settlement forming functions in the center's economy. The total population of a place is a function of both *settlement-forming* and *settlement-building functions*. Two centers may belong to the same level of the hierarchy (functional size) yet be somewhat different in population. The rank-size rule is based on the population of centers, not functional size. Population size produces a smooth rank-size curve; functional size produces a stepped hierarchy.

The discrepancy between the stepped and continuous curves may also be a function of scale. Rank-size distributions apply to large, fairly self-sufficient economic areas (United States, European Common Market, or the Portuguese Colonial System) and the central place model to their smaller subsystems (Upper Midwest).

Structural Elements of the Central Place Hierarchy

In this section we cite some of the empirical research that has focused on structural elements of the central place hierarchy. (see box) Our knowledge of structural elements of the central place hierarchy has been greatly extended by the work of Brian Berry (1967). His work is based on controlled field studies and the application of statistical techniques.

CENTRAL PLACE THEORY IS STRUCTURED

Central place theory is structured because all the elements of the theory are tied together in a logical and proportional way. Central place theory assumes, for example, that the population of a center is a function of the number of central functions it can support or that the size of a center's trade area is directly related to its functional size. In the text, we are interested in determining how accurately central place theory describes the actual structure of settlements as retail and service centers. To do this, we must determine whether or not empirical evidence supports the structural elements of central place theory.

Population Size and Functional Units Figure 6.31 shows the relationship between population and *functional units* in southwest Iowa (see box). Most centers fall very close to the regression line. Two centers, however, have larger populations than expected given the number of functional units in each. We can give a logical explanation for these two anomalies. Each town has relatively large settlement-building functions. Glenwood is the site of a state mental institution and Red Oak has a manufacturing plant. When the population of each town which is supported by these non-central functions is subtracted from their total populations, the number of people supported by settlement-forming functions can be estimated. These estimates fit the regression equation in Figure 6.30.

Evidence in Support of Central Place Theory

CENTRAL FUNCTIONS, ESTABLISHMENTS, AND FUNCTIONAL UNITS

A central function is a good or service offered by a central place. If a settlement has a gasoline station, then the addition of a second gasoline station will not increase the number of central functions in the center. The crossroads hamlet in the diagram has two general stores each of which is also a gas station. One store is a post office and the other sells liquor. The number of central functions is four: general store, gas, post office, liquor. Each central function, once offered, is counted only once, but two other measures of retail and service activity commonly are used in central place theory: establishment and functional unit. The term *establishment* refers to ownership and control. In our example, there are two establishments. The term *functional unit* refers to each separate time a central function is offered. The cross-roads hamlet has six functional units.

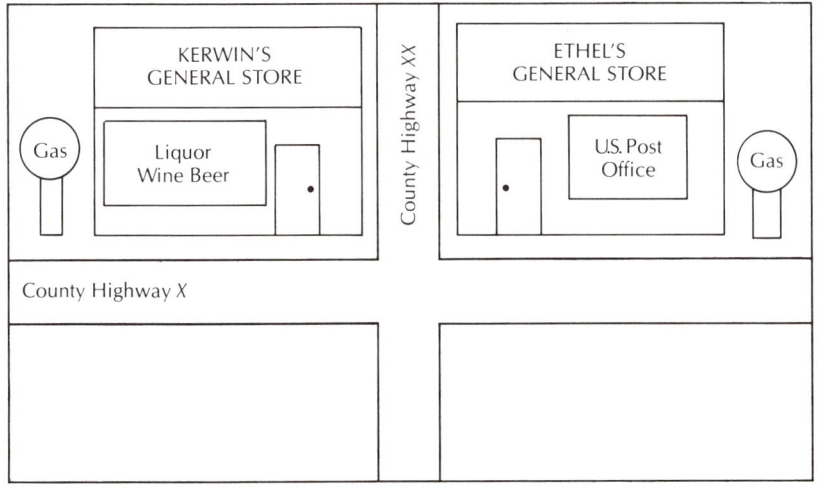

Population Size and Central Functions Several studies have shown a curvilinear or log-linear relationship between the population size and the number of *central functions* performed by centers (Figure 6.32). This relationship indicates that the population of a central place is a function of the total number of business types offered. Again there are deviations from the expected relationship. Some settlements have more central functions that expected (X-centers in Figure 6.32); they may be tourist centers like Reno or Las Vegas whose excess central functions are supported by transient populations. Other settlements (O-centers in Figure 6.32) fall above the best-fit line; they have larger populations than expected. This usually indicates the presence of settlement-building functions and is also typical of suburbs which may have large populations, but small functional sizes because of shopping opportunities in metropolitan areas.

Establishments and Population Size Increases in the number of *establishments* are proportional to increases in center sizes (Figure 6.33). By contrast the population/central function and the population/functional unit relationships are not

FIGURE 6.31 Relationship between population and functional units (southwest Iowa). SOURCE: Brian J. L. Berry and Harold M. Mayer, 1962, *Comparative Studies of Central Place Systems.* Final Report NONR 2121-18 and NR 389-126, Geography Branch, U.S. Office of Naval Research.

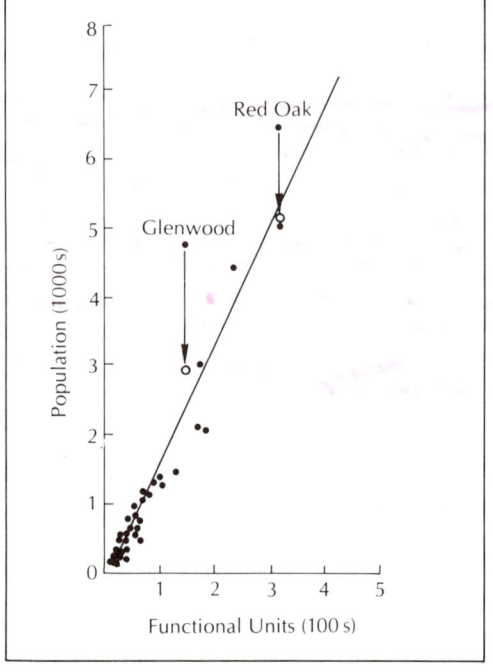

FIGURE 6.32 Anomalies and the relationship between central functions and population.

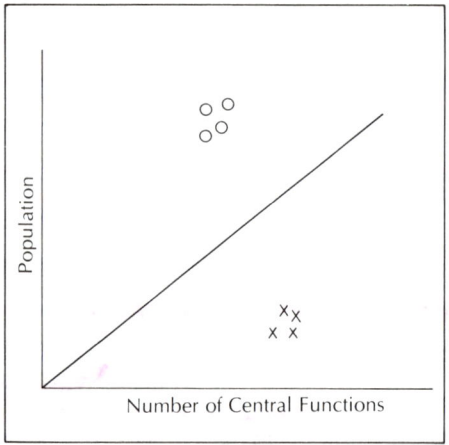

proportional and this observation raises the question of how centers meet increases in demand brought about by population changes. Existing establishments may expand; new establishments of the same functional type may be added; or some combination of the two may be used. The actual strategy adopted depends upon a number of factors, but empirical evidence indicates that increasing the number of establishments tends to happen more frequently. This is especially true of lower order functions and centers.

Trade Area Size and Population Density The size of a center's *trade area* determines the total population dominated by the center. The trade area must be

Evidence in Support of Central Place Theory

Reno, Nevada, has more central functions than predicted by the population size–central functions relationship.

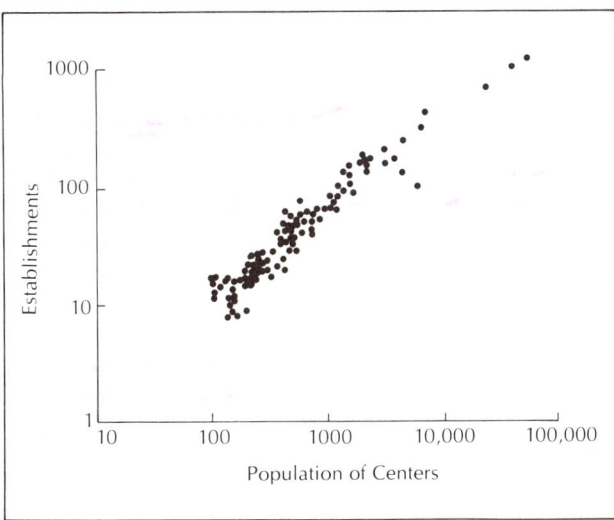

FIGURE 6.33 Relationship between establishments and population size.

large enough to meet the threshold of the highest order good offered by the center. Trade area size must be adjusted to meet changes in population density. Data collected by Brian Berry (1962) indicate a strong tendency toward adjustment to variations in population density (Figure 6.34). The 45° line in the figure indicates constant population density. Each level of center is arrayed along a line with a slope greater than 45°. Thus variations in trade area size are greater than variations in total population influenced by central places, suggesting density adjustment.

FIGURE 6.34 Density adjustment (southwest Iowa). SOURCE: Brian J. L. Berry and Harold M. Mayer, 1962, *Comparative Studies of Central Place Systems*. Final Report NONR 2121-18 and NR 389-126, Geography Branch, U.S. Office of Naval Research.

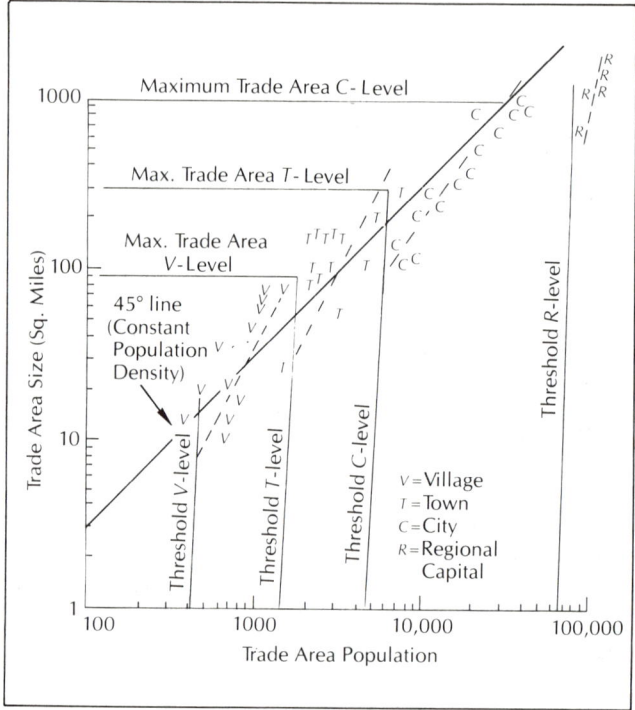

The central place hierarchy is sensitive to local variations in population density, but even more to regional variations. Figure 6.35 illustrates the relation of trade area sizes to total population serviced by central places in five contrasting regions in the United States. These regions range from sparsely settled areas influenced by "rural" central places (Iowa and North Dakota) to urban Chicago which has a population larger than most states. This population is serviced by a hierarchy of shopping centers ranging from corner grocery stores to the downtown shopping district. The forces controlling the structure and pattern of urban shopping centers are the same as those inherent in the "rural" central place hierarchy. Differences are merely those of scale and population density (Figure 6.34). In low density areas (corn belt in Figure 6.34), centers must service large areas to capture threshold populations, whereas in densely populated areas centers can meet threshold conditions with much smaller market areas.

Berry (1967) noted that different levels of the hierarchy in each of the rural areas and the levels of business centers within cities are so consistent that straight lines may be drawn linking the upper limits of each level (Figure 6.36). Notice, however, that the lines separating each level are not vertical, indicating that

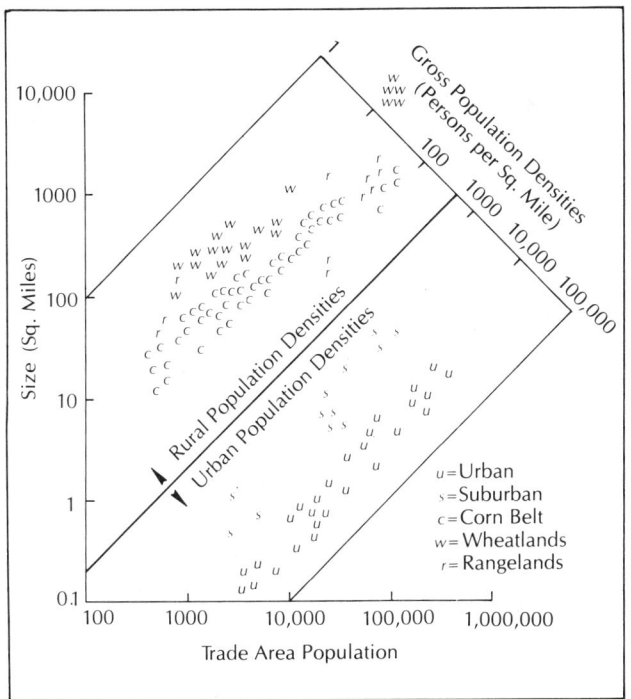

FIGURE 6.35 Density adjustment: large regional variations in population density. SOURCE: Brian J. L. Berry and Harold M. Mayer, 1962, *Comparative Studies of Central Place Systems*, Final Report NONR 2121-18 and NR 389-126, Geography Branch, U.S. Office of Naval Research.

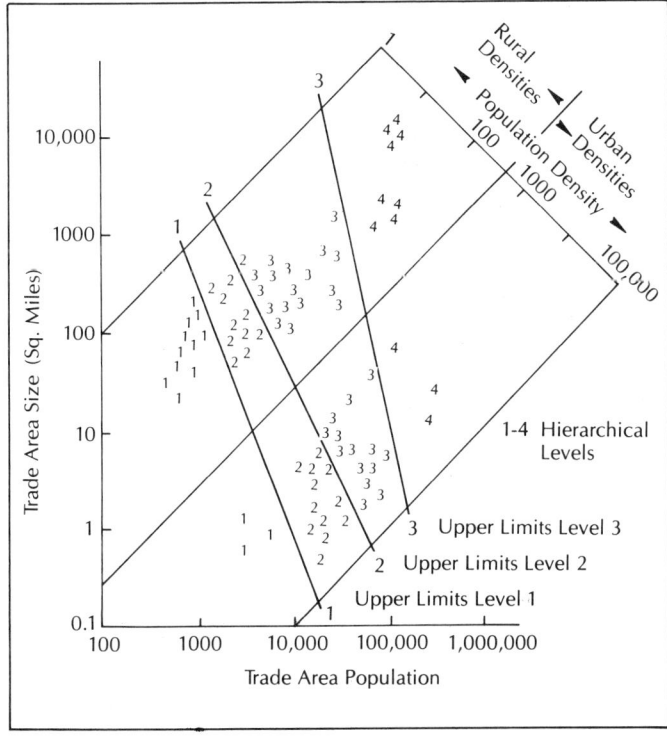

FIGURE 6.36 Hierarchical limits of settlements. SOURCE: Brian J. L. Berry and Harold M. Mayer, 1962, *Comparative Studies of Central Place Systems*, Final Report NONR 2121-18 and NR 389-126, Geography Branch, U.S. Office of Naval Research.

The population of a large city is serviced by a hierarchy of retail outlets: (A) corner "Ma and Pa" store; (B) supermarket (SOURCE: *Super Valu Stores, Inc.*); (C) neighborhood shopping center; (D) regional shopping center (SOURCE: *Dayton Hudson Properties*); and (E) downtown shopping street.

Evidence in Support of Central Place Theory

the adjustment to variations in density is not perfect. Figure 6.36 shows that level-1 centers in high density areas service larger populations than level-1 centers in low density areas. Some goods whose thresholds are met in level-1 centers in high density areas may not be offered until level-2 is reached in low density areas.

Spacing of Urban Centers Leslie King (1962) analyzed the distribution of urban places in a comparative study of twenty sample areas in the United States to determine the regularity in the spacing of urban centers. He applied the technique of *nearest-neighbor analysis* to measure the difference between actual and expected settlement arrangements. The nearest-neighbor index of spacing is obtained by comparing the observed pattern with a theoretical random distribution; that is,

$$R = \frac{D_{obs}}{D_{exp}}$$

where

R = the nearest-neighbor index of spacing;

D_{obs} = average observed distances between each urban center and its nearest-neighbor;

D_{exp} = expected average difference between each urban center and its nearest-neighbor

The expected average distance is given by:

$$D_{exp} = \frac{1}{2\sqrt{A}}$$

where

A = density of urban centers

The nearest-neighbor index of spacing ranges from a theoretical low of zero when the settlement pattern is clustered to a maximum value of 2.15 when the pattern is uniform. A value of 1.0 is obtained when the distribution is random.

King's results ranged from 0.70 in the case of the Utah sample area to 1.38 in Missouri. Most of the sample areas had R-values between 0.5 and 1.5. King concluded that the United States settlement pattern is not uniform, but random. Deviations from a uniform pattern are the result of environmental, economic, cultural, and historical factors.

Several researchers have claimed that a characteristic distance separates centers which function predominantly as central places. August Lösch (1954), for example, found a close correspondence in Iowa, a state with a relatively uniform environment, between observed and theoretical distances in a $K = 4$ system (Table 6.9). John Brush (1953) examined the spacing of hamlets, villages, and towns in an area of southwestern Wisconsin and noted a negligible difference between actual and theoretical settlement spacing. By contrast, Michael Dacey (1962), who selected the same areas studied by Brush, conducted a nearest-neighbor analysis, concluding the overall settlement pattern was more random than regular. We cannot, however, expect the distribution of central places to be regularly arranged in absolute space. Figure 6.25B revealed, for example, that regularities anticipated by

TABLE 6.9 Regional systems in Iowa: theory and reality correspondence with theoretical system for $K = 4$

Size Class of Regions	Centers			
	Number		Distance Apart (Miles)	
	Theory	Reality	Theory	Reality
1	615		5.6	
2	154	153	11.2	10.3
3	39	39	22.4	23.6
4	10	9	44.8	49.6
5	2–3	3	89.6	94.0
6	0–1		179.2	

SOURCE: August Lösch, 1939, *The Economics of Location*. Stuttgart: Gustav Fischer Verlag. The values actually obtained for class 1 were the starting point for the calculation of all theoretical values.

central place theory are more apparent when we use a transformation of distance based on population density.

Donald Bogue (1949) provided an empirical confirmation of the tendency of population to agglomerate around metropolitan centers by population density gradients from the center of 67 United States cities. Generalized cross-sections showed:

1. that population density declines with distance from the metropolis;
2. that density and the rate of decline vary with the size of the metropolitan community;
3. that density and the rate of decline vary with the region of the United States (Figure 6.37A);
4. that density and the rate of decline vary with the direction from the metropolis (Figure 6.37B).

Bogue recognized three types of sectors: a route sector which has a major highway leading from the city to other major metropolitan areas; a secondary sector which has at least one city of 25,000 or more people; and a local sector which has neither major highway nor major urban center. Density trends for the three sectors (Figure 6.37B) indicate that densities are greatest in the secondary sector. Densities along route sectors are lower than might be expected from Lösch's model of city-rich and city-poor sectors. Nonetheless, Bogue's empirical study does support Lösch's hypothesis concerning the arrangement of urban centers around the metropolis.

Consumer Travel as a Mirror of the Hierarchy

Thus far we have concentrated on the functional structure and arrangement of central places. A central place system can only result from consistent aggregate consumer behavior. Christaller's theory of central places postulates that consumers

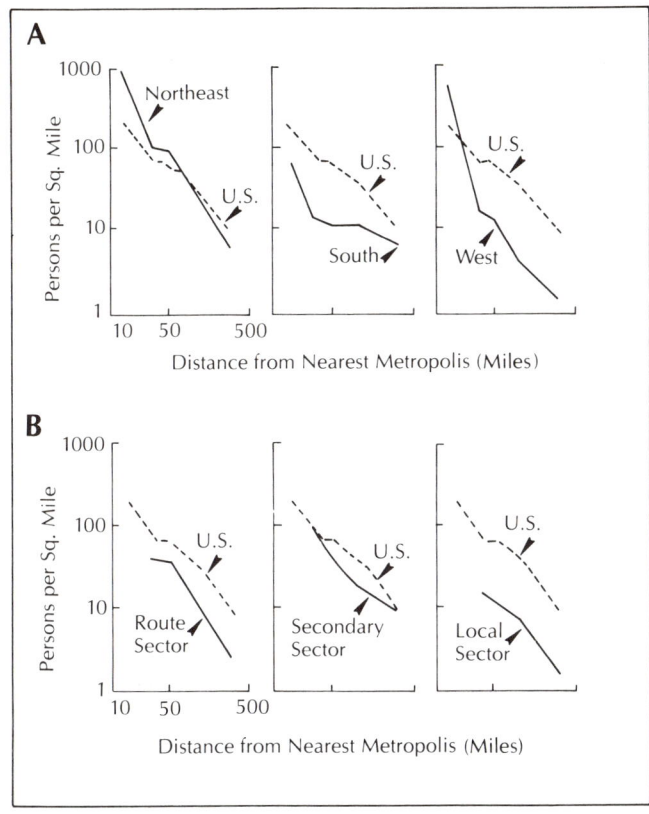

FIGURE 6.37 Intercity density-distance relationships by region (A) and by sector (B) in the United States. SOURCE: Donald Joseph Bogue, *The Structure of the Metropolitan Community: A Study of Dominance and Subdominance* (1950). New York: Russell & Russell, 1971.

behave predictably. They obtain goods and services from the nearest possible center. We will examine a few examples of low and high order goods to see whether theory matches reality.

Figures 6.38–6.41 show the primary purchase movements of both rural and urban consumers for four different goods in southwestern Iowa in the early 1960s (see box). Clothing is the highest level good (city-level) followed by furniture and dry cleaning (town-level). Groceries are the lowest level function (village-level). Consumers must consider the order of a good because it limits the number of possible purchase points. Within the framework of where goods are actually offered, however, consumers have some options about where the function is purchased. The distinction is primarily made between *convenience* and *shopping goods*. Consumers will generally travel to the closest possible place for convenience goods, but will often travel to higher-level centers for shopping goods even if they can be obtained locally.

Clothing is a city-level shopping good (Figure 6.38). Consumers generally go to the closest place which offers clothing, forming a clear trade boundary between Atlantic and Red Oak in both rural and urban preference maps. Note that Omaha-Council Bluffs, a regional level center, attracts consumers over much greater distances than do the two city-level centers. The few purchases made in Griswold, Oakland, and Elliot consist of work clothing, a lower-order good than general clothing.

FIGURE 6.38 Purchase movements of urban (A) and rural (B) consumers for clothing in southwestern Iowa, 1960. SOURCE: Brian J. L. Berry and Harold M. Mayer, 1962, *Comparative Studies of Central Place Systems,* Final Report NONR 2121-18 and NR 389-126, Geography Branch, U.S. Office Of Naval Research.

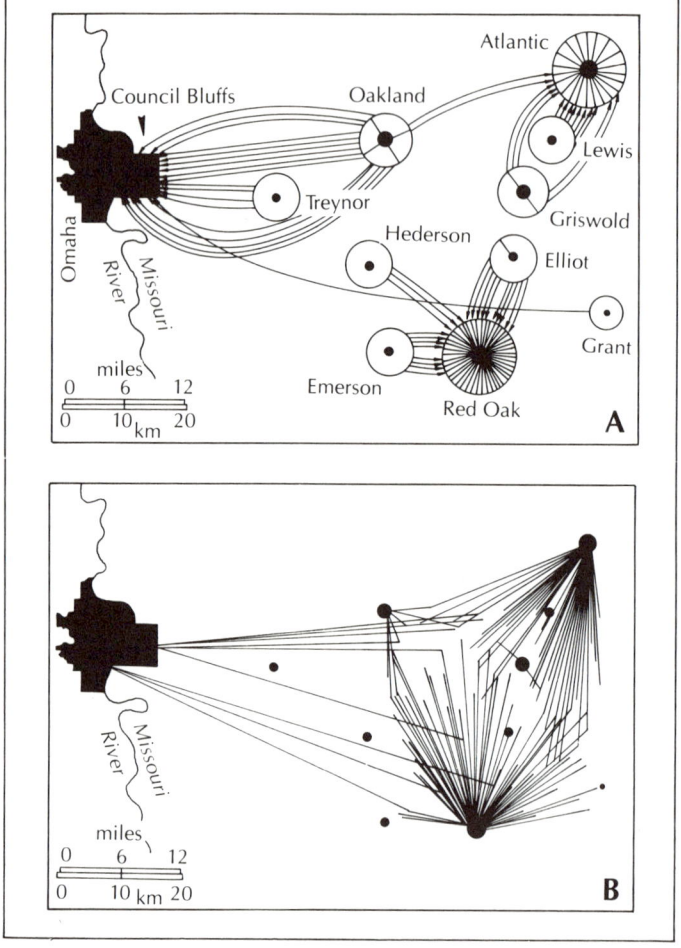

Furniture is a town-level shopping good (Figure 6.39). The most important feature of the figure is the emergence of Griswold as a central place. Once again, however, consumers are willing to travel much greater distances to Omaha-Council Bluffs to shop for furniture than to the lower order centers where selection is limited and prices may be higher.

Dry cleaning is also a town-level good, but it is a convenience good (Figure 6.40). Since one dry cleaner is much like any other, consumers go to the closest possible central place. Oakland is a good example. For furniture, many residents interviewed in Oakland traveled to Omaha-Council Bluffs, but all dry cleaning was done locally. This is also true of the rural residents of each center's hinterland. Note, however, that higher order centers like Red Oak and Atlantic are able to attract consumers over greater distances than lower-level Griswold. Consumers probably combine their dry-cleaning trips with other types of shopping travel.

Groceries are village-level convenience goods (Figure 6.41). Urban residents make almost all grocery purchases locally. Rural residents make a distinc-

Evidence in Support of Central Place Theory

> **SHOPPING PREFERENCES**
>
> Figures 6.38–6.41 show the shopping preferences of both rural and urban consumers for selected central functions. In each figure a line is drawn from the residence of a rural consumer to the central place where the good in question is purchased *most frequently*. A circle is drawn around each place in the maps for urban consumers. If the individual purchases the good most frequently in his own settlement, a ray is drawn from the circle to the settlement; if purchases are made more frequently in another town, an arrow is drawn from the residence settlement circle to the preferred central place circle.
>
>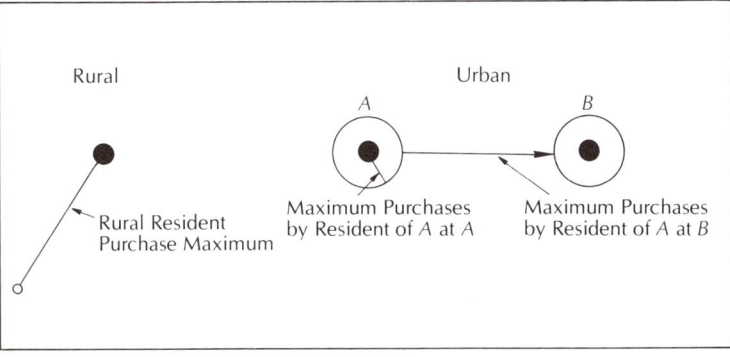

tion among the orders of centers, but once again are making multi-purpose shopping trips.

The maps of travel patterns in southwestern Iowa do not replicate the geometric precision of the central place model because the normative constraints are not met. Nonetheless, the central place model does help us to understand and

> **CONVENIENCE GOODS AND SHOPPING GOODS**
>
> Convenience goods are low in price, uniform in quality and style, and purchased frequently. They are often termed "short-run necessities" and include the goods and services we need on a day-to-day basis such as groceries, gasoline, and drugstore items.
>
> Shopping goods tend to be higher in price, vary considerably in quality and style, and are purchased infrequently. They are goods for which we "comparison shop." Furniture is an excellent example. We buy furniture infrequently and it is also an item for which we may visit several stores to compare prices, styles, and quality. Because furniture is a shopping good, consumers are more likely to visit a center where comparison shopping is possible (higher order center). The cost of a long-distance shopping trip as a proportion of total cost is much lower on a high priced good, and consumers are usually willing to pay this cost to obtain the satisfaction and utility of greater selection.

FIGURE 6.39 Purchase movements of urban (A) and rural (B) consumers for furniture in southwestern Iowa, 1960. SOURCE: Brian J. L. Berry and Harold M. Mayer, 1962, *Comparative Studies of Central Place Systems,* Final Report NONR 2121-18 and NR 389-126, Geography Branch, U.S. Office of Naval Research.

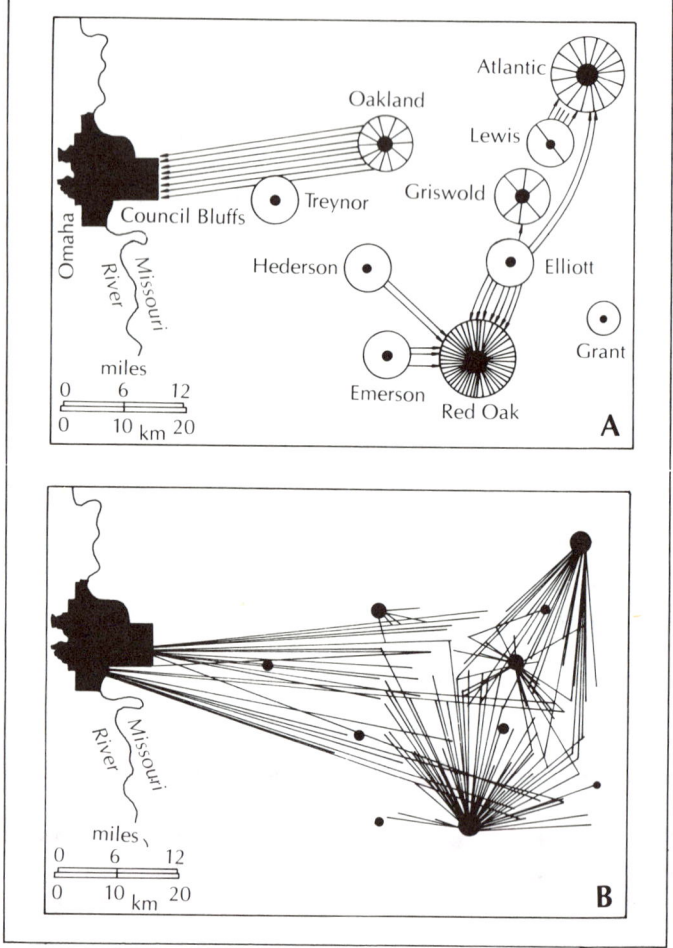

predict spatial patterns of consumer behavior. Although human beings are not economic optimizers, they do, to a limited extent, adhere to the principle of distance minimization. We can only understand the maps of consumer behavior in southwestern Iowa within the context of central place theory; the accuracy of our understanding is amplified by the model. That is the great utility of any model.

Summary

In this Chapter we outlined the assumptions, content, limitations, and extensions of classical central place theory, ending with examples of central place hierarchies in the United States. We observed that actual conditions distort and transform theoretical networks of central places.

We saw that central place theory stems from classical economic theory. It relies on three concepts to explain the spatial equilibrium of central places:

Summary

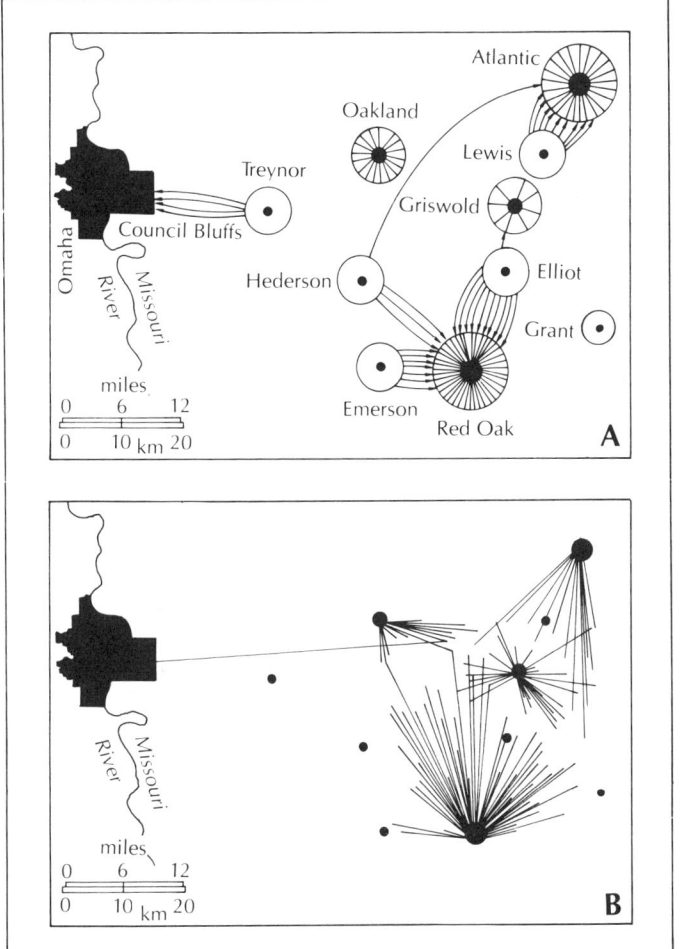

FIGURE 6.40 Purchase movements of urban (A) and rural (B) consumers for dry cleaning in southwestern Iowa, 1960. SOURCE: Brian J. L. Berry and Harold M. Mayer, 1962, *Comparative Studies of Central Place Systems,* Final Report NONR 2121-18 and NR 389-126, Geography Branch, U. S. Office of Naval Research.

threshold, range, and hierarchy. Central place activities are arranged into a hierarchy according to the functions they perform. High order places, the metropolitan wholesaling cities, weld regions of a national market exchange economy together. Within each metropolitan trade region a chain of lower-order centers—smaller cities, towns, villages, and hamlets—function as markets for the distribution of goods and services.

The theory of central places is not a dynamic theory. It does not explain the forces that underlie the growth and change of centers at specific locations. However, concepts of central place theory have been used for planning purposes. Many underdeveloped countries, for example, have primate city distributions. Western regional science usually recommends that planners streamline urban systems. They are advised to develop a "balanced" hierarchy of urban centers that link central cities with interstitial areas (see box). Central place notions have been used to design new market centers in the polders of the Netherlands and new settlements in Israel. They have been used to find new locations for educational and medical facilities, and for shopping centers. Since retailing and many other service activities

FIGURE 6.41 Purchase movements of urban (A) and rural (B) consumers for foodstuffs in southwestern Iowa, 1960. SOURCE: Brian J. L. Berry and Harold M. Mayer, 1962, *Comparative Studies of Central Place Systems,* Final Report NONR 2121-18 and NR 389-126, Geography Branch, U.S. Office of Naval Research.

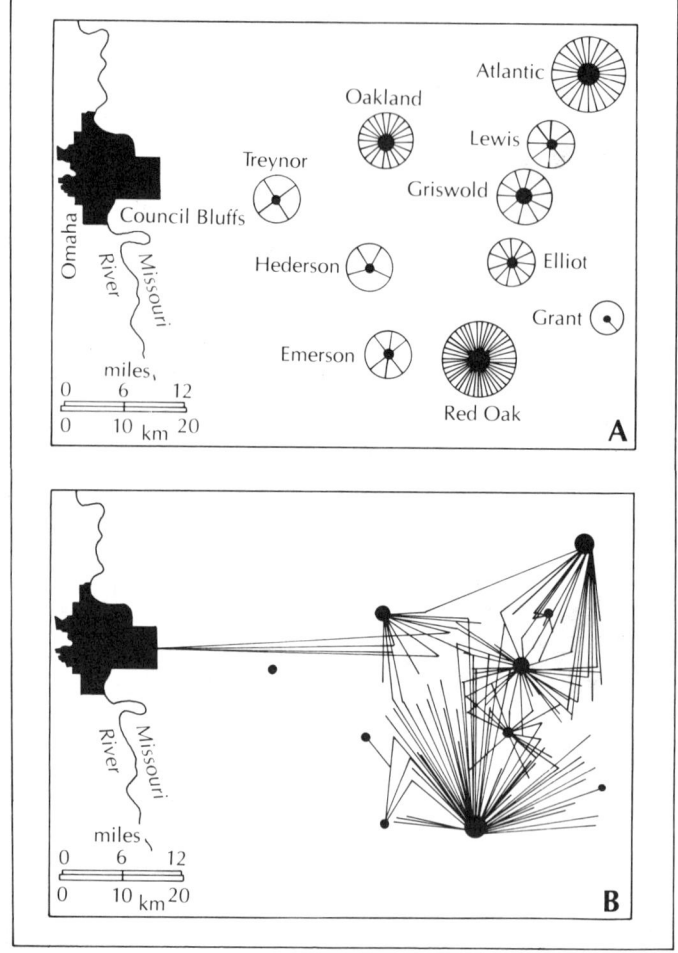

are highly sensitive to demand potential, planners in market societies select sites in areas of greatest unfilled demand. These sites are likely to be in high-income areas rather than low-income areas.

As a final point, the application of central place theory as well as other theories of spatial organization to planning is a great worry to some geographers. David Harvey (1972) feared that our theories of spatial organization may well be tools for the frustration of social change. E. Ralph (1976) is disturbed that much physical and social planning is divorced from places as we know them and experience them in our everyday lives. He argued that we reduce places to points or areas with their most important quality being (profitable) development potential. "This entire attitude is expressed by Richard Morrill (1970:p. 20): 'If there is an underlying attitude in human geography it is that man and society try to organize space efficiently, to locate activities and to use land in the "best way"; it is but a short jump from this to the idea that a major aim of planning is to overcome spatial incongruities and inefficiencies'" (Ralph, 1977: 87–88). This impersonal approach to both people

> **STREAMLINING CENTRAL PLACE SYSTEMS IN UNDERDEVELOPED COUNTRIES**
>
> Those who study central place systems in underdeveloped countries may be divided into three main groups: conservatives, liberals, and radicals. Conservatives, who may be described as classical economists and geographers, argue that no intervention is required in the process of spatial organization. Unarticulated central place systems are natural in the early stages of economic development, and corrected by natural processes with the achievement of development. By contrast, liberals feel that urbanization in underdeveloped countries has somehow gone wrong, and have devised corrective measures. In the interests of economic growth, they agree on the need to produce a balanced system of cities, but quarrel over specific policies.
>
> Radicals point out that central place systems in underdeveloped countries form part of a world network of cities. According to Gunder Frank (1969; 1970) central places in underdeveloped countries are centers of colonial domination. In the service of international capitalism, they subject regional and national hinterlands to economic "satellitization" and exploitation. Certain forms of international influence and manipulation condition the structure of capitalist-colonialist urban systems. For radicals, revolutionary institutional reform must precede regional planning.

and place is the basis for draining wetlands for the construction of new regional shopping centers, and for displacing single family residences by high rise offices. The places and people "affected are really quite incidental so long as the specific goal is achieved with a satisfactory level of efficiency. The narrowness of such an approach, the emphasis on the abstract, economic, public interest, rather than on individual or community life and values, is profoundly inauthentic" (Ralph, 1976:89). *We argue here that our theories of spatial organization, which do have relevance in national and regional development planning, must be applied with sensitivity if we are interested in bringing about humanizing social and economic change.*

DISCUSSION QUESTIONS

1. The ideal region is both the only way to learn about the essential, and the first step towards investigating the actual structure of any real economic region. Discuss this statement with reference to central place theory.
2. Discuss the relationship of a city to its hinterland.
3. Discuss: Cities are centers of dominance.
4. Briefly describe the differences between $K = 3$, $K = 4$, and $K = 7$ hierarchies.
5. Define the following: *threshold, range,* and *hierarchy.*

6. Do consumers shop at a hierarchy of centers for different types of goods and services? You may wish to answer this question for yourself by making a list of the establishments you patronize for convenience and shopping goods.
7. Compare and contrast central place models of Christaller, Lösch, and Isard.
8. Central place theory assumes that demand and supply are in equilibrium. Does a state of equilibrium exist within the retail sector of contemporary American cities?
9. Write a short essay on the mercantile model of settlement.
10. To what extent is there a correspondence between central place theory and the rank-size rule?

SUGGESTED READINGS

Location of Cities

Harris, C. D. and E. L. Ullman, "The Nature of Cities," *Annals of the American Academy of Political and Social science,* **242** (1945):7–17.

Hinterland Delimitation

Park, R. E., "Urbanization as Measured by Newspaper Circulation," *The American Journal of Sociology,* **35** (1929):60–79.

Ullman, E. L., *Mobile: Industrial Seaport and Trade Center.* Chicago: University of Chicago Press, 1943.

Central Place Theory

Berry, B. J. L., *Geography of Market Centers and Retail Distribution.* Englewood Cliffs, N.J.: Prentice-Hall, 1967.

Christaller, W., *Die Zentralen Orte in Suddentschland.* Jera: Gustav Fischer Verlag, 1933. Trans. C. W. Baskin, *Central Places in Southern Germany.* Englewood Cliffs, N.J.: Prentice-Hall, 1966.

Getis, A., and J. Getis, "Christaller's Central Place Theory," *Journal of Geography,* **65** (1966): 220–226.

Isard, W., *Location and Space Economy.* Cambridge, Mass.: The MIT Press, 1956.

Lösch, A., *The Economics of Location.* Trans. W. H. Woglom. New Haven: Yale University Press, 1954. Originally published by Gustav Fischer Verlag.

Valavanis, S., "Lösch on Location: A Review Article," *American Economic Review,* **45** (1955):637–644.

Vance, J. E., Jr., *The Merchant's World: The Geography of Wholesaling.* Englewood Cliffs. N.J.: Prentice-Hall, 1970.

Suggested Readings

Rank-Size Rule

Berry, B. J. L., "City Size Distributions and Economic Development," *Economic Development and Cultural Change,* **9** (1961):573–588.

Beckmann, M. J., "City Hierarchies and the Distribution of City Size," *Economic Development and Cultural Change,* **6** (1958):243–248.

Madden, C. H., "Some Indicators of Stability in the Growth of Cities in the United States," *Economic Development and Cultural Change,* **4** (1956):236–252.

Vining, R., "A Description of Certain Spatial Aspects of an Economic System," *Economic Development and Cultural Change,* **3** (1955):147–195.

Zipf, G. K., *Human Behavior and the Principle of Least Effort.* Reading, Mass.: Addison-Wesley, 1949.

Case Studies

Berry, B. J. L., H. G. Barnum, and R. J. Tennant, "Retail Location and Consumer Behavior," *Papers and Proceedings of the Regional Science Association,* **9** (1962):65–106.

Berry, B. J. L., *Geography of Market Centers and Retail Distribution.* Englewood Cliffs, N.J.: Prentice-Hall, 1967.

Borchert, J. R., *The Urbanization of the Upper Midwest: 1930–1960.* Upper Midwest Economic Study. Urban Report No. 2, Minneapolis, University of Minnesota, 1963.

Johnson, E. A. J., *The Organization of Space in Developing Countries.* Cambridge, Mass.: Harvard University Press, 1970.

Murdie, R. A., "Cultural Differences in Consumer Travel," *Economic Geography,* **41** (1965):211–233.

Ray, D. M., "Cultural Differences in Consumer Travel Behavior in Eastern Ontario," *Canadian Geographer,* **11** (1967):143–156.

Skinner, G. W., "Marketing and Social Structure in Rural China," *Journal of Asian Studies,* (1964):22–26.

Manufacturing

KEY TERMS

- agglomeration economies
- assembly costs
- basic cost
- conglomerate
- critical isodapane
- distribution costs
- economies of scale
- horizontal integration
- imperfectly divisible multiples
- isodapane
- isotim
- labor productivity
- locational costs
- locational inertia
- localized raw material
- market linkage
- massing of reserves
- material index
- orientation
- potential surface
- production linkage
- pure raw material
- service linkage
- space-cost curve
- spatial margins to profitability
- spatial monopoly
- spatial oligopoly
- technique
- technostructure
- transport cost surface
- ubiquitous raw material
- urbanization economies
- value added by manufacturing
- Varignon frame
- vertical integration
- weight-losing raw material

7

There have been two major "revolutions" in economic history. The first of these was the discovery of agriculture in prehistory, and the other was the *Industrial Revolution* which began in England in the late eighteenth century. The *Industrial Revolution* is the term applied to the aggregate of profound changes, which during the last 200 years, made industry, and later, service occupations, a more important source of employment than agriculture in developed countries. Like the domestication of plants and animals, the Industrial Revolution was not a sudden event. But compared with the centuries that had gone before, the social and economic changes of the eighteenth and nineteenth centuries were violent and revolutionary.

The Industrial Revolution brought about an unprecedented increase in productivity (labor output or efficiency). A series of inventions represented the mechanical basis for this increase. Some of the most significant inventions were in the development of textile machines such as the spinning jenny (1770) and the power loom (1787), the steam engine (1769), the steam locomotive (1825), and the hot blast furnace (1829). These and other innovations revolutionized the nature of production and employment. They led to the use of new materials (steel); the harnessing of inanimate energy sources (water power and fossil fuels); the mass production of goods in large factories with extreme division and specialization of labor; and the use of new forms of transportation which reduced the cost of assembling raw materials and distributing finished products.

The main cause for a "veritable outburst of inventive activity" in the late eighteenth and early nineteenth centuries was a rapidly increasing foreign demand for British manufactures, which was the outcome of the age of discovery and exploration. But without an economy with a well-developed market and one in which the traditional anti-capitalist market bias in attitudes had weakened, the Industrial Revolution would not have been possible. Profit-seeking was the motive that accounted for the extensive use of machines. The individualistic world view of classical capitalism created the atmosphere that fostered the growth of the factory system, and vaulted the capitalist class into a position of economic and political dominance.

From England the Industrial Revolution spread to Western Europe and North America. The early twentieth century witnessed the industrialization of the Soviet Union and Japan. Today the Industrial Revolution has diffused in some

Objectives

measure to almost every country in the world. In most Third World countries, however, machines and factories are restricted primarily to a few large urban centers.

One very important result of the diffusion of industrial capitalism was the creation of a world economy. Swept along by an immense growth of economic power, industrial nations drew nearly the whole world into a single system of dominant and dominated countries. This integrated system meant that international commerce was complementary. Its chief characteristic was the exchange of manufactured goods of developed countries for the foodstuffs and primary goods from the underdeveloped countries. We will discuss the impact of Western industrialism on the structure of underdeveloped countries in Chapters 10, 11, and 12.

Another feature of large-scale industry of great interest to economic geographers is the tendency for some types of manufacturing to scatter and for others to concentrate at a few locations. The pattern reflects spatial variations in the cost of production factors and markets and the ways in which different industries combine factors of production. In addition to these economic forces, manufacturing patterns are influenced by environmental, cultural and political considerations. In this chapter, however, we concentrate on the *spatial consequences* which influence locational patterns of manufacturing in market exchange societies.

This chapter introduces industrial location theory, illustrated by case studies. Many geographers and economists use industrial location theory to interpret spatial patterns of manufacturing. The principles of industrial location theory also have relevance in national and regional planning. We must remember, however, that industrial location theory derives from classical economics and shares its conservative ideology. Industrial location theory takes "*as given* the nature of economic organization (essentially that of capitalism, of both the nineteenth century and monopoly varieties), but ignores the historical context—and, therefore, the essential dynamic—of that form of organization" (Massey, 1973:33). Moreover, most industrial location theory, like other location theories we have considered (Chapters 4, 5, and 6) deals mainly with abstract space, and usually considers only one quality of space—distance—as locationally significant. As radicals remind us, the "space of industrial location is the product of a complex historical process. It is also a political and institutional space" (Massey, 1973:33).

OBJECTIVES

By the end of this chapter you should be able:

1. To discuss in detail the primary location factors developed by Alfred Weber.
2. To graph the Weberian solution to various location problems given in the text.
3. To discuss the important modifications of Weber's model.
4. To define *technique* and discuss briefly its effect on industrial location.

5. To list and discuss the factors that contribute to economies of scale and discuss the effects of scale on industrial location.
6. To discuss briefly the implications of demand on patterns of manufacturing.
7. To draw and discuss the "Ice Cream Vendor" analogy and to describe the concept of locational interdependence.
8. To list the important location factors for primary copper, steel, textile, soft drink, and ready mixed concrete manufacturing.
9. To discuss some of the factors important in the development of industrial regions.
10. To list some of the social problems which occur as the result of locational shifts of manufacturing.
11. To cite some of the criticisms of industrial location theory.

Spatial Forces Influencing Manufacturing

Phases of Manufacturing

Manufacturing involves three distinct phases: the collection of raw materials together at a point; the reworking and combining of raw materials to produce a finished product; and the distribution of the finished product. These three phases are identified as *assembly, production, and distribution*. Some industries assemble only a few raw materials whereas others collect hundreds of separate components to produce a finished product (for example, the auto industry).

The production of maple syrup is an excellent example of the manufacturing process. The raw material (sap) is collected from trees which are scattered over an area. The sap is brought together at a single point and boiled down into the syrup. The finished product must then be distributed to the market.

Classical location theory attempts to discover locations which minimize the transportation costs of raw material gathering and finished product distribution. Changing the form of a raw material involves all factors of production (land, labor, capital, and management skills) which vary widely in cost from point to point. All three steps of the manufacturing process, therefore, have a spatial or locational dimension.

Changing the form of a raw material increases its utility or value. Flour milled from wheat is more valuable than raw grain. This increase in labor power is termed *value added* by manufacturing. Bread, in turn, is worth more than flour. Value added may be quite low in an industry engaged in the initial processing of a raw material, but a few ounces of steel and glass changed into a watch yields a high value added (Table 7.1). The cost of labor or the availability of skills plays an important role in high value-added manufacturing; the cost of raw materials is the key variable in others. The relative importance of factors is called *orientation*. Terms such as "raw

Spatial Forces Influencing Manufacturing

TABLE 7.1 Value added by manufacturing as a percentage of total value of shipments

Industry	Percent
Food	30
Textiles	41
Apparel	48
Lumber and Wood Products	43
Furniture	53
Paper Products	46
Printing and Publishing	67
Chemical Products	56
Petroleum Products	20
Leather Products	50
Stone, Clay, and Glass Products	58
Primary Metal Products	39
Fabricated Metal Products	52
Nonelectrical Machinery	57
Electrical Machinery	57
Instruments	67

SOURCE: *1972 Census of Manufactures*

material-oriented" or "market-oriented" are used throughout this chapter to specify the key variable for a given industry. These have different geographical consequences in the patterns of industrial locations and concentrations.

Uneven Distribution of Raw Materials

One of the key constraints of Thünen's model of agricultural production is the assumption of evenly distributed resources. Points of manufacturing (cities) would develop even if all resources were ubiquitous. Manufacturing would operate at selected points and incur only two kinds of cost: production costs which involve the interrelationships among the other factors of production (labor, capital, and technical skills) and demand; and the cost of distributing the finished product to dispersed markets.

One of the most obvious features of reality, however, is that resources are *unevenly* distributed across space. This is especially true of the raw materials required for heavy manufacturing. Even those industries which use "producer's goods" as their raw material (see box) face an uneven distribution of material inputs.

> **PRODUCER'S GOODS**
>
> "Raw materials" are created by manufacturing rather than coming directly from the resource base. A firm which assembles electronic calculators may purchase all of its "raw materials" (integrated circuits, plastic, light-emitting diodes) from other manufacturers. Such a firm inputs only producer's goods.

Profit-seeking capitalists are therefore usually concerned with a third kind of cost: *assembly costs* or the price which must be paid to bring raw materials together from diverse locations to a single production point. Assembly costs are the main concern of classical industrial location theory.

ALFRED WEBER

Alfred Weber (1868–1958) was a German economist who taught at the University of Prague from 1904 to 1907 and at the University of Heidelberg from 1907 to 1933. His *Theory of the Location of Industries* was published in 1909 and has become the traditional treatise on many aspects of industrial location in a free enterprise economy. Subsequent conservative and liberal theories of industrial location have been modifications or extensions of Weber's general theory.

The Simple Weberian Model: Assembly Costs

Classical location theory is founded on the work of Alfred Weber (see box). Weber attempted to determine the patterns of manufacturing that would develop in a world of numerous, small, competitive capitalist enterprises given a certain set of normative constraints. Weber began by assuming that transportation costs are a linear function of distance. This simplification of transportation costs is a common criticism of Weberian analysis, but we shall preserve this assumption throughout this chapter. Transportation costs as they exist under capitalism and their effects on the Weberian system will be considered in Chapter 8. Weber required that producers, who face neither risk nor uncertainty, choose optimal locations. He also implied that the demand for a product is infinite at a given price. Producers can sell as many units as they produce at a fixed price. They can sell none at a higher price, and charging a lower price will not affect the total demand for a product. A producer's strategy is therefore to produce the product at the lowest possible cost, thus maximizing revenue. For this reason, Weber's system is called a "least-cost approach."

Weber's theory is also a "general theory" in that it can be applied to all types of industries. He was concerned with identifying "those forces which operate as economic causes of location" represented in each case by savings in cost as a result of producing in one place rather than some other (Weber, 1929:17–18.) These forces are called *location factors* (see box). Weber also distinguished between "general" factors which apply to all industries (transport costs, labor, and rent) and "special" forces which operate only on a specific industry. General and special factors are further subdivided into "regional" and "local" forces. Regional forces determine the general locational framework of manufacturing and include transportation and labor costs. Regional forces are, according to Weber, the result of spatial variations in raw material and labor costs. Local forces, on the other hand, cause the pattern of manufacturing to deviate from the optimum patterns produced by regional

LOCATION FACTOR

A location factor is any of the forces that influence industrial location. Many critical elements affect industrial location; some of the most important are summarized here.

Raw Materials Many raw materials are bulky. Instead of moving them over long distances, initial processing usually occurs near their source. In medieval Europe, for example, iron smelting was done as near as possible to the iron ore. Ore, which is heavy in relation to its value, would not bear cost of transport very far.

Power Large scale industry uses large amounts of energy, but, as a determinant of location, this element has declined in importance. Before the growth of steam-powered railway networks in Europe-North America, heavy industries became rooted to coalfield sites, and "black-country" industrial regions developed around Birmingham in England, Lille in France, the Ruhr in Germany, and Pittsburgh in the United States. Today transport improvements (pipelines, ocean-going tankers, high-tension power lines) have reduced the locational pull of power supplies for most industries. One exception is the aluminum industry, which requires the use of large amounts of electricity to convert bauxite into aluminum.

Market In the twentieth century, the market has increased in importance as a factor in industrial location. The market influences industrial location in three ways. First, some industries, to maximize profits, must locate at the market. This is especially true for newspaper and job printing, bakery goods, and the manufacture of bottles, containers, and cans. Second, many industries are attracted to large metropolitan areas. London and New York have the largest concentration of manufacturing plants in England and the United States, respectively. Third, firms that sell components to other firms tend to locate near their markets.

Labor Sometimes labor availability and costs affect industrial location. Labor-centered industries that produce high value goods may locate in regions where workers possess particular skills. Other industries may locate in an area to take advantage of cheap labor. The garment industry developed in New York in the nineteenth century to exploit low cost immigrant labor. Today, American multinational corporations have branch plants in areas of low labor cost such as Singapore, South Korea, Hong Kong and Taiwan.

Political Influences Government policies often affect industrial location. In Western Europe and North America, government assistance programs attempt to encourage industrial development in depressed industrial regions (coalmining areas of South Wales or Appalachia) and in underdeveloped regions (south Italy, northern Scotland). The political factor in industrial location is especially pronounced in socialist countries (Soviet Union, East Germany, China) and in many Third World countries.

> **Industrial Inertia** The phenomenon of industrial inertia refers to the tendency of industry to persist in outdated locations. Successful industry creates within a region conditions of capital and labor that tend toward stability. Even if the original industry declines in an area, similar or other industries often establish themselves to take advantage of underutilized capital and labor that the declining one leaves. The historical legacy of industrialization is a strong factor in industrial location.
>
> **Transport** Industrial location depends to a large degree on how to overcome the distance separating elements of the production process. Transport, therefore, is the all-important "general" location factor. Without improved means of communication, industries could not produce for export from their own districts. On the other hand, transport developments tend to weaken some of the factors conducive to localization.

forces alone and tend to be "economic" in origin, such as economies of scale and the high rent brought about by competition.

Transportation sets the general regional pattern of manufacturing. This pattern is in turn distorted by spatial variations in the cost of labor. The final solution considers the effects of local factors. Weber's approach is to consider each set of forces in sequence, increasing the complexity of analysis.

Weber's Raw Material Classes

Weber began with transportation costs. The first cost faced by manufacturers is the cost of assembling raw materials. Weber approached this problem by devising a simple classification system for raw materials. First, they are classified by their frequency-of-occurrence: *ubiquitous* raw materials are universally distributed and therefore always have a transportation cost of zero; *localized* raw materials are found only at specific locations. Transportation costs on localized raw materials are a function of the distance they must be moved. Second, Weber classified raw materials on the basis of the amount of weight lost during processing: *pure* raw materials lose no weight in processing. A 150-pound transmission entering an auto-assembly plant as a raw material adds 150 pounds of weight to the finished automobile; *gross* raw materials lose weight during processing. Weber dealt with weight loss through a *material index* which measures the ratio of raw material to finished product weight. The index is the weight of the raw material divided by its processed (finished) weight. Pure raw materials have a material index of one. Weight-losing raw materials have a material index of greater than one. Fuels have the highest material index because none of their weight enters the weight of the finished product.

Let us now consider the effects of transportation costs for a number of different kinds of raw materials. For each case we examine: the cost of assembling raw materials *(RM)*; the cost of distributing the finished product *(FP)*; and total transportation costs *(TTC)*. The optimum location in the Weberian system occurs where total transportation costs are minimized. All the cases with their final solutions are given in Table 7.2.

The Simple Weberian Model: Assembly Costs

Reserve Mining taconite plant, Silver Bay, Minnesota. The manufacture of taconite is an example of a weight-losing activity. In northern Minnesota, low grade iron ore, known as taconite, is beneficiated and pelletized near the mines and then shipped via the Great Lakes to iron and steel plants. SOURCE: *Reserve Mining Company.*

TABLE 7.2 Solutions to Weber's locational problems

Material Classes	Location
Ubiquities Only	Market
Localized and Pure	
One Pure	Anywhere Between Source of Raw Material and Market
One Pure and Ubiquities	Market
More Than One Pure	Market
More Than One Pure and Ubiquities	Market
Localized and Weight-Losing (Gross)	
One Weight-Losing	Source
One Weight-Losing and Ubiquities	Source or Market Depending on Relative Size of Input
More Than One Weight-Losing	Indeterminate (Mathematical Solution)
More Than One Weight-Losing and Ubiquities	Indeterminate (Mathematical Solution)

Ubiquities Only

Only *localized* raw materials attract production. Ubiquities merely add to the pull of the market. In all cases, we assume the existence of a single market point. Ubiquitous raw materials occur everywhere so the cost of their assembly is always zero. Only finished products costs are important and they are reduced to zero with a location at the market point. This is illustrated by Figure 7.1. Raw material costs *(RM)* are the line O–O'. Finished product distribution costs rise steadily away from the market. The cost line *FP* also marks total transportation costs which are minimized at the market.

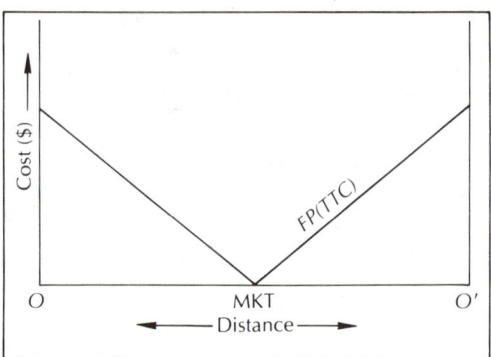

Figure 7.1 Weber's model: ubiquities only.

Localized, pure raw materials Figure 7.2 illustrates costs, given one pure localized raw material and a single market. The material is localized at *RM* and the market is at *M*. The line *RM* gives the assembly costs which increase as a function of distance from the source of the localized raw material. Similarly, the line *FP* gives the distribution costs for the finished product. Total transportation costs *(TTC)* is the sum of *RM* and *FP*. At *RM*, *TTC* = $7 (*RM* = $0, *FP* = $7, *TTC* = $7). At *O*, *RM* = $3.50, *FP* = $3.50, so that *TTC* = $7. Total transportation costs are exactly $7 everywhere along a straight line between mine and market, so that manufacturing can locate anywhere along this line and minimize costs.

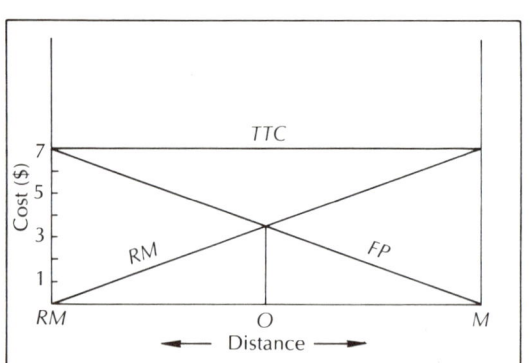

FIGURE 7.2 Weber's model: one pure, localized raw material.

One pure raw material plus ubiquities This case is graphed in Figure 7.3. The assembly costs for the localized raw material *(RM)* are minimized at *RM*. Ubiquitous assembly costs are zero everywhere and finished product distribution

The Simple Weberian Model: Assembly Costs

costs are minimized at M. Ubiquitous raw materials, once processed, add to the weight of the finished product so that total transportation costs (TTC) are minimized at the market (M). In other words, this location avoids the necessity of moving the ubiquitous material in its processed form. The optimum location is at M.

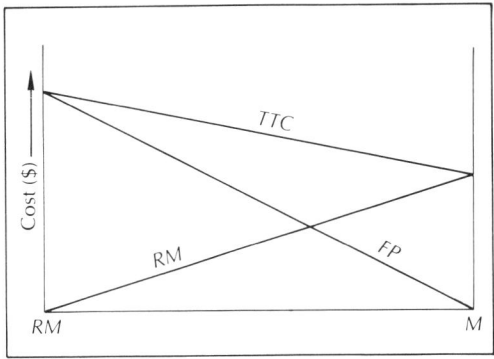

FIGURE 7.3 Weber's model: one pure, localized raw material plus ubiquities.

Several pure, localized raw materials Figure 7.4 shows the solution for two pure, localized raw materials, but the outcome is the same for more than two. Once again, the single market is at M; one pure raw material is localized at RM_1, and the other is localized at RM_2. The transportation cost for each raw material is given by the lines RM_1 and RM_2. It is assumed in Figure 7.4 that equal amounts of each raw material are used and that transport costs are $1 per ton-kilometer. Consider a location at RM_1; $RM_1 = \$0$, $RM_2 = \$6$ (one ton moved six kilometers), and a finished product which weighs *two* tons (both raw materials are pure). It costs $6 to ship the finished product back to M (two tons shipped three kilometers @ $1 per ton-km = $6) so that total transportation costs (TTC) at RM_1 equal $12. The same total transportation costs are also true of a location at RM_2. At M, however, total transportation costs equal $6 (one ton of RM_1 moved three kilometers + one ton of RM_2 moved

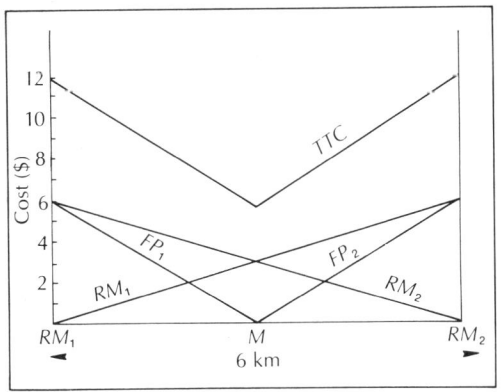

FIGURE 7.4 Weber's model: two pure, localized raw materials.

three kilometers @ $1 per ton-kilometer = $6). Total transportation costs are minimized at the market. Such a location eliminates the need to "back-haul" a raw material.

Several pure, localized raw materials plus ubiquities This case is illustrated in Figure 7.5. Remember that ubiquities always add to the pull of the market. In Figure 7.5 we assume that equal parts of RM_1, RM_2, and the ubiquitous raw material are used so that the finished product weighs three tons (assuming an input of one ton each of the raw materials). Finished product distribution costs at RM_1 and RM_2 are now $9. Localized raw material costs (RM_2) equal $6 and finished product distribution costs (FP_2) equal $9 (three tons moved three km) and total transportation costs equal $15 at RM_1 or RM_2 while they equal only $6 at M. The pull of the market is considerably strengthened by the addition of ubiquitous raw materials.

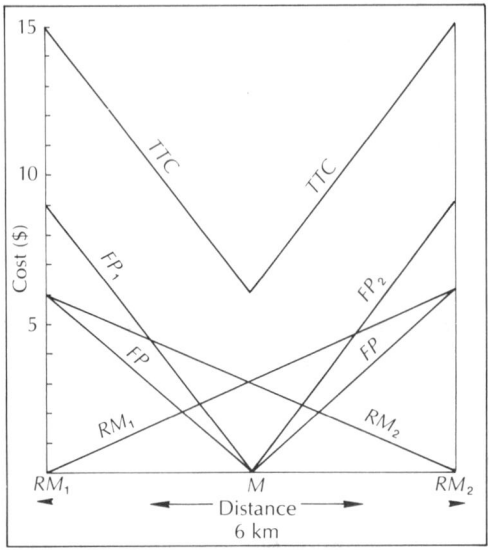

FIGURE 7.5 Weber's model: several pure, localized raw materials plus ubiquities.

Weight-Losing Raw Materials

Weight-losing raw materials have a material index greater than 1. We now consider several cases involving localized raw materials which lose weight in processing.

One localized, weight-losing raw material Figure 7.6 illustrates this particular situation. Assume that the raw material (located at RM) loses one-half its weight in processing ($MI = 2$). Each unit of the raw material shipped to the market (M) costs $10 (line RM), but each unit of the finished product shipped from the mine

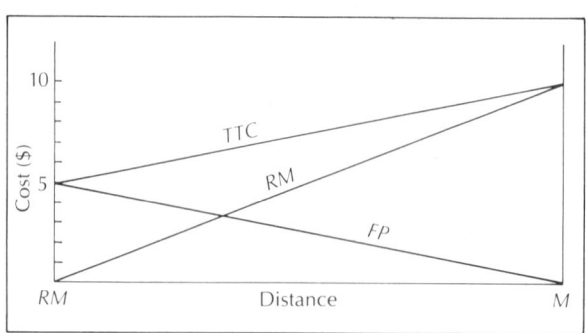

FIGURE 7.6 Weber's model: one localized, weight-losing raw material.

The Simple Weberian Model: Assembly Costs

costs only $5. Total transportation costs *(TTC)* are minimized at the raw material source.

One localized, weight-losing raw material plus ubiquities The solution to this case depends upon the ratio of weight lost through processing to the weight of the ubiquitous material. Two extreme cases are illustrated in Figure 7.7A and 7.7B. In Figure 7.7A, the weight-losing raw material is a fuel and all of its weight is lost in the manufacturing process. Assume that one ton of fuel (localized at *RM*) and 1000 kilograms of the ubiquitous raw material are required to produce 1000 kilograms of the finished product. Total transportation costs are minimized at the source. Figure 7.7B illustrates a weight-losing raw material with a material index of 2 (one-half its weight is lost in processing), but let us assume that the ratio of ubiquitous raw material to localized raw material (after processing) is 3:1. Two tons of the localized raw material plus three tons of the ubiquitous raw material are processed into a finished product weighing four tons. At *RM*, total transportation costs are $4 (weight of the finished product), but at *M*, total transportation costs are $2 (weight of the localized raw material required for one unit of the finished product). Total transportation costs are minimized at the market *(M)*. This last ratio typifies commercial brewing. Barley and hops are the localized raw materials and they lose weight in processing, but the major ingredient by weight (water) is ubiquitous. Brewers tend to be market rather than raw material oriented.

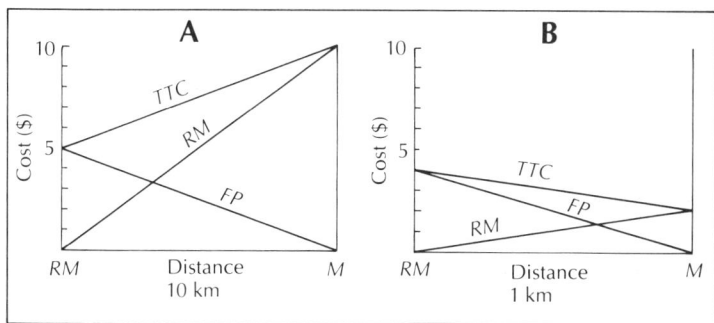

FIGURE 7.7 Weber's model: one localized, weight-losing raw material plus ubiquities (A) optimum location at raw material source; (B) optimum location at market.

Several localized, weight-losing raw materials The solution becomes more complex when several weight-losing raw materials are considered. Several mathematical solutions are possible, but a simple mechanical analogue known as the "Varignon frame" simplifies the problem. The localized raw material sites are pinpointed on a map mounted on a board (Figure 7.8). Holes have been drilled in the board at each site. A pulley (to reduce friction) is located at each hole. Each raw material is simulated by a weight proportional to the total weight of the raw material required to produce one unit of the finished product. Cords are run from the weights through the pulleys (raw material sites) and tied together into a single knot. When the weights are released, the final location of the knot will be the optimum location.

FIGURE 7.8 The Varignon frame.

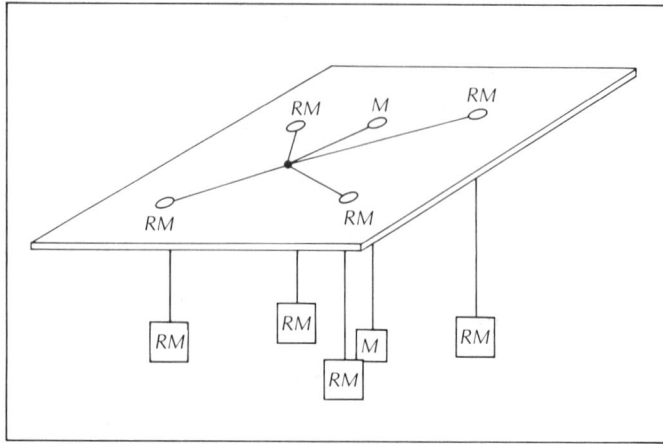

Finished product distribution costs are simulated by a weight (equal to finished product weight) running through a hole and pulley at the market point *(M)*. Ubiquitous raw materials can be simulated by adding to this weight.

This type of Weberian analysis of single firms has often been applied to the steel industry, which processes several weight-losing raw materials (Kennelly, 1954–55).

Extensions of Weber's Model: Transportation Costs

The emphasis of the Weberian model on transportation costs was modified by Walter Isard (1965). Isard treated transportation costs as just another input cost rather than considering them to be distinct from other factors of production. This treatment brings into focus the *total* location problem and allowed Isard to use sophisticated mathematical techniques to analyze locational problems.

Space-Cost Curves

Another extension of the basic Weberian system involves the use of *space-cost curves*, developed by David Smith (1966). Assume that equal amounts of two localized, weight-losing raw materials are required to produce one unit of the finished product. The material index of each is 2, so that one ton of RM_1 and one ton of RM_2 yields a one-ton finished product. In Figure 7.9A a series of concentric circles have been drawn around each raw material source and the market point. These are iso-cost lines for each transport input (called *isotims* by Weber).

Total transportation costs are the sum of all costs to all three points. At point X, (Figure 7.9B) for example, it costs $3 for XRM_1, $2 for RM_2, and $2 for transporting the finished product. We can find total transportation costs for as many

Extensions of Weber's Model: Transportation Costs

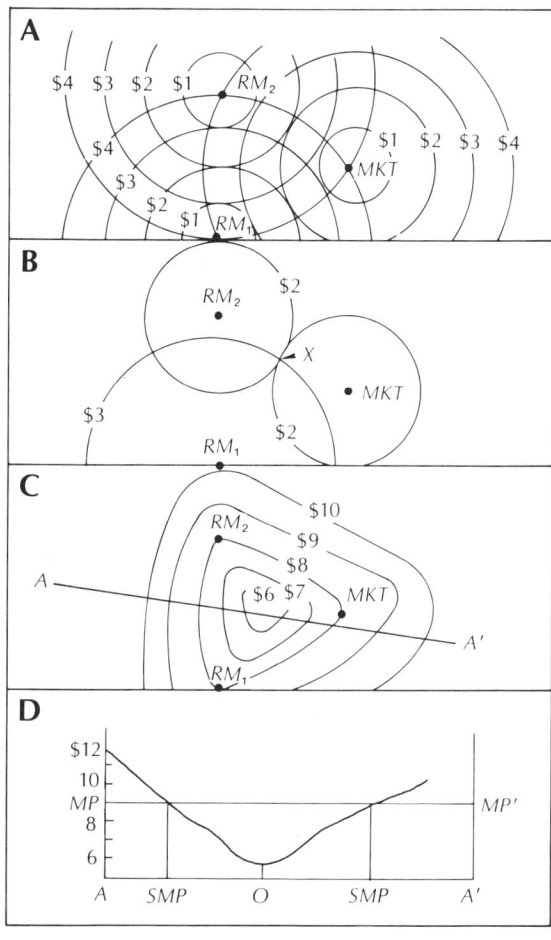

FIGURE 7.9 The development of a space-cost curve: (A) isotims; (B) total cost to a point; (C) isodapanes; (D) space cost along line A-A'.

points as we want and connect points of equal value to produce total cost isopleths which Weber termed *isodapanes*. If we visualize Figure 7.9C in three dimensional terms, we have mapped a depression. Smith then assumed that the market price for the finished product is a spatial constant (MP–MP' in Figure 7.9D). The intersections of the space-cost curve and the market price line gives the *spatial margins to profitability* and the optimum location (O) occurs at the lowest point on the space-cost curve.

Distortions of the Isotropic Surface: The Effects of Localized Resources

The assumption of the completely isotropic surface is modified when we consider the effects of *localized* resources in the Weberian model. This is the beginning of a transition from a normative to a descriptive model. Once localized resources are allowed, the regular patterns implied by central place theory are "distorted" to minimize the "pull" of non-ubiquitous resources. The role of the natural environment (localized resources) distorts the ideal patterns of an isotropic surface.

Geography has traditionally paid much more attention to the distorting effects of the environment. Although we are concentrating on the effects of space, we cannot ignore the role of the uneven distribution of resources.

Secondary Sector vs. Tertiary Sector

The tertiary sector provides and distributes goods and services. The secondary sector processes raw materials into finished products, but those products do not generally flow directly to consumers. They are channeled through the tertiary sector in the form of retail and wholesale trade. The tertiary sector is almost completely concerned with maximizing access to a market while minimizing distribution costs. It is, therefore, completely "market oriented." The orientation of the secondary sector, however, varies with the industry in question. Some types of manufacturing, as we have seen in the Weberian model, are market oriented. If all industries were of this type, the pattern of manufacturing would match the pattern of central places. Some industries, however, have a cost structure so dominated by localized input costs that they are "raw material oriented," thereby distorting the pattern.

This distortion is illustrated by Figure 7.10. Point *I* is the "ideal" location for a given order of central place. The shaded area is a major resource deposit. City A was established to exploit that resource and has become a center of manufacturing. City A also supplies central functions to the surrounding area. Because of its initial establishment and growth, it has superseded the establishment of service functions at a more ideal location (*I*). The purely spatial pattern has been "distorted" by the uneven distribution of resources.

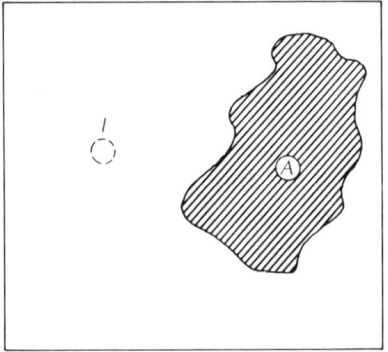

FIGURE 7.10 Distortion produced by localized resources.

Real world patterns are evolutionary and are not the result of decisions made by *optimizers*. Most real-world decisions do not result in optimum (most profitable) locations. Although we discuss spatial decision-making in Chapter 9, we should note here that locational decisions, once made, generate *inertia*. The inertia (investment in the non-optimal site) may be great enough to keep the pattern distorted even if more optimal locations are discovered in the future. We have today, for example, the analytical skills required to locate state capitals at the centroids of

Changes in Cost

state populations, but the investment we have in most state capitals precludes us from doing so. Tension develops between ideal spatial patterns and the patterns produced by localized resources. As technology (especially transportation) improves, ideal spatial patterns (from the point of view of the capitalist) become more possible, but the inertia imposed by past actions exerts a constant brake on their attainment.

Changes in Cost

To illustrate the effects of a change in the cost of an input on a location pattern, assume that two localized inputs are required to produce the finished product represented in Figure 7.11. Let RM_1 be a localized source of power such as coal (mine) and RM_2 another localized raw material. We are ignoring finished product distribution costs in this model so total costs are the sum of the two transport cost lines for the raw materials. At O, for example, RM_1 costs \$5, RM_2 costs \$7, so that total cost is \$12. At O', RM_1 costs \$10, RM_2 costs \$6, and total cost is \$16. We can find total costs for all points between O and O' (the line TC_a). Suppose that electricity is offered (technological change) at a spatially constant price of \$5. The new total cost curve will be TC_b (same as TC_a left of X). The optimum location in the first case is O_1, but the optimum location shifts to O_2 with the introduction of electricity. Whether or not the plant will actually shift depends upon the inertia (investment) at O_1 and the potential savings at O_2. Inertia, in many cases, has been the more powerful force. Gunnar Alexandersson (1961), for example, determined that the basic pattern of steel production in the United States remained relatively stable from 1948 to 1959 because it was cheaper to expand existing facilities than to construct

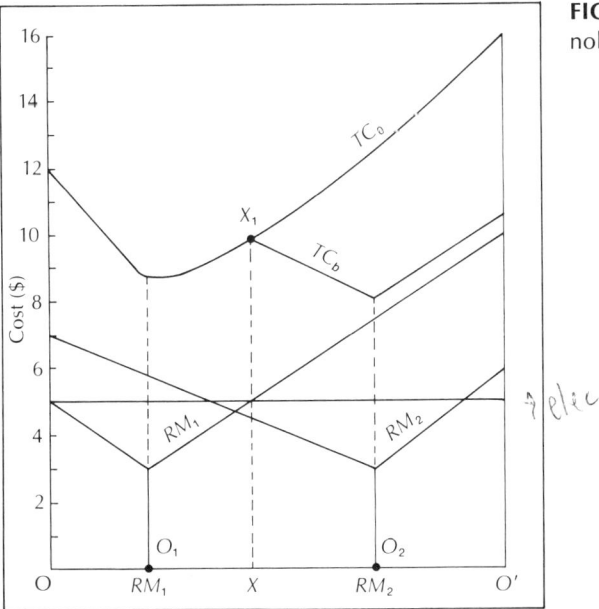

FIGURE 7.11 Changes in cost: technological innovation.

completely new ones at different locations, even though the new plants might represent more optimal locations if inertial investments were ignored.

Production Costs

The second set of costs faced by business firms is production costs. After raw materials have been assembled at a point, their form must be changed in the manufacturing process. Production costs include labor, capital, and technical and managerial skills. All of these are necessary for production, and exhibit spatial variations in both quantity and quality.

The Cost of Labor: Locational Impacts

Labor inputs are required for all forms of economic production, but the relative contribution of labor to value added by manufacturing varies considerably from industry to industry. Table 7.3 gives the relative importance of the labor input for

TABLE 7.3 The relative importance of labor

Industry	Contribution of Labor Costs*
Food products	7.0
Tobacco products	6.8
Textiles	17.1
Apparel	19.6
Lumber and wood products	16.5
Furniture	20.5
Paper products	15.3
Printing and publishing	18.1
Chemicals	8.3
Petroleum products	3.7
Rubber products	17.2
Leather products	21.3
Stone, clay, and glass products	18.7
Primary metal products	15.7
Fabricated metal products	18.4
Non-electrical machinery	17.3
Electrical machinery	16.5
Transportation equipment	13.6
Instruments	14.4

*Labor costs ($) as a percent of value of shipments ($).

selected industries in the United States. Both the supply and demand for labor vary across space, but those industries in which labor costs play a major role are much more sensitive to locational variations in the cost of this input. The cost of labor for the capitalist is determined in market economies by the relative *productivity* of labor rather than the dollar cost of wages and fringe benefits. It is the labor cost *per unit produced* rather than per hour that is of prime importance to business firms. Table 7.4

Changes in Cost

TABLE 7.4 Variations in labor productivity (hypothetical data)

Plant	Total Hourly Wages and Fringe Benefits (per Worker)	Output per Hour in Units (per Worker)	True Labor Cost per Unit Productivity
A	$5.50	100	5.5¢
B	$7.80	200	3.9¢
C	$4.20	76	5.5¢

Labor is necessary for all types of production. SOURCE: *Ford Motor Company.*

gives some hypothetical data illustrating differences in labor productivity. Notice that the labor cost per unit produced is lower in Plant B even though the hourly total of wages and fringe benefits is higher.

Weber considered the cost of labor to be a "regional" factor controlling patterns of manufacturing. The initial pattern is set by transportation costs and then "distorted" by spatial variations in the cost of labor. Weber's model assumed that an infinite amount of labor is available at different points, but that the cost of labor varies among the points.

Weber's analysis of the problem is given in Figure 7.12. The product in question involves two localized raw materials distributed to a single market (M). Isodapanes (TTC) are shown in the figure. Total transportation costs are minimized at Point T ($4). As we move away from T, total transportation costs increase. At Point L, labor costs are $2 per unit less than at T. This unit labor savings is then used to determine the value of a *critical isodapane*. No savings in total unit cost will result if the increased transportation costs encountered at another point are greater than the labor savings of that point. The move, in other words, must not exceed $2 per unit. Transportation costs at T ($4) plus labor savings at L ($2) give the amount which cannot be exceeded ($6). Point L lies inside this critical isodapane ($6) and is clearly an economic move. A point on the critical isodapane would result in zero savings and points outside the line represent higher total costs. It is in this way, within the limits established by critical isodapanes, that variations in labor costs "distort" the pattern established by general transportation costs.

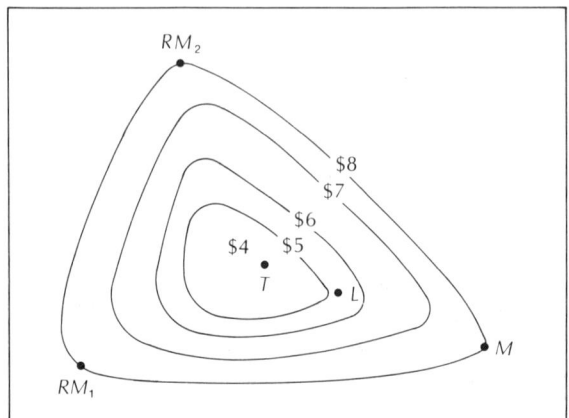

FIGURE 7.12 Critical isodapane for labor.

Equilibrium conditions should balance regional differences in the supply and demand for labor in a private free enterprise economy like the United States where mobility is high. Labor is theoretically a *mobile factor of production*. A high demand for labor in one place and an excess supply of labor in another should be brought into equilibrium through labor migration. Such migration has occurred in the United States. Massive rural to urban migration responsible for urbanization in the United States is an example, as are long run population shifts.

The response of labor, as in all factors of production, is not instantaneous. Labor, especially skilled labor, is relatively immobile (notably in the "short-run"). Labor has a degree of inertia. People are reluctant to pull up stakes, leave familiar places, family and friends, and perhaps lose local invested capital (homes, vested retirement plans), and move to unfamiliar places even if jobs are plentiful in another area. They tend to sit out short periods of unemployment or to accept a smaller net income than could be earned elsewhere because of this inertia. Liberal welfare policies such as unemployment payments and workmen's compensation have reduced the plight of the unemployed and underemployed in this century. However, it must be added that government welfare programs are not designed to reduce poverty and inequality.

The lack of instantaneous adjustment in labor demand and supply has resulted in regional variations in the cost of labor in the United States. These variations are illustrated in Figure 7.13, a chloropleth map of the average hourly earnings of production workers. Wage rates tend to be highest in the more densely settled areas, the prime manufacturing states, and in the more urbanized areas. Wage rates are lower in the South and Plains states.

The map in Figure 7.13 immediately suggests several factors which might affect the cost of labor in the United States. The level of industrialization seems to be

Changes in Cost

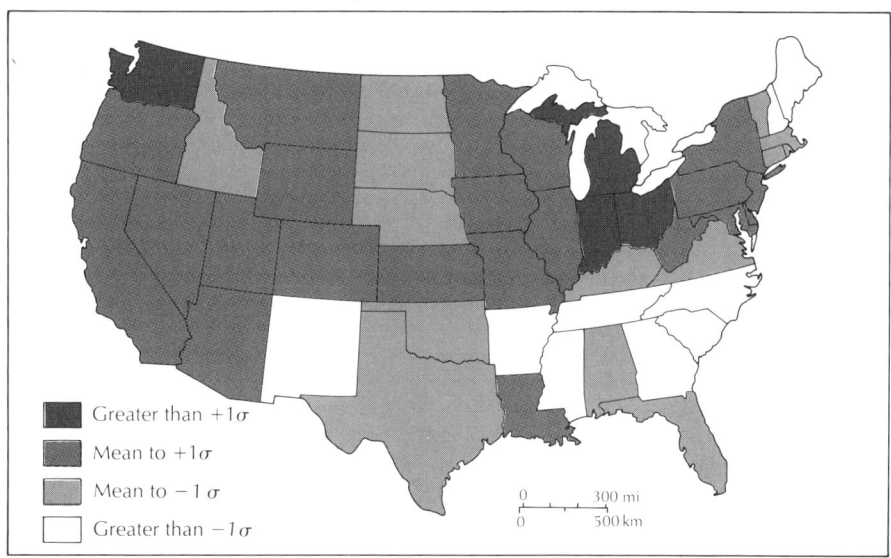

FIGURE 7.13 Variations in average hourly wages of production workers, 1974.

a primary factor. Older, established industrial areas have higher wage rates, but because of higher skill levels may also be more productive. Note that Figure 7.13 does not show productivity. Other factors involved include the level of unionization and the "industrial mix" of an area. Industry groups which have a high percentage of workers in unions and hence more bargaining strength will have higher wage rates than those which do not. Areas having a higher proportion of high wage industries will have higher wage rates than those which do not. Finally, the cost of living is another determinant of wage rates. If the cost of living is low, as in the South, bosses reason that workers do not have to earn as much to make ends meet. Other factors determine the *productivity* of labor and include the general educational level of the population, the commitment of state and local governments to training programs, job alternatives in the area, and tax reductions to companies to locate there.

Labor migration in response to supply/demand differentials is difficult to document adequately because it involves so many individual decisions. The response of individual industries to labor cost variations in the United States, however, has been the subject of numerous studies. Among the best known are the movement of textile manufacturing from New England to the Southern Piedmont, and the similar migration of the shoe and leather industry to the Southern Midwest. And the United States imports more and more textiles from Hong Kong and South Korea, and shoes and leather goods from Spain and Brazil.

Locational Impacts of the Cost of Capital

Capital is the third necessary factor of production. Capital takes two forms: fixed capital or money invested in buildings, equipment, and other tangible stocks; and liquid (variable) capital which is used to pay wages and meet other operating costs.

Liquid capital is theoretically the most mobile of all factors of production because its transportation costs are almost zero. Millions of dollars can be transferred across the United States almost instantly through the banking system. Fixed capital is much less mobile. Capital invested in buildings and other heavy equipment is obviously immobile and has been a primary reason for the previously mentioned stagnant pattern of steel production in the United States.

Any type of manufacturing which is profitable has an assured supply of liquid (operating) capital stemming from revenues or borrowing. Most types of manufacturing, however, require large amounts of fixed capital initially to establish the operation or periodically to expand, retool or replace outdated equipment, or to branch out into new products. The cost of this capital (interest) is paid from future revenues in the form of interest and dividends. Investment capital is not uniformly distributed nor does it display great mobility.

Investment capital can come from a variety of sources: personal funds, family and friends, lending institutions, and the sale of stocks and bonds. Most capital in the United States comes from the latter two sources. The *total* supply of investment capital is a function of total national wealth and the proportion of total income that is saved. "Savings" become the investment capital for future expansion.

Whether or not a particular type of manufacturing or a given entrepreneur can obtain an adequate amount of investment capital at an acceptable price (interest rate) depends upon several things: (1) The supply of capital in both a national and local context is important. At times the national supply of capital is low, postponing less profitable investments. Regional differences in the supply of capital also occur. Surplus capital tends to be concentrated in the older, more developed, and wealthier areas of the country. As long as profitable investments remain there, investment may be inadequate in areas of capital deficit. (2) The demand for capital is another determinant of the price of capital. As long as the demand for capital remains high in one area (such as an established industrial area), interest rates may preclude investments in less profitable regions and industries. (3) Capital can always be obtained if the user is willing to pay a high enough interest rate. Beyond supply and demand considerations, *investor confidence,* determined by fluctuating business expectations in a market economy, is the prime determinant of whether or not capital can be obtained at an acceptable rate. Investor confidence in a particular industry may be present in one area of the country and lacking in another. Many capitalists who failed to raise risk capital in one area of the country found it available in their home area (most notably Ford in Detroit and Douglas Aviation in Los Angeles).

Entrepreneurship and Technical Skills

Management and technical skills are required for any type of production process. Corporations are the primary agents responsible for the specific industrial pattern in the United States. The general (Weber's regional) pattern is, of course, determined by the localization of other factors of production, subsequent transportation costs, and spatial margins to profitability. Ford Motor Company was established in Detroit primarily because it was Henry Ford's home town and he was able to obtain risk

Changes in Cost

capital there, but any town in the Midwest accessible to the raw materials necessary for auto production (especially steel) could have supported automobile production. On the other hand, had Ford attempted to manufacture automobiles on a large scale in Butte, Montana, he would have failed. H. Hunker and A. J. Wright's study (1963) found that a majority of the manufacturing plants in Ohio were located in the home towns of their founders. The Midwest and the rest of American Manufacturing Belt establishes the regional pattern of profitable locations for most types of manufacturing, but the specific locations chosen within these margins are determined by the individual decisions of capitalists.

Management should be, theoretically, much more mobile than labor because fewer people are involved and the higher incomes of managers make moving less of a financial burden, but management skills, like labor, still tend to be highly concentrated. Figure 7.14 shows the location of the corporate headquarters of the 500 largest corporations in the United States. They are concentrated in the most densely urbanized areas of the country (see box). The high incomes of managers allow them to enjoy the advantages of American urban life while escaping the problems of the inner city through suburban living. The educational level of management makes the cultural attractions of large cities important also. Considerable financial inducements are necessary to persuade top managers to move to rural or less urbanized areas.

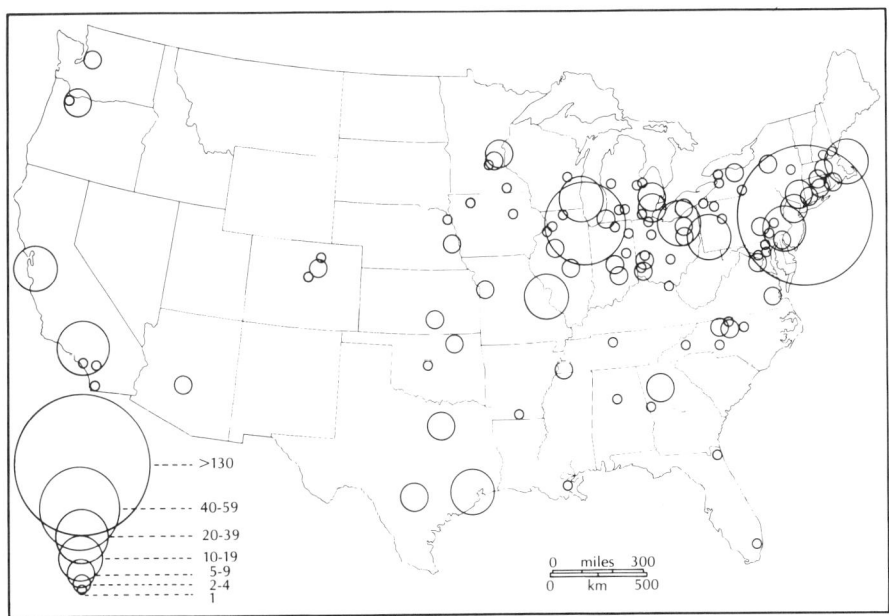

FIGURE 7.14 Corporate headquarters: 500 largest corporations, 1976.
SOURCE: *Fortune Magazine.*

Technical skills refer not to those required in the production process (*i.e.,* labor skills), but rather those necessary for continued innovation in terms of both new products and processes (see box). These skills in the United States are usually referred to as "research and development" (R and D). Research and development are

THE GEOGRAPHY OF LARGE, PRIVATE BUSINESS ORGANIZATIONS IN THE UNITED STATES

Several geographers have studied the locations of large private organizational headquarters in the United States (Goodwin, 1965; Semple, 1973; Pred, 1974; and Borchert, 1978). A study by John Borchert is especially interesting in that it surveys the changing geographical pattern of national headquarters, the *major control points in American economic geography*. A *control point* is an organization (household, corporation) that performs a production, consumption, and savings function. Large organizations control "a large share of extraction and production and they also aggregate savings from many smaller sources" (Borchert, 1978:215).

Borchert emphasized the geographical importance of major control points:

> ... [L]arge organizations shape the evolving settlement pattern of the nation. Meanwhile, at their control points, large organizations' administrative buildings and home plants dominate skylines and extensive land areas. The products of creative entrepreneurship, these organizational headquarters have been major shapers of the images of downtown districts, cities and regions. They have influenced regional differences in tax base and philanthropy. Their decisions are an essential part of any practical land use plan, and their headquarters expenditures reflect expansion or contraction in remote parts of their corporate networks (1978:215).

After mapping and describing the changing location of industrial corporations, investment corporations, major bank headquarters, and major transport headquarters over the half-century from the 1920s to the 1970s, Borchert concluded that:

> The share of national business assets controlled from the Northeast declined; the concentration of firms shifted somewhat toward regional centers. Thus the concentration within Megalopolis increased in the New York-Hartford axis; and in every other part of the country the shift was toward second, third, or fourth order regional or metropolitan areas. Political capitals emerged as major public business centers (1978:229).

Borchert observed that the existing pattern of corporate headquarters, which developed at points of optimum accessibility to the regional economy (entrepots and central places), reflects considerable inertia, but also a tendency toward instability. The historic concentration of corporate headquarters in Megalopolis is an example of inertia. Instability reflects the continued evolution of large business organizations. Cities like Houston, Minneapolis-St. Paul, Wilmington, Richmond, Akron, and Boise have more corporate headquarters than expected given their population sizes. Other cities have fewer headquarters than expected. "The wide variations among cities in their importance as control points is an expression of the instability of organizations, both individual and aggregate" (Borchert, 1978:231). Borchert, however, noted that the long-term tendency toward inertia in any system is always accompanied by a period of internal instability.

THE DECLINE IN RESEARCH AND DEVELOPMENT

For most of the twentieth century, the United States has been the world's leader in technological innovation. In the 1970s, however, the number of new inventions and patents granted declined. American inventions were granted 45,633 patents by major trading companies in 1966, but only 33,181 patents in 1976, a drop of more than 25 percent. Factors said to be retarding innovation in the United States include: a decline in federal support for basic research; an increase in government red tape; an increased managerial interest in improving existing products that bring quick returns; and difficulties of obtaining risk-capital, a problem that stems in part from high capital gains tax rates.

The lagging pace of research and development (R and D) is a great worry to many American economists: it is contributing to balance of payments problems; and it is dampening the domestic economy. The nation's business health may be impaired because new small companies grow on new inventions and create more jobs than mature firms. A United States Commerce Department study showed over a five year period that six large, mature firms (such as Bethlehem Steel and General Motors) added 25,000 workers, and that five new, high technology firms created 35,000 jobs.

The United States government is considering ways to arrest the retreat of R and D. One idea is to cut capital gains tax rates. Another is to set up research institutions that supply information on basic research to participating companies.

The Rand Corporation is a private institution engaged in research and analysis on national security and public welfare. SOURCE: *The Rand Corporation.*

much more important in some industries than in others. Industries such as wood products, textiles, and food have changed very little in the past decade, while others such as electronics have undergone sweeping changes. The proliferation of electronic calculators at lower and lower prices is a case in point. The amount of innovation necessary in an industry can be measured by the percentage of total value added by manufacturing which the industry spends on research and development (Table 7.5). Research and development skills tend to be localized also and focused

TABLE 7.5 Research and development funds as a percent of net sales: 1974

Industry	Percent
Food Products	0.4
Textiles and Apparel	0.4
Lumber and Wood Products	0.6
Paper Products	0.7
Chemicals	3.2
Petroleum Refining	0.5
Rubber Products	1.7
Stone, Clay, and Glass Products	1.5
Primary Metals	0.5
Fabricated Metal Products	1.1
Machinery	4.0
Electronic Equipment	6.9
Motor Vehicles	3.7
Aircraft and Missiles	12.5
Professional and Scientific Instruments	5.4

SOURCE: National Science Foundation

on major research university clusters and established areas of innovation. Two of the major growth industries of the past two decades, electronics and aerospace, have been heavily influenced by government action. The prime customers and supplies of capital for both of these industries have been the space and defense programs of the federal government. As such, government action has played a role in determining the major growth areas for the relatively *footloose* electronics industry. The location of military aircraft production was basically established during World War II, but specific locations have waxed or waned as a function of government contracts and the power of individual senators.

A Variable Cost Model

This section examines the influence of production costs on location in greater detail. Smith (1966) pointed out that the establishment of any manufacturing plant in a market economy involves three mutually interdependent decisions: *scale*—the size of the operation which will determine the volume of total output; *technique*—the particular *combination* of inputs that will be used to produce an output; and *location*. Here we will concern ourselves with location as a function of input costs, and therefore hold the influence of technique and scale constant. We will consider technique and scale in subsequent sections.

A Variable Cost Model

We assume also that variations in demand, if they exist, are solely a function of price. These assumptions allow us to portray three general industrial location cases, shown in Figure 7.15. In Case A, market price (revenue) is a spatial constant and costs vary across space. The optimum location is then the lowest point on the space-cost curve, and the spatial margins are where costs equal revenue. Total revenue (demand) exhibits spatial change in Case B while costs are a spatial constant. The optimum location is the highest point on the revenue curve, and the spatial margins to profitability are again where costs equal revenue. Variations in both cost and revenue across space are shown in Case C. The optimum location (O) will be the place where revenue exceeds costs by the greatest amount. For all three cases we can show that: *both* curves determine the spatial margins to profitability; the variable with the *steepest* gradient determines the optimum location; and the *slope* of the curve indicates the relative importance of locational costs.

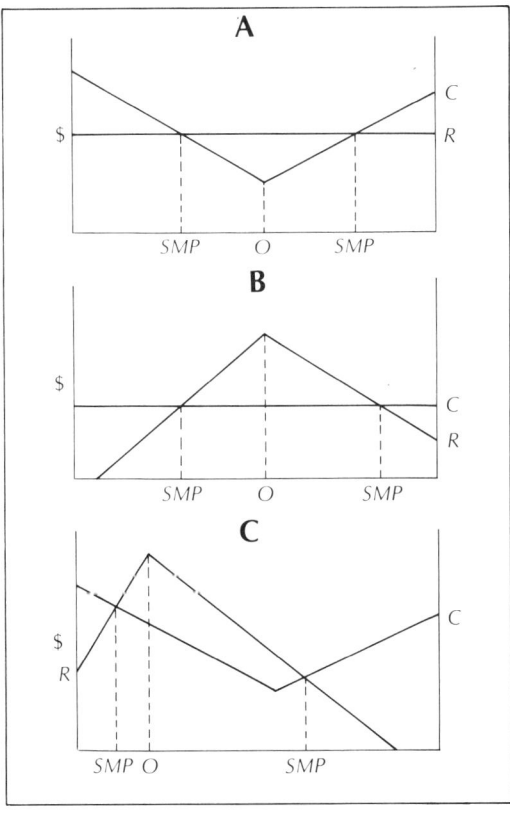

FIGURE 7.15 Spatial margins to profitability: (A) cost variable, revenue constant; (B) revenue variable, cost constant; (C) revenue and cost variable. Modified from D. Smith, 1971, *Industrial Location: An Economic Geographic Analysis*, New York: John Wiley & Sons.

Spatial margins to profitability are important because they incorporate *suboptimal* behavior. Profits are possible anywhere within these limits. The three graphs in Figure 7.15 are the most general statement that can be made about locational viability. Defining these margins in reality and determining specific locations to be occupied within them, however, is a much more difficult problem. We can still make one generalization about real-world patterns within spatial margins to profitability: *Industries which are clustered must face limited spatial margins to profitability and high location costs.* The situation is illustrated in Figure 7.16. Remember that any kind of cost and/or revenue may be the critical factor determining the spatial margins to profitability.

FIGURE 7.16 Spatial margins to profitability and clustering.

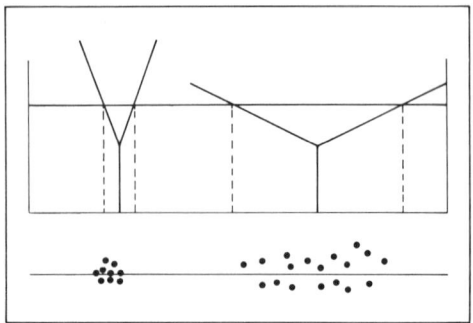

Weber's theory is preoccupied both with transportation costs and with finding least-cost (optimal) locations. A more general theory should consider total cost and the possibility of suboptimal decisions. Location theory has focused on transportation costs because they are easily calculated and can be treated as fairly simple functions of distance. The locational effects of other kinds of cost are more difficult to conceptualize. Walter Isard (1956) suggested that locational factors can be divided into three general classes on the basis of their geographic occurrence.

1. *Transfer charges:* costs that can be portrayed as a regular function of distance from some given point. The cost of acquiring a raw material from a single mine is an example of this kind of cost and is illustrated in Figure 7.17A.
2. *Spatially variable costs:* costs that vary across space (labor, power, capital, management skills), but which do not vary *systematically* with distance from a point (Figure 7.17B.).
3. *Aspatial costs:* factors which can influence costs but which are independent of location such as scale changes.

Geography has dealt with the problems associated with irregular variations in costs in a normative way through the use of models assuming an isotropic surface. These problems can be overcome, however, in two ways. First, they can be *conceptually* reduced. The cost of any input can be thought of as varying over distance in terms of dollars per kilometer. The least-cost point for labor can be determined, for example, and costs rise everywhere from this point. The exact *form* of the change may, of course, vary with direction. Second, we can deal with the practical aspects of the problem by determining the cost of an input at a large number of points and mapping variations in costs as a *surface.* The surface can be regularized by such techniques as *trend surface analysis* (see box). Each variable can be viewed as spatially continuous and the sum portrayed as a surface of total cost.

David Smith (1966) extended Weber's analysis to all types of cost through this type of conceptualization. He assumed that *each input* has a least-cost point. Least-cost points for materials may be mines or the factories of parts producers. There is a least-cost point for the particular kind of labor required and there is a point

A Variable Cost Model

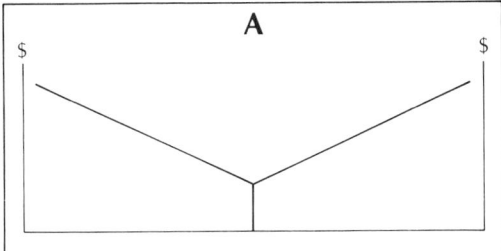

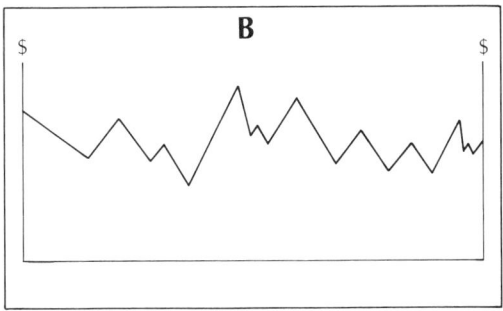

FIGURE 7.17 (A) Transfer charges; (B) spatially variable costs.

TREND SURFACE ANALYSIS

Trend surface analysis is a statistical method used to "smooth" or discover the general "trend" of a complex surface. Just as regression involves fitting a line through a scatter of data points, trend surface analysis is concerned with the fitting of a *surface* (or plane) through a set of data points.

Figure A below represents a complex surface such as wage rates in an area. Figure B shows the smoothed surface or general trend which might result from the application of trend surface analysis.

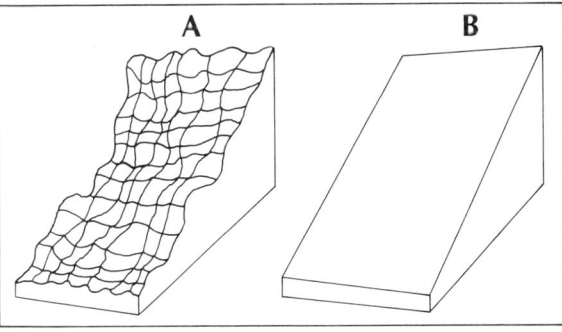

---

at which finished product distribution costs are minimized. Each of these points exerts a certain "pull" on location (remember the Varignon frame). The relative weight of all these pulls determines the least-cost location.

Smith also paid a great deal of attention to the distinction between *basic and locational* costs. Basic costs are the minimum that must be paid regardless of location and represent the lowest point on the cost surface of a particular input. The basic cost for labor, for example, would be the minimum wage. Locational costs are those incurred in overcoming distance. Figure 7.18 illustrates the two kinds of cost. We assume that some workers will accept the minimum wage. Their location represents the lowest point on the labor cost surface and basic cost. Away from that point, workers demand more than the minimum wage, but the additional amount takes the form of locational costs. Suppose an industry is covered by a national union wage-rate. The dollar amount paid to workers is the same everywhere. We might assume that ubiquitous basic costs prevail, but we must remember our previous discussion of productivity. Basic costs are found at the point of *highest* labor productivity. This represents the lowest *real* labor costs. As productivity falls away from that point, real labor costs rise, producing locational costs. The total cost of any input is therefore the sum of locational and basic cost. The relative "pull" of a given input then depends upon the slope of the (locational) space-cost curve and the percentage contribution of an input to the total cost of output. An input that accounts for a large proportion of total basic cost or has large variations in location cost should have the greatest influence on plant location.

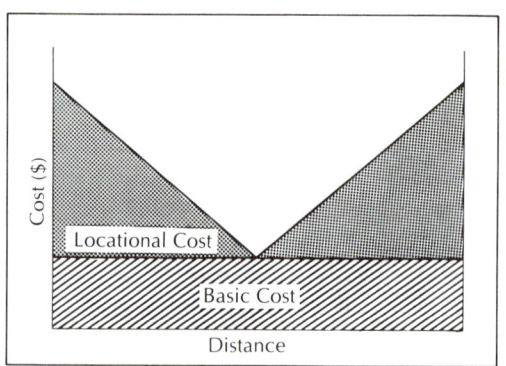

FIGURE 7.18 Basic and locational costs. After D. Smith, 1971, *Industrial Location: An Economic Geographic Analysis,* New York: John Wiley & Sons.

We now examine this proposition by a simple model. Assume that a particular product requires three inputs that have locational costs—a raw material, labor, and power. All other inputs have zero locational costs and do not influence the choice of sites. In Figure 7.19, the locational costs for the raw material, labor, and power are minimized at A, B, and C respectively.

Consider Case I in Table 7.6. Equal amounts (B) of each input are required. In each case we are dealing with the *cost* of the input so that in Case I, $20 will purchase the required amount of each input at the least-cost source. We must pay at least $60 in *basic cost*. Now we must determine the *locational cost* of each input. In Case I, locational costs are 10¢ per dollar per kilometer. Moving away from A for one kilometer, for example, will raise the cost of each dollar's worth of the raw material 10¢ so that the locational cost of the required quantity at one kilometer is $2 (10¢ × $20 = $2). The total cost of that input at one kilometer is $22.

In Figure 7.19, isocost lines are drawn around each input source at $20 intervals. Remember that basic cost is $20 at A so that the first isocost line is $40 and

A Variable Cost Model

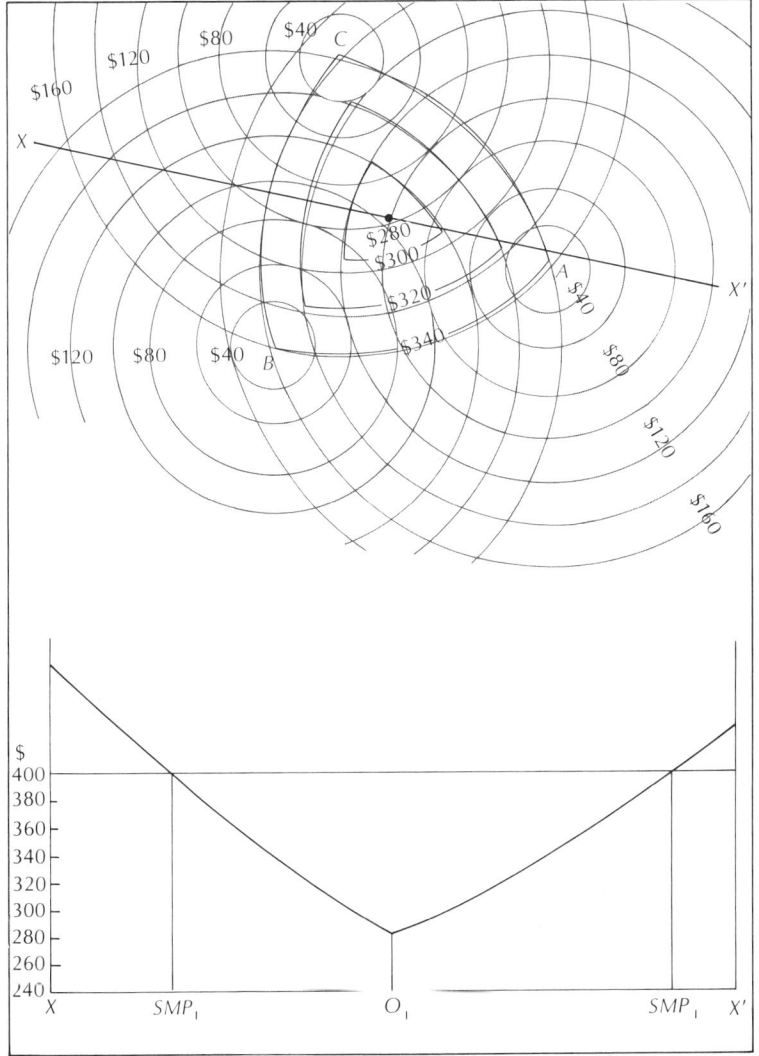

FIGURE 7.19 The variable cost model: Case I.

occurs 10 kilometers from A ($20BC + $20LC = $40; see Table 7.6). Notice that the isotims for each input are exactly the same. We can interpolate isodapanes (total costs for all inputs) from the isotims (heavy lines in Figure 7.19) and draw a space cost curve along line X'—X'. Assuming a spatially constant market price of $400, the optimum location is at O_1 and the spatial margins to profitability are SMP_1.

Case II examines the effect of variations in locational cost. The same amount (in dollars) of each input is required, but they have different locational costs in terms of the per kilometer cost per dollar unit. This produces a different set of isotims (Figure 7.20). Basic costs are still $20 at all three input sources, but the total cost (BC + LC) rises to $40 at only 6.5 kilometers from A, and at 10 kilometers from C. The slope of a space-cost curve for input A is much steeper than for input C, and input B is intermediate. The space cost curve for the isodapanes (sum of input costs) in Figure 7.20 is shifted from its position in Case I (the space cost curve from Figure 7.19

TABLE 7.6 Basic and locational costs of inputs (variable-cost model)

Case	Input	Least-Cost Source	Basic Cost of Quantity (B) Required Dollars (C) (BC)	Locational Costs per Dollar Unit per Kilometer (C) (C)	Space-Cost Curve Gradient (L) Dollars per Kilometer (LC)	Distance Between Total Cost Isolines at $20 Intervals ($20/LC)
I	Material	A	20	.10	2.00	10.00
	Labor	B	20	.10	2.00	10.00
	Power	C	20	.10	2.00	10.00
II	Material	A	20	.15	3.00	6.50
	Labor	B	20	.10	2.00	10.00
	Power	C	20	.05	1.00	20.00
III	Material	A	40	.10	4.00	5.00
	Labor	B	20	.10	2.00	10.00
	Power	C	10	.10	1.00	20.00

is also shown in Case II). The optimum location (O) and the spatial margins to profitability have shifted toward A.

Case III illustrates the effect of differences in basic costs. Notice in Table 7.6 that the quantity (B) of the material input required has increased whereas the required quantity of power has declined. The cost per dollar unit per kilometer (C) is the same for all inputs, but the increased quantity of the raw material leads to increased locational costs. Figure 7.21 gives the new set of isotims for Case III. The basic cost of the raw material at A is $40 and the first $20 isocost line would be $60 ($40 + $20) and would occur at 5 kilometers from A. (Many of the isotims around A have not been drawn to avoid clutter). The isotims around B and C are the same as for Case II. The locational costs of A are now much steeper. The space cost curve has now shifted toward A, the optimum location is now O_{III} and the spatial margins to profitability are considerably smaller than in Case I.

This series of examples demonstrated that locational costs can occur *either* because of high transportation costs per unit *or* because a large quantity (*basic cost*) is required even though the *per unit* locational costs are low. This last point is illustrated by coal which has had a profound effect on past industrial locational patterns of heavy industry. Coal is relatively cheap to move on a *per ton* basis, but the quantity (basic cost) of coal required in some types of manufacturing has produced high locational costs and "pulled" the industry toward coal deposits. This illustrates the difference between transportation costs *per unit* and locational costs.

The Locational Effects of Technique

As we have said, manufacturing requires three mutually interdependent decisions: location, scale, and technique. A decision made about any one of the three may

The Locational Effects of Technique

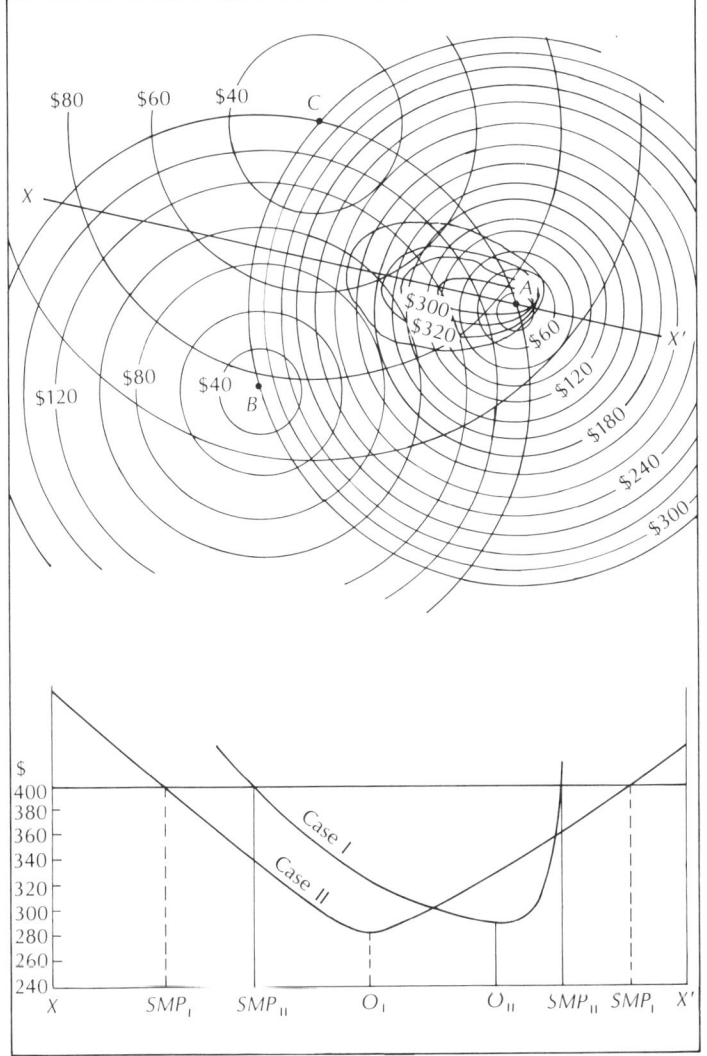

FIGURE 7.20 The variable cost model: Case II.

completely determine the limits of the remaining two. We will discuss scale in the next section, but technique can have a very important effect on a firm's locational decision. Technique is the *combination of inputs* used to produce a finished product. A certain amount of land (resources), labor, and capital is required to produce any finished product, but (within limits) labor may be substituted for capital, or labor for resources, or similar combinations.

Perhaps the most evident trend in large-scale manufacturing is the substitution of capital in the form of machinery for labor. More and more "automation" is being used to replace labor in many production processes. Whether or not substitution is used depends upon the relative cost of the two inputs and the scale and locational decisions already made by the firm. If, for example, labor costs rise at a given location, the firm may substitute capital for labor at that location or change

FIGURE 7.21 The variable cost model: Case III.

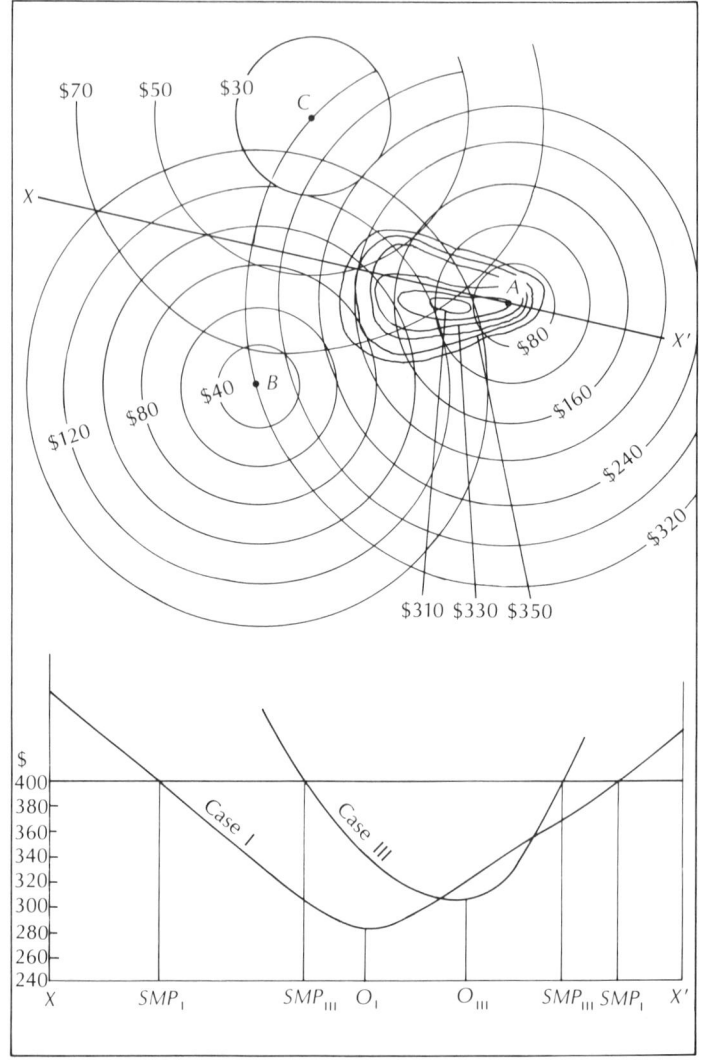

locations to take advantage of lower labor costs and maintain the same labor/capital ratio.

The limits set on substitution vary considerably from industry to industry. Petroleum refining, for example, can be readily automated, whereas the manufacture of garments cannot. The garment industry, therefore, should be much more sensitive to changes in labor costs than the refining industry. The textile industry which at one time required large amounts of labor shifted in the United States from New England to the Southern Piedmont as labor costs rose in the Northeast. This is an example of the influence of technique determining the location decision. Increased labor costs outweighed the costs of moving the industry. Had capital substitution been a viable option, the industry might have remained in place (location determined). Many times a firm may wish to change its *scale* to increase output and to produce extra profits. A change in scale may require a change in location and/or technique. The locational effects of scale are the subject of the following section.

Scale Considerations in Industrial Location

Scale is important not only because it forms one of the three interdependent production decisions, but also for two other reasons: (1) producers are concerned with the *unit cost* of production and adjustments in scale can produce considerable variations in unit cost; (2) scale is the means by which production is "tuned" to meet demand. This tuning may be done by the state in some types of economies and by private entrepreneurs in others.

We consider first the *scale economies* that can be realized by an individual firm, but later we will examine multi-firm economies that result from agglomeration.

Principles of Scale Economies

Division of Labor and Capital One of the two key ideas in mass production is the *division of labor* (the other is standardization of parts). As we saw in Chapter 1, workers performing one simple part of the production process are much more efficient (but their work is psychologically more dehumanizing) than those who carry out all phases of the process. Division of labor speeds up production for the capitalist and makes possible the use of relatively unskilled labor. A worker can be taught one simple task in a short time, whereas the skills required to master the entire operation may take years. Division of labor, however, requires a large scale in that more workers are generally necessary. A larger scale also makes possible the use of very specialized equipment (capital) which may only be available in large unit sizes or whose cost is only justified in large operations.

The efficiencies of labor division also apply to management. The owner of a small firm has to do the accounting, advertising, sales, and labor relations as well as manage production. As the firm increases in size, these roles can be handed over to specialists who are better trained to handle them.

The scale of a firm can be measured in many ways such as gross sales, size of capital investment, and others, but the most common measure is the number of employees. Capital, once invested in machinery or buildings, becomes fixed capital and only produces income when it is in operation. A firm using three shifts of workers makes much more profit than one employing a single shift. The three-shift firm is three times larger in scale (measured by employees) yet its fixed capital investment may be no more than the single-shift firm.

Massing of Reserves This principle states that large operations can maintain proportionally smaller inventories than small-scale firms, thereby reducing unit costs. Assume that a particular type of production requires a large, expensive, and complicated piece of machinery. The entire production process must stop if the machine breaks down. A plant shut-down even for an hour is an expensive proposition. Workers are idled, but must be paid while waiting, and other operational costs continue. A firm in this industry must maintain a reserve (inventory) of spare machine parts to prevent long term shut-downs. Firm A has only one machine in operation, but must maintain an inventory of almost one whole machine in equivalent spare parts. A capital investment of almost two machines must be counted as part of the cost of each unit. Firm B has ten machines in operation, but because it is unlikely that the same part will fail on all ten machines at the same time, it must maintain a reserve of parts only slightly larger than the smaller firm.

Suppose each machine costs $10,000 and the parts inventory that must be maintained is worth $8,000. Figure 7.22 shows the decline in (proportional) inventory cost as a firm increases in scale from a one-machine operation to ten. Total capital investment is part of unit cost. As a firm increases in size, massed reserves lower unit costs.

FIGURE 7.22 The massing of reserves.

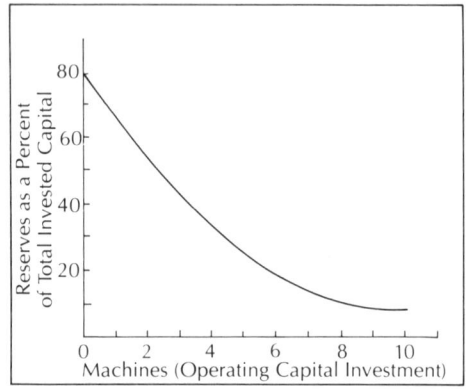

Imperfectly Divisible Multiples This principle of scale economies is much like our prior discussion of technique and involves the possibilities of input combination. Many inputs do not allow unitary combinations (one-to-one increases in scale).

Suppose we are considering the manufacture of hammers. Assume the machine (or process) which produces hammer heads can manufacture 300 heads per hour and the machine (or process) which manufactures hammer handles can produce 400 an hour. If we run both machines for one hour, we will have 300 complete hammers and 100 extra handles at the end of the hour. The production of hammers in this example involves imperfectly divisible multiples (400/300 does not produce a whole number).

One way to attack the problem of imperfectly divisible multiples is to run the head machine for the entire hour, but to shut down the handle machine after 45 minutes. Costs (labor, power, rent) go on, however, in the part of the plant devoted to handle production during the shut-down. A secondary strategy which can be employed is to increase the scale of the plant until we hit some unitary combination of head and handle machines. Suppose we increase the number of head machines to four and the number of handle machines to three. Now we produce 1200 heads and handles per hour. We have "tuned" the scale to reduce unit costs. We can see the kinds of savings that result from this principle in an industry such as automobile manufacturing where perfectly divisible multiples may be reached only in very large operations.

Bulk Purchases Large firms pay much less for material inputs than small firms. Stated simply, General Motors can obtain tires for a much lower unit price than

Scale Considerations in Industrial Location

an individual dealing with the same tire company because GM buys millions of tires per year.

Possible Scale Economies

As we saw in Chapter 5, the traditional economist portrays scale economies as a curve of *long-run* average costs (LRAC) which graphs these costs (per unit) as a function of scale. A typical (LRAC) curve for a firm is shown in Figure 7.23. Notice that unit costs fall (increasing marginal returns to scale), reach an optimum point, and then begin to rise. The rise in the curve is termed *diseconomies* of scale (diminishing marginal returns to scale) and occurs when a firm becomes too large to manage and operate efficiently. The *general* form of long-run average costs is the same for all types of production. Several possible long-run average cost curves are shown in Figure 7.24. The optimum scale is very small in Case A, very large in Case C, and covers a fairly wide range of scales in Case B. Firms in Industry A should be small; they should be large in Industry C; and range from small to large in Industry B.

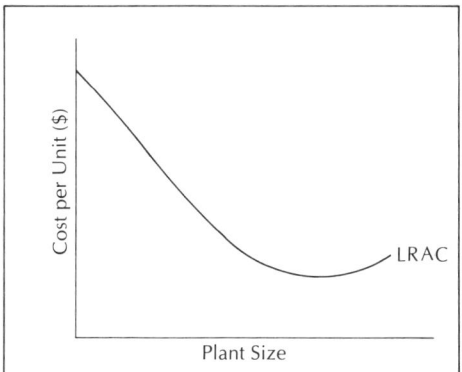

FIGURE 7.23 Economies of scale (long-run average cost).

Possible scale economies also give some indication of how firms in a given industry may expand production. A firm in Industry A, for example, should expand by building a branch plant; increasing the size of operations on the original site would produce diseconomies of scale. Firms in Industry B, however, could increase production by expanding existing plants or building new ones.

Spatial Implications of Economies of Scale

Let us now examine the locational implications of intra-firm scale economies. We will ignore the technique decision, but again remember that all three production decisions are interdependent.

Take the example of a company which operates two small breweries, each in a different town. The entire output of the firm is sold in the two towns. The long-run average costs (per barrel) for the firm are shown in Figure 7.25A. The firm operates the two breweries at scale S_1 and costs are $5 per barrel. The firm could reduce its cost per barrel by consolidating its operations into a single plant of scale S_2

FIGURE 7.24 Variations in long-run average cost.

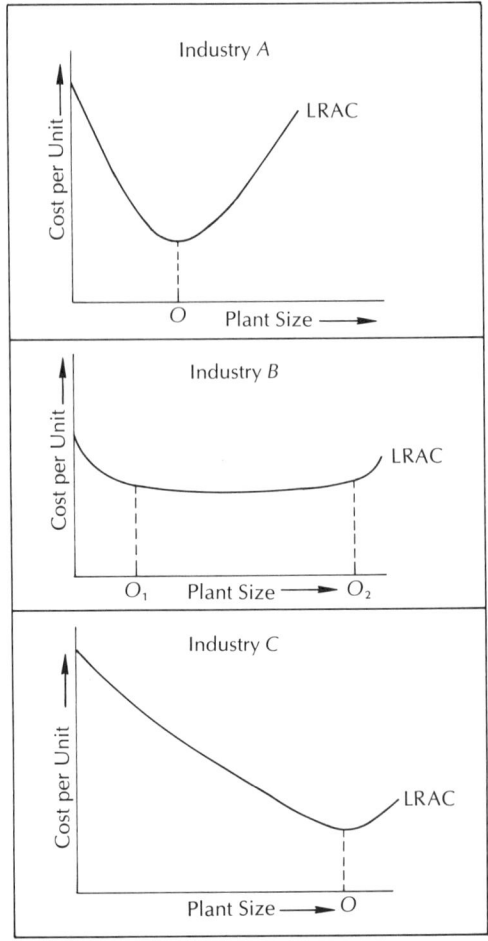

($2.50 per barrel). One plant could be closed and the remaining plant doubled in size, or both plants closed and a new, larger brewery built. However, the firm has minimized its finished product distribution costs by manufacturing beer in each town. Additional finished product transportation costs will have to be paid if a single brewery is used. The problem to be resolved is whether or not the savings from scale economies outweigh the increased transportation costs. These two items will balance at a transportation cost of $2.50 per barrel ($2.50 LRAC per barrel). In Figure 7.25B, the iso-cost line of $2.50 per barrel from each town has been drawn. Notice that the two lines intersect, indicating that the scale savings outweigh the increased transportation costs. The larger plant can be operated in either city or in an intermediate location with a lower cost per barrel than is possible with the two small-scale plants.

Vertical and Horizontal Integration

Intra-firm scale economies imply more than simply increasing plant size. Scale refers to anything that changes the size of the firm's inputs—labor, management, capital

Scale Considerations in Industrial Location

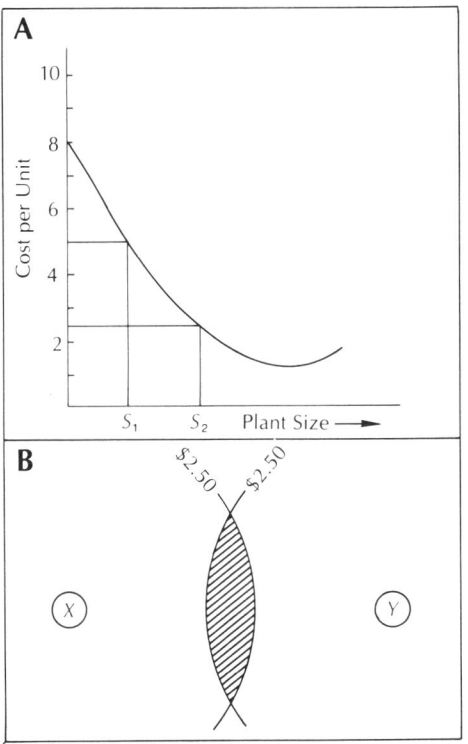

FIGURE 7.25 Spatial implications of scale economies: (A) long-run average costs; (B) transport cost isolines for break-even total cost with plant size of S_2.

investment, or raw materials. Firms use two common types of scale changes other than increasing plant size to increase their scale. Some firms may purchase raw material sources (mines, parts firms) or distribution facilities (retail outlets, advertising agencies, and trucking companies). This is called *vertical integration* (or vertical merger) because the firm is controlling more "up and down" from its initial niche in the total production process. Some large automobile manufacturing firms, for example, own iron and coal mines and produce their own steel ("down" in the process). They also may own dealerships and do their own transporting and marketing ("up" in the process). Large oil companies also tend to be vertically integrated; they control exploration, drilling, refining, and retailing.

Horizontal integration (or horizontal merger) occurs when a firm gains control of more and more of a given niche of a particular industry. Shoe manufacturing, for example, has gone from over 3,500 firms in 1900 to less than 1,300 firms in 1972 as a few companies have purchased small operations. Whether vertical or horizontal integration occurs (if either occurs at all) depends upon the economies to be gained from such a move. Monopolies are somewhat regulated in the United States in an attempt to control prices and the social cost of large-scale integration. Recent proposals to break up vertically integrated oil companies are a case in point.

Scale and the Modern Corporation

Vertical and horizontal integration generally refer to a single finished product. The vertical integration of Ford Motor Company, for example, is focused on controlling

The Ford Motor Company steel mill and auto assembly plants at River Rouge, Michigan, is a vertically integrated industrial complex.
SOURCE: *Ford Motor Company.*

the inputs and marketing required for automobile production. The horizontal integration of shoe manufacturing means consolidation of the plants in the industry within fewer and fewer firms. The *linkages* we will explore in the following section also apply to individual firms producing a single product. The trend, however, among corporations in the United States, Western Europe, and Japan has been a strategy of *diversification.* Large corporations, through *conglomerate* mergers, control the production and marketing of diverse products. A corporation may produce many unrelated finished products, each with elements of horizontal and vertical integration. Figure 7.26 shows the companies and products controlled by Tenneco. The products controlled by other diversified corporations would, of course, be different, but the figure adequately illustrates the great diversity of a modern company. Diversification spreads risk and increases profits. Diminishing demand for the products of one division may be offset by rising sales in another.

The social consequences of large-scale diversification have been hotly debated as have the implications of large size by a company producing a single product which is horizontally or vertically integrated. The economies produced by increasing scale have been previously discussed, but most large companies operate at a scale far beyond the initial optimum point on the long-run average cost curve. ". . . General Motors is not only large enough to afford the best size of automobile plant, but is large enough to afford a dozen or more of the best size; and . . . it is large

Scale Considerations in Industrial Location

Division	Products	Employees
Tenneco Oil	Crude oil, natural gas, refining, service stations	6,969
Tenessee Gas Transmission	Natural gas pipelines	2,792
J. I. Case	Two and four-wheel drive agricultural tractors and implements, loader/backhoes, crawler and wheel loaders, excavators, trenchers, industrial and materials handling cranes, skid steer loaders, forklift and compaction equipment.	25,424
Tenneco Automotive	Automotive exhaust systems, shock absorbers and ride control products, jacks and lifting equipment, filters, wheel oil seals, fans, pulleys, manifolds.	16,037
Tenneco Chemicals	Fine, intermediate, and hydrocarbon chemicals; plastic resins, stabilizers, plasticizers; paint colorants and dispersions. Chemical foam products and fabricated plastic materials. Synthetic and organic chemicals, paper and specialty chemicals.	3,825
Newport News Shipbuilding	Naval and merchant ship construction and repair, nuclear vessel refueling, components and services for the nuclear power industry, heavy castings and sheet metal products for industrial use.	25,351
Packaging Corporation of America	Corrugated containers, paperboard, folding cartons, molded pulp products.	7,997
Tenneco West	Agricultural products (fresh fruits, vegetables, almonds, pistachios, dates, raisins), commercial, recreational, and residential real estate.	3,535

FIGURE 7.26 Companies and products controlled by Tenneco Inc.

enough to produce things as diverse as aircraft engines and refrigerators, which cannot be explained by economies of scale" (Galbraith, 1967). John Kenneth Galbraith has suggested that firms expand for two reasons: survival and growth. Both goals are promoted by horizontal and vertical expansion and by diversification (see box).

Most location theory is based on the theory of the firm, which implies small, single-plant operations producing a single product. Large corporations are much more complex, but in terms of *individual* plants they face all the variables included in classical location theory. They still make locational decisions. Large firms, however, may seem to be more concerned with technique and scale decisions, but each location has scale and technique implications. We should consider two

GIANT CORPORATIONS IN THE UNITED STATES

As late as 1860 there were no giant corporations dominating an entire industry in the United States. Since that time, conditions have changed dramatically. By 1900, the share of incorporated business firms had grown to two-thirds. In this century, business concentration has proceeded rapidly. The accompanying table shows that the share of total manufacturing assets controlled by a few large firms is high indeed. Since large firms control most research in the United States, they are likely to continue to grow rapidly. A 1960 study showed that four firms accounted for 22 percent, and 384 firms accounted for 85 percent, of all industrial research and development (Galbraith, 1967:23).

SHARE OF 200 LARGEST MANUFACTURING CORPORATIONS

Year	Percentage of Total Manufacturing Assets
1929	45.8%
1938	48.7%
1949	47.1%
1959	54.8%
1969	60.2%
1973	60.3%

SOURCE: Federal Trade Commission reported and discussed in John Blair, 1972, *Economic Concentration*, New York: Harcourt Brace Jovanovich, p. 64. Data for 1973 from David Penn, Spring 1976, "Aggregate Concentration," *Anti-Trust Bulletin*.

Many economists are critical of the growth of giant monopolistic firms which regulate output and prices, and exercise enormous political control. Liberals assert that monopoly represents the most evil aspect of capitalism. Some economists believe, however, that the worst features of monopoly can be eliminated through enforcement of existing antitrust laws. Others, such as John Kenneth Galbraith, believe that change within the modern corporation is eliminating its most negative feature, the ruthless pursuit of greater and greater profits. In *The New Industrial State*, Galbraith argued that corporate control no longer resides with stockholders and top management, but with the *technostructure* (i.e. technical personnel, including scientists and technicians), which can use corporate resources in the best interests of all society.

Radicals disagree with Galbraith's view that the modern corporation is controlled by the technostructure. They argue that top management owns a large amount of corporate stock. As a consequence, the technostructure must worry about the return of capital. How can the technostructure control a corporation if its is hired and fired by top management? Surely, it is top management that makes the decisions and uses the advice of scientists and technicians to make more profitable decisions.

points: first, a large firm may be able to operate in less than optimal locations because it can control government policies, control the prices and sources of raw materials and make a significant impact on the market; conversely, large firms may be able to make more profitable locational choices because they have the scientists and technical personnel to help top management make more profitable decisions.

Inter-Firm Scale Economies: Agglomeration

We have been concerned solely with intra-firm scale economies and how the expansion of a single firm can lower unit costs. Scale economies also apply to clusters of firms in the same or related industries. By clustering together (increasing the *spatial* "scale"), costs per unit can be lowered for all firms. These economies are called *externalities, agglomeration economies,* or *linkages*. Regardless of the name used, such economies take four basic forms.

Production Linkages These economies accrue to firms which locate near other producers which manufacture their basic raw materials. The links between producers of aircraft components and aircraft producers (clustered in Southern California) and those between auto parts manufacturers and auto subassembly plants (concentrated in Michigan) provide examples. The output of one firm (or group of firms) becomes the input of another. By clustering together, distribution and assembly costs for both types of firms are reduced.

Service Linkages The garment industry, which includes a large cluster in New York City, is an example of service linkages. The firms in the garment industry are small, but they require specialized service and maintenance activities such as the repair of sewing and cutting machines. Individually, no firm is large enough to support the development of a service industry (repair, spare parts, preventive maintenance), but *collectively* they can support an extensive service industry. Clustering provides the scale economies necessary for this kind of service to operate profitably, thereby eliminating down-time for individual firms.

The clustering of the garment industry in Manhattan has also provided the impetus for the development of banking investment officers who deal almost exclusively with loans to this type of production. These investors who specialize in the garment industry understand its special needs, and are much more likely to advance risk capital than investors who do not understand the industry and its unique capital requirements. This specialization could not have developed, however, if small firms in the industry were not highly concentrated.

Market Linkages The garment industry also illustrates market linkages which occur when a cluster is large enough to attract specialized distribution services. The small firms of the industry in New York have collectively attracted advertising agencies, showrooms, buyer listings, and other aspects of finished product distribution which deal exclusively with the garment trade. Firms located within the cluster have a cost advantage over isolated firms which must provide these specialized services for themselves or deal with New York firms at a considerable distance and cost.

Urbanization Economies Some economies are not the result of interfirm linkages *per se,* but simply occur from locating in large cities. Firms in larger cities have an advantage, within limits, over similar firms in more rural areas. The city provides a market in which a small firm may be able to sell its entire output, thereby reducing finished product distribution costs. A city is more likely to provide the specialized labor force and service industries a firm may need and cities have the utilities (electricity, gas and water) which industry requires. Fire and police protection are more adequately provided in urban areas. Finally, cities are major nodes on the transportation networks (road, rail, and air) which are important to many kinds of manufacturing.

Demand and Industrial Location

Thus far we have been concerned almost exclusively with the supply side of manufacturing, examining ways in which firms could reduce unit costs. We implied that a firm could sell its entire output at a given market price and would be concerned only with reducing costs and increasing unit profits. This is one of the main assumptions of the conservative economists' model of *perfect competition* and many very small industrial enterprises operate within this framework. The level of market demand in a private enterprise economy, however, is an important aspect of industrial location for most firms.

Demand determines the scale of output and, in turn, determines the technique and location of a firm. Concentrations of high demand attract market-oriented industries and therefore, influence location patterns. Market demand is essentially a function of income and tastes—both of which change through time. Different industries must deal with different kinds of demand. Firms producing goods sold to general consumers face different location problems than those which produce a specialized product sold only to other manufacturers or to a select group of consumers. The demand pattern in the United States facing a producer of root beer is considerably different from that facing a manufacturer of snowmobile parts.

A Demand Potential Surface

Geographers have explored the problem of market demand through the concept of a *potential surface,* extensively developed by Chauncy Harris (1954). We may assume for a moment that tastes and incomes are the only factors determining demand. If tastes are uniform, the demand for a product is simply a function of income times population. If incomes are equal, the demand for a product will be high in densely populated areas and low where population is less. We could also allow income differences to play a role by weighting the population of an area by average income,

Demand and Industrial Location

total retail sales, or some other measure of the ability to consume. We also know the price of a good is a major determinant of demand. Price can be made a simple function of distance (finished product distribution costs) if we assume assembly and production costs are spatial constants. As always, we are holding some factors constant to simplify analysis.

What are the potential sales at Point j of a product produced at Point i? Assuming that demand is a function of population (or population weighted by income) and price (as a direct function of distance) we find:

$$D_{ij} = \frac{P_j}{d_{ij}}$$

where D_{ij} = demand at point j for a product produced at point i
P_j = the population of j (may be income weighted)
d_{ij} = distance between i and j

A large population at j increases demand, but a large distance between i and j raises the price and reduces demand. We can calculate the demand potential between point i and an infinite number of points j yielding:

$$D_i = \sum_{j=1}^{n} \frac{P_j}{d_{ij}}$$

where D_i = demand potential at i
P_j = population of j (may be income weighted)
d_{ij} = distance between i and j

the symbol $\sum_{j=1}^{n}$ means we take the *sum* of demand for all points j from the first point ($j = 1$) to the last point (n).

Demand potential is computed for a large number of points; all points with same values are connected (iso-lines) to produce a map of a demand potential surface. Figure 7.27A shows the potential surface of the United States produced by weighting population by retail sales per county for a number of sample points. The actual numbers produced by this sort of calculation have only a *relative* meaning, so the contours are expressed as a percentage below the highest point. Away from the point, potential demand drops off in all directions, as shown in the inset in Figure 7.27B which is a cross section drawn from New York to Los Angeles. We might assume that demand is maximized at the highest point of the surface and potential sales would be highest there. A producer might want to get as "near" as possible to total demand.

The problem can however, be viewed in another way. If all demand is concentrated at a single point, as in Weber's model, access to the market is maximized and transport costs are minimized at that point. Moving to one point, however, increases transportation costs (raises prices and lowers demand) to other points if demand is spread among a number of places. This is illustrated in Figure 7.28. Moving from Point B to Point C raises transportation costs to other points. A location at New York City maximizes the distance to a large part of the country.

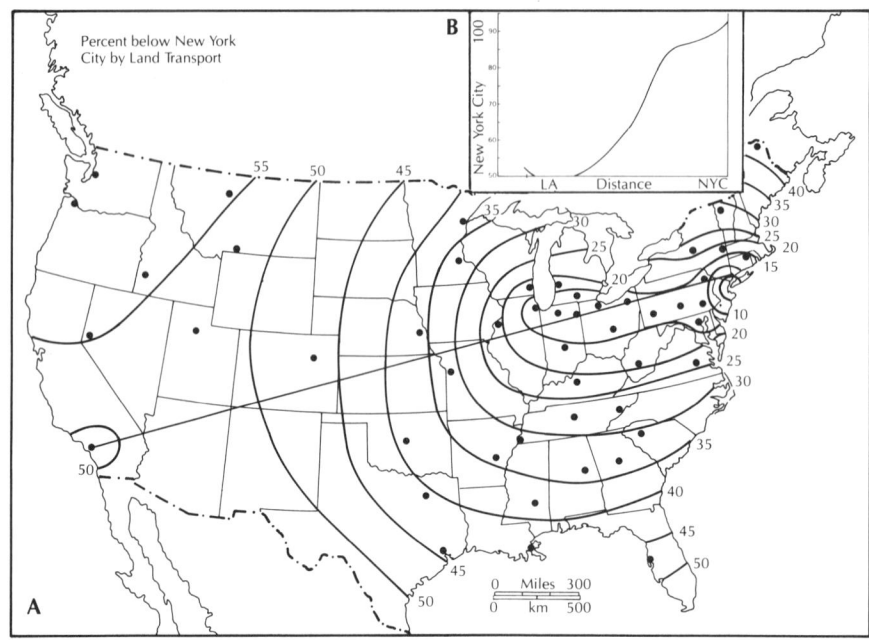

FIGURE 7.27 (A) Market potential, United States. SOURCE: "The Market as a Factor in the Localization of Industry in the U.S.," Figure 4, reproduced by permission of the *Annals* of the Association of American Geographers, Volume 44, 1954, C. D. Harris; (B) cross-section from New York City to Los Angeles (inset).

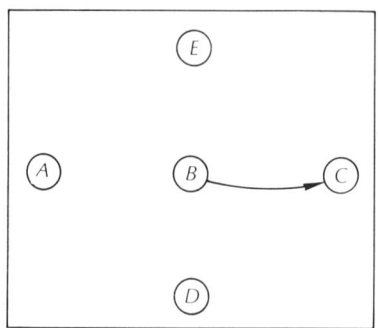

FIGURE 7.28 Changes in aggregate transportation costs.

A Transport Cost Surface

We can conceptualize a *transport cost surface* in much the same way as we did the demand potential surface:

$$TC_i = P_j d_{ij}$$

where
- TC_i is total transport costs at i
- P_j is the population of j (weighted)
- d_{ij} is the distance from i to j

Demand and Industrial Location

Notice that in the transport cost equation we *multiply* by distance while in the demand potential equation we *divide* by distance. A large distance will *lower* the value on the left-hand side of the equation in the demand model and *increase* it on the transport model. Figure 7.29A shows a transport cost surface based on the same sample of points as the demand model. The lowest point on the transport cost surface would be in the geometric center of the United States if population (and per capita income) were evenly distributed. The uneven distribution of population minimizes total cost at Fort Wayne, Indiana, and total cost rises in all directions as shown in the New York-Los Angeles cross-section in Figure 7.29B.

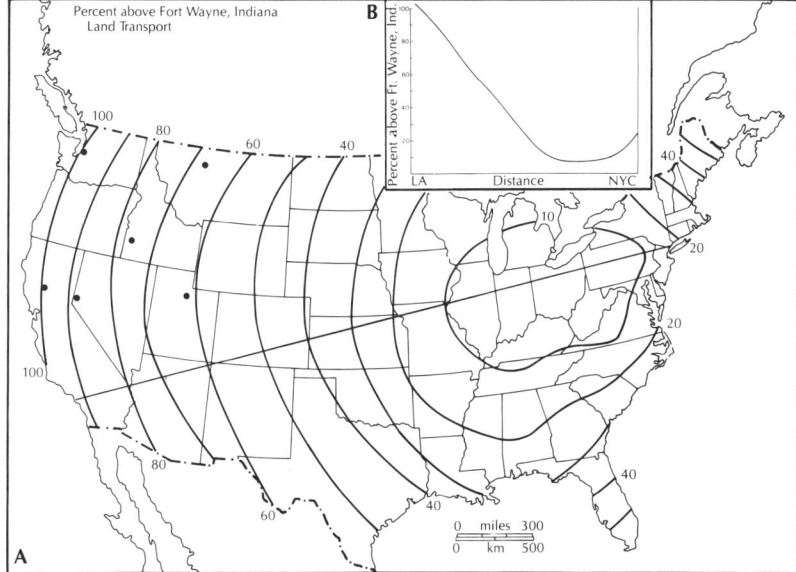

FIGURE 7.29 (A) Transport cost to the national market. SOURCE: "The Market as a Factor in the Localization of Industry in the U.S.," Figure 7, reproduced by permission of the *Annals* of the Association of American Geographers, Volume 44, 1954, C. D. Harris; (B) cross-section from New York City to Los Angles (inset).

The problem then is to determine the most profitable location. Is it the highest point on the demand potential surface or the lowest point on the transport cost surface? Harris (1954) summed the problem with an example. The West Coast comprised 11 percent of the U.S. market in 1954, but accounted for only 5 percent of the sales from Chicago firms (as a percent of total national sales), yet the West Coast accounted for 22 percent of the total transport costs incurred by Chicago firms. The potential model is useful because it allows us to visualize variations in demand. The more localized the market, the more nearly the optimum points on both surfaces coincide, but only for the distribution part of the manufacturing decision. We still would have to examine the surfaces for assembly and production costs.

The same model can be applied to industries which serve a more limited market. Figure 7.30 shows the potential demand surface faced by manufacturers.

Roughly 80 percent of all manufacturing in the United States uses some raw materials which have been processed by another producer. Some types of manufacturing sell their entire output to other manufacturers—machine tools as an example. In

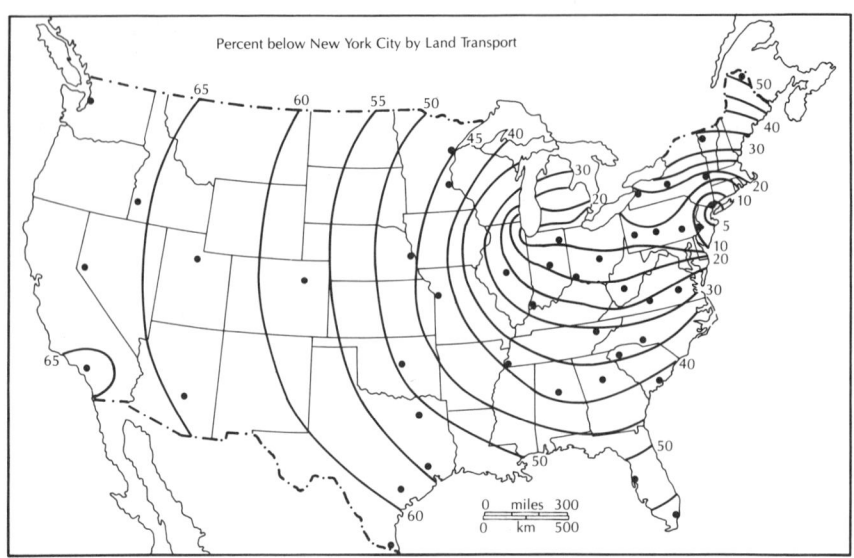

FIGURE 7.30 Manufacturing potential. SOURCE: "The Market as a Factor in the Localization of Industry in the U.S.," Figure 28, reproduced by permission of the *Annals* of the Association of American Geographers, Volume 44, 1954, C. D. Harris.

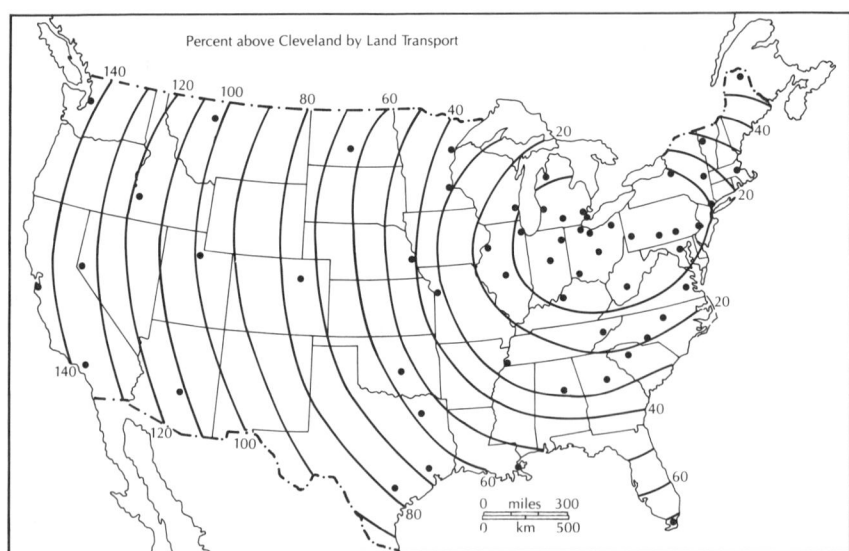

FIGURE 7.31 Transport cost to the national manufacturing market. SOURCE: "The Market as a Factor in the Localization of Industry in the U.S.," Figure 29, reproduced by permission of the *Annals* of the Association of American Geographers, Volume 44, 1954, C. D. Harris.

Demand and Industrial Location

Figure 7.30, the sample points have been weighted by employment in manufacturing. Figure 7.31 shows the transportation cost surface for the same producers.

Throughout much of this chapter we have assumed that demand (revenue) was a spatial constant and that optimum location for production was at the point of minimum cost (Figure 7.32). This figure assumes that we can sell as many units as we produce at the constant price and that revenue per unit and total revenue are maximized. Notice in Figure 7.32 that we minimize cost, and maximize the profit per unit and total profit at Point O. The reverse argument holds when price is a spatial constant and revenue varies across distance (Figure 7.33). At Point O, we maximize the profit per unit, total revenue, and total profit. We have also considered a situation in which both revenue and cost are spatial variables (Figure 7.34) and the optimum location occurs where the positive distance between revenue and cost is maximized. All three figures assume that the value of revenue and/or cost *at any given point* is constant. We can sell an infinite number of units at a price of R in Figure 7.32, for example. This assumption has been made to simplify analysis and to concentrate our attention on spatial variations in cost.

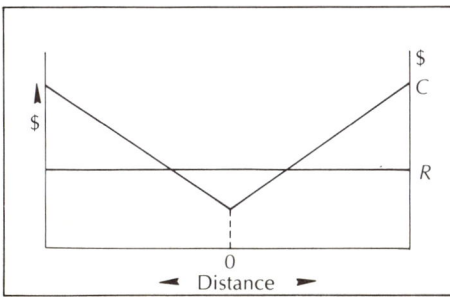

FIGURE 7.32 Optimum location: demand constant, costs variable.

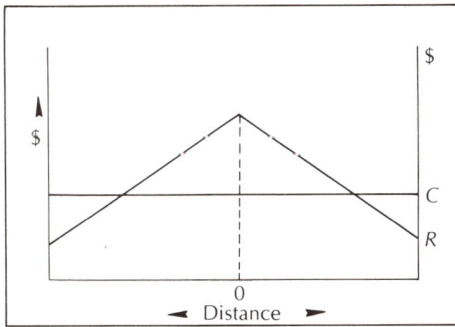

FIGURE 7.33 Optimum location: demand variable, costs constant.

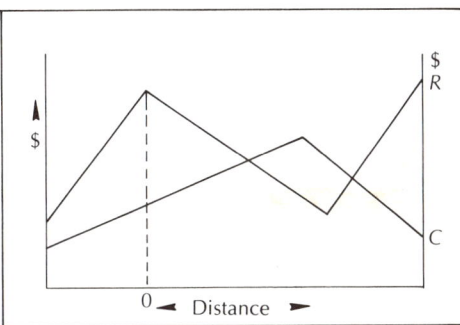

FIGURE 7.34 Optimum location: demand and costs variable.

The Cost of Competition: Locational Interdependence

We turn now to the problem of *locational interdependence*—the principle that says competition from rival producers can dramatically lower potential revenues at a given point in space. We have assumed in this chapter that each producer is a *spatial monopolist*. The capitalist is the sole producer of the particular product within his market area. Profit maximization occurs, under this assumption, at the level of output at which marginal cost equals marginal revenue. The profit maximizing strategy is different when non-monopoly conditions occur.

Locational interdependence implies a non-monopoly situation. Economic competition occurs, but not as in the classical model of perfect competition. The kind of market faced by spatial rivals is called an *oligopoly*, which occurs when more than one producer exists in the market, but the number is small enough so that the actions of one producer may have a considerable effect on the other. Economic (price) competition is lacking in an oligopoly, but intense non-price competition occurs.

An oligopoly often exists when producers are considered in a spatial context. A small manufacturing plant is only concerned with the actions of other firms within the *same market area*. A producer of ready-mixed concrete in Chicago, for example, is not concerned with the actions of similar firms in Los Angeles. Even if the Los Angeles firms lower their plant price to zero, they cannot capture the Chicago market because of the transportation costs involved. The individual Chicago producer is, however, concerned with the actions of other ready-mixed firms in the Chicago area because their actions can have a considerable effect upon his profits. *Locational interdependence*, therefore, is a term coined to refer to *spatial oligopolies*.

The Ice Cream Vendor Analogy

Let us consider a simple oligopoly model first developed by H. Hotelling (1929). Imagine a stretch of beach over which people are evenly distributed. On this beach are two ice cream vendors, each of whom sells an identical product at the same price. People on the beach, therefore, minimize the cost of their ice cream purchases by buying from the closer vendor. Initially the two vendors are located at the quartile points of the beach (Figure 7.35A). Each person buys from the closer vendor, so that the total market area is equally divided between the two. Vendor A can temporarily increase his share of the market by shifting the location of his stand to a site immediately adjacent to Vendor B (Figure 7.35B). The solid line in Figure 7.35B shows the division of the market under this condition. Vendor B's first countermove is shown in Figure 7.35C and the final solution is given in Figure 7.35D in which the market once again is evenly split between the two vendors. Neither can gain an advantage over his rival by moving, so each must turn to other forms of competition, such as advertising or product differentiation.

The Hotelling solution determines the equilibrium quantity sold by each producer and the equilibrium prices, but we must assume that demand is completely

The Cost of Competition: Locational Interdependence

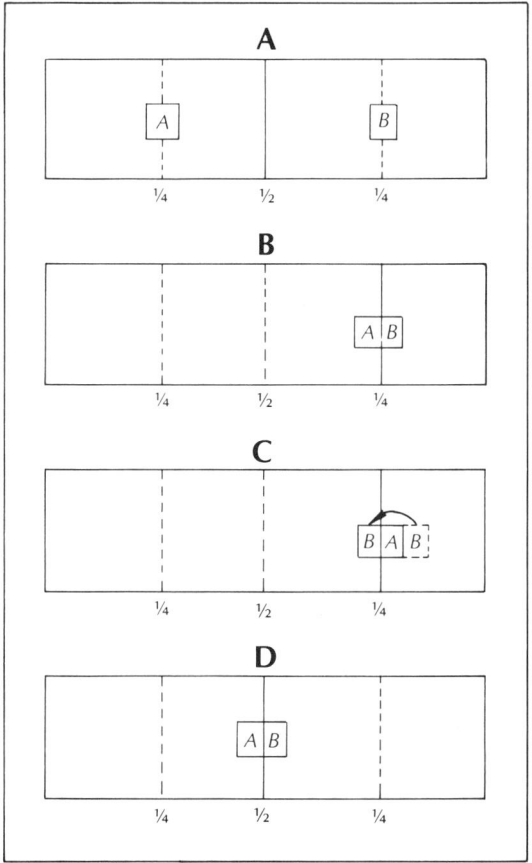

FIGURE 7.35 The "Ice Cream Vendor" Analogy. After H. Hotelling, 1929, "Stability in Competition," *Economic Journal*, **39**, 41–57.

inelastic at any price. If both producers charge the same price (plus the same transportation costs), total demand will be equally shared in the equilibrium situation. Hotelling assumed, in other words, that the demand of consumers at the edge of the market (who must pay a higher price) is the same as those near the common selling point. Both producers share the same production costs so that the common market price is that at which marginal costs equal zero. The distance to the most distant consumer is the same from both producers and neither can affect transportation costs. A producer who raises the market price will immediately lose the entire market, and neither producer can lower prices to a point where costs exceed the price per unit, so the equilibrium is uniquely determined. This is an optimum solution for each producer, but not for consumers because a location at the quartile points would minimize aggregate transportation costs.

Let us define the area of a spatial oligopoly more precisely. Consider Figure 7.36. A producer locates at X and sells at a mill price of $5 per unit. Transportation costs on the product are 10¢ per unit per kilometer. The producer at X need not be concerned with producers at Y and Y'. Although their mill price is lower, they cannot encroach on his market area because of their transportation costs. He will, however, be concerned with the actions of Z and Z' which do encroach on his potential market area. All producers must be concerned with the possibility of a rival producer locating at any point which could capture a portion of the shared market area.

Each producer (X, Z, and Z') will attempt to devise a strategy which will minimize the possibility that rivals can increase their share of the market and increase their profits.

The most important form of competition in the initial phase of a special oligopoly (before equilibrium) is price competition based on transportation costs. A producer is able to capture the part of the market area in which his delivered price is lowest. This outcome holds *only* if we assume that transport costs are charged to each consumer as a function of distance and until equilibrium conditions are reached. Other transportation pricing strategies are discussed in Chapter 8, but we should point out some other (non-technical) forms of competition here.

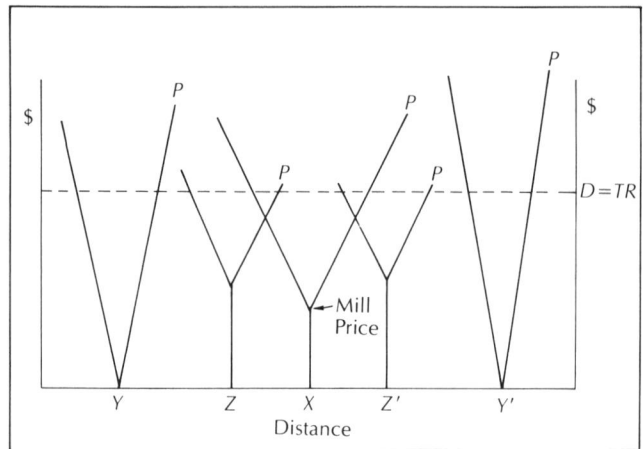

FIGURE 7.36 Spatial oligopoly.

Price differentials are the only form of competition allowed in technical economic analysis, but we popularly recognize several other types. Advertising, which adds to the cost of products, is the most important kind of non-price competition in the United States. A second strategy is to create perceived quality differentials among products, such as the wide range of automobile types (and prices) that all bear a given producer's name. Quality differentiation divides a broad market into a group of submarkets, thus meeting the demand for a wide variety of consumers. Design differences form a third technique of non-price competition. Tennis racket companies, for example, continually introduce new models which are purported to be "superior" to last year's design and to all competition.

Non-price competition should be the prevailing form if locational equilibrium prevails. The fact that this type of competition is the most common in the United States may imply some sort of short-run equilibrium, at least in certain industries.

Both long- and short-run locational equilibrium assume that producers can adjust instantaneously to changes in the location of competitors and other marginal changes in costs and revenues. A number of models, beyond the scope of this book, attempt to show the equilibrium reached after a series of adjustments by

Case Studies

spatial oligopolists. Locational inertia, however, prevents the instantaneous adjustment from taking place, and transportation costs prevent all factors of production from being as mobile as they are assumed to be in the models of classical economics.

Equilibrium adjustment also assumes economic rationality and perfect knowledge, which are not conditions of reality. Producers are reluctant to make major moves even if economically feasible because of risk and uncertainty. Spatial equilibrium, if it exists even in the short run, is the result of a trial and error process which has often resulted in great social costs.

Case Studies

The principles of industrial location theory can be applied to any industry, and they help us to understand the locational pattern of a given industry. To apply these principles, we have to determine the relative importance of the inputs used by an industry, the structure of transportation costs on inputs and outputs, and the historical development of the spatial pattern of the industry. For example, if a single, localized input accounts for 90 percent of the total input costs of Industry X, we can use a Weberian model to understand the locational pattern. For more complex patterns, we may have to examine the relative importance of localized and ubiquitous inputs, the cost of labor, and other factors. In this section, we examine several case studies of industries to illustrate the classical principles outlined in this chapter.

Copper Manufacturing

Copper is a valuable metal used in electrical and electronic industries. The metal is highly localized and rarely occurs in pure form. Most copper ores contain less than 3 percent pure copper. (*Ore* is an economic term. An ore is a material that contains enough of a mineral to pay for the cost of extraction.) Copper is so valuable that ores of 1–2 percent will pay for the cost of extraction, whereas materials containing the same percentage of iron would go untouched. Obviously, copper ore is a weight-losing raw material. The material index for most copper ore in the United States is nearly 100—for every 100 tons of ore mined, about one ton of pure copper is extracted. From mine to pure copper requires three distinct manufacturing phases: concentration, smelting, and refining, and the material index declines with each phase. We apply different elements of location theory to each step in the manufacturing process.

Concentrating Copper bearing materials are hauled from the mines to concentrators where the ore undergoes a process known as "froth-flotation." For every 100 tons of ore entering a concentrating plant, about 97½ tons are worthless waste. The remaining 2½ tons of concentrated copper also contains various impurities. The nation's copper concentrating capacity is highly localized in a copper belt running from Arizona to Montana (Figure 7.37). Copper concentrating takes place near copper mines to avoid the cost of shipping waste materials.

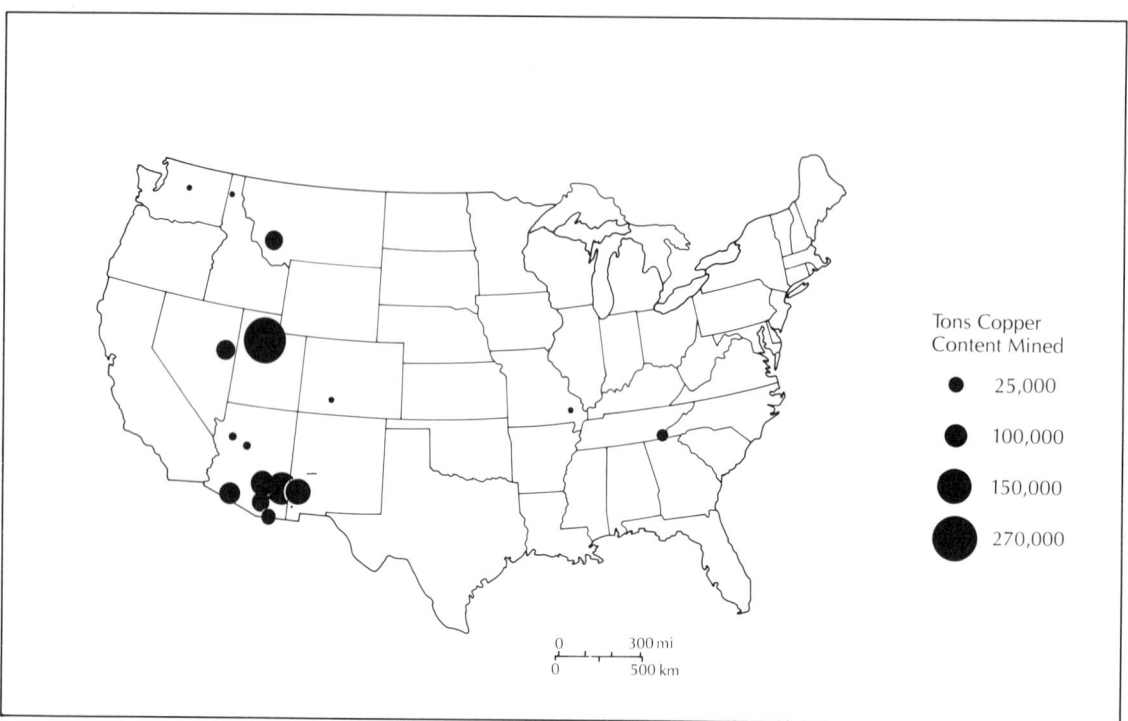

FIGURE 7.37 Copper mining and concentrating.

Smelting The next phase of the manufacturing process is to remove major impurities (mostly sulphur and oxygen) from the concentrated copper. Of the 2½ tons of concentrated copper entering a smelter, about 1½ tons are waste. This yields a material index of 1.66 (60% weight loss). The one ton of "blister copper" produced in the smelting process is 99% pure copper. Again, the high weight-loss ratio means that most copper smelting is done very near copper mines, usually in association with concentration, but the lower weight-loss ratio also means that some smelting can be done some distance from copper mines, especially if low transportation rates can be obtained. Figure 7.38 shows the lessening pull of the raw materials for copper smelting. Tidewater plants on the east and west coasts are able to smelt foreign ores which have been concentrated elsewhere. This pattern also illustrates the low cost of sea transportation.

Refining Blister copper emerges from the smelting process 99% pure, but its purity must be refined further before it can be manufactured into finished products. The material index is now very close to one (weight-loss ratio of 1%) and the pull of the raw material source has been considerably lessened. The material lost in the concentrating and smelting process was all waste, but the impurities removed from the copper in the refining phase consist of gold, silver, lead, and zinc—all of which are valuable and will pay for the cost of transportation. Blister copper is therefore a "pure" raw material in that no "waste" is transported. Some copper refining is done in the copper belt in conjunction with concentrating and smelting, but much of the nation's copper refining capacity is located elsewhere, especially on the northeastern seaboard close to the major markets for copper (Figure 7.39).

FIGURE 7.38 Copper smelting.

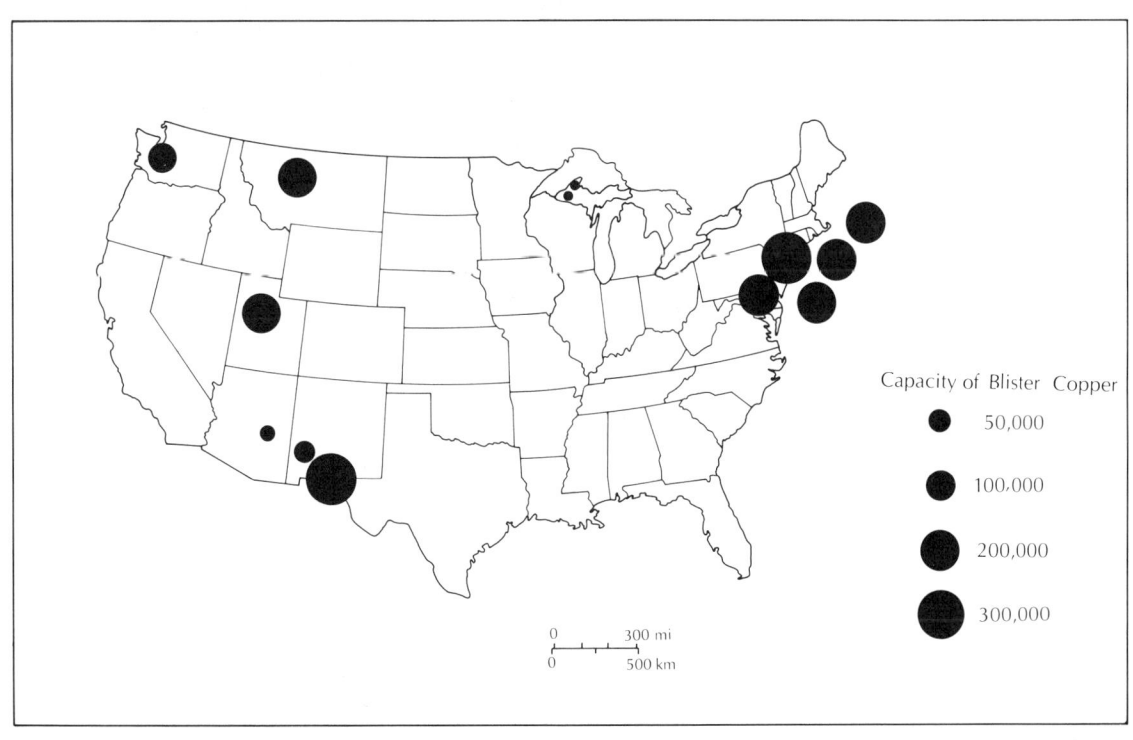

FIGURE 7.39 Copper refining.

359

Iron and Steel

Primary copper manufacturing is oriented toward a single raw material, but the steel industry requires three primary material inputs—iron ore, fuel (coal or electricity), and limestone. In recent years, the availability of scrap iron has become increasingly important as a raw material for the industry. The steel industry is important because it forms the primary raw material for other types of manufacturing. The steel industry produces few products directly for consumers. Most of its output flows to other manufacturing industries who fabricate the steel into other products (such as automobiles) or to the construction industry. Steel production, therefore, is the foundation upon which a modern industrial complex rests. For this reason, steel production is often used in market economies as a measure of industrial development and changes in steel prices are closely watched by economists as a barometer of price changes in other sectors of the manufacturing economy, and, ultimately, consumer price. Low-cost steel production was one of the prerequisites for the Industrial Revolution because steel was required for the steam and internal combustion engine, railroads, and other machinery. Large-scale production of steel, however, requires huge capital investments and large scale operations. Investments are usually so large that the pattern of steel manufacturing remains stable for many years. Most of the large industrial complexes in the world today reflect the development of

An open-pit iron ore mine, near Hibbing, Minnesota. Iron ore, the foundation of modern industry, is one of three basic resources necessary for steel making. The others are coal and limestone.

Case Studies

the steel industry in the nineteenth century. In England, the industrial complex dates back almost two hundred years. Early small-scale production relied on charcoal and small deposits of iron ore and were scattered throughout forest areas. The mass production of steel required coal as a fuel and was especially attracted to deposits of high-quality coking coal. A map of steel production today is still in many ways a map of coal.

Large scale steel production in the United States grew in response to the coal deposits of the Appalachian highlands; the vast iron ore deposits near Lake Superior; and the Great Lakes waterway which links these two raw material sources. The early pattern of steel manufacturing reflected coal deposits in the country, and much of the nation's steel capacity is still concentrated near Appalachian coal, illustrating the *inertia* of this capital-intensive industry. The pattern shown in Figure 7.40 can be broken down into several areas, each reflecting a different location factor and stage in the historical development of the steel industry:

1. old, coal oriented areas—Pennsylvania (Pittsburgh) and Ohio.
2. interior sites dependent on water transportation—the steel complexes located along the Great Lakes.
3. newer tidewater sites, especially Sparrow's Point, Maryland, and Morrisville, Pennsylvania, which utilize foreign ores and cheap ocean transportation.
4. smaller interior complexes utilizing localized deposits of coal and ore—especially Birmingham, Alabama.

Burns Harbor Plant located on the shores of Lake Michigan 55 kilometers southeast of Chicago. Since its beginning in 1962, the plant has become a complex that converts raw materials into plates, sheets, and tin mill products. The main market for steel products from the Burns Harbor Plant is Chicago which has an abundance of metal using industries. SOURCE: *Bethlehem Steel*.

A deepwater pier for ocean-going ore carriers at Bethlehem's Sparrow's Point, Md., plant. SOURCE: *Bethlehem Steel*.

5. the deep western complexes of Pueblo, Colorado, and Geneva, Utah, which were built during World War II by government action to supply the war effort on the West Coast.

The favorable location relative to coal and iron ore allowed the steel industry to prosper in the northeastern quarter of the United States. The production of steel in turn favored the development of a large and extensive manufacturing complex in the same area. The *American Manufacturing Belt* then became the major market for steel. Fuel exerts the major pull on the industry. Ore can be shipped a considerable distance if cheap water transportation is available. The pattern can be easily understood by relying on classical location theory, but the tremendous inertia must also be highlighted.

A modern steel plant requires a huge investment. Much of the expansion of the steel industry in the United States has taken place by adding to existing operations, which is generally cheaper than building at new sites (Alexandersson, 1961). The pattern today may be more reflective of the fixed capital inertia of the industry than the relative location of raw materials and markets.

The steel industry illustrates several locational principles. The initial location of the industry could be simulated using the Varignon frame with fuel (coal) showing the greatest amount of "pull" because of its high weight-loss ratio and contribution to total costs. Cheap water transportation can reduce the pull of any of the raw materials used to make steel, but water transportation is used basically to acquire ore rather than fuel. Once in place, however, the high fixed costs of plants hold the pattern stable for long periods of time. The costs of moving, therefore, outweigh the locational costs of raw materials.

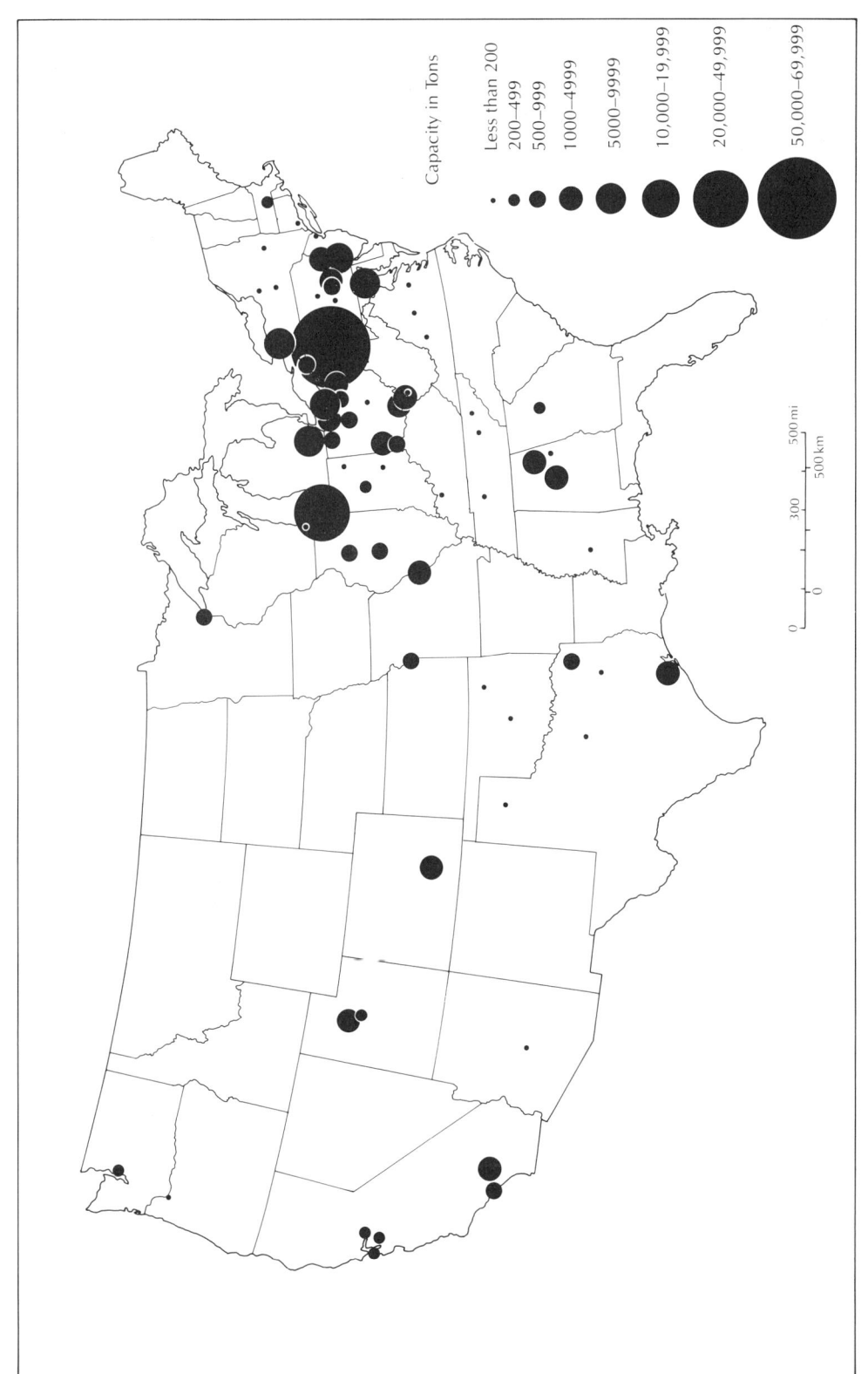

FIGURE 7.40 Steel manufacturing.

Coils of sheet steel awaiting shipment from mill to firms of the American Manufacturing Belt. SOURCE: *Bethlehem Steel.*

The Cotton-Textile Industry

The textile industry led the Industrial Revolution in Europe-North America. Textiles were the first product to be mass produced. The Industrial Revolution began in Great Britain with the mechanization of textile manufacturing with water power and later steam. The most influential inventions were mechanical spinning and weaving devices and the cotton gin which supplied large quantities of the raw material cheaply.

Power was the primary location factor in the early days of the industry. In the United States, for example, the industry was first localized along the small waterfalls of New England and the Middle Atlantic states. Greater water power was provided by damming streams, but, by 1860 steam became the major source of power for the industry. Coal had to be brought in by ship and the industry shifted to coastal locations—especially Fall River and New Bedford, Massachusetts. The industry required three major inputs, fiber, power, and labor, and labor quickly became a prime factor affecting the location of textile manufacturing. The industry started shifting southward. The South had some initial water-power sites and access to cheap coal, but it was an abundant supply of cheap labor that attracted textile manufacturing to the area. In the early part of the twentieth century, the industry switched to electric power, making possible single-storied plants which could be located in small towns, giving the South an advantage in terms of new plants and equipment. By 1925, the South had passed New England in output. The use of

Case Studies

electricity meant that the industry was no longer capital-intensive, and allowed it to follow cheap labor rather easily. Since World War II, the industry has stagnated somewhat because of foreign competition, again illustrating the importance of cheap labor determining the location of the cotton textile industry.

The three industries which we have discussed tend to be localized rather than ubiquitous. They are usually controlled by very large firms and each plant in the steel and copper manufacturing industries is very large. Other industries meet demand through the operation of hundreds of small plants, each controlled by a local manager or single entrepreneur. Case studies of these industries illustrate a different set of locational factors.

Soft Drinks

The manufacture of bottled and canned soft drinks is one of the most ubiquitous industries in the United States. The industry inputs one pure raw material (syrup) and one ubiquitous raw material (water). Water is the major raw material by weight. Furthermore, the finished product has a low value for its weight. Soft drink manufacture is therefore market-oriented and illustrates the classic Weberian principle; market orientation is the rule in industries processing one pure and one ubiquitous raw material. The output of each location is determined by the size of the local market, yielding a high correlation between output and population. This correlation is illustrated by the map in Figure 7.41.

Weight-gaining commodity: bottled soft drinks. SOURCE: Photograph courtesy *The Coca-Cola Company.*

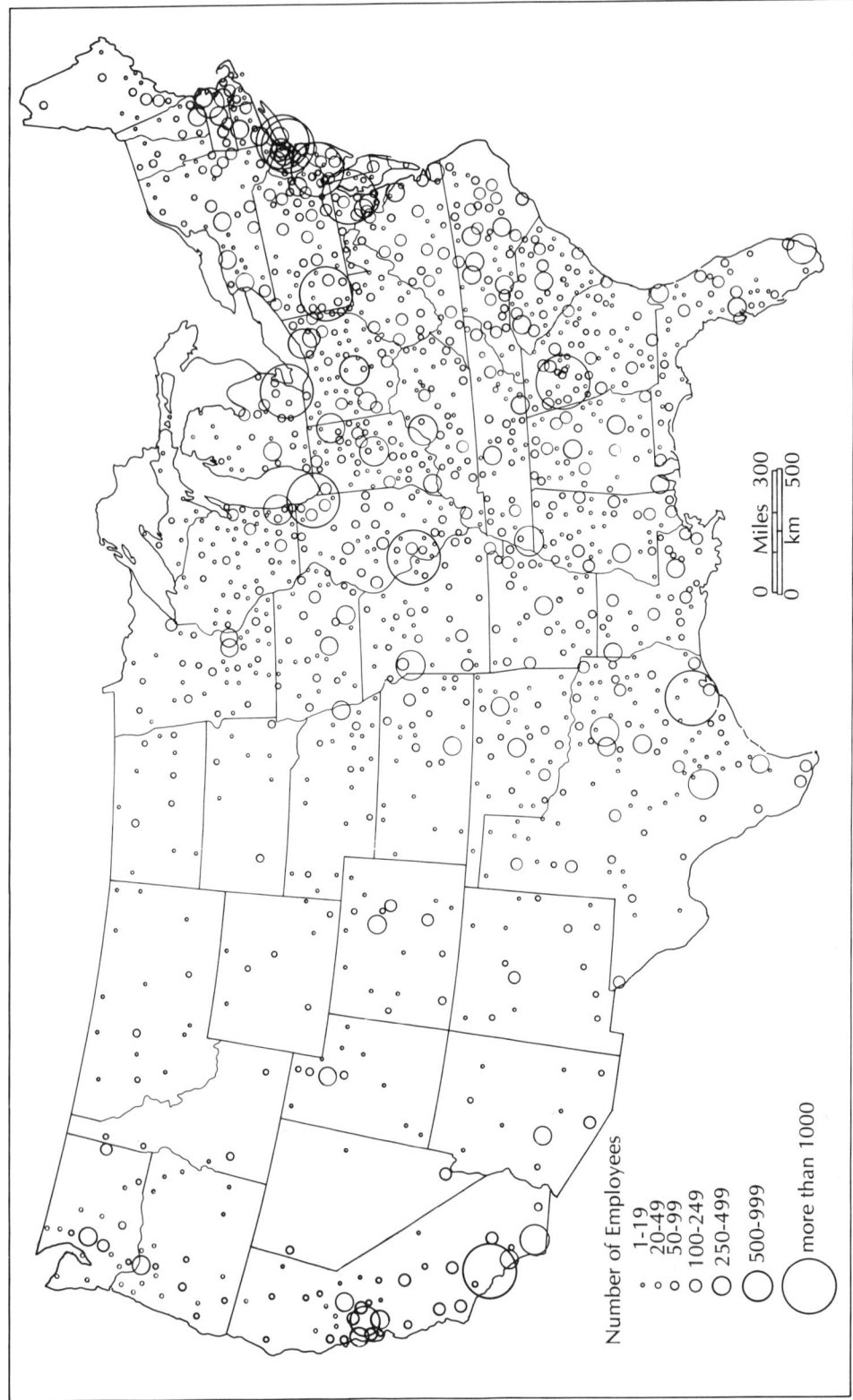

FIGURE 7.41 Location pattern of bottled and canned soft drink manufacturing, 1963.

Ready Mixed Concrete

This is another ubiquitous industry highly correlated with population. Three major raw materials are required: (1) portland cement which is pure; (2) water (ubiquitous); and (3) aggregate which is pure and often ubiquitous. Furthermore, the finished product is highly perishable and has a low value per unit of weight. Weberian theory states that the processing of more than one ubiquitous raw material plus a pure raw material yields a market orientation. The market orientation of the industry is shown in Figure 7.42.

The case studies all illustrate principles of classical location theory. The orientation of each industry toward raw materials, labor, markets, and/or other factors is relatively easy to determine in most cases. How specific locations are chosen, however, is a much more complex question and will be discussed in Chapter 9. The role of inertia and urbanization and industrial complex economies which lead to the development of industrial regions must now be introduced.

Industrial Regions

Most industrial location factors are essentially transportation problems. We may speak of an industry which is oriented toward coal, but what we mean is that coal is expensive to transport relative to other raw materials. If the transportation of coal were instantaneous and free, the industry would be oriented toward other factors. Locational costs exist because all movement costs, but locational costs vary among commodities, the level of technology, and the nature of the transportation net. For example, a water location or route may lower locational costs considerably. Once established, however, most industries face large fixed costs which generate inertia. Locational costs may change, but the industry remains in place because of inertia and because of the linkage and urbanization economies of a particular location.

A map of industrial regions in the world (Fig. 7.43) is a map of coal. The major industrial regions of the world were founded at a time when transportation costs were very high and the Industrial Revolution was oriented toward coal as a fuel source. The pattern has been somewhat modified by new energy sources (electricity), but the decisions of the past and the inertia of large industrial complexes produce a pattern that has been stable through time. The pattern of industrial regions also reflects cheap transportation systems (especially water), shown in the port and other water transportation locations.

The pattern of manufacturing in the United States illustrates these principles quite well. The map in Figure 7.44 shows that manufacturing is concentrated in the northeastern quarter of the country. This region is often called the "American Manufacturing Belt," and reflects three factors: (1) access to the coal of the Appalachian Highlands; (2) water transportation via the Atlantic and Great Lakes; and (3) the advantages of an early start in manufacturing, especially steel production. Once the steel industry was established, industries which used steel as a raw material located in the area, creating an industrial complex with linkages to many other types of manufacturing. Jobs created by industrialization created a market for goods and a

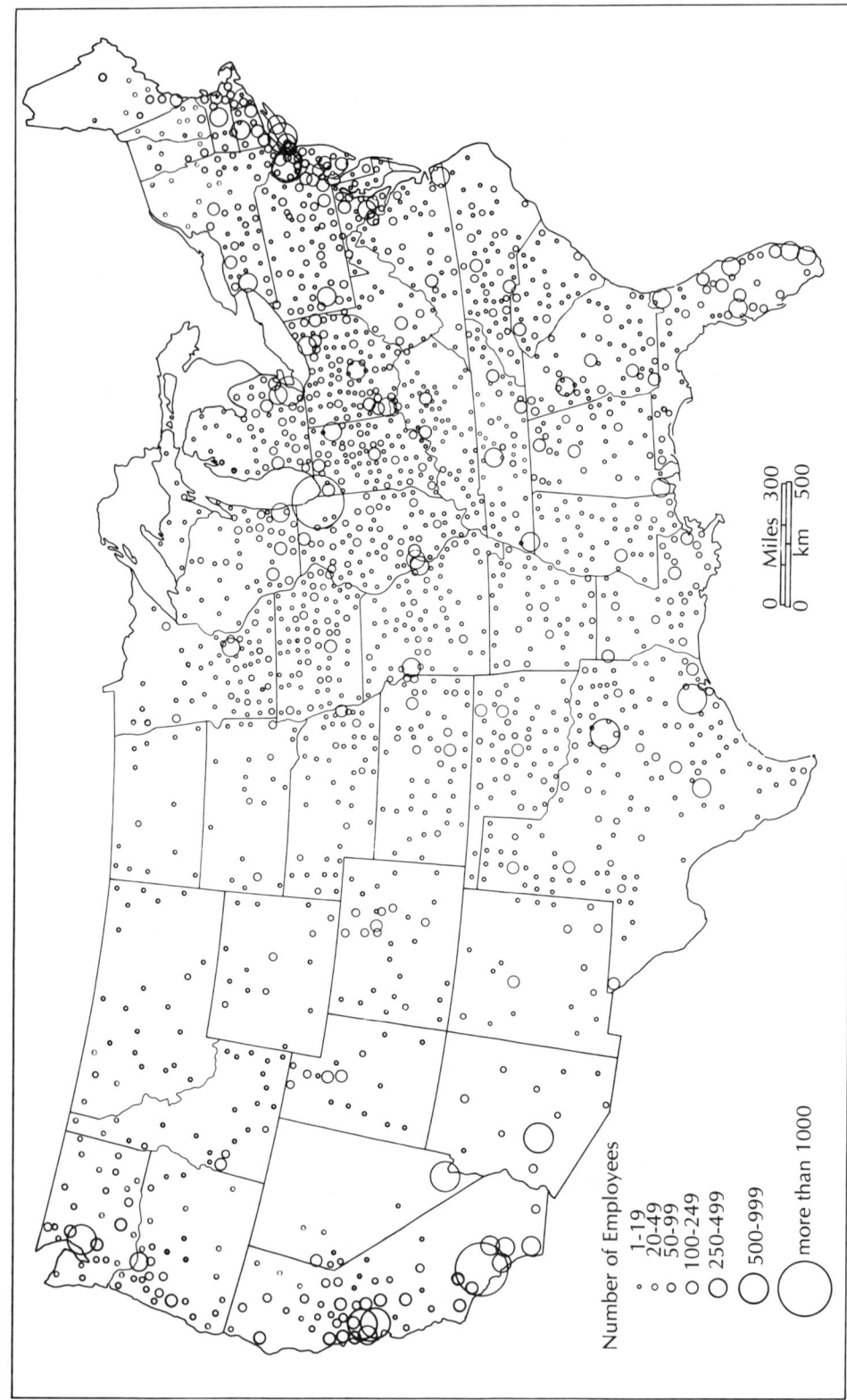

FIGURE 7.42 Location pattern of ready-mixed concrete production, 1963.

Social Consequences of Changes in the Location of Manufacturing

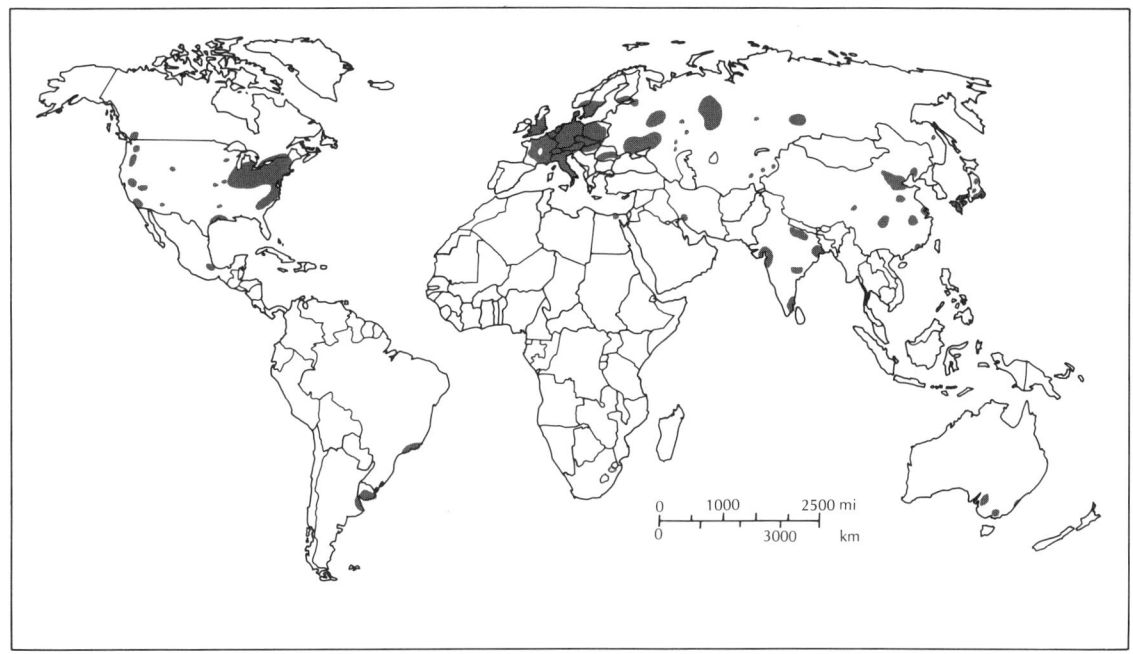

FIGURE 7.43 Major world industrial regions.

labor pool upon which other types of manufacturing could draw. Industrial development produced an urbanized region dominated by large manufacturing cities such as Baltimore, Cincinnati, Pittsburgh and Chicago. As technology changed, new transportation nets (rail, highway, and air) reinforced the centrality of existing cities.

Manufacturing is also important in other areas of the United States. The Southern Piedmont stands out on the map and, to a great extent, reflects the textile and furniture industries drawn to the area by cheap labor. The West Coast has developed considerable manufacturing, especially at coastal locations which can take advantage of water transportation.

Social Consequences of Changes in the Location of Manufacturing

Although manufacturing patterns tend to remain stable for long periods of time, long-run (and sometimes, abrupt) changes do occur. The pattern also may appear stable if we take a broad view, but at a different scale, changes may occur within manufacturing regions which have major social consequences. Long-run trends in the United States include: (1) a relative decline in the number of manufacturing jobs as the economy becomes more and more concentrated in the tertiary sector; (2) a decline in the number of manufacturing jobs in the older American Manufacturing Belt; (3) an increasing concentration of manufacturing jobs in newer industrial areas of the United States—especially in the "Sunbelt"; (4) a shift of manufacturing jobs to

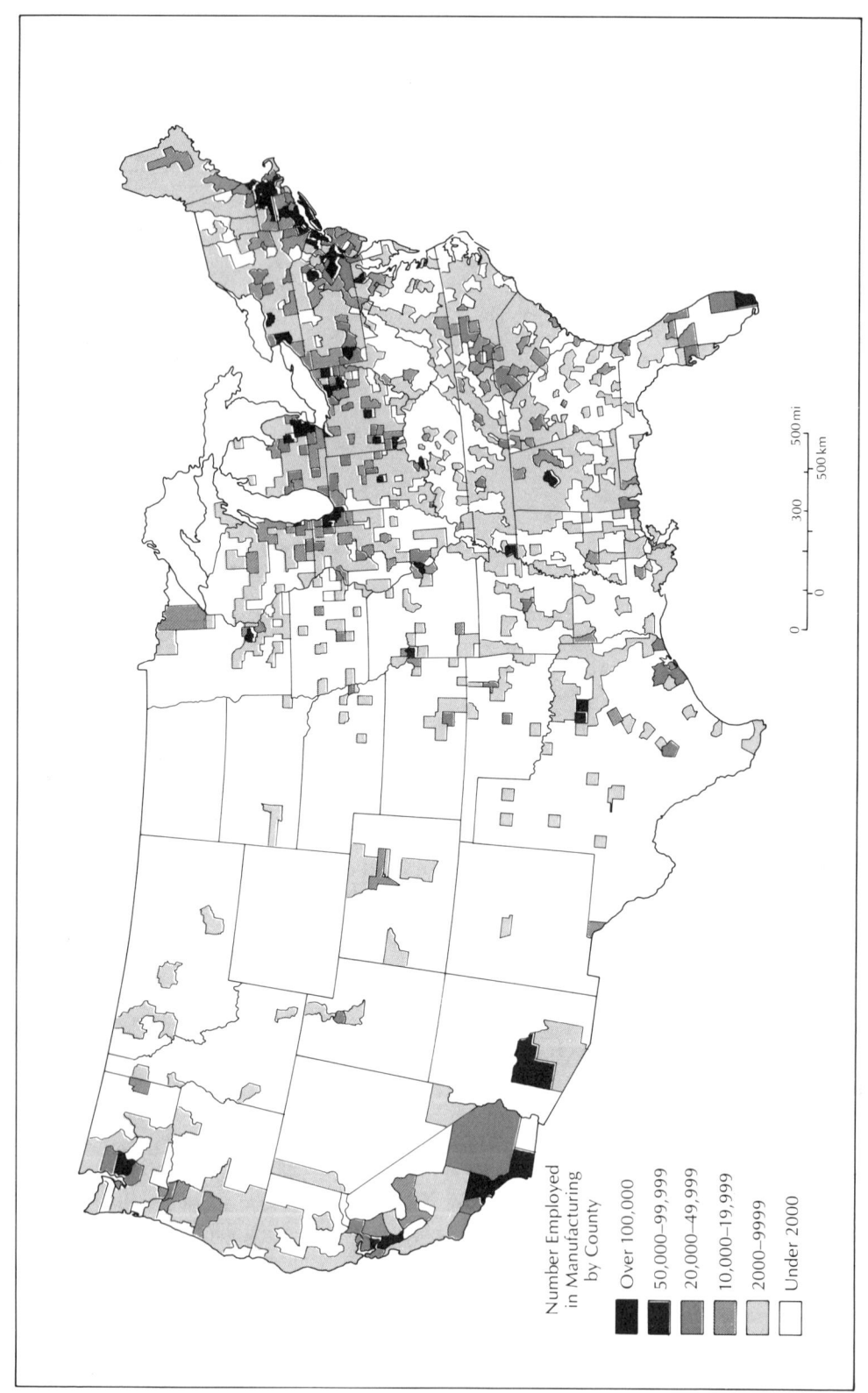

FIGURE 7.44 The pattern of manufacturing in the U.S. SOURCE: *County and City Data Book*, 1972.

foreign countries which offer cheaper labor, a move which can be easily accomplished by a multinational corporation. Both long- and short-run industrial shifts have social consequences. High unemployment, for example, occurs when a major employer moves out of an area. New England suffered high unemployment in the early 1900s as the textile industry moved southward.

An industry may shift by closing down one operation and opening a new plant somewhere else. Most multi-plant firms simply shift operations from older plants to newer branch plants. Shifts in the location of industry are the result of changing input costs (especially labor) at a given location or changing markets. The high wages of New England, for example, are usually cited as a primary reason for the industry's shift to the South. Organized labor in an area tends to drive up wages which, in turn, precipitates a move to an area where labor is less organized. On the other hand, some types of manufacturing which are highly capital-intensive, such as steel and automobile manufacturing, are not able to move easily and therefore are less able to withstand pressure for higher wages. These industries tend to have the highest wage rates. Labor organizations are moving toward nation-wide wage scales for specific industries, a trend which also has lessened the mobility of many types of manufacturing in terms of labor costs. Taxes, energy costs, and changing markets are other reasons for shifts in the industrial pattern.

When industry moves, workers lose jobs. They cannot easily follow the industry to another part of the country. Employees are reluctant to leave familiar places, family and friends, and the investment they may have in homes and schools. An industrial shut-down affects many more people than just laid-off production workers. Manufacturing, as we pointed out earlier, is a *settlement-building activity*. Wages earned in manufacturing support workers in other sectors of the economy such as wholesale and retail trade. The entire urban or regional economy may be adversely affected if the employment in a shifting industry is large enough. Many cities try to guard against such an event by trying to attract as many different types of manufacturing as possible. Diversification reduces the number of jobs lost if a single plant closes. The factors that make one plant in an industry viable in a given area, however, usually attract other producers of the same product or linked industries. Diversification tends to be the exception rather than the rule, especially in the old established industrial area of the American Manufacturing Belt. In a free-market economy, government action to stabilize employment patterns to replace employment opportunities lost to other areas, or to induce industrial development in underdeveloped regions or areas of high unemployment is generally lacking or ineffective. In planned economies, industrial shifts also take place in response to changes in material input costs, but regional unemployment can be reduced or industrial development stimulated much more easily. In either case, the relative difference in the mobility of industry and workers is a problem that must be faced.

Summary

The pattern of manufacturing in a market economy is determined by many factors. Assembly costs occur because of the uneven distribution of raw materials required for a particular kind of manufacturing. Production costs vary because of the areal differences in the cost of labor, capital, and technical skills. Finished product distribution costs occur if a producer must sell to dispersed or widely scattered markets. All these costs are collectively termed *locational* costs. Classical location theory (see box) has concentrated on finding production points at which locational costs are minimized.

SOME CRITICAL COMMENTS ON CLASSICAL INDUSTRIAL LOCATION THEORY

Although many of the ideas discussed in this chapter are important and useful conceptualizations, some criticisms of classical location theory have been noted:

1. The Nature of Abstraction Radicals point out that industrial location theory abstracts elements that form only a small part of reality so that the real structure and motive power is lost. We learn a great deal about producers and consumers, but nothing about capitalists, workers, imperialism, and private property (Massey, 1973:34).

2. Idealism Like other classical theories of location, industrial location theory is idealistic and lacks a historical perspective. The existence of either competitive maximizers (economic persons) or monopoly is assumed as given and unalterable. Relationships between the two, and the evolution of one from the other are ignored. "Static [harmonious] equilibrium is the rule and aim: internal contradictions and the dynamics of development are not apparent" (Massey, 1973:34).

Once the point of minimum locational costs is determined, however, other problems remain. The *scale* of the operation must be determined and the particular combination of inputs *(technique)* optimized. A producer must also be concerned with the actions of rival producers. The location problem, therefore, is very complex, but this complexity can be reduced with the concept of *spatial margins to profitability*. Locational costs, scale, technique, and locational interdependence together determine spatial margins to profitability. All viable manufacturing operations, by definition, must take place within these margins. How these limits are empirically determined and how locations within them are chosen, however, are usually discussed via a "behavioral" or decision-making approach. Decision-making in a market economy is the subject of Chapter 9.

DISCUSSION QUESTIONS

1. Show the graphical solution and optimum location for the following cases (use Weber's analysis) (A) ubiquities only; (B) one pure, localized raw material; (C) one pure, localized raw material plus ubiquities; (D) several pure, localized raw materials; (E) one localized, weight-losing raw material.

2. Show graphically the development of isodapanes through the construction of isolines. From the isodapanes construct a space cost curve.
3. Graphically show the concept of a critical isodapane for a least-cost labor point and a least-cost transportation point.
4. Define and discuss locational and basic costs.
5. Discuss the interrelationships among location, scale, and technique.
6. Discuss the reasons for scale economies and give a Weberian analysis of the possible effects of a change in scale.
7. Discuss some of the implications of spatial variations in demand on industrial location.
8. Write an essay on the geographical pattern of large private business organizations in the United States.
9. Using examples, show how the market influences the location of manufacturing plants in the United States.
10. Explain the location of the aero-space industry in the United States.
11. What factors have influenced the changing geographical pattern of the textile industry of the United States?
12. Critique classical industrial location theory.

SUGGESTED READINGS

Overview

Isard, W., *Location and Space-Economy.* Cambridge: The MIT Press, 1956.

Smith, D., *Industrial Location: An Economic Geographic Analysis.* New York: John Wiley & Sons, 1971.

Weber, A., *Alfred Weber's Theory of the Location of Industries,* trans. by C. J. Friedrich. Chicago: University of Chicago Press, 1929.

Critique of Industrial Location Theory

Massey, D., "Towards a Critique of Industrial Location Theory," *Antipode,* **5** (1973):33–40.

Case Studies

Borchert, J. R., "Major Control Points in American Economic Geography," *Annals* of the Association of American Geographers, **68** (1978):214–232.

Estall, R. E., *New England: A Study in Industrial Adjustment.* London: Bell, 1966.

Isard, W. and Cumberland, J. H., "New England as a Possible Location for an Integrated Iron and Steel Works," *Economic Geography,* **26** (1950):245–259.

Kennelly, R. A., "The Location of the Mexican Steel Industry," *Revista Geografica* (1954–5), **15**:109–29 and **16**:60–77.

Martin, J. E., *Greater London: An Industrial Geography.* London: Bell, 1966.

Parsons, G. F., "The Giant Manufacturing Corporations and Balanced Regional Growth in Britain," *Area,* **4** (1972):99–103.

Stafford, H. A., "Factors in the Location of the Paperboard Container Industry," *Economic Geography,* **36** (1960):260–266.

Smith, D., *Industrial Location: An Economic Geographic Analysis.* New York: John Wiley & Sons, 1971, Chapter 18.

Transportation

KEY TERMS

- accessibility index
- associated number
- back haul
- beta index
- break-of-bulk point
- core area
- cost-insurance freight (CIF) pricing
- cost-space convergence
- edges
- elasticity
- freight-on-board (FOB) pricing
- freight rates
- graph theory
- least-cost-to-build network
- least-cost-to-use network
- line-haul costs
- matrix
- negative deviations
- networks
- peripheral area
- positive deviations
- rate-break points
- Shimble index
- shortest path
- terminal costs
- time-space convergence
- transport costs
- vertices

8

The transportation industry increases the productivity of an economy. Like any other economic function, it creates utility (the quality of usefulness). Specifically, transportation creates time and space utility. Together with the concepts of complementarity, transferability, and intervening opportunity, the notions of place and time utility help us to understand and explain the movement of goods from place to place.

The concepts of time and space utility have been defined by G. L. Wilson (1954). "*Place utility* is the added economic value of a commodity created by

A woman carrying a bundle of tobacco grown near Lilongwe, Malawi. This mode of transport, which is prevalent in the underdeveloped world, is time consuming and greatly limits how far one travels. SOURCE: *World Bank Photo* by James Pickerell.

transporting it from the place or area in which it has little or no usefulness or value to a place or places in which it has greater usefulness or utility" (1954:5). For example, Newcastle coal has little or no utility to a London power station until the coal has been transported by North Sea freighter to the plant. "Transportation enhances the ability of goods to satisfy human wants by making goods available not only *where* they are needed but *when* they are needed. This results in time utility" (1954:7). Many goods have little or no usefulness in one location at one time, but may have great utility in another place at another time. For example, lumber may be of relatively little value in Oregon where it is plentiful; yet it may be extremely useful and valuable at a building site in Maryland at the time building is underway.

Log truck, Oregon. The motor truck is a flexible mode of transportation and moves goods efficiently over short distances. SOURCE: *Weyerhaeuser Company*.

Transportation is one of the most vital industries, essential for virtually every economic operation. It is impossible to operate a farm, grocery store, or brewery without transportation. And as the world's spatial economy becomes more complex, so the things that make up transportation systems become more indispensable.

We must remember, however, that a good transportation system is as personally important for an American senior citizen to get to a hospital as it is for a businessman to get from New York to New Orleans. Yet government transport policy in most developed and underdeveloped countries reacts unevenly to the needs of its people. Transport improvements contribute primarily to the well-being and convenience of the wealthy.

Previous chapters have shown that transportation plays a major role in structuring the space-economy. In our review of classical location models (Chapters 4, 5, 6 and 7), however, we deliberately simplified the nature of transportation routes and costs. Moreover, we assumed that transportation routes do not change over time. These constraints are relaxed in this chapter, which emphasizes traditional transport models. These models are concerned with the creation of profitable transportation networks, and with the spatial consequences of transport costs and improvements on locational patterns of activities under capitalism.

This chapter is divided into three sections. In it we first analyze the spatial structure of transport routes and networks. Attention then shifts to the nature and effects of transport costs. In the final section, we consider transportation improvements and their outcomes.

OBJECTIVES

By the end of this chapter you should be able:

1. To evaluate network connectivity and accessibility.
2. To discuss variations in the density and shape of transport networks.
3. To discuss ways in which transport routes deviate from straight line paths.
4. To describe the influence of terminal and line-haul costs on carrier rates.
5. To explain why transport cost curves vary from one carrier to another.
6. To identify and describe factors that produce variations in transport rates.
7. To consider the impact of transport improvements on the "tyranny of distance."
8. To describe an idealized stage model of transport development.

Network Analysis

In our review of classical location models we saw that even on an isotropic plain, movements of goods take place in a highly channeled form. But transportation routes do not exist all by themselves; they are organized into networks. Individual networks such as shipping lines, railroads, highways, and pipelines service transport demand and bind regions together.

Networks as Graphs

Networks are enormously complex spatial systems each with their own bundle of characteristics. This makes them difficult to describe, evaluate, and compare. One

Network Analysis

Transport networks are complex spatial systems: a freeway interchange, Milwaukee, Wisconsin. SOURCE: *University of Wisconsin—Extension*.

approach that examines the basic elements of networks and permits us to explore their common structural characteristics is provided by *graph theory*.

Graphs to Represent Networks To employ graph theory, we must reduce transport networks to graphs. This involves eliminating information, but retaining basic spatial elements. A network idealized as a graph consists of two elements: a set of *vertices* (V) representing sources, points, or nodes; and a set of *edges* (E) representing network branches, lines, or links. Figure 8.1 shows the reduction of a simple railway network to a system of vertices ($V_1 - V_5$) and edges ($E_1 - E_5$). Such a graph shows topological position only. The location of nodes is considered in terms of relative position on the graph regardless of their absolute location in the real world. Distance between nodes is determined in terms of intervals, not route length. Because a graph ignores the Euclidean concepts of distance and direction, it is possible to draw alternative topological forms for the graph mapped in Figure 8.1

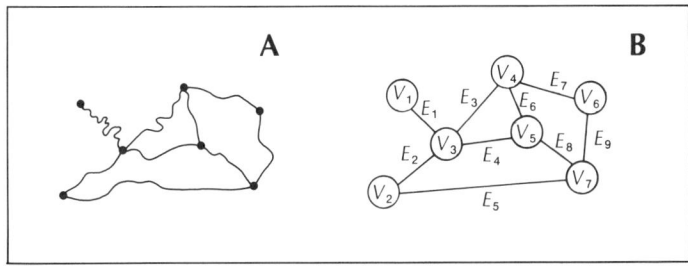

FIGURE 8.1 Reduction of a network (A) to a graph (B). SOURCE: P. Haggett and R. J. Chorley, 1969, *Network Analysis in Human Geography*, London: Edward Arnold, p. 5, Fig. 1.2.

that preserve the original pattern of interconnections between vertices and edges (Figure 8.2). Using the characteristics of edges and vertices, we can estimate the efficiency of networks by means of accessibility indices that measure the effort necessary to reach certain vertices of the network from one vertex, and by means of connectivity indices that evaluate the effort necessary to reach all vertices from all others.

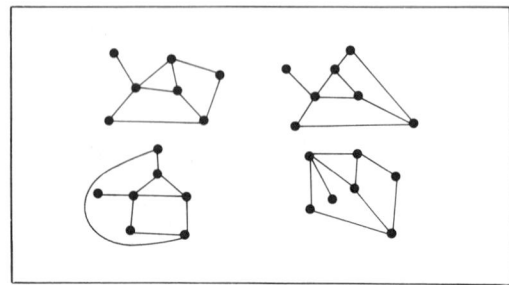

FIGURE 8.2 Alternative topological forms for the graph mapped in Figure 8.1. SOURCE: P. Haggett and R. J. Chorley, 1969, *Network Analysis in Human Geography*. London: Edward Arnold, p. 5, Fig. 1.3.

Network Connectivity A number of graph-theoretic measures may be used to evaluate the connectivity of networks; one of these is the *beta index*. The beta index expresses the ratio between the number of edges (E) in a system and the number of vertices (V) in that system:

$$\beta = \frac{E}{V}$$

Where the number of edges to vertices is large, the beta value will be large, indicating a well-connected network. Conversely, more vertices than edges signifies a poorly-connected network. Thus we can measure the differences in connectivity for a sequence of seven four-point graphs in Figure 8.3. In the simplest case we see four unconnected vertices, and the beta index is therefore zero. The index reaches unity when all vertices are connected by the same number of edges. It exceeds unity when there are more edges than vertices. Although the maximum value in Figure 8.3 is 1.75, larger graphs would yield higher beta values.

FIGURE 8.3 Beta values for seven four-point graphs.

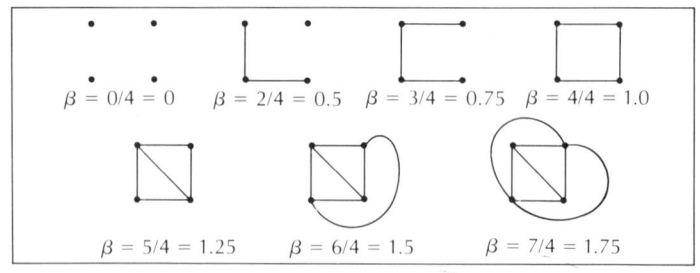

The beta index may be used to compare the structure of networks, either several different networks at the same time or a single network as it changes through time. Figure 8.4 portrays the beta index calculated for the railroad networks of several countries. The nomogram indicates that the size of the index value is

Network Analysis

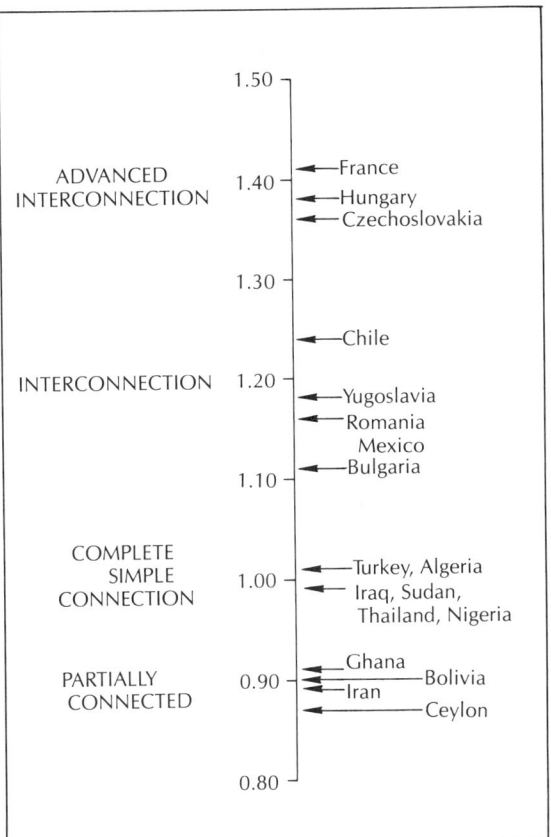

FIGURE 8.4 Beta values for the railroad networks of eighteen countries. After K. J. Kansky, 1963, *Structure of Transportation*, Department of Geography, Research Paper 84, University of Chicago, p. 99, Fig. 25.

generally high in developed countries like France, and low in underdeveloped countries like Ghana. Figure 8.5 shows the evolution of Ghana's road system. Beta values in Figure 8.6 indicate a steady improvement in the connectivity of the road network between 1910 and 1959.

One problem common to measures of network connectivity (including the beta index) is that they have low discriminatory power. They are unable to discriminate between networks having the same number of edges and vertices. The beta value for the two networks in Figure 8.7 is 1.92. Both networks have 48 edges and 25 vertices, but they have different internal spatial organization.

Network Accessibility The search for indices of higher discriminating power has led to various graph-theoretical measures of accessibility. One measure of network accessibility is the *associated number* of a vertex. The associated number is the topological distance between a vertex and the most remote place on the network as measured along the *shortest path* (Figure 8.8). In Figure 8.8 the associated number of place V_4 is 2 based on its shortest paths to V_2 and V_3. Likewise, V_3 and V_2 have associated numbers of 2. However, V_1 has an associated number of 1 because it is connected directly to all three vertices. Thus, the more accessible or central a place is, the lower is its associated number.

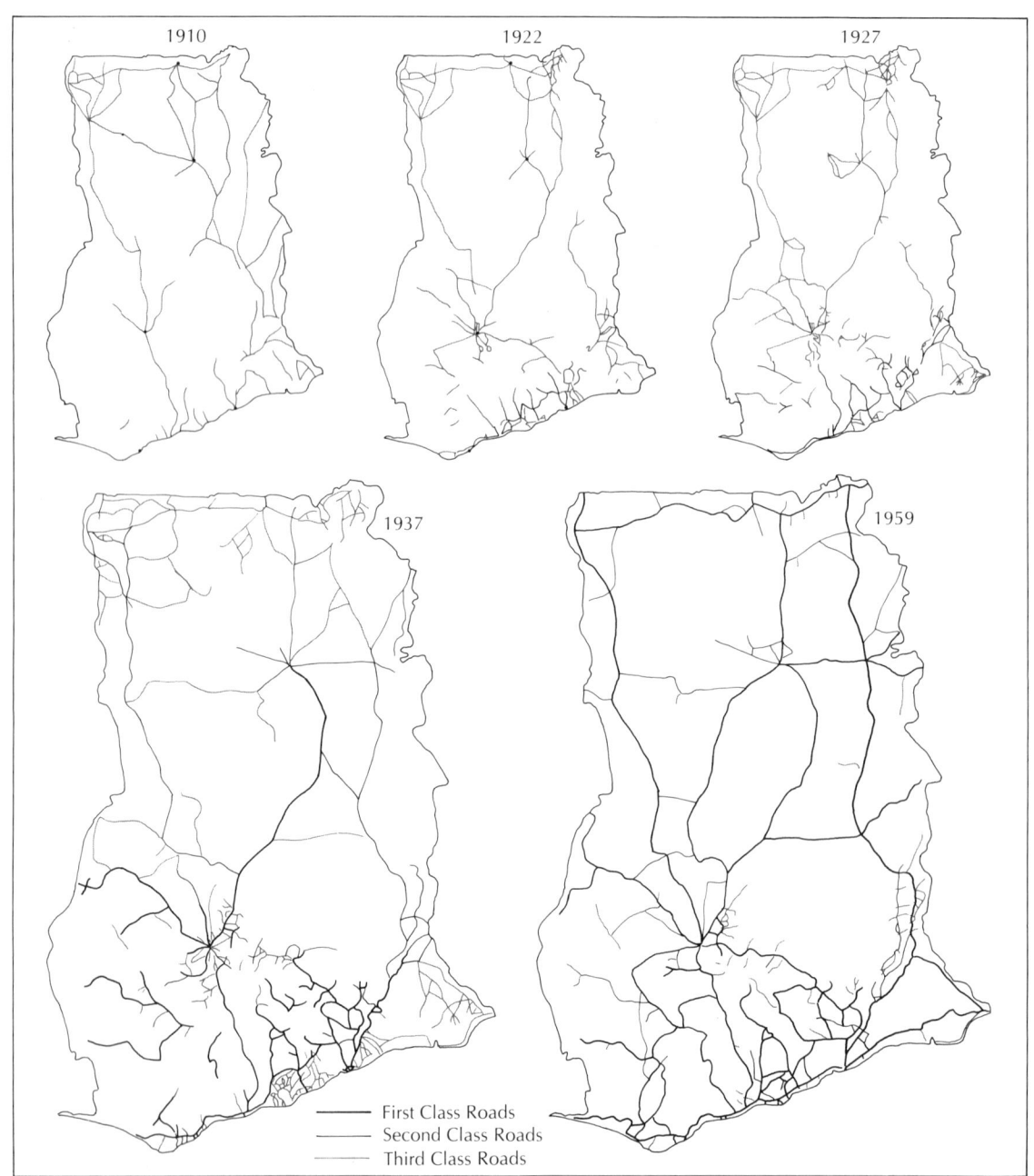

FIGURE 8.5 Evolution of Ghana's primary and secondary road system, 1910–1959. Based on Peter Gould, 1960, *The Development of the Transportation Pattern in Ghana*. Department of Geography, Studies in Geography, No. 5, Evanston, Ill., Northwestern University Press, Frontspiece, pp. 39, 41, 67, 69, Figs. 33, 34, 55, 56.

Network Analysis

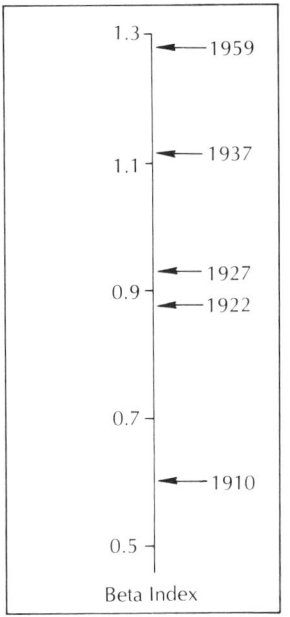

FIGURE 8.6 Increasing road connectivity in Ghana, 1910–1959.

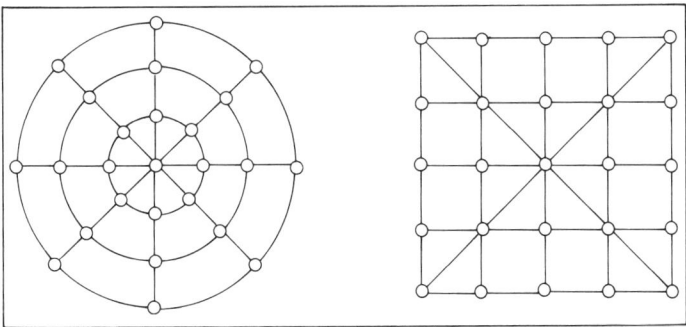

FIGURE 8.7 Networks with 48 edges and 25 vertices.

The associated number is a crude measure of vertex accessibility. Inspection of Figure 8.8 reveals that V_3 and V_2 are more accessible than V_4. Since the index does not use all the relevant information on the graph, it is often unable to differentiate between networks.

The *accessibility* and *Shimble indices*, which have full discriminating power, overcome the weakness of the associated number. The accessibility of a vertex is

$$Ai = \sum_{i=1}^{n} dij$$

where dij is the shortest path from vertex i to vertex j. Thus in Figure 8.8 the accessibility index for $V_1 = 3$, $V_2 = 4$, $V_3 = 4$, and $V_4 = 5$ (see box). These values correspond to our intuitive notions about vertex accessibility. The most accessible place is V_1; V_4 is the least accessible; and V_2 and V_3 have intermediate accessibility. If

FIGURE 8.8 A four-point network.

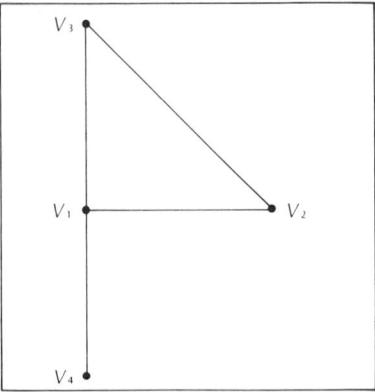

the index were applied to the United States' railroad system, we would find that Chicago has a low accessibility index compared to New York or Los Angeles, both of which are peripheral.

A MATRIX TO REPRESENT A GRAPH

When we deal with graphs larger than the simple four-point example in Figure 8.8, the accessibility value for a vertex cannot be obtained by visual inspection. Computer assistance is needed for very large graphs, but for medium size graphs a shortest path matrix is sufficient. A *matrix* is an array of numbers ordered in rows and columns. The shortest-path matrix for Figure 8.8 is:

TO:	V_1	V_2	V_3	V_4	Row Sum
FROM:					
V_1	0	1	1	1	3
V_2	1	0	1	2	4
V_3	1	1	0	2	4
V_4	1	2	2	0	5

The Shimble or dispersion index is defined as

$$D = \sum_{i=1}^{n} \sum_{j=1}^{n} d_{ij}$$

and it computes the accessibility of a network as a whole. For Figure 8.8 the value of the dispersion index is 16 (Table 8.1). This value provides a measure of the graph's compactness in terms of all the paths within it, and can be used for comparing one network with another. For example, when the dispersion value of an existing network is known, it can be used as a standard against which we can measure the impact of new links on total accessibility. Dispersion values are only an initial step in evaluating network change. Routes must be weighted in terms of their capacity and quality.

Account also must be taken of the cost of building and maintaining alternative links and their effectiveness in meeting given objectives.

TABLE 8.1 Connectivity matrix and dispersion value

TO:	V_1	V_2	V_3	V_4	Row Sum
FROM:					
V_1	0	1	1	1	3
V_2	1	0	1	2	4
V_3	1	1	0	2	4
V_4	1	2	2	0	5
				Total	16

Network Density and Shape

Viewing networks in terms of their basic topological properties ignores important aspects of their spatial structure. For example, topological analysis does not consider such important attributes of transport networks as density and shape.

Network Density By *network density we mean the total number of route kilometers per unit area*. This measure has been considered at all levels of observation from local to world scales.

Local Level At the local scale, variations in network density are closely related to central place theory. Examination of large scale maps or plans reveals strong variations of route density between villages and the surrounding countryside and between inner cities and suburbs. Table 8.2, for example, shows nearly 50 percent of the central area of Detroit is covered with highways, but the density declines with distance from the central business district. Similar distance decay density gradients have been noted for other American and British cities.

TABLE 8.2 Percent of land use devoted to roads

Cities	Downtown	1 km	2 km	3 km
Large U.S. Cities				
Detroit	47	42	37	34
Chicago	36	34	32	30
Medium-sized British Cities				
Nottingham	25	16	8	5
Luton	10	7	4	3

SOURCE: D. Owens, *Road Research Laboratory* Report LR 154 (1968), p. 9, Fig. 3.

Regional Level Several studies have examined the density pattern of route networks, especially in underdeveloped countries where transportation networks are regarded as vital agents of economic growth. Figure 8.9 shows variations in the density of the road network in Tanzania. Densities for main and secondary roads were calculated by measuring the length of such roads in grid squares of approximately 740 square kilometers. The appropriate length was then assigned to the center part of each square, and isolines were drawn to join places of equal density. Road density was positively associated with areas of high population density. It was also closely related to areas of intense commercial activity. For example, regions where crops are grown for the export market, such as the slopes of Mount Kilimanjaro and the areas around Lake Victoria, have high road densities.

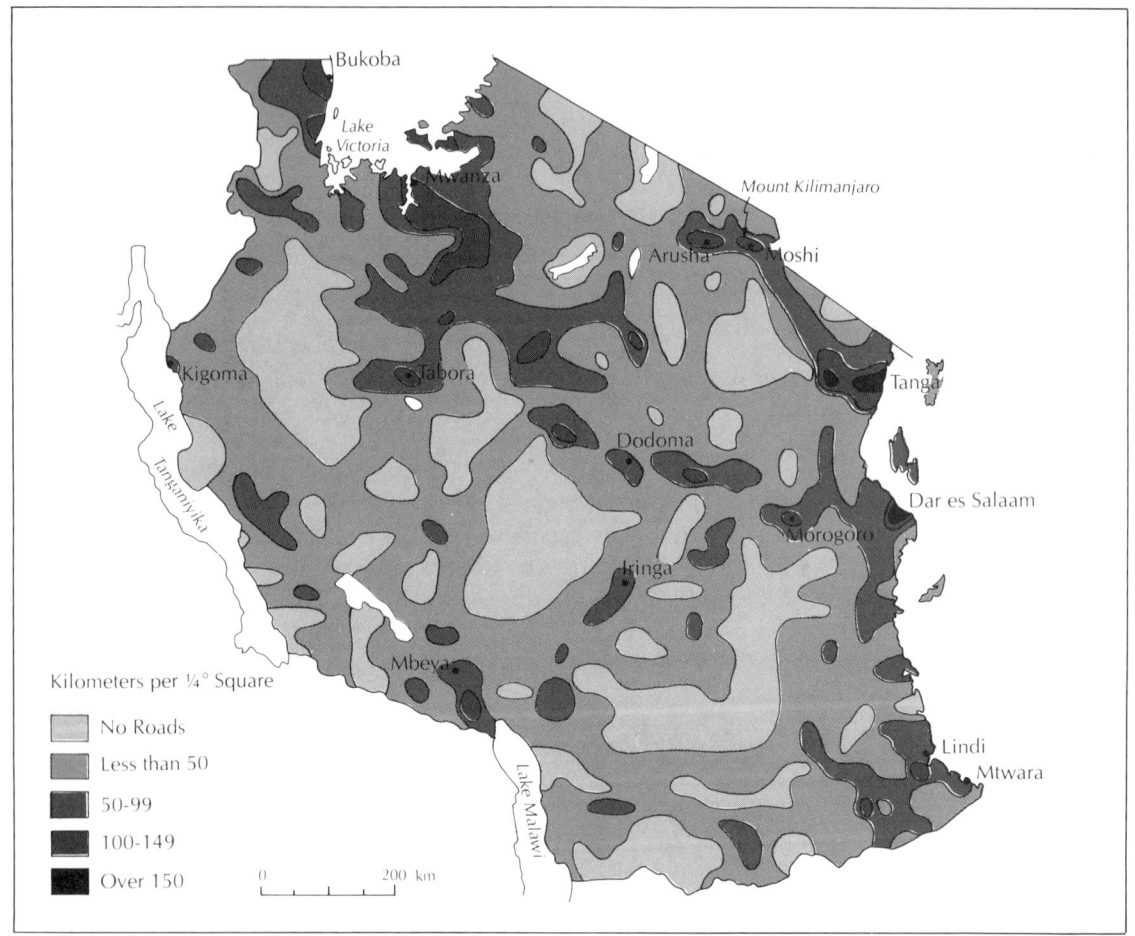

FIGURE 8.9 Road density in Tanzania.

International Level At the world level, the density of roads and railways provides an index of the differential intensity of urbanization and industrialization. The greatest intensity of surface transportation facilities, therefore, appears in Western Europe, the United States and southern Canada, Japan, and in western parts of the Soviet Union. Here, road and rail densities are so high that virtually no region is

Network Analysis

inaccessible. Somewhat less dense networks are found in parts of Uruguay, Argentina, eastern Brazil, eastern Australia, India and Pakistan (a colonial legacy), and in parts of the Mediterranean Middle East. Most underdeveloped countries are poorly served by roads and railways: for example, the vast tropical heartlands of South America and Africa, and the interior of China. They have limited funds to spend on transport development, and sometimes these are spent on wasteful projects such as underground railways. Although the world distribution of surface transportation is more highly articulated in rich industrial countries than in underdeveloped countries, the greatest contrast is between regions of dense and sparse population. In general, transport lines are thickest in densely populated regions and thinnest in sparsely populated regions of the world.

Network Shape Transport networks vary in shape from one region to another. Of great significance is the difference in shape between developed and underdeveloped countries. In many underdeveloped countries the shape of surface transport networks is a reflection of their colonial history. Resulting transport networks resemble drainage systems that converge on coastal ports which become the major cities. Railroad development in Uruguay, for example, centered on one port city, Montevideo. Port cities served as transshipment points for the export of primary products (meat, wool, copper, tin) and the distribution of imported finished goods. Transport networks, therefore, are typically fan-shaped (Figure 8.10). In developed countries, by contrast, the shape of transport networks is a fuller lattice, which by offering a high degree of internal spatial interchange allows a more even distribution of locations. In the United States federal and state governments have figured promi-

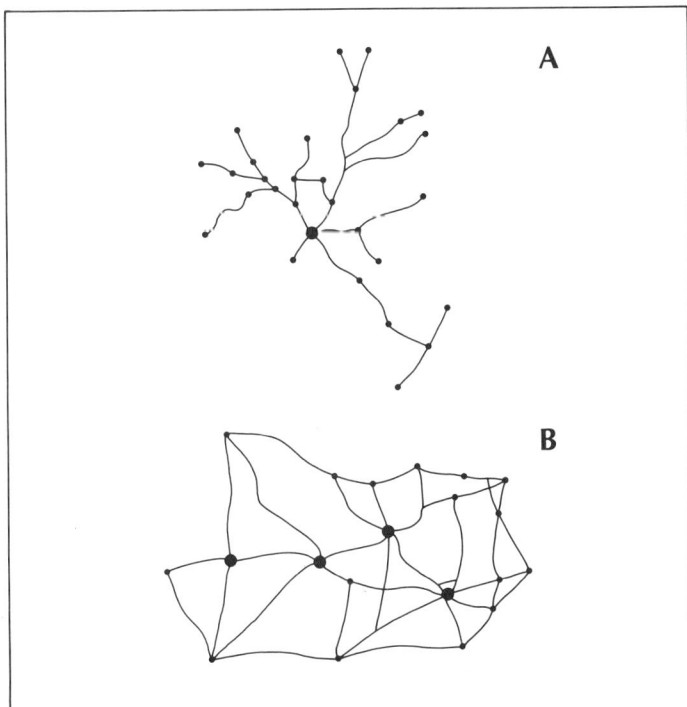

FIGURE 8.10 Schematic shapes of transport networks: (A) underdeveloped country; (B) developed country.

nently in the creation of an integrated transport network. After the Civil War, the federal government, for example, became a major source of railroad financing.

Location of Routes and Networks

Spatial interaction depends on the existence of a demand-supply relationship. If a demand-supply relationship exists between two unconnected places and is profitable, then it is likely that a transport route will be constructed. Choosing the actual location for a new route is a political task, but the procedures developed to aid decision-making are economic. Of critical importance in deciding where to construct a new route is the balance between fixed costs and variable transport costs. Fixed costs are construction costs and variable costs are operating costs that depend on the length of the routeway and the volume of traffic flowing along it.

A demand-supply relationship explains many, but not all, transport patterns. It does not, for example, account for the geographical pattern of Roman roads in England. Roman roads were built across the country to meet the needs of the administration, for fast communication between centers of civil administration in the south and east, and defense lines and fortresses in the north and west. Post-roads were constructed regardless of construction costs and local economic needs.

Minimum-Distance Networks As an example of the way cost ratios may influence the spatial pattern of a network, consider two extreme minimum-distance solutions to a problem in which demands exist between five towns (Figure 8.11). In Figure 8.11A operating costs are low, but fixed costs are high. The resulting network gives maximum benefit to the user because each of the five towns is directly linked to every other town. In Figure 8.11B fixed costs are dominant. The resulting network minimizes construction costs. This *least-cost-to-build network* has a lower degree of connectivity and is less convenient to the user (Table 8.3).

TABLE 8.3 Difference in connectivity between user optimum and builder optimum networks

Network	Number of Edges	Number of Vertices	E/V	B
User optimum	10	5	10/5	2.0
Builder optimum	7	8	7/8	0.87

The railroad pattern of the United States can be understood partly in terms of least-cost-to-use and least-cost-to-build motives (Figure 8.12). The *least-cost-to-user network* is characteristic of the eastern half of the country where cities are clustered and transport demands are high. In the West, where railway lines preceded settlement and where cities are scattered, the *least-cost-to-builder* solution dominates.

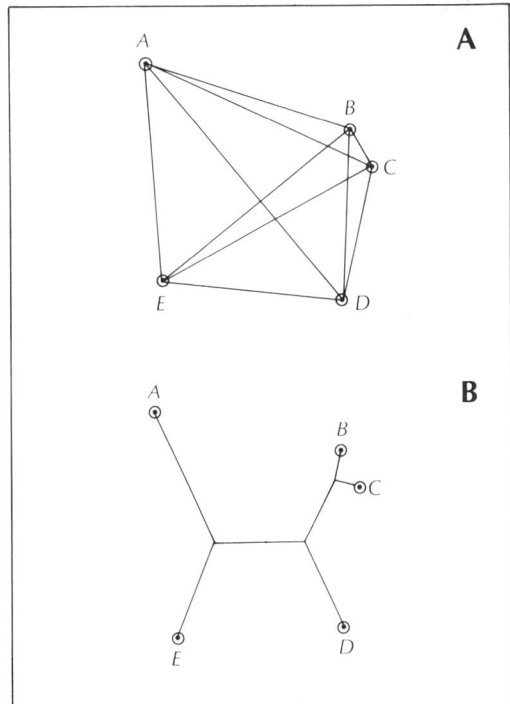

FIGURE 8.11 Alternative ways to connect five urban centers by a transportation network: (A) "least-cost-to-use" solution; (B) "least-cost-to-build" solution. After W. Bunge, 1962, "Theoretical Geography," *Lund Studies in Geography*, C., 1., p. 183, Fig. 7.10.

Deviations From Straight Line Paths Most transportation routes follow complex paths, and therefore deviate from the geometrical straight-line solution. Two types of distortion have been mentioned in traditional location theory. These are *positive deviations* and *negative deviations*.

Positive deviations occur when routes are made longer in order to increase traffic. Figure 8.13 shows an example in which the problem is to optimize the relationship between route length and the amount of revenue in a region consisting of eight towns. Two towns, X and Y, are large and generate more revenue than the others. In Figure 8.13A a direct connection between X and Y reduces construction and maintenance costs, but the net benefits are only 10 units (20 revenue units minus 10 cost units). A more indirect route connecting two additional settlements increases construction and maintenance costs and also raises revenues (Figure 8.13B). The greatest net benefit is not obtained when every settlement is connected, however (Figure 8.13C); this occurs when a route connects six centers and bypasses two of the smallest ones (Figure 8.13D). This hypothetical example of the costs and benefits in path design has counterparts in any situation in which routes must be designed to handle movements. When the United States' Interstate Highway System was built, it by-passed thousands of small towns, villages, and hamlets in favor of larger centers.

Negative deviations arise from the need to reduce the distance travelled through high cost areas. Lösch commented on this type of route distortion. He noted that as transport lines pass through space, they encounter varying degrees of resist-

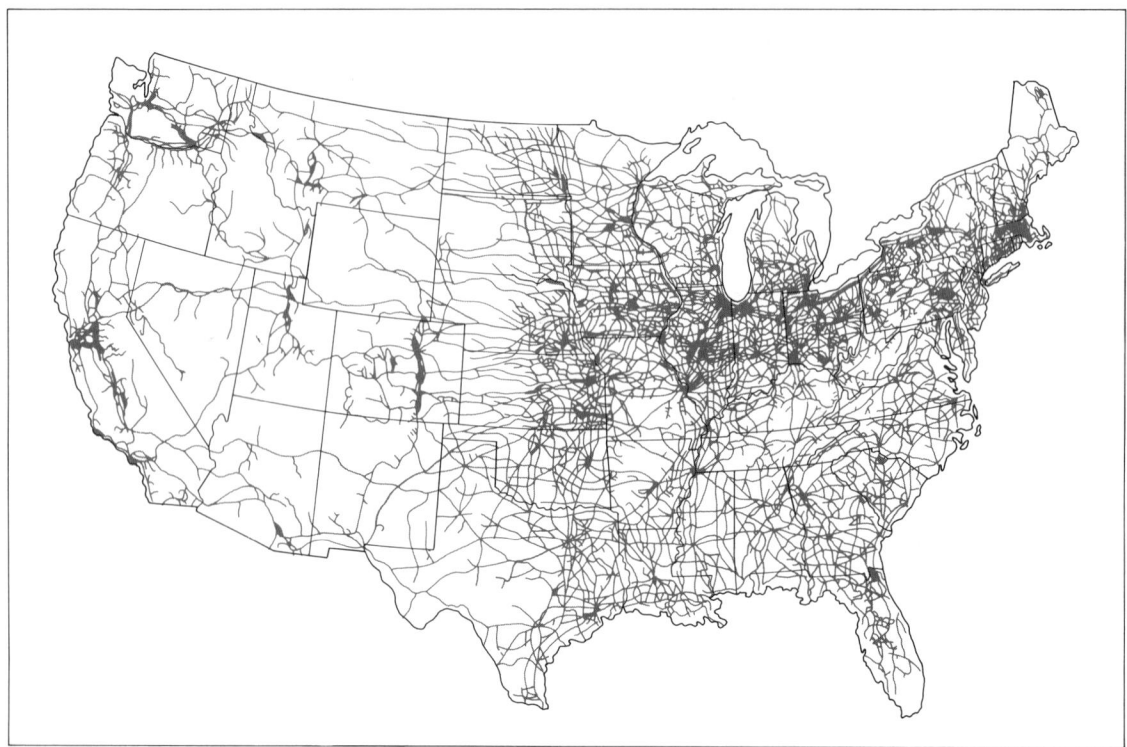

FIGURE 8.12 The railroad pattern of the United States. SOURCE: *Association of American Railroads.*

ance. He found this situation analogous to the way light rays are refracted as they pass from one medium to another (see box).

Figure 8.14 is an application of the law of refraction to route location. It illustrates the problem of determining the cheapest route to ship a product from A, which is a port, to B, which is an inland city in another country. In this example, transport costs are higher over land than over water ($2 per kilometer compared with $1 per kilometer). Figure 8.14 shows four ways of moving a product between A and B:

1. Route ADB is the path that minimizes the distance over water and maximizes the distance over land. Total transport costs are

$$(10 \times \$1) + (30 \times \$2) = \$70$$

2. Route ANB is the straight line path crossing equal distances over water and land. Total transport costs are

$$(20 \times \$1) + (20 \times \$2) = \$60$$

3. Route AEB is the path that maximizes the distance over water and minimizes the distance over land. Total transport costs are

$$(30 \times \$1) + (10 \times \$2) = \$50$$

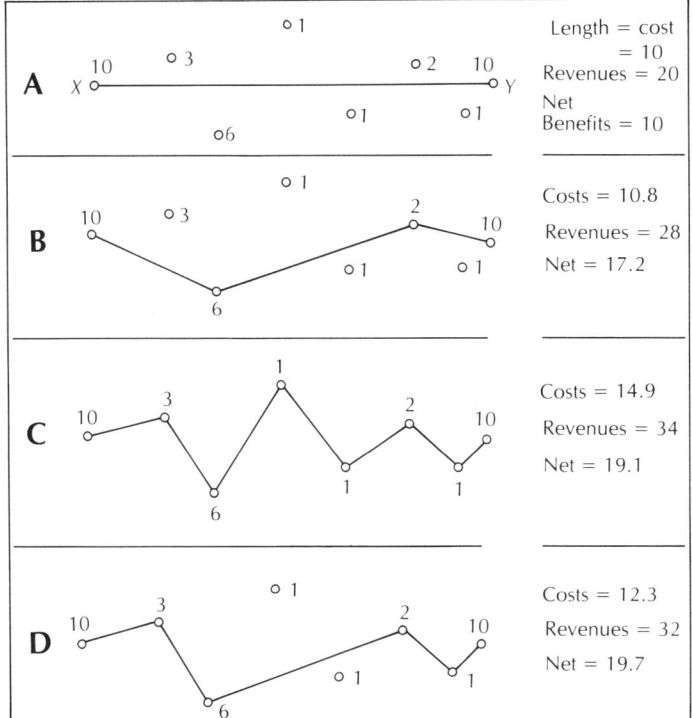

FIGURE 8.13 Alternative ways of locating a transport route to maximize net benefits. SOURCE: R. Abler, J. S. Adams, P. Gould, *Spatial Organization: The Geographer's View of the World*, © 1971, 275. Reprinted by permission of Prentice-Hall, Inc., Englewood Cliffs, New Jersey.

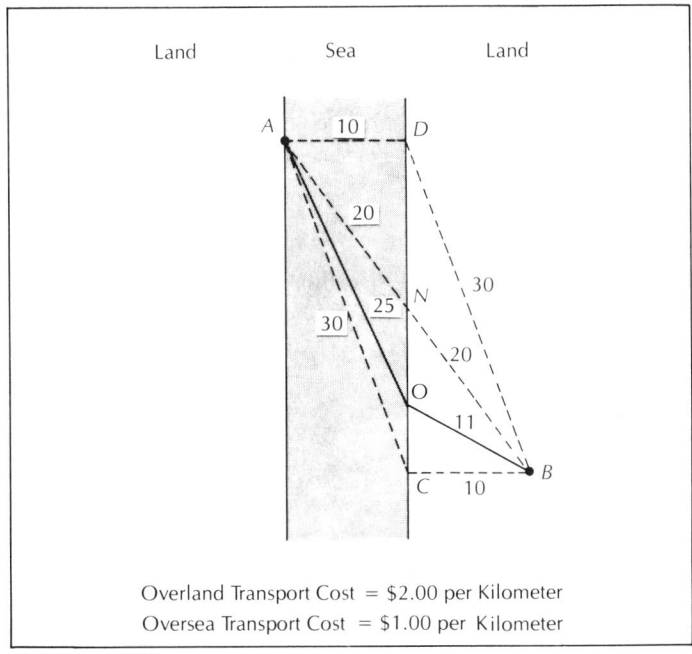

FIGURE 8.14 Application of the law of refraction to transport routes.

> **SNELL'S LAW OF REFRACTION**
>
> In 1620, Dutch mathematician Willebrord Snell discovered a relationship between the angle of incidence and angle of refraction for a ray of light crossing a boundary between two media. Snell's Law of Refraction has been used conventionally in physics, but August Lösch (1954) found that it could be extended to transport problems such as the location of a new freeway that has to cross a straight boundary line between two areas of different transport costs. "By analogy with Snell's Law," Peter Haggett said, "we can calculate a refractive index for any environmental zone simply by dividing the size of the angle of incidence between the route in zone 1 by the size of the angle of the route emerging within zone 2. Both angles are measured with respect to a perpendicular erected at a point where the route crosses the boundary between the two zones. For example, if the incoming route has an angle of 30° and the emerging route 18°, then the refractive index is given by the ratio of the size of these two angles: 0.50/0.30, or 1.67. The higher the index, the greater the relative resistance of the second zone in relation to the first" (1972:343).

4. Route AOB is the compromise path and total transport costs are

$$(25 \times \$1) + (11 \times \$2) = \$47$$

The least cost path crosses the coast at O. Note the path is deflected at sea in this instance and hence the analogy to the law of refraction, which was identified by August Lösch as the principle of least resistance or the "hypothesis that natural events reach their goals by the shortest route" (1954:184).

Although actual route locations are never as simple as the principle of refraction suggest, Lösch did provide an example of its influence. In the nineteenth century a great deal of trade between the east and west coasts of the United States was diverted via the Cape route, a diversion that added some 15,000 kilometers to the direct overland distance. Subsequently the degree of refraction was reduced with the construction of the Panama Canal, and today east-west movement across the United States is hardly refracted at all by overland barriers.

Route deviations are produced not only by variations in physical geography, but also by other barriers such as political boundaries. Maps of surface routes in North America reveal the effect of political differences. Figure 8.15 illustrates the effect of the international border between the United States and Canada on railroads, and the effect of the provincial border between Ontario and Quebec on road patterns.

International transport links are particularly weak in underdeveloped countries. For example, when European powers divided Africa into "artificial" political units, they established in each territory a circulation and communication system that facilitated external contact primarily with the mother country rather than with neighboring colonies. Thus a telling colonial legacy is the scarcity of transport and communication lines across international boundaries, especially between adjacent territories that were colonized by different European powers.

Our final example of the effect of political boundaries on transport networks comes from Tanzania, whose transport network is a reflection of British

Network Analysis

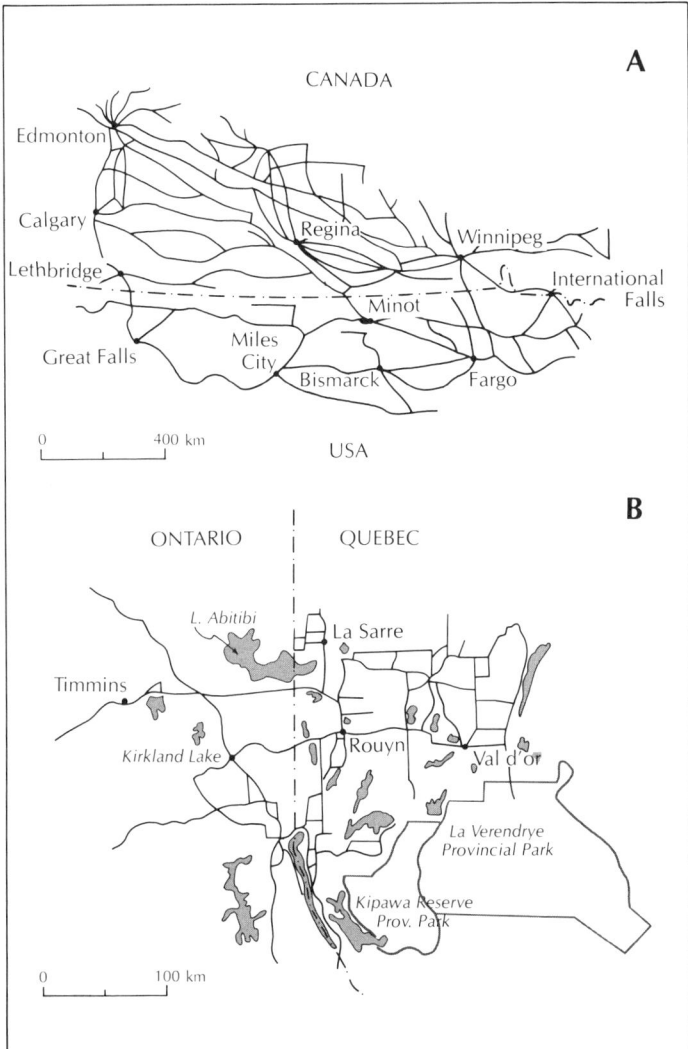

FIGURE 8.15 (A) Effect of the U.S.-Canadian border on railroad networks; (B) effect of the Ontario-Quebec border on road patterns.

colonial history in East Africa. The British treated transport in the territories of Kenya, Uganda, and Tanganyika in a regional context. Railroads were the backbone of the system and the connecting road and boat services linked areas with the rail system. The consequences of an integrated policy for Tanzania have been great. Figure 8.16 shows the status of road and rail transport for four dates: 1932, 1952, 1962, and 1971. Study of these maps shows that in 1962, after independence, Tanzania's transport network was not yet unified. Historically, Tanzania has had seven separate circulation subsystems: (1) the Northwest, Bukoba, and Mwanza areas, with exports and imports moving mainly through Kisumu and Mombasa; (2) Arusha-Moshi area, with exports and imports moving mainly through Mombasa, a saving of 86 kilometers over the line to Tanga; (3) the Tanga-Lushoto area; (4) the Central line, Dar es Salaam to Kigoma; (5) the Southern Highlands, with no rail links, but road services connecting with Dar es Salaam and with Arusha and Nairobi along the Great North

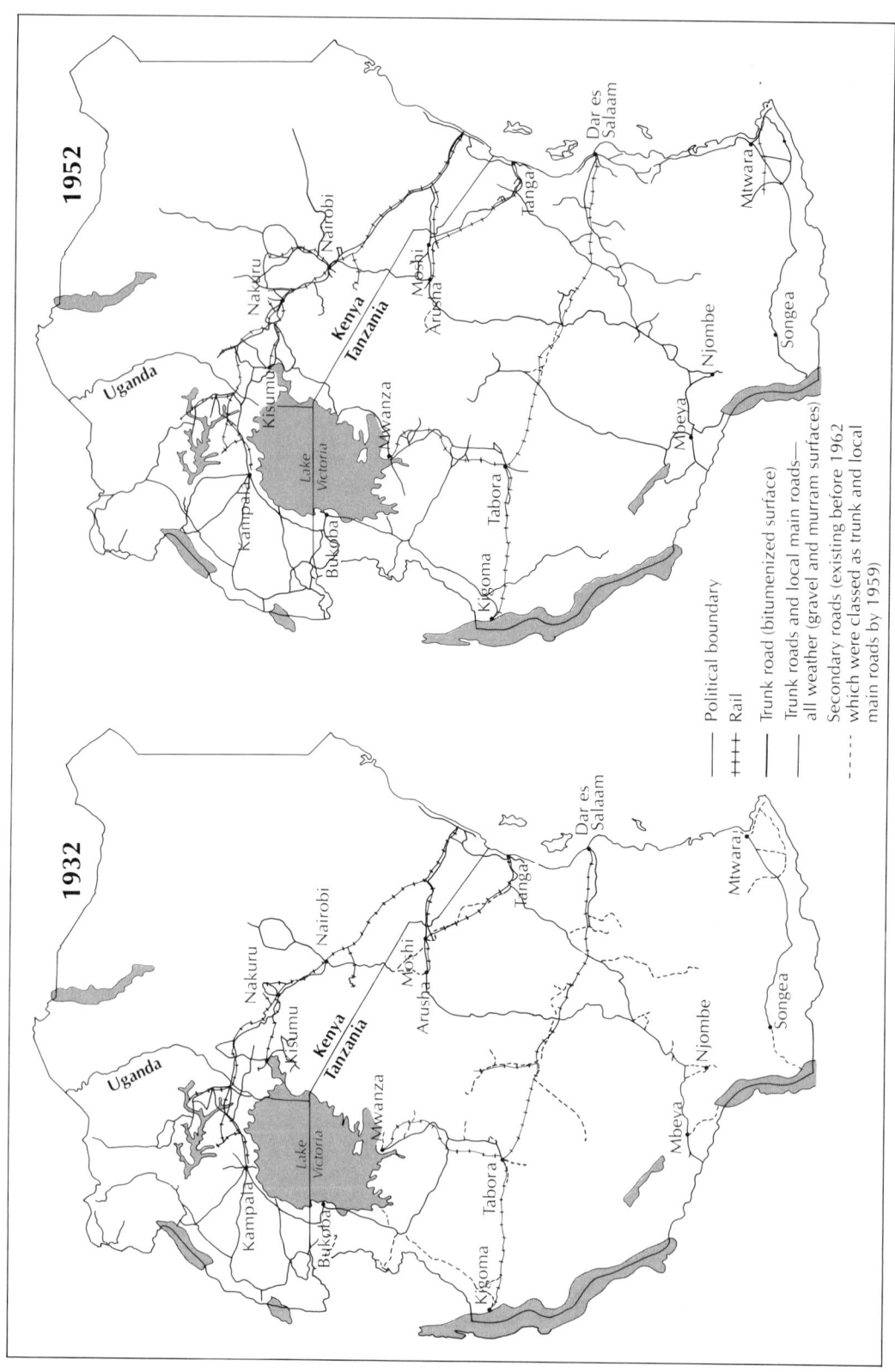

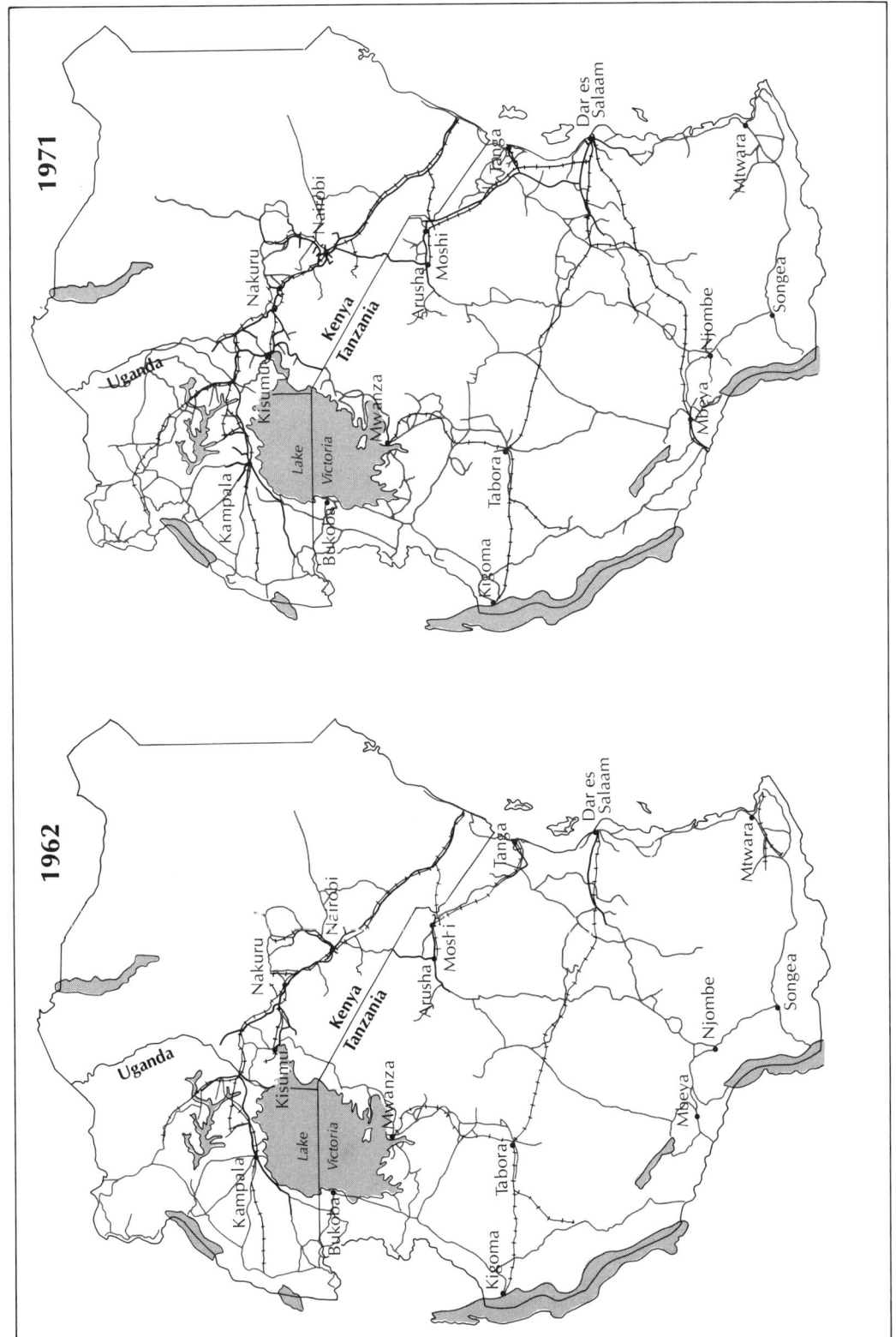

FIGURE 8.16 Development of the East African transport network. SOURCE: A. R. de Souza and P. W. Porter, 1974, *The Underdevelopment Modernization of the Third World*. Washington, D.C.: Association of American Geographers Commission on College Geography, Resource Paper No. 28, p. 45, Fig. 6.

Road; (6) the Southern Province, an area isolated from Dar es Salaam and the rest of the country during the rainy season by high water on the Rufiji River; and (7) Southwestern Tanzania, which is isolated from the rest of the country by a lack of roads.

Only in the early 1960s was Northwest Tanzania linked with the rest of the country by all-weather road, when the Nzega-Singida section was built. By 1971, a hard-surface road finally linked the Tanga-Dar es Salaam systems by a shorter route than those formerly made through Morogoro and Handeni, reducing the journey from 574 kilometers in 1952 to 470 kilometers by 1962, to 272 kilometers by 1971. By 1973, the Mbeya-Dar es Salaam road was completely surfaced, the Tanzam Railway line was completed in Tanzania, and an agreement had been negotiated for construction of a bridge across the Rufiji River.

One consequence of the political disruption and distortion of transport networks is a reduction in the intensity of movement and interaction. Ross Mackay (1958) studied telephone traffic between Montreal and Quebec cities, other Canadian cities, and United States cities (Figure 8.17). Mackay predicted the intensity of telephone traffic from the gravity model and tested the results against actual telephone traffic. He found that telephone traffic between Montreal and other cities in Quebec was from five to ten times greater than traffic between Montreal and Ontario cities. American cities interacted with Montreal as if they were fifty times as distant (see box).

THE EFFECT OF A POLITICAL BOUNDARY UPON FLOWS OF TELEPHONE CALLS

When telephone calls are plotted against distance, the intensity of interaction declines (diagram **A**). If a political barrier is placed across the area, then the amount of interaction falls way below what could be expected from the distance-decay effect (diagram **B**). The effect of a political boundary upon flows of telephone calls can be measured by aligning the two pieces of the graph. This involves displacing the lower segment to the right (diagram **C**). The barrier effect can then be measured in distance terms; and we could conclude that a political barrier has the same retarding influence on interaction as, say, thirty kilometers of distance.

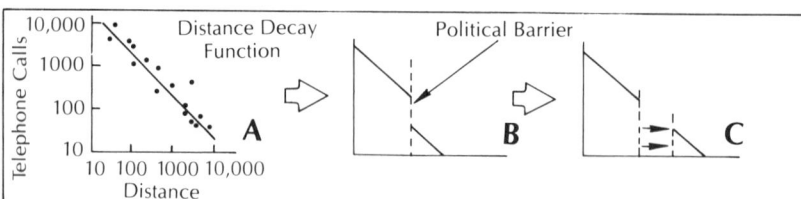

SOURCE: P. Gould, 1975, *Spatial Diffusion: The Spread of Ideas and Innovations in Geographic Space*. Learning Package Series Number 11, p. 18, Fig. 10. Consortium for International Studies Education, The Ohio State University.

Transport Costs

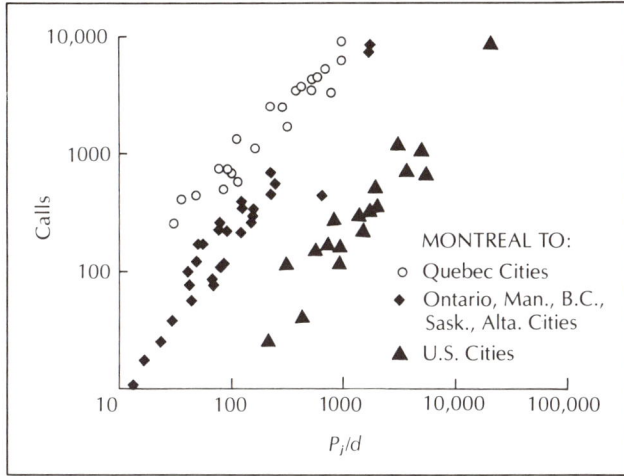

FIGURE 8.17 Telephone calls from Montreal to three sets of cities in a ten-day period. SOURCE: J. R. Mackay, 1958, "The Interactance Hypothesis and Boundaries in Canada," *Canadian Geographer*, 11, p. 4, Fig. 2.

Transport Costs

Terminal Costs and Transport Gradients

Throughout our discussion of classical location models we assumed that *transport costs* are proportional to distance. This normative constraint, which reduced the complexity of the models, is illustrated in Table 8.4 and Figure 8.18. The cost of transporting a commodity 200 kilometers is exactly twice the cost of transporting it 100 kilometers. Of course, this hypothetical situation does not prevail. The cost curve "tapers off" with distance for a number of reasons.

First, certain transport costs must be paid regardless of *line-haul* or over-the-road costs. These *terminal costs* include the cost of preparing shipping documents, loading, packing and unloading, capital investment, and line maintenance. Terminal costs are fixed in the short run, but they may be altered by technolog-

TABLE 8.4 Linear transport costs

Kilometers	Cost $
0	0
100	1
200	2
300	3
400	4
500	5
600	6
700	7
800	8
900	9
1000	10

FIGURE 8.18 Linear transportation costs as a sole function of distance.

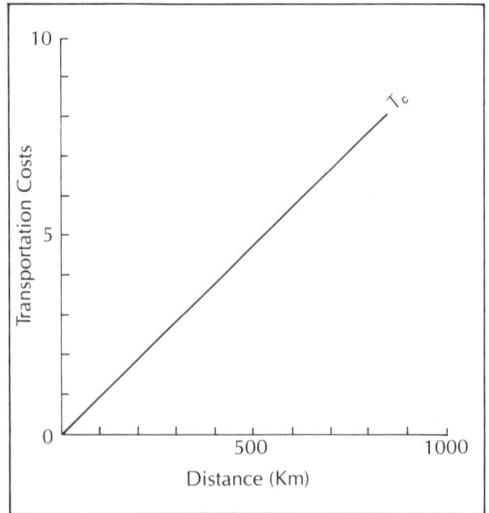

Discharging tea boxes by crane. This conventional cargo handling technique incurs high terminal costs. SOURCE: *Brooke Bond Oxo Ltd.*

Transport Costs

ical changes. For example, efforts have been made in the last twenty years to reduce high loading and unloading costs and excessive turnaround time involved in operating cargo ships by transporting loaded highway trailers by containership. An added benefit is reduced labor requirements and costs.

Container terminal, New York. SOURCE: *The Port Authority of N.Y. and N.J.*

Terminal costs greatly influence transport costs per kilometer. For very short trips, they are the major cost components. But as the length of haul increases, they are spread over a broader and broader area. Consider a hypothetical example in which terminal costs for a commodity are twenty cents and line-haul costs are one cent per kilometer (Table 8.5 and Figure 8.19). The total per kilometer cost—terminal plus line-haul costs divided by distance—declines rapidly and then flattens out with distance (Figure 8.20).

Tapering transportation costs are mainly the consequence of spreading terminal costs over a large number of kilometer units; they are also the result of curvilinear line-haul costs (Figure 8.21). The rate increases with distance, but at a decreasing rate. The distance from O to D_2 in Figure 8.21 is twice that from D_1 to D_2, but does not involve twice the cost (C_1 to C_2). As the distance increases, the average cost per kilometer constantly decreases.

Transportation costs taper with distance, but the degree of tapering varies from one mode of transportation to another, depending on their terminal and line-haul costs. Figure 8.22 shows variations in terminal and line-haul costs among three competing types of transportation: highway, railroad, and waterway. Trucks have low terminal costs partly because they do not have to provide and maintain

TABLE 8.5 Tapering freight structure

Distance (Kilometers)	Terminal Costs	Line-Haul Costs	Total Costs	Per Kilometer Costs
0	.20	0.00	.20	—
1	.20	0.01	.21	.21
5	.20	0.05	.25	.05
10	.20	0.10	.30	.03
20	.20	0.20	.40	.02
30	.20	0.30	.50	.016
40	.20	0.40	.60	.015
50	.20	0.50	.70	.014
100	.20	1.00	1.20	.012

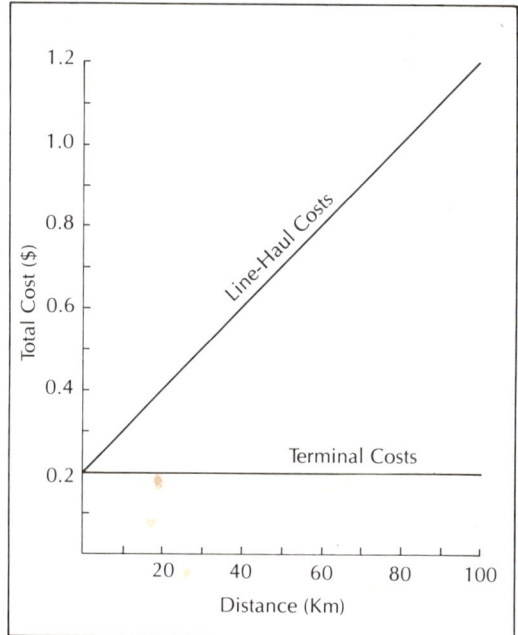

FIGURE 8.19 Terminal and line-haul costs.

their own highways, and partly because of their flexibility. If provisions for parking are adequate, they can load and unload almost anywhere. However, trucks incur relatively steep line-haul costs. They are not as efficient in moving freight on a ton-kilometer basis as the other two modes of transportation. With three competing forms of transportation, trucks involve the least cost only out to distance D_1. Railroad carriers have intermediate terminal costs between truck and water carriers and a competitive advantage through the distance D_1–D_2. Water carriers, such as barges, have the highest terminal costs, but they achieve the lowest line-haul costs, giving them an advantage over longer distances. An indication of comparative distances for different modes of transportation is given in Table 8.6, which shows the average kilometers per ton shipped for manufacturing commodities in the United States.

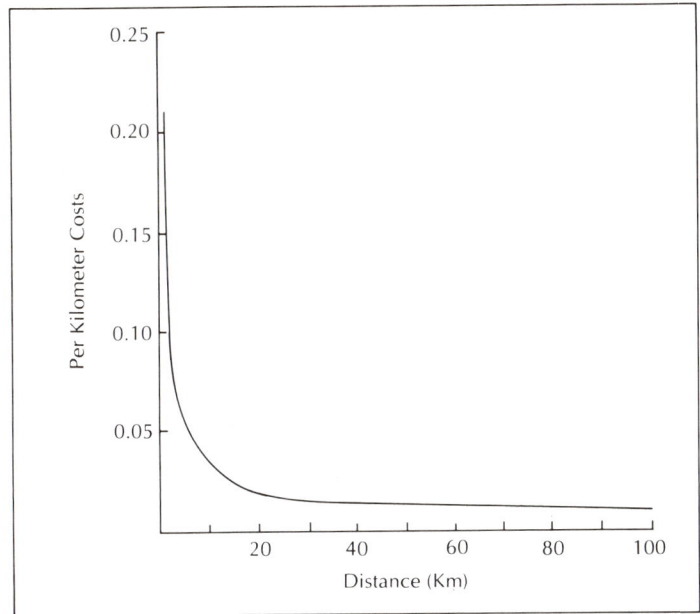

FIGURE 8.20 Per kilometer transport costs.

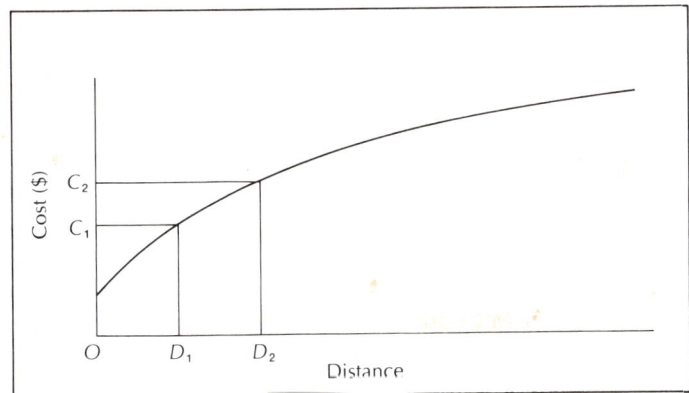

FIGURE 8.21 Curvilinear line-haul costs.

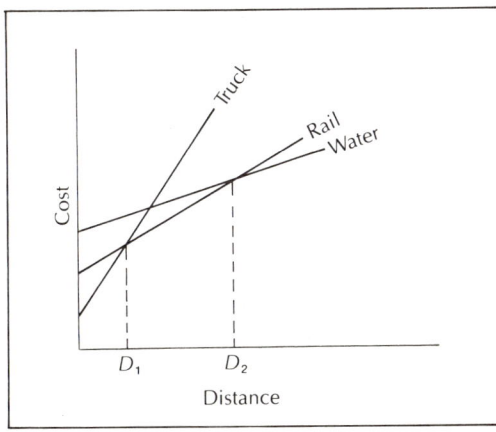

FIGURE 8.22 Variations in terminal and line-haul costs among different transport media.

401

TABLE 8.6 Average line-haul distance for manufacturing commodities as shipped by different modes

Mode	Average Kilometer per Ton Shipped
Rail carrier	824
Motor carrier	405
Private truck	181
Air carrier	1600
Water carrier	1352

SOURCE: F. S. Pardee et al., *Measurement and Evaluation of Transportation System Effectiveness*, Rm-5869-DOT. The Rand Corporation, September, 1969.

VARIATIONS IN TRANSPORT RATES

Actual transport rates reflect the cost profiles in Figure 8.22, but other factors produce variations in transportation costs. These include grouping *freight rates* into zones; variations in *freight rates* according to *commodity characteristics*; and variations in *freight rates* according to *traffic characteristics*.

Grouping Freight Rates into Zones Theoretically, every point along a line from a given origin should pay a slightly different rate based on the actual distance involved. But computing large numbers of rates is both time-consuming and expensive to administer. Consequently, it is common among transport companies to operate zonal-rate systems. For example, railroads group stations into areas, and charge a single rate for all stations within the same zone. In general, group-rates are set in relation to "control" points, often the largest centers in each zone, thus reinforcing their urban dominance.

Railroad rate zones are step functions that retain the tapering principle and favor long haul movements (Figure 8.23). The total transport bill per unit of delivered material from station R to Y should be only slightly more than to X, but because of the nature of the rate zones, Y pays a much higher price than X. Station Z pays the same price as Y because it is in the same rate zone. Station X has a competitive advantage over Y, but Y does not have a cost advantage over Z despite

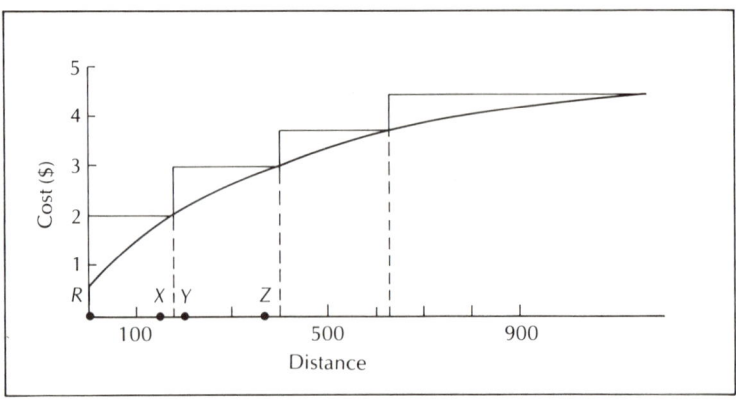

FIGURE 8.23 Stepped freight rates.

the greater distance of Z from R. Historically, cities such as Chicago, St. Louis and some Missouri and Ohio River crossings have occupied and benefited from strategic positions in railroad rate groupings.

Variations in Freight Rates According to Commodity Characteristics Carriers charge different transport rates on different products to cover fixed costs. The result is variation between commodities in the level of freight rates and the existence of many rates which are higher or lower than can be justified on the basis of transportation costs alone. This is shown in Table 8.7, in which freight revenue from a large number of carload shipments is expressed as a percentage of the fully distributed cost of transporting these commodities. When figures in the table are less than 100, as in the case of flour, lettuce, potatoes, and iron ore, they were transported at rates below the fully distributed cost. Conversely, commodities above 100 exceeded the fully distributed cost. Carriers, therefore, practice a degree of cross-subsidization; the "losses" on transporting such commodities are counter-balanced by "gains" on others.

TABLE 8.7 Comparison of carload freight revenue from selected commodities as a percentage of fully distributed cost, 1959*

Commodity	Percent of Fully Distributed Cost	Commodity	Percent of Fully Distributed Cost
Lettuce	67	Sugar	122
Oranges and grapefruit	72	Pig iron	143
		Agricultural implements	154
Potatoes	73	Boots and shoes	158
Iron ore	73	Automobiles	171
Flour	76	Cigarettes	196
Bituminous coal	81	Machinery and machines	212
Gasoline	84		
Anthracite coal	93	Alcoholic liquors	216
Butter	109		

* Includes variable costs together with an allocation of constant costs, including an allowance for a return on investment.

SOURCE: Interstate Commerce Commission, Bureau of Accounts, Statement No. 2–61, *Distribution of Rail Revenue Contribution by Commodity Groups—1959*, Washington, D.C., 1961.

In the United States carriers have ample opportunity to charge unfair rates between commodities. However, differences in rates may also be reasonable. The usual method of determining the reasonableness of rates on a particular commodity is to compare the rate with the rates on commodities that have similar transportation characteristics. Six main factors enter into any comparison of rates:

Loading and Packaging Costs Of particular importance in determining the reasonableness of rates is the weight density of a commodity. Light, bulky commodities usually incur higher freight charges per carload than heavy, compact articles. This explains why rates generally favor "knocked down" over "set-up" commodities. For example, parts for a complete automobile are shipped for a much lower rate than a finished car.

A low weight-density is not the only reason why some commodities load cheaply. Ability to load commodities compactly must also be considered. Articles of odd shape like furniture may not load efficiently. Sometimes cars cannot be filled without damage to commodities. Melons, for example, cannot be loaded more than a few layers deep without crushing those on the bottom. Furthermore, some articles cost more to load. Wheat can be loaded rapidly and cheaply by conveyor. Television sets must be handled with care to avoid damage. Coal requires little advance preparation for shipment, but furniture requires special packing which adds to terminal costs (Figure 8.24).

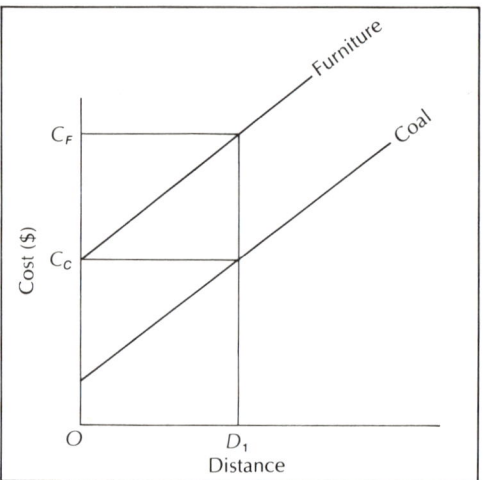

FIGURE 8.24 Variations in loading and packaging costs.

Damage and Risk Variations The cost of transporting commodities is affected by the possibility of damage in transit. Except for ocean carriers of freight, most transport companies are liable for loss and damage during transit and must assume a greater risk for some commodities than others. Sand, gravel, brick, and iron ore are not subject to damage, but fresh fruits and vegetables are perishable or fragile.

Shipment Size The size of a shipment is another factor in determining the reasonableness of rates on particular commodities. Some commodities are shipped in bulk, whereas others must be carried in small quantities. Railroads charge higher rates for less-than-carload (LCL) lots than for carload (CL) shipments. Rates are lower for commodities transported in volume over a period of time because carriers can better organize operation and handling methods and thus reduce costs. Large consignments should lower per-ton costs because terminal charges become a smaller proportion of total costs, and a high volume of a single commodity should lower line-haul costs per ton. Striking examples are complete trains carrying coal or iron ore.

Transport Costs

Regularity of Movement If traffic moves regularly, carriers can operate at lower costs and should charge lower rates. Schedules are worked out more easily and vehicles and labor needs can be planned. Irregularity of movement increases rates. This is often true of seasonal movements of fruits, vegetables, or wheat. Many railroad cars have to be supplied over a short period. These cars may have to stand idle for much of the time or be diverted from other routes, disrupting regular service.

Special Equipment and Services The type of equipment or the provision of special services for some commodities affects the cost of transportation. Refrigerated cars cost more to operate and maintain than ordinary boxcars. Some articles require insulated cars. Special sidings or terminal facilities have to be maintained for commodities such as livestock. Shipments of fresh fruit require expedited transfer. Any of these special services can command a higher freight rate on the commodity involved.

Elasticity of Demand Previous factors related to the relative cost of transporting different articles, but the *elasticity* of demand for transportation must also be considered (see box). It is generally accepted that goods of high value per unit of weight are better able to "bear" higher transportation rates than goods of lower value per unit value. Compared to coal, television sets have a very high value per unit of weight. A high freight rate on television sets accounts for only a small percentage of the total cost of the item. A small increase in the transportation rate per ton of coal may mean a significant rise in the total cost per ton at the delivery point. In the United States carriers generally charge what the market will bear and may exercise considerable flexibility in setting rates within the limits imposed by the Interstate Commerce Commission. Commodity A (television sets) in Figure 8.25 illustrates transportation price inelasticity. An increase in the rate from P_1 to P_2

PRICE ELASTICITY

The price elasticity of a good is the relative change in the quantity demanded in response to a change in price or, in other words, the percentage change in quantity resulting from a one percent change in price. For most goods the relationship is *inverse*—a price increase causes a decrease in the quantity demanded and vice versa. Economists usually designate the coefficient of price elasticity by the lower case Greek eta (η) and have identified three classes of price elasticity:

1. *unitary elasticity:* a one percent change in price brings about a one-percent change in quantity demanded ($\eta = 1$);
2. *price elasticity:* a one percent change in price results in a *greater* than one percent change in quantity demanded ($\eta > 1$);
3. *price inelasticity:* a one percent change in price results in a change in quantity demanded of *less* than one percent ($\eta < 1$).

produces only a slight change in the quantity of shipments. Commodity B (coal), however, exhibits a great change in the quantity of shipments with only a small change in the transportation rate (P_1 to P_2).

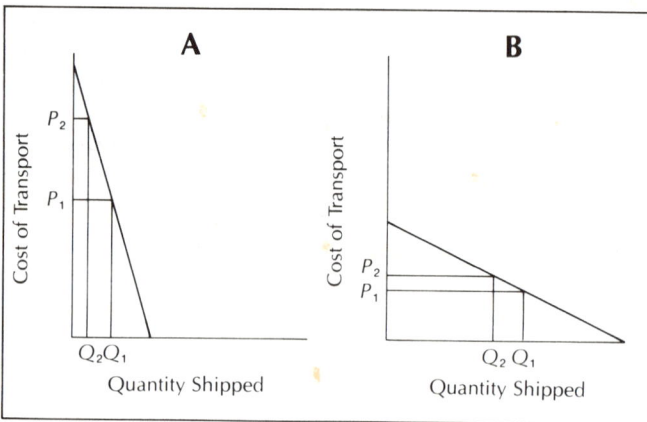

FIGURE 8.25 Demand elasticity for transportation.

The value of an article does not completely determine a commodity's ability to bear a higher freight rate. Transportation services are not purchased simply for the sake of consuming ton-kilometers. Assume two products each with a very high value. One product is produced at points A and B; the second is produced only at A. The product at A may be able to bear a high freight rate from A to B but the commodity produced at both locations will not be shipped from A to B even if a very low rate is offered. Transportation is a means of distributing localized commodities. The most localized commodities can usually bear higher rates within the framework of loading, shipment size, and damage and risk characteristics.

Variations of Freight Rates According to Traffic Characteristics Just as rate comparisons are used to judge the reasonableness of rates between different commodities, they also are used to judge the fairness of rates between particular points. At least three factors influence rates between points. They include:

Carrier Competition An absence of competition between transport modes means a carrier can set rates between points to cover costs, and in the absence of government control, a carrier may set unjustifiably high rates. Such practices are more unlikely in the United States today than in the past when there was less regulation and intermodal competition. The effect of competition between carriers is to reduce rate differences between competitors. For example, the opening of the St. Lawrence Seaway in 1959 resulted in lower rail freight rates on commodities affected by low water transport rates.

Route Demand An important factor influencing the cost of haul is traffic density. A large volume of traffic moving over a particular route may lower transportation rates, because the higher the demand, the lower the line-haul and terminal costs per unit. Areas or routes of sparse traffic may result in higher rates. For the first half of this century, the United States' Interstate Commerce Commission allowed railroads to vary freight rates according to traffic density. The country was divided into five major zones. Figure 8.26 shows how average railroad freight rates varied from region to region. Disparities were enormous; for example, the difference between the Mountain-Pacific, an area of low traffic density, and the Eastern Region, an area of high traffic density, was an average 66 percent. These differences in rate levels were abandoned in the 1950s, but their effects continue to exert an impact on the organization of the space-economy, because of the stimulus they gave to economic activities in favored regions.

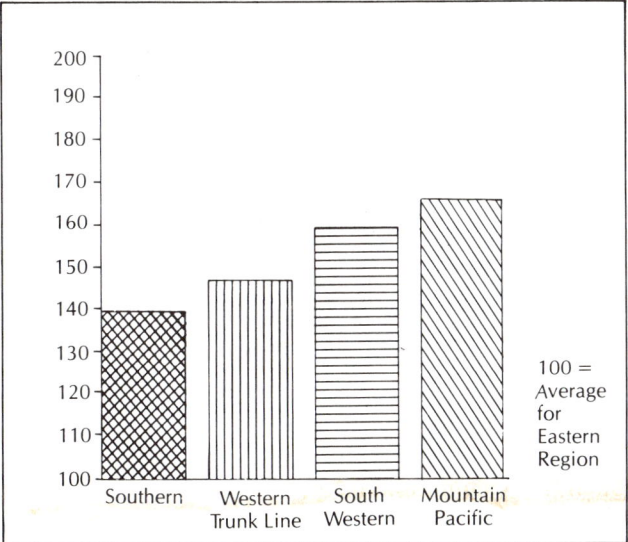

FIGURE 8.26 Relative freight rate levels by major freight rate region, United States.

Back-hauling Many carriers face heavy demand only in a specific direction. Consider the large volume of produce shipped from Florida to New York. Trucks must often return empty for the next load. The cost of the total trip, however, is used to determine the transportation rate. Because carriers must make return trips anyway, they are willing to charge very low rates on the *back-haul*. Any revenue on the back-haul is preferred to returning empty. Rates are higher where there is little or no possibility of backhauling; most such runs occur in the transportation of raw materials from resource points to production points. An example is the railroad that carries iron ore pellets from Labrador to the port of Sept Illes, Quebec. This railroad may be likened to a huge conveyor belt operating in one direction only. By contrast, the distribution of finished products generally involves traffic between many large urban points, creating a reciprocal flow and lower rates.

Transport Costs and Location

Consideration of more realistic transportation rates for a market society revealed some of the complexities of transport costs. With our revised view of transport costs, let us now consider some of their effects on classical location theory.

Iron ore pellets produced in Labrador are transported over 350 kilometers to the port of Sept Iles, Quebec. SOURCE: *Bethlehem Steel.*

Effect on Location Figure 8.27A shows Weber's solution for one pure raw material localized at M and sold as a finished product at MKT. Terminal costs are zero and line-haul costs are linear. What happens to the Weberian solution when terminal costs are added? The solution is given in Figure 8.27B. At either mine or market, one set of terminal costs is paid, but at any intermediate location, two sets of terminal costs must be paid. This raises total transportation costs by an amount equal to one set of terminal costs. Mine or market locations have a clear advantage because terminal costs do not favor intermediate points.

Curvilinear line-haul costs also encourage terminal locations (Figure 8.28). For simplicity the diagram eliminates terminal costs. It shows how curvilinear line-haul costs stimulate long-hauls. Shipping the raw material from M to D_1 costs C_1; shipping the finished product from D_1 to MKT costs C_2. Shipping the raw material all the way to MKT, however, only involves a cost of C_4. Total transportation costs are minimized at either mine or market. The Weberian solution for both terminal costs and curvilinear line-haul costs is shown in Figure 8.29.

Raw materials tend to be easier to load and less subject to damage and risk than finished products, so transportation rates are lower on raw materials than finished products, favoring market locations. This is illustrated in Figure 8.30 in which linear transportation costs are retained for simplicity. The lower raw material transportation rate minimizes total transportation costs *(TTC)* at the market.

We have seen that tapering freight rates encourage plants to locate at material sources or markets rather than at some intermediate orientation. Nonetheless, many manufacturing activities do locate at intermediate places. In the transport

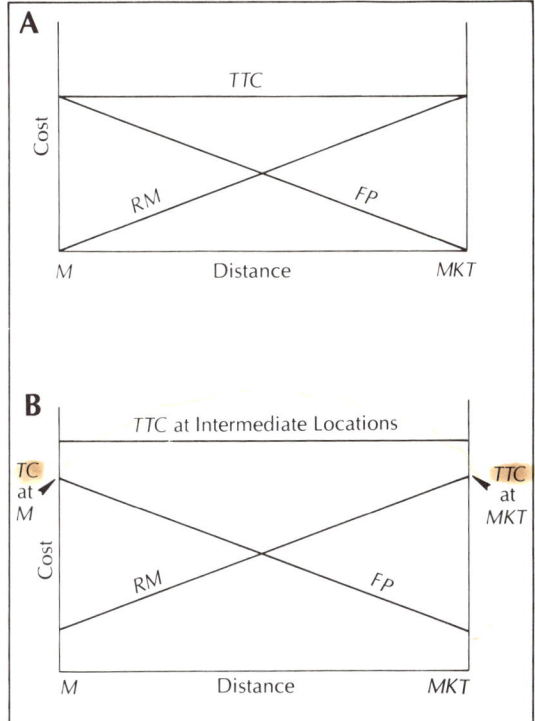

FIGURE 8.27 Weber's model: the effects of terminal costs.

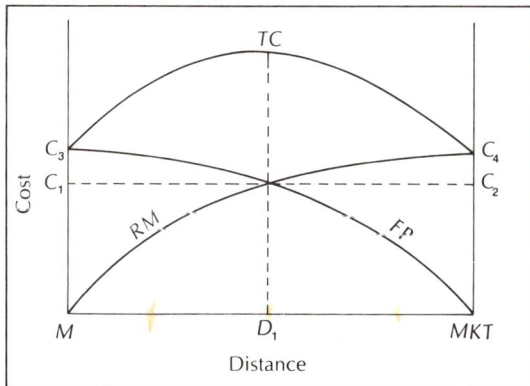

FIGURE 8.28 Weber's model: the effects of curvilinear line-haul costs.

context, locations between material sources and markets may arise for two important reasons.

First, and most important, some industrial plants locate at necessary transshipment points. A change in carrier must occur, for example, when goods produced in the interior of the United States are shipped to Europe—land transportation to water. Materials moved from A to C in Figure 8.31 must pay additional terminal costs at the intermediate location B, which is called a *"break-of-bulk"* point. Although transportation costs usually disfavor processing at intermediate locations because of additional costs, these must be paid anyway at break-of-bulk points. This

FIGURE 8.29 Weber's model: terminal and curvilinear line-haul costs.

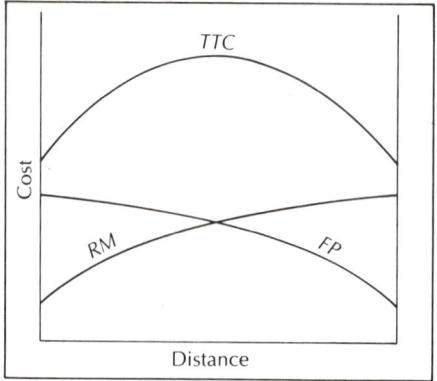

FIGURE 8.30 Weber's model: variations in commodity rates.

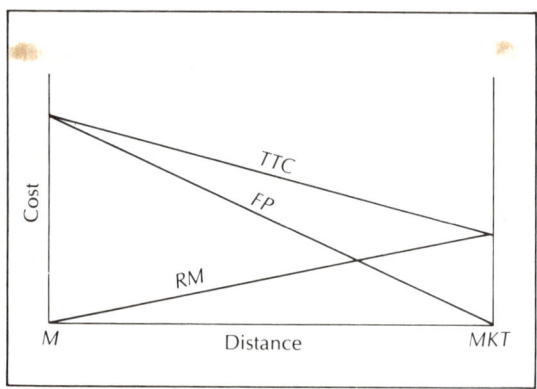

FIGURE 8.31 Break-of-bulk point between land and water transportation.

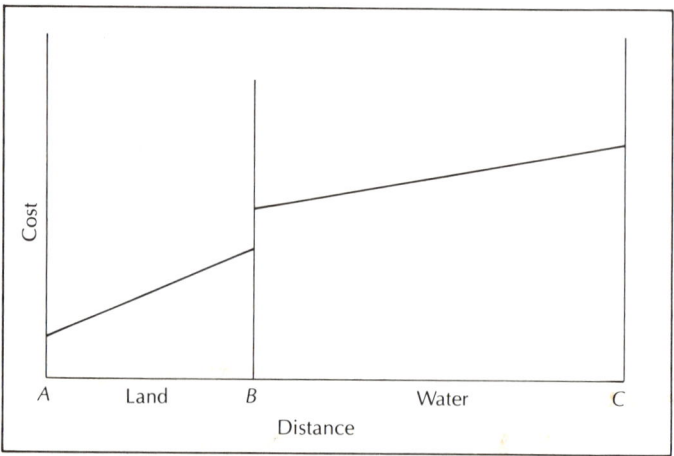

simple fact helps to explain why processing often takes place in port cities. Oil and sugar refineries, for example, often lie at tidewater.

Second, industrial plants sometimes locate at *rate-break points*. Figure 8.32 shows three freight-rate zones. Costs are $3 per ton in Zone 1, $5 per ton in Zone 2, and $6 per ton in Zone 3. A wheat growing region is located at W and a market for flour is located at M. The cost of shipping from W to M is the composite of

Transport Costs

Sugar refinery. SOURCE: *Tate and Lyle, Ltd.*

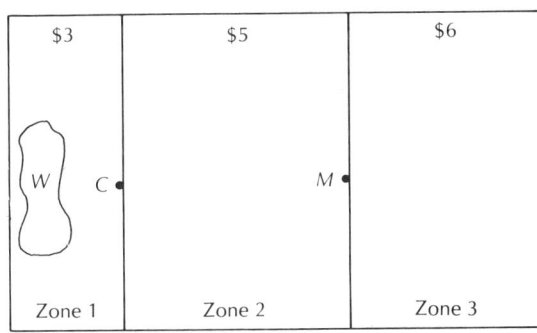

FIGURE 8.32 Rate-break point.

the two rates or $8 per ton. A city located at C may have an advantage for flour milling because of its location at the rate-break point. At intermediate point C the distances moved at the $3 and $5 rates are maximized. Such a location may compete favorably with mills located in the wheat area or at the market.

Effect on Supply and Market Areas Tapering freight rates extend supply and market areas for different kinds of products—agricultural, central place goods, and manufacturing. Consider the effect of tapering freight rates on agricultural rent curves (Figure 8.33A). Instead of being linear they become curvilinear. As a result, zones of agricultural production, especially the outer ones, spread outward. Moreover, if commodities have different transport costs, some production zones may disappear altogether (Figure 8.33B).

FIGURE 8.33 Effect of: (A) tapering freight rates on agricultural rent curves; and (B) differing levels of transportation on agricultural land-use zones.

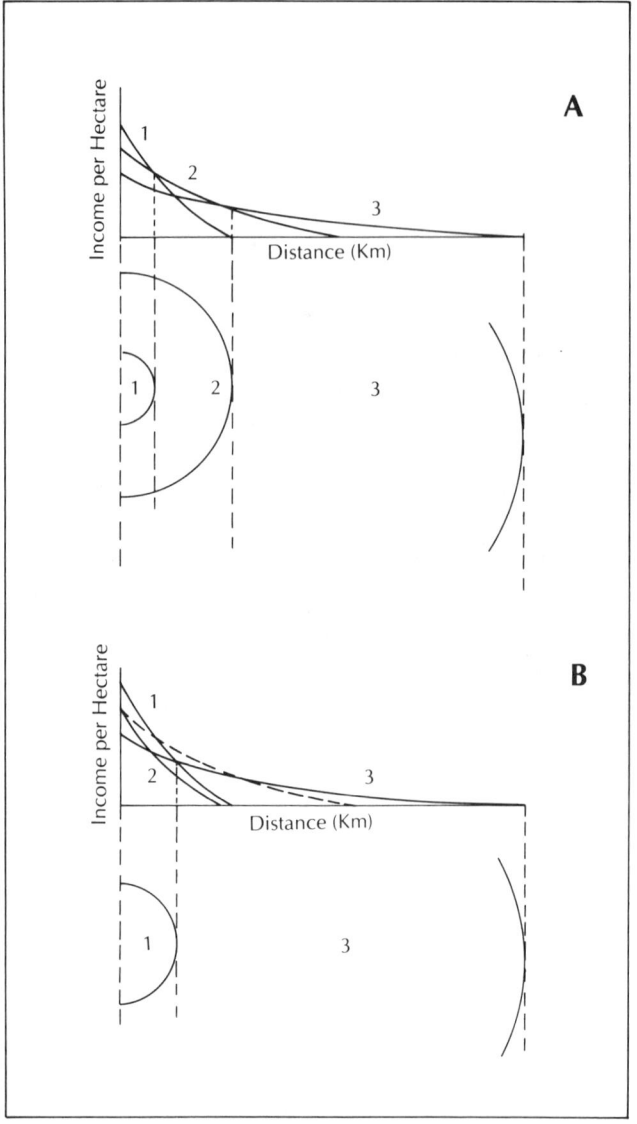

Long haul economies also extend market areas of producers. Suppose we have two producers of the same good. Firms A and B have the same terminal and line-haul costs, but A has lower production costs. With linear transportation costs, the market boundary between the two occurs at D_1 (Figure 8.34A). The situation changes, however, when curvilinear line-haul costs are introduced (Figure 8.34B). Because of long-haul economies, A is able to capture some of B's market area.

Pricing Policy Thus far, we have portrayed transportation rates charged by producers as being a function of distance from the production point. This is called *freight-on-board* or FOB pricing. The consumer pays the plant price plus the cost of transportation. Consumers close to the plant pay less than more distant consumers

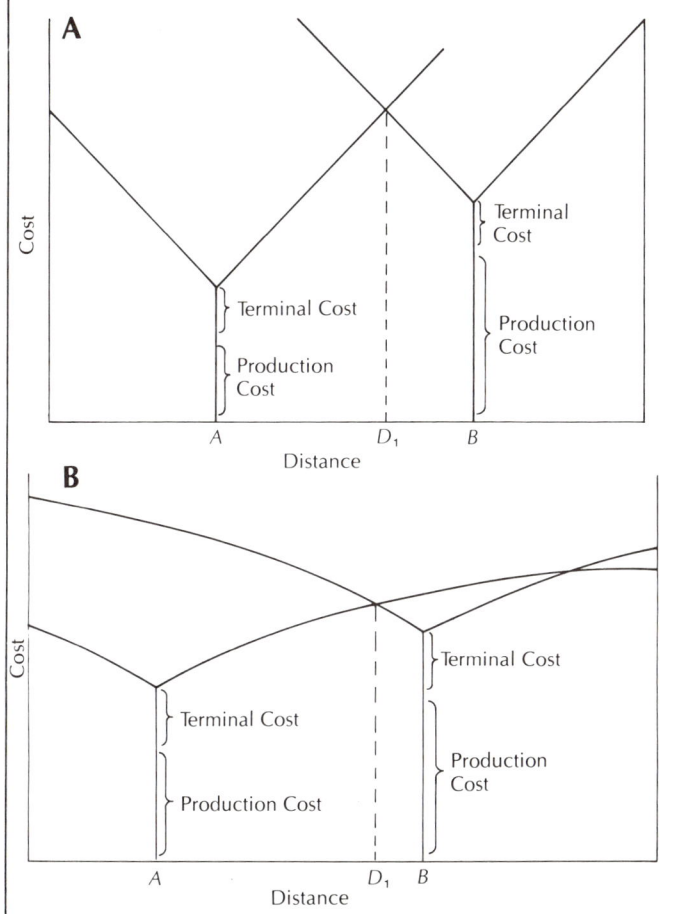

FIGURE 8.34 Market areas: (A) with linear line-haul costs; and (B) with curvilinear line-haul costs.

(Figure 8.35). Many producers adopt a pricing policy known as *cost-insurance-freight* or CIF pricing in which each consumer is charged production costs plus a flat mark-up to cover transportation charges. CIF pricing is illustrated in Figure 8.36. Each consumer is charged a CIF price of C_1. Consumers from A to B are charged more than the actual cost of transportation. Consumers from X to A and B to Y are charged less than the actual cost. Near customers pay the distribution costs of more distant consumers.

What effect does CIF pricing have on the market areas of producers? The FOB prices of Producers A and B are shown in Figure 8.37. The market area boundary is at X_1 with FOB pricing. If B adopts a CIF pricing strategy, the market area boundary shifts to X_2. Of course, Producer A can counter by also adopting CIF pricing. Each consumer then pays the same price to each producer, and price-competition disappears. Producers must now compete through other means such as advertising. For finished products in the United States, CIF pricing tends to be the rule rather than the exception. This is especially true of consumer goods such as clothing, liquor, and small appliances which are offered at a uniform price throughout the nation.

FIGURE 8.35 FOB pricing.

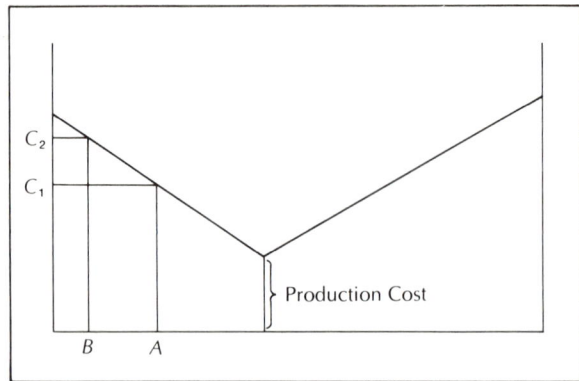

FIGURE 8.36 FOB and CIF pricing.

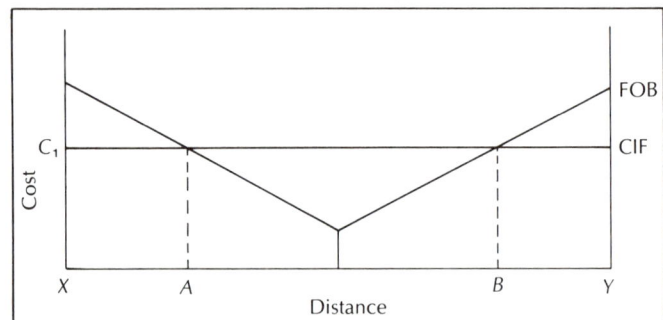

FIGURE 8.37 The effect of CIF pricing on market area boundaries.

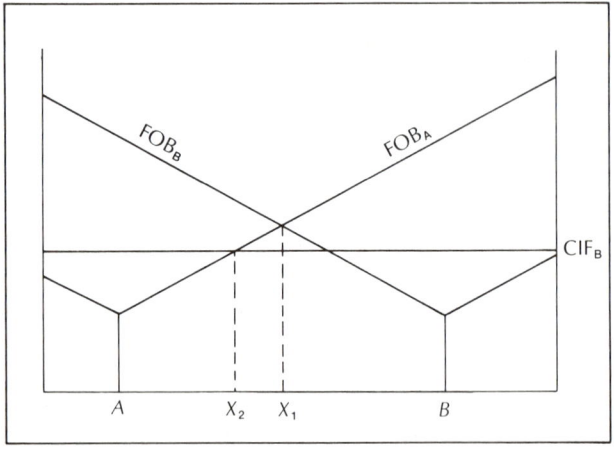

In this section we have seen that transportation costs are complex. We can summarize with respect to industrial location the effects of tapering transportation costs and varying transportation rates:

1. Transportation costs tend to favor terminal locations over intermediate locations.
2. Transportation rates tend to be lower for many raw materials than for finished products, favoring production at market locations.

Transport Improvements

3. Transportation rates tend to be lower where demand for transportation is high. High demand, in turn, increases the supply of transportation routes and carriers.
4. Transportation is required for localized commodities which are produced at few locations and demanded at others. High transportation costs, however, can make the cost of local production competitive with localized production plus transportation costs, producing a ubiquitous production of some commodities with high transportation costs.

Transport Improvements

Improved Transport Facilities

During the last 150 years the need to move goods and people from place to place as rapidly and cheaply as possible has resulted in successive improvements in transport facilities. Let us take an over-all look at the major transport innovations before commenting on their significance.

Prior to the development of railroads, overland transportation of heavy goods was slow and costly. Moving freight by water, however, was much cheaper than by land. For this reason, most of the world's commerce was carried by water transportation, and the important cities were maritime cities. The invention of the steam engine in 1765 paved the way for improved transportation facilities. Its application to water in 1807 and to land in 1829 through the development of the steam locomotive heralded the era of cheap transportation. The steamboat reduced the cost of transportation by water, but the steam railroad had a revolutionary effect on land transportation. It enabled Americans to unite regional markets and to conquer the continental dimensions of the United States. In England, the railways exterminated all regional building styles and all local building materials. In Third World countries railway lines linked export centers more firmly to the economies of Europe and North America.

Technological improvements made since the introduction of steam locomotives reduced the cost of rail transportation. But transport improvements have not been confined to the railroads. Automobile and air transport have also dramatically improved. Highways and waterways have been improved, with the assistance of massive federal aid. Pipelines have been developed to move petroleum and its products, and electrical transmission lines have been constructed to transfer energy.

The introduction of different modes of transportation altered the competitive position of existing types of transportation. This is partly because each new innovation represented an improvement in speed or efficiency of service, and partly because each new mode offered particular advantages over certain distance ranges or for particular types of freight. Table 8.8 shows for the United States trends in the distribution of freight and passenger traffic among the principal modes of transport. In 1940, railroads carried 61 percent of the total ton-kilometers of freight; by 1970

(A) The steam locomotive was invented in England in 1825 partly as a response to the need to transport raw materials to factories and finished products to markets. In the 1950s and 1960s, British Rail replaced steam locomotives with (B) diesels and (C) diesel electrics.

the railroad share had declined to 40 percent. By contrast, motor transport accounted for about 8 percent of the total ton-kilometers in 1940 and over 21 percent in 1970. Airlines have become important people-movers, especially between metropolitan areas; but the shipment of cargo by air is still in its embryonic stage. The airway share of freight traffic is likely to increase sharply as soon as the economy shifts to the containerization of low-weight and/or high value manufactured goods. (Note in reading Table 8.8 that the increasing share of total traffic which is carried by highways arises partly from the creation of new traffic and not entirely from the diversion of traffic from other modes of transport.)

Transport improvements of the last two hundred years required enormous supplies of capital. Recognizing the importance of efficient transportation

TRANSPORT IMPROVEMENTS

Cargo plane. SOURCE: *The Port Authority of N.Y. and N.J.*

networks for economic development, governments and aid agencies such as the World Bank have subsidized canals, roads, railways, port facilities, and air transportation. In the twentieth century, the American federal government, for example, has provided billions of tax dollars for building freeways, remodeling airports, and developing supersonic transportation. Private enterprise has profited handsomely from government transportation aid.

TABLE 8.8 Trends in the distribution of freight and passenger traffic among the principal modes of transport

Agency	Percent of Total Ton-Kilometers				Percent of Total Passenger-Kilometers			
	1940	1950	1960	1970	1940	1950	1960	1970
Railroads	61.34	58.69	43.51	39.97	8.71	8.12	2.86	0.92
Highways	7.91	12.39	22.50	21.44	90.46	89.57	92.37	88.73
Inland Waterways	19.13	16.19	16.76	15.98	0.46	0.30	0.27	0.34
Oil Pipelines	11.62	12.70	17.18	22.43	—	—	—	—
Airways	*	0.03	0.06	0.18	0.37	2.01	4.50	10.01

*Less than 0.01 percent
SOURCE: Interstate Commerce Commission

COST-SPACE CONVERGENCE

Transport improvements have brought significant cost reductions to shippers. For example, the opening of the Erie Canal in 1825 reduced the cost of transport between Buffalo and Albany from $100 to $10 and ultimately to $3 per ton. Railroad freight rates in the United States dropped 41 percent between 1882 and 1900. Between the 1870s and 1950s the real cost of ocean transport fell by about 60 percent. The most important effects of cost-space convergence may be summarized briefly.

Transportation and Availability of Goods Cheap transportation based on cheap energy enables communities to obtain goods which must be produced elsewhere. For example, fresh fruits can be brought into a community when the season is not suitable for the local product or when the local supply is short. Crop failures in a region are less serious if supplies can be brought in from another.

Transportation and the Extent of the Market Cheap transportation widens the zone of profitable production for a given market. For example, during the nineteenth century, American railroads increased the profitability of agricultural production in areas remote from the national market. The effect of cheap railroad transportation in the United States was also experienced in England where grain prices fell up to 50 percent, and posed a problem for English farmers and landowners.

Transportation and Prices Cheap transportation may reduce the price of goods if transportation savings are passed on to consumers by lowering the costs of producing them. This is accomplished in several ways. First, cheap transportation reduces the cost of distributing finished products to consumers. Second, it reduces the costs of assembling raw materials. Third, it allows increased geographical division of labor at national and international scales. In other words, it encourages communities to specialize in the production of goods for which they have the greatest advantages (the law of comparative costs). Fourth, cheap transportation reduces prices by encouraging large-scale production. In many instances, large-scale production means that either raw materials or finished products must be transported long distances. The flour milling industry, for example, could not persist in Minneapolis-St. Paul if millers had to rely on local supplies of grain or on a local market for their products. The mills are remote from their sources of wheat, and on the far northwestern margin of the national market.

Transportation and Urbanization Cheap transportation contributes to the growth of cities. It enables cities to obtain food products from distant places. It facilitates urban concentration by stimulating large-scale production and geographical division of labor.

Transportation and Cities Transportation improvements change patterns of urban accessibility. In the contemporary American city, for example, urban freeways and high performance rapid transit systems such as the Bay Area Rapid Transit (BART) have tended to serve high-income groups and to increase the isolation of the poor. The poor have been powerless to prevent the carving up of city neighborhoods for freeways and the flight of industry and jobs to the suburbs. They have also been unable to prevent the neglect of short-haul central city mass transportation, which could benefit most low-income groups.

TRANSPORT IMPROVEMENTS

TIME-SPACE CONVERGENCE

Developments in transportation have not only meant cost reductions, but also great increases in speed. As a result of increases in speed, relative distances between places have been melting away. The notion of a "shrinking world" has been elaborated by Donald Jannelle (1968, 1969), who introduced the term *time-space convergence*. He showed that the travel time between Edinburgh and London decreased from 20,000 minutes by stagecoach in 1658 to under 60 minutes by airplane today (Figure 8.38). Over the 300 year period, he calculated that the average annual rate of time-distance convergence has been about 29 minutes. It is clear from Figure 8.38 that time-space convergence is marked in a period of rapid transportation development; for example, the change from stagecoach to railroad. In the 1840s travel time between Edinburgh and London by stagecoach was 2000 minutes, but by the 1850s with the arrival of the steam locomotive the travel time had been reduced by two-thirds to 800 minutes. Subsequently, the rate of time-space convergence by train levelled off.

A

B

Travel effort and the journey to work: (A) downtown Chicago during the morning rush hour (SOURCE: *U.S. Department of Transportation/Urban Mass Transportation Adm.):* (B) downtown Minneapolis on a Sunday afternoon. These two pictures emphasize that if more and more people insist on driving to work by automobile, then time-space divergence and increased congestion will result. A solution to the problem is to induce people to use such conventional movers as buses and trains.

FIGURE 8.38 Reduction in journey times as a result of progressive transportation improvements. SOURCE: "Central Place Development in a Time-Space Framework," reproduced by permission from *The Professional Geographer* of the Association of American Geographers, Volume 20, 1968, D. Janelle.

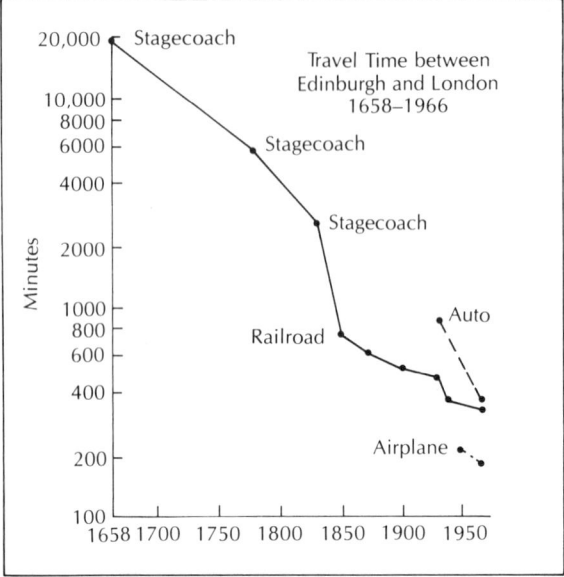

The friction of space has diminished over time, but the process has been uneven: some places have benefited more than others. Economically developed areas have benefited most from time-space convergence. The consequences of this differential process have had a notable effect on regional economic development. In underdeveloped countries, for example, towns located in the foreign enclaves or on the colonial transport arteries that linked the most productive regions of the space-economy to the port cities grew rapidly, while other centers bypassed by road or rail stagnated or lost ground. Transportation networks in the colonial Third World were built to provide easy access for resources which European countries and companies wanted, not what might benefit the local peoples.

Idealized Model of Network Change

The impact of transportation improvements on regional economic development is captured in Edward Taaffe, Richard Morrill, and Peter Gould's (1963) stage model of network change. Studies in Nigeria, East Africa, Brazil, and Malaya provided the basis for their model, but it is generally applicable to the United States. They assumed implicitly a macro-region with an unexploited interior. They defined the extension of transport in terms of penetration from the coast. Transport links reflect "(1) the desire to connect an administrative center on the sea coast with an interior area of political and military control; (2) the desire to reach areas of mineral exploitation; [and] (3) the desire to reach areas of potential agricultural export production" (1963:506).

The model illustrates through six stages how the interplay between the evolution of a transport network and urban growth is self-reinforcing (Figure 8.39). The ideal-typical sequence begins (stage 1) with a series of small scattered ports along the sea coast. In stage 2, two major lines of penetration, which reduce

Transport Improvements

A passenger train pulls into the Terminus at Lagos, Nigeria. The railway network in Nigeria is a colonial legacy. It serves the mines and the specialized crop-producing areas, and carries their products mainly to the port of Lagos for export. SOURCE: *World Bank Photo* by Federation of Nigeria.

transport costs, link major ports (P_1 and P_2) and their inland centers (I_1 and I_2). Feeder routes begin to develop and they focus on the major ports. Agglomeration economies permit the major ports to expand their hinterlands by capturing the hinterlands of smaller adjacent ports, which decline or disappear. In stage 3, feeder routes focus on major ports and inland centers and new urban centers grow at strategic points along the main routes. By stage 4 there is lateral route development which enhances the competitive position of the major ports and inland centers. A few nodes along the original lines of inland penetration, for example N_1 and N_2, become focal points for feeder networks of their own, and they begin to capture the hinterlands of smaller centers on each side. Eventually a transport network interconnects all the major centers (stage 5). The last stage shows the development of high-priority linkages reinforcing the advantages of urban centers that have come to dominate the economic landscape.

The ideal-typical sequence of transport development illustrates how a space-economy tends to root itself ever more firmly as early locational decisions that shaped the system are reinforced subsequently by others. The result is an increased

FIGURE 8.39 Model of transport development. From E. J. Taaffe, R. L. Morrill, and P. R. Gould, 1963, "Transport Expansion in Underdeveloped Countries: A Comparative Analysis," *Geographical Review,* 53, p. 504, Fig. 1.

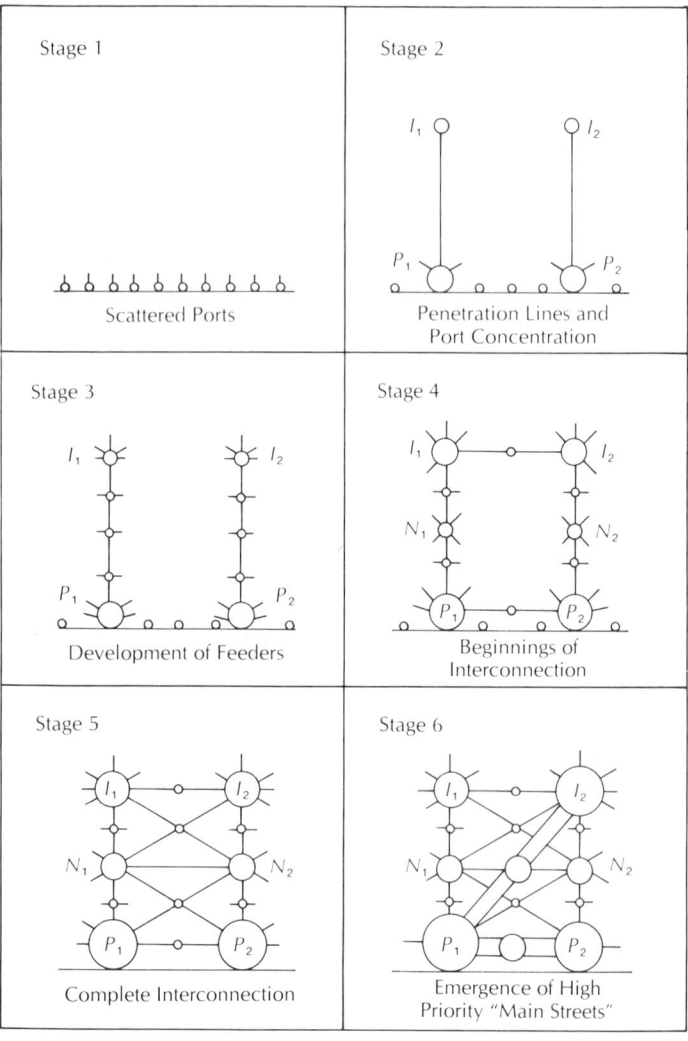

CORE AND PERIPHERY

The concepts of core-region and periphery were introduced to Western regional analysis by John Friedmann:

> ... core regions are territorially organized subsystems of society which have a high capacity for innovative change; peripheral regions are subsystems whose development path is determined chiefly by core region institutions with respect to which they stand in a relation of substantial dependency.

> Peripheral regions can be identified by their relations of dependency to a core area.

> Core and periphery together constitute a complete spatial system (1969, 18–19).

concentration of economic development and increased polarization between *core* and *peripheral areas* of the space-economy (see box). The final three chapters of this book examine in greater detail the theme of unequal development.

Summary

Movements of goods, people, and information take place over and through transport *networks*. In analyzing transport networks, geographers often employ *graph theory*, which involves reducing networks to a set of *vertices* and a set of *edges*. We showed how graph theoretic measures may be used to determine nodal accessibility and network connectivity. We also considered other properties of networks, their shapes and densities.

In our review of classical location models we assumed, for simplicity, that *transport costs* are proportional to distance. But in the real world, transport costs are complex, and these complexities were considered to obtain a better understanding of production, exchange, and consumption patterns. We showed, for example, how differential transport rates influence industrial location.

The final section of the chapter was devoted to transport improvements, which have resulted in *cost-space* and *time-space convergence*. Although the friction of space has diminished over time, the process has benefited some places and groups more than others. The orientation and organization of the transport system in American cities favors affluent suburbanites and the trucking industry. In 1969, the federal government allocated 85 percent of its budget for transportation to highways and aviation, but less than 3 percent of this budget for mass transit, the system which could potentially be of greatest benefit to the poor.

DISCUSSION QUESTIONS

1. What are the advantages and disadvantages of reducing a transport network to a graph?
2. Compare and contrast the orientation of transport networks in developed and underdeveloped countries.
3. Discuss the relationship between physical and economic factors in the development of transport routes.
4. Define fixed costs and give some examples from the transportation industry.
5. Define variable costs and give some examples from the transportation industry.
6. What factors must a carrier take into account in pricing transportation?
7. Explain why transportation rates are only indirectly related to distance.
8. Comment on the influence of terminal and line-haul costs on carrier rates.
9. Why are there more trucklines than airlines?

10. The automobile industry, for long centered in the Detroit area, has now established assembly plants and branch manufacturing plants in market areas. Why?
11. What factors govern the location of intraurban expressways?
12. Discuss the relationship between network structure and levels of economic development.

SUGGESTED READINGS

Overview

Lowe, J. C., and S. Moryadas, *The Geography of Movement.* Boston: Houghton Mifflin Company, 1975.

Taaffe, E. J., and H. L. Gauthier, *Geography of Transportation.* Englewood Cliffs, N.J.: Prentice-Hall, Inc., 1973.

Network Analysis and Graph Theory

Haggett, P., "Network Models in Geography" in *Models in Geography,* eds. R. J. Chorley and Peter Haggett. London: Methuen and Co. Ltd., 1967, pp. 609–68.

Haggett, P., and R. Chorley, *Network Analysis in Geography.* New York: St. Martin's Press, 1970.

Harary, F., *Graph Theory.* Reading, Mass.: Addison-Wesley, 1967.

Kansky, K., *Structure of Transport Networks.* Department of Geography Research Papers 84, University of Chicago, 1963.

Werner, C., "The Law of Refraction in Transportation Geography: Its Multivariate Extensions," *Canadian Geographer,* **12** (1968):28–40.

Wolfe, R. I., "Transportation and Politics: The Example of Canada," *Annals* of the Association of American Geographers, **52** (1962):176–190.

Transportation Cost Structures

Alexander, J. W., S. E. Brown, and R. E. Dahlbery, "Freight Rates: Selected Aspects of Uniform and Nodal Regions," *Economic Geography,* **34** (1958):1–18.

Locklin, D. P., *The Economics of Transportation,* 7th ed. Homewood, Ill.: Richard D. Irwin, 1972.

Sampson, R. J., and M. T. Farris, *Domestic Transportation: Practice, Theory and Policy.* Boston: Houghton Mifflin Company, 1966.

Transport Improvements and Network Change

Janelle, D. G., "Spatial Reorganization: A Model and a Concept," *Annals* of the Association of American Geographers, **59** (1969):348–364.

Taaffe, E. J., R. L. Morrill, and P. R. Gould, "Transport Expansion in Underdeveloped Countries," *Geographical Review,* **53** (1963):503–529.

9

Decision-Making

KEY TERMS

- behavioral matrix
- catastrophe theory
- game theory
- global solution
- local solution
- mean information field
- Monte-Carlo simulation
- psychic income
- saddle-point
- satisficer
- simulation
- spatial diffusion
- technostructure
- zero-sum game

9

Classical location models assume that the economic landscape is the work of optimizers under conditions of perfect competition. Optimizers can foresee the outcomes of all possible actions and always act to maximize profits. The landscape created by optimizers does not go through any intermediate adjustment stages, but rather goes from undifferentiated to optimal instantly.

Today, economists and geographers recognize that the classical assumptions of perfect competition and perfect economic persons are inadequate. They have attempted to improve upon classical location theory by developing behavioral theories that take into account that many firms are large, complex corporations with hierarchical managerial bureaucracies, and that decisions are made in the face of uncertainty. Behavioral approaches to the study of economic systems owe much to the work of R. Cyert and J. March (1963) and the Carnegie Institute of Technology. Although they are accepted as being descriptively more realistic, behavioral theories have not replaced their classical counterparts, because behavioral theories are more complex. They do not always yield more accurate predictions about behavior and patterns of resource allocation than traditional theories.

Radicals point out that behavioral approaches have not produced a new theory of the market economy. Descriptive behavioralism has merely replaced the *optimizer* with the *satisficer*. Like classical theories, behavioral ones are a-historical. They isolate human decision-making from the overall development of capitalist society.

This chapter offers no further critique of the behavioral approach in economic geography. Its purpose is to introduce some of the behavioral models used by geographers to discuss decision-making in a market economy. As a preface to that discussion, let us present the main assumptions advanced by behavioral economic geographers.

First, the behavioral economic geographer would argue that economic landscapes are created by fallible and unequal human beings. People do not foresee the outcomes of all possible actions; their knowledge is imperfect. Neither do they have the ability to synthesize large amounts of information instantly. Economic landscapes are created by a trial-and-error process. They are strongly structured by existing patterns of production, exchange, and consumption in a capitalist society.

Objectives

Decision-making: a committee meeting. SOURCE: *University of Wisconsin—Extension*.

Second, decision-makers who have created the existing economic landscape are not optimizers. To gain a better understanding of real-world patterns, a model of the decision-maker called the *satisficer* must be utilized. Satisficers make decisions which are "good enough" or satisfactory. In a capitalist society, the best decision is one which results in profits or, at least, zero loss. These decisions may be optimal, but only if decision-makers are lucky enough to choose an optimal location. Satisficers may choose sub-optimal locations even when more profitable locations are known if they are strongly motivated by non-economic factors (or protected by monopolistic industries and/or government subsidies). This concept is termed "psychic income." *Psychic income* is the non-economic satisfaction which may come from operating in one's home town, in a specific physical environment, or away from other environments such as high-crime urban areas. The behavioral geographer would argue that understanding of the economic landscape of reality must incorporate this view of human decision-making.

OBJECTIVES

By the end of this chapter you should be able:

1. To draw and label an elementary behavioral matrix and to discuss the implications of various locations within the matrix.
2. To describe the game theoretic approach to agricultural decision-making.

3. To describe the game theoretic approach to the diffusion of innovations.
4. To discuss in detail Morrill's model of the spread and growth of urban settlements.
5. To list and discuss the three major points of Alchain's discussion of the "random hypothesis."

The Behavioral Matrix

A conceptual approach to the problem of non-optimal decision-making involves the use of a "behavioral matrix" (Pred, 1967), shown in Figure 9.1. The origin of the matrix is the top, left-hand corner. The reliability and quantity of information increases to the right and the ability and speed with which that knowledge is utilized increases downward. A perfect optimizer would be located in the extreme lower right-hand corner. A purely "random" decision-maker would be located at the origin. The individual capitalist in a small, one-plant firm may make the locational decision. In the real world, the information and synthesizing ability of individual firms is necessarily limited and unequal. The personnel and data-gathering ability possessed by large corporations, on the other hand, allows them to make much more precise locational decisions. In the large corporation, such decisions are made not by an individual, but by a collective of middle-level managers each of whom brings specialized knowledge and skills to the decision-making process. This group of specialists has been labeled the "technostructure" by Galbraith (1967). The specialized knowledge and skills of the technostructure allow large corporations to operate close to the optimum position on the behavioral matrix because they have largely eliminated the competition.

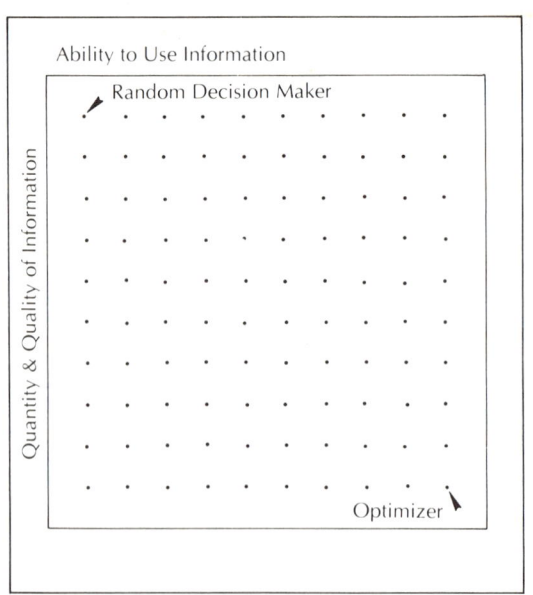

9.1 A behavioral matrix. After A. Pred, 1967, "Behavior and Location: Foundations for a Geographic and Dynamic Location Theory, Part I," *Lund Studies in Geography, Series B*, 27, p, 25, Fig. 1.

Agriculture

An elementary application of the behavioral matrix is shown in Figure 9.2. The isolines represent spatial margins to viability. Any location chosen within those margins is a viable location. Decision-makers in the lower right quadrant of the behavioral matrix are most likely to choose viable locations, but they may also select non-viable sites and disappear from the landscape. Decision-makers from the upper left quadrant are more likely to choose non-viable locations, but they may be lucky enough to select viable or even optimal sites.

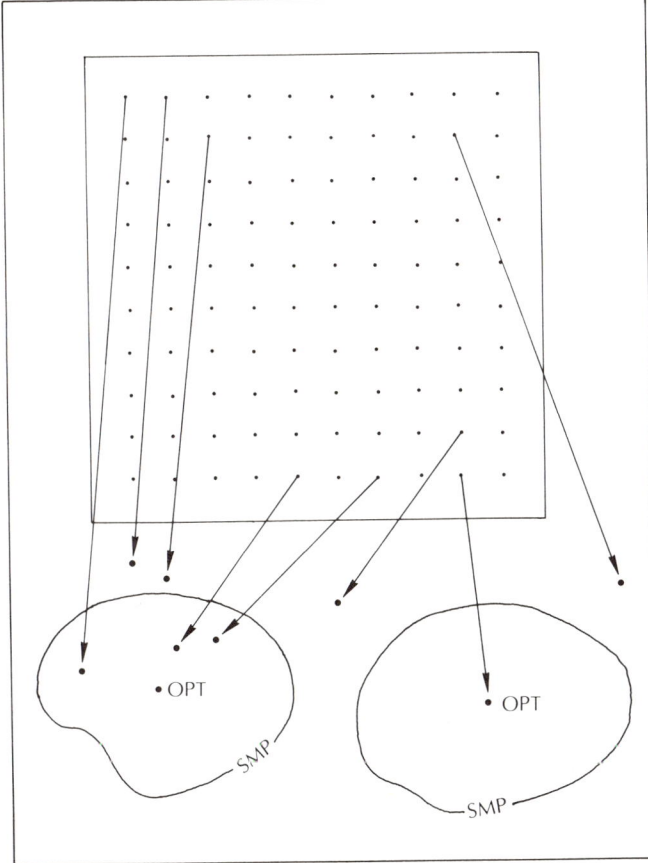

FIGURE 9.2 A behavioral matrix and locational choice. After A. Pred. 1967, "Behavior and Location: Foundations for a Geographic and Dynamic Location Theory, Part I," *Lund Studies in Geography, Series B,* 27, p. 92, Fig. 11.

Agriculture

The behavioral matrix may be applied to the Thünen model of agricultural land use. Growing the optimum crop in a given location is a trial-and-error process. The Thünen model helps us to understand the *prevailing* form of agriculture over large areas, especially when the environmental aspects of Ricardian rent theory are added. Within the prevailing pattern of agriculture, however, individual farms or larger sub-regions may use other forms of agriculture. This may result from suboptimal decision-making as illustrated in Figure 9.3. Better decision-makers have, with few exceptions, chosen the more profitable form of agriculture for a given location. Less knowledgeable decision-makers have, in many cases, chosen less profitable, but still viable forms of agriculture. Most of the less profitable decisions occur near the boundary of the two prevailing crops where the decision is less clear-cut and information often conflicting.

FIGURE 9.3 A behavioral matrix and agricultural regions.

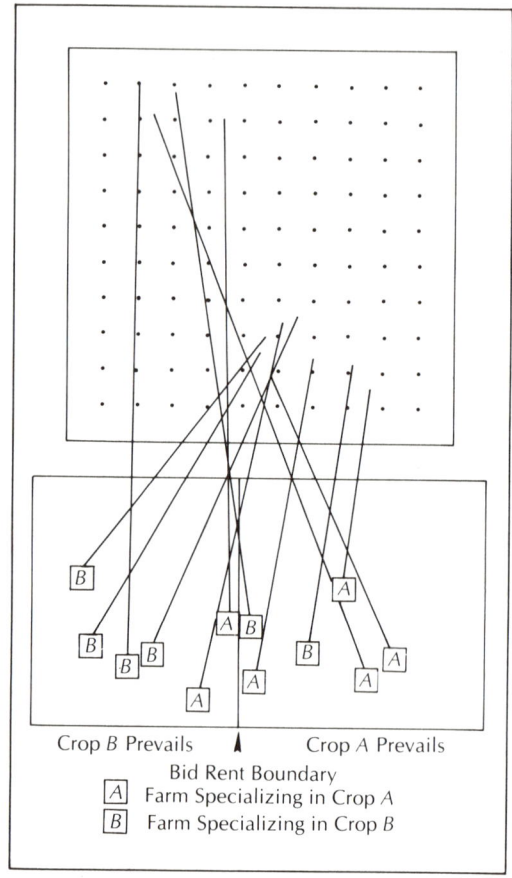

Many types of agriculture and farming practices are the result of different cultural values which often prevail even in a predominant market ideology. In the United States, the horse-powered agriculture of Amish farms in the midst of tractor-based farming, the persistence of wheat farming in the margins of dry lands during the 1930s, and the continuation of tobacco as a secondary crop in parts of the South are examples. Residual farms surrounded by suburban housing at the margins of cities are another example. How can they persist in the face of much more profitable forms of land use? The answer is partly the result of the time period involved and partly the result of the basis of agriculture. Residual farms cannot persist in the *long-run,* but for a short period of years they can hold out in the face of much higher income which would result from selling the land for housing purposes. Owners reap psychic income from remaining in farming and increased real income when they

Agriculture

sell. The psychic income from such action outweighs the pecuniary income which would come from selling. Land is the basis for agricultural wealth. A farmer who owns the land controls the means of production and can persist against more competitive forms of land use. No beginning farmer, however, could afford to buy a residual farm for agricultural purposes. The same is true of secondary forms of agriculture in the midst of more profitable types of farming. We must assume, however, that such decisions produce favorable results in the short run.

Environmental Space: A Game Theory Approach

Environmental conditions provide a partial explanation for broad patterns of prevailing agricultural conditions. The boundary between wheat farming and livestock ranching, for example, is basically a function of precipitation. If rainfall could be predicted accurately over the long run, the boundary between the two types of

Livestock ranching in Paraguay. The boundary between grain farming and livestock ranching is basically a function of precipitation. For example, north and west of the great grass plains (*pampa*) of Argentina, Uruguay, and Paraguay, rainfall decreases. As environmental conditions become increasingly unfavorable for maize, alfalfa and wheat, the predominant land use becomes commercial stock raising on improved pastures, and then the grazing of low-quality cattle on unimproved pastures. SOURCE: *Brooke Bond Oxo Ltd.*

agriculture would be much less transitional. The uncertainty of environmental conditions plays a considerable role in agricultural decision-making. Some areas are too dry for wheat, whereas other areas always have enough moisture. In a middle zone, between wet and dry, however, some years will support wheat while others will bring severe losses to anyone attempting to grow wheat. Farmers in this middle zone may practice only ranching, risk everything on wheat with its potentially high rewards or losses, or mix the two types of agriculture as a hedge against the uncertainty of the environment.

Environmental decision-making has been approached in a *game-theoretic* framework (Gould, 1963). Although the environment is uncertain, knowledge of the probabilities of normal and extreme conditions based on past experience can be used to develop a strategy of action using game theory. We will give two abstract examples of the use of game theory. The values of both environmental conditions and net incomes per hectare in the examples are hypothetical, but real values could be provided through field work. We will first assume that farmers must maximize their net income per hectare with a minimum of uncertainty in order to survive. We further simplify the problem by assuming only two environmental possibilities: drought and abnormally wet years.

The first example involves only two possible types of agriculture: wheat and livestock ranching. The net income of each type is shown in Figure 9.4. Wheat ranges from $30 per hectare in the wet years to zero in the dry years; livestock ranching yields a net income per hectare of $20 in the wet years and $10 in the dry years. These values can be placed in matrix form as in Figure 9.5, yielding a "two-person-two-strategy-zero-sum game." The agriculturist represents one person in the game and the environment the opposing player. The two types of agriculture are the two strategies. The game is a "zero-sum" game because the "pay-off" to one player is exactly the value "lost" by the opponent. In Figure 9.5, for example, it is assumed that the farmer chooses the strategy of ranching. If the "environment"

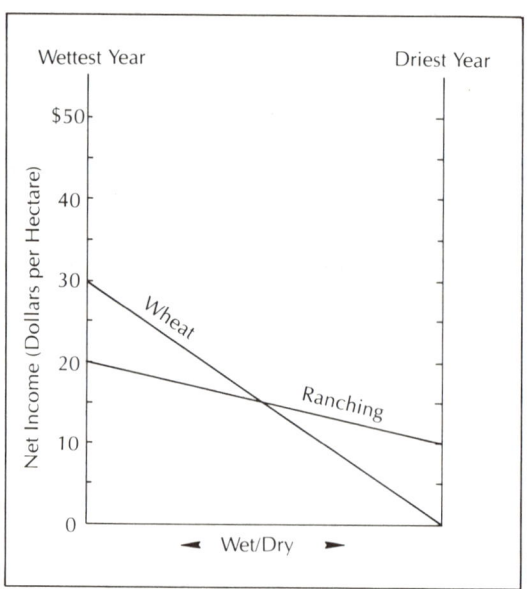

FIGURE 9.4 Wheat and ranching yields: extreme years.

Agriculture

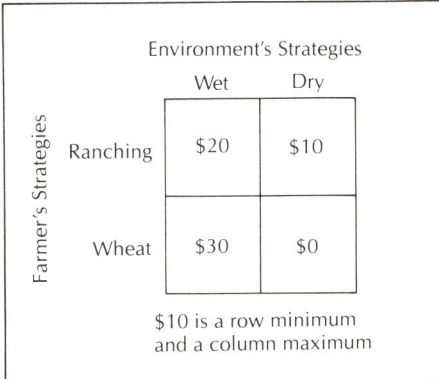

FIGURE 9.5 Pay-off matrix: wheat and ranching.

chooses the strategy of a wet year, he will "lose" $10 ($20 − $10) compared to a dry year strategy, but the farmer will gain $10 over a dry year. In the matrix of Figure 9.5, the value of $10 is a minimum value of a row and a maximum value in a column. This is called a *saddle-point* or *minimum-maximum* in game theory. The "minimax" can also be seen in Figure 9.4 in which the value of $10 is the lowest point on the highest strategy curve. The farmer will always win by practicing livestock ranching and the environment will always "lose." The environment will "win" some of the time if a strategy of wheat farming is chosen.

In the second example, we consider a more humid area in which four strategies are possible:

1. livestock ranching based on natural vegetation;
2. wheat farming;
3. corn with all income based on the sale of corn as grain;
4. feeder livestock with all income derived from animals fattened on corn.

Which strategy (or combination of strategies) will yield the highest net income per acre over the long run with the least risk? The graphical solution to this question is given in Figure 9.6. The lowest point on the uppermost boundary in the figure gives the two crops on which farmers should concentrate. "Mixed farming" is a combination of corn-for-grain and feeder livestock. The two crops are then placed in a pay-off matrix (Figure 9.7). The difference between each pair of values is calculated and assigned (regardless of sign) to the alternate strategy to determine the proportion of each type of agriculture which should be planned for sale. Corn should be the primary cash crop 20 percent of the time and feeder cattle should account for sales 80 percent of the time. The type of agriculture which will be the primary sale item must be planned ahead. Feeder cattle must be purchased early in the year for fattening and a farmer cannot switch from feeder cattle sales to selling corn for grain without first dumping livestock on the market or losing his total investment in the cattle by not feeding them at all.

How should the solution in Figure 9.7 be used? Should corn be the sole source of income 20 percent of the years and feeder cattle the remainder? Should total income be based on these proportions each year? In game-theory terms and over the long run, it makes no difference.

FIGURE 9.6 Locating a critical pair of strategies.

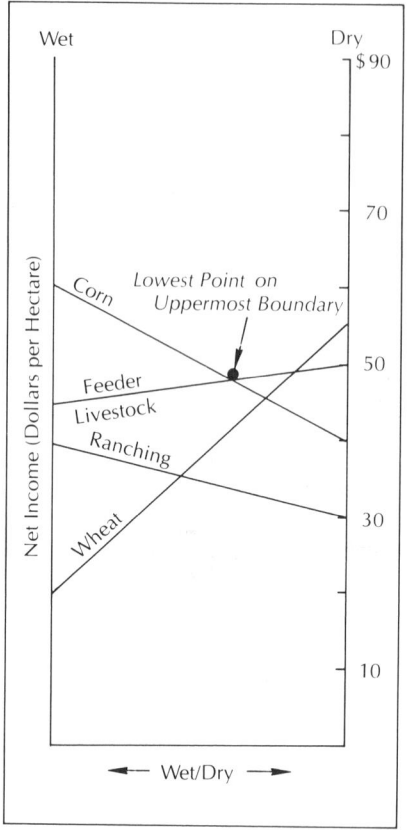

FIGURE 9.7 Pay-off matrix: corn and feeder livestock.

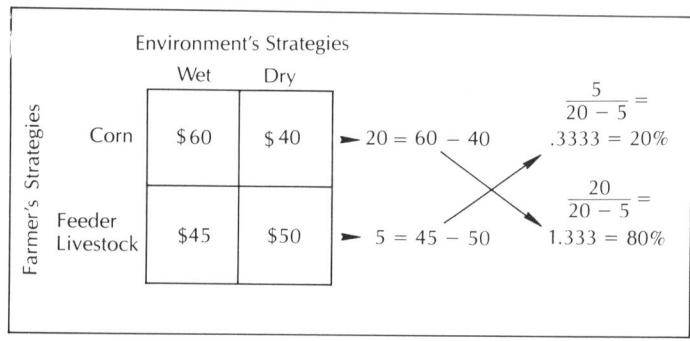

Assume that dry years occur 50 percent of the time and the farmer uses 20 percent of his land for corn (for grain) and 80 percent for feeder cattle each year. Income per hectare ($48.00) will be the same whether the year is wet or dry (Figure 9.8). The same average will result if the land is used exclusively for corn 20 percent of the years, and for feeder livestock for the remainder. The individual farmer, however, must be concerned with short-run results. A below average income will result if all income is derived from corn in a dry year or feeder livestock in a wet year. We assume that each farmer desires at least an "average" income each year and will therefore obtain the best results if the specific proportions of each type of agriculture are adopted every year.

FIGURE 9.8 Determination of long-run average income per hectare.

```
ASSUME:      Dry years occur 50% of the time
             20% of land used for corn for grain
             80% of land used for feeder livestock

WET YEAR:    Corn = $12.00 = ($60.00 • 20%)
             Livestock = $36.00 = ($45.00 • 80%)
             Total (per hectare) = $48.00

DRY YEAR:    Corn = $8.00 = ($40.00 • 20%)
             Livestock = $40.00 = ($50.00 • 80%)
             Total (per hectare) = $48.00

AVERAGE:     $48.00 = $48.00 + $48.00 ÷ 2
             (dry years occur 50% of the time)
```

Spraying coffee trees with a copper solution on an estate in Kenya. The copper solution helps coffee trees to retain their leaves and with a larger area for photosynthesis larger coffee berries are produced. However, spraying is only a successful strategy if there is sufficient moisture. Under drought conditions, a coffee tree protects itself by dropping its leaves, but when it is sprayed with the copper solution it cannot use this natural mechanism and gradually dies through evapotranspiration. Thus estate owners must decide whether to spray or not to spray on the basis of knowledge about precipitation. They will spray in areas where there is a high probabiliity of receiving adequate rainfall. They may also spray if they irrigate their land. Irrigation reduces the uncertainty of the natural environment. SOURCE: *Brooke Bond Oxo Ltd.*

Game theory provides only a framework within which the problem of uncertainty can be approached. We must assume that patterns of production are the result of a trial-and-error process which has been modified over time. Agriculture is always a gamble and random shocks are caused by environmental extremes. The water shortages and severe winter of 1976–77 in the United States are examples.

The Diffusion of Technological Innovations

The margins of a particular kind of agriculture can shift because of changes in demand which shift the boundary into less profitable areas if demand is high and diminish the area of the crop if demand falls; and changes in technology which allow the crop to shift into areas once limited by environmental conditions. We used the example of hybrid corn, a technological innovation which shifted the margins of corn-based agriculture. Less than one-third of the corn planted in the United States in 1940 was of the hybrid variety, but by 1954 almost 90 percent was hybrid and the percentage was over 97 percent in the North Central States which make up the "Corn Belt." The use of hybrid corn increased the yield per hectare by as much as 20 percent and made the use of mechanical harvesters much more efficient, but the greatest advantage of hybrids was the great increase in the speed of maturation. Older varieties of corn required at least 140 days for maturation while the hybrids mature in as little as 90 days. Rapid maturation made corn a profitable crop in formerly marginal areas and a marginal crop in areas where it could not be grown for grain before the introduction of hybrids. In other words, the environmental margins of the crop were shifted northward in the United States. H. Roepke (1959) found that the introduction of hybrids resulted in (1) an increase in the intensity of corn production in the core region of the "Corn Belt"; (2) a significant increase in the intensity of production in areas formerly marginal for corn; and (3) little change in the amount of production in areas newly marginal for corn. Roepke also found evidence that "Corn Belt" type farming had shifted northward into southern Wisconsin. The introduction of hybrid corn, therefore, produced a change in the pattern of agricultural production in the United States.

Because changes in technology induce changes in agricultural patterns, geographers are interested in the forces that control the spread and adoption of technological innovations. Innovations are not adopted instantly by all potential users. The rate of adoption does, however, follow a consistent and predictable sequence. Once the innovation is introduced in an area, it is accepted very early by a small percentage of the potential users. A short period of rapid adoption then follows, which falls off once the rate of adoption has reached 90 percent or more. The change in the cumulative percentage of adoption is shown in Figure 9.9 which is a generalization of acceptance curves for most types of innovation.

Geographers have used *simulation* to analyze the process of the adoption of technological innovations in a spatial context. They assume that an innovation *diffuses* outward from an initial core. The core is a given distribution of people who have already accepted the innovation. The problem then becomes one of determining the key variable(s) which control(s) the diffusion or spread of the innovation. As with all models, numerous factors cannot be or are not included among the variables

Agriculture

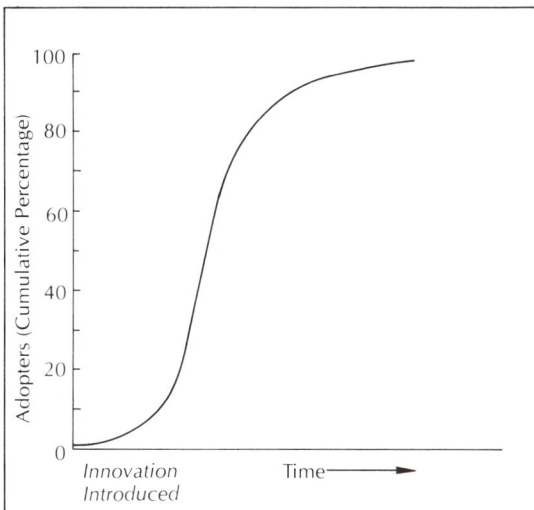

FIGURE 9.9 Adoption of an innovation over time.

selected for controls. These other factors which might influence the spread of innovation are considered to interact *randomly* in the diffusion model. This is the first model which we have considered that attempts to represent real decision-making by suggesting that people behave randomly within a given set of rules.

Some geographers would argue that the technique of simulation has been used to illustrate the *speed* of diffusion rather than decision-making. Further, a few geographers who have studied decision-making in the Third World have suggested that some of the assumptions upon which innovation diffusion research is based may be incorrect. Data from East Africa and Thailand, for example, show that ideas, plans, and innovations sent down from the core to the local level and to the people are often ignored. Ideas are accepted more readily at the village level if they are first introduced by local change agents.

Most of the initial work in geography on the simulation of diffusion was done by Torsten Hägerstrand (1953). The Hägerstrand model assumes that innovation spreads through personal contacts and that the frequency of personal contact is an *inverse* function of distance. The problem, therefore, is to determine the exact form of the relationship between distance and the frequency of personal contact. Hägerstrand first applied the techniques of simulation to an analysis of the diffusion of a government subsidy program in Sweden. The government program was designed to encourage farmers to improve pastureland and to discourage grazing in open woodland. Figure 9.10 shows the number of acceptors in the area of Hägerstrand's study in the first year after the introduction of the subsidy program in 1929. Personal contact was especially important in promoting the acceptance of the program in the 1930s before the widespread use of radio, television, telephones, and automobiles in rural areas. Hägerstrand used the distances over which people in the area migrated as an estimate of the distance/personal contact relationship. Most migrants settled close to home and, as distance increased, the number of migrants tailed off in the familiar distance-decay curve (Figure 9.11).

The migration/distance curve then was used to develop a *mean information field* (MIF) which gives the probability of personal contact from a given point in

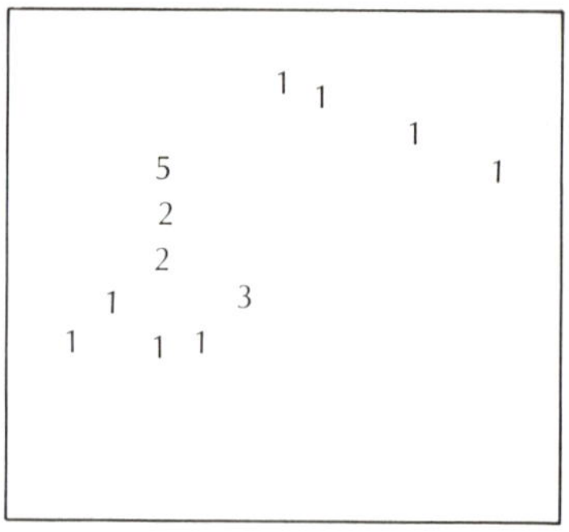

FIGURE 9.10 Initial acceptors in 1929. Adapted from T. Hägerstrand, 1965, "A Monte Carlo Approach to Diffusion," *European Journal of Sociology,* 6, 43–67 by permission of author and publisher.

FIGURE 9.11 Migration as a function of distance.

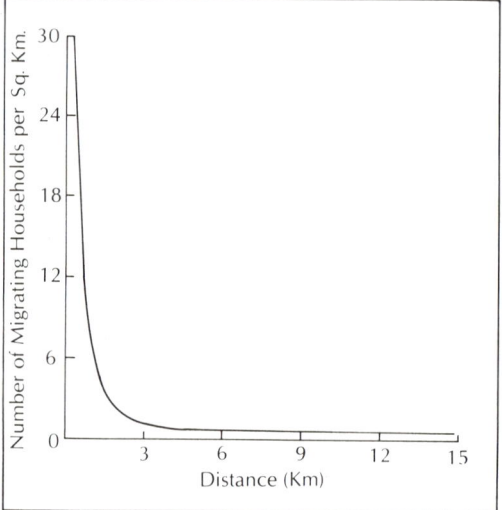

all directions. The MIF is calculated by rotating the migration/distance curve 360° (Figure 9.11). The MIF developed by Hägerstrand was an area 25 km by 25 km (Figure 9.12A) in which the value of each cell was determined by the curve in Figure 9.11. For example, a cell whose center is 10 km from the center square has a value of 0.167 (interpolated from Figure 9.11). These values were then translated into migrant households per cell by multiplying by 25. The value 0.167 (10 km from center) is an estimate of the number of migrant households per square kilometer. Each cell contains 25 square kilometers so that 0.167 times 25 is an estimate of the number of households migrating from the center cell (4.17). The distance-decay function for migration overestimates the number of migrants at very short distances, so the value of the center cell was determined by using the actual number of migrants over this distance. The result is Figure 9.12B. The values in Figure 9.12B were then converted into probabilities by dividing each value by the sum of all values (Figure 9.12C). The probabilities in Figure 9.12C sum to 1.00. The probabilities were then accumulated from 0.0000 to 0.9999 with the interval assigned each cell determined by its respective probability (Figure 9.12D). Each of the corner cells in Figure 9.12D, for example, has a probability of .0096 and an interval of 96.

The simulation proceeds by centering the mean information field over an acceptor and drawing a random number. Suppose the first random number drawn is

Agriculture

A						B				
.095	.139	.167	.139	.095		2.38	3.48	4.17	3.48	2.38
.139	.299	.543	.299	.139		3.48	7.48	13.57	7.48	3.48
.167	.543		.543	.167	→	4.17	13.57	110.00	13.57	4.17
.139	.299	.543	.299	.139		3.48	7.48	13.57	7.48	3.48
.095	.139	.167	.139	.095		2.38	3.38	4.17	3.48	2.38

C						D				
.0096	.0140	.0168	.0140	.0096		.0000 / .0096	.0097 / .0236	.0237 / .0404	.0405 / .0544	.0545 / .0640
.0140	.0301	.0547	.0301	.0140		.0641 / .0780	.0781 / .1081	.1082 / .1628	.1629 / .1929	.1930 / .2069
.0168	.0547	.4431	.0547	.0168	→	.2070 / .2237	.2238 / .2784	.2785 / .7215	.7216 / .7762	.7763 / .7930
.0140	.0301	.0547	.0301	.0140		.7931 / .8070	.8071 / .8371	.8372 / .8918	.8919 / .9219	.9220 / .9359
.0096	.0140	.0168	.0140	.0096		.9630 / .9455	.9456 / .9595	.9596 / .9763	.9764 / .9903	.9904 / .9999

FIGURE 9.12 Calculation of a mean information field.

.6000. It is then assumed that information on the farm subsidy is passed from an initial acceptor to someone living in the center cell (Figure 9.13). This process is repeated for each initial acceptor. Given the probabilities, most information (gaining new acceptors) will be passed to people living a short distance from someone already using the innovation, but the possibility of drawing any random number from .0000 to .9999 allows the innovation to diffuse to more distant farmers. The process is continued for a series of rounds with the mean information field centered on all acceptors from the preceding round. Figure 9.14 shows the actual and simulated pattern of acceptance for three years. Although there are differences, simulation accurately predicts the actual pattern of diffusion of this particular innovation.

The diffusion model can be modified to simulate non-uniform transportation routes and variations in population density. Furthermore, all farmers do not accept new ideas instantly, but the model can be altered to account for the relative speed of acceptance. It may be decided that a given cell must be "hit" two or three times before the innovation is accepted. A cell's probability can be changed to accurately reflect its population density and movements in certain directions can be limited to simulate the inadequacy of transportation routes.

New technology is one of the prime forces operating to change agricultural patterns. Innovations may allow the farmer to increase the gross income per hectare, lower the cost per hectare, or both. New technology may lower the risk the

FIGURE 9.13 The simulation process.

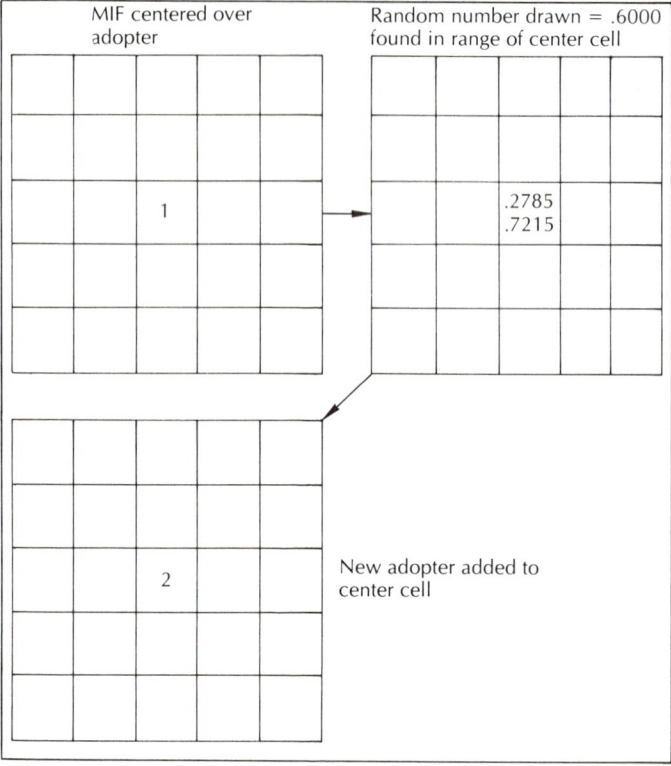

farmer must face in terms of weather or soil fertility. Hybrid corn is an excellent example of an innovation which allowed the expansion of a higher net income agriculture into a new area and lowered the risk farmers faced from shortened growing seasons. Irrigation systems lower risk, whereas herbicides, pesticides, and fertilizers increase yields per hectare. To understand how patterns of agricultural production change, we need to have some understanding of how innovations spread, and the diffusion model increases that understanding. The diffusion model also allows the simulation of non-optimal human decision-making and portrays the landscape as evolutionary rather than instantaneous, which is typical of descriptive (as opposed to normative) models.

Agricultural patterns also shift in response to changes in demand. The growing importance of meat in the American diet over the past 100 years has resulted in increased emphasis on feeder livestock in the Midwest, for example. Most agricultural pattern shifts take years to occur. They reflect slowly changing demand and the spatial restraints on the diffusion of information, and the unwillingness of farmers to accept risks they cannot afford to take. Today agriculture in the United States requires a large capital investment. Machinery may be so specialized that it can be used for only one particular kind of agriculture. A given kind of agriculture may therefore remain in an area because farmers are limited by the investments of the past (inertia). Other agricultural boundary shifts are much more rapid.

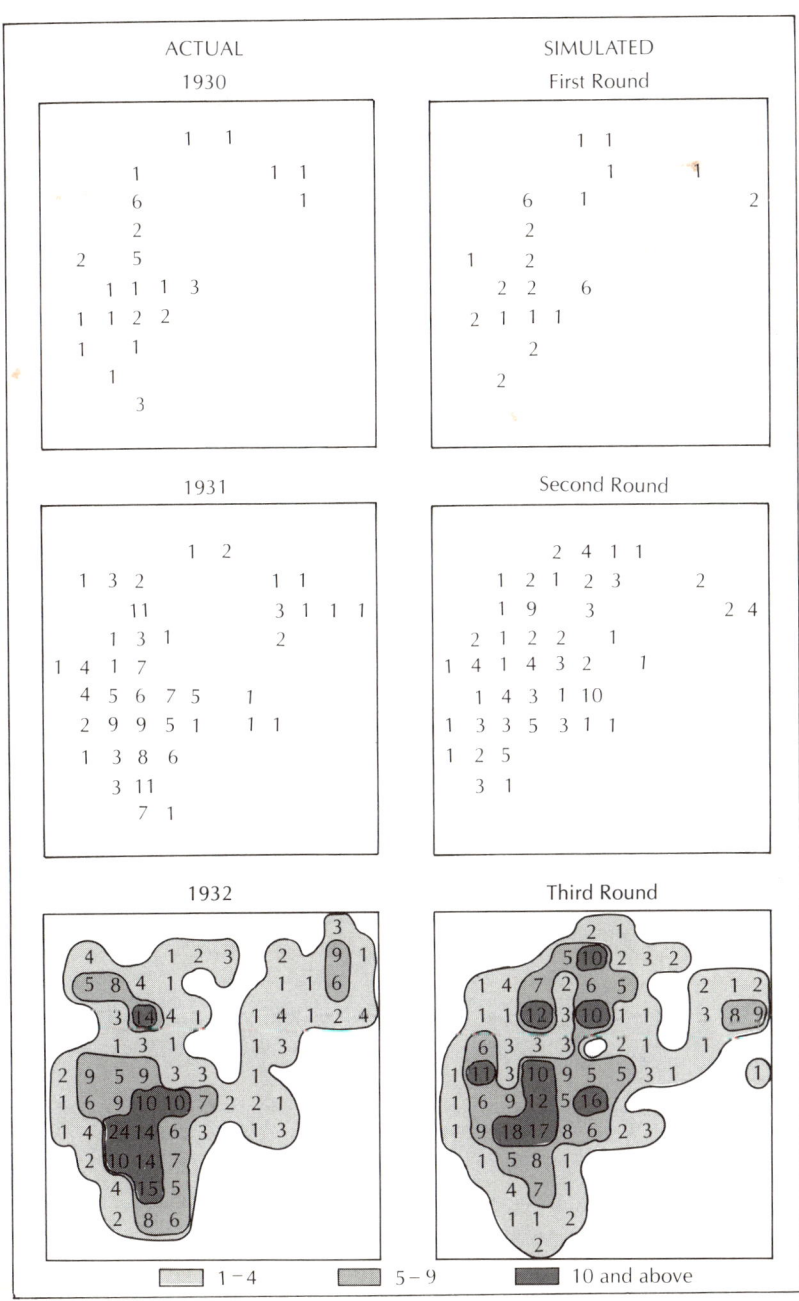

FIGURE 9.14 Actual simulated patterns. Adopted from T. Hägerstrand, 1965, "A Monte Carlo Approach to Diffusion," *European Journal of Sociology*, 6, 43–67 by permission of author and publisher.

Catastrophe Theory: Possible Applications

The rate-of-acceptance curve in Figure 9.9 represents a continuous or "smooth" process. The gradual migration of an agricultural boundary is the same type of phenomenon, but a sudden boundary shift is a discontinuous or "abrupt" process. *Catastrophe theory* is a new technique which has widespread applications in many areas of geography. Catastrophe theory can deal with abrupt or discontinuous phenomena. In this section, we give an elementary application of catastrophe theory to a geographic event.

Catastrophe theory deals with events not only numerically, but also visually by representing discontinuous events with certain geometric shapes. The rapid shift of the western boundary of wheat production as the prevailing form of agriculture is illustrated in Fig. 9.15. Rainfall increases along one axis and risk increases along the other. The surface of the graph is folded, however, to produce a "cusp." (A *cusp* is a point of meeting of two similar curves.) A movement from the upper surface of the cusp to the lower surface is a discontinuous event or a "catastrophe." The upper surface represents wheat farming and the lower surface represents livestock ranching. Wheat farming expanded westward during the early part of the twentieth century in the United States into land that was climatically better suited to livestock ranching. The expansion was a gradual process made possible by abnormally wet years which lowered risk. This is represented by the smooth progression from livestock ranching to wheat farming along the continuous edge of the graph in Figure 9.15

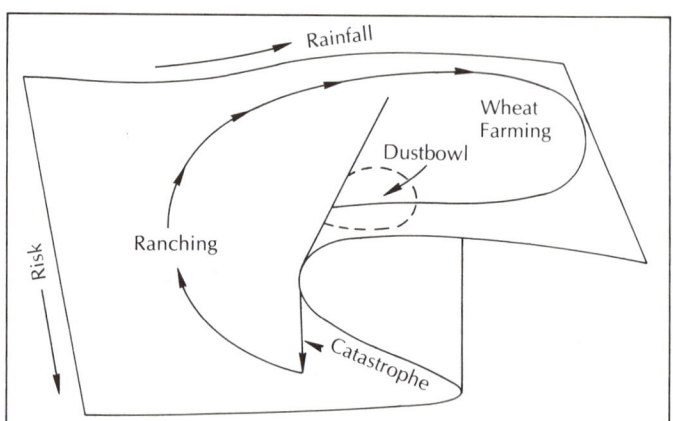

FIGURE 9.15 A "cusp" catastrophe surface.

Wheat was planted using "dry farming" techniques which proved to be disastrous in the long run. As rainfall declined and conditions moved toward the drought of the 1930s, the risk involved in wheat farming increased. The drought and dry farming (capital-centered) techniques resulted in the "Dust Bowl" conditions experienced throughout much of the Plains States during that time. Farmers held out as long as possible in an attempt to amortize their investment in wheat farming equipment and mortgages on the land. Finally the situation was no longer tenable.

Agriculture

Agriculture conditions shifted almost instantly from wheat agriculture to ranching, and the western boundary of wheat cultivation (as the prevailing form) retreated many kilometers eastward. This shift is respresented by the drop from the upper part of the cusp to the lower part.

A rapid change in the type of agriculture always involves risk because of the new and different kind of investment required but, as rainfall remained low, the amount of risk represented by livestock ranching declined. The same process could be repeated if abnormal wet conditions prevailed over a long period of time. The transition from ranching to wheat farming would occur because of the relatively high income per hectare for wheat farming compared to ranching, and the transition would be smooth because there are no conditions inducing rapid change.

The smooth (continuous) part of a catastrophe cusp has all the elements of both game theory and innovation diffusion. Game theory deals with the final result of a long trial-and-error process which attempts to minimize risk. Diffusion deals with the spread of information over time and space. If a wheat farmer has a good income per hectare over a period of years, the information spreads most readily to adjacent land-holders and they may adopt this type of agriculture. This passage of "successful" information leads to a gradual and continuous migration of an agricultural boundary over a period of years. The cusp part of the catastrophe model, however, deals with the discontinuous or abrupt change which can occur under adverse conditions. Game theory and diffusion theory in many cases represent evolutionary and short-run solutions to the problem of the best type of agriculture in an area. Catastrophe theory may represent a long-run solution and simulate conditions which require an "either-or" decision to be made.

The agriculturist engaged in "mixed farming" often faces an either-or decision. He can concentrate his investment for the year on feeder livestock or on corn grown for grain. Which he chooses depends upon the relative price of each, but once committed, the farmer cannot easily change back to the alternative type of agriculture during the year. This situation is represented by the "swallow-tail" surface in Figure 9.16. The lower surface on the right represents corn for grain, whereas the lower surface on the left represents an investment in feeder livestock. The middle of the upper surface represents equality between the price of feeder livestock and corn grown for grain (potential net income per hectare). The price of corn increases relatively to the right and the net income of feeder livestock increases to the left. The other dimension of the upper surface represents time, with the outermost edge of the surface being the exact time at which the decision must be made as to which type of agriculture will be chosen. As we move along the time axis, we come closer and closer to the time at which some decision must be made. The individual farmer swings to the right or left of the equality line depending upon the relative prices of corn and feeder livestock. At the decision-making time, there is an abrupt shift to one of the two lower surfaces (agricultural types). Movement from the corn-for-grain surface to the feeder livestock surface is not possible.

These two elementary examples represent some possible applications of catastrophe theory to geographical problems. Some elements of the theory are especially applicable to decision-making and explaining sudden trends or shifts in patterns.

FIGURE 9.16 A "swallow-tail" catastrophe surface.

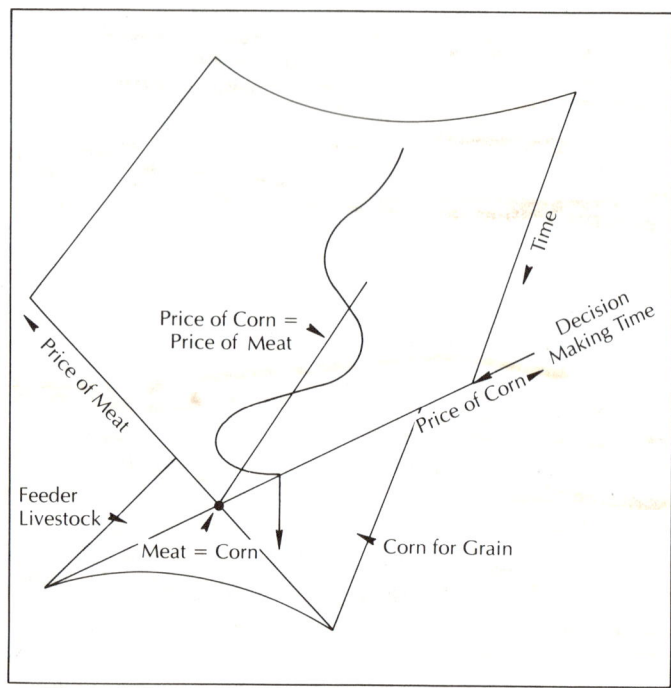

The Size and Spacing of Cities

A partial explanation of the size and spacing of cities was discussed in detail in Chapter 6, but in a normative context. The normative assumptions of the central place model include: an even distribution of population *and* resources; and instantaneous adjustment of the hierarchy to produce a stable system. These two assumptions produce a static and precise geometric arrangement of cities in terms of size and spacing. The size and spacing arrangement of cities in reality, however, is the result of many complex forces. An understanding of the arrangement of urban places must take into account the following factors: (1) the economic and social conditions which allow and/or encourage the concentration of all economic activities in settlements. The central place model deals only with central functions, but settlements are also the localization points for most manufacturing and other "settlement-building" activities; (2) the spatial or geographic conditions which influence the spacing and size of settlements. These include the heterogeneous nature of the physical environment which determines the transportation routes, the economic base of an area, and the distribution of resources; (3) the fact that the development of the urban pattern is an *evolutionary* process in which the structure of the past exerts a powerful influence on subsequent growth and change; and (4) the fact that the urban system is the result of human decisions based on imperfect knowledge. This last point recognizes that the elements of uncertainty and indeterminancy induced by human decision-making play a major role in the formation of the urban system.

The Size and Spacing of Cities

Central place theory deals primarily with the economic links between a settlement and its hinterland while industrial location theory treats activities which serve national or regional markets and depend upon a complex of localized and ubiquitous raw materials, transportation routes, labor supplies, and management skills as well as variations in demand. The "settlement-building" aspect of manufacturing has been a key factor in urban growth and change. Urbanization has been primarily the result of industrialization. Cities have grown because the population has migrated from rural areas in response to changing employment opportunities.

Evolutionary aspects of the urban system are also of consequence. It is important to recognize that technology changes; urban populations and the physical aspects of cities are constantly being modified; and social and economic conditions often undergo major change after a locational decision is made. Technological change is extremely important. Transportation innovations change our evaluation of distance. Hinterlands expand or contract as transportation costs change. Technology forces a constant reevaluation and assessment of the variable resource base. An area that had no resource base on which to develop at one time period may be a rapid growth area in another time period because changing technology allowed the exploitation of a local resource. Also take into account the uncertainty and indeterminancy of human decisions. Human decisions are rarely optimum. At a given time, there may be many possible locations for a given level of central place, many viable locations for a particular type of manufacturing, or many settlements to which an individual might migrate in search of employment. Once a decision is made, however, it affects subsequent decisions. Faced with many alternatives, decision-makers choose the action that they think has the greatest probability of success, but the probability is determined by the information available and the circumstances under which the decision is made. The actual choice may be considered a "random" action strongly conditioned by the probabilities of the moment. Many other smaller forces also have a random effect. In this section, we are concerned with the effect of the random and cumulative effects of human decision-making.

In Chapter 6 we dealt briefly with the "distortion" of ideal locations (in the sense of central place geometry) by the existence of localized resource deposits. Thus, human decision-making plays a role in all aspects of the urban system because central places, manufacturing, transportation routes, and migration are all the results of human action. The initial sites of many settlements were chosen for reasons that had nothing to do with spacing geometry. Many settlements were initially located to take advantage of natural routeways such as mountain passes, stream fords, or the head of navigation on rivers. Others were located for completely random reasons such as where the horse died on the way West. Whether or not such settlements survived depended upon the subsequent development of the region, including the size and spacing of other centers. Settlements which were able to exploit a localized resource base might have become the highest level central place in an area simply because of the large population and consequent central function size initiated by the population supported by manufacturing.

This is illustrated in Figure 9.17. Point *I* is the ideal location for the highest order central place in the region shown. The shaded area represents a

The choice of urban site is frequently influenced by the physical environment: (A) Paris originated on a small island in the Seine River (SOURCE: *Walton Photographic Supplies Ltd.*); (B) The site for London was chosen at the lowest point on the River Thames where an easy crossing point (London Bridge) could be built (SOURCE: *Woodmansterne Ltd.*). All cities have sites, but the key to understanding their growth is not so much site as relative location.

localized power resource such as coal. The isoline is a spatial margin to viability for the highest order central place in the region. Because of spacing geometry, places outside that isoline can never attain the highest level. The first settlement in the area is located at A to exploit the resource base. That city prospers, increases in population through migration, and grows in functional size. A subsequent settlement locates at *I*, but is a pure central place. Because of the early growth and subsequent size of A, it assumes the primate central place role in the region. The final pattern is

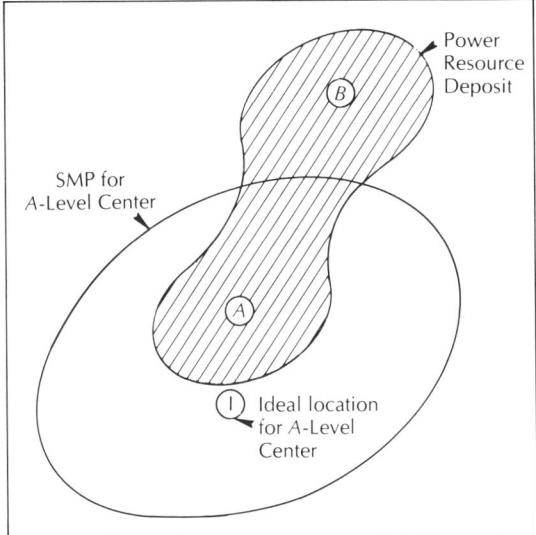

FIGURE 9.17 Actual and ideal locations: distortion by localized resources.

the result of both the unpredictability of human decision-making and the evolutionary nature of the urban system. It is assumed that the localized resource can only support one large manufacturing city. The initial site chosen for development could have been at *I* which would have optimized the spacing arrangement of the highest order central places or at point *B*. Point *B*, however, is outside the spatial margins to viability for *A*-level centers and could never have developed to that level. Its population would be supported by manufacturing (resource exploitation) and a lower-level central place role.

Richard Morrill (1963) developed an extensive model incorporating all aspects of a developing urban system including the "randomness" of human decision-making. The model applies the same approach as the simulation introduced in the discussion of the diffusion of an innovation. Human decisions are assumed to be random within probability restraints. Probability or "stochastic" models are used when it is necessary to evaluate an indeterminate situation. A range of possibilities is built-in rather than various forces converging to a unique solution. Some possibilities are given a higher probability than others, but the final choice is determined by the drawing of random numbers as in the diffusion model. This type of simulation is called a *Monte-Carlo* model and was first used extensively in geography by Hägerstrand. The probabilities used in Morrill's analysis were determined by prior developments and the random choices of a given stage were used in turn to establish probabilities for subsequent stages. In this section, Morrill's model is discussed to demonstrate the effects of both random decision-making and the structures imposed by development over time.

Morrill began by defining a study region, dividing it into component areas, and choosing time periods (Figure 9.18). To simulate the development of an actual urban system, it would be necessary to collect information on net growth rates during the chosen time period, the demand for new transportation, the amount of economic activity which could be supported, and the number of migrants that the

FIGURE 9.18 The simulation of an urban system: original situation.

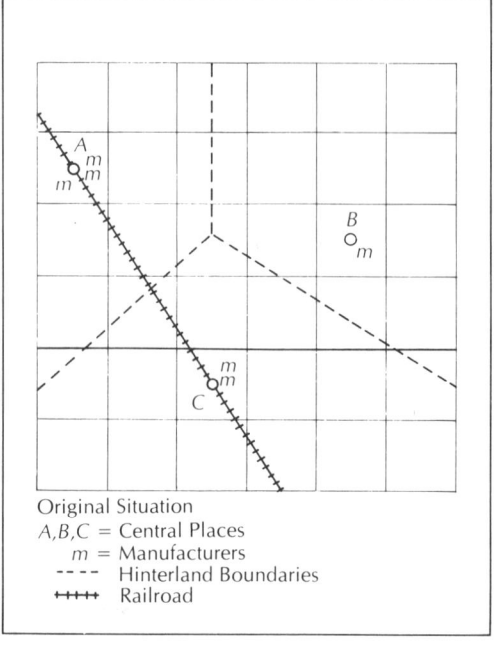

economic activity would be likely to attract. In this example, these levels are chosen arbitrarily.

The first step in the model is to assign transportation routes. In Figure 9.19, for example, point C can be connected by several possible links. Possible connections may be limited by assuming that any alternative route can be only a given percentage longer than the shortest possible route or certain routes can be excluded from consideration by physical barriers. Each possible route is then given a probability of being chosen based on its distance, the population of the areas through which it passes, and the costs of building such a route. A specific route is then chosen by random numbers to simulate the uncertainty of human decision-making. Transport routes are important because a place, once connected, has a much better chance of becoming a higher order central place and of attracting other "settlement-building" economic activities.

The second step in the model is the assignment of non-central place (settlement-building) activities such as manufacturing. The demand for these activities is determined by population, income, resources, and other factors. The total number of plants and their output would be determined from an economic analysis of the area if one were to simulate an actual urban system. The possibility of each sub-area in the study region attracting manufacturing is then determined. All sub-areas may be considered possibilities or some areas may be excluded from analysis because the cost of production is prohibitive or because they lack the necessary labor force or resource base. The probability of each sub-area attracting a manufacturing plant is then determined. Ineligible areas have a probability of zero. Eligible areas have probabilities determined by resources, transportation links, labor force, and other factors considered by traditional industrial location theory (Figure 9.20). The total number of manufacturing plants required to meet the demand of a given time period is then assigned, using the Monte-Carlo technique as in Figure 9.21.

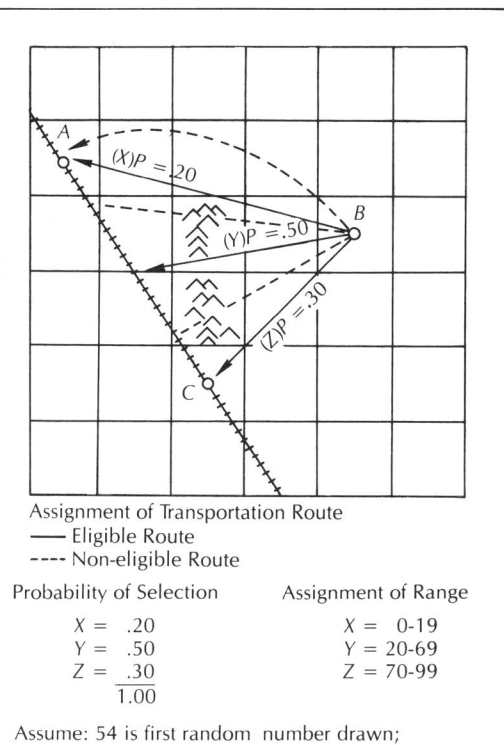

FIGURE 9.19 The simulation of an urban pattern: assignment of transportation routes.

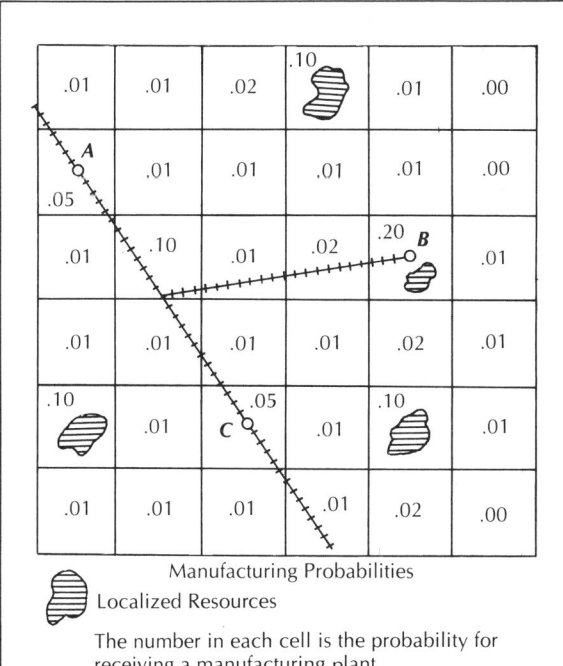

FIGURE 9.20 The simulation of an urban system: assignment of manufacturing probabilities.

449

FIGURE 9.21 The simulation of an urban system: assignment of manufacturing plants.

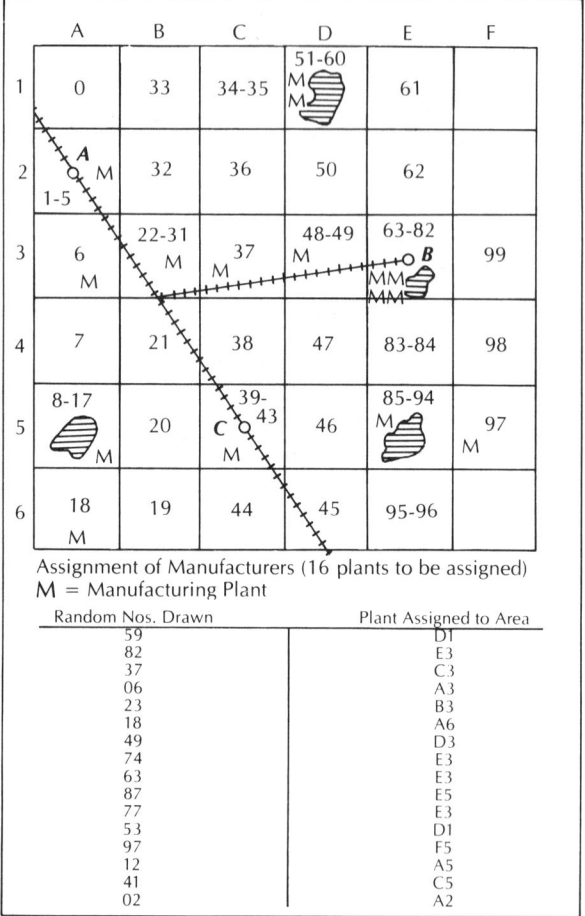

The assignment of central place activities is the third step of the model developed by Morrill and determines which areas will be successful in capturing a local hinterland as the economy of the study area grows and is able to support more and more central functions. The probability of a place attaining a given level in the central place hierarchy is strongly conditioned, however, by the presence or absence of transportation connections and manufacturing. The assignment of central place activities involves determining the total number of central places of a given level which can be supported in the region. This is determined by dividing the total population of the area by the threshold of each central function. The possibility of new central places is conditioned by the minimum hinterlands (thresholds) of existing central places. Higher order central functions may be added at successively fewer central places and their thresholds met by the consolidation of smaller hinterlands. Lower order central places, on the other hand, can only squeeze in if sufficient threshold population can be found for them within the limits posed by existing central place hinterlands. Any hinterland, old or new, must therefore: (1) contain at least a threshold population for the good in question; (2) contain no area which is closer to an existing center; and (3) contain no area which is farther than some closer

The Size and Spacing of Cities

existing intervening area. A given place, in other words, has the possibility of becoming a central place of several different levels. Once the level is determined, however, the hinterland of the place and of surrounding places is determined by the necessary threshold market area a place must have to exist at that level.

The probability of a settlement becoming a given level of central place is dependent upon many factors, including the population of the place (determined by the prior assignment of manufacturing activities and transportation connections). A place which is not in the best geometric position for a given level may have a better probability of success because its resident population is supported by manufacturing and requires a certain range of service functions, and because of its superior connections via the existing transportation network. Each settlement and its theoretical hinterland is assigned a probability based on these criteria (Figure 9.22). Monte-Carlo simulation is then used to determine which points actually succeed as central places of a given level. The selection of the first central place eliminates many others from consideration because hinterlands of a given level must be mutually exclusive. All possible central places contained in the first hinterland selected are eliminated. In Figure 9.23 the first random number chosen is 20 which selects hinterland 1 (place X) and eliminates the possibility that places Y and Z will become places of the level in question.

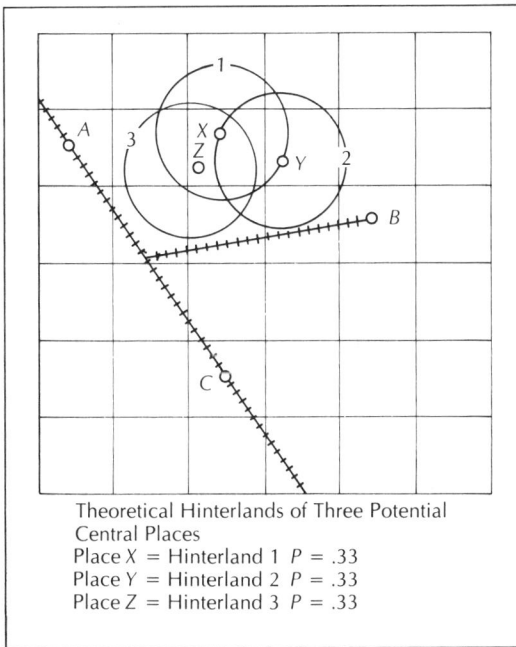

FIGURE 9.22 The simulation of an urban system: theoretical central place hinterlands.

The Monte-Carlo process continues until all possible hinterlands have been selected. Some areas may remain outside the theoretical hinterland of a chosen central place; these are assigned to the nearest viable central place. The process is then repeated for higher levels of the hierarchy, but, to be selected, a place must already be a central place of the next lower order. Prior simulation, therefore, sets rigid limits on the next step of the simulation process.

FIGURE 9.23 The simulation of an urban system: assignment of central place hinterlands.

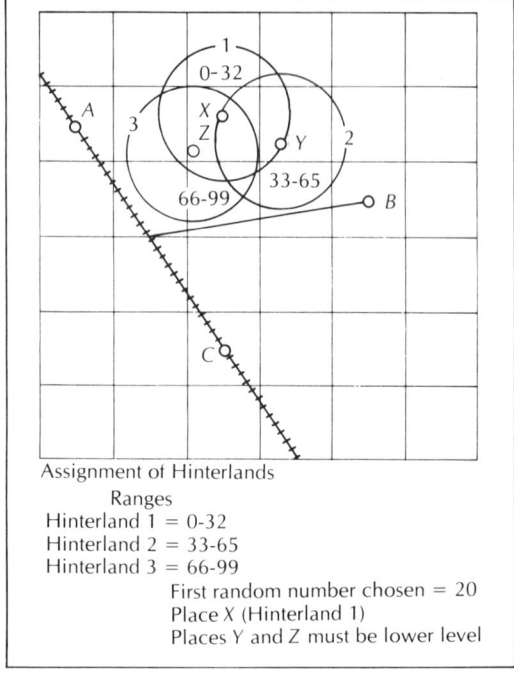

The fourth step of Morrill's model is a simulation of migration which redistributes population and provides the basis for urban growth and decline. The expected volume of migration from a given area is determined by employment conditions, resource base, and socioeconomic characteristics. The probability of other areas receiving migrants from a source area is then determined by three factors: (1) the distance from a source region; (2) the attractiveness as determined by growth and employment potential; and (3) previous migration from the source region (friend/family contacts). Each area is then assigned a probability range for attracting migrants from a given source region and Monte-Carlo simulation is used to assign migrants. The sequence of the model is shown in Figures 9.24A through 9.24D. The losses or gains of a given area through migration are used to adjust the level of urban development in each area to give a constantly adjusted feedback.

Morrill's model is an important departure from the static and geometric central place models of Christaller and Lösch because of its built-in flexibility and its evolutionary (feed-back) elements. We have presented the model in an abbreviated form, but the required data for a given area can be collected and the model run to determine whether or not it adequately results in an urban system corresponding to reality. The most important feature of the model is the incorporation of non-optimal and indeterminate human decision-making.

Morrill's model also assumes a "free economy" in which the development of the urban system is the result of the decisions of many individual entrepreneurs. Each decision-maker must operate within the structure imposed by the past and within the confines of the existing market economy. Within these limits, however, is enough "slack" to allow for random decision-making. In a planned economy,

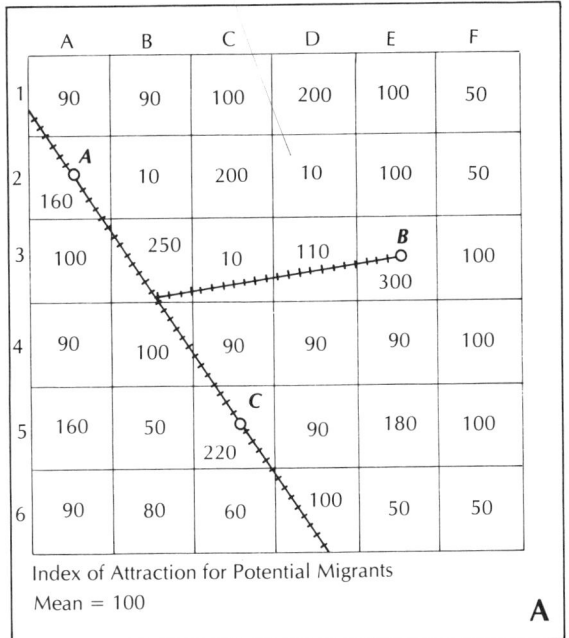
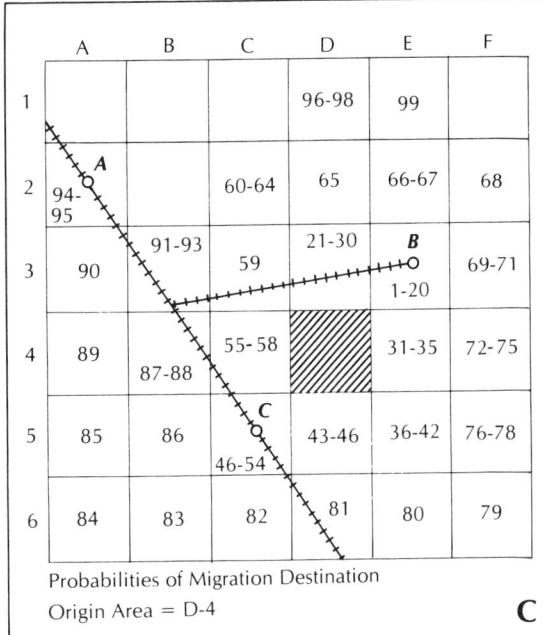
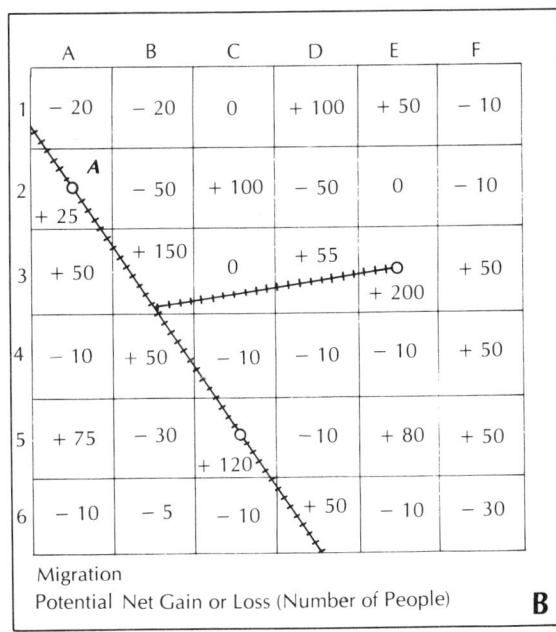
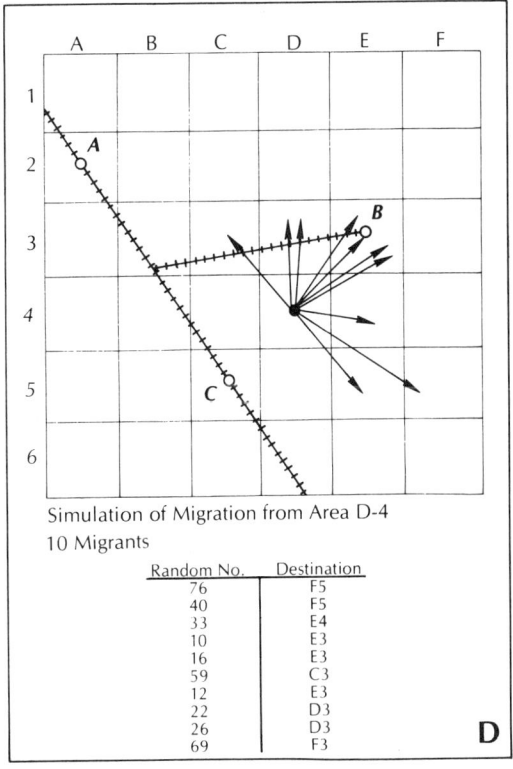

FIGURE 9.24 The simulation of an urban system-migration: (A) indexes of attraction; (B) potential gains or losses; (C) migration probabilities; (D) assignment of migrants from area *D*-4.

453

the state acts as a decision-maker and may regulate the space-economy to achieve a variety of goals. Central economic planners may decide, for example, to spur the development of a depressed or underdeveloped area. This can be achieved by building transportation lines or developing a heavy industrial complex to serve the area. Such events may not be possible in a capitalist economy because the underdeveloped area could not bring the profits required by private development. This is not to say that controlled economies are not concerned with the economics of development, but rather that long-run social goals may outweigh the short-run losses that such a policy may bring. In the long-run, the development of the depressed area may be "profitable," in both an economic and social welfare sense, but its development can only come about in a controlled economy. In an economy dependent upon many private decision-makers, each entrepreneur must wait for the development process to begin before acting. Development may then never proceed. Even in the United States, government action often occurs. The Tennessee Valley Authority of the 1930s is a case of direct intervention in the regional economy.

Manufacturing

Manufacturing requires a decision to operate at a particular scale with a particular input combination at a given *location*. This decision must be made without perfect knowledge. The reliability of an individual decision depends upon the location of the decision-maker within the behavioral matrix. We have dealt with the problem of industrial decision-making in a limited way in the discussion of the location of settlement-building functions in Morrill's model of the urban system. In this section we explore the industrial decision-making process in greater detail.

A study of locational behavior is one part of the problem of understanding the patterns of the economic landscape. We have previously discussed the *structure* of viable locations—the conditions which make certain locations viable and/or optimal and other locations non-viable. With a perfect knowledge of this structure, the optimizer would choose only optimal locations. The concept of spatial margins to viability was introduced to allow the inclusion of sub-optimal decision-making. The second part of the problem is a consideration of how actual locational decisions are made. These are two different aspects of the same problem. The first approach is concerned with economic forces, whereas the second is concerned with the behavioral aspects of decision-making.

The deterministic models which make up much of location theory ignore the second aspect of the problem. In them, the behavior of optimizers is completely predictable. If an optimal location exists, the optimizer will always choose that particular point. The behavioral matrix (see Figure 9.1) introduces a *stochastic* element in an attempt to stimulate non-optimal behavior. Stochastic models predict the *probability* of a certain outcome. The behavioral matrix determines the probability of a decision-maker choosing a viable (or optimal) location from the individual's store of information and ability to use that information. The behavioral matrix assumes that the store of knowledge (and ability) is information about the economic structures which determine the viability of a given location or many possible loca-

Manufacturing

Aerial view of The Maytag Company's Plant 2 manufacturing complex. The Maytag Company was founded in 1893 in Newton, Iowa, as a maker of farm implements. In 1907 it entered into the washer manufacturing field partly to offset seasonal slumps in the farm implement business and partly to meet the perceived need for a washing machine for home use. In 1974 The Maytag Company launched an expansion program that included the construction of new storage, dryer assembly and painting facilities with the goal of increasing production capacity 75 percent by 1980. SOURCE: *The Maytag Company*.

tions. A third appraoch would be to assume that all industrial location decisions are made by individuals who fall in the extreme upper left-hand corner of the behavioral matrix. In other words, people have no relevant information (or ability) concerning the spatial structure of economic viability. The actions of such decision-makers can be characterized as completely random. A question is then raised concerning the difference between the industrial landscape created by perfect knowledge and one created by random decision-makers or the difference between random decision-makers and those possessing some information (and ability) concerning the spatial structure of viability.

A. Alchain (1950) and C. Tiebout (1957) explored this question in detail. The following discussion is based mostly on Alchain's ideas and terminology. His major points are as follows:

1. If the number of random decisions is large enough, the probability of some decision-makers selecting viable and optimal locations is also large. Alchain likened the process to betting on a horse race. Some bettors may use the most rational handicapping system possible and select the winning horse. Other gamblers may select the same horse for "non-rational" reasons

such as its name or a "lucky number." If we know nothing about the decision-making process, both bettors are correct in the sense of perfect foresight. Therefore, it does not matter whether the decision-making process is rational in the economic sense or completely random in that viable locations will be chosen if enough random decisions are made.

2. Individual behavior based on foresight and rational motivation does not necessarily imply a *collective* pattern of behavior different from collective random action. Judgments differ even when based on the best available evidence and with each individual weighing each variable, but the aggregate set of actions may be indistinguishable from a set of random actions.

3. Even if all decision-making is random, we can still specify the conditions and structures which determine viability. With a knowledge of the viability structure, we can state the types of locations which will be more viable relative to other types even if the decision-makers themselves do not know the locational conditions of success or try to achieve them by readjusting locations. If they do know the conditions, there will be a tendency toward a locational equilibrium. This point is illustrated in the following example. Suppose that the location pattern of the plants in an industry is fixed for a given period, but during that period the potential viability of many locations is altered (perhaps through differential migration). Some plants will be located closer to the new, but unknown, optimum locations. These firms now have a greater probability of survival and growth. Such locations will prosper relative to others and will come to dominate the locational pattern. Survival conditions may push the location pattern of the set of survivors toward the unknowable optimum location pattern by either repeated trials or survival of more of those who happened to be near the optimum locations (as determined subsequently). If this new viability structure lasts very long, the pattern will be different from that which prevailed or would have prevailed under other spatial economic structures. Even if the viability structure cannot be forecast, the locations having a higher probability of availability or adoption may be stated, given alternative potential viability structures. If a consideration of past patterns rather than the prediction of future patterns is the task, a critical variable which was significant in facilitating survival can be identified, even though the individual decision-makers were not aware of it.

4. Prediction of viable locations does not assert that every (or any) firm change its location. It only asserts that the pattern of a new *set* of locations, or possibly a set of new locations, will differ from the pattern produced by a preceding viability structure. As the conditions of viability and optimality change, some firms which were once optimal may now be merely viable and vice versa.

5. A final implication which can be drawn from the random hypothesis is that empirical investigations like questionnaires may be incapable of evaluating the hypothesis that traditional location factors exert a "pull" on an industry or "cause" certain location patterns. Suppose that for a certain industry the

presence of low-wage labor is the critical (structural) variable determining viable locations. We poll the founder of each plant in order to validate this hypothesis. Each plant founder, however, asserts that the presence of low-wage labor had absolutely no influence on his choice of a plant site. Nonetheless, those who chose locations near pools of low-wage labor have a greater probability of success and, through time, a pattern may evolve which is in harmony with those conditions. Questionnaires may reveal that the location decision of each entrepreneur was different and based on amenity (non-economic) factors. In this example, the spatial margins to profitability were determined by economic-demographic conditions (low-wage labor pools) which are independent of the decision-making process, but a researcher using questionnaires might conclude that the differential pattern of amenities determined the pattern. In fact, the pattern is the result of subjective (non-economic) decisions which founded plants on sites which happened to coincide with viable space-economic conditions. Only successful plant founders are polled; the ones which chose non-viable sites have disappeared from the landscape. This is not to suggest that individuals do not consider spatial-economic conditions, only that it is not necessary. All that is required to produce a given location pattern is a particular viability structure and a group of participants who submit various locations for the structure's selection and adoption. Non-economic reasons for locational decisions are numerous and difficult to quantify. They may be considered in aggregate as "random" as in Morrill's model of urban system evolution.

The congruency between a space-economy produced by optimizers and one produced by the random process can be amplified by a simple simulation model. In Figure 9.25, the spatial margins to profitability for a particular industry have been drawn. These margins are small and the exact center of each viable area represents the optimum location for a manufacturing plant in the industry. The spatial margins to viability and the optimum locations are determined by economic conditions which are independent of locational decisions. In other words, we are ignoring the possible changes in profitability which might result from locational interdependence.

A sheet of plywood is placed over the map and holes are cut in the covering sheet which exactly match the spatial margins to profitability on the map

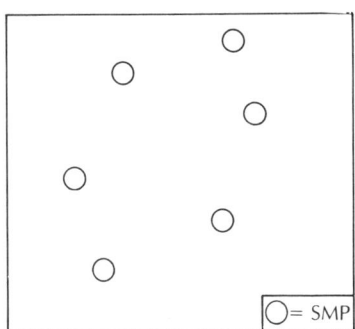

FIGURE 9.25 Spatial margins to profitability for industry X.

below (Figure 9.26). With only six possible viable locations, it is assumed that only six manufacturing plants (one in each area) are required to serve total demand. The decision-making process is simulated by throwing darts at the plywood sheet, removing the sheet after all darts have been thrown, and observing the resultant pattern.

FIGURE 9.26 Map covered by plywood sheet (holes correspond to spatial margins to profitability).

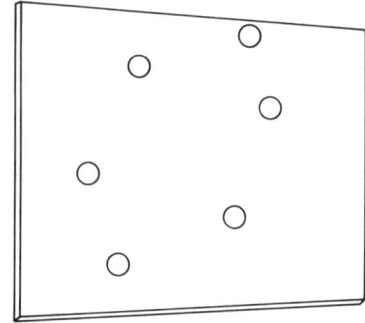

The actions of optimizers is simulated by the darts champion of an English pub. The champion is given only six darts to throw and the pattern which results is shown in Figure 9.27.

FIGURE 9.27 (A) Simulation by "optimizer"; (B) resultant pattern.

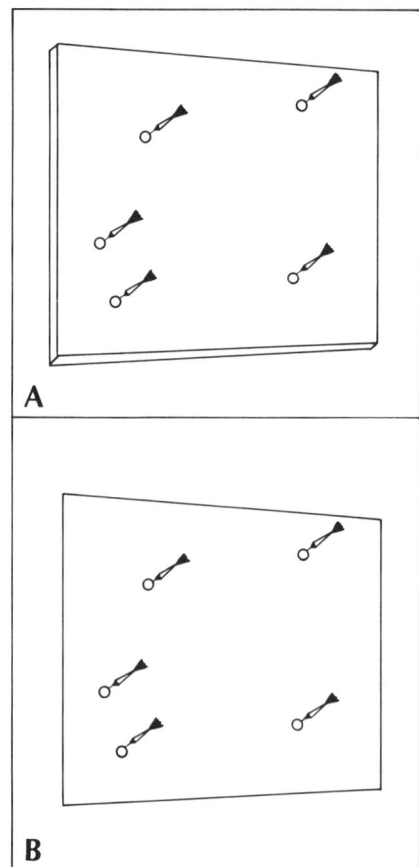

Manufacturing

The actions of random decision-makers is simulated by someone with little experience at darts. This individual is given a hundred darts to throw. The pattern produced by random action is shown in Figure 9.28. Optimizers and random decision-makers have produced exactly the same pattern.

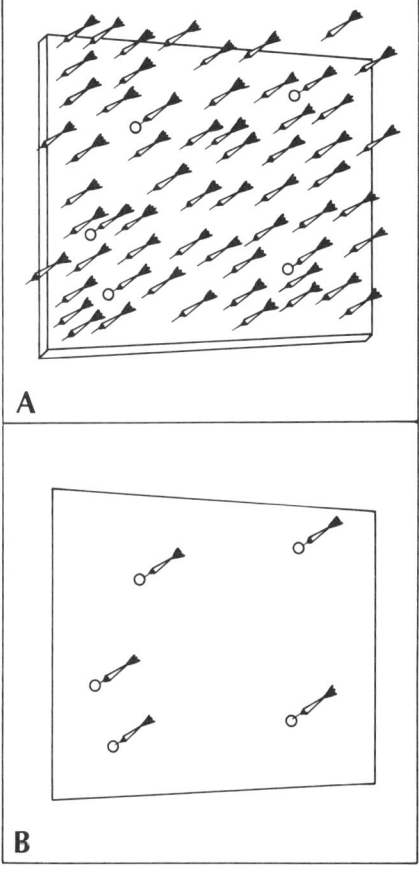

FIGURE 9.28 (A) Simulation by "satisficer"; (B) resultant pattern.

The process in reality, of course, is much more complicated because of the problem of locational interdependence. The structure of viable locations is constantly altered each time a new producer establishes a production site, but, if demand is stable, the final outcome is much the same. One can never be sure that current producers are in *optimal* sites, however; only that they are in viable sites during the current period.

Even producers who pay careful attention to the spatial structure of economic conditions can never be certain they have selected an optimal site although they may be certain of its viability because of the large amount of information facing most producers. Shortages of time and money preclude the examination of all possible sites. A producer may identify one set of spatial margins to profitability and the optimum location within these limits. This is a "local" solution to the location problem, while the "global" solution may present locations where higher profits are possible. This is illustrated in Figure 9.29. A producer examines only the area to the right of the vertical line. Within that area he determines the spatial margins to profitability and selects an optimal location. In a global sense, however, more profitable locations are possible. Total demand may be met by an aggregate of locations which are merely viable rather than optimal.

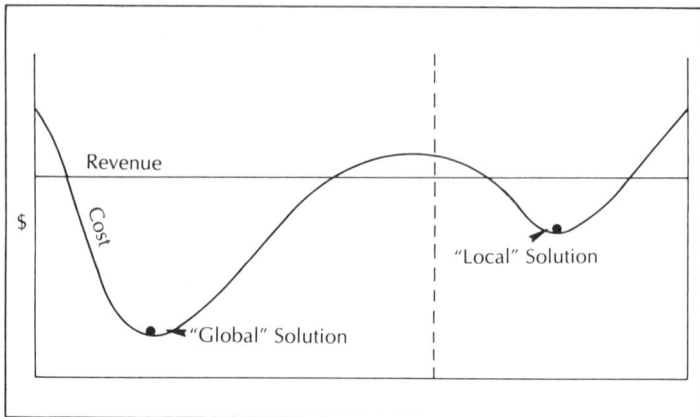

FIGURE 9.29 "Local" and "global" solutions.

Summary

The behavioral economic geographer argues that most location models of the space-economy assume the existence of optimizers who produce rigid location patterns based on perfect knowledge. Such models are *deterministic* in that a given set of data always yields a specific pattern. But human decisions are merely satisfactory choices and are often made with non-economic motives in mind. This forces a reliance on *stochastic* models which specify only the probability of a certain set of actions producing a particular pattern. Monte-Carlo simulation is an example of a stochastic model. We have demonstrated, however, that the patterns produced by *non-optimal* decision-makers may not be appreciably different from those produced by *optimizers*, especially if the limits of choice are small and if the number of individual decision-makers is large enough. The problem is complicated by the actions of other producers and by history.

DISCUSSION QUESTIONS

1. Discuss the concept of a "behavioral matrix" and the implications of non-optimal decision-making and spatial margins to profitability.
2. Show how the concept of the diffusion of innovations has been a major part of most geographical discussions of decision-making.
3. Discuss the variables used in Monte-Carlo simulation.
4. Graphically show Morrill's Monte-Carlo approach to: (A) the development of a transportation route; (B) the location of manufacturing plants; and (C) migration.

5. List and discuss each of Alchain's points concerning random decision-making.
6. Show how Alchain's ideas are essentially "Darwinian."

SUGGESTED READINGS

Spatial Diffusion

Gould, P., *Spatial Diffusion,* Washington, D.C.: Association of American Geographers Commission on College Geography, Resource Paper No. 4, 1969.

Hägerstrand, T., *Innovation Diffusion as a Spatial Process* (trans. and postscript by A. Pred). Chicago: University of Chicago Press, 1967.

Behavioral Aspects of Locational Decision-Making

Pred, A., "Behavior and Location: Foundations for a Geographic and Dynamic Location Theory, Part 1," *Lund Studies in Geography,* 1967, Series B, 27.

Pred, A., "Behavior and Location: Foundations for a Geographic and Dynamic Location Theory, Part 2," *Lund Studies in Geography,* 1969, Series B, 28.

Catastrophe Theory

Zeeman, E. C., "Catastrophe Theory," *Scientific American,* **234** (1976):65–83.

Simulation of an Urban System

Morrill, R. L., "Migration and the Spread and Growth of Urban Settlement," *Lund Studies in Geography,* 1965, Series B, 26.

Game Theory

Gould, P., "Man Against His Environment: A Game Theoretic Framework," *Annals* of the Association of American Geographers, **53** (1963):290–297.

Random Decision-Making

Alchain, A. A., "Uncertainty, Evolution, and Economic Theory," *Journal of Political Economy,* **58** (1950):211–221.

Tiebout, C. M., "Location Theory, Empirical Evidence, and Economic Evolution," *Papers* of the Regional Science Association, **3** (1957):74–86.

Underdevelopment

10

KEY TERMS

- "backward"
- capital shortage
- colonial division of labor
- colonial organization of space
- development
- development continuum
- disguised unemployment
- economic (technological) dualism
- environmental factors
- historical dialectical method
- imperialism
- land alienation
- limiting factors
- low labor productivity
- modernization
- *n*-Achievement value
- proletariat
- social dualism
- social evolution
- stages-of-growth model
- statistical index numbers
- unilineal evolution
- underdevelopment
- vicious circle

10

The following three chapters examine the themes of (inequality and of unequal development) We begin by examining *underdevelopment,* concentrated on the continents of Africa, Asia, and Latin America. Although underdevelopment also exists in Europe and North America, the great core of the problem of underdevelopment occurs in the southern and eastern continents.

What does the word *underdevelopment* mean? To answer the question, it is helpful first to define the word *development*. In conventional usage, <u>development</u> has been treated as a (synonym for economic growth) But growth is not development. During the last thirty years many underdeveloped countries have been growing at unprecedented rates, but they have also experienced increases in poverty, unemployment, and inequality. Although the concepts of growth and development are related, they deal with different matters. Growth is essentially a matter of output; development is a historical process which encompasses not only production, but the entire economic and social life of a nation.

According to some scholars, substituting the term *growth* for *development* has not been accidental. An emphasis on economic growth perpetuates the imbalance between underdeveloped and developed countries. The imbalance concerns the existing international division of labor in which developed nations concentrate on high technology and manufactured products, while underdeveloped nations produce raw materials and luxury goods.

(Economists and political theorists in many poor countries believe that economic growth to maintain the world division of labor is not development but underdevelopment) In this context, underdevelopment is not an original state that traces to internal causes in environment and culture. Rather it is an active process that emerged historically when expanding European capitalism began to penetrate pre-capitalist societies.

In this chapter we present some controversial ideas on underdevelopment. We will first consider some of the adjectives used to describe poor nations. Then we will consider some explanations for underdevelopment as expressed by members of different social sciences including geography. Finally, we present a summary of a study that traces the underdevelopment of Rhodesia. (The case study supports the *contention that underdevelopment is an active process that prevents underdeveloped countries from developing.*)

From Primitive to Underdeveloped

OBJECTIVES

By the end of this chapter you should be able:

1. To distinguish between underdevelopment as an original state and underdevelopment as an active process.
2. To explain why reliance on statistical indices alone may lead to unwarranted conclusions about the development of underdevelopment.
3. To discuss underdevelopment as an aggregate of limiting factors.
4. To pass in review sociological or psychological theories of underdevelopment.
5. To review the ideas of social and technological dualism.
6. To identify and describe Rostow's stages of economic growth.
7. To assess Rostow's version of history.
8. To discuss world views in geography.
9. To describe the measures used to create the labor force in Rhodesia's export sector.

From Primitive to Underdeveloped*

Many terms have been used in Western countries to describe poor countries in the past half century. Each of the following adjectives has been employed: *primitive, backward, undeveloped, underdeveloped, less developed, emerging, developing,* and *rapidly developing*. The blunt terms "primitive" and "backward" were used until President Truman's Point IV Program which was set forth in 1949. Subsequently, the poor countries of the world were described as "undeveloped" and "underdeveloped." By the late 1950s and during the 1960s, most tropical colonies gained independence and seats in the United Nations General Assembly. The need to consider the feelings of the new representatives, who were disturbed to hear their countries called *undeveloped* led to the search for more optimistic sounding words. The new terms were *developing* and *rapidly developing*. The polite epithet *rapidly developing* was hastily abandoned, but Western social scientists continue to use the word *developing,* and, increasingly, the word *less developed.*

The last three decades have seen most developed countries advance and prosper. But the capitalist world economy has not worked to the advantage of countries of Africa, Asia, and Latin America. The development gap between rich and poor countries, as measured by per capita income figures, is widening (Figure 10.1).

---

*This section is a slight modification of de Souza and Porter, 1974, pp. 1–2.

FIGURE 10.1 Gross National Product for developed and underdeveloped countries, 1960–2000. SOURCE: Figures for 1960 through 1980 are based on *Bureau of Intelligence and Research, Department of State,* "The World's Product at the Turn of the Decade: Recessional," September 12, 1972. Projections for 1990 and 2000 were arrived at by computing annual growth at 5 percent for developed countries and 6 percent for underdeveloped countries.

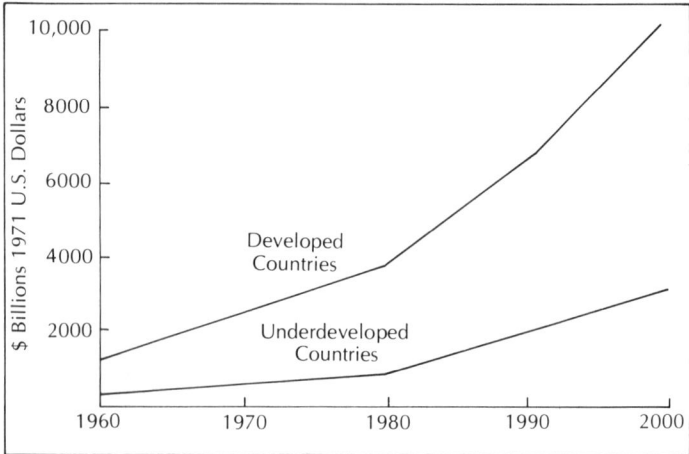

As the gap between rich and poor countries grows wider, economic and political theorists in poor countries are giving more attention to the historical processes which have brought their countries to their present condition. They see the process as part of a worldwide network of intrusion by the rich countries into the poor, of neoimperialist penetration which forecloses most opportunities for development because of the hold foreign interests and their local counterparts have on trade and investment. In trying to describe the underlying historical processes, they have refashioned one of the words formerly used to describe poor countries. The word is *underdeveloped*. *Underdeveloped* was formerly used to refer to a situation wherein resources had not yet been developed. People and resources were seen as existing, respectively, in a traditional and natural state. It was assumed that if people adopted Western technology and accepted Western help and advice they could rise from their underdeveloped condition. Economists and political theorists are now using the word *underdeveloped* to mean not an initial state, but a condition arrived at through the agency of imperialism. Instead of underdevelopment being conceived of in a static fashion as a state, it is viewed as an active process. Hence in some recent titles, the verb *"underdevelop"* is made active: *I underdevelop you* (Rodney, 1972).

The assertion that underdevelopment is a process brought about in large measure by exogenous forces is not widely accepted in Western social science. Western scholars usually adopt a "blaming the victim" approach to explain underdevelopment. They believe that economic "backwardness" traces mainly to internal rather than to external causes.

The next five sections describe and evaluate some of the common explanations for underdevelopment that are represented in the social sciences of the West. According to Marxists, Western interpretations of underdevelopment are deficient because they do not go to the origin of the problem. To illustrate the Marxian or radical perspective, the last section of this chapter provides some detailed evidence for underdevelopment-as-process. A dialectical historical approach is used to describe the transformation of the Rhodesian peasantry into a new working class that lives by selling its labor power. (This transformation process is called *proletarianization*.)

Statistical Index Numbers and Underdevelopment

Single and Multiple Measures of Underdevelopment

It is common to define underdevelopment on the basis of *statistical index numbers* that are created from various indicators of income, industry, agricultural productivity, commerce, trade, housing, health, education, nutrition, urbanization, and occupational structure. Such data are often used to illustrate development differences or to support various explanations for underdevelopment.

As noted in Chapter 2, the most usual index applied to measure the economic achievement of countries is gross domestic product per capita (Figure 10.2). The cartogram makes the height of each region proportional to per capita income. Compared to Central and South America, North America appears as an unscalable wall.

Some Western experts argue that a variety of factors other than income should be taken into account before progress in "development" can be properly computed. For example, Brian Berry (1960) combined sets of indices, each defining an aspect of the interlocked socio-economic structure of nations. After obtaining 43 indices for 95 countries, he reduced this mass of data and obtained two new indices: a *technological index,* which was closely associated with measures of gross national product, energy production, consumption, industrialization, transportation and trade; and a *demographic index* which was related to a number of population measures including birth and death rates, population densities, and rates of population growth. He then plotted on a graph the distribution of countries on technological and demographic scales (Figure 10.3). What emerges from the graph is that underdeveloped countries tend to rank low on the technological scale, but high on the demographic scale. The graph also shows that countries are arranged fairly evenly along the technological scale from the most to the least "developed."

Importance of Qualitative Differences

Quantitative measures of underdevelopment are extremely interesting and informative. They tell us something about what it means to be poor. They do not help us to understand the *causes* of underdevelopment, however, because they exclude qualitative differences between countries. For example, a list of countries arranged in order of the size of their national income per person reflects actual levels of productive forces at a given time, but it conceals differences in production and social relations between countries, and their relations to the world economy (Table 10.1). From the figures in Table 10.1 we would think that Kuwait, with a national income per capita of $15,270 is the "most developed" nation in the world. It appears that Libya ($5,530) is "more developed than the United Kingdom ($3,780). It appears that Tanzania with an income figure of $170 is at an earlier stage of development than a

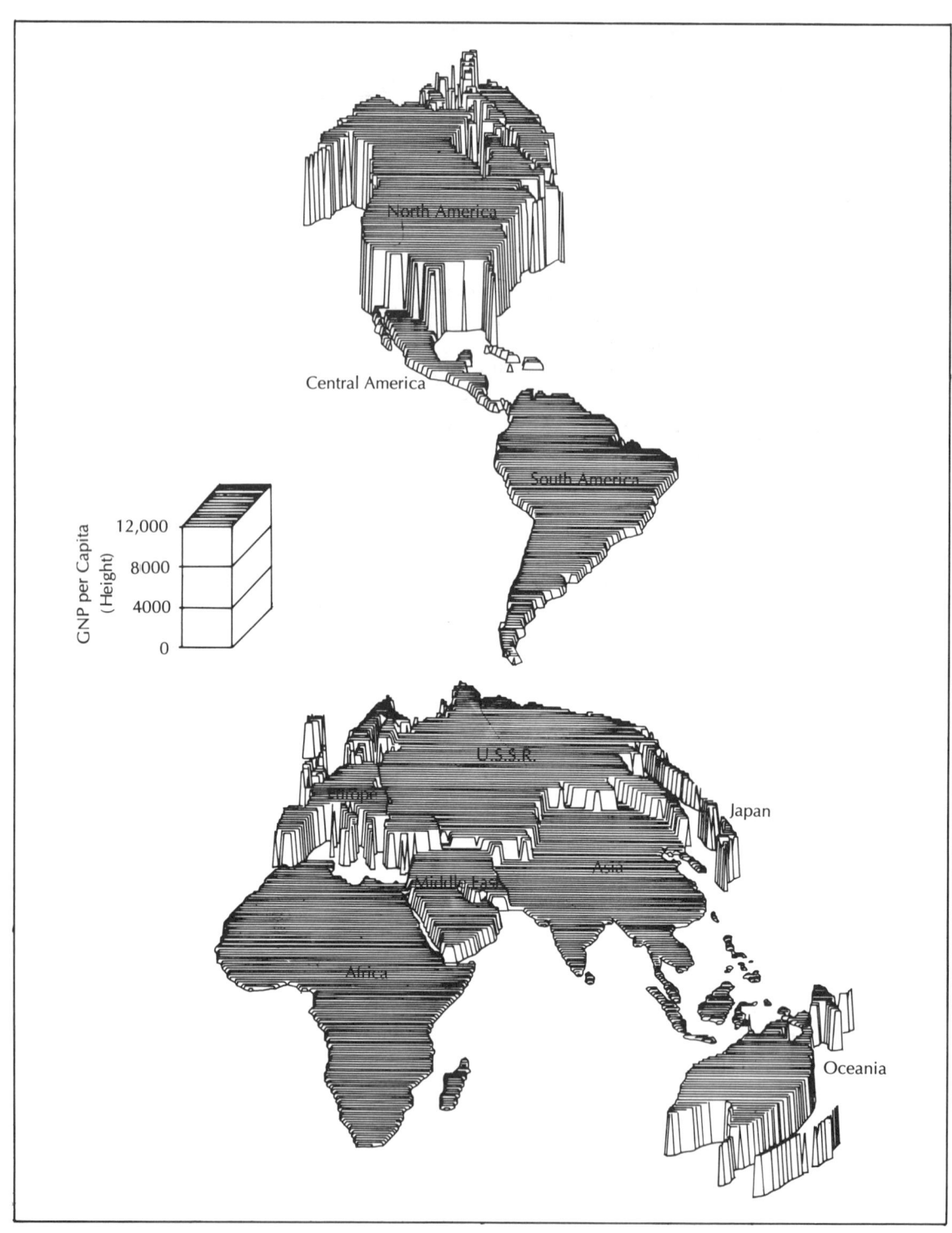

FIGURE 10.2 GNP per capita by major regions, 1975. (The height of each region is proportional to per capita income.) SOURCE: *World Bank Atlas,* The World Bank, Washington, D.C., 1977.

Limiting Factors and Underdevelopment

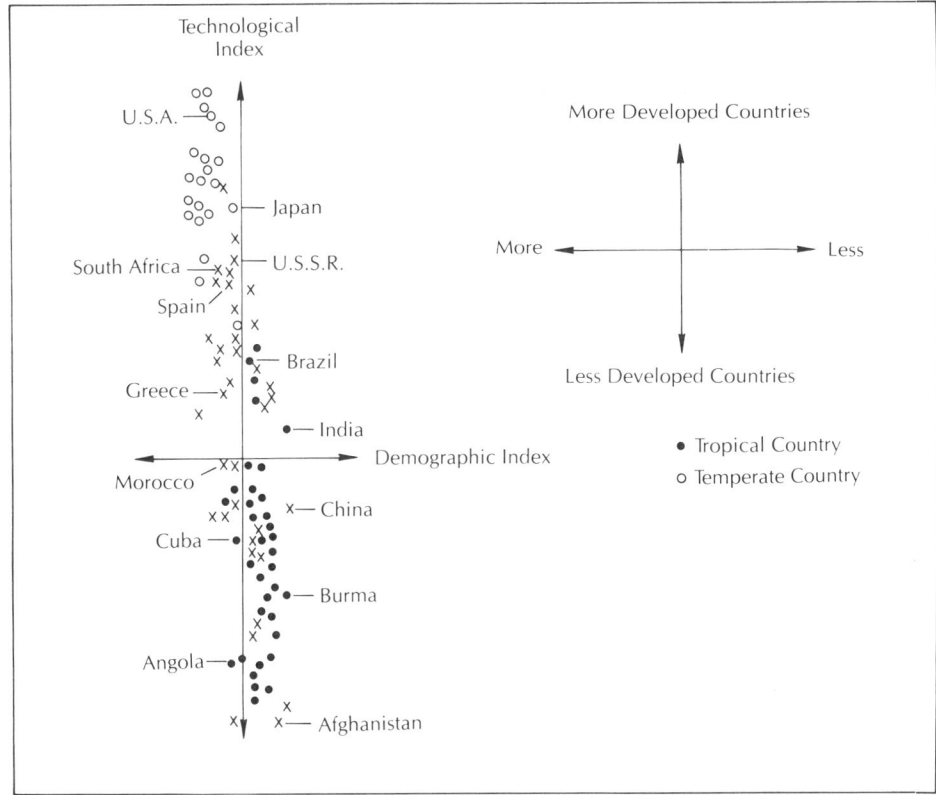

FIGURE 10.3 The distribution of countries on economic and demographic scales. Adapted from N. Ginsburg, 1961, *Atlas of Economic Development,* Chicago: The University of Chicago Press, p. 113, Fig. 3.

host of underdeveloped countries like Venezuela ($2,280) and Jamaica ($1,110). But it is largely foreigners and a tiny ruling elite who enjoy the prosperity of Venezuela and Jamaica. Most Venezuelans and Jamaicans remain poor, and lack the status and dignity, and often even the material satisfactions available to Tanzanians. From these examples we see that reliance on statistical indices may lead to superficial or untrue conclusions about underdevelopment.

Limiting Factors and Underdevelopment

Lists of factors limiting development are frequently seen in books dealing with underdevelopment. The specification of factors may serve as an illustration of the gravity of the problem of underdevelopment. But some Western writers go further and use *limiting factors,* just as they also use statistical index numbers, as a starting point for certain theories of underdevelopment. For example, "typical" factors hindering development often serve the view that underdevelopment is an original state or a lagging behind in the development of production forces.

TABLE 10.1 Per capita Gross National Product at market prices (1975)

Income Group	Country	Amount (U.S. $)
Less than $200	Bhutan	70
	Bangladesh	90
	Lao People's Democratic Republic	90
	Mali	90
	Ethiopia	100
	Rwanda	100
	Burma	110
	Burundi	110
	Maldives	110
	Nepal	110
	Somalia	110
	Upper Volta	110
	Chad	120
	Guinea-Bissau	120
	Benin (Dahomey)	130
	Guinea	130
	Malawi	130
	Niger	130
	India	140
	Zaire	140
	Afghanistan	150
	Lesotho	160
	Pakistan	160
	Tanzania	170
	Gambia, The	180
	Mozambique	180
	Haiti	190
	Sri Lanka	190
$200–$499	Yemen Arab Republic	200
	Comoros	200
	Madagascar	200
	Sierra Leone	200
	Central African Empire	220
	*Indonesia	220
	Kenya	220
	Botswana	230
	Uganda	230
	Solomon Islands	250
	Togo	250
	Yemen, People's Democratic Republic	250
	Egypt, Arab Republic of	260
	Sudan	270
	Cameroon	280
	Equatorial Guinea	320
	Mauritania	320

Limiting Factors and Underdevelopment

TABLE 10.1 (continued)

Income Group	Country	Amount (U.S. $)
	Western Samoa	320
	*Nigeria	340
	Thailand	350
	Bolivia	360
	Honduras	360
	Senegal	360
	Angola	370
	China, People's Republic of	380
	Philippines	380
	Grenada	390
	Liberia	410
	St. Vincent	420
	Zambia	420
	Swaziland	440
	Korea, Democratic People's Republic of	450
	El Salvador	460
	Jordan	460
	Sao Tome and Principe	460
	Morocco	470
	Papua New Guinea	470
$500–$1,999	Albania	510
	Congo, People's Republic of the	510
	Guyana	510
	Ivory Coast	540
	Rhodesia	550
	Dominica	560
	Korea, Republic of	560
	Guatemala	570
	Columbia	580
	Paraguay	580
	Seychelles	580
	St. Lucia	580
	*Ecuador	590
	Ghana	590
	Mauritius	610
	St. Kitts-Nevis	640
	Belize	670
	Nicaragua	700
	Dominican Republic	720
	Syrian Arab Republic	720
	Tunisia	730
	Malaysia	760
	Peru	760
	Macao	780
	Cuba	800

TABLE 10.1 (continued)

Income Group	Country	Amount (U.S. $)
	Antigua	840
	Mongolia	860
	*Algeria	870
	Turkey	900
	China, Republic of	930
	Costa Rica	960
	Namibia	980
	Chile	990
	Brazil	1,030
	Mexico	1,050
	Lebanon	1,070
	Fiji	1,090
	Jamaica	1,110
	Cyprus	1,240
	Romania	1,240
	*Iraq	1,250
	South Africa	1,270
	Panama	1,290
	Surinam	1,370
	Malta	1,390
	Barbados	1,410
	Guadeloupe	1,500
	Argentina	1,550
	Yugoslavia	1,550
	Portugal	1,570
	*Iran	1,660
	French Guiana	1,680
	Netherlands Antilles	1,680
	Hong Kong	1,760
	Reunion	1,920
	Djibouti	1,940
$2,000–$4,999	Trinidad and Tobago	2,000
	Bulgaria	2,110
	Hungary	2,150
	Bahrain	2,210
	*Venezuela	2,280
	Oman	2,300
	Puerto Rico	2,300
	Greece	2,340
	Martinique	2,350
	Ireland	2,390
	Singapore	2,450
	*Gabon	2,540
	U.S.S.R.	2,550
	Poland	2,600
	Spain	2,750

TABLE 10.1 (continued)

Income Group	Country	Amount (U.S. $)
	Italy	2,810
	Bahamas	3,110
	Uruguay	3,600
	Czechoslovakia	3,610
	United Kingdom	3,780
	Israel	3,790
	German Democratic Republic	3,910
	*Saudia Arabia	4,010
	New Zealand	4,280
	Japan	4,450
	Austria	4,870
$5,000 + over	Virgin Islands	5,050
	Finland	5,420
	*Libya	5,530
	Australia	5,700
	Netherlands	5,750
	Iceland	5,930
	France	5,950
	Luxembourg	6,020
	Belgium	6,270
	Germany, Federal Republic of	6,670
	Norway	6,760
	Bermuda	6,770
	Denmark	6,810
	Canada	6,930
	United States	7,120
	Sweden	8,150
	Switzerland	8,410
	*Qatar	10,970
	United Arab Emirates	13,600
	*Kuwait	15,190

KEY: * Opec Countries
  _____ Underdeveloped Countries
SOURCE: *World Bank Atlas,* The World Bank, Washington, D.C., 1977.

Leibenstein's List of Attributes of Underdevelopment

According to H. Leibenstein, whose list is one of the most comprehensive, the characteristics of underdeveloped countries are:

  I. *Economic*
     A. General
        1. A high proportion of the population in agriculture, usually 70 to 90 percent.

Is underdevelopment a lagging behind in the development of productive forces? (A) Two Ethiopian villagers dig a trench for a pipeline which will bring water from a spring to their village (SOURCE: *World Bank Photo* by Ray Witlin), and (B) Heavy machinery for highway construction in the United States (SOURCE: *University of Wisconsin—Extension*).

2. "Absolute over-population" in agriculture; that is, it would be possible to reduce the number of workers in agriculture and still obtain the same total output.

3. Evidence of considerable "disguised unemployment" and lack of employment opportunities outside agriculture.

4. Very little capital per head.

5. Low income per head and, as a consequence, existence near the "subsistence" level.

6. Practically zero savings for the large mass of the people.

7. Whatever savings do exist are usually achieved by a landholding class whose values are not conducive to investment in industry or commerce.

8. The primary industries, that is, agriculture, forestry, and mining, are usually the residual employment categories.

9. The output in agriculture is made up mostly of cereals and primary raw materials, with relatively low output of protein foods. The reason for this is the conversion ratio between cereals and meat products; that is, if one acre of cereals produces a certain number of calories, it would take

between five to seven acres to produce the same number of calories if meat products were produced.

10. Major proportion of expenditure on food and necessities.
11. Export of foodstuffs and raw materials.
12. Low volume of trade per capita.
13. Poor credit facilities and poor marketing facilities.
14. Poor housing.

B. Basic characteristics in agriculture

1. Although there is low capitalization on the land, there is simultaneously an uneconomic use of whatever capital exists due to the small size of holdings and the existence of exceedingly small plots.
2. The level of agrarian techniques is exceedingly low, and tools and equipment are limited and primitive in nature.
3. Even where there are big landowners as, for instance, in certain parts of India, the openings for modernized agricultural production for sale are limited by difficulties of transport and the absence of an efficient demand in the local market. It is significant that in many backward countries a modernized type of agriculture is confined to production for sale in foreign markets.
4. There is an inability of the small landholders and peasants to weather even a short-term crisis, and, as a consequence, attempts are made to get the highest possible yields from the soil, which leads to soil depletion.
5. There is a widespread prevalence of high indebtedness relative to assets and income.
6. The methods of production for the domestic market are generally old-fashioned and inefficient, leaving little surplus for marketing. This is usually true whether or not the cultivator owns the land, has tenancy rights, or is a sharecropper.
7. A most pervasive aspect is a feeling of land hunger because of the exceedingly small size of holdings and small diversified plots. The reason for this is that holdings are continually sub-divided as the population on the land increases.

II. *Demographic*

A. High fertility rates, usually above 40 per thousand.
B. High mortality rates and low expectation of life at birth.
C. Inadequate nutrition and dietary deficiencies.
D. Rudimentary hygiene, public health, and sanitation.
E. Rural overcrowding.

III. *Cultural and Political*

A. Rudimentary education and usually a high degree of illiteracy among most of the people.
B. Extensive prevalence of child labor.

C. General weakness or absence of the middle class.

D. Inferiority of women's status and position.

E. Traditionally determined behavior for the bulk of the populace.

IV. *Technological and Miscellaneous*

A. Low yields per acre.

B. No training facilities or inadequate facilities for the training of technicians, engineers, etc.

C. Inadequate and crude communication and transportation facilities, especially in the rural areas.

D. Crude technology (1957:40–41).

Any social scientist could add to and take issue with Leibenstein's mixed and heterogeneous list of facts and observations; but social scientists would generally agree that the list cites many of the attributes of underdeveloped countries. A crucial question, however, is whether inhibiting internal factors either separately or in their aggregate provide a logical and acceptable explanation of underdevelopment. Tamás Szentes (1971) examined some of the common explanations for underdevelopment which are based on lists of characteristics. The explanations considered population, climate and resources, capital and labor, and the circle of poverty into which the poor countries seemed to be locked.

Rapid Population Growth

Szentes considered arguments that underdeveloped countries are in a *less advantageous demographic position*. He agreed that rapid population growth fritters away any gains in real economic growth, that it poses difficulties of too many mouths to feed and too many hands to employ. He pointed out that the population problem in underdeveloped countries is a fairly recent phenomenon, and attributable, largely, to the diffusion of Western medicine and public health. He concluded that population growth is an important symptom, but not a cause of underdevelopment.

Climate and Resources

Szentes agreed that debilitating heat, insufficient or sporadic rainfall, poor soils, and a lack of resources of other kinds such as navigable rivers and accessible deposits of coal and iron, of tin and bauxite, pose obstacles for development. He rejected the idea that underdevelopment traces to *environmental factors*, however.

Environmental conditions are extremely diverse in the underdeveloped world. Great heat reduces crop yields, and the efficiency of people and animals. Some parts of the tropics experience extreme heat, but most of the tropics are not that hot. Furthermore, not all underdeveloped countries are tropical. Korea, for example, is temperate. Large areas of Africa wash away under torrential downpours or parch under drought. Parts of Asia have unreliable monsoons. By contrast, South America as a whole has a much more favorable distribution of annual rainfall. Vast tracts of

Limiting Factors and Underdevelopment

Does underdevelopment trace to environmental conditions? (A) Large areas of East Africa have poor soils and low, unpredictable rainfall. This dry wooded steppe in the rainshadow of Mount Meru, Tanzania, is on the arid margins of agriculture and supports Masai pastoralists at low population densities. (B) Large numbers of East African farmers, however, live in better watered areas—along the coast, near the lakes (especially around Lake Victoria), and in the highlands. This picture is of an agricultural landscape in the Kigezi district of southwest Uganda. Fertile volcanic soils and ample rainfall make agriculture highly productive on these carefully terraced hillsides. Small holders cultivate maize, millet, sorghum, potatoes, and a variety of vegetables. In many densely populated areas of East Africa, the main problems are not so much those of climate and resources, but of land shortage, marketing difficulties for domestic crops, and unfavorable terms of trade for commodities sold on world markets.

India have poor soils, but Indonesia has fertile volcanic soils. Tanzania has a small mineral potential, but Zaire and Nigeria have great underground wealth.

Szentes pointed out that vagaries of weather, exposure to natural disasters such as flood and drought, and danger of soil erosion are not exclusive to the underdeveloped world. Despite technical advances, climate still poses recurring problems for farmers in North America, Europe, and the Soviet Union. As a further point, some developed countries have unfavorable natural conditions. Japan, Switzerland, and the Netherlands are examples. What explains the Netherlands' ability to obtain the natural resources it needs? What part of the explanation lies in its history of trade and colonial exploitation in the centuries since the Renaissance?

Capital and Labor

Szentes considered that *capital shortage* and *low labor productivity* are two of the principal obstacles to development. To illustrate just how unproductive labor is in underdeveloped countries, comparisons are often made with developed countries. Use agriculture as an example. The average American farmer supports 24 non-food

Aluminum production at Reynolds Metals Company's Longview, Washington, plant. Capital abundance and high labor productivity are characteristic of developed countries. SOURCE: *Reynolds Metals Company.*

producing citizens. By contrast, in Africa agricultural productivity is "still so low that it takes anywhere from two to ten people—men, women, and children—to raise enough food to supply their own needs and those of one additional non-food growing adult" (Kimble, 1960, I:572).

In the opinion of some Western economists, low labor productivity in the underdeveloped world is attributable to the small scale of operations, the poor quality of the working population, and in particular to the absence or shortage of capital. Most underdeveloped countries lack the machines, engines, power lines, and factories that enable people and resources to produce more than is possible with bare hands and simple tools. Szentes concluded that capital shortage and low labor productivity are universal characteristics of underdevelopment, but not causes of underdevelopment. An important question for Szentes is: What concrete historical factors prevented capital from accumulating and labor productivity and quality from improving in underdeveloped countries?

Vicious Cycles of Poverty

Szentes rejected the idea that underdeveloped countries exist in an "initial state" of equilibrium which is characterized by a *vicious circle of poverty.* Vicious circle explanations emphasize the multi-causality of underdevelopment. These explanations suggest that it is not "just" a lack of ambition, or "just" an absence of specialization, or "just" a low output per capita, or "just" a population problem, or even "just" a political problem that holds back underdeveloped countries. It is a combination of interwoven limiting factors that thwarts development. An example of a vicious cycle is: low output → low incomes → low demand levels → low investment → capital deficiency → low output (Figure 10.4). Szentes concluded:

> The main weakness of the vicious cycle theories is that they reveal neither the historical circumstances out of which the assumed "magic" circle originated, nor the underlying socio-economic relations and the fundamental, determinant causes (1971:54).

Vicious cycle theories are also unable to explain how the now developed countries managed to escape the low income equilibrium trap.

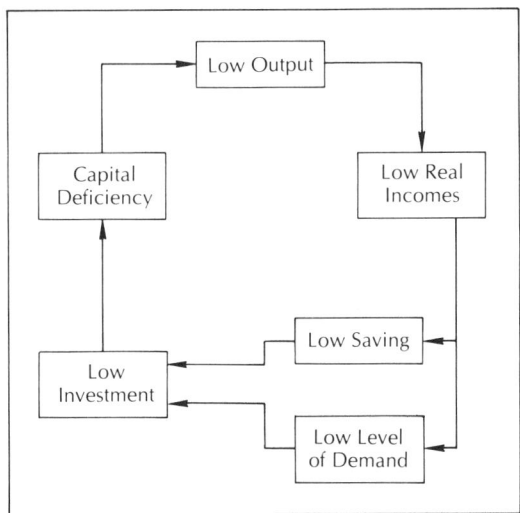

FIGURE 10.4 Closed cycle of poverty.

Sociological Theories of Underdevelopment

Two major types of sociological interpretations of underdevelopment are commonly cited in the literature: the *idea of a stagnant, traditional society*, and the *idea of social and economic dualism*.

The Idea of a "Stagnant, Traditional Society"*

When Western social scientists speak of the "backwardness of people" they are referring to a traditional society that lacks the qualities, propensities, motivations, and incentives of advanced capitalist societies. H. Leibenstein listed the following as

---

*This sub-section is a slight modification of de Souza and Porter, 1974, pp. 16–18.

desirable attitudes that should be created in underdeveloped countries if development is to take place:

1. a strong profit incentive
2. a willingness to take entrepreneurial risks
3. an eagerness to be trained for industrial jobs
4. an eagerness to engage in and promote scientific and technical progress.

In his view, developed countries are characterized by incentives directed toward "the creation of entrepreneurship, the expansion of productive skills, and the increase in productive knowledge" whereas underdeveloped countries are marked by activities "directed toward the maintenance of existing economic privileges through the inhibition and curtailment of potentially expanding economic opportunities; the conservative activities of both organized and unorganized labor directed against change; the resistance to new ideas; (and) increases in essentially non-productive conspicuous public or private consumption" (1957:188–189).

Probably the best known sociological or psychological theories of underdevelopment appear in the works of Everett Hagen (1962) and David McClelland (1961). They say one cannot account for the lack of development in a "stagnant, traditional society" on the basis of the economic situation in the underdeveloped country; after all, other countries were once poor and they developed. The answers must lie in personality and behavior, in values and needs expressed, and roles played by people in society.

Hagen explored psychological roots of cultural change and growth, as well as the underlying causes of resistance to change. After surveying economic theories of growth, he concluded that "economic theory has rather little to offer toward an explanation of economic growth, and that broader social and psychological considerations are pertinent" (1962:8). He emphasized the environment of childhood, parental behavior toward children, and the personality traits which emerge as a result.

Hagen postulated an "internal state" consisting of anxiety, rage, various needs, and aggression. He believed childhood experiences modify the original "internal state" and create personality, and in later life external stimuli "trigger" processes which result in observable behavior patterns. According to Hagen, the immediate social environment (the family) and the more distant social context (the structure of society) have small effects on behavior. Explanation of human behavior requires, in his view, knowledge of the operation of the "internal state."

Hagen applied his model of development first to "traditional" societies, and then to societies which experience economic growth, using a number of case studies. The last part of Hagen's book is devoted to the effects of the colonial experience on personality formation and subsequent behavior. Diverse reactions to tensions introduced by colonialism include: rage among adults, retreatism among their children, dependency, ritualism, identification with the aggressor, and messianism (Hagen, 1962:415–424). Hagen searched for those conditions useful for the development of creativity and innovativeness in personality, traits which can emerge out of retreatism and repression of needs.

Sociological Theories of Underdevelopment

McClelland advanced the thesis that development depends upon the degree to which entrepreneurial propensity measured by *n-Achievement Value* (or need to achieve) is mobilized or permitted to flower. He said that need achievement, one of a series of human needs, is established in childhood through family and school socialization, and is expressed in subsequent behavior. Entrepreneurial motivation—risk-taking in a semi-controlled environment where there is a chance of failure, but also a chance of success—is the key to development for McClelland. People with high need achievement motives feel within themselves a strong desire to excel. How well one has done the job becomes the reward. Profit, the traditional goal of capitalism, is simply a measure of how well one has performed (see box).

McCLELLAND AND THE NEED TO ACHIEVE

McClelland's "need achievement" is illustrated in a film he prepared, *The Need to Achieve* (1963). It shows, in one episode, a kindergarten or first grade class being introduced to a new game. The game is to toss a ring onto an upright peg on the floor; but there is no rule as to how far away to stand when throwing. The children decide for themselves. Little Willie, conformist, stands practically over the peg and always makes a ringer. Smart Alec stands at the other end of the room giving a care-free fling of the ring and misses by several feet. He never succeeds. But Edward, entrepreneur, and Norman, *n*-Achiever, tomorrow's captains of industry, back away from the peg to that exquisite position that gives the game some challenge, and a degree of risk, and some probability of success. People assess themselves. "What can I achieve as a person, to what degree should I challenge myself in life?" Those with a high *n*-Ach seem to raise the ante through life (SOURCE: de Souza and Porter, 1974:17).

The theories of Hagen and McClelland assume that early childhood socialization predetermines future behavior. Thus fundamental social and economic change cannot be expected to occur rapidly in underdeveloped countries. Behavioralists disagree. John Kunkel (1965) said that psychological principles cannot account for the data from small development projects in Pakistan and Peru where "progressive" behavior changes occurred over a few years. He said that development can occur at any time in a traditional society through new learning experiences.

Psychological and behavioral observations hardly comprise a coherent theory of underdevelopment. People in underdeveloped countries define themselves as "backward" when measured against the model of advanced capitalist societies. "This definition [of backwardness] . . . , by including the lack of entrepreneurship, an entrepreneurial class and individualism in general among the criteria of backwardness of people, labels, as a matter of fact, every society as backward that is not characterized by individualism and capitalist private interest" (Szentes, 1971:63).

The Idea of Social and Economic Dualism

The idea of dualism or disintegration is popular in studies of underdevelopment. The theory appears in two main variants: *social dualism,* and *economic* or *technological dualism.*

The theory of the dual society originated with the Dutch economist, J. Boeke (1953). He based his ideas on his experiences in Indonesia and presented it as a theory of Eastern societies. According to his cultural explanation, "Social dualism is the clashing of an imported social system with an indigenous social system of another style. Most frequently the imported social system is high capitalism" (1953:103). The intrusion of the capitalist society of the West into the precapitalist agrarian societies of the East resulted in a form of disintegration. Since the two societies are opposed in character, and "neither of them becomes general and characteristic for that society as a whole," therefore "as a rule, one policy for the whole country is not possible,... and what is more beneficial for one section of society may be harmful for the other" (1953:103). Boeke concluded that the penetration of Western capitalism into Eastern society has been useless. Easterners, he thought, were disinterested in profit, and incapable of adopting Western means.

Benjamin Higgins (1956) attacked Boeke's theory for its defeatism. He said some degree of dualism is present in every country, and the challenges of changing a traditional society into a modern Western one can be met. Instead of social dualism, Higgins advocated a theory of technological and economic dualism differentiating *capital-intensive* and *labor-intensive* sectors. He concluded that the "backward" labor-intensive sector could be transformed by the gradual diffusion of Western capitalism supported by transplantations of technical assistance.

The theory of dualism helps us to understand the mechanism of underdevelopment. However, Boeke's and Higgin's variants of the theory of dualism can be criticized. Both variants assume the labor-intensive sector is something given against which the intrusion of the capital-intensive sector will be either ineffective (as in Boeke's view) or effective (as in Higgin's view). Neither variant examines the interlocked nature of the two sectors. Neither variant considers dualism as a complex integrated socio-economic phenomenon. Finally, neither variant regards dualism as a product of a specific historical development, derived from the development of the capitalist world economy.

Historical Explanations of Underdevelopment

In the last quarter-century, historical models of socio-economic development have excited Western scholars. They evolved in response to the quickening pace of world economic expansion and integration, the collapse of colonial power structures, the emergence of new social systems, and the Cold War, but also in opposition to Marxist critical analysis of world capitalism. Western "historical" models relate the present state of underdeveloped countries to the past of developed countries, and their future to the present state of developed countries. Based on the same Western liberal philosophy that justified the historical process of colonial expansion, these models

Historical Explanations of Underdevelopment

assume that underdeveloped countries can achieve development through European political forms, science, and technology, and that their path to progress from traditional to modern will be more or less unilinear.

Rostow's Historical Scheme

The classic example of a historical model that states that the development history of the West will be repeated in the underdeveloped world is contained in Walt Rostow's study *The Stages of Economic Growth,* sub-titled "A Non-Communist Manifesto" (see box). Rostow wrote his book when he was a political and economic advisor to the United States government, and he wanted to provide a rebuttal to *The Communist Manifesto* of 1848, written by Marx and Engels. He argued that the highest stage of evolution is *not* socialism, but developed capitalism.

Rostow's study sees the economic development of all societies as lying within one of five levels: the traditional society, the pre-conditions necessary for growth, the take-off, the drive to maturity, and the age of high mass-consumption (Figure 10.5).

> **WALT WHITMAN ROSTOW (1916–)**
>
> Rostow is an economic historian who was educated at Yale and at Oxford, as a Rhodes Scholar. He has taught at Cambridge University and the Massachusetts Institute of Technology. He was appointed special assistant to the President in 1966. His major publication, *The Stages of Economic Growth,* has had a pervading influence on Western study of the processes of change. Although Rostow's concepts of growth have been attacked, his subsequent rejoinder to his critics showed that he has not changed his central thesis. The progressive diffusion of new technologies remains the basis for economic growth (Rostow, 1971).

The Traditional Society In this society, knowledge of modern technology and science is lacking. Productivity levels are low. At least 75 percent of the population is engaged in food production. Upper classes spend available capital on unproductive ends. Society is conservative and resistant to change. It is hierarchically organized: political power is either in the hands of a land-owning aristocracy or is embodied in a central authority supported by the military and civil servants.

The Preconditions for Take-Off When this stage occurs, revolutionary changes overcome obstacles to growth. Outside influences usually stimulate the initial growth of productive investment, the installation of roads, railways, and utilities, and the emergence of a new elite. Agriculture surrenders its dominance to secondary and tertiary activities. Society develops a new mentality; a propensity to accept new techniques, and a freedom for a new class of businessmen to operate. People believe that economic growth creates conditions necessary for the attain-

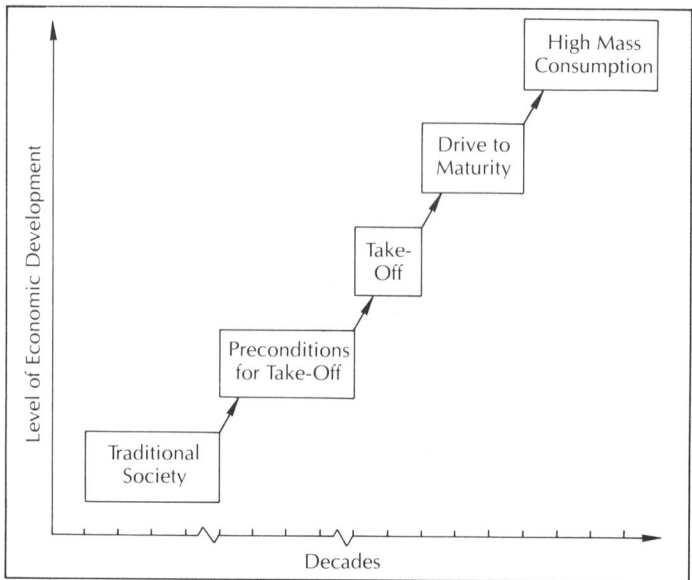

FIGURE 10.5 Rostow's five stages of economic growth.

ment of certain goods, greater national power, improved social welfare, and a higher material standard of living. Rostow dated this phase in Western Europe as the seventeenth and eighteenth centuries. Among the Western European states, Britain, favored by natural resources, trading possibilities, and social and political structure, was the first to develop fully the preconditions for take-off. In the underdeveloped world, the idea of economic progress usually came with European intervention and diffused within and through social elites.

The Take-Off Stage The crucial third stage marks the "great watershed in the life of modern societies" (Rostow, 1960:7). In a critical decade or two the forces of economic progress expand and dominate society. Growth becomes more or less automatic. The rate of effective investment and savings increases from 5 percent of national income to more than 10 percent. One or more substantial manufacturing sectors expand rapidly and they become "leading sectors" of growth. A political, social, and institutional framework emerges quickly; it exploits the impulses to expansion in the modern sector; and it gives the growth an on-going character. "One can approximately allocate the take-off of Britain to the two decades after 1783; France and the United States to the several decades preceding 1860; Germany, the third quarter of the nineteenth century; Russia and Canada, the quarter century or so preceding 1914; while during the 1950s India and China have, in quite different ways, launched their respective take-offs" (Rostow, 1960:9; and Figure 10.6).

Drive to Maturity After take-off, a long interval of fluctuating progress follows. The society becomes a force in the international economy, and begins to import raw materials and export finished products. Economic growth extends to all sectors of the expanding economy. It comes to technologically complex industries; for example, in the twentieth century it has spread from leading sectors such as iron,

Historical Explanations of Underdevelopment

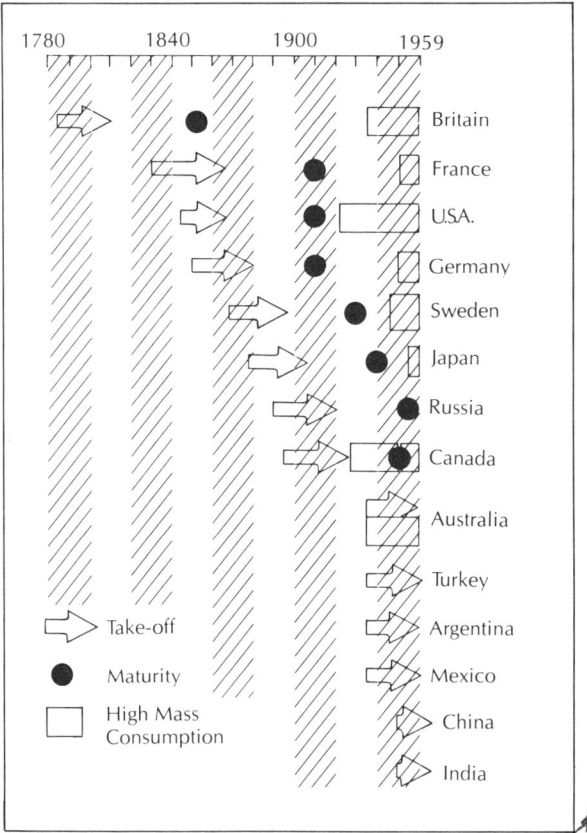

FIGURE 10.6 Stages of economic growth applied to selected countries. SOURCE: W. W. Rostow, 1960, *The Stages of Economic Growth: A Non-Communist Manifesto*, Cambridge, England: Cambridge University, p. xii.

steel, and coal toward machine tools and electronics. Some 10 to 20 percent of the national income is reallocated for reinvestment each year, permitting output to outstrip population growth. Society has the technological skills and the industrial leadership necessary to produce almost anything it chooses to produce. Britain completed the drive to maturity by 1850, the United States, Germany, and France 50 years later, and the Soviet Union more recently.

The Stage of High Mass Consumption Leading sectors of a technically and technologically mature society shift toward durable consumer goods and services. Per capita income is so high that a large number of people gain a command over consumption which transcends basic food, shelter, and clothing. They buy automobiles, sewing machines, electric-powered household gadgets. Urbanization and the proportion of the population working in offices and in skilled factory jobs increases. Society turns its attention to superior objectives such as increased resources allocated to social welfare and security. For the United States it was in the 1920s, and again in the decade, 1946–1956, that this stage of growth was pressed to its logical conclusion. In the 1950s, Western Europe and Japan entered this phase, and the Soviet Union is technically ready for it.

A Closer Look at Rostow's Second Stage

Of particular interest in the study of underdeveloped countries is Rostow's second stage in which the preconditions for take-off are developing. Rostow distinguished between two examples of the second stage: the general case, and the specific case. He said the general case fits the evolution of Europe, Asia, Africa, and Latin America. In this case, major changes in an entrenched traditional society are required, resulting in alterations of the socio-political structure as well as techniques of production. Rostow said the specific case fits the evolution of a small group of nations created out of British civilization, which were far along in the transition process: the United States, Australia, New Zealand and Canada. According to Rostow, these countries, founded on the periphery of the dynamic transitional process that was proceeding within Britain, were never deeply enmeshed in the structure, politics, and values of the traditional society. Thus their transition to modernity was merely economic and technical. For example, the United States, in Rostow's view, was "born free." Except for the South, it had a socio-economic system that adapted easily to industrialization.

A crucial question in Rostow's model is, "How did Britain outgrow the traditional stage?" For Rostow the answer springs from two features of post medieval Europe: the discovery of regions beyond Western Europe, and the accelerating development of modern science. An important factor that permitted the first "take-off" to occur in Britain and not in a neighboring country like the Netherlands was the political, social, and religious revolution fought out in Britain by 1688.

Rostow considered the present traditional state of underdeveloped countries as a natural stage of growth which every country except Britain had or has to undergo. He said that the penetration of ideas of developed countries into traditional societies represents the "positive demonstration effect" of colonialism, an important element of the preparation for take-off. He admitted that colonialism also generates a "negative demonstration effect," the way developed countries impose their will on underdeveloped countries. Even this effect, however, is beneficial in Rostow's thinking. Without the intrusion of advanced nations, the pace of modernization would have been much slower than it has been.

Rostow's model provides the theoretical basis for the use of the term "economically backward." Since underdeveloped countries pass through the same stages of development as the developed countries passed through earlier, then their present state is backwardness, and colonialism cannot be responsible for that state. Indeed Rostow argued that colonialism is an accelerator of progress (see box).

MARX AND COLONIALSIM

Marx believed that colonialism was a progressive force. Colonialism would help to break down feudalism, nurture capitalism, and develop a revolutionary proletariat. After a climactic struggle between the proletariat and the bourgeoisie, Marx prophesied that the proletariat would emerge victorious.

Development: Evolutionary or Revolutionary?

Rostow's *stages-of-growth model* is a typical example of a *theory of social evolution* that dominated late nineteenth century thinking following publication of Darwin's idea of biological evolution. It assumes that development is a trend by which underdeveloped countries gradually acquire ways of life characteristic of technological civilization. The notion of a *development continuum* has been heavily criticized; for instance, Robert Heilbroner (1963) argued that the path to progress to be followed in Africa, Asia, and Latin America will be fundamentally different from the history of the West. To countries of the underdeveloped world, development will come not as the culmination of a long process of *unilineal evolution*, but as a discontinuous jump from one type of society to another. Whereas a long period of preparation was necessary for the Industrial Revolution to start in the West, the underdeveloped nations must begin their "Great Ascent" without these preconditions. According to Heilbroner, the "Great Ascent" will get into motion by a profound social and political transformation. "At the heart of the development process lurks a revolutionary potential—revolutionary not in the sense of a gradual redistribution of power and wealth such as accompanied the Industrial Revolution, but in the sense of a drastic, rapid, and painful redistribution such as accompanied the French or Russian revolutions (Heilbroner, 1963:17). Heilbroner, a liberal economist, argued that the price of development is likely to be political and economic authoritarianism. He said the development process promises the appearance of socialism on a world scale, an assumption that presents the capitalist world with a new environment (1963:134–158).

Marxists and Rostow's Version of History

Marxists reject Rostow's version of history. They dismiss Rostow's claim that the present state of "backwardness" of underdeveloped countries is an original state or is one of the natural transitional stages of the evolution from the original primitive state toward development. They reject Rostow's claim that the now developed countries were once underdeveloped. They argue that these interpretations are not consistent with history. For example, Andre Gunder Frank noted that Rostow's model "attributes a history to the developed countries but denies all history to the underdeveloped ones" (1967:37). Moreover, Frank said that Rostow's model "simply disregards the historical fact... that the economic and political expansion of Europe since the fifteenth century has come to incorporate the now underdeveloped countries into a single stream of world history, which has given rise simultaneously to the present development of some countries and the present underdevelopment of others" (1967:37).

A Global World View*

Marxists, therefore, do not accept Rostow's isolated or independent interpretation of underdevelopment and development. They insist that the world has been one at least

---

*This sub-section is a slight modification of de Souza and Porter, 1974, pp. 20, 41–44.

since the fifteenth century; and all that time the European trading powers have been transferring the surpluses of the countries with whom they have traded back to Europe to invest in development there. Their trading activities enriched Europe, but impoverished the underdeveloped world.

> The Dutch, for instance, exacted an annual tribute in spices; for other crops they enforced compulsory deliveries at favourable prices. The English destroyed the Indian textile industry and then proceeded to supply India with cotton goods from Great Britain. How Britain was to finance the imports of tea from China presented great problems for as the Chinese emperor said to George III, "our celestial empire possesses all things in prolific abundance" and, presumably therefore, China had little need for English goods. This knotty problem was finally resolved by forcing opium on the Chinese and encouraging addiction. This created a large demand for the drug which the East India Company was able to supply from Bengal. The Chinese made many vain attempts to restrict the trade. Finally, Britain forced China to permit the trade and forget the Opium War of 1839–43— "a war that was precipitated by the Chinese government's effort to suppress a pernicious contraband trade in opium, concluded by the superior firepower of British warships, and followed by humiliating treaties that gave Westerners special privileges in China" (Griffin, 1969:35).

The intrusion of Europeans not only impoverished the people, it sometimes eliminated them. " 'It has been reckoned that at the approach of the Spaniards in 1492, total Carib population in Hispaniola was about 300,000. By 1508 it was reduced to about 60,000 . . . and by 1548 it had reached a figure which indicated virtual extermination, about 500' " (Griffin, 1969:45). The coming of the Spaniards to Mexico meant the destruction of Aztec civilization, and population declined from 13 million to about two million by the end of the sixteenth century (Griffin, 1969:46) (see box).

MIDDLE AMERICAN AND CARIBBEAN POPULATION DECLINE

Widely different figures have been estimated for Middle American and Caribbean populations as of 1492, and for subsequent population decline. Keith Griffin did not note that the inadvertent introduction of diseases by the Spaniards was a major cause of population decline.

COLONIALISM: MYTH AND REALITY

John Kenneth Galbraith put it nicely when he said "Colonialism . . . was possible only because the myth of higher moral purpose regularly concealed the reality of lower economic interest" (1977:259). The civilizing mission, patriotic destiny, and Christian Evangelism are some of the elevated motives for justifying the "rightness" of colonial penetration. The underlying reasons for colonialism, such as the need to make colonies export commodities required by the mother country, were altogether too selfish and uncouth to be revealed.

Historical Explanations of Underdevelopment

In Africa, the slave trade greatly reduced population and reduced the territory occupied in large parts of the Congo Basin and in the West African forest. The slave trade was followed in the late nineteenth century by the establishment of colonies (see box). The "mad-scramble" for colonies brought 96 percent of Africa's territory and perhaps 92 percent of the people into colonial status by 1914 (Figure 10.7).

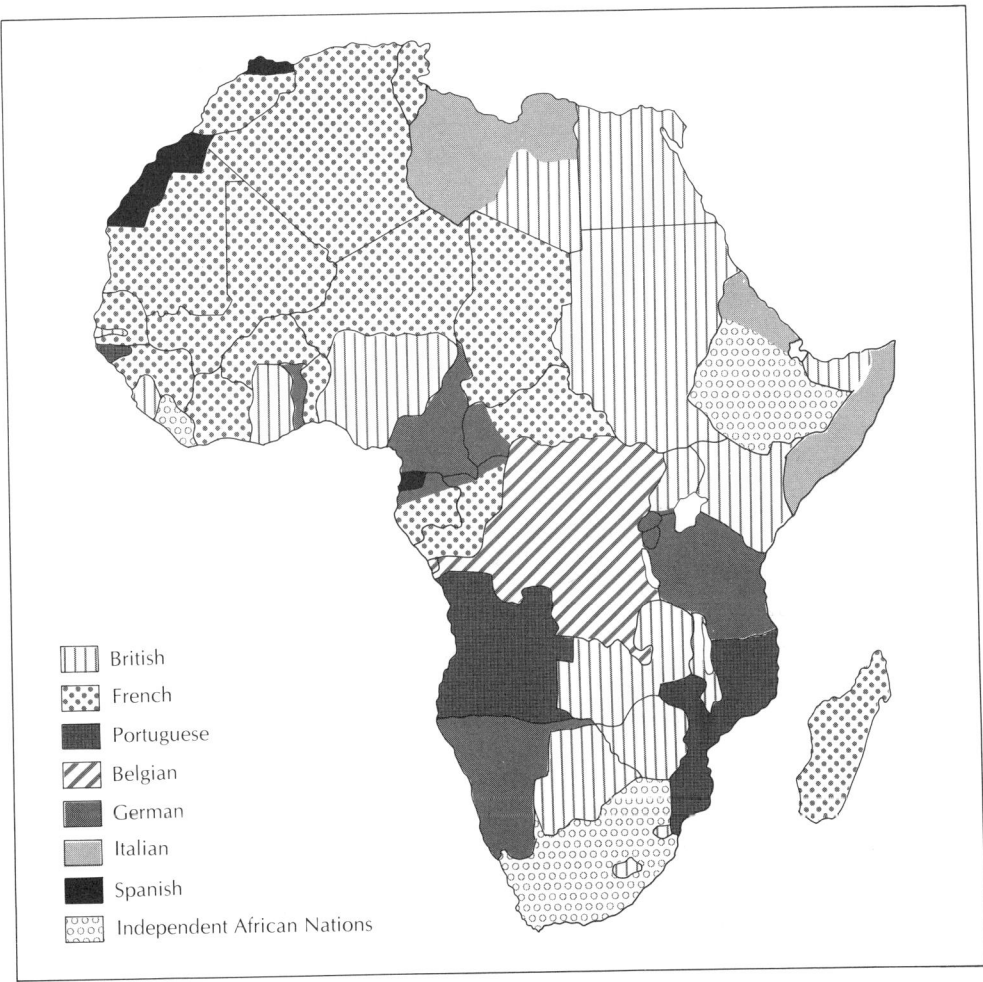

FIGURE 10.7 The mad scramble for Africa.

Europeans settled in East, Central, and South Africa with a colonial organization of space that served settler interest. For example, in Kenya a complex classification governed who could use a given piece of land and how that land could be used. *The Kenya Political and General Map* (1957) summarizes the long process of land allocation which evolved over a period of about 60 years (Figure 10.8). The four main land types were Native Land Units for Africans, Kenya Highlands for Europeans, Alienated Land Outside the Highlands for Asians, Europeans, and Coastal Arabs, and Crown Land whose use was reserved at the pleasure of the Crown (Morgan, 1963). Crown Land was not developed, and neither was a large part of the

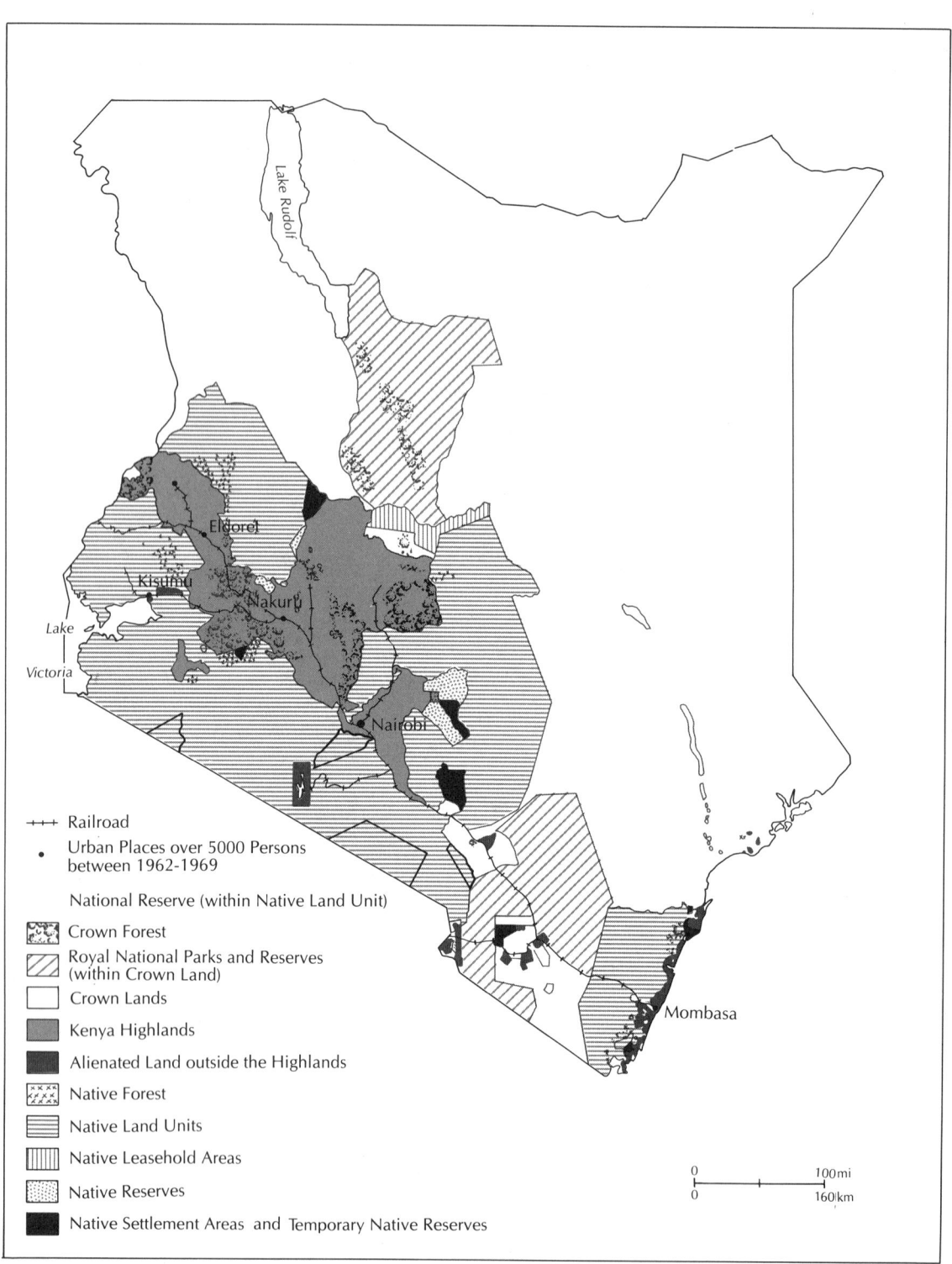

FIGURE 10.8 Land allocations in Kenya, 1957. SOURCE: A. R. de Souza and P. W. Porter, 1974, *The Underdevelopment and Modernization of the Third World*. Washington, D.C.: Association of American Geographers Commission on College Geography, Resource Paper No. 28, p. 42, Fig. 5.

immense acreage of land allocated to European settlers. Keith Griffin noted that the setting aside of large areas of land "led to underemployment both of land (in the European areas) and labour (in the African areas)" (1969:43–44). Europeans occupied the most favorable farming areas, and they enjoyed considerable infrastructural advantages with regard to marketing their produce. Rail development served the alienated land, but rarely the native land units. As a result, most of the urban development in Kenya has taken place within alienated land (Table 10.2).

TABLE 10.2 Urban development and alienated land in Kenya

Urban Places	Served by Rail (1969 Population in Brackets)		
	Yes	No	Total
In Areas of Alienations	13 [897,980]	2 [20,901]	15
In Native Land Units	2 [37,181]	6 [42,483]	8
Total	15	8	23

From the colonial system emerged the distorted structure of world imperialism: colonies with foreign enclaves and an underdeveloped indigenous sector, and an international division of labor. In West Africa, small holders were drawn into export agriculture by large trading companies, which forced local people to make considerable adjustments in their farming practices, land tenure arrangements, settlement and trading patterns. In Eastern and Southern Africa, the indigenous population was forced into low-paid wage labor in mines, plantations, and European farms. The measures used to create the labor force were many, but, basically consisted of actions that made it difficult for the indigenous population to earn a living.

The Geographer's Perspective on Underdevelopment and Modernization*

The World View in Western Geography

Geographers usually ascribe the "backward" status of underdeveloped countries to internal obstacles, sometimes to physical isolation from the West, and rarely to the nature of the world's political economy. The absence of a global view that considers the relational nature of underdevelopment in much of Western geography traces to:

1. our faith that industrial capitalism could, would, and should develop the underdeveloped world

---

*Based on de Souza and Porter, 1974, pp. 20–23, and de Souza and Porter, 1978, pp. 26–46.

2. our aid to imperialism today but also in the past, in the era of European exploration and discovery
3. our interest in systems maintenance
4. our psychic investment in the region.

Our penchant for dividing the world into regions to simplify the problem of description has impaired our vision of the interrelatedness of events in world history. For example, colonialism is usually considered when we discuss Africa, but not when the development of Europe is considered.

Let us illustrate the world view in Western geography with a few examples. Preston James (1964) considered that differences in economic development stem partly from differences in the natural resource base and partly from time lags in the spread of industrial and democratic revolutions to places "remote" in some way from the origins of these revolutions. He suggested that Rostow's five stages of

A city created by Europeans out of the African "wilderness": Nairobi, capital of Kenya. Nairobi originated in 1899 as a railway camp during the building of the Mombasa-Lake Victoria railway line. To the north and west of Nairobi, the fertile "White Highlands" were alienated to European farmers who specialized in wheat, corn, pyrethrum, sheep, and cattle. Land was also alienated along the coast for Europeans, many of whom had a holiday place on the Indian Ocean to use as a change from the "White Highlands." Since independence colonial land ownership and use has been modified. For example, much of the land in the "White Highlands" has been acquired by Africans and divided into small holdings. SOURCE: James W. King for the *National Council for Geographic Education.*

economic growth are a guide to the future development of underdeveloped countries. In his book, as in many others by geographers and economists is an implicit assumption of initial equality among countries. For example, H. Leibenstein said:

> We begin with a set of economies (or countries), each 'enjoying' an equally low standard of living at the outset . . . Over a relatively long period of time (say, a century or two) some of these countries increase their output per head considerably whereas others do not (1957:4).

The question, for Leibenstein, is how to apply the lessons learned by those countries which have escaped the "low level equilibrium trap" to those countries which have not.

Similarly, Jan Broek and John Webb (1973) gave considerable attention to Rostow's stages of economic growth, and in their discussion of underdevelopment they cited four general causes for economic stagnation: racial differences (or at least beliefs concerning racial differences), natural resource endowment, isolation and "that favorite scapegoat—colonial rule." They concluded that no factor itself sufficed as an explanation. In their view, "an underdeveloped country can derive great benefits from selling raw materials and investing the profits in enterprises that push the economy upward, such as education, land reform or public utilities" (1973:342).

J. Barry Riddell (1970) expressed a similar interpretation of the benefits of colonialism. In his geography of *modernization* he said:

> Although it has been characterized as many things, [the colonial era] was essentially a period of modernization, a time in which the ideas, methods, and techniques of European society were imposed upon or melded into traditional ways of life. In Africa, it brought dramatic and often painful changes. Yet, at the same time, Western medicine was slowly introduced; missionaries brought European forms of education, as well as Christian theology; the European administrators imposed peace and security; and the roads and rails they built brought commercial and other secular values, and occasionally prosperity (1970:3).

Peter Gould (1970) and Edward Soja (1968) argued that the diffusion of Western elements of modernization will promote the downfall of traditional societies. Gould, for example, studied the diffusion of modernization across Tanzania. He interpreted modernization, as defined by a host of infrastructural variables such as roads, railways, telephones, postal stations, hospitals, schools, and administrative offices, as diffusion outward from foreign enclaves. His "modernization surface" maps (Figure 10.9), and accompanying descriptions indicate that beyond towns, and in some cases their rich agricultural hinterlands, levels of modernization decrease sharply. Peripheral areas are illustrated in the sequence of maps as shrinking areas of "no modernization." Gould noted that in the 1920s there were a few islands of development focused on Dar es Salaam and the lower order centers of Tanga, Mwanza, and Tabora that "float in the still mill-pond of traditionalism" (1970:156). By the 1960s, the spatial pattern of modernization was more widespread and intense, but the larger towns remained the major centers of change.

Our final example comes from J. Spencer and W. Thomas (1969). They presented a world view which is one of cultural convergence as European political

Akosombo Dam on the Volta River in Ghana generates low-cost hydroelectric power for aluminum smelting and urban-industrial needs in Accra. VALCO (Volta Aluminum Company) consumes nearly 75 percent of the electricity produced from the Akosombo power plant. Is modernization in the Third World merely a process of diffusing Western technology? SOURCE: I. Vogeler.

forms, technical inventions, and values spread throughout the world. In addition, they dismissed the claim that colonialism underdeveloped poor countries:

> In the present brief era of emergent political colonialism and strongly contrasting sociopolitical systems it has become popular in some quarters to describe advanced cultures as malignant exploiters that have preyed upon the regions of the earth . . . Such a procedure is easily adopted, for it shifts responsibility for human development, initiative, and progress from the shoulders of the exploited and places it wholly on the shoulders of the exploiters. However, this procedure disregards both the physical-biotic environmental differentiation of the earth and the very nature of cultural evolution (1969:367, 369).

The Dialectical Historical View

The world view in Western geography must be contrasted with a growing radical dialectical literature on underdevelopment and modernization. The emergence of a radical literature was delayed until some years after the wholesale achievement of political independence by former colonies. In the 1960s it became clear to some geographers that political independence had in most cases not changed the dependency relations between former colony and former mother country.

The Geographer's Perspective on Underdevelopment and Modernization 495

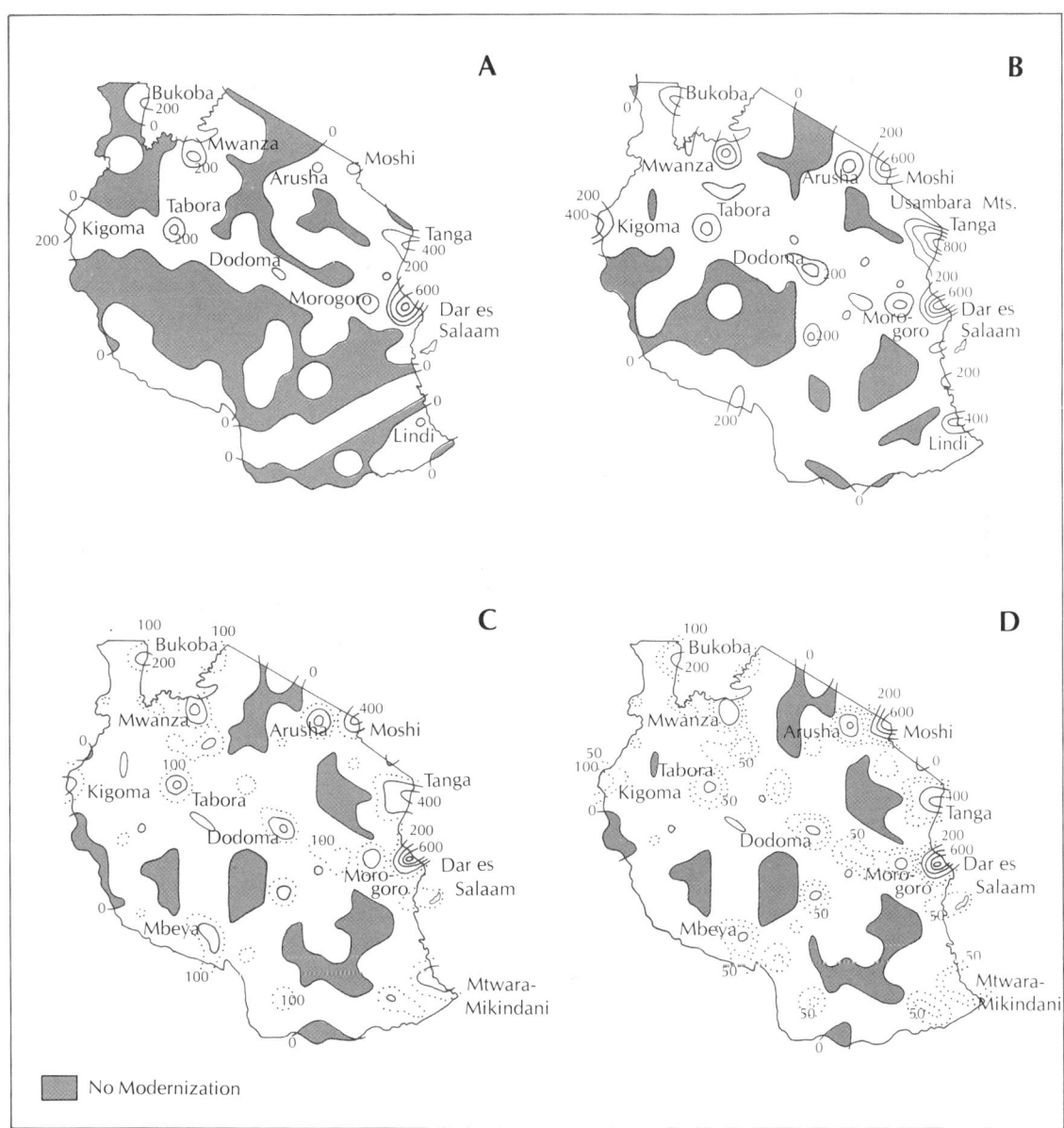

FIGURE 10.9 The diffusion of "modernization" in Tanzania: (A) early twenties; (B) late twenties and early thirties; (C) late forties and early fifties; and (D) late fifties and early sixties. SOURCE: Peter R. Gould, "Tanzania 1920–63: The Spatial Impress of the Modernization Process," *World Politics,* 22, No. 2 (January 1970) copyright © 1970 by Princeton University Press. Figures 2, 3, 5, 6 reproduced by permission of Princeton University Press.

An early example (1964) of a radical approach to the study of the underdeveloped world was Keith Buchanan's "Profiles of the Third World." He showed in a series of cartograms that maldistribution is the central fact of underde-

Salisbury, the capital and primate city of Rhodesia. Many researchers believe that the city is the gateway for Third World nations because it can transmit economic change to smaller centers. SOURCE: *Rhodesia Department of Information*.

velopment. For example, he argued that hunger in underdeveloped countries is not in any way predestined by a hostile environment (Figure 10.10). Rather it has been "perpetuated, even aggravated, by generations of Western exploitation which have distorted and twisted the economies of the dependent territories" (1964:103). Buchanan provided several illustrations of the ways in which developed countries underdevelop poor countries. For instance, he described the general pattern of earnings from American overseas investments (Figure 10.11).

The importance of investment in oil comes out clearly, as does the relevance of Latin America to the United States business economy; equally striking is the relatively small scale of investment in Africa and Monsoon Asia. That these investments, however massive they may appear, bring only "fringe" benefits to the underdeveloped countries is illustrated by American investments in Latin America, where, in 1959, United States firms "made 775 million (dollars), only reinvested 200 million and sent 575 back to the United States. In the last seven years, Latin America lost, because of these shipments of money, $2,679,000,000." Under these conditions, overseas investment is a powerful factor making for a widening gap between the rich nations and the poor, rather than a factor making for real economic progress (1964:114).

In the last several years, a few geographers have been writing overviews of underdevelopment and modernization, many of which argue for a historical dialectical approach and a global world view when explaining dependency rela-

A rural general store (*duka* in Swahili) in East Africa represents the impress of modernization. Farmers who grow crops for national and international markets have cash to purchase a variety of goods they do not produce. SOURCE: James W. King for the *National Council for Geographic Education*.

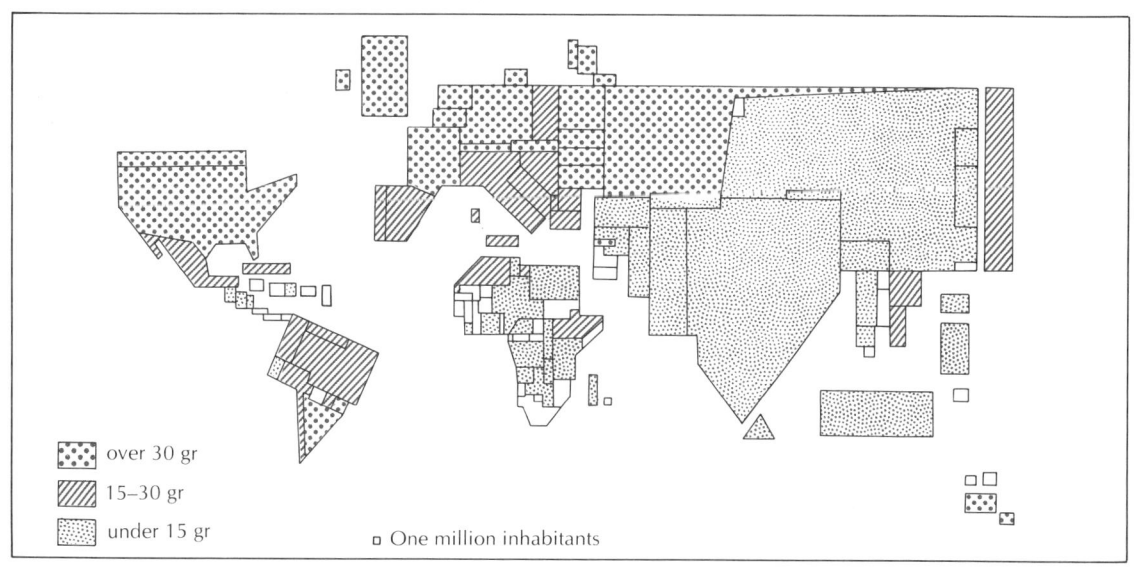

FIGURE 10.10 Daily intake of animal protein, 1962. SOURCE: K. M. Buchanan, 1964, "Profiles of the Third World," *Pacific Viewpoint*, Vol. 5, p. 102, Fig. 4.

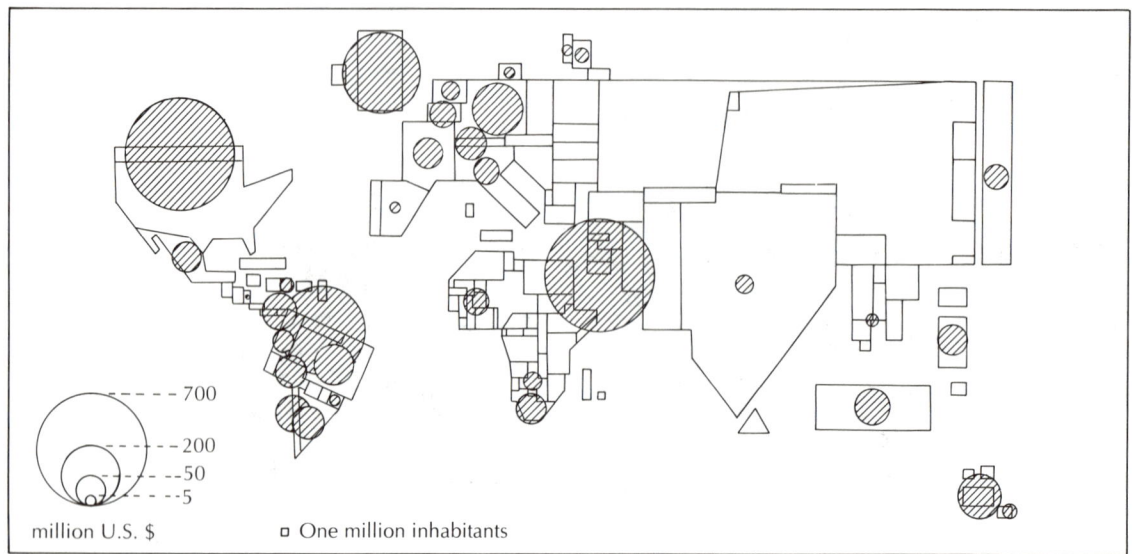

FIGURE 10.11 Earnings of U.S. investments, 1960. SOURCE: K. M. Buchanan, 1964, "Profiles of the Third World," *Pacific Viewpoint,* Vol. 5, p. 115, Fig. 15.

tionships (Slater, 1974; Blaut, 1975; Santos, 1975; and Brookfield, 1975). Their works may be characterized as wide-ranging literature surveys and critiques.

A strong theme in the dialectical approach has been the increasing dependency of people in underdeveloped countries. Geographers taking this approach argue that poor people in underdeveloped countries are becoming increasingly marginalized. The people are more interdependent and linked with developed countries, and in consequence more "disaster prone." (see box). When drought or earthquakes hit, they are less able to help themselves, and suffer more severe losses than was formerly the case (Baird, *et al.* 1975).

WHY FAMINE THREATENS THE SAHEL

The United Nations estimates that 450 million people worldwide were seriously malnourished in 1976. The World Bank puts it closer to one billion.

This massive hunger has perhaps been most vividly illustrated by the drought and famine in the Sahel region of Africa. There, on the southern edge of the Sahara desert, about 100,000 people, mostly elderly and children, starved to death in the early 1970s.

Why can't these countries produce enough food for their needs? The amazing fact is that they do. That food, however, is not for those who grow it. The Sahel is a net exporter of barley, beans, peanuts, fresh vegetables, and beef, despite protein malnutrition among its children that is about the worst in the world, even in normal years.

The problem of malnutrition in the Sahel is rooted in the class structure of the region. There are differences in class structure among the seven Sahel countries (parts of Senegal, Mauritania, Mali, Upper Volta, Chad, Nigeria, and Niger), but the broad outlines are depressingly similar: legacies of French colonial rule.

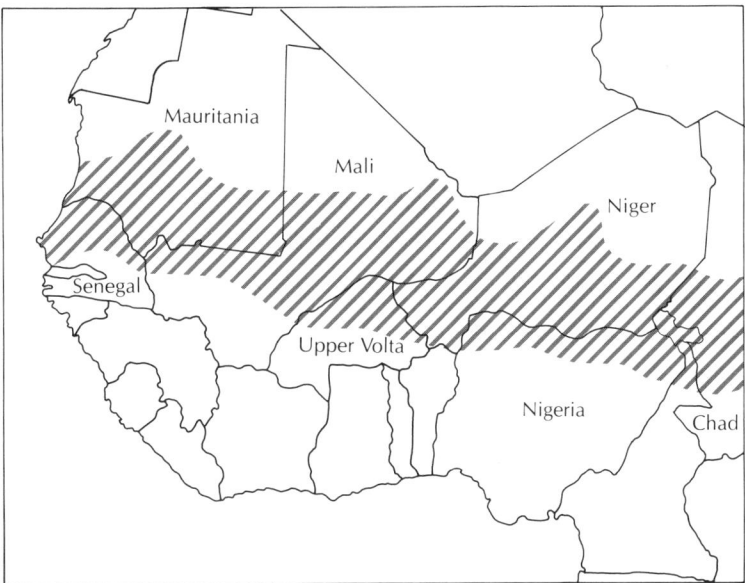

The shaded area indicates that part of Africa known as the Sahel, or fringe of the desert. SOURCE: *Dollars and Sense*, 1978, No. 33, p. 5.

Before colonialism, or where colonialism had not reached, desert farmers left land fallow for up to twenty years between plantings. They used a variety of crops to maintain soil quality. Nomads drove their mixed herds over vast areas of arid grazing land. In what is now Mali, there were granaries for storing good harvests against bad years.

Then came the French. They conquered the area gradually, against native opposition, beginning with Senegal in the 1860s and reaching Lake Chad in 1900. The French introduced export crops to the area, particularly cotton, to compete with British textiles, peanuts for the oil, and beef, a meat that Europeans preferred to camel.

The cheapest way to grow these exports was generally to make the peasants do it, using a method that the British pioneered in India—imposing taxes on land, buildings, and even people that had to be paid in the colonial power's currency. French trading companies, the sole buyers in their areas, could depress the prices paid. The lower the prices paid, the more the peasants had to grow to pay the taxes.

The pressure of the taxes forced peasants to abandon land-conserving farming techniques—to sell the future to pay for the present. Intensive cotton cultivation, for example, depletes the Sahelian soil, leaving it too poor for food production when cotton moves on. The much-publicized advance of the desert results. It is not a natural calamity, but one created by colonialism.

Although the colonial era has ended for the Sahel, the class structure evolved under colonialism continues. Local elites of landowners, tax collectors, food traders, and government functionaries live off the exported surplus and continue to encourage it. The taxes also continue. In 1970, in the midst of the drought, Mali's tax forced small farmers to come up with 106 pounds of cotton each. In Senegal, peanut exports alone pay one-third of the government budget, and one-half of that budget is for salaries.

The system channels the Sahel's production through local elites and then out to the world export markets, regardless of the desperate need of the Sahel people. During the drought, as relief food came in, peanuts, cotton, vegetables, meat and fish went out, sometimes on the same boats and planes. In Mali, cottonseed, peanut and rice exports actually reached new highs.

As herdsmen sold off cattle they could not feed or water, cattle exports rose 41% from 1968 to 1971, and local elites grew richer. Traders and moneylenders prospered in the bad years as peasants borrowed and then sold their harvests cheap, all to avoid losing their land. Towns now feature "chateaux de la secheresse," or mansions of the drought—homes of the local elite that for the first time rival in splendor the homes of the wealthy Europeans there.

There are glimmers of peasant organization in the Sahel. A National Liberation Front operates in Chad, and there have been sporadic peasant revolts in Senegal. In response to these, the Senegal government, which calls itself "socialist," has hired agricultural experts from capitalist countries to help introduce labor saving technology, so that peasant resistance cannot affect exports. An example is Bud Antle, Inc., a California-based vegetable grower and marketer.

Back in 1972, around the time Bud Antle was suing to have Cesar Chavez jailed for the United Farm Workers' lettuce boycott, it formed a joint enterprise with the Senegalese government, called Bud Senegal. Bud Senegal grows vegetables using a virtually labor-free drip irrigation system whose plastic tubes individually water each plant continuously.

The Senegalese government paid for the system. The World Bank provided a loan, one of only three the bank made to private business in 1974. It's supposed to be a showcase development project.

All production is for Europe. It's flown there by jet. Senegalese don't have the money to buy what Bud makes, and few peasants were helped by getting jobs. Many were hurt when Bud, in laying out its plantation, uprooted the baobob trees that villages had been treating as common property. The trees had provided rope, building materials, fuel, and wind erosion protection. In 1974, as Senegalese starved, European governments reacted to a vegetable "glut" at home by buying up and destroying $53 million worth of produce.

In July 1977, the Senegalese government took over Bud Senegal. But beyond providing new high-level jobs for the country's elite, Bud Senegal's policies have not changed. Bud Antle still controls the export end of the business. And domestically, Bud Senegal is taking over the sale of small farmers' crops; half of all produce sold in the capital city is sold at Bud stands.

Meanwhile, the American parent firm has moved into Gambia, Nigeria, the Ivory Coast, and Mali and intends to expand into the rest of West Africa as well. It has announced plans to merge with the giant Cooke and Castle company (owner of

> the Dole pineapple business) to create a truly world-wide empire. West German, Italian, and Belgian agribusinesses are also showing interest in West Africa.
>
> The interest of companies like Bud gives a glimpse of the potential for food production in the Sahel.... [T]he region could increase its agricultural production sixfold to become a "bread-basket of Africa," thanks to extensive underground lakes and an excellent sunny growing season.
>
> Technology and weather do have some influence on the Sahel's food problems. It is an area of periodic drought, and the drought of the early 1970s was the most severe since 1910. The farmers do lack methods to conserve water, and do engage in over-grazing and over-cultivation that makes matters worse.
>
> But it is essentially the class structure of the Sahel countries, together with eager multinationals like Bud Antle, that breed short-sighted farming practices for windfall profits. Under these conditions, even such valuable inventions as drip irrigation can benefit the people very little. The most advanced agricultural technique can co-exist with the most miserable poverty.
>
> Source: *Dollars and Sense*, 1978, No. 33, pp. 4–5.

Several geographers such as David Harvey (1975) are making efforts to forge a theory of *imperialism* capable of explaining the dynamics of capitalism at both center and periphery, and capable also of including an analysis of class. In their view, it is insufficient to provide a picture of imperialism related only to the experiences of dependent underdeveloped countries. "International relations are not to be reduced to relations between the Western world (advanced) and the 'Third World' for the internal relations of the Western World occupy an essential place in those relations, and one that is qualitatively much more important" (Amin, 1973:5).

Now that broad critical surveys of the development literature have been completed, more scholars are using the dialectical historical method. The results are case studies, usually of nation states (Arrighi, 1970; Amin, 1973a; and Wolff, 1974). Detailed historical case studies are intended to increase our understanding of the underdevelopment process in poor and rich countries.

Underdevelopment-As-Process: The Colonial Division of Labor*

The argument that underdevelopment is a process is supported by Giovanni Arrighi's dialectical historical study on the proletarianization of the African peasantry in Rhodesia (1970). The article is a critique of W. Barber's (1961) use of Arthur Lewis's (1963) two-sector model for labor differentiation in development theory. Lewis advanced the thesis that in the "subsistence sector" of underdeveloped countries there is a surplus of labor often termed *disguised unemployment* by economists. This labor is thought to be surplus since part of the labor force could be taken away from the "subsistence economy" without reducing the usual productivity of the "subsis-

---

*This section is a slight modification of de Souza and Porter, 1974, pp. 47–52.

tence sector." This labor supply is regarded as "unlimited" provided "that average productivity in the subsistence sector does not increase, pushing up the conventional subsistence income" (Arrighi, 1970:198). Arrighi attempted to show that Lewis's model of economic development has far more limited application to the Rhodesian experience than Barber claimed.

Our interest in Arrighi's study is (1) in the details of the actions taken by the colonial government and the European settlers to insure the development of mines and European agriculture; (2) in the initial responsiveness of the African population to participate in the growing economy; and (3) in the way historical analysis reveals the weakness of statistical indices and conclusions drawn from them alone. A brief summary of Arrighi's main points follows:

Instead of starting off with a situation of normal labor abundance and ending with one of normal labor shortage, the Rhodesian capitalist sector seems to have moved in the opposite direction. From 1896 to 1903 real wages rose markedly and then became sticky so that by 1922 wages were lower than in 1904. The reason lies not in market forces, but in changes in the Rhodesian capitalist sector during the 1903–04 crisis. Before the crisis, production was oriented toward immediate speculative gains, especially from the gold fields. After the collapse of the speculative boom in London (1903) attention was directed toward enhancing the profitability of those enterprises which had survived the crisis.

In Rhodesia "the tradition of a subsistence wage" emerged—a wage fixed at a level that would support a single worker while he worked in the capitalist sector plus a small margin to meet urgent cash income requirements of his family, whose members continued to reside and support themselves on the reserve. No provision for retirement income was included in the subsistence wage, since the worker was supposed to spend his old age back on the reserve. Since changes in wages were not the equilibrating factors in the labor market, political mechanisms became crucial in closing the gap between labor need and supply. This was achieved in a number of ways.

Prior to 1904, the European farming sector was small and African farmers supplied food stuffs required by the mines. The Africans responded quickly to these opportunities for trade. Later, when the European farmers began to develop mixed farming and ranching, Africans were also quick to sell large numbers of cattle. They also derived income by hiring out bullocks to the mines for transport. These income-increasing responses were achieved through expanded farming and trade, not through hiring out labor.

The notion of "disguised unemployment" can be criticized since it tends to ignore the nonagricultural activities which Africans are often engaged in during the agriculturally slack season. House building, well digging, iron working, weaving, net making, carpentry—all these activities are essential although time consuming. Even such activities as discussing crops, weather, village relocation, or land disputes, which economists might classify as leisure, are vitally necessary.

Arrighi's study tries "to demonstrate [that] 'disguised unemployment' was itself the result of the process of capitalist development which steadily restructured and eventually disrupted 'traditional' African societies" (202). (At each point henceforth in this summary when we encounter an action on the part of the colonial power that had a consequence in the life of the indigenous people, we have begun the paragraph with a number. To the degree possible we have made the list of points chronological.)

1. British rule threw upper caste Ndebele men out of work, since it deprived them of their role of fighting and expropriating land and cattle. They became structurally unemployed rather than join the peasant sector in farming and livestock tending.

Underdevelopment-As-Process: The Colonial Division of Labor

> **THE NDEBELE**
>
> The Ndebele (or Matabele in English) are one of about 40 ethnic groups in Rhodesia. Their location in relation to other major ethnic groups is illustrated in the accompanying map. Unlike many African peoples, the Ndebele are divided into castes or classes. During the nineteenth century, the Ndebele were a strong military force, and had developed the rudiments of a nation.
>
>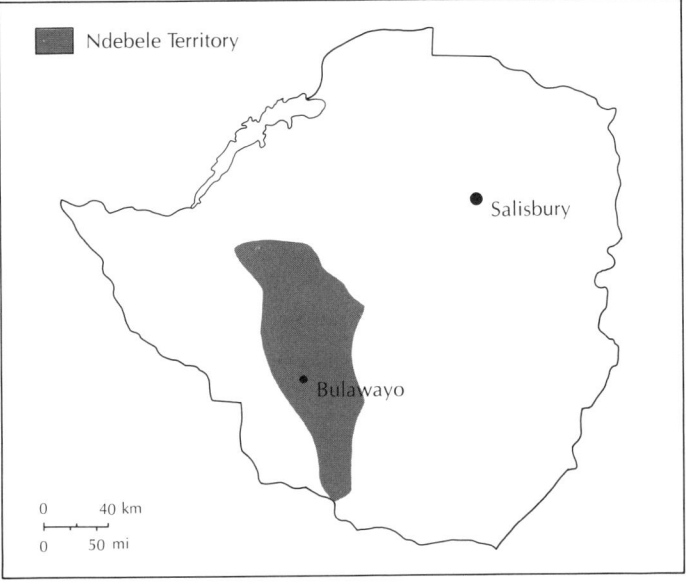

2. British rule also released the lower caste Ndebele who formerly had served the upper cast Ndebele.

3. Land was expropriated, but people were not moved from their ancestral lands. The people were needed where they were. Land without people was of no value to the Europeans at the time. "It would be very shortsighted policy to remove these natives to reserves, as their services may be of great value to future European occupants," noted the Native Affairs Committee of Enquiry (1911) (208).

4. Taxation was introduced to force Africans to earn cash. A hut tax of ten shillings was introduced in 1894. This was replaced in 1904 by a poll tax of one pound sterling. But taxation did not discriminate as to the way money was earned, so the effect was to increase and intensify agricultural production. Taxation, however, did have the desired effect in areas which were remote from mines and other areas of European development where African produce could be sold. Thus a spatial or locational discrimination forced some Africans into the wage-employment sector. At first, "payment in kind was accepted but it was soon discouraged in order to induce Africans to earn their tax by wage labour" (208).

5. In the early days of settlement, forced labor was used. Later this practice was largely abandoned as a result of the African Rebellions of 1896–97, though the Native Commissioners still resorted to it in an informal way even into the 1920s.

6. Land expropriation was the major measure responsible for the creation of Rhodesia's African wage-earning population. By 1902 more than three-quarters of the land had been expropriated, but this did not immediately restrict land available to Africans for cultivation. African farmers were "generally allowed to remain on their ancestral lands, upon payment of rent or commitment to supply labour services" (208). In other words, they entered a semifeudal status with the European landowners (Roder, 1964:51).

    In 1903, it was three times more profitable for an African farmer to participate in the Rhodesian economy by growing produce than selling his labor. Only in areas with structurally disguised unemployment (as for example among the Ndebele) did men participate in the wage employment sector. Indeed, so long as the capitalist agricultural sector did not expand parallel with the mining sector, prices for produce from African farmers would tend to rise, thus further discouraging Africans to seek wage employment. But political rather than market mechanisms were to be "the equilibrating factor in the African labour market" (200). The wage rate was to remain fixed by "the tradition of the subsistence wage."

    The low rate of African participation in the wage employment sector in the years before 1922 lies in the "discretionary" character of African participation in the money economy. People could earn money through the sale of produce. "The comparatively small effort-price of cash income earnable through the sale of produce was in fact the main factor restraining African participation in the labour market" (207). With an increasing need for African labor on European farms and in the mines, a series of actions by the government forced the labor into being.

7. In 1903, a Department of Agriculture was set up to assist European agriculture, and it expanded its technical work: distributing improved seeds and plants, boring water holes, and conducting agricultural experiments.

8. European farmers received financial assistance at subsidized rates.

9. In 1905, the major burden of taxation shifted from the European to the African population. (African share: 1904 equalled 27 percent, 1905 equalled 41 percent of a tax base that remained nearly at 453,000. The European share declined in the same period from 33 to 27 percent.)

10. In 1909 the British South Africa Company imposed a rent on unalienated land (land outside reserves, but not yet sold to Europeans); all Africans living on these lands had to pay a rent. In addition, European landowners exacted various grazing, dipping, and other fees from Africans living on their farms.

11. It became customary for European landowners to market the produce of their tenants, a practice which prevented these Africans from underselling the Europeans.

12. European-grown maize was a success and the capitalist sector had become largely self-sufficient by 1915. Production rose from 46,000 bags in 1904 to 1,001,000 bags in 1921; the effect of this increase in production was to depress grain prices (by 30 to 50 percent between 1903–04 and 1911–12), making it less economic for Africans to grow and sell it. The depressing effect on African participation in maize sales was increased by the fact that only 30 percent of African-owned land was within 40 kilometers of a railhead, compared with 75 percent of European-owned land. In general, beyond a 24-kilometer ox-wagon journey, it was not economic to produce grain for sale. This same displacement process would have occurred with regard to African and European-owned livestock, had not the external demand for

cattle brought on by World War I carried both groups through to 1920. Maize also made a comeback during the war years. A big slump in both maize and cattle prices came in 1921–23, "which radically altered the position of the African peasantry in the structure of the Rhodesian economy" (216). In 1920 the price was ten shillings per bag and Africans sold 198,000 bags. In 1921 the price was five shillings per bag and Africans, despite a good harvest, sold only 43,600 bags. An immediate effect of the slump in the produce market was to increase African participation in the labor market. Sale of produce, which accounted for 70 percent of African earned cash income in the early 1900s, accounted for less than 20 percent of such earnings by 1932. As Giovanni Arrighi emphasized: *"this change cannot be considered as merely a cyclical phenomenon. It rather was an 'irreversible' change in the sense that subsequent recoveries could not restore the previous position of the African peasantry vis-à-vis the capitalist economy"* (216).

13. Extraterritorial labor, largely from Zambia, Malawi, and Mozambique, made possible rapid capitalist developments in a transitional period in the first two decades of this century. By 1922, extraterritorial laborers accounted for 68 percent of the total work force. This kept wage levels low.

14. The "discretionary" cash requirements of earlier years had gradually become "necessary" ones. A decade of intense participation in the produce market significantly changed the African farmers' living requirements. These expanded to include "hoes, picks, cutlery, blankets, clothing, salt, beads, etc., with occasionally such luxuries as coffee, sugar, golden syrup, and corned beef" (211). In periods of falling incomes, farmers were compelled to find alternate ways to continue to enjoy their new necessities of life. One way was to seek wage work. Many of the articles demanded were substitutes for nonagricultural hand-crafted products formerly made by the farmers themselves in periods of non-agricultural work. "The African peasantry underwent an 'unlearning process' whereby they gradually lost their ability to produce nonagricultural goods" (212). Education became one of the new elements in the farmers' lives that assumed increasingly a necessary character. "[A]s wage employment became more and more a source of means of subsistence, expenditure on education also lost its discretionary nature, and was to become one of the major expenditure items in African families' budgets" (212).

    The slumps following 1921 and 1929 accelerated the movement of Africans into the reserves. The result was increased population pressure on the land, a shorter fallow period and, as a consequence, lower yields, which induced compensatory planting of larger acreages, thus reducing still further the fallow period. People began to find it "'impossible,' not just 'uneconomic'" (217) to produce a marketable surplus, and they began to seek wage employment in large numbers.

    Adjustments to these new conditions in African agriculture were reflected in the farmers turning increasingly to grade stock, but they did not shift to production of purely export crops, such as tobacco. They were in a poor position to invest in such a changeover to newly demanded crops. Before the slump of 1921 the good prices for cattle and maize discouraged cultivation of commercial crops and labor-saving investment. After the 1920 slump, the smallness of the surplus impeded change.

15. The insecurity of African wage labor in the European sector, however, led adult men to keep an interest in the land and kinship groups on the reserve, who increasingly came to depend on their remittances. Land fragmentation increased and traditional structures of land holding hampered innovation in farming techniques. Land con-

Tobacco estate near Salisbury, Rhodesia. Before Rhodesia became a rebel state in 1965, tobacco grown on European-owned farms was its main export crop. As a result of UN sanctions, production was cut by 50 percent and tobacco farmers were forced to diversify into other commodities. SOURCE: *Rhodesia Department of Information.*

These white-owned Mazoe citrus estates near Salisbury are dependent on cheap African labor and foreign markets. SOURCE: *Rhodesia Department of Information.*

solidation and centralization were resisted because it would undermine social cohesion. "[E]ither the family landholdings had to be fragmented, or the family itself" (218). An added problem was the Africans fear that "any success (in raising land productivity) [would] be a reason for depriving them of a portion of the Reserves set aside for them or a ground for refusing their demands, which [were] insistent, for an extension of the Reserves" (220).

16. The terms of the Land Apportionment Act (1931) barred Africans from purchasing land outside designated areas at a time when they might have done so. During the period 1931–41, 50,000 Africans moved to the reserves, while an equal or greater number moved there between 1941 and 1945.

17. By the 1930s the European farmers were in positions of political influence, and they reversed a previous government policy of nondiscrimination in commodity prices, replacing it with a two-price system for maize and for cattle which protected the small European producer.

18. The "effort-price" of African participation in the produce market increased because of increasing land pressure and a high rate of population growth. From 1936 to 1946 the rate was 2.7 percent per annum; from 1945 to 1956, it was 3.4 percent per annum. This forced the farmers increasingly to bring inferior land into cultivation. Further, higher rents and more stringent labor clauses on European-owned land forced other farmers onto the reserves. The proportion of Africans living on reserves rose from 54 percent in 1909 to 64 percent in 1922. Because poorer land was brought into production, average yields fell.

19. The "effort-price" also increased because of the increasingly unfavorable position of the African farmer vis-à-vis the capitalist sector. The capitalist sector: (a) tended to bring a short-term increase in African farmer per capita output; but (b) the Europeans appropriated much of the surplus in the form of rents, fees, and taxes; (c) it increased African dependence on purchase of goods from the capitalist sector; and (d) it substituted market uncertainty for ecological uncertainty for the African people.

20. Though considerable productive investment was made by African farmers in the form of carts, maize mills, and plows (440 plows in 1905 to 133,000 in 1945), one effect was to expand greatly the land a farmer cultivated. By 1926 overcrowding on the reserves was being noted. In 1943 the Department of Native Agriculture estimated that 62 out of 98 reserves were overpopulated, and of those remaining, 19 were in or dangerously close to tsetse fly zones and not suitable for cattle keeping.

21. From this point on, market forces worked to widen the gap between African and European producers and only the latter had sufficient surpluses to enable them to reinvest, innovate, and increase their productivity. From the 1920s onward African participation in the wage-employment sector increased whether real wages were increasing or not. "[D]isguised unemployment in the peasant sector was no longer due to a lack of incentives to apply unutilized labor-time to agricultural production within the peasant sector, but to a structural disequilibrium between means of production and subsistence requirements of the peasantry" (221).

Arrighi continued the analysis through World War II up to 1962. After the war, although real wages continued to rise, employment opportunities did not. The increase in real wages was mainly a result of upgrading and stabilizing African labor. It replaced the tradition of providing a wage for a single man whose family lived on the reserve to which he would return unpensioned in his old age, with a wage intended to support the worker and his family, and to provide for his eventual retirement. This upgrading of labor occurred mainly in manufacturing, transportation, and communication types of employment, not in agricultural employment. By the later 1940s "[f]oreign controlled oligopolies, characterized by considerable 'international mobility,' had come to dominate important sectors of the economy (mining and secondary industries)" (225). The recession of the late 1950s caused a fall in rates of accumulation and labor demand, and an outflow of investment capital from Rhodesia.

A

B

Foreign controlled companies dominate mining and manufacturing industries in Rhodesia. (A) Asbestos mine, Pangani. The picture shows tailing dumps and the processing plant. Today Rhodesia is the world's largest producer of crysotile asbestos, and asbestos is the leading mineral export. SOURCE: *Rhodesia Department of Information*. (B) Bata shoe factory in Gwelo. In Rhodesia wages for African industrial workers are set below the poverty line. SOURCE: *Rhodesia Department of Information*.

This summary has served at least two useful purposes. One is that it has carried the reader through the intricate story of political and economic actions that established the hegemony of the capitalist sector in Rhodesia, and enabled it to create a low paid, proletarian labor force to serve the needs of the capitalist sector. The list of actions, *i.e.*, forced labor, taxes, land alienations, land rents, expulsions of Africans from alienated lands, subsidies for European farmers through extension services, provision of transport facilities and agricultural credit, marketing controls, use of extraterritorial labor, and introduction of marketing controls including discriminating dual pricing systems, illustrates the manner in which the European capitalist sector served its own ends. These actions, as well as others, operated in Kenya and in most other colonies which experienced European settlement.

The other purpose has been to show how a careful historical account helps one to understand the underdevelopment process. Such an understanding is unlikely to emerge if the researcher relies mainly on statistical indices, such as wage employment and wage levels, and their changes through time. Reliance on such indices can lead to unwarranted conclusions, if unsupported by inquiry into the underlying economic, social, political, demographic, and geographical processes which created the conditions summarized by the indices.

SUMMARY

In this chapter we considered the question of underdevelopment in Third World countries. Underdevelopment often is defined on the basis of statistical index numbers and on the basis of distinguishing characteristics. To define underdeveloped countries on the basis of GNP per capita is misleading. For example, there is no relationship between level of income and social development. Ancient Egypt had a highly developed culture and a low average income. Moreover, GNP per capita hides wide disparities in individual incomes. Kuwait has the highest level of GNP per capita in the world, but most of the income is concentrated in the hands of a few very rich people.

Dissatisfaction with the use of single economic measures of underdevelopment has led some scholars to list typical characteristics of Third World countries. These typical characteristics (overpopulation, lack of resources, capital shortage) are often cited as causes of underdevelopment. We concluded that they may be important symptoms, but not causes of underdevelopment.

In this chapter, we explored several models that geographers have used for the understanding of underdevelopment. These included the ideas of a "stagnant, traditional society," economic and social dualism, and Rostow's Stages of Economic Growth. We argued that such models have in some ways obscured important aspects of underdevelopment.

We suggested that underdevelopment is a *process* not a condition. People in underdeveloped countries are kept poor because they are controlled by an artificial world division of labor and because they are ruled by elites who benefit from the way things are. Since the view that underdevelopment is a process is opposite to traditional views, we ended the chapter with a case study of the colonial division of labor in Rhodesia.

DISCUSSION QUESTIONS

1. Discuss theories of underdevelopment, and select one which gives, in your opinion, the best explanation.
2. Describe and evaluate Rostow's stages of economic growth.
3. Is per capita income a reliable index of progress in development? Why or why not?
4. Why are poor people poor?
5. Underdeveloped countries must generate most of their own development. Do you agree?

6. Discuss: The most pressing problem for poor countries is to eliminate the development gap.
7. Discuss: Rostow's theory of economic growth "attributes a history to the developed countries but denies all history to the underdeveloped ones" (Frank).
8. Write an essay on the world view in Western geography.
9. Write an essay on the colonial organization of space.
10. Some degree of dualism is present in virtually every country. Discuss with reference to the United States.
11. Is the state of high development of some countries a cause of the underdevelopment of others?
12. Economic development is not primarily an economic but a political and social process. Discuss.
13. Write an essay on difficulties of economic development in one underdeveloped country.

SUGGESTED READINGS

General Statements on Underdevelopment and Development

Baran, P., *The Political Economy of Growth.* New York: Monthly Review Press, 1962.

Barratt Brown, M., *The Economics of Imperialism.* Harmondsworth, England: Penguin Books, Ltd., 1974.

Galbraith, J. K., *Economic Development.* Cambridge, Mass.: Harvard University Press, 1964.

Heilbroner, R. L., *The Great Ascent.* New York: Harper and Row Publishers, 1963.

Higgins, B., *Economic Development: Principles, Problems and Policies.* New York: Norton, 1968.

Lewis, W. A., *The Theory of Economic Growth.* London: George Allen Unwin, 1955.

Myint, H., *The Economics of the Developing Countries.* London: Hutchinson, 1964.

Szentes, T., *The Political Economy of Underdevelopment.* Budapest: Akademiai Kiadó, 1971.

Reviews of the Concept of Underdevelopment

Amin, S., *Accumulation on a World Scale.* New York: Monthly Review Press, 1973.

Frank, A. G., *Capitalism and Underdevelopment in Latin America.* New York: Monthly Review Press, 1969.

Griffin, K., *Underdevelopment in Spanish America.* London: George Allen Unwin, 1969.

Rodney, W., *How Europe Underdeveloped Africa.* Dar es Salaam: Tanzania Publishing House and Bogle-L'Overture Publications, 1972.

Suggested Readings

Cross-section of the Literature of Underdevelopment and Modernization in Geography

Buchanan, K. M., "The Third World—Its Emergence and Contours," *New Left Review,* **18** (1963):5–23.

Brookfield, H. C., "On One Geography and a Third World," *Transactions,* Institute of British Geographers (1973), No. 56, pp. 1–20.

———, *Interdependent Development.* Pittsburgh: University of Pittsburgh Press, 1975.

Connell, J., "The Geography of Development," *Area,* **3** (1971):259–265.

Gould P., "A Note on Research into the Diffusion of Development," *Journal of Modern African Studies,* **2** (1964):123–125.

——— "Tanzania 1920–63: The Spatial Impress of the Modernization Process," *World Politics,* **22** (1970):149–170.

Harvey, D., "The Geography of Capitalist Accumulation: A Reconstruction of the Marxist Theory," *Antipode,* **7** (1975):9–21.

Riddell, J. B., *The Spatial Dynamics of Modernization in Sierra Leone: Structure, Diffusion and Response.* Evanston: Northwestern University Press, 1970.

Slater, D., "Contribution to a Critique of Development Geography," *Canadian Journal of African Studies,* **8** (1974):325–354.

Soja, E. W., *The Geography of Modernization in Kenya.* Syracuse: Syracuse University Press, 1968.

Soja, E. W. and R. J. Tobin, "The Geography of Modernization: Paths, Patterns, and Processes of Spatial Change in Developing Countries" in Ronald Brunner and Gary Brewer (eds.), *Political Development and Change.* New York: Free Press, 1975.

International Trade and Aid

KEY TERMS

- aid
- capital-output ratio
- comparative advantages
- Development Assistance Committee (DAC)
- debt payments
- European Economic Community (EEC)
- Engel's Law
- factor endowments approach
- free trade
- Generalized System of Preferences (GSP)
- General Agreement on Tariffs and Trade (GATT)
- group of 77
- infant industry
- International Monetary Fund (IMF)
- import substitution
- Lomé Agreement
- multinational
- New International Economic Order (NIEO)
- non-tariff barriers
- Official Development Assistance (ODA)
- Organization of Petroleum Exporting Countries (OPEC)
- price instability
- production-possibilities curve
- productivity theory
- profit repatriation
- regional integration
- structural rigidity
- export earnings stabilization scheme (STABEX)
- tariffs
- terms of trade
- trade
- transnational system
- United Nations Conference on Trade and Development (UNCTAD)
- World Bank

11

11

The most important external relationship of underdeveloped countries is *trade*. But the role of international trade in the development of underdeveloped countries is a subject of controversy. The traditional view, based on classical economics and the history of developed countries, is that international trade can benefit every society. Some observers, without contradicting this view, argue that the gains of trade are unlikely to be significant among underdeveloped countries because of their heavy dependence on a few specialized primary products that are highly vulnerable to changes in international demand and prices. A more radical view is that international trade underdevelops poor nations, because it takes place at their expense. Development of poor nations will be enhanced by a strategy that increases individual and collective self-reliance and reduces dependence on developed countries.

A second contact between developed and underdeveloped countries is the flow of resources—capital, labor, knowledge, food, commonly called *aid*. Like trade, the aid relationship is highly controversial. For example, liberals argue in favor of official government aid on the assumption that aid promotes increased welfare in underdeveloped countries. Conservatives and radicals, from quite different viewpoints, argue against official development assistance. Conservatives believe that aid is a system of doles that damages the development prospects of its recipients. Radicals believe that "aid" is imperialism. Critics of aid, however, generally agree that development, if it is to be sustained, is essentially an indigenous process.

In this chapter, we argue that international trade can promote the development of underdeveloped countries, but only if they get a fairer share of world markets for their exports (Figure 11.1). We also argue that international aid acts as a drag on development. In the discussion, we first indicate the traditional case for international trade; and second, suggest some of the reasons for the failure of trade to act as generator of development in the Third World. Thereafter, we examine the possibility of effecting a reversal of the worsening trade situation for the underdeveloped countries. The final section is devoted to a discussion of "aid" as an instrument for development.

The Apapa Wharves, part of the port of Lagos, Nigeria, suggest that trade is the most important element linking underdeveloped countries with the world. SOURCE: G. Gerster for *World Bank Group.*

FIGURE 11.1 Unjust terms of trade prevent the poor nations from developing (cartoonist Claudius). SOURCE: *Development Forum,* December 1975, Vol. 3, No. 9, p. 7.

OBJECTIVES

By the end of this chapter you should be able:

1. To discuss the benefits to be derived from the international exchange of goods and services.
2. To outline a simple Ricardian model of trade.
3. To examine the view that the world division of labor is biased against underdeveloped countries.
4. To describe the trade structure of underdeveloped countries.
5. To account for commodity price instability.
6. To present the theoretical causes for the decline in the terms of trade for primary products.
7. To indicate problems of import substitution.
8. To suggest strategies for improving the trade position of underdeveloped countries.
9. To state the avowed purposes of aid.
10. To examine the view that foreign aid is ineffective as an instrument for development.

The Conventional Case for Trade

Most nations do not produce all the goods they need. They must, therefore, trade with others. An underdeveloped country must import machinery, building materials, and other capital goods to increase income and raise production. And in years of crop failure, it must import food. These imports must be paid for. Foreign aid may be a short-term solution, but it will not be enough. The only way out is for the underdeveloped country in question to finance imports for development with income from exports.

A need for foreign goods, however, gives no indication as to how far a country can rely on international trade. The decision to engage in trade depends on the possibility of exchanging domestically produced goods for foreign goods. If this possibility exists, then any nation, even one that is self-sufficient, can benefit from participating in trade and specializing in response to the international market. According to traditional theorists, the potential gains from trade may be divided into two categories, those which improve the allocation of resources and those which lead to an increase in the quantity of available resources. The former are direct or static, once-for-all gains postulated by the theory of *comparative advantage*. The latter are indirect or cumulative gains postulated by *productivity theory*.

The Conventional Case for Trade

Direct Gains from Trade

Theory of Comparative Advantage The theory of comparative advantage developed by eighteenth and nineteenth century English economists—notably David Ricardo—describes how the people of, say, two countries benefit from the free flow of trade between them. It asserts that countries will export the goods they can produce at the lowest relative cost. For example, Country A specializes in the export of raisins because it can produce them at less cost compared to other goods than Country B, and Country B exports paper because it can be produced at less cost than other goods. Raisins may be cheaper than paper in both countries, but the cost difference is wider in Country A than in Country B. To explain the structure of foreign trade of a particular country, we must identify its comparative advantage, which involves studying its endowment of natural and human-made resources.

Natural and Human-Made Resources Resource differences between countries result in differences in their comparative advantage. One country is rich in iron ore, and another has tremendous oil deposits. Some countries have populations large enough to support industrial complexes, whereas others do not. People are not only a natural resource, they are also a precious human-made resource with differential skills. One country has a large number of workers adept at running modern machinery, and another has an abundance of scientists and engineers specializing in research-laden products. An important part of a nation's capital is embodied in its labor force skill, but another part is embodied in its physical equipment that has been created by past output. Some countries have a large number of roads, power stations, factories, and office buildings, whereas others do not.

A Simple Model To show how a difference in natural and human-made resources can lead to international trade, consider a classical labor-cost model like the one used by Ricardo early in the nineteenth century. The model excludes economies of scale and ignores transport costs. It assumes *free trade*, full employment of productive resources, and that technology and tastes are the same everywhere. To make things even easier, it assumes that there are only two countries, A and B, and these two countries produce only two commodities, coal and corn.

Countries A and B are the same in every way except one. Both countries have 120 person-days of labor at their disposal. Both countries require two person-days of labor to produce a ton of corn, and they have enough arable land to employ all their workers in corn farming. In Country A, however, coal deposits are much nearer the surface than in Country B. As a result, Country A requires only one person-day of labor to mine a ton of coal, whereas Country B needs four person-days.

We see that if Country A decided only to grow corn or only to mine coal, then it could produce either 60 tons of corn or 120 tons of coal. It is also clear that Country A could produce both corn and coal by choosing from various production opportunities, as Table 11.1 shows. Each opportunity point represents a mutually exclusive combination of corn and coal. Thus if Country A selects any one combination, it must reject all other combinations. The opportunity points in Table 11.1 are graphed in Figure 11.2. The output of coal is plotted on the horizontal axis and the output of corn is plotted on the vertical axis. The sloping line *AE* connecting the various points on the graph is called the *production-possibilities curve*. Without international trade, Country A would have to select one combination of corn and coal.

TABLE 11.1 Production-possibilities schedule for Country A

Opportunity Points	Corn	Coal
A	60	0
B	45	30
C	30	60
D	15	90
E	0	120

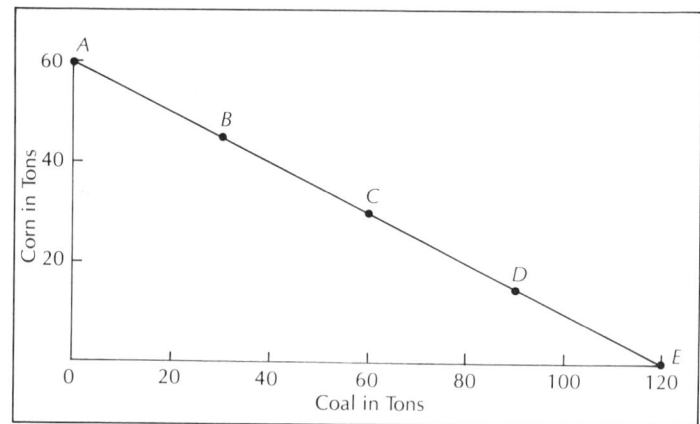

FIGURE 11.2 Production-possibilities curve for Country A.

Table 11.2 and Figure 11.3 describe the production-possibilities schedule and curve for Country B. Note that the maximum output of corn is the same as in Country A because both countries have the same amount of labor and they are equally efficient in growing corn. But maximum coal output in Country B is smaller than in Country A because its mines are deeper and therefore more expensive to operate. In the absence of international trade, Country B would have to select some combination of coal and corn along its production-possibilities curve.

Suppose that Country A and Country B are no longer isolated, and that they are now allowed to trade with one another. An opportunity for trade creates a

TABLE 11.2 Production-possibilities schedule for Country B

Opportunity Points	Corn	Coal
A_1	60	0
B_1	45	7.5
C_1	30	15
D_1	15	22.5
E_1	0	30

The Conventional Case for Trade

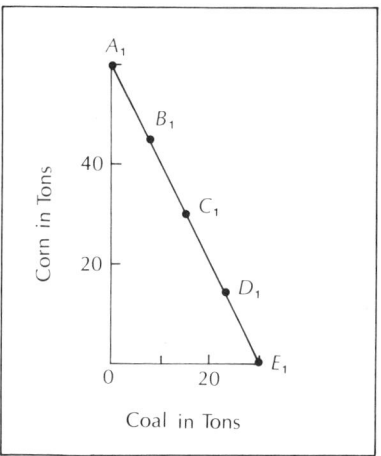

FIGURE 11.3 Production-possibilities curve for Country B.

single market, and a common price for coal comes into being. Let this new price for coal be less than the previous price in Country B, but more than it was in Country A. Country B can now obtain a ton of coal without giving up so much corn as in the past when it had to produce coal domestically. It can now specialize in growing corn and use some of its corn to buy coal from Country A. Similarly, Country A can now obtain more corn for its coal. It can now specialize in mining coal and use some of its coal to buy corn from Country B.

Figure 11.4 illustrates one possible rearrangement of production where the common price for coal is set at one ton of corn for one ton of coal. The left hand triangle is the production-possibilities curve for Country A, and the "upside down" triangle is the production-possibilities curve for Country B. Before trade, when each country was confined to its own production-possibilities curve, Country A produced 60 tons of coal and 30 tons of corn, and Country B produced 22.5 tons of coal and 15 tons of corn. After trade is allowed both countries can rearrange production and consumption to mutual advantage. Country A can specialize in coal production and

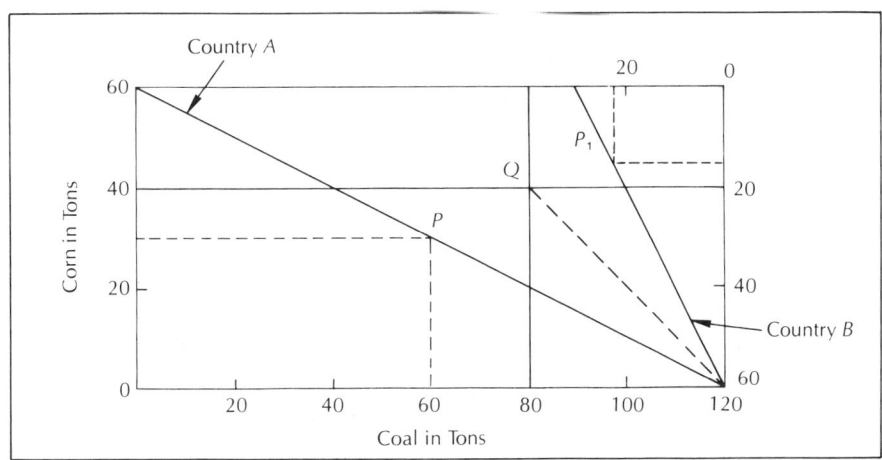

FIGURE 11.4 Trade between Country A and Country B.

mine 120 tons and Country B can specialize in corn production and grow 60 tons. Reading from the graph in Figure 11.4, we see that Country A now consumes 80 tons of coal and exports 40 tons to buy corn, and Country B now consumes 20 tons of corn and exports 40 tons to buy coal. Country A's consumption shifts from P to Q, and Country B's consumption shifts from P_1 to Q.

According to this simple Ricardian model, both countries enjoy a higher level of consumption than they did before trade. Moreover, trade has enlarged world output of coal and corn by allowing both countries to specialize. Before trade, coal output was 82.5 tons (60 tons for Country A plus 22.5 tons for Country B). With trade coal output increases to 120 tons. Before trade, corn output was 45 tons (30 tons for Country A plus 15 tons for Country B). With trade, corn output increases to 60 tons. This increase in output leads to a fundamental principle in orthodox trade theory: *free trade* is best, because it allocates economic tasks to maximize world output and income (see box).

MODERN TRADE THEORY

Modern orthodox theorists consider Ricardo's two-country, two-product, labor-cost model as too simple. A major criticism is that it emphasizes one factor of production, labor. Modern trade theory, much of which is derived from work by two Swedish economists, Eli Heckscher (1919) and Bertil Ohlin (1933), allows for several factors of production—land, labor, capital, and entrepreneurship—and thereby shows how trade arises from international differences in factor endowments. One country may have more abundant labor than another, but few machines and land. As a result of differences in factor supplies, countries will vary in their ability to produce the many goods they want to consume and will benefit from trade. In brief, the Heckscher-Ohlin *factor endowments approach* to trade theory predicts that a country should specialize in the production of goods that make the lightest demands on its scarce factors of production. It should export its specialities in order to obtain goods it is ill-equipped to make. For example, Switzerland, well-endowed with machines and skilled labor but little land, exports watches and scientific instruments and imports raw materials and foodstuffs.

Indirect Gains from Trade

Comparative advantage theory shows that trading partners benefit directly from the exchange of goods and from specialization. In addition to these static benefits, however, *productivity theory* postulates dynamic gains from free trade. Wider markets and increased specialization of production that result from trade may have the effect of encouraging technological innovation and raising labor skills. Trade may also create new industries and higher productivity. In these ways, trade should not only provide a country with a range of goods better than the best it can produce, but also stimulate economic growth.

Costs of Protection

All orthodox trade theories illustrate the same proposition: Free trade is best because it maximizes world economic output. They also show that trade, which is a substitute for *factor movements,* benefits each participating nation. It follows directly that any deviation from free trade will reduce production, leaving less to go around. And yet, many countries, especially rich industrial countries, have had a long history of constructing barriers to trade. Barriers to trade include *protective tariffs* (import duties), *quotas,* and *commodity agreements.*

What are some of the major arguments for *tariffs?* We hear some fallacious arguments, one of the most common of which is the "cheap foreign labor" argument that contradicts the principle of comparative advantage. It suggests that a country like the United States with its high union wages must protect itself against a country like Brazil with its low-paid workers. Other arguments appeal to national gain and are based on sound grounds. One argument asserts that a country with market power can improve its *terms of trade* with a tax that forces down the price at which other countries sell to it. Another argument is that tariffs may be used to divert demand from foreign to domestic goods in order to shift a country's employment problem onto foreign nations. Still another argument is that tariffs may be used to protect an "infant industry" which is less efficient than a well established industry in another country. Although there is merit in these arguments for protective tariffs, traditional theorists argue their use sacrifices efficiency, invites retaliation, and reduces world output. They recommend other approaches to attain desired goals. For example, they suggest that if there are grounds for protecting an infant industry until it has grown large enough to take advantage of economies of scale, protection could be given through a subsidy rather than through a protective tariff.

Direct and indirect benefits from trade are based on the uneven international distribution of resources. Each country's endowment of natural resources and humanmade stock of skill and physical infrastructure equips it to produce some goods more efficiently than others. Trade based on comparative advantage means that resources are allocated in the most efficient manner. Tariffs and quotas are barriers that impede the flow of trade and sacrifice efficiency.

Limited Gains from Trade

Standard trade theory states that in a *laissez-faire* environment, everyone playing the international trade game benefits from specialization and exchange. Beyond indicating that free trade is efficient, the theory neglects to consider whether it is fair. The current structure of world trade which has been in force over the past 200 years has left most Third World countries poor (low per capita income, low living standards) and promoted great wealth in Europe and lands of overseas European settlement (North America and Oceania). The purpose of this section is to consider some of the reasons for the failure of international trade to act as a generator of development in most countries of the underdeveloped world.

The World Division of Labor

Implicit in the early nineteenth century argument for free trade was the notion that "what was good for Britain was good for the world." Free trade was established with inequality between nations. Free trade and competition was agreeable to Britain only after it had become the world's most technically advanced industrial country. Until the middle of the nineteenth century, many of Britain's infant industries developed behind the protection of tariff walls. The cotton mills of Lancashire, for example, owed their preeminence to the near annihilation of the Indian textile industry. From 1815 to 1832 "prohibitive duties ranging from 10 to 20, 30, 50, 100 and 1000 percent were levied on articles from India" (Clairmonte, 1960:86).

Having established an initial advantage over other manufacturers, Britain repealed the Navigation Laws in 1849, and threw open its markets to the rest of the world. Other countries were instructed or lured to do the same. The pattern of specialization that resulted was obvious. Britain, the first industrial power—the "workshop of the world"—concentrated on manufacturing goods and exporting them in exchange for primary products. Although many countries gained from the application of an apparently "fair" system of free trade, none gained more than Britain.

The only way for other countries to break out of this artificial division of labor was to interfere with free trade. In the 1870s, the United States and Germany challenged British hegemony, and adopted protectionist policies. France and a few other European countries with embryo industries did the same. Underdeveloped countries, however, failed to escape from the artificial form of specialization. Even newly independent Latin American countries that could begin to develop their own economies made no attempt to break out of the artificial division of labor. It was not in the interests of their ruling groups to do so; they depended on exports to Britain, and on British and, ultimately, on United States support for their rule.

In underdeveloped countries the world division of labor bred an "enclave" type of development (Figure 11.5). Although these "enclaves" or "islands of development" brought gains of a static nature, they did not generate widespread growth and development. A number of factors support this contention. First, the capital, techniques, and skilled personnel were imported, and the recipient economy provided the unskilled labor. (But as we saw earlier in the case of Rhodesia, the creation of an indigenous labor force to serve the needs of the export economy helped to underdevelop the rest of the economy). Second, profits from the sale of primary products were repatriated. Third, income generated in the enclaves tended to be diverted to the purchase of imported luxury goods rather than local products. Fourth, there was only a limited diffusion of skills and production techniques from the export to the traditional sector.

These four factors apply mainly to underdeveloped countries that experienced capital-intensive development of mines and plantations. But in other countries peasants were drawn into export production by large chartered trading companies (e.g. Royal Niger Company). These enclaves did not generate widespread dynamic gains either; peasant export production was not usually accompanied by any notable increase in labor specialization and productivity per person hour. Cocoa farmers in Ghana and rice farmers in Thailand, for example, responded to new

Limited Gains from Trade

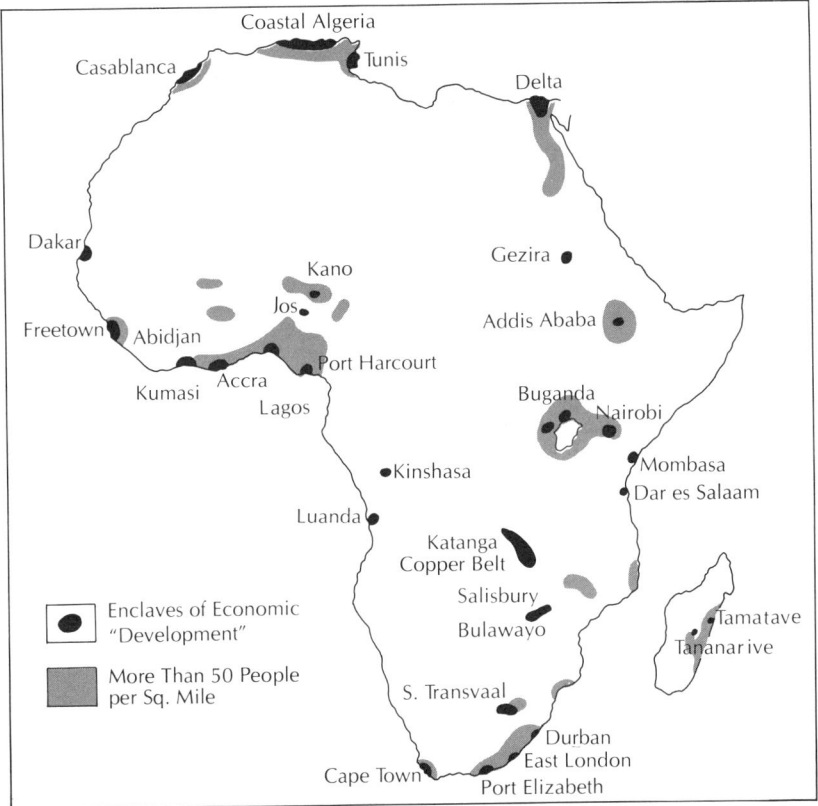

FIGURE 11.5 "Islands of development" in Africa.

market opportunities by either extending the amount of land under cultivation or farming the existing land more intensively.

Structure of Trade

Over the years relatively little has changed in the classic division of labor between primary and secondary producers. As a result, economies of Third World countries remain heavily dependent on the export of primary commodities (Figure 11.6). Thus, primary products amounted to two-thirds of the export earnings of underdeveloped countries in 1973, half the value of primary commodities exported by developed countries. Table 11.3 shows that more than 50 Third World countries gain half or more of their trading receipts from agricultural commodities, and in more than 30 of these, the bulk of the revenues comes from three or fewer products.

Exports of underdeveloped countries are usually concentrated in one or two products, and they also are sold in few foreign markets. Developed capitalist countries are the most important export market. Roughly 75 percent of the exports of underdeveloped countries are sold in developed market economies. Sales to other

The chief characteristic of the export trade of underdeveloped countries is the importance of one or two commodities. (A) Forty-seven percent of Ghana's export earnings come from unprocessed cocoa. SOURCE: *Chocolate Manufacturers Association*. (B) Coffee accounts for fifty-nine percent of Uganda's export earnings. SOURCE: *Brooke Bond Oxo Ltd*. (C) Meat exports are of considerable importance in the national economies of Paraguay and Uruguay. SOURCE: *Brooke Bond Oxo Ltd*. (D) Liberia is overwhelmingly dependent on export of iron ore. SOURCE: *Bethlehem Steel*.

underdeveloped countries, even neighboring countries, are small. In return for primary commodities, underdeveloped countries import manufactured goods, particularly engineering products. Some 70 percent of their imports are purchased from developed capitalist countries.

Limited Gains from Trade

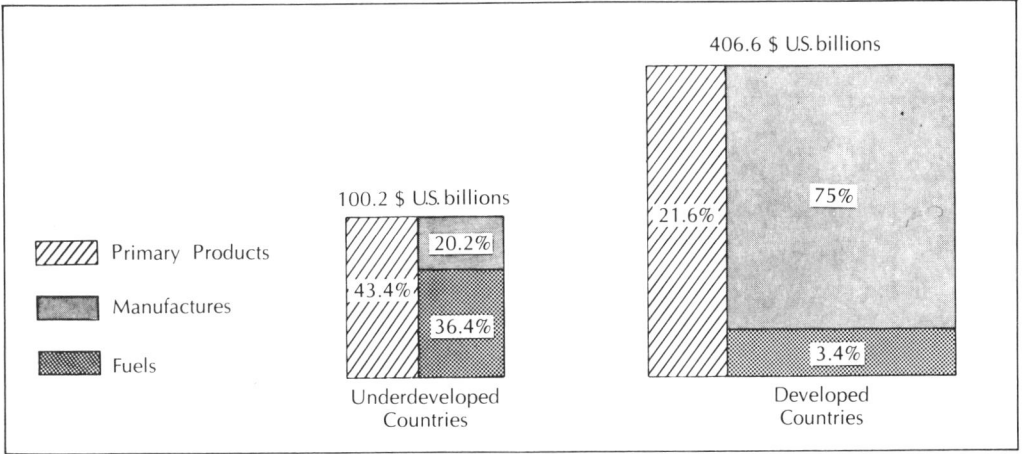

FIGURE 11.6 Developed market economy and underdeveloped market economy countries' exports, 1973. SOURCE: *UNCTAD* TD/B/530 Add 1; *U. N. Yearbook Int. Trade Stat.* 1972–1973.

On first thought, it may seem that the division of labor between developed and underdeveloped countries is fair. Economic growth in developed countries ensures a greater demand for commodities from the underdeveloped world. From growing export earnings underdeveloped countries can import manufactured goods to increase their rates of employment and to build up their industrial sectors. In reality, this integration between the developed and the underdeveloped world creates a widening gap between the trading nations, weighted against the underdeveloped world.

Fluctuations of Commodity Prices

The argument that international economic transactions are biased against underdeveloped countries would lose much of its strength if export prices for primary commodities were subject to small year-to-year fluctuations. Instead of being able to count on a steady and reliable flow of earnings underdeveloped countries find the prices for their major exports subject to large and sometimes disastrous changes (Figure 11.7). For example, sugar prices shot up to record levels during the 1973–74 economic boom, and then collapsed dramatically. Sugar rose to $1.45 a kilogram in 1974, but sold for 22¢ a kilogram in 1978. Such price instability makes it extremely difficult for primary producers, excluding oil producing states, to predict their future revenues and to plan development programs.

Fluctuations and Trends of Export Prices: The Tanzanian Case Like many underdeveloped countries, Tanzania has experienced declines and large fluctuations in prices for its major agricultural export commodities. Five crops—cotton, coffee, sisal, cashew nuts, and tea—comprised 63.5 percent of Tanzania's exports in 1960 and 44.3 percent in 1971. (Trends in volume, value, and prices may be seen in Table 11.4.) During this period, cotton production increased significantly,

TABLE 11.3 Underdeveloped countries arranged by share of agricultural products in total exports (1959–60 and 1969–70) or nearest available

Agricultural Goods			Three Main Agricultural Products		
	Share of Total Exports			Share of Total Exports	
Country	1959–60	1969–70	Country	1959–60	1969–70
1 Gambia	99.9	99.2	Gambia	96.3	98.9
2 Sudan	99.9	98.9	Guadeloupe	96.3	96.0
3 Cambodia	96.7	98.7	Mauritius	98.7	94.8
4 Mauritius	99.8	98.5	Reunion	85.6	91.2
5 Ethiopia	93.3	98.2	Somalia	81.9	87.8
6 Sri Lanka	98.3	98.0	Ethiopia	76.3	86.5
7 Malawi	98.3	96.3	Sri Lanka	89.3	85.2
8 Chad	94.0	96.1	Ecuador	90.9	83.7
9 Guadeloupe	96.3	96.9	Uganda	81.5	81.6
10 Upper Volta	91.8	96.0	S. Vietnam	91.7	81.4
11 Niger	99.5	94.6	Cuba	84.9	80.8
12 Somalia	92.7	94.1	Niger	91.8	80.4
13 Martinique	97.5	93.9	Ghana	81.4	80.0
14 Ecuador	98.5	92.7	Chad	81.4	79.8
15 Ivory Coast	97.2	92.4	Uruguay	70.9	78.4
16 Reunion	85.6	91.5	Ivory Coast	90.5	78.3
17 Uruguay	95.2	91.4	Malawi	75.4	77.4
18 Burma	94.6	91.3	Sudan	75.2	77.3
19 Paraguay	92.1	91.2	Martinique	84.9	75.8
20 Mali	96.3	91.1	Dom. Republic	70.9	72.5
21 Dahomey	95.2	90.3	Burma	77.2	71.4
22 Uganda	90.7	90.1	Colombia	78.3	76.4
23 Mozambique	89.6	88.7	Panama	91.9	67.4
24 Dom. Republic	92.0	87.5	Cambodia	84.6	64.9
25 Cuba	91.8	87.0	Cameroon	61.9	63.0
26 Argentina	55.1	85.4	Costa Rica	84.9	61.8
27 S. Vietnam	96.0	84.7	Egypt	77.7	60.5
28 Madagascar	91.0	83.8	Honduras	77.9	60.0
29 Honduras	93.6	82.8	El Salvador	86.6	60.0
30 Nicaragua	95.9	82.1	Mali	73.7	58.8
31 Cameroon	76.9	81.5	Philippines	69.1	58.5
32 Ghana	83.3	80.8	Rwanda	14.3	57.1
33 Costa Rica	95.8	80.0	Togo	77.3	54.6
34 Colombia	79.6	78.6	Congo	76.8	52.5
35 Brazil	89.2	78.2	Syria	61.3	52.3
36 Afghanistan	87.9	77.9	Senegal	85.7	51.7
37 Tanzania	86.8	76.9	Paraguay	55.7	51.9
38 Panama	99.6	75.3	Guatemala	85.1	51.4
39 Syria	81.6	75.3	Upper Volta	82.1	51.4
40 Kenya	86.6	74.8	Kenya	53.5	49.6
41 Guatemala	96.1	73.3	Malaysia	60.9	49.4

TABLE 11.3 (continued)

Agricultural Goods			Three Main Agricultural Products		
	Share of Total Exports			Share of Total Exports	
Country	1959–60	1969–70	Country	1959–60	1969–70
42 Thailand	91.1	72.6	Barbados	95.0	48.7
43 Philippines	85.4	70.7	Afghanistan	61.0	47.7
44 El Salvador	94.8	68.4	Brazil	67.6	46,0
45 Egypt	83.1	68.3	C.A.R.	72.1	42.8
46 Congo	84.2	68.2	Guyana	61.0	42.0
47 Senegal	91.4	64.6	Tanzania	55.0	39.3
48 Malaysia	75.6	61.6	Angola	51.7	37.9
49 Rwanda	18.8	61.2	Dahomey	85.0	36.8
50 Togo	96.2	60.1	Indonesia	52.3	35.0
51 Barbados	98.3	59.9	Gabon	60.7	33.2
52 Morocco	54.5	57.6	Mozambique	56.0	32.3
53 Cyprus	48.0	56.7	Pakistan	57.2	30.4
54 Angola	75.4	54.3	Liberia	50.3	18.8
55 C.A.R.	85.4	53.5	Nigeria	54.1	18.1
56 Mexico	63.7	51.2	Mauritania	69.3	3.8
57 Indonesia	61.2	48.3			
58 Guyana	70.7	45.4			
59 Peru	52.2	44.1			
60 Jordan	59.6	44.1			
61 Pakistan	73.8	40.9			
62 Singapore	62.7	40.5			
63 Lebanon	59.1	37.2			
64 Tunisia	64.7	36.0			
65 Gabon	61.7	33.6			
66 Nigeria	91.1	27.8			
67 Liberia	51.7	22.9			
68 Mauritania	69.9	9.3			

SOURCE: Adapted from GATT, *International Trade*, 1973–74, Table F.

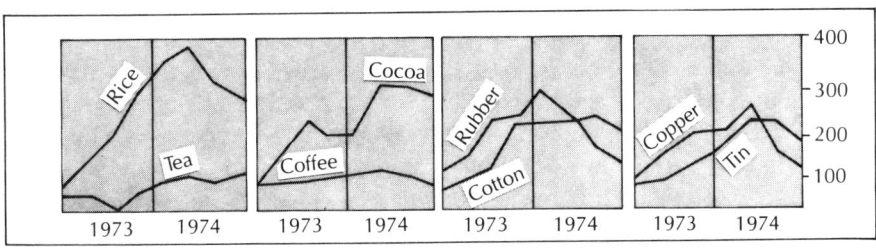

FIGURE 11.7 Commodity price fluctuations (Quarterly Indices Market Prices—1972 = 100). SOURCE: *UNCTAD Monthly Commodity Price Bulletins.*

Sugar beet arriving at the Monitor Sugar Company factory in Bay City, Michigan. Sugar comes from sugar beet produced in temperate areas of Europe and North America, and from sugar cane produced in tropical areas such as Jamaica, India, Fiji, Mauritius and East Africa. Rich countries growing sugar beet and poor countries growing sugar cane are thus in direct competition. Sugar beet farmers in many countries would like to obtain a larger share of the world sugar market. But people in underdeveloped countries who depend on selling sugar would find it even more difficult to make a decent living. Other commodities in which exports of underdeveloped countries compete directly with products in developed countries include foodgrains and oilseeds, vegetable oils and meat. SOURCE: *Farmers and Manufacturers Beet Sugar Association.*

and prices remained relatively stable; but they averaged only 80 percent of the 1954 price. Coffee prices fluctuated markedly from year to year. Although the volume of production generally rose during the 1960s, coffee prices in the early 1970s were only about one-half those of the mid-1950s. Sisal experienced a serious decline, both in production and value. In 1971, prices had dropped to less than two-thirds of values in the 1950s. Cashew nuts—although production more than doubled in the decade 1960–1970—had fluctuating market prices. Cashew prices varied as much as plus or minus 30 percent of the 1960 index. Tea, whose export value more than doubled in ten years, had generally declining prices in the eight-year period 1964–1971. In summary, all commodities except cashew nuts experienced a worsening price situation over the 11 to 18 years before 1971. These falling prices cost the Tanzanian economy millions of dollars in export receipts.

TABLE 11.4 Trends in volume, value, and prices of main export crops, Tanzania (1960–1971)

	1960	1961	1962	1963	1964	1965	1966	1967	1968	1969	1970	1971
Coffee												
Volume*	25.1	24.6	26.1	26.0	33.0	28.2	50.6	44.4	49.2	49.5	44.8	32.3
Value*	147	135	132	137	221	171	301	237	265	257	312	221
Price*	5750	5498	5116	5262	6698	6134	5920	5264	5392	5194	6962	6400
1960 = 100*	100	96	89	91	108	103	102	92	94	90	121	111
1954 = 100*	55	53	47	50	60	58	57	51	52	49	67	61
Percentage increase or decrease: (1960–1971) Volume: +42 Value: +22												
Cotton												
Volume	38.9	29.7	33.1	47.8	44.5	56.2	86.2	60.8	62.9	56.7	60.7	55.3
Value	177	135	148	214	198	244	350	251	283	235	247	217
Price	4470	4610	4538	4480	4444	4420	4062	4140	4500	4130	4075	4396
1960 = 100	100	102	101	100	99	99	91	93	101	92	91	98
1954 = 100	81	84	83	81	80	80	74	75	83	74	74	79
Percentage increase or decrease: (1960–1971) Volume: +28 Value: +50												
Sisal												
Volume	207.2	200.9	223.0	214.4	208.9	213.6	198.9	204.4	189.1	171.9	217.2	162.0
Value	309	281	315	453	437	286	235	201	159	160	179	136
Price	1467	1396	1434	2116	2094	1358	1179	983	839	728	823	833
1960 = 100	100	95	98	144	142	92	80	67	57	63	56	57
1954 = 100	112	107	110	162	161	104	90	75	64	71	63	64
Percentage increase or decrease: (1960–1971) Volume: −22 Value: −56												
Cashew nuts												
Volume	36.7	40.0	59.9	42.5	55.8	64.6	72.2	70.9	79.7	82.2	77.4	95.0
Value	43	36	47	41	66	83	100	92	107	119	115	127
Price	1140	824	798	952	1180	1296	1384	1301	1276	1447	1487	1237
1960 = 100	100	75	70	84	104	114	122	114	112	127	130	109
Percentage increase or decrease: (1960–1971) Volume: +159 Value: +195												
Tea												
Volume	3.2	3.2	4.0	3.9	4.4	4.3	6.3	6.1	6.7	7.6	6.9	8.1
Value	23	27	32	31	31	30	45	43	45	48	42	48
Price	7167	8452	8268	7894	7020	7160	7123	7131	6707	6360	6085	5930
1960 = 100	100	118	116	110	98	100	99	99	94	89	85	83
Percentage increase or decrease: (1960–1971) Volume: +153 Value: +109												

*Volumes in thousands of tons; values in millions of shillings (E.A.); prices in shillings (E.A.) per ton; unit price indexes: 1960 = 100 and 1954 = 100.

SOURCE: *The Economic Survey, 1971–72,* Dar es Salaam: Government Printer, 1972, and *Statistical Abstract, 1966,* Dar es Salaam: Government Printer, 1968. There are minor discrepancies between these two sources in values given for volumes, values and prices for the export commodities.

Sisal gone to seed near Morogoro, Tanzania, reflects the serious decline in prices for this commodity. Sisal, which originated in Central and South America, is a fiber-producing plant. The fibers are processed into rope, sacks, and rough clothing. The future of sisal and other fibers including cotton remains uncertain because of the availability of more and more synthetic fibers.

Reasons for Price Instability Most world prices for commodities vary over short periods with changes in supply and demand. Commodities exported by underdeveloped countries may be divided into (1) those for which demand is fairly stable but supply fluctuates, (2) those for which both demand and supply fluctuate, and (3) those for which demand fluctuates more than supply. The first group includes crops such as sugar, coffee, tea, cocoa, and food grains. Their supply is more variable than demand. Supply is greatly affected by variations in weather and other conditions of farming, and small changes in world prices. The second group includes most agricultural raw materials such as sisal, jute, cotton, oilseeds, timber, and rubber. As with the first group, supply is highly sensitive to farming conditions. Demand, however, is less stable, and varies directly with the rate of economic growth in importing countries. The last group includes most metals and minerals. With the exception of a war or some other catastrophic event, supply is fairly stable. Demand, however, tends to fluctuate with changes in the level of economic activity in the importing country.

Share of World Trade

The total value of world trade increased enormously between 1953 and 1975, but the increase has not been shared equally (Table 11.5). Until 1970, the developed

Limited Gains from Trade

Cocoa research center in Brazil. National and international research institutions exist to improve crop productivity. Research is undertaken, for example, to find ways to reduce the destructive effects of diseases and insects which could ruin harvests and the economy of an underdeveloped country. Although research organizations have been established in many underdeveloped countries for export crops, central items of food and internal commerce such as cassava, beans, millet and yams are without benefit of much scientific study. SOURCE: *Chocolate Manufacturers Association*.

capitalist countries' share of world trade increased steadily from 63.0 to 71.6 percent. The trade of members of the European Economic Community (EEC)—Belgium, Denmark, France, West Germany, Ireland, Italy, Luxembourg, the Netherlands, United Kingdom—grew especially fast in this period. The share of the underdeveloped countries in world trade decreased from 27.0 to 17.7 percent. This drop reflected a relatively slow increase in demand for primary products since the Korean War boom in the early 1950s, and a worsening price situation of primary products relative to the price of manufactured goods.

After 1970, the trend changed, mainly as a result of a four-fold increase in oil prices imposed by OPEC members at the end of 1973. The share of developed capitalist countries in world trade declined from 71.6 percent in 1970 to 66.0 percent in 1975, whereas the underdeveloped countries share increased from 17.7 to 24.1 percent. During this period, however, the share of underdeveloped countries excluding OPEC countries actually declined from 12.2 to 11.1 percent.

Except for OPEC countries and some others like Hong Kong and Taiwan which supply developed countries with consumer goods, the majority of underdeveloped countries have experienced a declining share in world trade. Between 1953

TABLE 11.5 World exports, 1953–74 and 1975

	1953		1960		1970		1973		1974		1975	
	$m fob	%	$m fob	%	$m fob	%	$m fob	%	$m fob	%	$m fob	%
Total exports of which:	78,300	(100.0)	128,660	(100.0)	313,100	(100.0)	577,490	(100.0)	838,890	(100.0)	879,120	(100.0)
Developed market economies*	49,300	(63.0)	85,950	(66.8)	224,290	(71.6)	407,810	(70.6)	544,250	(64.8)	579,920	(66.0)
Centrally planned economies	7,900	(10.1)	15,260	(11.9)	33,360	(10.7)	57,890	(10.0)	71,990	(8.6)	86,800	(9.9)
Underdeveloped countries	21,000	(21.3)	27,450	(21.3)	55,450	(17.7)	111,790	(19.3)	222,650	(26.5)	212,400	(24.1)
OPEC	n.a.		n.a.		17,250	(5.5)	43,440	(7.5)	123,920	(14.8)	113,940	(13.0)

*Including Australia, New Zealand, and South Africa.

SOURCE: GATT, *International Trade*, 1965 and 1975–6.

Limited Gains from Trade

and 1974, world trade in foodstuffs and industrial raw materials (excluding fossil fuels) fell from 40.2 to 20.0 percent. Meanwhile, the share of semi-finished and finished goods increased from 48.6 to 57.1 percent.

Terms of Trade

The worsening world trade position for poor nations is one of the most intractable problems of underdevelopment. Since the end of the Second World War, prices of raw materials have risen relatively little or not at all, whereas prices of manufactures have increased at a higher rate. Thus the *terms of trade*—prices received for exports relative to prices paid for imports—have declined steadily: underdeveloped countries have to sell more raw materials for the same amount of manufactured goods (see box). According to United Nations Conference on Trade and Development (UNCTAD) statistics, the terms of trade for primary products declined from 126 to 84 or at an average rate of 2.5 percent per year between 1953 and 1972 (Table 11.6). Some countries have been hit harder than the average. For example, between 1963 and 1970, the amount of sisal that Tanzania had to sell in order to import a tractor increased from 5 tons to 10 tons.

Keith Griffin (1969:110–116) provided an account of the theoretical causes for the decline in the terms of trade for export commodities. He said that for

---

Twenty Five Tons of Rubber = ? Tractors

For 25 tons of exported rubber an underdeveloped country could import six tractors in 1960 but inflation has taken its toll. Some years ago it was not too bad; in 1964 and 1969 you could still get three-and-a-half tractors. But the recent inflation (1975) has reduced the value to only two. The effect depends not just on the year chosen but also on the raw material in question.

(SOURCE: *Development Forum,* June-July 1975, Vol. 3, No. 5, Dossier 7.)

SOURCE: F.A.O. *Production Yearbooks* and UNCTAD *Monthly Commodity Bulletins.*

TABLE 11.6 Comparison of World Bank and UNCTAD indices of terms of trade of primary commodities, 1953–1972

| | Terms of trade | |
Year	UNCTAD*	World Bank
1953	126	122
1954	138	137
1955	133	130
1956	123	128
1957	116	118
1958	111	111
1959	107	110
1960	106	106
1961	101	98
1962	96	97
1963	100	100
1964	105	109
1965	100	109
1966	99	109
1967	95	100
1968	99	102
1969	100	104
1970	98	102
1971	86	89
1972	84	87

*Based on unit values of developing countries' exports of coffee, cocoa, tea, maize, rice, sugar, bananas, copra, coconut oil, groundnut oil, cotton, jute, sisal, natural rubber, wool, copper, tin, lead, zinc, bauxite, alumina, aluminum, iron ore, phosphate rock, managanese and on values of world exports of oranges (and tangerines) and tobacco. The index has been weighted by 1963 values of exports from developing countries. In 1963 the total export value of these selected commodities from underdeveloped countries represented 67.5 percent of the total value of all primary commodities (excluding petroleum) exported from underdeveloped countries.

SOURCE: Taken from UNCTAD, "Indexation: Report by the Secretary-General of UNCTAD," (TD/B/563), July 7, 1975, Table 3.

any country, the cause of a decline in the terms of trade depends on three factors: the nature of the product exported, the degree of structural rigidity in the economy, and the bias of technical progress. Following is a summary of Griffin's account.

The Nature of the Product Exported A statistical finding, known as *Engel's Law*, is that as incomes increase beyond a certain point, the proportion of income spent on food declines. The idea extended to international trade argues that as consumption of manufactured goods increases, agriculture will form a decreasing proportion of total trade, and income elasticity of demand will be greater for manufactured goods. Thus there is built-in structural disequilibrium which will result in worsening terms of trade for countries which export largely agricultural produce. Further, unless the supply of primary products grows at a rate slower than the demand of industrialized countries for these products, the terms of trade will deteriorate for this reason as well. Most primary products, however, are produced in many countries, and it has been politically impossible for them to agree to restrain growth and control the supply.

Limited Gains from Trade

The Degree of Structural Rigidity Economies of many underdeveloped countries are characterized by inflexibility, and a consequent inability to alter the composition of exports rapidly in response to changing relative prices. For example, an underdeveloped country may have been exporting a high-priced commodity for several years, when demand conditions suddenly change, and export prices fall. Since the economy of the country in question is *structurally rigid*, it will have no alternative but to accept a decline in its terms of trade.

Griffin said that

> "Structural rigidities sometimes take the form of asymmetrical reactions to price changes. A rise in price may lead to an increase in investment and an eventual expansion of output, whereas a fall in price will not necessarily lead to a reduction of output. In other words, long-run world supply curves may be kinked: supply may be elastic for favourable shifts in demand and inelastic for unfavourable shifts in demand. If this is so, then fluctuations of demand will lead to a gradual decline in the average price of the commodity concerned. This argument is illustrated (Figure 11.8).

> Assume, for example, that the price of coffee is initially P_0—as determined by the intersection of the supply and demand curves—S_0S and D_0 respectively. Assume further, that there is an increase in demand to D_1 caused, say, by the outbreak of war in Asia. The price of coffee will at first rise very sharply due to the fixed capacity of the existing coffee plantations. These extraordinary high prices will encourage people to invest in this sector; output will eventually increase substantially, and the price will settle at P_1" (112).

Increased prices may encourage expansion of output among established producers, and may encourage new competitors to enter the market. This happened in Africa with respect to coffee after World War II (113).

> "If, now, demand falls, say, to its original level, it will move along a new supply curve, S_1S. Price will not return to its initial level but, on the contrary, will fall considerably below this, to P_2. Once capacity has been installed in new plantations with long lines, variable costs of production may be very low and, hence, supply may be quite insensitive to price reductions. Once resources have become fixed in specific and long-lived capital—in this case, coffee trees—the economy becomes inflexible and is unable to transform resources from declining-price to rising-price sectors" (114).

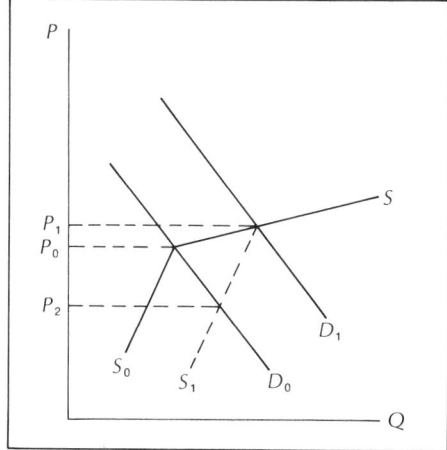

FIGURE 11.8 Structural rigidity and commodity price changes. SOURCE: Keith Griffin, 1969, *Underdevelopment in Spanish America*. London: George Allen and Unwin, Ltd., p. 113, Fig. II: 2.

The Bias of Technical Progress Technical advances help to solve economic problems of developed countries. They do not seem to occur randomly, but, rather, appear to reflect relative factor and commodity scarcities. Such technical advances do not necessarily help underdeveloped countries. Indeed they may well make matters worse.

Griffin noted:

> Continuous increases in technical knowledge in the industrialized countries enable capital to be substituted for labour and primary materials—the factor of production and the commodities which the less developed countries possess in abundance. This is part of the bias or non-random development of technical progress. As is generally recognized, these increases in knowledge (i) enable the industrial economies to reduce the primary content of final products, such as the reduction of the tin content of tin cans, (ii) enable the wealthy nations to produce high quality finished products from less valuable or lower quality primary products, such as a reduction in the quality of coffee used to produce instant coffee, and (iii) enable the advanced economies to produce entirely new manufactured products which are substitutes for existing primary commodities, such as the development from plastics of a synthetic leather which "breathes" (114–115).

Tappers using a conveyor system to move rubber latex to a collecting station on a Firestone rubber plantation, Harbel, Liberia. After iron ore, rubber is Liberia's most important export. Though production has increased in recent years, prices have declined partly because of the development of synthetics. SOURCE: *The Firestone Tire and Rubber Company.*

> These technological developments are irreversible and asymmetrical . . . The demand for many primary goods may be inelastic for price decreases but in the long-run it may be very elastic for price increases. A rise in the price of a raw material provides an incentive to undertake industrial research into ways of economizing on the commodity or substituting something else for it or producing it in the importing country. A price decline appears to provide no such incentive for investigating new ways of using the commodity. For example, a fall in the world price of copper may lead to a very small increase in the quantity demanded, but a rise in the price of copper may result in its permanent substitution by aluminum. Under these circumstances there will be a long-run tendency for the price of unprocessed raw materials to fall (115).

Limited Gains from Trade

Griffin concluded that one of the major factors that explains the inflexibility of economies of underdeveloped countries is their slow rate of technical development. Terms of trade difficulties of poor nations are based upon their inability to shift resources from declining to expanding industries. Until underdeveloped countries reduce structural rigidities by transforming their economic, social and institutional frameworks, they will continue to experience trade difficulties.

Protection and Preferences

Foreign trade problems of poor nations, although mainly the result of their underdeveloped condition, are also caused by the restrictions imposed by developed countries. To avoid the enormous reduction of trade that followed protectionist policies of the interwar years, developed countries came together after the Second World War to discuss the need for trade liberalization. Out of these meetings emerged three major international institutions—the *International Monetary Fund (IMF)*, the *General Agreement on Tariffs and Trade (GATT)*, and the *World Bank*. None of these institutions has worked primarily in the interests of underdeveloped countries. For example, GATT demanded that any trade liberalization introduced by one country must be offered in return for a concession from another. In other words, tariff reductions must be on the basis of reciprocity. As noted earlier, a reciprocal trading system works to the relative disadvantage of underdeveloped countries.

On top of measures to liberalize trade in the post Second World War period, developed countries established a tariff structure that discriminated against poor nations. A profile of *tariffs* faced by underdeveloped countries is shown in Table 11.7 and Figure 11.9. They encounter low tariffs on traditional primary commodity exports, higher tariffs on exports of semi-manufactured products, and still higher tariffs on manufactures. This system of tariffs discourages the development of processing industries in underdeveloped countries.

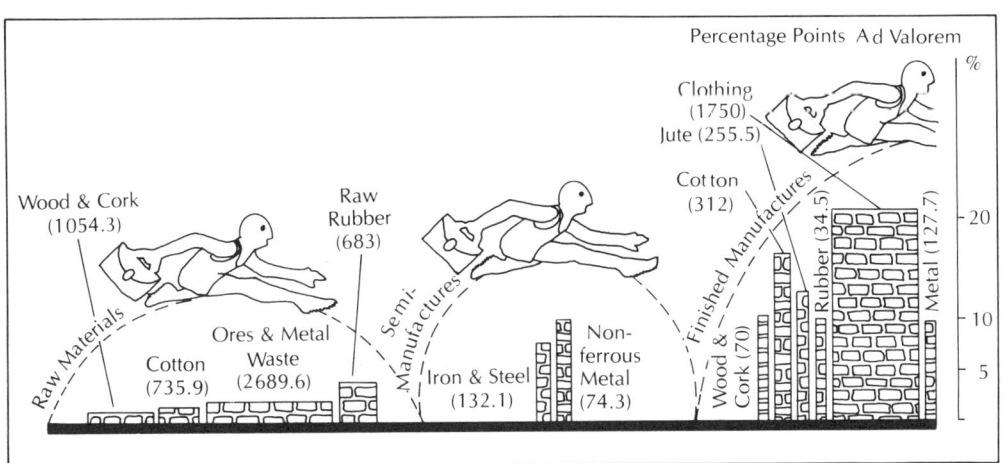

FIGURE 11.9 Tariff barriers (1973 tariff profiles—importation values in million $ U.S.—for underdeveloped country products imported into developed market economy countries). SOURCE: *GATT*.

TABLE 11.7 Average nominal tariffs, by country and product group (percentage)

Country	Product Group		
	Raw Materials	Semi-manufactures	Manufactures
EC			
Arithmetic average*	1.7	8.9	8.3
Weighted average†	0.7	7.7	9.2
Japan			
Arithmetic average*	2.2	9.6	11.3
Weighted average†	6.0	9.6	11.5
US			
Arithmetic average*	5.6	9.8	13.1
Weighted average†	3.8	9.1	8.2

*Simple (unweighted) arithmetic average of all most-favored-nation duty rates applying to tariff lines within a commodity group.

†This average has been calculated in two steps. First, a simple (unweighted) arithmetic average of tariff lines was computed for each BTN (Brussels Tariff Nomenclature) heading. Then, each of these averages was weighted by the total combined imports of the eleven industrialized countries covered by the tariff study.

SOURCE: General Agreement on Tariffs and Trade (GATT), *Basis Documentation for the Tariff Study. Summary by Industrial Product Categories, Tariff 1973, Import 1970/71* (Geneva: GATT, 1974).

A textile mill in India. A problem for underdeveloped countries is the imposition of tariff and non-tariff barriers by developed countries who want to protect their own textile industries. SOURCE: *International Labor Organization.*

Limited Gains from Trade

It has to be noted that in recent years the relative importance of tariff barriers has decreased whereas *non-tariff* barriers have become more significant (Figure 11.10). Measures like quantitative restrictions, discretionary licensing standards, and health and sanitary regulations impede the export of products that compete with products of developed countries, such as processed agricultural goods, textiles, clothing, and electrical and mechanical appliances. For some countries, these restrictions affect their major export items, thus causing balance-of-payments, employment, and economic growth problems.

Health regulations—Tight limits may be set on insecticide or other preservative chemicals on foodstuffs exported by developing countries. These have been accused of being partly protectionist in intent.

Quotas, ceilings and calendriers—restrictions as to the quantity of exports are common; example, cotton textiles from India to UK, protection for the Lancashire cotton industry. Many foodstuffs that compete with EEC products are allowed in only at certain seasons to avoid competing with the peak production of the importers. The producing nation cannot therefore control its own trade timetable.

Packaging—increasingly loose or 'break bulk' cargo is unacceptable to developed country mechanized transport handlers. Dockers and longshoremen often demand bonuses for handling such things as unpacked skins and hides. Consumers too demand agricultural products in packing that requires more investment on the part of the exporting developing country.

Other barriers may include discretionary licensing, variable levies, labelling and 'certificate of origin' regulations.

FIGURE 11.10 Non-tariff barriers. SOURCE: *Development Forum,* June–July 1975, Vol. 3. No. 5, Dossier 7.

Tariff and non-tariff barriers to trade are reinforced by the policies of Western and Japanese transport carriers who charge discriminating freight rates. Bulky raw materials incur lower rates than manufactures and highly processed goods. Thus the tariff policies of developed countries and the freight rates charged by international shippers introduce a strong bias against the industrialization of Third World nations. Factories are located near final markets (in developed countries), rather than near their sources of raw materials (in underdeveloped countries).

Another problem related to the developed country domination of world trade stems from the existence of regional groupings such as the *European Economic*

Community (EEC). Underdeveloped countries who are associated with the Community are given preferential access for their exports of primary products to Common Market countries. The existence of such groupings discriminates against underdeveloped nations that are not associated members. It also divides underdeveloped countries into different interest groups, which makes it difficult for them to present a uniform front against developed countries.

Import Substitution

Even without tariff barriers, it would be difficult for most underdeveloped countries to export manufactured products to developed countries. Their acquired comparative advantage does not lie in these goods. And without preferential treatment from developed countries, they are unlikely to acquire a comparative advantage for manufactures. Thus in the last twenty years many underdeveloped countries opted for *import substitution* at the national level. This development strategy does not rely on the export of manufactured goods to Europe and North America. Import substitution became fashionable in the early 1950s in Latin America. New industries, established behind protection tariffs in Argentina, Chile, Mexico, and Brazil, met with some success. By the late 1950s, however, policies of import substitution were running into difficulties, and governments began to consider a new policy of regional coordination of industrial development and the erection of common tariffs against third nations.

Some problems of import substitution at the national level have been noted by Griffin. He said:

> The internal markets in these countries frequently are too small even to justify the erection of one efficient sized plant. Monopolies with strong vested interests, uncontrolled by the state, were created. Prices of manufactured products rose substantially and affected a redistribution of income toward the monopolistic producers. There was little chance that these "infants" would ever grow up, and in any case, the limited market soon stopped this "development from within."

> Moreover, there are inherent difficulties of import substitution for small nations. Such a strategy is almost inevitably biased, first, in favour of small plants and, second, toward the consumer goods industries. The first bias tends to lower the level of income by creating inefficiency, and the second bias tends to retard the rate of growth. Indiscriminate protection of consumer goods industries usually is combined with liberal import policies for raw materials and capital goods. This tends to discourage export promotion as well as backward linkage import substitution into capital goods, yet one or both of these activities is essential for sustained rapid growth (1971:223–224).

The narrowness of internal markets in most underdeveloped countries and their general lack of technological dynamism imposes severe constraints on their economic growth possibilities if they opt out of international trade. And yet there are a number of limits to underdeveloped countries' gains from trade. These limitations result from the underdevelopment of poor countries, dependence on primary product exports, and the predominance of developed countries among their trading partners. For some 200 years, developed countries have created and reinforced

Improving the Status of Trade

tendencies toward unequal exchange through the adoption of trade policies based on self-interest.

Improving the Status of Trade

Increased international trade can make an important contribution to the development of poor countries. Such trade is a source of foreign exchange earnings required to import goods and to service foreign debt. Trade is also important as a supplement to inadequate domestic markets.

What can be done to improve trade prospects for poor countries? First, ways must be found to reduce price instability and improve terms of trade for raw commodities. Second, economies of underdeveloped countries diversify their export and production structure. Lopsided concentration on a few raw commodities—too often of only one commodity per country—causes economic vulnerability and instability. In countries with minerals, mineral processing industries need to be developed to raise the value-added in the countries in which the exploitation is

The development of Gabon's manganese deposits is expected to diversify the Republic's export products and provide a new source of foreign exchange. SOURCE: *United Nations*.

done. The same vertical diversification is necessary for agricultural products. With the possible exception of further regional groupings of poor countries *(regional integration)*, these efforts will be in vain unless developed countries are prepared to reform the existing world trade system.

GATT and UNCTAD

Can international organizations assist in the process of improving the status of trade for the underdeveloped countries? Thus far, the accomplishments of two global organizations, the *General Agreement on Tariffs and Trade (GATT)* and the *United Nations Conference on Trade and Development (UNCTAD)* do not give much cause for optimism. At present, these institutions appear to be huge debating societies wherein nations of the world discuss the problems of world trade and development, and developed countries fight to preserve the *status quo*.

GATT was born in 1947, and now consists of 83 developed and underdeveloped member nations. To begin with, GATT demanded reciprocal negotiations on tariff reductions which favored developed countries. Not until the mid-1960s did GATT begin to consider the trade problems of underdeveloped countries and to allow them to participate in negotiations. As a result of their efforts in GATT, underdeveloped countries gained acceptance of the principle of non-reciprocity and the General System of Preferences (GSP). Under GSP, which was adopted by developed countries in 1971, tariffs charged on imports of manufactured and semi-manufactured products are granted preferential treatment. However, one of the most striking features of GSP schemes so far is the low proportion of manufactured goods that are eligible for preferential treatment. Because most GSP schemes are restrictive, few underdeveloped countries have benefited.

UNCTAD, which was formed in 1964, operates side by side, but not always in harmony, with GATT. Its area of operations often overlaps with GATT, as for example in the GSP which was an UNCTAD idea. An important feature of UNCTAD is the "Group of 77." The "Group of 77" (named after the number of nations initially involved) is comprised of more than 100 underdeveloped countries. One of the objectives of this caucas is to formulate uniform positions and strategies on trading and marketing to help negotiations with the developed countries, which also attend UNCTAD. When it comes to specific proposals, however, this group has seldom spoken with a single voice. For example, when anything meaningful is at stake, African countries find no common ground. One country will refuse to give up any preferential treatment it enjoys with a developed country.

The committee structure of UNCTAD shows with which aspects of world trade and development it concerns itself:

1. *Committee on Commodities,* which attempts to improve the terms on which commodities are exported by underdeveloped countries, through international commodity agreements.
2. *Committee on Manufactures,* which attempts to promote the export of manufactured products from underdeveloped to developed countries. Its main concern thus becomes tariff barriers.

3. *Committee on Invisibles and Financing Related to Trade.* This committee deals with tourism, banking, insurance and reinsurance, and aid goals for underdeveloped countries.

4. *Committee on Shipping.* The underdeveloped nations' share of the world's merchant fleet (Liberian and Panamanian registration excluded) is 6 percent. Thus underdeveloped countries are at the mercies of the large shipping lines.

Despite the efforts of poor countries in UNCTAD, most really important decisions (for example, world monetary policy, devaluation, and drawing rights in the International Monetary Fund) continue to be made by the developed countries. The GSP and some individual commodity agreements such as Cocoa (1973) are about the only real gains underdeveloped countries have made under UNCTAD auspices.

Since 1974, the "Group of 77" has been trying to obtain an international agreement for an integrated commodity program. This integrated program to combat price deterioration, price instability and growing foreign debt consists of five elements:

1. The establishment of internationally owned buffer stocks covering major food and raw material commodities (see box).

2. The institution of a system of medium- to long-term commitments to purchase and sell commodities at agreed prices;

3. The establishment of a common financing fund that will make resources available for the acquisition of stocks;

4. The institution of measures to provide compensating financing to producers to cover shortfalls in export earnings;

5. The initiation of an extensive program of measures to further the processing of commodities by primary producers.

INTERNATIONAL COMMODITY STOCKS

Eighteen commodities are, at present, considered suitable for internationally owned buffer stocks. They include certain foodstuffs (wheat, maize, rice and sugar), tropical beverages (raw coffee, cocoa beans, and tea), agricultural raw materials (cotton, jute and manufactures, wool, hard fibres, and rubber), and some industrial minerals (copper, lead, zinc, tin, bauxite, alumina, and iron ore).

The integrated program is not likely to be accepted by developed countries in the near future. Each time the Group of 77 has put forth its integrated commodity program, it has been rejected by the United States and other developed countries.

A low point was reached at the 1976 meeting in Nairobi, Kenya of the U.N. Conference on Trade and Development (UNCTAD) when then-Secretary of State Kissinger took a particularly stiff line in presenting a flat-out rejection of the poor countries' proposals.

Negotiations in various U.N. and independent forums dragged on, however, until at the end of 1977 the Group of 77 suspended talks, declaring that it was "utterly futile" to continue "until the developed countries demonstrate the necessary political will to make the negotiations meaningful."

From the point of view of the rich nations' governments, demands for a major alteration of trade patterns and prices would threaten their own prosperity, a particularly unwelcome prospect in light of their experience with imported oil *(Dollars and Sense,* 1978, 37:17).

The EEC and the Lomé Convention

Since the Second World War, several inter-governmental agreements on trade have been made. Among Western countries, the most significant trading bloc to emerge is the *European Economic Community (EEC).* There have also been several "North-South" agreements, or agreements between developed and underdeveloped countries. These agreements have three main characteristics. First, they are usually made along "regional" lines (e.g. agreements between EEC and African countries). Second, they tend to involve the offer of more concessions by the developed countries than by the underdeveloped countries. Third, they tend to involve the offer of official aid by developed countries.

The most comprehensive and most important "North-South" agreement is the Lomé Convention signed in 1975 by the EEC and 46 states in Africa, the Caribbean and the Pacific (ACP states). The ACP countries have a population of about 268 million living predominantly in rural areas. Among these countries are 18

MAJOR BENEFICIARIES OF THE STABEX SCHEME

The STABEX scheme is likely to be an important income-stabilizing factor for the following countries who earn at least 25 percent of their foreign currency by exporting the STABEX products (lower percentages in brackets):

Groundnuts:	Gambia, Niger, Senegal.
Coffee:	Burundi, Rwanda, Ethiopia, Uganda, Ivory Coast, Kenya, Madagascar.
Cocoa:	Ghana, Equatorial Guinea, Grenada, Togo, Cameroon, Western Samoa.
Cotton:	Chad, Sudan
Palm Oil:	Dahomey.
Hides and Skins:	Ethiopia (9%), Botswana (7%).
Bananas:	Somalia, Grenada.
Wood:	Congo, Gabon
Tea:	Malawi (22%), Kenya (16%).
Sisal:	Tanzania (10%).
Iron Ore:	Swaziland.

SOURCE: *Development Forum,* April 1975, Vol. 3, No. 3, p. 4.

of the world's poorest, averaging a per capita income of only $148. For all Africa, the Caribbean and the Pacific, the EEC is the first trading partner as it absorbs (1970 figures) about 54 percent of their exports and provides 44 percent of their imports (for Africa, 60 percent).

The Lomé Agreement has been eulogized as a "historical event" and a "new model." This praise is based on a commodity price-support system known as the *STABEX* mechanism. The STABEX scheme applies to thirteen commodity groups (bananas, coffee, cocoa, cotton, coconut oil, copra, groundnuts, hides, palm products, sisal, tea, timber excluding plywood, and iron ore). Many ACP states are dependent on STABEX products for their export earnings (see box), but several important products are not covered by the STABEX scheme (Table 11.8). In order to benefit from the STABEX scheme, the products must constitute at least 7.5 percent of the total of any particular country and average annual export revenues must have dropped by at least 7.5 percent in comparison with a chosen reference period.

TABLE 11.8 Important export products of selected ACP countries not covered by the STABEX scheme: proportion of total exports (percentages)

Country	Product	Country	Product
Central African Republic	Diamonds 44	Senegal	Cereals 17.4 Phosphates 8.5
Congo	Diamonds 14.8	Sierra Leone	Diamonds 71
Gabon	Wood 36.8	Somalia	Live cattle 50.1
Guyana	Bauxite 47.9	Togo	Phosphates 29.2
Jamaica	Bauxite 22.7	United Republic of Cameroon	Aluminum 9.5
Malawi	Tobacco 34.6		
Mali	Live cattle 48.2 Fish 14.1	United Republic of Tanzania	Diamonds 10.7 Vegetables and fruit 9.2
Niger	Live cattle 14.3	Upper Volta	Live cattle 36.9
Nigeria	Tin 4.4	Zaire	Diamonds 5.3
Rwanda	Tin 31.1		

SOURCE: UNCTAD, "Commodities: Preservation of the Purchasing Power of Developing Countries' Exports, Report by the UNCTAD-Secretariat" (TD/184/Supp. 2), March 5, 1976, Annex II, p. 6.

The Lomé Agreement provides a framework for continuing a colonial type relation, and for discriminating against non-ACP states. It is, however, a commodity price support system. The STABEX mechanism does not deal with the terms of trade problems, but it is a model case for stabilizing export earnings on a world-wide basis.

A New International Economic Order

In the late 1960s and early 1970s, underdeveloped countries began to demand structural changes in the organization of the world political economy (see box). This demand stemmed partly from stresses and strains within the existing international system as revealed by world-wide recession and inflation, food crises, and oil price increases, and partly from the wish of underdeveloped countries to redress the growing inequality between developed and underdeveloped countries. Demands for reconstructing the basis of economic exchange in the interests of equity and justice became amalgamated at the Sixth Special Session (see box) of the United Nations General Assembly in 1974 into a call for the establishment of a *New International Economic Order (NIEO)*. At least in the short run, a NIEO has little or no chance of becoming a reality.

THE TANZANIAN MANIFESTO

The Manifesto presented by the government of Tanzania at the Conference of Non-Aligned States in September 1970 in Lusaka, Zambia, is a proposal to restructure the basis of world trade and aid.* The Manifesto notes that joint development between rich and poor countries, and aid channeled through international agencies, tend to reinforce the present world economic system, which promotes inequality. It notes, further, that the "poverty of the Third World, and the economic dependence of the nations of the Third World, are an integral part" of that system. The Manifesto proposed a multilateralization of aid recipients, rather than a multilateralization of aid sources. It "identifies the absence of technical economic expertise as being the chief bottleneck in defining and developing the necessary tactical proposals." It suggested that a source of

> . . . technical cadres possessing the necessary empathy would be found in the formation of some kind of UN-sponsored Peace Corps which would recruit younger economists and lawyers from throughout the industrial world. Unlike national, unilateral Peace Corps efforts, such a Progress Corps cadre would be explicitly tailored to respond to the political wills of the 'poor' nations. . . . Any new directions in expatriate manpower assistance programs must ensure that expatriates so transformed be made vulnerable to the will, expectations and strategies of the poor (Gappert, 1971:35–36).

By reconstructing the basis of economic exchange, and by gaining control of some international institution such as regional development banks or the United Nations Development Program, underdeveloped countries would achieve a position from which they could bargain with the developed world for new institutions based on a new international political economics.

*Tanzania appreciates the importance of international trade and does not propose to opt out of international trade, despite its policy of self-reliant development. Tanzania seeks ways to avoid being dependent on a few developed countries.

The call for a NIEO, which took developed countries by surprise, was made at a time when many underdeveloped countries perceived a golden opportunity to tip the balance of international power in their favor. Commodity producers thought they might be able to emulate *OPEC* in bidding up prices for their primary products. It soon became clear to most commodity producers (excluding oil producers), however, that they had less bargaining power than they first thought. As a consequence, relations between developed and underdeveloped countries shifted

> **WHAT IS A SPECIAL SESSION?**
>
> "Special sessions" are extraordinary meetings of the full United Nations membership called to discuss urgent and important world problems. The Sixth Special Session on Raw Materials and Development in 1974 was the first called to consider an economic problem.

from confrontation at the Sixth Special Session in 1974 to conciliation at the Seventh Special Session in 1975. At the Seventh Special Session a United States inspired resolution was accepted. It called for patching up the existing system rather than reconstructing the international economic and political order.

Trade Among Underdeveloped Countries

One strategy for improving the status of trade that does not require the cooperation of developed countries is to focus on interdependent relations among underdeveloped countries. This strategy involves regional integration schemes with a high degree of common protection against products of developed countries. In recent years, underdeveloped countries have moved toward greater economic cooperation (Table 11.9). Underdeveloped countries should choose strategies of collective self-reliance for two main reasons. First, regional integration enlarges the market, and second, it may enable participants to use complementary resources to build up national and regional specializations. But unless there are concessions to the weaker partners of a common market, the benefits from cooperation will pile up in the economically more prosperous and powerful countries. Thus without planning policies, measures for increasing trade among underdeveloped countries pose similar problems to those arising from developed/underdeveloped country trading relations.

Trade Prospects

Underdeveloped countries face gloomy international trade prospects. Their comparative advantage is in primary goods for which demand is inelastic. Developed countries have produced substitutes for many primary products, and they continue to impose tariffs on semi-processed and fuel goods. Underdeveloped countries will continue to experience price deterioration, price instability, and growing foreign debt unless developed countries agree to a reorganization of the world trade system. Eventually such reorganization may be forced on developed countries through major defaults by underdeveloped countries on their foreign debts (Table 11.10). Massive defaults are likely to occur during a major recession in the rich countries. Without expanding markets, the poor countries will be unable to earn the foreign exchange needed to meet scheduled debt payments to large United States and European banks.

TABLE 11.9 Selected economic groupings of underdeveloped countries

Organization	Member States	Date of Establishment	Main Provisions of Agreement
Latin America and Caribbean			
1. Latin American Free Trade Area (LAFTA)	Bolivia, Chile, Colombia, Ecuador, Peru, Argentina, Mexico, Paraguay, Uruguay, Venezuela, Brazil	1960	Free Trade Area leading to establishment of Latin American Common Market by 1985. Distinguishes relatively developed countries (Argentina, Brazil, Mexico), less developed countries (Colombia, Chile, Peru, Venezuela) and underdeveloped countries (Bolivia, Ecuador, Paraguay, Uruguay). Less developed and underdeveloped members can obtain preferential treatment from others and have a longer timetable for reduction of tariffs among LAFTA members. No common external tariff. Joint industrial planning through 'complementarity' agreements whereby production is shared among countries.
2. Andean Common Market and Community (ACM)	Bolivia, Chile till 1976, Colombia, Ecuador, Peru, Venezuela	1969 (Cartagena Agreement): Venezuela joined in 1973	Common external tariff by 1980: internal free trade by 1981. Bolivia and Ecuador (less developed members) have longer timetable for removal of customs duties. Common policy on foreign investment stipulates 51 percent local control within 15 years (20 years for Bolivia, Ecuador) of initial investment. Andean Development Corporation (1967) serves as common development bank. Agreements on merchant shipping and on treatment of migrant workers.
3. Central American Common Market (CACM)	Costa Rica, El Salvador, Guatemala, Honduras,* Nicaragua. (*Honduras, while still officially a member, has re-imposed tariffs on other members)	1960	Common external tariff and internal free trade (largely achieved). Intra-regional trade increased tenfold 1963–73. Aims at common customs administration, fiscal policy, industrial policy, etc.

4. Caribbean Community (CARICOM)	Antigua, Barbados, Belize, Dominica, Grenada, Guyana, Jamaica, Montserrat, St. Kitts—Nevis—Anguilla, St. Lucia, St. Vincent, Trinidad and Tobago	1973 (Treaty of Chaguaramas)—succeeding CARIFTA (1968)	Common external tariff and protective policy against imports from outside. Common scheme for incentives for industry envisaged. Joint planning in agriculture, aiming at greater self-sufficiency and intra-regional trade, covers most items produced in the region for regional consumption. Slower timetables for integration of less-developed members (all those except Guyana, Jamaica, Trinidad and Tobago, and Barbados). Caribbean Development Bank (1970) lends to public and private development projects.

Africa

5. East African Community (EAC)	Kenya, Tanzania, Uganda	1967	Intra-Community free trade, modified by 'transfer taxes' (internal import duties) imposed by deficit countries (Uganda and Tanzania against Kenya). Common external tariff inherited and adopted from colonial administration. Common exchange control, posts, railways, harbours and shipping and airlines administrations through independent regional corporations. East African Development Bank aims to invest 77 percent of funds in Uganda and Tanzania.
6. Economic Community of West African States (ECOWAS)	Dahomey, The Gambia, Ghana, Guinea, Guinea-Bissau, Ivory Coast, Liberia, Mali, Mauritania, Niger, Nigeria, Senegal, Sierra Leone, Togo, Upper Volta	1975	Staged reduction to zero of internal customs duties and establishment of common external tariff by 1990. Free movement of labour and, ultimately, of capital. Harmonisation of agricultural, industrial, economic, and monetary policies and promotion of joint agricultural, marketing, research, and agro-industrial projects, together with schemes for joint development of infrastructure. Elimination of inter-state disparities in development: establishment of ECOWAS fund for cooperation, compensation, and development.
7. Union Douanière et Economique de l'Afrique Centrale (UDEAC)	Cameroon, Central African Republic, Congo (Brazzaville). Gabon	1966	Customs union with common external tariff, with preferences for EEC and 'French African' countries. Common investment code. Common central bank based in Paris. All countries members of the Franc Area.

549

TABLE 11.9 (continued)

Organization	Member States	Date of Establishment	Main Provisions of Agreement
8. Communauté Economique de l'Afrique de l'Ouest (CEAO)	Ivory Coast, Mali, Mauritania, Niger, Senegal, Upper Volta, (Observers: Benin, Togo)	1974 (formerly West African Customs Union—(UDEAO)	Customs union with common external tariff. Joint policies to be developed on transport and communications, cattle and beef, industry, trade, tourism, etc. Intra-Community free trade in crude products: Regional Co-operation Tax on intra-trade in manufactures. Community Development Fund to be established. Common central bank based in Paris.
9. Maghreb Permanent Consultative Committee	Algeria, Morocco, Tunisia	1964–70	Permanent intergovernmental committee aiming at strengthening Maghreb cooperation. In abeyance since 1970.

Asia

10. Association of South-East Asian Nations (ASEAN)	Indonesia, Malaysia, Philippines, Singapore, Thailand	1967	Not customs union. Gradual relaxation of barriers to regional trade. Joint negotiations with other countries (e.g. EEC) and within GATT. Private-sector consultation through Chambers of Commerce and Industry. Joint highway projects, tourist promotion. Consideration of Asian shipping line.

Middle East

11. Regional Co-operation for Development (RCD)	Iran, Pakistan, Turkey	1964	Intergovernmental discussion and cooperation in fields of industrial cooperation (joint regional agreements on establishment of certain industries), transport (RCD shipping services on internal routes), joint public/private enterprises, trade expansion. No common tariff or free-trade area.

SOURCE: Kathryn Morton and Peter Tulloch, 1977, *Trade and Developing Countries.* New York: John Wiley & Sons, Inc., (London: Croom Helm Ltd. Publishers), Table 8.2, pp. 305–308.

TABLE 11.10 Debt burden: Ratio of debt-service payments plus profits to exports of goods and services in selected countries

Country	1965	1968	1975	Average 1965–1971
Iraq	39.2	40.0	38.2	39.9
Mexico	36.9	42.2	40.5	39.3
Iran	31.8	36.3	39.7	36.2
India	22.8	28.7	29.7	29.4
Trinidad and Tobago	28.2	28.0	21.8	27.8
Venezuela	29.7	29.7	25.4	27.6
Argentina	20.7	33.2	23.8	27.5
Chile	20.4	33.5	27.6	27.0
Nigeria	21.7	27.1	19.1	23.2
Uruguay	11.4	27.4	22.2	22.4
Jamaica	14.6	22.6	23.0	22.2
Pakistan	15.0	21.7	24.8	22.2

NOTE: Most underdeveloped countries pay a high proportion of their export earnings back in interest and other debt service. In the case of Mexico and India, around a third of their export earnings flow out again in such a way.

SOURCE: UNCTAD TD/B/C.3/AC.8/6 p. 21.

Aid

We have seen that international trade has not worked in the best interests of underdeveloped countries. But trade is just one element in the relationship between rich and poor countries. In addition, there is the transfer of resources, which is commonly called *aid*. In this section we consider the question: Can aid supply underdeveloped countries with what they need for economic growth and development?

Origins and Amount of Aid

International trade has been going on since the beginnings of civilized life, but the deliberate transfer of wealth from rich nations to poor is new. It is a concept dating from after the Second World War. In this period, at least three factors were at work directing developed countries to provide aid to underdeveloped countries. First, the colonial system collapsed, and could no longer serve as a protective shield for the developed capitalist world's conscience. Developed countries were forced to acknowledge poverty and international inequality. Second, aid was seen as a strategic weapon for winning the Cold War. Finally, it was thought that if Europe could recover from the ravages of the War through Marshall Aid—the injection of American capital—then aid could also stimulate the development of underdeveloped countries.

Against this background, aid programs developed in the post war years, with the total flow of resources from developed capitalist to underdeveloped countries reaching $38 billion in 1975 (Table 11.11). That figure, which was 40 percent higher than it was in 1974, was equal to 1.02 percent of donor countries' combined GNP. In other words, it appears from the figures supplied by the *Development Assistance Committee (DAC)* secretariat, the main source of information concerning aid, that developed capitalist countries are devoting one day's production out of every hundred days' to aid the poor in Africa, Asia, and Latin America.

TABLE 11.11 The flow of financial resources from DAC countries to underdeveloped countries and multilateral institutions: 1970–75 (U.S. $000 millions)

Net Disbursements	1970	1971	1972	1973	1974	1975†
Total, offical and private*	15.66	17.85	19.69	24.66	27.98	38.83
As share of GNP (%)	0.78	0.80	0.77	0.79	0.82	1.02
Total official	7.93	8.95	10.08	11.85	13.50	16.27
Official Development Assistance	6.79	7.69	8.54	9.38	11.32	13.61
As share of GNP (%)	0.34	0.35	0.33	0.30	0.33	0.36
Total private*	7.73	8.90	9.61	12.81	14.48	22.57

Details may not add to totals because of rounding.
*Includes grants by private voluntary agencies.
†Preliminary.
SOURCE: *World Bank Annual Report,* 1976, p. 10.

Total capital flow figures, however, do not give an accurate assessment of the amount of development assistance that actually flows from the developed into the underdeveloped world. The amount of aid is considerably less than $38 billion. As Table 11.11 shows, the total movement of resources is an aggregate of two broad categories: (1) Official Development Assistance (ODA) consisting of grants, multilateral contributions, and bilateral loans made available by governments and international institutions such as the World Bank and agencies of the United Nations, and (2) private foreign investment. It is highly misleading for the DAC secretariat to include private flows with official flows. Private flows constitute commercial transactions. Investors set up businesses in underdeveloped countries in the hope that they will turn a profit. When private flows are subtracted from official flows, the amount of aid in 1975 totalled $13.61 billion or 0.36 percent of DAC members' combined GNP.

Even DAC official aid statistics must be qualified. First, much aid for underdeveloped countries has strings attached to it. It is estimated that "three quarters of world aid and 64 percent of British aid is 'tied,' which means that it must be spent on goods provided by the aid-giving country, even when the same goods can be bought far more cheaply elsewhere. A study of tied credits for twenty projects in Pakistan showed that the prices paid were over 50% higher than if the materials had been bought from the cheapest sources" (Cavadino, 1973:17–18). Second, much aid extended by developed countries is politically motivated. France, for example, has used aid as an instrument of foreign policy. "When Guinea chose independence rather than associate status with France, France immediately with-

Aid

Aerial view of the Quai Mineralier under construction at Nouadhibou (formerly Port Etienne), Mauritania in the early 1900s. Large deposits of high quality iron ore were deposited near F'Derick (formerly Ft. Gouraud) in the Sahara, 640 kilometers from the sea, in Mauritania. In 1960 the World Bank lent $66 million for the development of these deposits, involving the building of a township at the mine, the construction of a railway to the sea, and the building of port and other facilities at Nouadhibou. Until 1974 when this development was nationalized, it was controlled by European and local interests. It is important to note that the World Bank and other international development agencies usually provide loans for major infrastructural projects which are proven money earners and which reinforce the modern export sector. SOURCE: *World Bank Photo* by Marc and Evelyne Bernheim.

drew her assistance programme, taking with her everything moveable, including records, statistics, and even telephones. When aid is dealt out in this way, . . . it is the coercive arm of the strong exerting control over the weak" (Cavadino, 1973:21). Third, much aid extended by developed capitalist countries is used to promote private investment. For example, "at a time of acute famine in India, the U.S. threatened to cut off food shipments unless India granted certain concessions to the Standard Oil Company of Indiana. 'For a long time, India insisted that it handle all the distribution of fertilizer produced in that country by the U.S. companies and that it also set the price. Standard of Indiana understandably refused to accept these conditions. AID put food shipments to India on a month-to-month basis until the Indian government let Standard of Indiana market its fertilizer at its own prices'" (Cavadino, 1973:19).

This is not where matters end, however. We still do not know what the total *net* flow of resources from developed to underdeveloped countries amounts to.

In order to find out, reverse flows of capital—flows from underdeveloped to developed countries—must be subtracted from the aid total. The main outflows of capital are: (1) the payment of interest on past loans, and (2) repatriated profits from private investments. These reverse flows, which worsen the balance of payments for underdeveloped countries, have grown to such an extent that they are thought to be of the same dimension as the total flow of financial resources (private and official) from developed countries, or not much smaller. For some countries, particularly Latin American, outflows exceed inflows by more than four times. Myrdal quoted United States Republican Senator Charles Mathias Jr., Maryland, as saying that "Capital flows *from* Latin America and into the United States are now over four times as great as the flow south. The countries of Latin America, in a way, are actually giving foreign aid to the United States, the wealthiest country in the world" (1971:322–323).

The Classical Model and Private Investment

During the last 30 years, governments in developed countries have begun to allocate a small part of the national budget to aid poor countries. The *liberal* philosophy of the need to extend aid is in strong contrast to traditional thinking on international economics. The traditional view is that natural forces work to promote material progress and to reduce international inequalities.

The traditional economist would argue that developed countries have expensive labor, and an abundance of capital. The situation is reversed in underdeveloped countries: labor is abundant and cheap, but capital is in short supply. Under free market conditions labor and capital will flow into areas where it is most needed (Figure 11.11). Capital will flow to underdeveloped countries, and labor to developed countries. Perfect factor mobility does not exist, but the movement of capital and labor will tend to exercise an equalizing effect throughout the world.

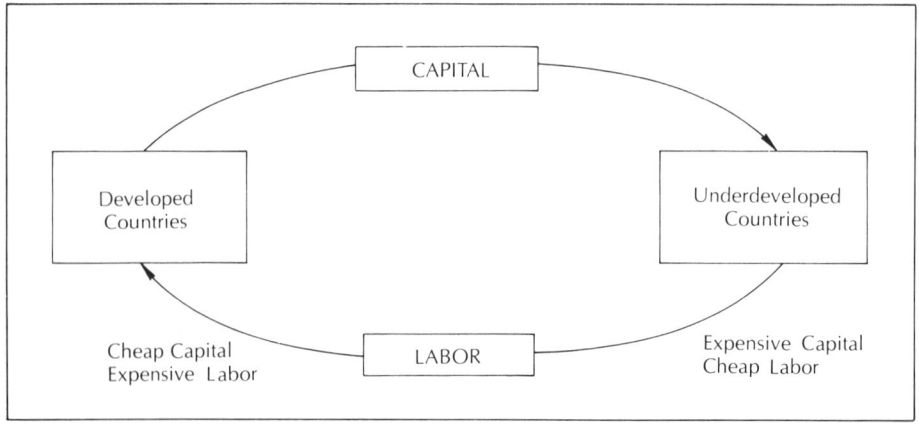

FIGURE 11.11 The flow of capital and labor under free market conditions.

This classical picture of a harmonious world does not accord with reality. Private capital goes where investors think they can make money, and that is seldom in underdeveloped countries. Labor does move from less to more prosperous countries, but it is generally capital-intensive labor which has received a good deal of education and training.

Let us look at the classical argument of likely capital movements in relation to the experiences of underdeveloped countries in both the colonial and post-independence periods. Consider the colonial period first. During the last third of the nineteenth century, British capitalists invested huge sums abroad each year. This capital investment went principally to other advanced capitalist nations, to newly-independent Latin American countries, especially Argentina and Mexico, and to European settler colonies of Canada, Australia, and New Zealand. British foreign investment in Africa and Asia was limited, and directed mainly to specific areas such as South Africa and India. Most parts of Africa and Asia received little capital investment. And when private capital did flow to African and Asian colonies, it went into foreign enclaves where the returns were substantial and fairly secure and where reliance on indigenous resources was minimized. During the colonial period, therefore, capital did not flow to where the need was greatest. Overseas private investment did not lead to an equalization of world income; rather it led to a widening of the gap between rich and poor.

In the past-independence era, flows of private capital continue to concentrate in the modern sectors of underdeveloped countries. Most of the private investment is carried out by a few multinational firms. One estimate is that some 250 United States-based firms control more than 70 percent of America's foreign investment, and that some 165 firms in the United Kingdom control more than 80 percent of its overseas private investment. The distribution of West German, French, British, and American companies with subsidiaries in Africa, Asia, and Latin America is shown in Figure 11.12.

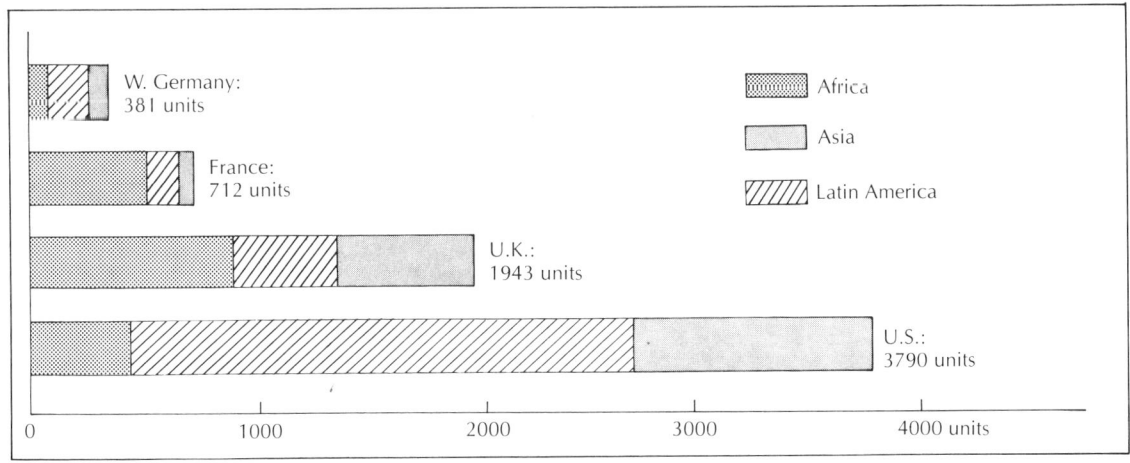

FIGURE 11.12 Selected countries: companies with underdeveloped country subsidiaries, 1969. SOURCE: *Yearbook of International Organizations* 1968/69.

John Kenneth Galbraith provided a clear account of the function of the multinational firm:

> It is, simply, the accommodation of the technostructure to the peculiar uncertainties of international trade. It transcends the market internationally as it does nationally. It accomplishes over a world of multiple national sovereignties what it first accomplishes within any one. It minizes the need for tariffs, quotas, and embargoes to reduce uncertainty in national markets. And, needless to say, it is not peculiarly American. It is the common accommodation of all nonsocialist planning, whatever the country of origin, to the special problem of international trade (1973:167).

The *transnational system* is dominantly a relationship between developed countries (Figure 11.13). Nonetheless, multinational corporations have entered underdeveloped countries to secure sources of raw materials, to find outlets for manufactured products, and to produce components for American and European products cheaply.

The transnational system: (A) Ford Motor's headquarters in Great Britain; and (B) Ford Motor's assembly plant in South Africa. SOURCE: *Ford Motor Company*.

Aid

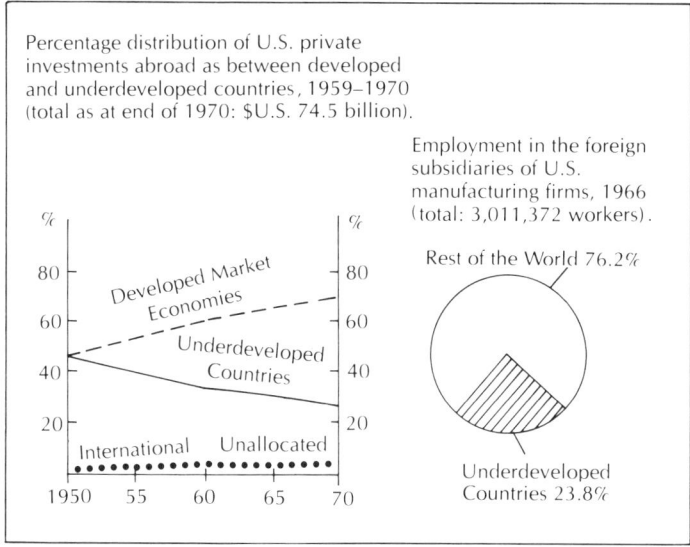

FIGURE 11.13 United States private foreign investments. SOURCE: S. Amin, 1973, "Growth is not Development," *Development Forum*, Vol. 1, No. 3, p. 2.

Many Third World scholars say that the multinational corporation is counterproductive to development (see box). Modern capital-intensive industry "does not rapidly increase employment. Its development as an enclave with limited links with the surrounding economy reduces its effectiveness in propagating change . . ." (Livingstone, 1971:244). Further, monopolistic firms often produce balance of payment problems because of heavy profit repatriations. Figures show (Table 11.12) that "as a result of direct overseas investments between 1950 and 1965 . . . there was a *net* capital flow of $16 billion to the United States . . ." (Horowitz, 1969:19). For the years 1950–1965, the United States repatriated from underdeveloped countries nearly three times as much money as was invested. Although the balance of payments problem would be avoided, in part, if multinational firms reinvested more of their profits in the host country, it is not certain that the national interest would be served. Reinvestment causes "growing foreign control of the economy and the denationalization of local industry" (Griffin, 1969:148). National elites see the multinational firm as an assault on political sovereignty. Equally important, they may resent the multinational corporation because "the transnational system internationalizes the tendency to unequal development and to unequal income" between developed and underdeveloped countries (Galbraith, 1973:174).

The argument that private foreign capital is not an instrument for development provides a rationale for official aid. But since developed capitalist countries see aid as a means of promoting private foreign investment, how can official aid promote development? Why can't poor countries generate their own development? After all, developed countries progressed without government-to-government aid? What is the purpose of aid?

TWO VIEWS ON THE ROLE OF MULTINATIONAL CORPORATIONS IN UNDERDEVELOPED COUNTRIES

There are two polar attitudes about the presence of multinationals in the underdeveloped world. In one view, the multinational firm has a high potential to aid the process of economic development. According to Herman Kahn, who is director of the Hudson Institute, New York, "the transnational corporation is probably the most efficient social, economic and political institution ever devised to accomplish the following tasks for the less developed nations:

1. Raising, investing, and reallocating capital.
2. Creating and managing organizations.
3. Innovating, adopting, perfecting and transferring technology.
4. Distribution, maintenance, marketing, and sales (including trained personnel and providing financing).
5. Furnishing local elites with suitable—perhaps ideal—career choices.
6. Educating and upgrading both blue collar and white collar labour (and elites).
7. In many areas, and in the not-so-distant future, serving as a major source of local savings and taxes and in furnishing skilled cadres (i.e., graduates) of all kinds to the local economy (including the future local competition of the TNC).
8. Facilitating the creation of vertical organizations or vertical arrangements which allow for the smooth, reliable, and effective progression of goods from one stage of production to another. In many cases, while such organization is a partial negation of the classical Free market, it is still often a very efficient and useful method of stable and growing production and distribution.
9. Finally, and almost by themselves, providing both a market and a mechanism for satellite services and industries that can stimulate local development much more effectively than most (official) aid programmes.

... Of course, the transnational corporation is not doing any of this for altruistic or public interest reasons (though sometimes elements of such motivations are important), nor do TNCs always operate in the best interest of the host country. I am simply saying that under proper conditions the above nine points should, and in fact often do, hold—at least to an important degree" (1973:2).

In the other view, the multinational corporation blocks existing or potential development opportunities. According to Samir Amin, Director of the African Institute for Economic Development and Planning, multinational corporations do not transfer technology.

> "They sell technology and they sell it under highly monopolistic conditions. In a world where everything is bought and sold, technology is a merchandise like any other, although perhaps an unusually complex one. Its constituent parts are machinery and equipment, skilled labour which knows how to use them, knowledge of processes and markets, raw materials and other imports. The market for technology is a highly controlled one, which gives the multinationals a large element of monopoly in their field. They use it to draw the maximum profit from their dealings with the peripheral countries.
>
> ... The highly centralized research and development of the multinational companies is not primarily directed at the conditions obtaining on the periphery. When it comes to

> developing countries, the right questions are not asked. Among them is the important one on how the technology will affect the broad mass of the people.
>
> The inadequacy of the technology bought makes itself felt in different ways. Growing unemployment is in many cases associated with new technical processes. Moreover, it is by no means the highest kind of technology that is transferred. The multinationals follow the well-known pattern under which the industries which need low-paid labour are sent abroad while the highly skilled, high return industries—software, electronics, space, atomic and solar energy, to name a few—are kept at home. The experience of countries like Taiwan, Hong Kong and Singapore, which have received 'runaway industries,' shows that the multinational corporations merely serve to deepen the inequalities in the already existing international division of labour.
>
> The answer clearly is that the developing countries must create their own research and development, not to imitate, but to assimilate and invent the processes that are suitable to their needs. Such an initiative will undoubtedly run into the opposition of the multinationals" (Amin, 1973b:2).

TABLE 11.12 Direct investments transferred to the United States (1950–1965)

	Europe	Canada	Latin America	All Other Areas
	(in billions of U.S. dollars)			
Flow of direct investments from U.S.*	8.1	6.8	3.8	5.2
Income on capital transferred to U.S.†	5.5	5.9	11.3	14.3
	+2.6	+0.9	−7.5	−9.1

*The figures represent net capital movements of direct investments.

†The figures represent the sum of dividends, interest, and branch profits (not profits of corporate subsidiaries whose earnings are retained abroad) after taxes.

SOURCE: Harry Magdoff, 1970, "The American Empire and the U.S. Economy," in Robert I. Rhodes, ed., *Imperialism and Underdevelopment*. New York: Monthly Review Press, p. 39. Copyright © 1970 by Monthly Review Press. Reprinted by permission of Monthly Review Press.

Aid and National Development

Advocates of foreign aid generally argue that it *accelerates the rate of economic growth; eases balance of payments difficulties;* and *acts as a vehicle for transferring knowledge*. Let us examine each of these functions of aid briefly.

Aid and Economic Growth. Many people say foreign aid is a supplement to inadequate domestic capital formation, and will, therefore, accelerate an underdeveloped country's rate of economic growth. Keith Griffin (1971) found no support for the view that foreign aid encourages growth. A scatter diagram for 12

Latin American countries revealed a loose, but, nonetheless, an inverse relationship between foreign aid and the average rate of growth of gross national product between 1957–64 (Figure 11.14). Foreign aid *may* deter economic growth for two reasons. First, it alters the composition of investment in favor of less desirable, highly capital-intensive projects with long gestation periods—roads, dams, power stations, and hospitals—and, therefore a higher *capital-output ratio*. Second, and more important, foreign aid reduces the propensity to save (Figure 11.15). Griffin argued that "given a target rate of growth in the developing country, foreign aid will permit higher consumption and domestic savings will simply be a residual, *i.e.* the difference between required investment and whatever amount of foreign aid is available" (1971:122).

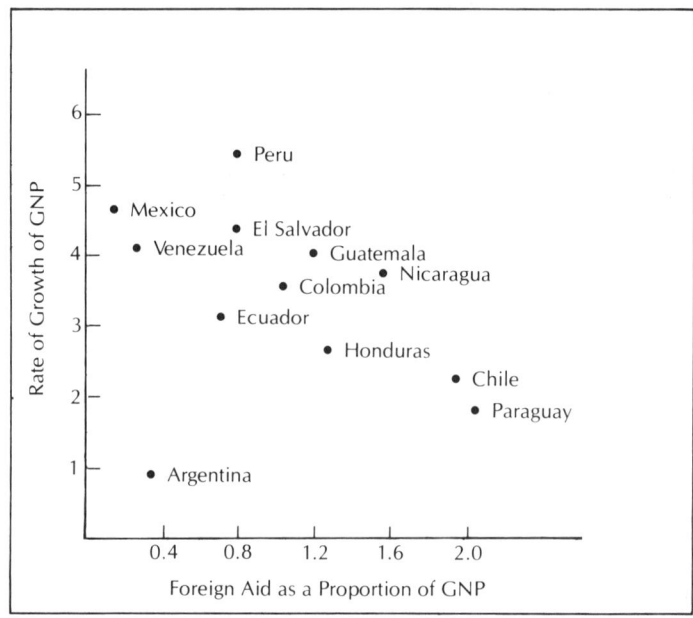

FIGURE 11.14 Relationship between foreign aid and the average rate of growth of Gross National Product, 1957–64. SOURCE: K. B. Griffin and J. L. Enos, 1970, "Foreign Assistance: Objectives and Consequences," *Economic Development and Cultural Change*, Vol. 18, p. 319, Fig. 1.

Aid and Balance of Payments Another argument for aid is that it may ease the balance of payments problem, *i.e.*, difficulties in earning enough foreign exchange to meet debt payments and to pay for necessary imports. Aid brings new debt, but it can provide a means for paying back old debt. Through new and larger borrowings to pay debts from earlier loans, however, bankrupt countries like Zaire become increasingly controlled by the lending developed nations and their "international" lending institutions.

Aid also can provide a means for purchasing goods that are essential for development. The usefulness of such aid, however, depends on its form. The best type of aid is "free" or "untied" foreign exchange, which, as we have seen, is in short supply.

Aid and the Transfer of Knowledge Proponents of aid stress that aid is an important vehicle for transferring techniques and know-how. Those who make such an assertion imply that such a transfer is of value to the recipients. In general this may be true, but not all such transfers are useful. Personnel from developed countries

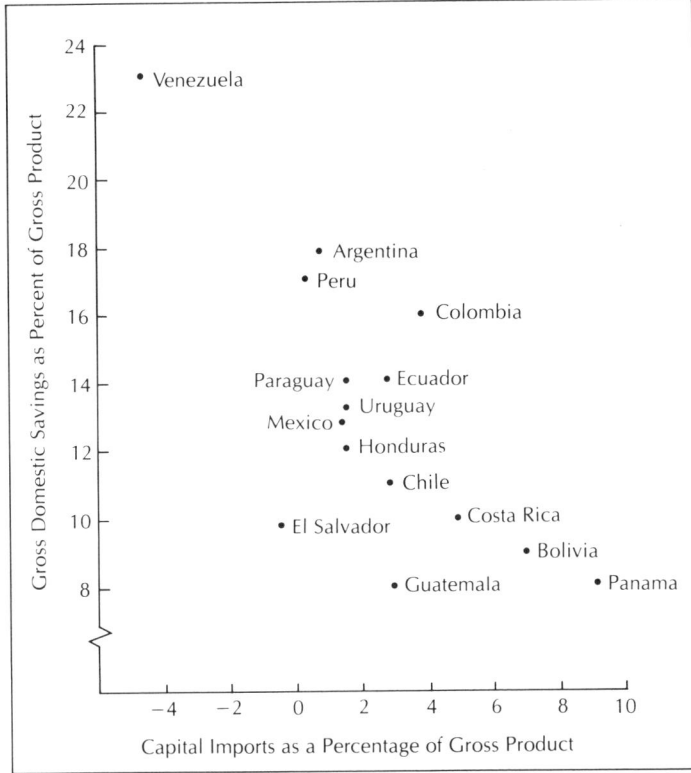

FIGURE 11.15 Relationship between gross domestic savings and foreign aid, 1958–64. SOURCE: Keith Griffin, 1969, *Underdevelopment in Spanish America*. London: George Allen and Unwin, Ltd., p. 123, Fig. III: 3.

may introduce inappropriate attitudes, techniques and methods into the host country. Western attitudes may prejudice indigenous development. Imitation of Western techniques and methods may increase unemployment and landlessness and reduce the rate of economic growth. Capital-intensive techniques may retard the rate of growth because they may not be the most profitable ones, given the prevailing prices of labor and capital.

Opposition to Aid In developed countries today, lay persons are increasingly skeptical about the liberal philosophy of aid-giving. Their opposition to aid, however, is often based on ignorance about the Third World (Figure 11.16). To many Americans, United States foreign aid is altruistic in the sense that it deprives its citizens:

> ... we have too much of a "give-away" policy. I think we should take care of our own first.
>
> So many people are out of jobs here and the country is helping other countries ... Our own people should be helped before foreign countries.
>
> I don't want the taxpayers of the U.S. to feed the rest of the world forever. We would go broke. (Free and Cantril, 1968:73).

In the academic world the most severe critics of foreign aid are conservative and radical economists and geographers. From the conservative viewpoint, P. Bauer is perhaps the most effective critic. Believing in the efficacy of free market

FIGURE 11.16 It isn't just in the Third World that we're fighting ignorance. SOURCE: *Development Forum,* March 1975, Vol. 3, No. 2, p. 11. Note: This illustration is a poster produced by United Kingdom's "War on Want," and brings home the need for development education.

forces, Bauer (1966) argued that foreign aid is a system of unearned doles that leads to the pauperization of its recipients. He stressed that foreign aid is neither a necessary condition for material progress nor a sufficient condition for economic advance. If people's faculties, attitudes, motivations, and institutions are incompatible with economic development, then the provision of aid alone is unlikely to lead to development. Moreover, Bauer noted that aid encourages comprehensive development planning which increases the concentration of power. It encourages governments to dissipate their foreign exchange reserves. And aid supplied gratis tends "to influence the recipient's values, and indeed the whole development process in a direction copied from external prototypes. This pattern is often uncongenial to . . . the peoples of the recipient countries and may have to be imposed forcibly. And the resulting coercion is often ineffective, and it not only sets up acute tensions but also leads to frustration" (1966:38).

Teresa Hayter (1971) and Keith Griffin (1971) are representative of the radical viewpoint. Hayter argued that aid is the "smooth face of imperialism" (1971:7). It continues to tie the poor countries into a relation of dependence. The availability of aid helps to "create and sustain, within Third World countries, a class which is dependent on the continued existence of aid and foreign private investment and which therefore become an ally of imperialism" (1971:9). Griffin said that foreign aid retards economic growth, and leads to wastefully high capital-output ratios. "Foreign savings often tend to supplant rather than supplement (let alone increase) domestic savings" (1971:122). Griffin also considered that aid is used to pursuade underdeveloped countries to accept private foreign capital aid and to accept the free enterprise system.

Both conservative and radical critics agree that existing aid programs do not promote development. They also agree that development must be primarily an indigenous process. For Bauer, development "is a social process requiring much more than the supply of money from aboard" (1966:37). And for Griffin "the development process requires a strong ideological foundation . . . Foreign investment, however, is not the type of activity which generates and sustains an ideological fervour; this is something which only domestic efforts can produce" (1971:132).

We can see that foreign aid has been used by many underdeveloped countries as an easy substitute for decisions to generate domestic development. It is also apparent that aid has been used by donor countries as an instrument of both economic and foreign policy. In many respects, aid from developed countries and international organizations like the World Bank is a palliative designed to give support to the continuation of an unequal world division of labor. A genuine transfer of resources from rich to poor countries is possible, but only if the existing division of labor is replaced with a more equitable one.

Summary

In this chapter, we looked at the *classical case for trade*. The classical model shows that trade is based on *comparative advantage*, not absolute advantage, and that *free trade* is best because it maximizes world output.

Beyond predicting that everyone gains something from trade, orthodox theory neglects to consider the distribution of benefits. Free trade was established in the nineteenth century within a framework of inequality between countries. An *artificial division of labor* was established between developed and underdeveloped countries. Third World countries as primary producers became dependent on foreign demand and, therefore, vulnerable to the business cycle of expansion and contraction in developed countries.

Today, underdeveloped countries continue to export raw and semi-processed primary goods. In return, they import mostly manufactured goods. Since the Korean War boom, the trend in prices for raw materials has been down, whereas the trend in prices for manufactured goods has been up, resulting in a worsening in the *terms of trade*. Declining prices of raw materials cause serious economic problems for underdeveloped countries (unemployment, balance of payments difficulties).

Increased international trade can make an important contribution to the development of Third World nations. But can international institutions such as

UNCTAD effect a reversal of the worsening trade situation for the underdeveloped countries? At present, developed countries are not prepared to scrap the existing trade system and replace it with one that is more equitable.

In the last section of the chapter we explored foreign aid and investment. We discovered that multinationals extract more profit each year than they put into the Third World in investment, and that much official aid is "tied." We also discovered that aid may not accelerate the rate of economic growth. Finally, we saw that conservatives and radicals oppose the liberal philosophy of aid-giving, but for different reasons, and agree that development is essentially an *indigenous* process.

DISCUSSION QUESTIONS

1. Although Country A can produce commodity X more efficiently than Country B, it continues to import X from B. Can you explain why?
2. Why do nations trade among themselves?
3. Evaluate the "infant industry" argument in favor of tariffs.
4. "Western countries should refuse to allow a reorganization of trade relations which would favor poor countries' exports." Comment.
5. Why have underdeveloped countries experienced great price instability for their major exports?
6. Explain in detail why most underdeveloped countries cannot rely upon expanding foreign trade as the main means of achieving development.
7. Discuss: Foreign aid is not a necessary condition of economic advance.
8. Discuss: "Aid is imperialism."
9. Why are many underdeveloped countries leery of direct private foreign investment?
10. Explain why the OPEC-conjured idea of "commodity power" is an illusion as far as most commodities are concerned.

SUGGESTED READINGS

Foreign Trade

Griffin, K., *Underdevelopment in Spanish America*. London: George Allen Unwin, 1969, Chapter 2.

Kenen, P. B., *International Economics*. Englewood Cliffs, N.J.: Prentice-Hall, Inc., 1964.

Haberler, G., *A Survey of International Trade Theory*. Princeton: International Finance Section, 1961.

Suggested Readings

Morton, K., and P. Tulloch, *Trade and Developing Countries.* New York: John Wiley & Sons, 1977.

Myint, H., "The Classical Theory of International Trade and Underdeveloped Countries" in I. Livingston (ed.), *Economic Policy for Development.* Harmondsworth, England: Penguin Books, 1971, pp. 85–111.

Myrdal, G. M., *Economic Theory and Underdeveloped Regions.* London: Duckworth, 1957.

Thoman, R. S., and E. C. Conkling, *Geography of International Trade.* Englewood Cliffs, N.J.: Prentice-Hall, 1967.

Foreign Aid

Bauer, P. T., "Foreign Aid: An Instrument for Progress?" in B. Ward and P. T. Bauer, *Two Views of Foreign Aid.* London: Institute of Economic Affairs, Occasional Paper No. 9, 1966, pp. 31–58.

Cavadino, P., *Get Off Their Backs.* Oxford: Third World First, 1973.

Gappert, G., "Cooperation Against Poverty," *Africa Today,* **18** (1971):35–51.

Griffin, K., *Underdevelopment in Spanish America.* London: George Allen Unwin, 1969, Chapter 3.

Hayter, T., *Aid as Imperialism.* Harmondsworth, England: Penguin Books, 1971.

Ward, B., "The Decade of Development—A Study in Frustration?" in B. Ward and P. T. Bauer, *Two Views of Foreign Aid.* London: Institute of Economic Affairs, Occasional Paper No. 9, 1966, pp. 7–29.

Urban and Regional Differences in Income and Welfare

12

KEY TERMS

- backwash effects
- bazaar economy
- center-periphery
- dependency
- deviation-amplification
- deviation-counteraction
- dual economy
- firm-centered economy
- internal colonialism
- involution
- lower-circuit
- modern-traditional dichotomy
- multiplier
- peripheral economy
- polarization effects
- proto-proletariat
- rural development
- self-centered economy
- spread effects
- squatter settlements
- trickling-down effects
- *Ujamaa*
- underemployment
- unemployment
- upper circuit

12

International economic inequalities have grown to their present dimensions only recently. In the mid-eighteenth century, the world as a whole was economically much poorer, but the distribution of wealth among nations was more even than it is today. In 1850, developed countries, with a quarter of the population, produced about one-third of the world's output, but by 1960 they accounted for roughly four-fifths of world income.

The existence of affluence amidst poverty is to be found not only at the international level. It exists within countries, as the following index reveals:

Disparities in Regional Income per Capita
(per capita income, average of the country = 100)

Country	Year	Average per Capita Income of Region with Highest Level		Average per Capita Income of Region with Lowest Level		Ratio
Brazil	1960	State of Guanabara	291	State of Piaui	29	10
Colombia	1953	Dept. of Curdimarca	185	Dept. of Choco	17	11
U.S.A.	1960	Delaware	126	Mississippi	53	2.5

SOURCE: C. R. Hensman, 1975, *Rich Against Poor* © C. R. Hensman, 1971. Harmondsworth: Penguin Books Ltd., p. 130. Reprinted by permission of Penguin Books Ltd.

The figures show that the ratio of the income of the richest and the poorest states is low in the United States, but high in Brazil and Colombia. A low ratio indicates that affluence is dispersed. Conversely, a high ratio indicates that affluence is concentrated.

How can disparities in income and welfare be reduced, especially in underdeveloped countries? Opinions differ. According to conservatives, convergence is inevitable; it will occur gradually within a free market system. Liberals find little evidence to support the conservative viewpoint. They believe that government action can lead to an eventual reduction in the gap between rich and poor regions.

Center-Periphery Relations

For radicals, problems of inequality cannot be solved within a capitalist system. The only solution is a revolutionary reform of society based on human needs, not individual profits.

In this final chapter, we consider some aspects of economic inequality within underdeveloped countries. The chapter is divided into three sections. First, we examine center-periphery relations, and review some of the theoretical literature on regional differences in income. Second we take a look at the proto-proletariat, a marginal social group in Third World cities. Like the peasants in the countryside, their poverty is a consequence of the unequal deployment of power at national and international levels. Finally, we consider Tanzanian strategies for national and rural development. Tanzania is one of several underdeveloped countries that has attempted to equalize extremes of wealth among regions and among people.

OBJECTIVES

By the end of this chapter you should be able:

1. To discuss the center-periphery model.
2. To describe models of spatial polarization of societies.
3. To discuss the relationship between development and interregional inequality.
4. To distinguish between spread effects and backwash effects.
5. To explain the difference between deviation-amplification and deviation-counteraction.
6. To state the major characteristics of the modern-traditional dichotomy.
7. To discuss the dualistic model of the structure of a Third World city.
8. To delineate the proto-proletariat and describe its main features.
9. To define and discuss the concept of urban involution.
10. To describe the Tanzanian development process.

Center-Periphery Relations*

The Center-Periphery Concept

The *center-periphery* concept is an idea presented by regional analysts to explain the persistence of disequilibrium within underdeveloped countries (see box). In its

---

*This section is modified from de Souza and Porter, 1974, pp. 60–64.

> **THE CENTER-PERIPHERY PHENOMENON**
>
> The center-periphery concept has been variously stated by social scientists. One view of the center-periphery phenomenon was presented by John Friedmann (1966). He divided the world into a dynamic center and a stagnating periphery, and proposed four regions, as follows:
>
> 1. *Core-regions* are concentrated metropolitan economies with a high capacity for innovation and change. They exist as nested hierarchies from the national metropolis down to the hamlet. At the world level, Europe-North America is the core development region in the Western world.
>
> 2. *Upward-transition regions* are peripheral to the core, and suitable for resource exploitation and development. A special type of upward-transition region is the *development corridor* which exists between two major cities. An example is the corridor between Rio de Janeiro and Sao-Paulo.
>
> 3. *Resource-frontier regions* are peripheral areas of new settlement. An example is settlement on the north slope of Alaska.
>
> 4. *Downward-transition regions* are stagnating or declining areas. Rural economies and uncontrolled urban settlements of the underdeveloped world are examples.
>
> An alternative view of the center-periphery concept was presented by Andre Gunder Frank (1969, 1970) in his schematic system of *transfer of exploitation*. His dichotomy has been criticized for being too concerned with "spatial dominance." It assumes exploitation occurs only at the periphery, and not at both center and periphery. It does not pay sufficient attention to relations among capitalists, workers, and peasants. According to N. Poulantzas, the essence of the chain of exploitation is that "each link of this chain reflects the chain as a whole in the specificity of its own social formation" (1975:42).

Marxist form, the center appropriates to itself the surplus of the periphery for its own development. The center-periphery phenomenon can be seen as a multiple system of nested centers and peripheries. At the world level, the global center (rich industrial countries) drains the global periphery (most of the underdeveloped countries). But within any part of the international system, within any national unit, is another center and periphery. That center, although of considerably less power, is of sufficient strength to appropriate to itself a smaller, but still sizable, fraction of remaining surplus value. The center may be a single urban area, or a region encompassing several towns that stand in an advantageous relation to the hinterland. Even in remote peripheral areas there are likely to be local, regional imbalances, with some areas growing, and others stagnating or declining.

There are reverse flows from the various centers to the peripheries—to peripheral nations, to peripheral rural areas—but these flows may accentuate further center-periphery differences. They may increase the rate at which the economic

Center-Periphery Relations

surplus can be accumulated at the center. For example, most infrastructural projects supported by Western and international development agencies diffuse to underdeveloped countries those things which are necessary to the functioning of international capitalism (Hayter, 1971). Such aid generally is used to improve harbors, construct roads and dams, increase levels of health and education, improve urban housing, and train administrators, doctors, and scientists. Moreover, factories established by international companies are often built for the assembly and reexport of prefabricated parts at low labor cost. These developments tend to reinforce the status quo of the world economy.

A World Bank loan of $20 million is being used to help finance the cost of upgrading squatter areas in Lusaka, the capital of Zambia. In some cases, home owners are building new houses around their old ones. New housing developments, however, do not help to solve the unemployment problem in the Third World city. SOURCE: *World Bank Photo* by Edwin G. Huffman.

Yet many social scientists see core-regions of underdeveloped countries as centers from which the benefits of modernization flow outwards to "develop" the stagnating periphery. Such a vision could confine social scientists to the role of aiding the growth of national, regional, and individual inequalities in underdeveloped countries.

Neo-Classical Theories of Regional Development

One view of regional development stems from *equilibrium models,* which are extensions of classical location theory. Equilibrium models focus on deviation-counteracting systems, and hypothesize that the advantage of the center is only temporary (see box). The underlying assumption is that economic processes steer a system "naturally" toward an optimal equilibrium state. Thus, regional development inequalities are corrected by a free flow of factors of production which eventually bring about an equalization between center and periphery. No government intervention is required in the periphery; economic development will spread automatically from center to peripheral areas. Little historical evidence supports this assumption, however, while considerable evidence refutes it. *Polarizing effects* accentuating differences between center and periphery are the norm.

DEVIATION-COUNTERACTION AND DEVIATION-AMPLIFICATION

The term *deviation-counteraction* refers to any process that operates to reduce differences with a system. Conversely, *deviation-amplification* refers to any process that amplifies an initial "kick" or "trigger" to growth, and increases deviation and divergence from an initial condition. In the context of regional economics, deviation-counteracting forces narrow disparities in income and standards of living among regions, and deviation-amplifying forces widen the gap between rich and poor regions. For a detailed discussion of deviation-counteracting and deviation-amplifying forces, see Magorah Maruyama, 1963, "The Second Cybernetics: Deviation-Amplifying Mutual Causal Processes," *American Scientist*, **51**:164–179.

Polarized Development: Models of Myrdal and Hirschman

Gunnar Myrdal (1957) and Albert Hirschman (1958) attacked equilibrium notions in economic theory and suggested basic ideas about polarized development. In Myrdal's view, core regions of the space-economy are self-reinforcing magnets of progress. Rather than deviation-counteracting forces, deviation-amplifying forces increase the differences between center and periphery. Myrdal began his book with a discussion about the widening gap between rich and poor nations and between rich and poor people. He then sketched a model of cumulative change. He argued that during the early stages of development, increasing economic inequalities are generated through the operation of *circular* or *cumulative upward causation* (Figure 12.1). He reasoned that "change does not call forth contradicting forces" as equalization models suggest, "but, instead, supporting changes; which move the system in the same direction as the first change but much further" (1957:13). Myrdal said that once growth has been initiated in favored locations in a free economy, inflows of labor, skills, capital, and commodities develop spontaneously to support them. These flows, however, include *backwash effects,* amplifying inequalities between expanding and other regions (see box). Myrdal argued that if events follow an uncontrolled course, backwash effects perpetuate growth in expanding regions and retard growth elsewhere. For development to occur throughout a country, centrifugal *spread effects* of expansionary momentum must, on the average, be stronger than backwash effects.

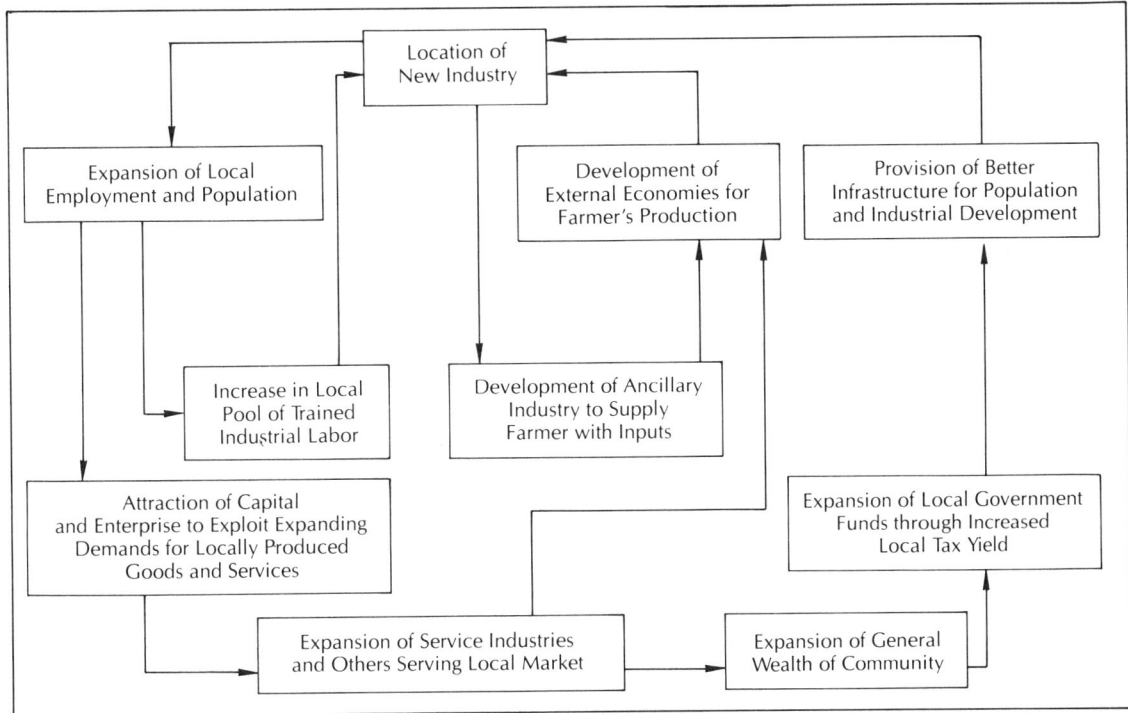

FIGURE 12.1 Myrdal's model of circular or cumulative upward causation. From D. E. Keeble, 1967, "Models of Economic Development," in Richard J. Chorley and Peter Haggett, eds., *Models in Geography*, London: Methuen & Co. Ltd., p. 258, Fig. 8.4.

Myrdal recognized that backwash effects are stronger in depression than in boom, so that down-turns of the business cycle affect stagnating or regressing communities more than vigorous growth centers. He noted that spread effects in rich industrial countries have not been strong enough to draw whole national economies into a more-or-less equal and simultaneous expansion process.

> In the United States, for example, almost the whole of the region usually referred to as the South was until recently largely a stagnating one. Similarly, the emergence some generations ago of the great new opportunities in agriculture in the western frontier left large rural areas in New England in a decay from which some of them have not yet emerged (1957:32–33).

Albert Hirschman advanced a similar model of economic development, and pointed out that *polarization effects* are "natural" in the early stages of development. He argued more persistently than Myrdal, however, in favor of massive investment in the urban-industrial core-region, realizing full well that such a policy would accentuate differences between the center and the periphery.

His model shows that once an initial decision is made to locate a particular industry at a specific point, it has an initial *multiplier* effect (Figure 12.2). New local demands are generated by the factory and by the purchasing power of its labor force. The labor force creates a demand for housing and for a set of services. The new factory attracts additional industries producing complementary goods.

> **SPREAD EFFECTS AND BACKWASH EFFECTS**
>
> Growing regions influence other regions through two opposing forces which, in the Myrdal model, are called *spread effects* and *backwash effects*. Spread effects refer to the beneficial impact prosperous regions have on less prosperous regions. These may include: increased demand for primary commodities, increased investment, and the diffusion of ideas and technology. In most underdeveloped countries, spread effects are restricted to areas around major centers of the urban hierarchy.
>
> "Backwash effects" refer to negative effects prosperous regions have on less prosperous regions. In underdeveloped countries the construction of roads is one example of negative effects. New roads may permit industrial plants in growing regions to supply lagging regions with goods formerly supplied by the poor regions' own craft industries. Migration of the most enterprising and educated people from lagging to growing regions may have a negative effect on production and productivity in poor regions. Finally, a further illustration of the forces creating "backwash" is exploitation through monopolies. An example is profit repatriation between the *Sierra* (periphery) and the coastal regions (center) of Peru. According to Alan Gilbert, "the *Sierra* has a trade surplus in its dealings with the more prosperous coastal regions. It gains little benefit from this surplus, however, because most of the trade is controlled by a small number of agricultural, mining and commercial enterprises operating from Lima. Consequently the profits from this trade are not reinvested in the *Sierra* but are transferred to banks in Lima and abroad" (1974:231–232).

Linked industries either provide needed inputs (backward linkages) or purchase semi-finished products (forward linkages) from the initial factory. The entire process has a cumulative self-generating momentum; after the first cycle of growth is complete, a new round of growth is initiated at a higher threshold. As Figure 12.2 illustrates, the cycles of growth can be carried through any number of times, at least until the process is arrested by diseconomies or interrupted by the competitive advantages of other growth points. Figure 12.2 also shows that the initial multiplier stimulates expansion of non-industrial activities and they in turn trigger a second multiplier which induces further growth and still higher thresholds.

Hirschman argued that it was natural for entrepreneurs to select and to concentrate their activities at growth points. Development becomes increasingly unbalanced. Growth of the developing region—"North" according to Hirschman's terminology—restricts the capacity for growth elsewhere—"South." The North attracts skilled labor and savings from the South. The income elasticity of demand is greater for Northern manufactured goods, and hence terms of trade turn against Southern producers of primary commodities.

The central idea of Hirschman's model is that these polarization effects are offset eventually by *"trickling-down effects,"* the equivalent of Myrdal's spread effects. Trickling down effects include the Northern purchase of commodities produced in the South, and the southward movement of capital. In addition, the North may attract enough southern labor to ensure an increase in the South's marginal

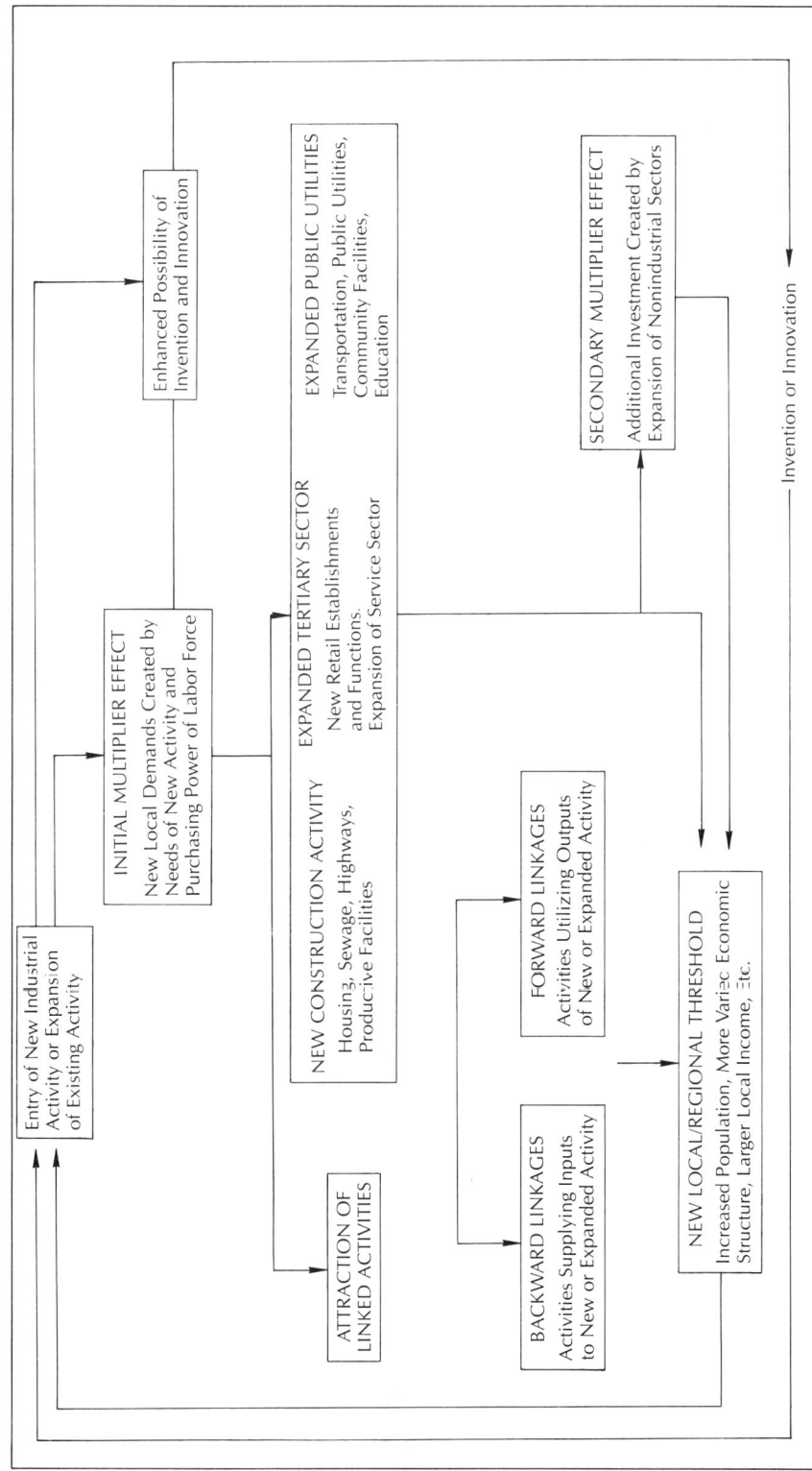

FIGURE 12.2 Initial multiplier effect and the process of cumulative upward causation. Based on Allan R. Pred, 1966, *The Spatial Dynamics of U.S. Urban-Industrial Growth*, p. 25, Fig. 2.1. By permission of The MIT Press, Cambridge, Massachusetts.

productivity of labor and per capita consumption levels. Hirschman insisted that trickling-down effects can only take place if the North needs the South for its own expansion. He presumed that if in the course of development inequalities between North and South do not melt away in the course of time through unrestrained market forces, then the "visible" hand of the state would have to intervene and introduce remedial measures.

Both Myrdal's and Hirschman's models of spatial polarization of economies suggest that in a free enterprise economy, increasing disparities between more developed and less developed areas are typical of early stages of economic development. On the question of later convergence, Myrdal was pessimistic and did not carry his analysis beyond a discussion of the vicious cycle of backwash effects. He said that most governments in underdeveloped countries were elitist, and their actions only succeed in accentuating inequalities between rich and poor regions and between rich and poor people. On the other hand, Hirschman insisted that eventual convergence is the norm. He believed that once government starts to play a role in planning development, it intervenes to reduce inequalities by applying progressive taxation programs or by giving subsidies to rural areas.

Convergence, or the idea that with increasing economic development comes greater regional economic equality was explored empirically by J. Williamson (1965). He concluded that regional income inequalities are greater in underdeveloped countries and smaller in developed countries. Further, he suggested that "during the course of development, some or all of the disequilibrating tendencies diminish, causing a reversal in the pattern of interregional inequality" and the likely result is that "a statistic describing regional inequality will trace out an inverted 'U' over the national growth path" (1965:9–10). The relationship between regional income inequality and national economic growth is shown in Figure 12.3.

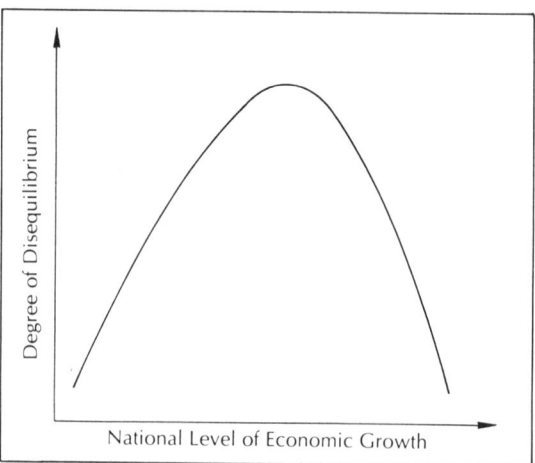

FIGURE 12.3 Relationship between the degree of disequilibrium and level of national economic growth.

Friedmann's Models of Regional Development

The name of John Friedmann is closely associated with the development of Western regional science. We will review his work in center-periphery relations from 1964 to

Center-Periphery Relations

1970. Like Hirschman, Friedmann assumed that government action can lead to eventual solution of regional-income disparities. Unlike Myrdal and Hirschman, he related the problem of unequal development to the process of urbanization and to the interaction between cities and their surroundings.

In an early statement on urban-regional development Friedmann (jointly with William Alonso) stated:

> Spatial patterns will change with shifts in the structure of demand and of production, in the level of technology, and in the social and political organization of the nation. The economic and social development of the nation is reflected in its patterns of settlement; its patterns of commuting and migration; and its reticulation of areas of urban influence. And if there is a spatial pattern corresponding to each 'stage' of economic development, it may be further suggested that there is an optimal strategy for spatial transformation from one stage to the next. In the early period of development, marginal returns to the factors of production differ greatly between regions. With economic advancement, economic functions become more differentiated in space, and the relevant scale of many functions will increase. At an advanced stage of development, the national economy will appear as a fully integrated hierarchy of functional areas, with most of the population and activities polarized in metropolitan areas and, in effect, with national markets for labor, capital and commodities (1964:2).

The authors then proposed their version of the center-periphery model:

> ... centers not only grow so rapidly as to create problems of an entirely new order, but they also act as suction pumps, pulling in the more dynamic elements from the more static regions. The remainder of the country is thus relegated to a second-class, peripheral position. It is placed in a quasi-colonial relationship to the center, experiencing net outflows of people, capital and resources, most of which redound to the advantage of the center where economic growth will tend to be rapid, sustained, and cumulative (1964:3; By permission of The MIT Press.).

Two years later, Friedmann devised a descriptive four stage model of spatial evolution in his book, *Regional Development Policy*. It draws on the nineteenth century North American experience to impose stages onto the continuum of economic growth countries are supposed to experience as they develop. Friedmann recognized the following stages of spatial evolution (Figure 12.4):

1. *A pre-industrial phase*, which is characterized by a number of small independent urban centers spread throughout a large region. There is no urban hierarchy, the possibilities for growth are soon exhausted, and the economy tends to stagnate. Friedmann assumed the system to be in balance, because each center serves, by and large, only its local area.

2. A period of *incipient-industrialization* is characterized by a primate city (C) which dominates a large region, and exploits the natural resources of its periphery (P). Local economies in the periphery are undermined in consequence of a mass movement of would-be entrepreneurs, intellectuals, and labor to the primate city. Friedmann viewed the primacy-dominated organization of space as unstable, because the system is generated by exogenous forces.

3. During the *transitional stage* toward industrial maturation the primate city (C) still dominates the large region, but not as much as previously. The

construction of strategically located urban centers or growth centers (SC_1 and SC_2) reduces the influence of the large city. Friedmann regarded the third stage as still unstable, because pockets of "backwardness" in peripheral areas persist (P_1, P_2, P_3 and P_4).

4. The last stage consists of a *full-fledged spatial organization* based on the hierarchy principle which covers the entire national territory. According to Friedmann, this functionally interdependent system of cities will fulfill essential goals of internal spatial organization such as national integration, efficiency of location, maximum growth potential, and a high degree of interregional balance.

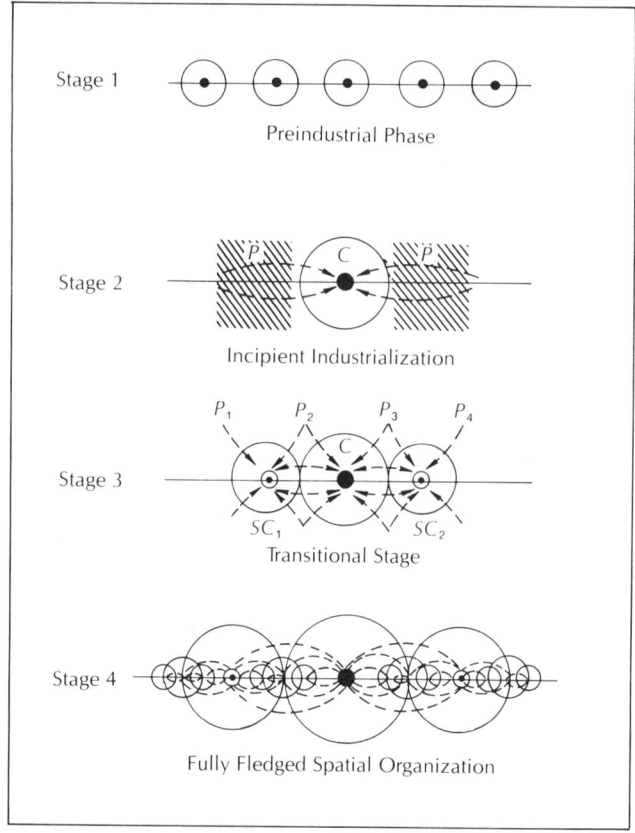

FIGURE 12.4 Friedmann's stages of spatial evolution. Reprinted from *Regional Development Policy: A Case Study of Venezuela* by J. Friedmann, p. 36, Fig. 2.1, 1966. By permission of The MIT Press, Cambridge, Massachusetts.

Friedmann's evolutionary model posits ultimate convergence between center and periphery. However, he stressed that empirical evidence points to persistent disequilibrium (1966:14). He noted that even after 150 years of sustained urban-industrialization, the United States still has problems of depressed and backward regions. Figures 12.5 and 12.6 demonstrate unequal development in the United States. Note the inverse relationship between low income and extent of commuting fields. The heartland has the greatest complexity of interpenetrating and coalescing commuter fields, and the hinterlands, with the widest spacing of metropolitan urban centers and the most extensive inter-urban peripheries, have the greatest concentration of low-income counties.

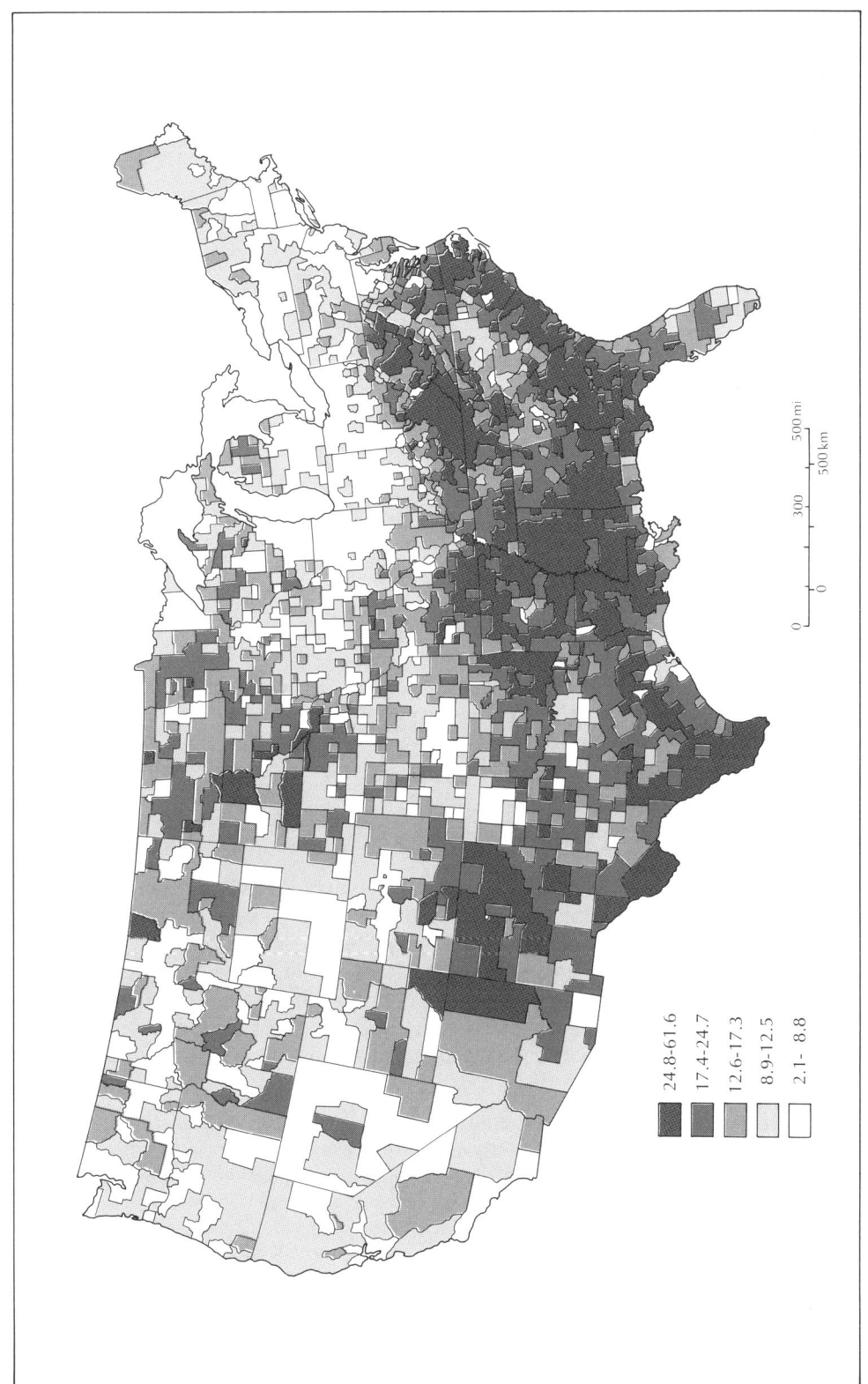

FIGURE 12.5 Percentage of families below low income level in the United States, 1969. SOURCE: *County and City Data Book*, 1972.

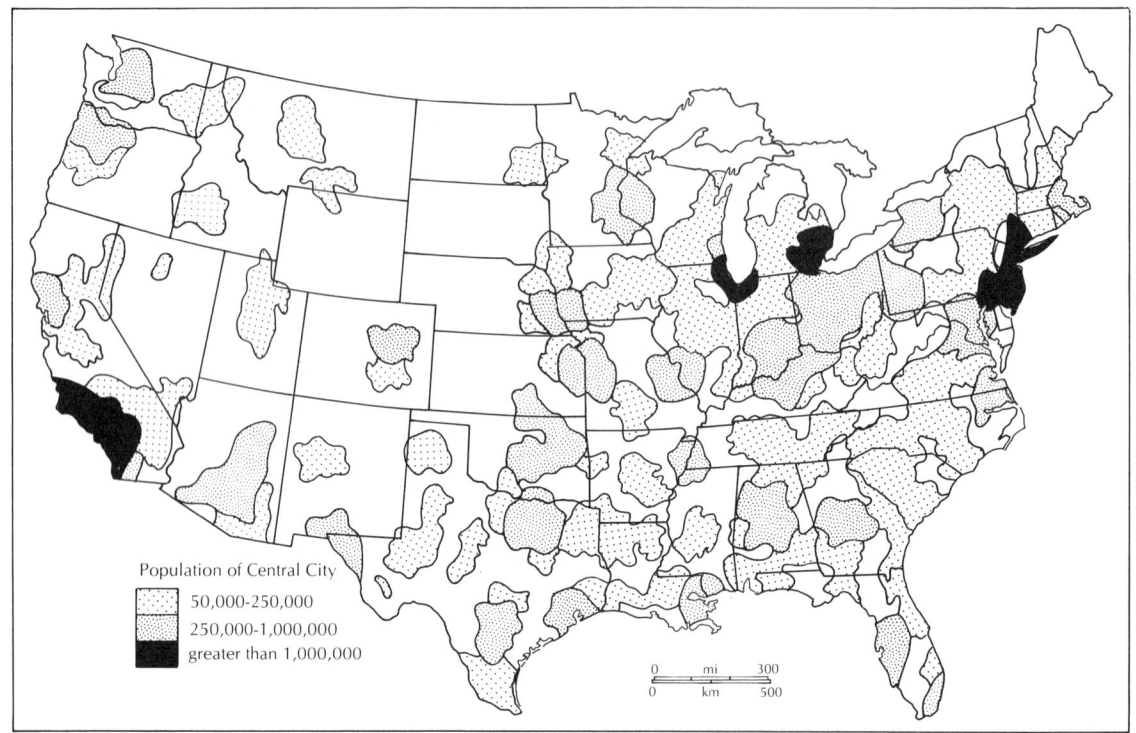

FIGURE 12.6 Extent of commuting fields in the United States in 1960. SOURCE: B. J. L. Berry, 1968, *Metropolitan Area Definition: A Re-evaluation of Concept and Statistical Practice,* Washington, D.C.: Bureau of the Census, Working Paper No. 28.

Friedmann went on to remark that convergence is an extremely drawn-out process, and he thought it would come only when a society reached an advanced stage of the industrialization process. He suggested, however, that continued urban-industrial expansion in major metropolitan areas should lead to catalytic impacts on surrounding regions. He offered a number of propositions which reflect the ongoing urban-regional development process in the United States. The propositions, which have an explicit link with central place theory and innovation diffusion theory, are as follows:

> Economic growth takes place in a matrix of urban regions through which the space economy is organized . . . Cities organize the space economy. They are centers of activity and of innovation, focal points of the transport network, locations of superior accessibility at which firms can most easily reap scale economies and at which industrial complexes can obtain the economies of localization and urbanization. Agricultural enterprise is more efficient in the vicinity of cities. The more prosperous commercialized agricultures encircle the major cities . . . There are two major elements in this organization of economic activities in space:
>
> (a) A system of cities, organized in a hierarchy according to the functions performed by each;

Center-Periphery Relations

(b) Corresponding areas of urban influence or urban fields surrounding each of the cities in the system.

Generally we can argue the following about this system of spatial organization:

(a) The size and function of a central city and the size of the urban field are proportional.

(b) The spatial incidence of economic growth is a function of distance from the central city. Troughs of economic backwardness lie in the most inaccessible areas along the intermetropolitan peripheries.

(c) Impulses of economic change are transmitted in order from higher to lower centers in the urban hierarchy, in a "size-rachet" sequence, so that continued innovation in large cities remains critical for extension of growth over the complete economic system.

(d) The growth potential of an area situated along an axis between two cities is a function of the intensity of interaction between them (Berry, 1969:288). (See box.)

RADICALS AND THE CITY DOMINANT THESIS

According to John Friedmann, Third World cities, as centers of influence over regional and national hinterlands, are catalysts to development. This article of faith is to radicals, who see Third World cities as capitalist structures, nothing more than colonialism thinly disguised. For Andre Gunder Frank (1969, 1970), cities in underdeveloped countries are centers of colonial domination. This view calls into question Friedmann's assumption that urbanization is necessarily coupled with development.

Radicals emphasize how important it is to see *dependency* relationships clearly. The Marxist mode of analysis approaches underdevelopment historically, seeing urbanization in underdeveloped countries, since the birth of industrial capitalism, as a dependent process. By contrast, the standard Western regional science approach, which is reflected in the work of Friedmann, tends to neglect the past; to underestimate effects of world economy on urban and regional patterns; and to misjudge the resistance of institutions and cultures in underdeveloped countries to the standard Western regional model. The usefulness of the established model for radicals is reduced by its limited historical and cultural perspective.

Friedmann became critical of his own emphasis on economic forces propelling change. In *A General Theory of Polarized Development,* he sought a linkage between regional interaction theory and a theory of social change. He stated:

> The General Theory treats economic growth as a function of changes in the structures that inevitably limit a system's capacity for expansion and, in the specific case of growth based on the application of science to problems of economic production, also of the system's capacity for continuous generation and absorption of innovations. This formulation assigns a decisive influence to the institutional and organizational framework of society and, specifically to the patterns of authority and dependency that result from the unusual capacity of certain areas to serve as cradles of innovation (1969:29–30).

Adopting a non-Marxist conflict theory of social change, Friedmann reformulated his center-periphery model:

> Dominant core and dominated periphery together constitute a relatively stable spatial system in which the latter is successfully "colonized" chiefly to sustain the continued growth of the former.
>
> The further growth of core regions, however, is in the final analysis constrained by the tensions that tend to build up from the ever more visible discrepancies in the rates of expansion and modernization between core and periphery. The increasing flow of information from core to periphery, together with aroused awareness of potentially modernizing elites in the periphery of the conditions of their own dependency, produce conflict with core-region authorities over the extent of permissible autonomy (Friedmann, 1969:30).

Friedmann identified four possible resolutions of dualism between center and periphery: (1) the suppression of peripheral elites by the center, (2) neutralization of peripheral elities, (3) replacement of center by peripheral elites, and (4) selection of peripheral by center elites. These outcomes lead either to further deviation-amplification, or to the appearance of deviation-counteracting forces. If conflict resolution between center and periphery results in further deviation-amplification, the center becomes progressively more and more rigid *vis-a-vis* the periphery, and "growth without development" is the consequence.

The critical planning problem then becomes: how and when to change authority-dependency relations if "progress" is to occur. There is little agreement as to when to transform authority-dependency relations. Liberals argue that in the early stages of economic development the center works to mobilize the periphery, and therefore, the most effective development policy is to leave things as they are. Yet it is recognized that this course might create an overly entrenched center, and it might decrease the likelihood of peaceful transformation.

Although the problem of "when" to act is unresolved, "how" to change is, in Friedmann's view, more clear. Several interrelated transformations are required. The transformations are isomorphic and include:

1. *Socio-cultural patterns.* The evolutions of spatial structure proceeds from isolated "islands of innovation" to a completely "modernized" surface.

2. *Locational patterns of economic activity.* The evolution of spatial structure proceeds from intense center concentration of "modern" activities to a more dispersed pattern.

3. *Settlement patterns.* The evolution of spatial structure proceeds from primacy to log-normality in a hierarchy of central places.

4. *Political organization.* The evolution of spatial structure proceeds from a centralized to a decentralized system for making political and economic decisions (Friedmann, 1970:33–34).

These isomorphic transformations suggest a relationship between the degree of disequilibrium and the level of "development." In the early phases of "development," backwash effects dominate. The degree of disequilibrium reaches a peak in the middle phases of "development," after which spread effects begin to propel the system toward an equilibrium state.

Center-Periphery Relations

To summarize our discussion of center-periphery relations, we note that classical economists argue that no intervention is required in processes of spatial organization. Convergence is likely to occur within a free market economy. By contrast, liberals like Friedmann urge active intervention because of the inability of "invisible hands" to reduce disequilibrium. He advocated that planners should "act upon social and economic processes . . . to guide society towards desired objectives" (Friedmann, 1967:229). For Friedmann, the desired objectives were a high rate of growth and economic efficiency.

Friedmann's concept of the center-periphery model is close to a Marxian view of the world (see box). His notion of dominated periphery by dominant core corresponds with the idea of the center appropriating the economic surplus of the periphery for its own development. Marxists, however, would prefer to view the problem of unequal development not primarily in terms of spatial relations, but of class relations. According to Marxists, the process of unequal development is assisted by the concentration of political and economic power in the hands of a minority seeking advances for itself or the class to which it belongs. The monopoly of power over the production process by the few prevents the mass of people from increasing what they create and produce for themselves. Poor people may know what they lack and how to get it, but they are powerless to get the economy moving in the proper direction. The wealthy own the land, control development policies, and direct the production process at a minimum cost to themselves and their associates at home and abroad. In consequence, Marxists would argue that deep rooted structural change is necessary to redress inequalities generated by the capitalist mode of production.

JOHAN GALTUNG AND THE CENTER-PERIPHERY CONCEPT

Johan Galtung (1971), concerned about the tremendous inequalities within and between nations, based his concept of the center-periphery model on a theory of imperialism. Although his analysis of center-periphery relations may be described as radical, he preferred to adopt a non-Marxist interpretation of imperialism. Marxists conceive of imperialism as "an economic relationship under private capitalism, motivated by the need for expanding markets. . . . According to this view, imperialism and dominance will fall like dominoes when the capitalistic conditions for economic imperialism no longer obtain (Galtung, 1971:81). Galtung viewed imperialism as a more "general structural relationship between two collectivities. . . . Briefly stated, imperialism is a system that splits up collectivities and relates some of the parts to each other in relations of *harmony of interest,* and other parts in relations of *disharmony of interest,* or *conflict of interest."* (Galtung, 1971:81).

Galtung illustrated his discussion of imperialism with a simple two-nation world, a world in which the center nation has power over the periphery nation, so as to bring about a condition of disharmony of interest between them. According to Galtung:

Imperialism is a relation between a Center and a Periphery nation so that

(1) there is *harmony of interest* between the *center in the Center* nation and the *center in the Periphery* nation,

(2) there is more *disharmony of interest* within the Periphery nation than within the Center nations,

(3) there is *disharmony of interest* between the *periphery in the Center* nation and the *periphery in the Periphery* nation [see diagram].

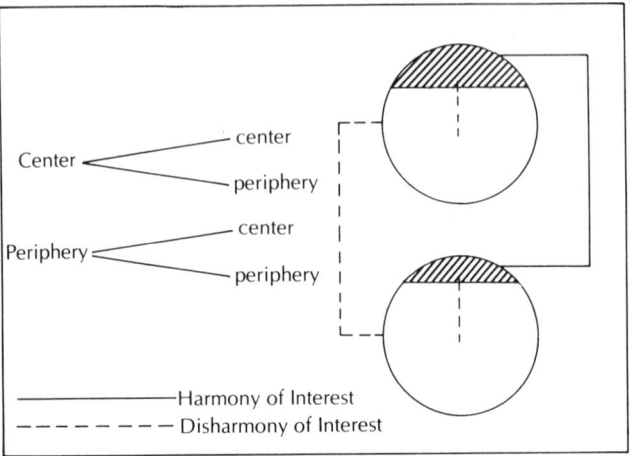

The structure of imperialism. SOURCE: J. Galtung, 1971, "A Structural Theory of Imperialism," *Journal of Peace Research*, No. 2, p. 84, Fig. 1.

This complex definition, borrowing largely from Lenin, needs spelling out. The basic idea is, as mentioned, that the center in the Center nation has a bridgehead in the Periphery nation, and a well-chosen one: the center in the Periphery nation. This is established such that the Periphery center is tied to the Center center with the best possible tie: the tie of harmony of interest. They are linked so that they go up together and down, even under, together. . . .

Inside the two nations there is disharmony of interest. They are both in one way or another vertical societies with LC [Living Condition] gaps—otherwise there is no possibility of locating a center and a periphery. Moreover, the gap is not decreasing, but is at best constant. But the basic idea, absolutely fundamental for the whole theory to be developed, is that *there is more disharmony in the Periphery nation than in the Center nation*. At the simplest static level of description this means there is more inequality in the Periphery than in the Center. At the more complex level we might talk in terms of the gap opening more quickly in the Periphery than in the Center, where it might even remain constant. Through welfare state activities, redistribution takes place and disharmony is reduced for at least some LC dimensions, including income, but usually excluding power.

If we now would capture in a few sentences what imperialism is about, we might perhaps say something like this:

In the Periphery nation, the center grows more than the periphery, due partly to how interaction between center and periphery is organized. Without necessarily thinking of economic interaction, the center is more enriched than the periphery. . . . However, for part of this enrichment, the center in the Periphery only serves as a transmission belt (e.g. commerical firms, trading companies) for value (e.g. raw materials) forwarded to the Center nation. This value enters the Center in the center, with some of it drizzling down to the periphery in the Center. Importantly, there is less disharmony of interest in the Center than in the Periphery, so that the total arrangement is largely in the interest of

> the periphery in the Center. Within the Center the two parties may be opposed to each other. But in the total game, the periphery see themselves more as the partners of the center in the Center than as the partners of the periphery in the Periphery—and this is the essential trick of that game. Alliance-formation between the two peripheries is avoided, while the Center nation becomes more and the Periphery nation less cohesive—and hence less able to develop long-term strategies.
>
> Actually, concerning the three criteria in the definition of imperialism as given above, it is clear that no. (3) is implied by nos. (1) and (2). The two centers are tied together and the Center periphery is tied to its center: that is the whole essence of the situation. If we now presuppose that the center in the Periphery is a smaller proportion of that nation than the center in the Center, we can also draw one more implication: *there is disharmony of interest between the Center nation as a whole and the Periphery nation as a whole*. But that type of finding, frequently referred to, is highly misleading because it blurs the harmony of interest between the two centers, and leads to the belief that imperialism is merely an international relationship, not a combination of intra- and inter-national relations (Galtung, 1971, 83–84).
>
> Galtung then examined the mechanisms of imperialism (the relations between center and periphery), the types of imperialism (the types of exchange between center and periphery nations—economic, political, military, communication and cultural), and the phases of imperialism in history (colonialism in the past, and neo-colonialism today and in the future). Finally, he generalized his center-periphery scheme to several nations, and considered strategies for structural change of the international dominance system.

The Proto-Proletariat

Center-periphery relationships are features of the evolving world economy which contribute strongly to the underdevelopment of poor people. This is particularly true of peasants and their urban counterparts, the *proto-proletariat,* in those countries of Africa, Asia, and Latin America that have experienced capitalist systems emanating from the cores of Anglo-America and Western Europe. In a world viewed as a set of Thünen rings, they exist at its outer fringe—poor and discriminated against in the use and control of the world's resources (Figure 12.7). For example, 33 percent of the population of Chile have a per capita income one fortieth or one fiftieth of that enjoyed by their rulers, the top two percent. In Peru, large landowners and capitalists (0.1 percent of the active population) and peasants (59 percent) take 20 percent and 13 percent, respectively, of the national income.

The purpose of this section is to describe and analyze the *proto-proletariat*. The proto-proletariat is a peripheral social group which makes up a substantial proportion of the occupational structure of cities in most underdeveloped countries. The people in this group are engaged primarily in the economic activity of the "traditional" as opposed to the "modern" sector, and, therefore, they are neither salary nor regular wage earners. In underdeveloped countries, urban and rural areas have a *dual-economy*—one sector "traditional" and the other sector "modern"—tied through export, organization, capital support, and use of technology to the de-

FIGURE 12.7 The world's stratified society. SOURCE: A. R. de Souza and P. W. Porter, 1974, *The Underdevelopment and Modernization of the Third World.* Washington, D.C.: Association of American Geographers Commission on College Geography, Resource Paper No. 28, p. 81, Fig. 13.

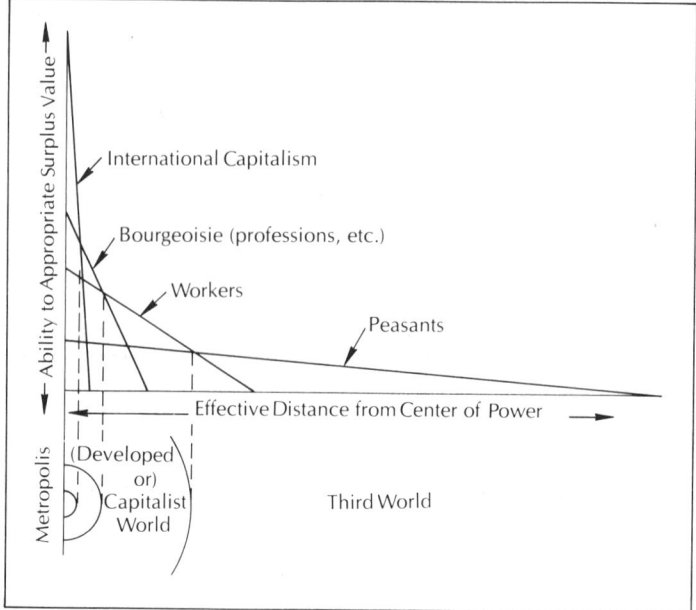

veloped countries of Europe and North America. These two sectors do not exist independently side by side; they are interlaced and unequal.

Urban Growth with Dependent Industrialization

The key to the development of the United States was its emphasis on the domestic requirements of the national economy. The first need to be met was food, followed by the establishment of producer goods and mass consumption goods industries. By contrast, the allocation of economic resources in most underdeveloped countries today is topsy-turvy. Urban-industrial growth takes priority over rural development. Industrial growth is oriented toward export-processing and luxury goods industries; the former producing for an external market and the latter for a limited internal market and export. The chief beneficiaries of this kind of development are the already wealthy people of developed and underdeveloped countries. Except for a few privileged industrial workers, usually under five percent of the work force, the broad mass of the population is more or less excluded from the export-luxury economy. This is easily confirmed by a few visits to cities of the underdeveloped world. For example, in many African cities, the inhabitants of "uncontrolled" or "squatter" settlements, who provide a reservoir of cheap labor for the modern industrial sector, have increased from one-fifth to one-half of the urban population in recent years.

Although urban areas have achieved remarkable industrialization since 1945, industrial employment has not kept pace with population growth. Urban population growth rates are frequently in excess of eight percent annually, but industrial employment rate increases are generally less than four percent annually.

The Proto-Proletariat

Center-periphery contrast: (A) luxurious corporate headquarters of Continental Oil Company in the prestigious suburban office estate of High Ridge Park, Stamford, Connecticut (SOURCE: Continental Oil Company); and (B) a peasant preparing for spring planting in the Ecuadorian Andes. SOURCE: *World Bank Photo* by Edwin G. Huffman.

The employment situation has been aggravated by the introduction of advanced technology which permits high worker-output ratios. As a consequence, the proto-proletariat are absorbed by small-scale family enterprises, personal services, and *unemployment*. They are victims of urban growth without industrialization. More precisely, they are victims of the world's spatial economy whose center (rich industrial countries) encourages an export-luxury economy in underdeveloped countries.

A Neglected Occupational Element

Today alarm is voiced about massive *unemployment* and *underemployment* among the proto-proletariat of Third World cities. But until the late 1960s, most social scientists neglected to examine the proto-proletariat, who were dismissed out of hand as inefficient and unproductive. The question of whether the proto-proletariat contributed to development was ignored. At least three reasons may be given for the lack of research attention.

A

B

Traditional-modern contrast. (A) Small villages in Central Karamoja, Uganda. SOURCE: J. H. Blower for *UNESCO* (B) Employees of the Mali Electrical Works on a high tension line near Bamako. SOURCE: J. C. Bois for *UNESCO*.

First, most systems of official data collection in underdeveloped countries record activities only of the wage-earning population of the "modern" sector. Second, during the United Nations' Development Decade (the 1960s), most development models emphasized activities of the "modern" sector which were assumed to be growth promoting. Third, the *modern-traditional dichotomy,* a major evolutionary theory of social and economic change, encouraged social scientists to view development as the penetration of traditional systems by Western elements of "modernization" (see box). Major characteristics of this theory may be summarized as follows:

> **MODERN-TRADITIONAL DICHOTOMY**
>
> The study of the urbanization and modernization of underdeveloped countries has been dominated by the assumption of incompatibility between "modern" and "traditional" societies. Modernization is viewed as a process of diffusing Western culture. In this theme, modernization becomes a problem of changing a "traditional" society into a "modern" one.
>
> The conception of the "modern-traditional" dichotomy arose in the nineteenth century, when European scholars were asking questions about the revolutionary change brought by industrial urbanization. Students of the problem assumed that with industrialization came a "modern" urban-industrial society as distinguished from a "traditional" preindustrial society. These ideas are contained in the classic works of Maine, Tonnies, Durkheim, Simmel, Weber, and Marx. Their ideas were to influence many of the world's practical urbanists until the late 1960s.
>
> Urbanists are now coming to realize that modernization is not an evolutionary process of diffusing Western culture. In the diverse cultures of the underdeveloped world, there are numerous modernization processes each producing different results. H. Singer (1971) in "Beyond Tradition and Modernity in Madras" said that there are fundamentally different attitudes toward modernization and they arise out of differences in philosophies, world views, and value systems. He also stated that traditional societies are not dominated by unchanging traditions, values, and beliefs. Rather they are highly flexible and able to change. But the adaptability of traditional societies cannot be treated adequately if "traditional" is made synonymous with "indigenous," and "modern" with "foreign." Singer preferred to view modernity as a permanent dimension of any culture and not a collection of foreign imports recently adopted by the people of that culture.

Theory of Social Change The study of modernization has been dominated by the idea that Western culture, more than any other, invented or perfected most things associated with modernization (for example, television, supermarkets, and freeways), and that in due course people in underdeveloped countries will enjoy them too.

Conceptualizing the Modern A theory of social change needed a beginning and an end to the process. The influential ideas come from the nineteenth and early twentieth century sociologists and social philosophers, who proposed ideal polarities—barter and credit, sacred and secular—which can be subsumed under the more general "traditional-modern" dichotomy. Table 12.1 provides a good summary of the polar distinctions between traditional and modern society. The stimulus for these polarities was provided by the history of English urbanization and industrialization.

Evolutionary Schema An evolutionary rationale is implicit in studies examining the process of transformation from traditional to modern. It is assumed that the path of change is a unitary process governed by the linear laws of history.

TABLE 12.1 Polar distinctions between pre-industrial and urban-industrial societies

	Pre-Industrial Society	**Urban-Industrial Society**
Demographic	High mortality, fertility.	Low mortality, fertility.
Behavioural	Particularistic, prescribed. Individual has multiplex roles.	Universalistic, instrumental. Individual has specialized roles.
Societal	Kin-group solidarity, extended family, ethnic cohesion. Cleavages between ethnic groups.	Atomization. Affiliations secondary. Professional influence groups.
Economic	Non-monetary or simple monetary base. Local exchange. Little infrastructure. Craft industries. Low specialization.	Pecuniary base. National exchange. Extensive interdependence. Factory production. Capital intensive.
Political	Non-secular authority. Prescriptive legitimacy. Interpersonal communications; traditional bases.	Secular polity. Elected government. Mass media participation. Rational bureaucracy.
Spatial (geographical)	Parochial relationships. Close ties to immediate environment. Duplication of socio-spatial groups in a cellular net.	Regional and national interdependence. Specialized roles based upon major resources and relative location within urban-spatial system.

SOURCE: Brian J. L. Berry, 1973, *The Human Consequences of Urbanization,* London and Basingstoke: The MacMillan Press, p. 13, table 1.

Achieving Development A major idea is the transition from tradition to modernity. Study of the transitional phase has focused on identifying and analyzing the circumstances and consequences of change. The transition has been treated either with a negative emphasis in terms of removing obstacles to development, or with a positive emphasis of creating the cultural environment necessary for development.

Elites The role of elites is considered crucial for the evolution of a modern society. Leadership groups—political, bureaucratic, entrepreneurial, intellectual, and military—are charged with the responsibility of providing the conditions needed for "take-off."

The most important *limitation of the modern-traditional dichotomy,* apart from the assumption of the unilineal evolution of societies, is that *it views traditional society as static* and opposed to modernization and therefore a blockage to development. It views modernity as an accretion of recently adopted foreign elements rather than as a permanent dimension of any society (Singer, 1971).

In the late 1960s, economists became aware of the size and activities of the proto-proletariat in Third World cities. We suggest three main factors for this recognition. First, a group of writers drew attention to the emergence of the proto-proletariat as a major element in the class structure of urban areas (Worseley, 1972; Fanon, 1963; Frank, 1969).

The Proto-Proletariat

A traditional Swahili house and bicycle repair shop contrast strongly with a modern office building in Dar er Salaam, Tanzania.

Second and belatedly, social scientists and members of international organizations such as the United Nations and International Labor Office drew attention to the grotesque employment problem in most cities. High urban underemployment and unemployment was noted as a feature of not only countries with modest rates of economic growth such as Indonesia, but also countries with rapid rates of growth such as Brazil. Explanations for massive urban labor surpluses varied. Some asserted that the problem was caused by defective manpower planning. Others said the problem was caused by rural-urban migration, and noted that the lure of the towns stems from the substantially higher wage rates earned by those fortunate enough to find industrial employment—earnings kept high by minimum wage legislation and union bargaining strength. Others pointed to the bias of governmental development planning towards capital-centered techniques of production. More correctly, still others indicated that the unemployment problem is a reflection of the underdevelopment of industrialization.

Third, some social scientists began to question their own work and recommendations for development. They were increasingly disenchanted with development being treated as synonymous with Western economic growth. Some of this disillusionment traced to the ecological and energy crises in developed countries. Researchers showed more interest in labor-centered systems of production that produce little industrial waste and pollution, and that do not rely on high energy consumption of fossil fuels.

Those who now study the proto-proletariat in urban economies in underdeveloped countries may be divided into two main groups: one that sees the process of occupational formation as *evolutionary,* the other that sees it as *involutionary.* Writers who subscribe to the evolutionary concept say that the problem posed by the proto-proletariat is temporary. In the belief that labor market conditions in underdeveloped countries are the same as those in nineteenth century Europe and North America (which they are not), they assume that occupational mobility and economic growth will correct the problem eventually. Writers who subscribe to the involutionary concept point out that high rates of population increase in town and country and a large volume of urban migration pose a constraint on labor absorption in capital-intensive enterprises which combine the power of machines (automatic tools) and the skill of machines (computers). The result is a proliferation of low productive, low pay, mainly tertiary service, activities. This process of occupational formation indicates an urban involution. The process of *involution* is characterized by: (1) a tenacity of basic pattern; (2) internal elaboration and ornateness; (3) technical hair-splitting; and (4) unending virtuosity (McGee, 1971:74).

Demographic projections support the involutionary concept. Trends indicate that cities in the underdeveloped world will absorb nearly a billion additional people between 1970-2000. A continuation of the kind of dependent economic development currently being fostered in most underdeveloped countries will ensure that urban unemployment and underemployment will remain acute for at least a couple of generations, especially in countries with large, dense populations such as India.

Defining the Proto-Proletariat

Thus far we have noted that the proto-proletariat are an enduring and expanding group who are not engaged in the economic activity of the "modern sector." Now let us define their economic characteristics more clearly. Terry McGee (1974) defined this peripheral class in terms of three dimensions. Let us look at each of them in turn. (Before proceeding, however, it is important to note that not all members of a family necessarily belong to the proto-proletariat. In the African situation, for example, family members who support and sustain one another, could be classified as belonging to all different categories of class: this one peasant, that one proto-proletarian, that one proletarian, and that one a member of the sub- or semi-elite.)

One approach to defining the proto-proletariat is *structural*. They conduct their economic activities within one sector of the dualistic structure of a Third World city (Figure 12.8). Clifford Geertz (1963) divided the structure of a poor world city into a *firm-centered* (modern and capital-intensive) economy "where trade and industry occur through a set of impersonally-defined social institutions which organize a variety of specialized occupations with respect to some particular or distributive ends, and into a *bazaar* (traditional and labor-intensive) economy based on "the independent activities of a set of highly competitive commodity traders who relate to one another, mainly by means of an incredible volume of ad hoc acts of exchange" (1963:28).

The Proto-Proletariat

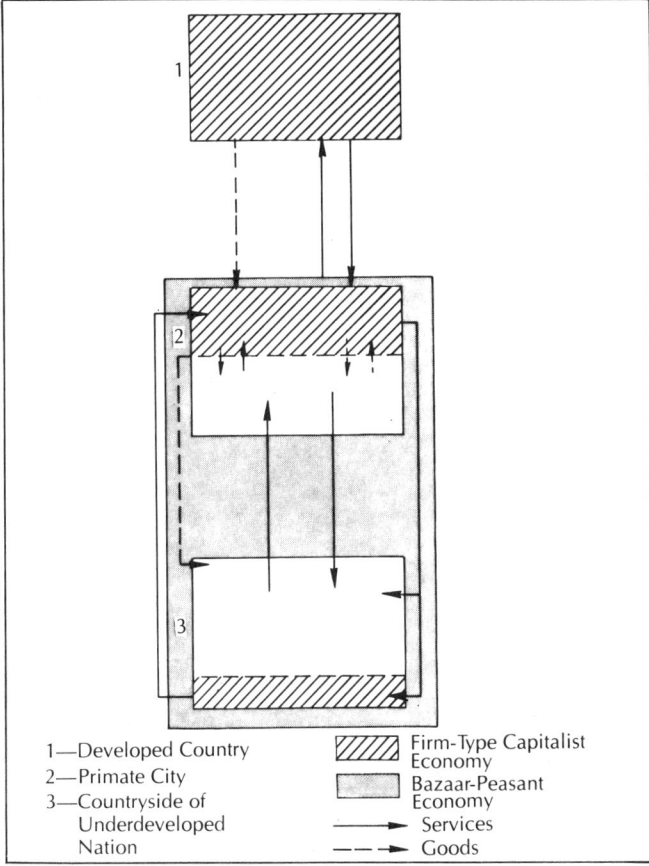

FIGURE 12.8 The economic setting of the third world primate city. SOURCE: T. G. McGee, 1971, *The Urbanization Process in the Third World—Explorations in Search of a Theory.* London: Bell & Hyman, Ltd., p. 70. Fig. 3.

Recently, this model has been improved by Milton Santos (1971, 1972, 1977) and G. Missen and M. Logan (1977). Santos emphasized the interlocking nature of the bazaar economy and the firm-centered economy. He viewed these as circuits, each with their own internal flows. The firm-centered economy, the *upper circuit,* and the bazaar sector, the *lower circuit,* have characteristics respectively as follows: capital-intensive vs. labor-intensive technology; bureaucratic vs. family organization; abundant vs. scarce capital; fixed vs. negotiable prices; regulated vs. unregulated hours of work; bank vs. noninstitutionalized credit; indirect vs. direct client relations; significant vs. insignificant government aid; and great vs. small dependence on foreign countries. The proto-proletariat participate in the lower circuit of the urban economy.

Missen and Logan noted that the upper circuit is a network of enterprises enjoined in the urban hierarchy, whereas the lower circuit is a swelling "globule" of small-scale enterprises functioning within each town, but not directly related with other towns (Figure 12.9). They further pointed out that

> At the national scale, the upper circuit reaches into the rural areas to link with the estates, loggers, and mines of the capitalist enterprises and with the more productive of the small farming regions. While the urban field of the modern distribution system is greatest

Retailing in the Third World city. (A) The "Western" shopping district in Nyeri, Kenya. (B) A street market in Kumasi, Ghana. Here vendors are selling groundnuts. SOURCE: I. Vogeler.

Industry in the Third World city. (A) Modern manufacturing plants using mechanical power in the Pugu Road industrial district of Dar es Salaam, Tanzania. (B) Small scale industry: a metal works in Kano, Nigeria. SOURCE: I. Vogeler.

around the main cities, the significant feature of this circuit is that it is selective in its spatial links: thus, in the main field there may be pockets of local farmers isolated from the national circuit, while in the poor peripheral areas the modern sector may tap isolated mines and logging camps. Beneath this circuit lies the lower circuit localized by regions. The energy which drives the local circuit is partly derived from its connections with the upper circuit . . . and is partly fed by local commodity production and abundant local labor (1977: 60–61 and Figure 12.10).

Transport in the Third World city: (A) bus terminal in Salisbury, Rhodesia. SOURCE: *Rhodesia Department of Information*; and (B) human transport, Niamey, Niger. SOURCE: I. Vogeler.

Another approach to defining the proto-proletariat is *institutional*. As noted in Chapter 4, there are three systems of economic production: capitalist, socialist, and peasant. The proto-proletariat engage in a peasant system of production within the urban environment.

A third approach concerns the *income opportunities* available to the proto-proletariat. Table 12.2 lists the income opportunities in a Third World City. Formal income opportunities are associated with activities of the upper circuit. Informal income opportunities, both legal and illegal, are associated with activities of the lower circuit. The proto-proletariat gain income mainly from informal opportunities.

On the basis of structural, institutional, and income dimensions, it is possible to delineate the proto-proletariat as a substantial group engaged in a peasant system of production in the lower circuit and deriving their income mainly from informal income opportunities (McGee, 1974). From a definition of the proto-proletariat, let us now review economic, ecological, and political features of this population. Finally, we will consider the issue of planning.

FIGURE 12.9 Urban system. SOURCE: G. I. Missen and M. I. Logan, 1977, "National and Local Distribution Systems and Regional Development: The Case of Kelantan in West Malaysia," *Antipode*, 9, No. 3, p. 61, Fig. 1.

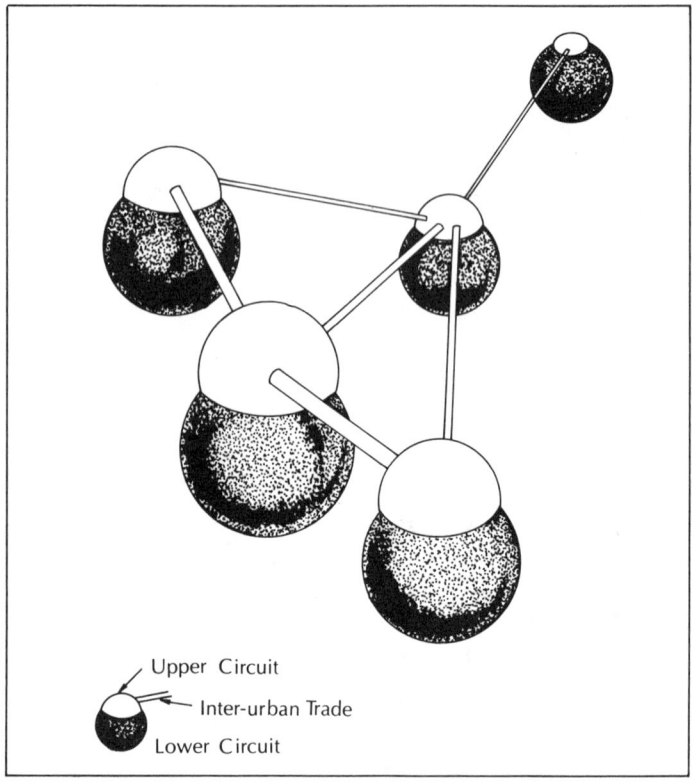

FIGURE 12.10 National and regional trade. SOURCE: G. I. Missen and M. I. Logan, 1977, "National and Local Distribution Systems and Regional Development: The Case of Kelantan in West Malaysia," *Antipode*, 9, No. 3, p. 62, Fig. 2.

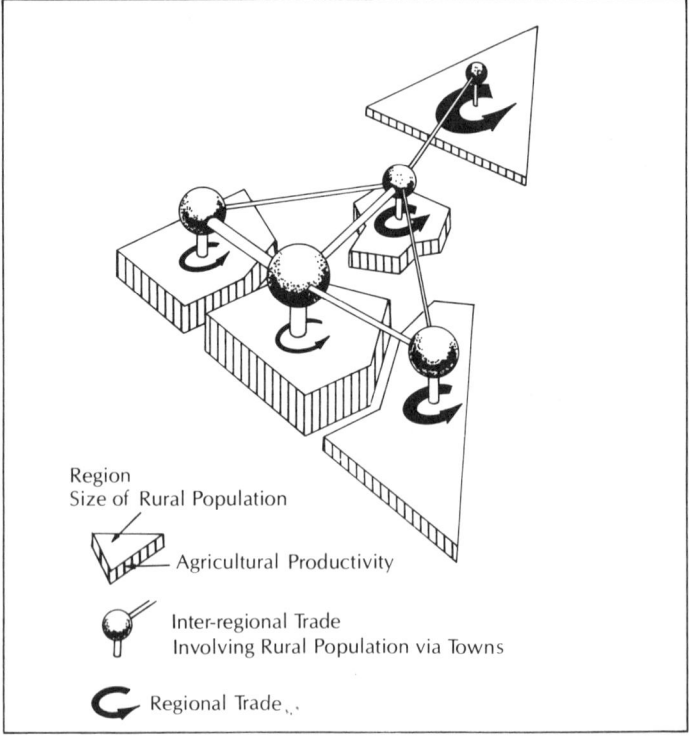

TABLE 12.2 Income opportunities in a Third World city

Formal Income Opportunities
   (a) Public sector wages.
   (b) Private sector wages.
   (c) Transfer payments—pensions, unemployment benefits.

Informal Income Opportunities: Legal
   (a) Primary and secondary activities—farming, market gardening, building contractors and associated activities, self-employed artisans, shoemakers, tailors, manufacturers of beers and spirits.
   (b) Tertiary enterprises with relatively large capital inputs—housing, transport, utilities, commodity speculation, rentier activities.
   (c) Small-scale distribution—market operatives, petty traders, street hawkers, caterers in food and drink, bar attendants, carriers, commission agents, and dealers.
   (d) Other services—musicians, launderers, shoeshiners, barbers, night-soil removers, photographers, vehicle repair and other maintenance workers; brokerage; ritual services, magic, and medicine.
   (e) Private transfer payments—gifts and similar flows of money and goods between persons; borrowing; begging.

Informal Income Opportunities: Illegal
   (a) Services—hustlers and spivs, receivers of stolen goods; usury, and pawnbroking (at illegal interest rates); drug-pushing, prostitution, poncing, smuggling, bribery, political corruption Tammany Hall-style, protection rackets.
   (b) Transfers—petty theft (e.g. pickpockets), larceny (e.g. burglary and armed robbery), embezzlement, confidence tricksters (e.g. money doublers), gambling.

SOURCE: T. G. McGee, 1974, *The Persistence of the Proto-Proletariat: Occupational Structures and Planning for the Future of Third World Cities.* Department of Geography, Monash University, Mimeographed.

Economic, Ecological and Political Features of Urban Third World Masses

Economic   Many economists assume that the economic activities of the proto-proletariat are incompatible with economic development. Activities of the lower circuit are believed to be unproductive and stagnant. For example, Arthur Lewis observed:

> These occupations usually have a multiple of the number they need, each of them earning very small sums from occasional employment; frequently their number can be halved without reducing output in this sector. Petty trading is also exactly of this type; it is enormously expanded in over-populated economies; each trader makes only a few sales; markets are crowded with stalls, and if the number of stalls were greatly reduced the consumers would be no worse off—they might be better off, since retail margins might fall (1958:402).

Lewis' description advances the idea that a surplus of labor exists in the traditional sector of underdeveloped countries. As we saw in Chapter 10, this labor is thought to be surplus since part of the labor force can be taken away from the traditional sector without decreasing the productivity of the traditional sector. Although "hidden unemployment" or "disguised unemployment" is a nearly ubiquitous feature of the underdeveloped world, Lewis' portrayal does not represent a very precise assessment of the productivity of the proto-proletariat.

Only the acquisition of hard data will make it possible to judge the contribution of the traditional sector to total income generated in the city, or to show the volume and value of goods flowing between upper and lower circuits. Although knowledge of the actual contribution of the proto-proletariat to the urban economy is still limited, we can see that they are engaged in an immense range of activities that may be grouped under four headings:

1. Trade and transportation activities such as taxi and truck operators, wholesalers, market vendors, and street traders;
2. Services such as self-employed mechanics, car washers, shoe cleaners, and bicycle tire pumpers;
3. Industrial activities such as food preparation, beef production, furniture-making, carving, and pottery; and
4. Financial activities such as money-lending.

Some economic activities of the proto-proletariat: (A) street market trader. SOURCE: *Braniff International*; (B) beauty parlor. SOURCE: I. Vogeler; (C) rubber tire sandalmaker. SOURCE: I. Vogeler; and (D) blacksmith. SOURCE: I. Vogeler.

The Proto-Proletariat

The relative importance of lower circuit economic activities compared to the upper circuit varies inversely with *city size* (Figure 12.11). In absolute terms, however the volume and degree of specialization of activities varies directly with the *importance* of cities. Whereas in the small city, the economic activities of the proto-proletariat sometimes replace non-existent modern services, in the large city their activities serve growing populations that do not have regular access to upper circuit activities, and also may function as external economies for upper circuit activities (Santos, 1977: 53–54).

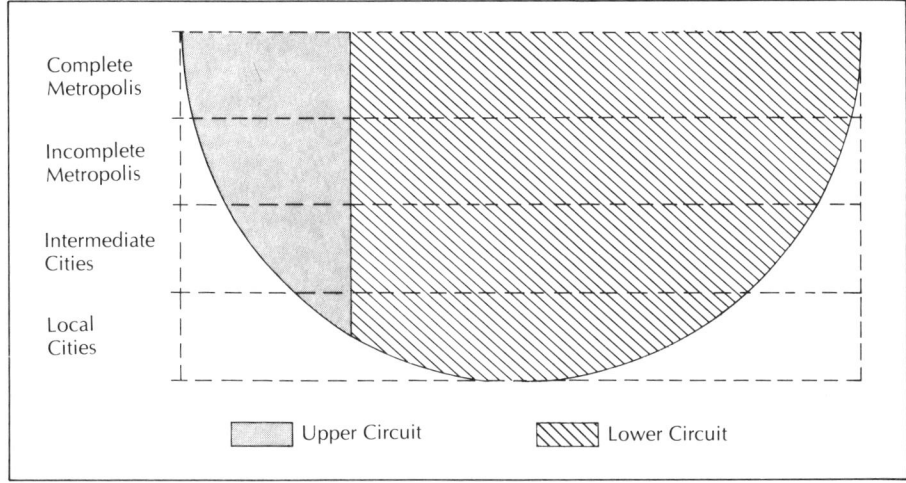

FIGURE 12.11 Relative importance of the two circuits in the systems of cities. SOURCE: M. Santos, 1977, "Spatial Dialectics: The Two Circuits of Urban Economy in Underdeveloped Countries," *Antipode*, 9, No. 3, p. 54, Fig. 3.

Ecological The proto-proletariat inhabit streets and waterfronts, inner city "slums," and "uncontrolled" or squatter settlements located in peripheral parts of most cities of the underdeveloped world (Table 12.3). "Squatter" settlements which favor activities of the proto-proletariat have sprung up in response to high rates of urban growth and low rates of industrialization in countries that cannot or will not provide housing for the increasing population.

"Squatter" settlements are commonly viewed as being malignant tumors growing on otherwise more or less healthy cities (Juppenlatz, 1970). For example, one sociologist referred to a Colombian *tugurio* as a human cesspool, and stated:

> It is the rudest kind of slum, clustering like a dirty beehive around the edges of any principal city in Latin America. In the past two decades poor rural people have flocked to the cities, found no opportunities but stayed on in urban fringe shanty-towns, squatting squalidly upon the land . . . Living almost like animals, the *tugurio's* residents are overwhelmed by animality. Religion, social control, education, domestic life are warped and disfigured (Schulman, 1967:1,004).

The conventional view is that "squatters" experience problems of adjustment to urban ways of life. Living in a "culture of poverty," the deprived and frustrated residents experience social disorganization. The "squatter" settlement is

TABLE 12.3 Size of uncontrolled settlements in underdeveloped countries

Country	City	Year	City Population (Thousands)	Population Living in Uncontrolled Settlements Total (Thousands)	As Percentage of City Population
Latin America					
Brazil	Rio de Janeiro	1961	3,326	900	27
	Belo Horizonte	1965	872	120	14
	Porto Alegre	1962	680	86	13
	Recife	1961	792	396	50
	Brasilia	1962	148	60	41
Chile	Santiago	1964	2,184	546	25
Colombia	Cali	1964	813	244	30
	Buenaventura	1964	111	89	80
Ecuador	Guayaquil	1968	730	360	49
Mexico	Mexico City	1966	3,287	1,500	46
Panama	Panama City	1968	373	63	17
Peru	Lima	1969	2,800	1,000	36
	Arequipa	1961	135	54	40
	Chimbote	1957	33	7	20
Venezuela	Caracas	1964	1,590	556	35
	Maracaibo	1966	559	280	50
	Barquisimeto	1968	31 (d.u.)*	13 (d.u.)*	41
	Ciudad Guayana	1966	86	34	40
Africa					
Senegal	Dakar	1969	500	150	30
Tanzania	Dar es Salaam	1967	273	93	34
Zambia	Lusaka	1967	194	53	27
Asia					
Afghanistan	Kabul	1968	475	100	21
India	Calcutta	1961	6,700	2,220	33
Indonesia	Djakarta	1961	2,906	725	25
Iraq	Baghdad	1965	1,475	500	29
Malaysia	Kuala Lumpur	1961	400	100	25
Pakistan	Karachi	1968	2,700	600	27
South Korea	Seoul	1970	440 (d.u.)*	137 (d.u.)*	30
Singapore	Singapore	1966	1,870	280	15
Taiwan	Taipei	1966	1,300	325	25

Note: Date quality poor. For details see source cited.
*d.u. = dwelling units.
SOURCE: United Nations General Assembly, *Housing, Building and Planning,* 1970, pp. 55–57, Annex III.

stereotyped as a haven of disruptive social behavior—crime and violence, bitterness, despair, juvenile delinquency, alcoholism, and prostitution.

In a more positive view, William Mangin (1967) and Terry McGee (1974) showed that "squatter" settlements make several contributions to the urban

Residential areas in Third World cities. (A) Luxurious house in an elite, low density hilly suburb of Nairobi, Kenya. (B) Densely packed one-storied African housing near the commercial center of Dar es Salaam, Tanzania. (C) Squatter houses near the center of Guatemala City, Guatemala. (D) Squatters on the outskirts of Guatemala City, Guatemala. (E) A high-rise public housing development in Hong Kong, where land is scarce. These apartments were built to house the urban poor, many of whom were refugees from mainland China.

economy. They contribute to capital formation in the housing sector, and add to social overhead in the form of schools, churches, and halls. They offer the proto-proletariat work, full-time and part-time. They support economic activities—bars, restaurants, repair shops, groceries, and fruit stores. They aid in the growth of markets. Their strong social organization provides a degree of support in times of crises. They enable the proto-proletariat to live close to work, to carry out activities such as food preparation that are subject to legal restriction in the modern sector, to employ labor of all ages, and to conceal illegal activities such as the preparation of certain alcoholic beverages. In theory, they also enable residents to live tax and rent free.

Political Some observers (Fanon, 1963) see the proto-proletariat as representing a revolutionary force. They argue that the unequal distribution of power and wealth within cities of the underdeveloped world creates frustration, anger, and alienation among the urban poor. But McGee (1971:64–94) in one of the most interesting applications of Geertz' (1963) involutionary construct argued "that the dualist economic structure of the Third World city and its relationship with the rural hinterland will prevent the emergence of . . . a revolutionary demand among the urban poor in the short term" (1971:28). He showed how a system of reciprocity spreads available income, and facilitates the absorption of an ever larger proto-proletarian population.

According to McGee, the traditional sector acts as a safety valve and maintains the social and political status quo; but the traditional sector in a poor

The proto-proletariat depend on a traditional agricultural resource base, and sometimes also on a free resource base. Here are two bags of charcoal processed from "free" wood collected on the Masai steppe to be sold in Moshi, Tanzania. Charcoal is used mainly for cooking and heating, especially in urban centers.

The Proto-Proletariat

world city is heavily dependent upon the existence of a traditional agricultural resource base, and the activities and policies of the modern sector (McGee, 1971:85). He argued that "under conditions of penetration of the traditional structure—whether in the city or in the countryside—by capitalist modes of production and/or appropriation, traditional labour absorptive capacity would fall and the polarization between the modern capital-intensive sector" and the unemployed proto-proletariat "would come out into the open" (McGee, 1971:85 and Figure 12.12).

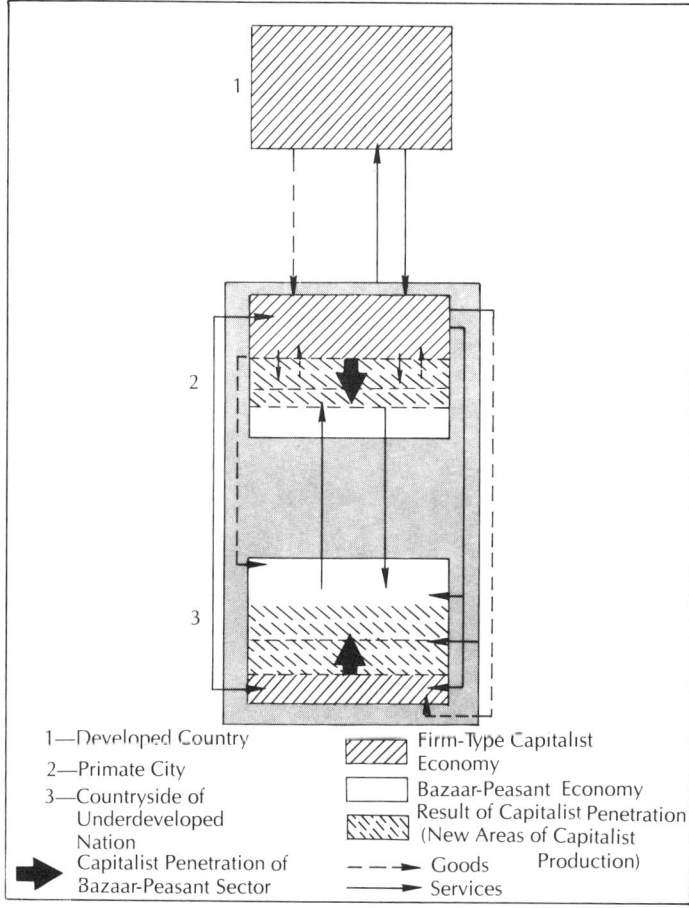

FIGURE 12.12 The economic setting of the third world primate city (dynamic model). SOURCE: T. G. McGee, 1971, *The Urbanization Process in the Third World—Explorations in Search of a Theory*. London: Bell & Hyman Ltd., p. 87. Fig. 7.

It "came out into the open" in Cuba during the late 1950s. Western imperialism penetrated to such an extent that indigenous urban-rural involution was unable to develop further, and a revolutionary situation was reached. Such a situation was averted in Jamaica and Puerto Rico where an additional safety valve, external migration to Britain and the United States, was operative. Of course, other "Cubas" are not inevitable. Underdeveloped countries are at various stages of capitalist penetration. Much will depend on the degree of penetration by Western capital, the ability of political leaders to set the terms under which that capital penetrates, and the ability of political leaders to solve internal problems of development within their own societies.

Policy Issues

We have suggested the proto-proletariat is a direct result of the export-luxury economic model pursued in most underdeveloped countries. This model prescribes that the mass of people of the underdeveloped world work for others, not for themselves. It ensures a continuing process of underdevelopment that will encourage the growth of population in most poor world cities. Planning strategies will be necessary to cope with exacerbating unemployment and poverty. If the traditional perjorative view of the proto-proletariat prevails, policies will be designed to eliminate their activities. Conversely, if more positive views prevail, policies may be designed to increase income and growth of the traditional sector.

The International Labor Office (1972) report on Kenya made the following suggestions for solving problems of unemployment and poverty: (1) increase links between traditional and modern sectors by a massive redistributon of income to be achieved by taxing the wealthy; (2) ease or repeal laws that stymie the economic activities of the proto-proletariat; and (3) encourage corporate enterprises to place orders and utilize economic enterprises of the traditional sector. This kind of approach, however, denies class struggle and the need for political change.

In neighboring socialist Tanzania, political and economic theorists insist that the only way to solve the employment problem is a radical redistribution of political power and wealth. Tanzanian socialism is an excellent example of such redistribution, as we shall see in the next section.

Tanzania's Development Strategy*

Tanzania is one of several underdeveloped countries whose policies are deliberately directed toward improving rural life and reversing, or at least slowing, the trend toward urban development at the expense of the rural areas. Under the subtitle "Let Us Pay Heed to the Peasant," Julius Nyerere remarked:

> Our emphasis on money and industries has made us concentrate on urban development . . . Yet the greater part of the money that we spend in the towns comes from loans. Whether it is used to build schools, hospitals, houses or factories, etc., it still has to be repaid. But it is obvious that it cannot be repaid just out of money obtained from urban and industrial development . . . Where, then shall we get it from? We shall get it from the villages and from agriculture. What does this mean? It means that the people who benefit directly from development which is brought about by borrowed money are not the ones who will repay the loans. The largest proportion of the loans will be spent in, or for, the urban areas, but the largest proportion of the repayment will be made through the efforts of the farmers (1968: 26–27).

---

*This section is a slight modification of de Souza and Porter, 1974, pp. 64–68.

Tanzania's Development Strategy

Nyerere argued that, with over 90 percent of Tanzania's population living in rural areas, the best opportunity for improving the well-being of the average citizen lies in rural development.

In the years following independence (December, 1961), the government has pursued policies consistent with developing Tanzania, which ranks among the world's 25 poorest countries, in a way that avoids extremes of wealth among regions and among people. The government has not yet succeeded, but it has made notable progress.

> Rough estimates of the range of real income differentials in the public sector wage and salary group for 1961 might place it at a level of 80 or 100 to 1. M. A. Bienefeld estimates that ten years later, after the introduction of various taxes, levies, and wage and salary adjustments, these ratios may have fallen to as low as 9 or 14 to 1 (Arrighi and Saul, 1973:243).

A brief summary of events and decisions taken by the Tanzanian government since independence will indicate the overall strategies being followed to build a socialist society, to prevent great inequalities in wealth, to eliminate poverty, hunger, and unemployment, and to reach people in rural areas.

Colonialism bequeathed privileged classes, and a dependent, but underdeveloped, economy to Tanzania. Unlike many other African countries, however, Tanzania was one of the least transformed by international capitalism, and its favored domestic classes were less evolved and entrenched. These conditions provided Tanzania with a better opportunity for breaking out of the syndrome of underdevelopment. The country also began its years of independence with a common language, Swahili, and with a multitude of small tribes—about 120—which prevented any one or more from emerging as dominant. These factors helped to guarantee a relatively unified population.

The main events and decisons since independence can be summarized as follows:

1963 The Ministry of Development Planning was established, and in 1964 the Ministry introduced the first Five Year Plan. The plan was intended to begin a period of development that would take fifteen years to complete. Its main objectives were to raise annual per capita income from $55 to $126; to substitute citizens for expatriates in all professional and managerial posts; and to raise life-expectancy from around 35 to 50 years. The plan was later criticized because of its emphasis on "more is better" and its failure to present a coherent development strategy. No attempt was made to specify what parts of the country or what sectors of the economy should be given priority in development help.

1967 On February 5, 1967, the Arusha Declaration was released. The declaration, which is amplified in a series of papers written by President Julius Nyerere (1967a, 1967b, and 1967c) is the central document in Tanzania's efforts to build socialism. The declaration (1) states the goals of socialism and the methods to be used in achieving it, (2) provides special guidance for the leadership, and (3) provides for public ownership of major financial, commercial, and industrial enterprises. President Nyerere was aware that a social and economic elite was emerging composed of such people as ministers, party officials, civil servants, merchants, property-owners and those engaged in the professions. He was aware that common people mockingly referred to government officials, who drove around in large luxurious Mercedes-Benz cars, as a new tribe called the *Wa-Benzi*. The Arusha Declaration limited government officials as to ownership of houses and other kinds of property and participation in business enterprises. To realize goals of structural transformation, the government nationalized (with full and fair compensation) banks, insurance companies, food processing factories, and certain other manufacturing firms. The eight largest import-export and wholesaling enterprises became the nucleus of the State Trading Corporation. The government took controlling shares of major manufacturing industries and the sisal industry. The resulting public/private firms are known in Tanzania as "parastatals." Between 1967 and 1972 the large-scale manufacturing, commercial, and financial sector had been changed from 90 percent foreign owned to 80 percent public-sector majority owned.

1968 A policy of *Ujamaa Vijijini* (roughly, "family-hood in the villages") has been adopted for the transformation of the rural areas, although it is intended eventually to apply the idea to urban neighborhoods. *Ujamaa* is a way to mobilize labor and help people through education and practice to live in a socialist way. The *Ujamaa* village is a nucleated settlement for which it is more economic to provide such things as safe water, a primary school, a day-care center and a dispensary, than for an area of dispersed settlement. Ideally, the land is held communally, labor is contributed, and the proceeds of the harvest and other economic activities are shared equally. Decisions or investments of proceeds (e.g. for a tractor) are made by adult members through discussion and vote. In practice, each family retains some land to cultivate for itself. People also contribute labor to the *Ujamaa* farm, whose proceeds are used to finance village developments, such as a furniture shop or tinsmithy. Initially, migration to *Ujamaa* villages was voluntary, but few responded. Then, in 1973, the Tanganyikan African National Union (TANU) ordered peasants in the countryside to the villages. Despite coercion, only three million or eighteen percent of Tanzanians lived in *Ujamaa* villages by 1976.

1969 The Ministry of Economic Affairs and Development Planning (DEVPLAN), in its second Five Year Plan, concentrated on decentralization of the economy. The plan recognized the overwhelming attraction that Dar es Salaam has as a location for industry, to the exclusion of most other cities (Table 12.4). DEVPLAN, therefore, proposed to redress the imbalance by designating Tanga, Arusha, Moshi, Mwanza, Tabora, Dodoma, Morogoro, Mbeya, and Mtwara as *growth centers* (Figure 12.13). Industrial investment, housing projects, and other aids to growth were channelled to these towns in an attempt to spread development more equally over the country and among the regions.

1971 In February, 1971, new TANU guidelines were published and widely discussed. These guidelines were intended to provide for greater worker participation in policy formation and to make management in government, parastatals, and business more accountable to the people they serve. Two major tasks facing TANU are to keep the leadership from becoming a ruling class and to raise the level of national consciousness and participation of people living in rural areas.

Tanzania's Development Strategy

TABLE 12.4 Percentage share of manufacturing in African capital cities

City	Percentage
Bangui (Central African Republic)	100
Bathurst (Gambia)	100
Bukavu (Rwanda)	100
Libreville (Gabon)	100
Monrovia (Liberia)	100
Dakar (Senegal)	81
Bujumbura (Burundi)	80
Freetown (Sierra Leone)	75
Blantyre (Malawi)	73
Abidjan (Ivory Coast)	63
Dar es Salaam (Tanzania)	63
Khartoum (Sudan)	60
Conakry (Guinea)	50
Douala (Cameroon)	50
Addis Ababa (Ethiopia)	47
Nairobi (Kenya)	42
Lagos (Nigeria)	35
Lusaka (Zambia)	35
Brazzaville (Republic of Congo)	33
Accra (Ghana)	30
Kinshasa (Democratic Republic of the Congo)	30
Kampala (Uganda)	28
Cotonou (Dahomey)	17

SOURCE: Akin L. Mabogunje, 1973, "Manufacturing and the Geography of Development in Tropical Africa," *Economic Geography*, Vol. 49, p. 11, table 3.

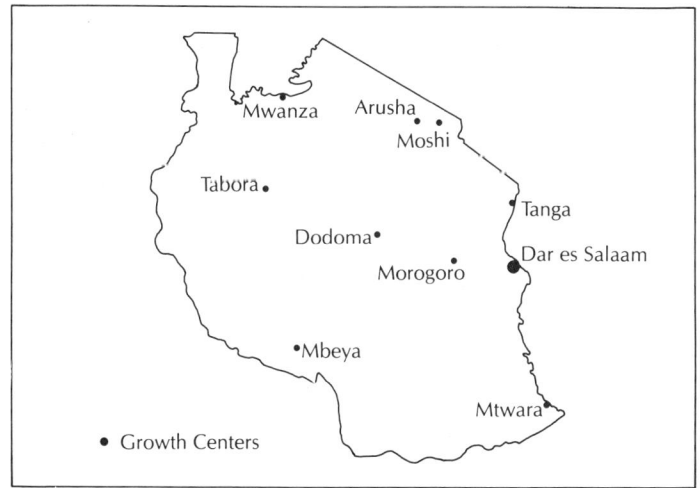

FIGURE 12.13 Tanzanian growth centers.

1972–1973 A policy of decentralization to administrative regions was being pursued with the creation of regional development directors, regional planning officers, and at a lower level, district development directors. Their duties included both planning and implementation. Thus the sectoral approach, which dominated administration and economic planning in the colonial era and the first

Dar es Salaam, with a population of over 500,000 is the commercial, industrial, and primate city of Tanzania. Shown here is part of the central business district. SOURCE: James W. King for the *National Council for Geographic Education*.

decade of independence, had its importance reduced. Under the old sectoral system, each separate ministry had a hierarchical system of penetration to regional and district levels. They often functioned separately from one another, and at times even at cross-purposes. Furthermore, the ideas and plans were formulated mainly at the top and sent down the chain of command to the district level and to the people who were supposed to carry out the ideas. This meant that local participation in providing information, assessing the feasibility of projects, and in expressing local wishes regarding development priorities was not sought. It often happened that ideas sent from above were ignored at the village level. People would not contribute their labor and resources. One of the objectives of decentralization was to reach people in the villages and to engage them in more self-reliant development.

In 1973, a decision was reached, after long public discussion, to move the capital to Dodoma, which is situated in the poor, semi-arid central part of the country. Dodoma (30,000), located 400 kilometers west of Dar es Salaam, has the highest degree of transport connectivity of any city in Tanzania, and the mean center of Tanzania's population lies only 96 kilometers to the north. The development of Tanzania's new capital, however, has required a great deal of investment in buildings, roads, airport improvements, water supply, and a host of social and economic services.

Tanzania's strategies with respect to export crops and world trade are to rely less and less on export commodities, to prevent further expansion of, and

Tanzania's Development Strategy

dependence on, such crops as sisal and coffee, and to promote schemes, such as dairying and beef production, geared more toward internal and African markets. Its strategies with respect to tourism (see box), external financial links, and industrialization are not clear. Consider industrialization, for example. Beyond the recognized task of dismantling dependency relationships caused by links to Western capitalism, Tanzania has yet to decide "how capital formation should be divided between the capital goods sector and the consumer goods sector or, again, between the sectors servicing the rural areas and those servicing the urban areas, or how agricultural policy should be expected to fit into this pattern" (Arrighi and Saul, 1973:36).

TOURISM AND THE THIRD WORLD

Third World countries account for one-eighth of all international tourist arrivals. But metropolitan tourism in countries of the Third World has contributed to the development of underdevelopment. It has done little to solve their foreign exchange shortages because a high proportion of tourism profits and expenditures flow back to metropolitan investors.

> For instance, in order to develop the type of tourist industry that will attract those willing to spend their dollars freely, an underdeveloped country must import most building and maintenance materials. Luxury hotels require imported materials both as part of the initial capital investment and as part of their normal operation. Typically, imports absorb about 25% of the initial investment and normal operating costs.
>
> Added to this, the hotel sector, which generally takes in over half of tourist expenditures, is largely foreign-owned. Many of the major hotel chains are, in fact, linked to the large airlines and multinational corporations. One survey of Latin America in 1971 found the Intercontinental Hotel Corporation, owned by Pan Am, with 17 hotels; Western International, owned by United Airlines, with 41; Hilton Hotels, owned by TWA, with 11; Sheraton Hotels, owned by IT&T, with 10; and Holiday Inns with 23.

Luxury tourist hotels, Acapulco, Mexico. SOURCE: *Braniff International.*

> And because the hotels are foreign-owned, the foreigners make the profits. The World Tourism Organization estimates that a minimum of 40 percent of gross hotel revenue goes to pay for imports, interest, and profits if the hotel is foreign-owned, and that the figure can run as high as 75 percent or more.
>
> A country may also have to invest in airport and road construction and power facilities to accommodate tourist development. All these projects require imported materials (*Dollars and Sense*, 1978, No. 36, p. 14).
>
> It is also pointed out that
>
>> . . . the richer classes of underdeveloped countries often use the luxury facilities of the tourist industry in their own countries for all sorts of social occasions . . .
>
> While the rich minority of a country enjoy the local highrise hotel, the majority of people in underdeveloped countries do not benefit from international tourism. The industry does not provide the local populace with the jobs it is commonly thought to supply; recent studies have demonstrated that the number of jobs created by money invested in tourism is less than in the manufacturing and agricultural sectors of the economy.
>
> The allocation of local resources, too, tends to favor the international tourist over the local resident. In one Tunisian city, for example, 20 percent of the water supply goes to the large hotels, while 80 percent of the dwellings remain without water. In 1977, in anticipation of the World Bank and International Monetary Fund Conference, the Philippine government loaned $500 million for luxury hotels in Manila alone. During that same year, the government spent only $13 million for public housing for the whole country (*Dollars and Sense*, 1978, No. 36, p. 15).
>
> Tourism promotes underdevelopment in other ways too. Metropolitan promoters of tourism view Third World countries as
>
>> socially uninhabited *places* where metropolitan visitors can unwind amid an abundance of sun, sand, sea, sex, and servility. Travel brochures reveal very little about the culture, history or problems of the destination country . . . [B]ecause of the pervasiveness of the playground attitude, local residents begin to view themselves as part of the holiday culture, thus abandoning their own values and traditions (Matthews, 1977:25).
>
> What can be done about Third World tourism? Can tourism become a more meaningful intercultural experience for visitors and local residents, and a stronger force for local development?

Tanzania is determined to develop a society in its own image. Its efforts are directed toward internal self-transformation and preservation of elements of traditional African culture. Tanzania's reform movement is basically unorthodox in structure, a grass roots proliferation of *Ujamaa* villages as major sources of growth and change, and *politics,* a socialist strategy. Tanzania, however, is also experimenting with growth centers to strengthen its urban system, which is more in line with the Western development model. Tanzania's growth center strategy is a specific policy to counter the dominance of Dar es Salaam. Tanzanian politicians and policy advisers, like many others throughout the underdeveloped world, have a distinct anti-primate-city bias (Alonso, 1968). The "gigantism" of Dar es Salaam (500,000) is something to be feared, and rightly so, because of its colonial impact.

Tanzanians have faced many problems in implementing socialism based on Africa's traditional extended family, and her people cannot yet be said to have

Tanzania's Development Strategy

achieved it except in isolated instances. Many vested interests are resistant to change: the farmer on Mount Kilimanjaro who owns a hectare or so of mature coffee trees, the Asian shopkeeper, the university graduate, the government official. The inheritance of a colonial structure of administration is a barrier to achievement of socialist goals, since residual external and internal structures of colonial and neocolonial days stand in the way of achievement. In addition, the country is nearly

(A) Chagga farmers raise coffee, bananas, vegetables, some grain and root crops and dairy cows on the slopes of the snow-capped mountain of Kilimanjaro, which rises from a dry plain at 1000 meters to a summit of nearly 6000 meters. Shown here are coffee bushes interplanted with bananas, whose large leaves provide shade. (B) Before the introduction of coffee in the 1920s, the Chagga were poor and lived in rude beehive huts. (C) From the proceeds of coffee sales the Chagga have been able to modernize their dwellings. Note the corrugated roofing in this picture. Moreover, the Chagga have been able to send their children to school, and to afford consumer durables such as radios, and in some instances motor vehicles. It is, therefore, quite understandable why the prosperous Chagga have been reluctant to live in a socialist way and join Ujamaa villages.

bankrupt and depends on aid from the United States, Western Europe, China, and the Soviet Union to remain solvent. The government is having second thoughts about some of its economic policies, and has recently endorsed a World Bank study that calls on Tanzania to (1) spend less on social services and more on industrial and agricultural development, (2) pay peasants more for crops to spur productivity, and (3) stop forcing peasants to join *Ujamaa* villages. Nonetheless, the direction of change is clear, and the accomplishments of Tanzanians in the face of immense difficulties have been significant. Tanzania in the 17 years since independence from Britain has moved some distance from a *peripheral* and *dependent economy* characterized by the centrality of primary exports and the dominance of luxury consumption, but it has yet to disengage itself completely from international capitalism and to construct a thoroughly *self-centered* economy which matches production with internal needs.

Summary

In this chapter, we considered some aspects of inequality among regions and among people in underdeveloped countries. The *absolute gap* between rich and poor regions is widening, just as it is between wealthy and poor people. We noted that progressive development concentration is primarily the result of a pattern of *deviation-amplification* which is contingent upon locational advantages derived during earlier periods of growth. Conservatives contend that eventual convergence between rich and poor regions is the norm. Liberals believe greater regional economic equality requires government intervention. Neither conservatives nor liberals seriously question that unequal development and inequality of income are the direct products of capitalism. Radicals argue that revolutionary institutional reform must precede regional planning, because underdeveloped countries exhibit *dependency* on core-regions, and spread from *center* to *periphery* is limited.

To illustrate the unequal distribution of power and wealth generated by capitalism in underdeveloped countries, we examined the *proto-proletariat*. Like the peasants in the countryside, they are poor and discriminated against with respect to the use and control of resources. Liberals urge that ways must be found to solve problems of urban unemployment and underemployment. One suggestion is to encourage *multinationals* or *global* firms to place orders and utilize enterprises of the traditional sector. Radicals contend that the proto-proletariat are victims of the *world's space-economy* whose center (rich industrial countries) encourages an export-luxury economy in underdeveloped countries. This point may be illustrated with a problem. Connect the following nine points with a single line of four (not five) straight segments:

As long as you stay within the square of points there is no solution to the problem. The solution is that we must emerge from this limited frame:

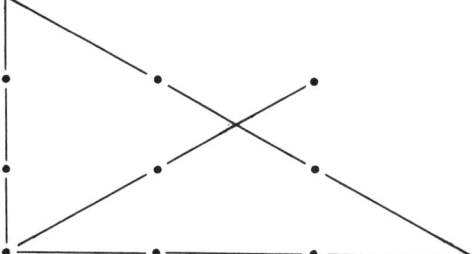

Thus to solve the unemployment problem in Third World cities, radicals contend that we must begin with the world system that created it.

Tanzania is one of several underdeveloped countries that believes that it has to disengage itself from international capitalism if it is to experience authentic national development. The Tanzanian development process, with its emphasis on decentralization, self-help, and *ujamaa*, is rural; and social and economic change, embodied in the idea of *ujamaa* is intended finally to spread a human-oriented concept of development to the urban areas. Tanzanians have faced immense difficulties in implementing democratic socialism, and they have not yet succeeded in creating a *self-centered economy*.

DISCUSSION QUESTIONS

1. Analyze regional differences in per capita income in the United States.
2. How does out-migration from poorer regions to richer regions affect regional-income differentials?
3. Write an essay on the dualistic structure of the urban economy in underdeveloped countries.
4. Why have few governments in underdeveloped countries attempted a policy of industrial dispersal?
5. Is it true that urban primacy is a handicap to the economic development of poor nations?
6. Discuss: Cities of the underdeveloped world are growing but not developing.
7. How does the center-periphery formulation help to explain unequal development?
8. Describe and analyze the main features of the proto-proletariat.
9. Describe Myrdal's model of cumulative change.
10. What are the pros and cons of the peripheral-dependent model of development?

11. Compare policies of national development in Kenya and Tanzania.
12. Critique Friedmann's stages of spatial evolution.
13. "Given the limited possibilities for fundamental structural changes in most underdeveloped countries, policies designed to aid the proto-proletariat should be encouraged." Comment.

SUGGESTED READINGS

Center-Periphery Phenomenon

Amin, S., *Accumulation on a World Scale*. New York: Monthly Review Press, 1974.

Frank, A. G., *Latin America: Underdevelopment or Revolution*. New York: Monthly Review Press, 1970.

Friedmann, J. R. P., *Regional Development Policy: A Case Study of Venezuela*. Cambridge, Mass.: The MIT Press, 1966.

Galtung, J., "A Structural Theory of Imperialism," *Journal of Peace Research*, No. 2 (1971):81–107, 110–116.

Poulantzas, N., *Classes in Contemporary Capitalism*. London: New Left Books, 1975.

Dualistic Structure of Third World Cities

Geertz, C., *Peddlers and Princes: Social Change and Economic Modernization in Two Indonesian Towns*. Chicago: The University of Chicago Press, 1963.

McGee, T. G., *The Urbanizaton Process in the Third World—Explorations in Search of a Theory*. London: Bell, 1971.

Santos, M., "Economic Development and Urbanization in Underdeveloped Countries. The Two Flow Systems of the Urban Economy and Their Spatial Implications." Unpublished paper, University of Toronto, 1972.

Santos, M., "Spatial Dialectics: The Two Circuits of Urban Economy in Underdeveloped Countries," *Antipode*, **9** (1977):49–60.

Features of the Proto-proletariat

Hart, K., "Informal Income Opportunities and Urban Employment in Ghana," *The Journal of Modern African Studies*, **11** (1973):61–89.

International Labor Organization, *Employment, Incomes, and Equality: A Strategy for Increasing Productive Employment in Kenya*, Geneva, 1972.

McGee, T. G., "Peasants in the Cities, A Paradox, A Paradox, A Most Ingenious Paradox," *Human Organization*, **32** (1973):135–142.

———. "The Persistence of the Proto-Proletariat: Occupational Structures and Planning for the Future of Third World Cities," Department of Geography, Monash University, Mimeographed, 1974.

Mangin, W., "Latin American Squatter Settlements: A Problem and A Solution," *Latin American Research Review*, **2** (1967):65–98.

Suggested Readings

Oshima, W., "Labor Force Explosion. The Labor Intensive Sector in Asian Growth," *Economic Development and Cultural Change,* **19** (1970–71):161–183.

Turnham, D. and I. Jaeger, *The Employment Problem in Less Developed Countries. A Review of Evidence.* Paris: Development Center of the Organization for Economic Cooperation and Development, 1971.

Tanzania's Strategy for National and Rural Development

Nyerere, J. K., *Ujamaa—Essays on Socialism.* Dar es Salaam: Oxford University Press, 1968.

Saul, J. S., "African Socialism in One Country: Tanzania" in G. Arrighi and J. S. Saul (eds.), *Essays on the Political Economy of Africa.* New York: Monthly Review Press, 1973, pp. 237–335.

Bibliography

Abler, R., J. S. Adams and P. Gould. *Spatial Organization: The Geographer's View of the World.* Englewood Cliffs, N.J.: Prentice-Hall, 1971.

Adams, J. S., ed. *Contemporary Metropolitan America: Twenty Geographical Vignettes.* Cambridge, Mass.: Ballinger Publishing Company, Association of American Geographers, Comparative Metropolitan Analysis Project, 1976.

———. *Urban Policy-Making and Metropolitan Dynamics: A Comparative Geographical Analysis.* Cambridge, Mass.: Ballinger Publishing Company, Association of American Geographers, Comparative Metropolitan Analysis Project, 1976.

Ackerman, F. and A. MacEwan. "Energy and Power." *Monthly Review,* **25** (1974):1–14.

Alchian, A. A. "Uncertainty, Evolution, and Economic Theory." *Journal of Political Economy,* **58** (1950):211–221.

Alexander, J. W., S. E. Brown and R. E. Dahlberry. "Freight Rates: Selected Aspects of Uniform and Nodal Regions." *Economic Geography,* **34** (1958):1–18.

Alexandersson, G. "Changes in the Location Pattern of the Anglo-American Steel Industry: 1948–1959." *Economic Geography,* **37** (1961):95–114.

Allaby, M. *The World Food Problem. Can We Solve It?* London: Tom Stacey, Ltd., 1972.

Alonso, W. *Location and Land Use: Toward a General Theory of Land Rent.* Cambridge, Mass.: Harvard University Press, 1964.

———. "Urban and Regional Imbalance in Economic Development." *Economic Development and Cultural Change,* **17** (1968):1–14.

Amin, S. *Accumulation on a World Scale.* New York: Monthly Review Press, 1973a.

———. "Growth is not Development." *Development Forum,* 1, No. 2, (April 1973b):1–3.

Arrighi, G. "Labour Supplies in Historical Perspective: A Study of the Proletarianization of the African Peasantry in Rhodesia." *Journal of Development Studies,* **6** (1970):197–234.

Arrighi, G. and J. S. Saul. *Essays on the Political Economy of Africa.* New York: Monthly Review Press, 1973.

Averitt, P. *Coal Resources of the United States—January 1, 1967.* U.S. Government Printing Office, U.S. Geological Survey Bulletin, 1275 (1969).

Baird, A. et al. *Towards an Explanation and Reduction of Disaster Proneness.* University of Bradford, Disaster Research Unit, Occasional Paper No. 11 (1975).

Baran, P. *The Political Economy of Growth.* New York: Monthly Review Press, 1962.

Baran, P. and P. M. Sweezy, *Monopoly Capital.* New York: Monthly Review Press, 1966.

Bibliography

Barber, W. Y. *The Economy of British Central Africa: A Case Study of Economic Development in a Dualistic Society.* Stanford, Calif.: Stanford University Press, 1961.

Barnbrock, J. "Prologomenon to a Methodological Debate on Location Theory: The Case of von Thünen." *Antipode,* **6** (1974):59–66.

Barratt Brown, M. *The Economics of Imperialism.* Harmondsworth, England: Penguin Books, 1974.

Bauer, P. T. "Foreign Aid: An Instrument for Progress?" in B. Ward and P. T. Bauer, *Two Views of Foreign Aid.* London: Institute of Economic Affairs, Occasional Papers No. 9 (1966).

Beckmann, M. J. "City Hierarchies and the Distribution of City Size." *Economic Development and Cultural Change,* **6** (1958):243–248.

Berry, B. J. L. "An Inductive Approach to the Regionalization of Economic Development." in *Essays on Geography and Economic Development* edited by Norton Ginsburg. Chicago: University of Chicago, Department of Geography Research Paper, **62** (1960):78–107.

———. "City Size Distributions and Economic Development." *Economic Development and Cultural Change,* **9** (1961):573–588.

———. *Geography of Market Centers and Retail Distribution.* Englewood Cliffs, N.J.: Prentice-Hall, 1967.

———. "Relationships between Regional Economic Development and the Urban System—The Case of Chile." *Tijdschrift voor Economische en Sociale Geografie,* **60** (1969):283–307.

———. *The Human Consequences of Urbanization.* London: The Macmillan Press, 1973.

———, H. G. Barnum and R. J. Tennant. "Retail Location and Consumer Behavior." *Papers and Proceedings of the Regional Science Association,* **9** (1962):65–106.

———, E. C. Conkling and D. M. Ray. *The Geography of Economic Systems.* Englewood Cliffs, N.J.: Prentice-Hall, 1976.

Blaike, P. M. "Spatial Organization of Agriculture in Some North Indian Villages: Part 1." *Transactions* of the Institute of British Geographers, **52** (1971):1–40.

Blair, J. *Economic Concentration.* New York: Harcourt Brace Jovanovich, 1972.

Blaut, J. "Imperialism—The Marxist Theory and its Evolution." *Antipode,* **7** (1975):1–19.

Boeke, J. H. *Economics and Economic Policy of Dual Societies—As Exemplified by Indonesia.* New York: Institute of Pacific Relations, 1953.

Borchert, J. R. *The Urbanization of the Upper Midwest: 1930–1960.* Upper Midwest Economic Study, Urban Report No. 2. Minneapolis: University of Minnesota, 1963.

———. "American Metropolitan Evolution." *Geographical Review,* **57** (1967):301–332.

———. "Major Control Points in American Economic Geography." *Annals* of the Association of American Geographers, **68** (1978):214–232.

Boserup. E. *The Conditions of Agricultural Growth.* Chicago: Aldine, 1965.

Breckenfield, G. " 'Downtown' Has Fled to the Suburbs." *Fortune,* October, 1972, pp. 80–87, 156, 158, 162.

Brobst, D. A., W. P. Pratt and V. E. McKelvey. *Summary of United States Mineral Resources.* U.S. Geological Circular 682, 1973.

Broek, J. O. M. and J. W. Webb. *A Geography of Mankind.* 2nd ed. New York: McGraw-Hill, 1973.

Bibliography

Brookfield, H. C. "On One Geography and a Third World." *Transactions,* Institute of British Geographers, **56** (1973):1–20.

———. *Interdependent Development.* Pittsburgh: University of Pittsburgh Press, 1975.

Brown, L. R. and G. W. Finsterbusch. *Man and His Environment: Food.* New York: Harper and Row, 1972.

Brown, R. N. *Principles of Economic Geography.* London: Pitman, 1920.

Brush, J. E. "The Hierarchy of Central Places in Southwestern Wisconsin." *Geographical Review,* **43** (1953):380–402.

Buchanan, K. M. "The Third World—Its Emergence and the Contours." *New Left Review,* **18** (1963):5–23.

———. "Profiles of the Third World." *Pacific Viewpoint,* **5** (1964):97–126.

Bunge, W. *Fitzgerald: The Geography of a Revolution.* Cambridge, Mass.: Schenkman Publishing Co. Inc., 1971.

Burgess, E. W. "Growth of the City." In *The City,* edited by R. E. Park, E. W. Burgess, and R. D. McKenzie. Chicago: University of Chicago Press, 1925.

Callahan, D., ed. *The American Population Debate.* Garden City: Doubleday and Co., 1971.

Cavadino, P. *Get Off Their Backs.* Oxford: Third World First, 1973.

Chisholm, G. G. *Handbook of Commercial Geography.* London: Longmans, Green, 1889.

Chisholm, M. D. I. "Agricultural Production, Location, and Rent." *Oxford Economic Papers,* **13** (1961):342–359.

———. *Rural Settlement and Land Use.* London: Hutchinson, 1966.

Christaller, W. *The Central Places of Southern Germany.* Translated by C. W. Baskin. Englewood Cliffs, N.J.: Prentice-Hall, 1966.

Cipolla, C. M. *The Economic History of World Population.* Harmondsworth, England: Penguin Books, 1970.

Clairmonte, F. *Economic Liberalism and Underdevelopment: Studies in the Disintegration of an Idea.* Bombay: Asia Publishing House, 1960.

Clarke, J. I. *Population Geography.* Elmsford, New York: Pergamon, 1966.

Clarkson, W. *Energy for Survival: The Alternative to Extinction.* New York: Doubleday and Co., 1974.

Coale, A. J. "The History of the Human Population." *Scientific American,* September, 1974, pp. 40–51.

Cole, H. S. D., C. Freeman, M. Jahoda, and K. L. R. Pavitt, eds., *Models of Doom.* New York: Universe Books, 1973.

Commoner, B. *The Closing Circle: Nature, Man and Technology.* New York: Knopf, 1971.

———. "How Poverty Breeds Overpopulation." *Ramparts,* August/September, 1975, pp. 21–25, 58–59.

Connell, J. "The Geography of Development." *Area,* **3** (1971):259–265.

Cook, E. *Energy: The Ultimate Resource.* Washington, D.C.: Association of American Geographers Commission on College Geography, Resource Paper No. 77-4, 1977.

Curry, L. "Quantitative Geography." *Canadian Geographer,* **11** (1967):265–279.

Bibliography

Cyert, R. M. and J. G. March. *A Behavioral Theory of the Firm.* Englewood Cliffs, N.J.: Prentice-Hall, 1963.

Dacey, M. F. "Analysis of Central Place and Point Patterns by a Nearest Neighbor Method." *Lund Studies in Geography, Series B, Human Geography,* **24** (1962).

Datoo, B. A. "Toward a Reformulation of Boserup's Theory of Agricultural Change," Dar es Salaam: University of Dar es Salaam, Department of Geography, 1976.

Demko, G. I., H. M. Rose, and G. A. Schnell, eds. *Population Geography: A Reader.* New York: McGraw-Hill, 1970.

de Souza, A. R. and P. W. Porter. "Modernisation des environnements Africains: Perspectives des géographes." *Revue Tiers-Monde,* **19** (1978):15–46.

———. *The Underdevelopment and Modernization of the Third World.* Washington, D.C.: Association of American Geographers, Commission on College Geography, Resource Paper No. 28, 1974.

Dollars and Sense. "Why Famine Threatens the Sahel." No. 33 (1978):4–5.

———. "Tourism Travels to the Third World." No. 36 (1978):14–15.

———. "Terms of Trade Squeeze Third World Nations" No. 37 (1978):16–17.

Dowd, D. F. "Thorstein Veblen and C. Wright Mills: Social Science and Criticism." In *The New Sociology: Essays in Social Science and Social Theory in Honor of C. Wright Mills,* edited by I. L. Horowitz. New York: Oxford University Press, 1964.

Dunn, E. S. *The Location of Agricultural Production.* Gainsville: University of Florida Press, 1954.

Ehrlich, P. R. and A. H. Ehrlich. *Population, Resources and Environment: Issues in Human Ecology.* San Francisco: W. H. Freeman and Company, 1970.

Encyclopedia Brittanica. "Domestication, Plant and Animal." *Macropaedia,* **5** (1974):936–942.

Engels, F. *The Condition of the Working Class in England.* Stanford, Calif.: Stanford University Press, 1958.

Estall, R. C. *New England: A Study in Industrial Adjustment.* London: Bell, 1966.

Evans, A. "The Pure Theory of City Size in an Industrial Economy." *Urban Studies,* **9** (1972):49–77.

Fagan, J. J. *The Earth Environment.* Englewood Cliffs, N.J.: Prentice-Hall, 1974.

Fanon, F. *The Wretched of the Earth.* New York: Grove Press, 1963.

Found, W. C. *A Theoretical Approach to Rural Land Use Patterns.* Toronto: Macmillan, 1971.

Frank, A. G. "Sociology of Development and Underdevelopment of Sociology." *Catalyst 3,* Buffalo, N.Y.: State University of New York at Buffalo, (1967):20–73.

———. *Capitalism and Underdevelopment in Latin America.* New York: Monthly Review Press, 1969.

———. *Latin America: Underdevelopment or Revolution.* New York: Monthly Review Press, 1970.

Franklin, S. H. "Systems of Production: Systems of Appropriation." *Pacific Viewpoint,* **6** (1965):145–166.

Free, L. A. and H. Cantril. *The Political Beliefs of Americans: A Study of Public Opinion.* New Brunswick, N.J.: Rutgers, 1967.

Bibliography

Freedman, R. and B. Berelson. "The Human Population." *Scientific American,* September, 1974, pp. 30–39.

Fried, M. *The Evolution of Political Society.* New York: Random House, 1967.

Friedmann, J. and W. Alsonso. *Regional Development and Planning: A Reader.* Cambridge, Mass.: M.I.T. Press. 1964.

Friedmann, J. *Regional Development Policy: A Case Study of Venezuela.* Cambridge, Mass.: M.I.T. Press, 1966.

_____. "A Conceptual Model for the Analysis of Planning Behavior." *Administrative Science Quarterly,* **12** (1967):225–252.

_____. *A General Theory of Polarized Development.* Los Angeles: University of California School of Architecture and Urban Planning, 1969.

Fusfield, D. *The Age of the Economist.* Glenview: Scott, Foresman and Co., 1966.

Galbraith, J. K. *Economic Development.* Cambridge, Mass.: Harvard University Press, 1964.

_____. *The New Industrial State.* Boston: Houghton Mifflin, 1967.

_____. *Economics and the Public Purpose.* Boston: Houghton Mifflin, 1973.

_____. *The Age of Uncertainty.* Boston: Houghton Mifflin, 1977.

Galtung, J. "A Structural Theory of Imperialism." *Journal of Peace Research,* No. 2 (1971): 81–107, 110–116.

Gappert, G. "Cooperation Against Poverty." *Africa Today,* **18** (1971).

Geertz, C. *Agricultural Involution: The Processes of Ecological Changes in Indonesia.* Berkeley and Los Angeles: University of California Press, 1963.

_____. *Peddlers and Princes: Social Change and Economic Modernization in Two Indonesian Towns.* Chicago: University of Chicago Press, 1963.

George, S. *How the Other Half Dies—The Real Reasons for World Hunger.* Montclair, N.J.: Allanheld, Osmun and Co. Publishers, 1977.

Getis, A. and J. Getis. "Christaller's Central Place Theory." *Journal of Geography,* **65** (1966): 220–226.

Gilbert, A. *Latin American Development—A Geographical Perspective.* Harmondsworth, England: Penguin Books, 1974.

Goldsmith, E., ed. *Blueprint for Survival.* Harmondsworth, England: Penguin Books, 1973.

Good, C. M. "Periodic Markets: A Problem in Locational Analysis." *Professional Geographer,* **24** (1972):210–216.

Goodwin, W. "The Management Center in the United States." *Geographical Review,* **55** (1965):1–16.

Gordon, D. *Problems in Political Economy.* Lexington, Mass.: D. C. Heath, 1971.

Gottmann, J. *Megalopolis.* Cambridge, Mass.: The MIT Press, 1964.

Gould, P. "Man Against His Environment: A Game Theoretic Framework." *Annals* of the Association of American Geographers, **53** (1963):290–297.

_____. "A Note on Research into the Diffusion of Development." *Journal of Modern African Studies,* **2** (1964):123–125.

_____. *Spatial Diffusion.* Washington, D.C.: Association of American Geographers, Commission on College Geography, Resource Paper No. 4, 1969.

Bibliography

―――. "Tanzania 1920–63: The Spatial Impress of the Modernization Process." *World Politics,* **22** (1970):149–170.

Gourou, P. *The Tropical World: Its Social and Economic Conditions and Its Future Status.* New York: John Wiley & Sons, 1953.

Gray, H. and S. Tangri, eds. Economic Development and Population Growth, A Conflict? Lexington, Mass.: Raytheon/Heath, 1970.

Gregor, H. F. *Geography of Agriculture: Themes in Research.* Englewood Cliffs, N.J.: Prentice-Hall, 1970.

Griffin, K. *Underdevelopment in Spanish America.* London: George Allen Unwin, 1969.

―――. *Land Concentration and Rural Poverty.* New York: Macmillan, 1976.

Grove, D. J. and L. I. Huszar. *The Towns of Ghana.* Accra: Ghana Universities Press, 1964.

Haberler, G. *A Survey of International Trade Theory.* Princeton: International Finance Section, 1961.

Hagen, E. E. *On the Theory of Social Change.* Homewood, Ill.: The Dorsey Press, 1962.

Hägerstrand, T. "The Propagation of Innovation Waves." *Lund Studies in Geography, Series B,* **4** (1952).

―――. *Innovation Diffusion as a Spatial Process.* Translation and postscript by A. Pred. Chicago: University of Chicago Press, 1967.

Haggett, P. *Locational Analysis in Human Geography.* New York: St. Martin's Press, 1965.

―――. "Network Models in Geography." In *Models in Geography,* edited by R. J. Chorley and Peter Haggett. London: Methuen and Co. Ltd., 1967.

―――. *Geography: A Modern Synthesis.* New York: Harper and Row, 1972.

―――, and R. Chorley. *Network Analysis in Geography.* New York: St. Martin's Press, 1970.

Hall, A. D. and R. E. Fagen. "Definition of System." *General Systems Yearbook,* **1** (1956):18–28.

Hall, P. G., ed. *Von Thünen's Isolated State.* London: Pergamon, 1966.

Harary, F. *Graph Theory.* Reading, Mass.: Addison-Wesley, 1967.

Hardin, G. "The Case Against Helping the Poor." *Psychology Today,* **38** (September, 1974): 124–126.

Harris, C. and E. L. Ullman. "The Nature of Cities." *Annals* of the American Academy of Political and Social Science, **242** (1945):7–17.

Harris, C. "The Market as a Factor in the Localization of Industry in the U.S." *Annals* of the Association of American Geographers, **44** (1954):315–348.

Hart, K. "Informal Income Opportunities and Urban Employment in Ghana." *The Journal of Modern African Studies,* **11** (1973):61–89.

Hartshorne, R. *The Nature of Geography.* Washington, D.C.: Association of American Geographers, 1939.

Harvey, D. "Locational Changes in the Kentish Hop Industry and the Analysis of Land Use Patterns." *Transactions* of the Institute of British Geographers, **33** (1963):123–144.

―――. "Theoretical Concepts and the Analysis of Agricultural Land Use Patterns in Geography." *Annals* of the Association of American Geographers, **56** (1966):361–374.

Bibliography

_____. *Society, the City and the Space-Economy of Urbanism.* Washington, D.C.: Association of American Geographers, Commission on College Geography, Resource Paper No. 18, 1972.

_____. *Social Justice and the City.* London: Edward Arnold, 1973.

_____. "Population, Resources, and the Ideology of Science." *Economic Geography,* **50** (1974):256–277.

_____. "The Geography of Capitalist Accumulation: A Reconstruction of the Marxist Theory." *Antipode,* **7** (1975):9–21.

Hayter, T. *Aid as Imperialism.* Harmondsworth, England: Penguin Books, 1971.

Heckscher, E. "The Effects of Foreign Trade on the Distribution of Income." *Ekonomisk Tidskrift,* 21 (1919). Trans. in H. S. Ellis and L. A. Metzler, eds., *Readings in the Theory of International Trade.* Philadelphia: Blackiston, 1949.

Heilbroner, R. L. *The Economic Problem.* Englewood Cliffs, N.J.: Prentice-Hall, 1972.

_____. *The Great Ascent.* New York: Harper and Row, 1963.

Hensman, C. R. *Rich Against Poor.* Harmondsworth, England: Penguin Books, 1975.

Higgins, B. "The Dualistic Theory of Underdeveloped Areas." *Economic Development and Cultural Change,* **4** (1956):99–115.

_____. *Economic Development: Principles, Problems and Policies.* New York: Norton, 1968.

Hirschman, A. O. *The Strategy of Economic Development.* New Haven, Conn.: Yale University Press, 1958.

Horowitz, D., ed. *Corporations and the Cold War.* New York: Monthly Review Press, 1969.

Horvath, R. J. "Von Thünen's Isolated State and the Area Around Addis Ababa, Ethiopia." *Annals of the Association of American Geographers,* **59** (1969):308–323.

Hotelling, H. "Stability in Competition." *Economic Journal,* **39** (1929):41–57.

Hoyt, H. *The Structure and Growth of Residential Neighborhoods in American Cities.* Washington, D.C.; Federal Housing Administration, 1939.

Hughes, J. W., ed. *Suburbanization Dynamics and the Future of the City.* New Brunswick, N.J.: Rutgers University, Center for Urban Policy Research, 1974.

Hunker, H. and A. J. Wright, *Factors of Industrial Location in Ohio.* Columbus: The Ohio State Press, 1963.

Hunt, E. K. and H. F. Sherman. *Economics.* New York: Harper and Row, 1978.

International Labor Organization. *Employment, Incomes and Equality: A Strategy for Increasing Productive Employment in Kenya.* Geneva, 1972.

Isard, W. and J. H. Cumberland. "New England as a Possible Location for an Integrated Iron and Steel Works." *Economic Geography,* **26** (1950):245–259.

Isard, W. *Location and Space-Economy.* Cambridge, Mass.: M.I.T. Press, 1956.

Issac, E. *Geography of Domestication.* Englewood Cliffs, N.J.: Prentice-Hall, 1970.

James, P. E. *One World Divided—A Geographer Looks at the Modern World.* Waltham, Mass.: Blaisdell, 1964.

Janelle, D. G. "Central Place Development in a Time-Space Framework." *Professional Geographer,* **20** (1968):5–10.

Bibliography

_____. "Spatial Reorganization: A Model and a Concept." *Annals* of the Association of American Geographers, **59** (1969):348–364.

Jefferson, M. *Recent Colonization in Chile.* New York: American Geographical Society, Research Series, **6** (1921).

Johnson, E. A. J. *The Organization of Space in Developing Countries.* Cambridge, Mass.: Harvard University Press, 1970.

Johnson, S., ed. *The Population Problem.* New York: John Wiley & Sons, 1973.

Juppenlatz, M. *Cities in Transformation.* St. Lucia: University of Queensland Press, 1970.

Kahn, H. "If the Rich Stop Aiding the Poor . . . ," *Development Forum,* **1,** No. 2 (March, 1973):1–3.

Kansky, K. *Structure of Transport Networks.* Chicago: University of Chicago, Department of Geography Research Papers, 84 (1963).

Kenen, P. B. *International Economics.* Englewood Cliffs, N.J.: Prentice-Hall, 1964.

Kennelly, R. A. "The Location of the Mexican Steel Industry." *Revista Geografica,* **15** (1954–5):109–129 and **16**:60–77.

Keynes, J. M. *The General Theory of Employment Interest and Money.* New York: Harcourt, Brace, 1936.

Kimble, G. *Tropical Africa.* New York: The Twentieth Century Fund (1), 1960.

King, L. J. "A Quantitative Expression of the Pattern of Urban Settlements in Selected Areas of the United States." *Tijdschrift voor Economische en Sociale Geografie,* **53** (1962):1–7.

_____. "Alternatives to a Positive Economic Geography," *Annals* of the Association of American Geographers, **66** (1976):293–308.

Knight, C. G. "Prospects for Peasant Agriculture." In *Contemporary Africa: Geography and Change,* edited by C. G. Knight and J. L. Newman. Englewood Cliffs, N.J.: Prentice-Hall, 1976.

_____, and R. P. Wilcox. *Triumph or Triage? The World Food Problem in Geographical Perspective.* Washington, D.C.: Association of American Geographers, Commission on College Geography, Resource Paper No. 75-3, 1976.

Kolars, J. F. and J. D. Nystuen. *Human Geography: Spatial Design in World Society.* New York: McGraw-Hill, 1974.

Kunkel, J. H. "Values and Behavior in Economic Development." *Economic Development and Cultural Change,* **13** (1965):257–277.

Lappé, F. M. and J. Collins. "More Food Means More Hunger." *Development Forum,* **4,** No. 8 (1976):1–2.

_____. *Food First: Beyond the Myth of Scarcity.* Boston: Houghlin Mifflin, 1977.

Lecomber, R. *Economic Growth Versus Environment.* New York: John Wiley & Sons, 1975.

Leibenstein, H. *Economic Backwardness and Economic Growth.* New York: John Wiley & Sons, 1957.

Leonard, J. N. *The First Farmers.* New York: Time-Life, 1973.

Lewis, W. A. *The Theory of Economic Growth.* London: George Allen Unwin, 1955.

_____. "Economic Development with Unlimited Supplies of Labour." In *The Economics of Underdevelopment,* edited by A. N. Agarwala and S. P. Singh. New York: Oxford University Press, 1958.

Livingstone, I. "Agriculture Versus Industry in Economic Development." In *Economic Policy for Development,* edited by Ian Livingstone. Harmondsworth, England: Penguin Books, 1971.

Bibliography

Locklin, D. P. *The Economics of Transportation.* 7th ed. Homewood, Ill.: Richard Irwin, 1972.

Lord Ritchie-Calder. "UNICEF's Grandchildren." *UNICEF News,* **78** (December 1973/January 1974), 4 pages.

Lösch, A. *The Economics of Location.* New Haven: Yale University Press, 1954.

Lowe, J. J. and S. Moryadas. *The Geography of Movement.* Boston: Houghton Mifflin, 1975.

Mabogunje, A. L. "Manufacturing and the Geography of Development in Tropical Africa." *Economic Geography,* **49** (1973):1–20.

McClelland, D. *The Achieving Society.* New York: Van Nostrand, 1961.

Mackay, J. R. "The Interactance Hypothesis and Boundaries in Canada." *Canadian Geographer,* **11** (1958):1–8.

McGee, T. G. *The Urbanization Process in the Third World—Exploration in Search of a Theory.* London: Bell, 1971.

———. "Peasants in the Cities, A Paradox, A Paradox, A Most Ingenious Paradox." *Human Organization,* **32** (1973):135–142.

———. "The Persistence of the Proto-Proletariat: Occupational Structures and Planning for the Future of Third World Cities." Melbourne: Monash University, Department of Geography, 1974.

Madden, C. H. "Some Indicators of Stability in the Growth of Cities in the United States." *Economic Development and Cultural Change,* **4** (1956):236–252.

Magdoff, H. "The American Empire and the U.S. Economy." In *Imperialism and Underdevelopment,* edited by Robert I. Rhodes. New York: Monthly Review Press, 1970.

Malthus, T. R. *An Essay on the Principle of Population and a Summary View of Principle of Population.* Harmondsworth, England: Penguin Books, 1970.

Mamdani, M. *The Myth of Population Control.* New York: Monthly Review Press, 1973.

Mangin, W. "Latin American Squatter Settlements: A Problem and a Solution." *Latin American Research Review,* **2** (1967):65–98.

Martin, J. E. *Greater London: An Industrial Geography.* London: Bell, 1966.

Maruyama, M. "The Second Cybernetics: Deviation-Amplifying Mutual Causal Processes." *American Scientist,* **51** (1963):164–179.

Masotti, L. H. and J. K. Hadden, eds. *The Urbanization of the Suburbs,* Urban Affairs Annual Review 7. Beverly Hills: Sage Publications, 1973.

Massey, D. "Towards a Critique of Industrial Location Theory." *Antipode,* **5** (1973):33–40.

Matthews, H. G. "Radicals and Third World Tourism." *Annals of Tourism Research,* **5** (October/December 1977):20–29.

Meadows, D. et. al. *The Limits to Growth.* New York: The New American Library, 1972.

Mesarovic, M. and E. Pestal. *Mankind at the Turning Point.* New York: Signet, 1976.

Mikesell, M. W. "Patterns and Imprints of Mankind," from *The International Atlas.* Chicago: Rand McNally, 1969.

Miller, G. T., Jr. *Living in the Environment: Concepts, Problems and Alternatives.* Belmont: Wadsworth, 1975.

Mishan, E. J. *Technology and Growth: The Price We Pay.* New York: Praeger, 1969.

Missen, G. I. and M. I. Logan. "National and Local Distribution Systems and Regional Development: The Case of Kelantan in West Malaysia." *Antipode,* **9** (1977):60–74.

Morgan, W. T. "The 'White Highlands' of Kenya." *Geographical Journal,* **129** (1963):140-155.

Bibliography

Morrill, R. L. "The Development and Spatial Distribution of Towns in Sweden." *Annals* of the Association of American Geographers, **53** (1963):1–14.

———. "Migration and the Spread and Growth of Urban Settlement." *Lund Studies in Geography, Series B,* **26** (1965).

———. *The Spatial Organization of Society.* Belmont, Calif.: Wadsworth, 1970.

Morton, K. and P. Tulloch. *Trade and Developing Countries.* New York: John Wiley & Sons, 1977.

Muller, P. "Trend Surfaces of American Agricultural Patterns: A Macro-Thünen Analysis." *Economic Geography,* **45** (1973):228–242.

Muller, P. O. *The Outer City.* Washington, D.C.: Association of American Geographers, Commission on College Geography, Resource Paper No. 75-2, 1976.

Murdie, R. A. "Cultural Differences in Consumer Travel." *Economic Geography,* **41** (1965): 211–233,

Murphy, R. *Patterns on the Earth.* Chicago: Rand McNally College Publishing Company, 1978.

Muth, R. *Cities and Housing.* Chicago: University of Chicago Press, 1969.

Myint, H. *The Economics of the Developing Countries.* London: Hutchinson, 1964.

———. "The Classical Theory of International Trade and Underdeveloped Countries." In *Economic Policy for Development,* edited by I. Livingstone, Harmondsworth, England. Penguin Books, 1971.

Myrdal, G. *Economic Theory and Underdeveloped Regions.* London: Duckworth, 1957.

———. *The Challenge of World Poverty.* New York: Vintage Books, 1971.

Notestein, F. W. "Zero Population Growth: What is it?" *Family Planning Perspectives,* **2** (1970):20–24.

Nyerere, J. K. *The Arusha Declaration.* Dar es Salaam: Government Printer, 1967a.

———. *Education for Self-Reliance.* Dar es Salaam: Government Printer, 1967b.

———. *Socialism and Rural Development.* Dar es Salaam: Government Printer, 1967c.

———. *Ujamaa—Essays on Socialism.* Dar es Salaam: Oxford University Press, 1968.

Nystuen, J. D. "Identification of Some Fundamental Spatial Concepts." In *Spatial Analysis: A Reader in Statistical Geography,* edited by B. J. L. Berry and D. F. Marble. Englewood Cliffs, N.J.: Prentice-Hall, 1968.

Odun, H. T. *Environment, Power, and Society.* New York: John Wiley & Sons, 1971.

Ohlin, B. *Interregional and International Trade.* Cambridge: Harvard University Press, 1933.

Oshima, W. "Labor Force Explosion. The Labor Intensive Sector in Asian Growth." *Economic Development and Cultural Change,* **19** (1970–71):161–183.

Owens, D. *Road Research Laboratory,* Report LR 154, 1968.

Paddock, W. and P. Paddock. *Time of Famines—America and the World Food Crisis.* Boston: Little, Brown and Co., 1976.

Pardee, F. S., et. al. *Measurement and Evaluation of Transportation System Effectiveness,* RM-5869-DOT. Santa Barbara, Calif.: The Rand Corporation, September, 1969.

Park, R. E., E. W. Burgess and R. D. McKenzie. *The City.* Chicago: University of Chicago Press, 1925.

Park, R. E. "Urbanization as Measured by Newspaper Circulation." *The American Journal of Sociology,* **35** (1929):60–79.

Bibliography

Parsons, G. F. "The Giant Manufacturing Corporations and Balanced Regional Growth in Britain." *Area,* **4** (1972):99–103.

Parsons, J. J. "Corporate Farming in California." *Geographical Review,* **67** (1977):354–357.

Peccei, A. "Controlling the Population Will Be the Rule." *Development Forum,* **2,** No. 7 (1974):4.

Peet, J. R. "The Spatial Expansion of Commercial Agriculture in the Nineteenth Century: A von Thünen Interpretation." *Economic Geography,* **45** (1969):283–301.

Pelzer, K. J. *Pioneer Settlement in the Asiatic Tropics.* New York: American Geographical Society, Special Publication No. 29, 1945.

Penn, D. "Aggregate Concentration." *Anti-Trust Bulletin,* Spring, 1976.

Pickard, J. P. "U.S. Metropolitan Growth and Expansion, 1970–2000 with Population Projections." In *Population Growth and the American Future.* Washington, D.C.: U.S. Government Printing Office, 1972.

Platt, R. H. *Land Use Control: Interface of Law and Geography.* Washington, D.C.: Association of American Geographers, Commission on College Geography, Resource Paper No. 75-1, 1976.

Porter, P. W. "Environmental Potentials and Economic Opportunities: A Background for Cultural Adaption." *American Anthropologist,* **67** (1965):409–420.

Poulantzas, N. *Classes in Contemporary Capitalism.* London: New Left Books, 1975.

Pred, A. "Behavior and Location: Foundations for a Geographic and Dynamic Location Theory, Part 1." *Lund Studies in Geography, Series, B,* **27** (1967).

_____. "Behavior and Location: Foundations for a Geographic and Dynamic Location Theory, Part 2." *Lund Studies in Geography, Series B,* **28** (1969).

_____. *Major Job Providing Organizations and Systems of Cities.* Washington, D.C.: Association of American Geographers Commission on College Geography, Resource Paper No. 27, 1974.

Price, A. G. *White Settlers in the Tropics.* New York: American Geographical Society, Special Publication No. 23, 1939.

Prothero, R. M. "Land Use at Soba, Zaria Province, Northern Nigeria." *Economic Geography,* **33** (1957):72–86.

Ralph, E. *Place and Placelessness.* London: Ron Ltd., 1976.

Ravenstein, E. G. "The Laws of Migration." *Journal of the Royal Statistical Society,* **48** (1885):167–227.

_____. "The Laws of Migration." *Journal of the Royal Statistical Society,* **52** (1889):241–301.

Ray, D. M. "Cultural Differences in Consumer Travel Behavior in Eastern Ontario." *Canadian Geographer,* **11** (1967):143–156.

Reilly, W. J. *The Law of Retail Gravitation.* New York: The Knickerbocker Press, 1931.

Riddell, J. B. *The Spatial Dynamics of Modernization in Sierra Leone: Structure, Diffusion and Response.* Evanston: Northwestern University Press, 1970.

Ridker, R. G. "To Grow or Not to Grow: That's Not the Relevant Question." *Science,* **182** (1973):1315–1318.

Robinson, J. "Introduction" to *The Accumulation of Capital,* by R. Luxembourg. New Haven: Yale University Press, 1951.

Bibliography

Roder, W. "The Division of Land Resources in Southern Rhodesia." *Annals* of the Association of American Geographers, **54** (1964):41–52.

Rodney, W. *How Europe Underdeveloped Africa.* Dar es Salaam: Tanzania Publishing House and Bogle-L'Overture Publications, 1972.

Roepke, H. G. "Changes in Corn Production on the Northern Margin of the Corn Belt." *Agricultural History,* **33** (1959):126–132.

Rostow, W. W. *Politics and the Stages of Growth.* Cambridge, England: Cambridge University Press, 1971.

———. *The Stages of Economic Growth: A Non-Communist Manifesto.* Cambridge, England: Cambridge University Press, 1960.

Sampson, R. J. and M. T. Farris. *Domestic Transportation: Practice, Theory and Policy.* Boston: Houghton Mifflin Co., 1966.

Santos, M. *Les Villes du Tiers Monde.* Paris: Editions M-Th. Génin, 1971.

———. "Economic Development and Urbanization in Underdeveloped Countries. The Two Flow Systems of the Urban Economy and Their Spatial Implications." Toronto: University of Toronto, Unpublished Paper, 1972.

———. "Space and Domination: A Marxist Approach." *International Social Science Journal,* **27** (1975):346–363.

———. "Spatial Dialectics: The Two Circuits of Urban Economy in Underdeveloped Countries." *Antipode,* **9** (1977):49–60.

Sauer, C. O. *Agricultural Origins and Dispersals.* New York: American Geographical Society, 1952.

Saul, J. S. "African Socialism in One Country." In *Essays on the Political Economy of Africa,* edited by E. Arrighi and J. S. Saul. New York: Monthly Review Press, 1973.

Schulman, S. "Latin American Shantytown." In *Taming Megalopolis. Vol. II,* edited by H. Westworth Eldredge. New York: Doubleday, 1967.

Schumacher, E. F. *Small is Beautiful.* London: Blond and Briggs, 1973.

Scott, E. P. "Agricultural Marketing in Northern Nigeria: Some Observations on Rural Economic Development." Unpublished paper presented at the annual meeting of the African Studies Association, Philadelphia, 1972.

Semple, E. C. *The Influences of Geographic Environment.* New York: Henry Holt, 1911.

Semple, R. K. "Recent Trends in the Spatial Concentrations of Corporate Headquarters," *Economic Geography,* **49** (1973):309–318.

Simon, H. A. "On a Class of Skew Distribution Functions." *Biometrika,* **42** (1955):425–440.

Sinclair, R. "Von Thünen and Urban Sprawl." *Annals* of the Association of American Geographers, **57** (1967):72–87.

Singer, M. "Beyond Tradition and Modernity in Madras." *Comparative Studies in Society and History,* **13** (1971):160–195.

Skinner, G. W. "Marketing and Social Structure in Rural China." *Journal of Asian Studies,* (1964):22–26.

Slater, D. "Contribution to a Critique of Development Geography." *Canadian Journal of African Studies,* **8** (1974):325–354.

Smith, A. *Wealth of Nations,* 6th ed. London: Methuen, 1950.

Bibliography

Smith, D. M. "A Theoretical Framework for Geographical Studies." *Economic Geography,* **42** (1966):95–113.

_____. *Industrial Location: An Economic Geographic Analysis.* New York: John Wiley & Sons, 1971.

Soja, E. W. *The Geography of Modernization in Kenya.* Syracuse: Syracuse University Press, 1968.

_____, and R. J. Tobin. "The Geography of Modernization: Paths, Patterns, and Processes of Spatial Change in Developing Countries." In *Political Development and Change,* edited by R. Brunner and G. Brewer. New York: Free Press, 1975.

Spencer, J. E. and W. L. Thomas. *Cultural Geography—An Evolutionary Introduction to Our Humanized Earth.* New York: John Wiley & Sons, 1969.

Sprague, G. F. "Agriculture in China." *Science,* **188** (May, 1975):549–555.

Stafford, H. A. "Factors in the Location of the Paperboard Container Industry." *Economic Geography,* **36** (1960):260–266.

Stanford Research Institute. *Patterns of Energy Consumption in the United States.* Prepared for the Office of Science and Technology, Executive Office of the President, 1972.

Steinhart C. and J. Steinhart. *Energy: Sources, Use, and Role in Human Affairs.* N. Scituate, Mass.: Duxbury Press, 1974.

Stewart, C. T., Jr. "The Size and Spacing of Cities." *Geographical Review,* **48** (1958):222–245.

Stigler, G. "The Division of Labor is Limited by the Extent of the Market." *Journal of Political Economy,* **59** (1951):371–385.

Stine, J. H. "Temporal Aspects of Tertiary Production Elements in Korea." In *Urban Systems and Economic Development,* edited by F. Pitts. Eugene, Oregon: University of Oregon School of Business Administration, 1962.

Suyin, H. "Controlling the Population is Not the Cure." *Development Forum,* **2,** No. 7 (1974):5.

Szentes, T. *The Political Economy of Underdevelopment.* Budapest: Akademiai Kiadó, 1971.

Taaffe, E. J., R. L. Morrill, and P. R. Gould. "Transport Expansion in Underdeveloped Countries." *Geographical Review,* **53** (1963):503–529.

_____, and H. L. Gauthier. *Geography of Transportation.* Englewood Cliffs, N.J.: Prentice-Hall, 1973.

Teitelbaum, M. S. "Relevance of Demographic Transition Theory for Developing Countries." *Science,* **188** (1975):420–425.

Thoman, R. S. and E. C. Conkling. *Geography of International Trade.* Englewood Cliffs, N.J.: Prentice-Hall, 1967.

Thomas, W. L., Jr., ed. *Man's Role in Changing the Face of the Earth.* Chicago: University of Chicago Press, 1956.

Thünen, J. H. von. *The Isolated State.* Hamburg: Perthes, 1826.

Tiebout, C. M. "Location Theory, Empirical Evidence, and Economic Evolution." *Papers of the Regional Science Association,* **3** (1957):74–86.

Turnham, D. and I. Jaeger. *The Employment Problem in Less Developed Countries. A Review of Evidence.* Paris: Development Center of the Organization for Economic Cooperation and Development, 1971.

Bibliography

Ullman, E. L. "A Theory of Location for Cities." *American Journal of Sociology,* **46** (1940–41):853–864.

_____. *Mobile: Industrial Seaport and Trade Center.* Chicago: University of Chicago Press, 1943.

_____. "The Role of Transportation and Bases for Interaction." In *Man's Role in Changing the Face of the Earth,* edited by W. L. Thomas. Chicago: University of Chicago Press, 1956.

_____. "The Nature of Cities Reconsidered." *Papers and Proceedings of the Regional Science Association,* **9** (1962):7–23.

United States Department of Agriculture (Cooperating with the United States Agency for International Development). *The Marketing Challenge,* Foreign Economic Development Report No. 7, 1970.

U.S. Geological Survey. *Mineral Resource Perspectives, 1975.* U.S. Geological Survey Professional Paper 940, 1975.

Valavanis, S. "Lösch on Location: A Review Article." *American Economic Review,* **45** (1955):637–644.

Vance, J. E., Jr. *The Merchant's World: The Geography of Wholesaling.* Englewood Cliffs, N.J.: Prentice-Hall, 1970.

Vining, R. "A Description of Certain Spatial Aspects of an Economic System." *Economic Development and Cultural Change,* **3** (1955):147–195.

Vogeler, I. and A. R. de Souza. *Dialectics of Third World Development.* Montclair, N.J.: Allanheld, Osmun and Co., forthcoming.

Walker, R. A. "Urban Ground Rent: Building a New Conceptual Framework." *Antipode,* **6** (1974):50–58.

Ward, B. "The Decade of Development—A Study in Frustration." In *Two Views of Foreign Aid,* edited by B. Ward and P. T. Bauer. London: Institute of Economic Affairs, Occasional Paper No. 9, 1966.

Warner, S. B., Jr. *The Private City.* Philadelphia: University of Pennsylvania Press, 1968.

Weber, A. *Alfred Weber's Theory of the Location of Industries.* Trans. by C. J. Friedrich. Chicago: University of Chicago Press, 1929.

Wells, H. G. *Anticipations: The Reaction of Mechanical and Scientific Progress on Human Life and Thought.* London: Harper and Row, 1902.

Werner, C. "The Law of Refraction in Transportation Geography: Its Multivariate Extensions." *Canadian Geographer,* **12** (1968):28–40.

Whittlesey, D. "Major Agricultural Regions of the Earth." *Annals of the Association of American Geographers,* **26** (1936):199–240.

Williamson, J. C. "Regional Inequality and the Process of National Development: A Description of the Patterns." *Economic Development and Cultural Change,* 13, Part II (1965).

Wilson, G. L. *Transportation and Communications.* New York: Appleton-Century Crofts, 1954.

Wolfe, R. I. "Transportation and Politics: The Example of Canada." *Annals of the Association of American Geographers,* **52** (1962):176–190.

Wolff, R. D. *The Economics of Colonialism: Britain and Kenya, 1870–1930.* New Haven: Yale University Press, 1974.

Bibliography

Wolpert, J., A. Mumphrey, and J. Seley. *Metropolitan Neighborhoods: Participation and Conflict over Change.* Washington, D.C.: Association of American Geographers, Commission on College Geography, Resource Paper No. 16, 1972.

Worseley, P. "Frantz Fanon and the 'Lumpenproletariat.'" In *The Socialist Register,* edited by R. Milbrand and J. Savile. London, 1972.

Zeeman, E. C. "Catastrophe Theory." *Scientific American,* **234** (1976):65–83.

Zelinsky, W. *Prologue to Population Geography.* Englewood Cliffs, N.J.: Prentice-Hall, 1966.

Zipf, G. K. *Human Behavior and the Principle of Least Effort.* Reading, Mass.: Addison-Wesley, 1949.

Zwerdling, D. "The Day of the Locust—How Pesticides Have Created Monsters Out of Previously Harmless Insects." *Mother Jones,* August, 1977, pp. 35–38.

Index

Absolute distance, 23
Absolute location, 24
Abstract space, 20–23
Accessibility, 22, 24
Accessibility index, 380, 383
Ackerman, F., 129 (see also MacEwan A.)
Administrative principle, 258, 262
Age composition, 49, 53
Agglomeration, 22
Aggregate distance, 22
Agribusiness, 162, 193
Aid, 514, 551–54, 557–61
Alchian, A., 455
Alexandersson, G., 321, 362
Alonso, W., 577, 610
Amin, S., 501, 558–59
Areal differentiation, 3, 27, 29, 32
Arrighi, G., 12, 501–2, 507, 609 (see also Saul, J. S.)
Assembly costs, 310, 312, 314, 351, 371
Associated number, 381, 383
Average productivity, 167, 169
Average total costs, 204

Back-haul, 407
Backwash effects, 572, 574, 582
Baird, A., 498
Baran, P., 12 (see also Sweezy, P. M.)
Barber, W., 501
Barnbrock, J., 193
Basic cost, 334–36
Basic employment, 216
Basic firms, 215, 217
Bauer, P. T., 561–63
Behavioral matrix, 428–29, 454–55
Berry, B., 271, 281–82, 285–86, 289–90, 467, 581 (see also Pred, A.)
Beta index, 380–81
Bid rent curve, 175

Birth rate, 74
Blaikie, P. M., 184
Blaut, J., 498
Boeke, J., 482
Bogue, D., 294
Borchert, J., 272, 279, 328
Boserup, E., 155
Break-of-bulk point, 409
Break-point model, 249–50
Broek, J., 493 (see also Webb, J.)
Brookfield, H. C., 498
Brown, R. N., 28
Brush, J., 293
Buchanan, K., 495–96
Bunge, W., 215
Burgess, E., 217, 219, 223–24

Cantril, H., 561 (see also Free, L. A.)
Capital accumulation, 6, 11
Capital-intensive, 164
Capital-output ratio, 560
Capital shortage, 477
Carrying capacity, 95
Catastrophe theory, 442–43
Cavadino, P., 552–53
Ceiling rent, 209
Center-periphery, 569–70, 576–77, 582–85
Central business district, 196–97, 208, 219, 222
Central city, 239
Central function, 251, 287, 297
Central place, 244–46, 251–301
Central place theory, 385
Chisholm, G. G., 27
Chisholm M. D. I., 183–84
Christaller, W., 29, 254–61, 265–67, 271–72, 294, 452
City-rich and city-poor sectors, 264
Clairmonte, F., 8, 522

Cole, H. S. D., 96
Collins, J., 111–14, 140 (see also Lappé, F. M.)
Comparative advantage, theory of, 516–20, 563
Comparative costs, law of, 8
Competitive bidding process, 208
Complementarity, 25–26
Components of population change, 63
Concentric zone model, 217, 219, 241
Concrete space, 20, 23, 25
Conglomerate, 344
Connectivity, 20, 22–24
Convenience good, 295–97
Convergence, 576
Core area, 422–23
Cost-insurance-freight (CIF), 413
Cost of labor, 322–24, 371
Cost-space convergence, 417–18, 423
Cowboy life-style, 93, 137–38
Critical isodapane, 323
Cultural preferences, 157–58
Cyert, R., 426 (see also March, J.)

Dacey, M. F., 293
Datoo, B., 155
Death rate, 74
Debt payments, 547
Deevey, E. S., 73
Demographic index, 467
Demographic transition, 80–82
Dependence, 13
Dependency, 581, 612
Dependency ratio, 49
Dependent economy, 612
Depletion curve, 115–16
de Souza, A. R., 155, 166, 481 (see also Porter, P. W.)
Development, 2, 464
Development Assistance Committee (DAC), 552
Development continuum, 487
Deviation-amplification, 572
Deviation-counteraction, 572
Dialectical approach, 31
Diminishing returns, law of, 76, 166, 204
Direction, 20, 22–23
Diseconomies of scale, 205
Disguised unemployment, 501–2, 598
Dispersion index, 384
Distance, 20, 22–23

Distribution costs, 312, 314–16, 318
Division of labor, 4, 339, 522–23, 525
    artificial, 522, 563
    colonial, 501–8
Domestication hearths, 147
Dowd, D. F., 2
Dual-economy, 585
Dunn, E. S., 173
Durkheim, E., 589

Economic base, 215–16
Economic dualism, 482
Economic liberalism, 4
Economic rent, 166, 169, 170–71, 191, 193
Economies
    agglomeration, 347
    external, 205
    industry, 205
    internal, 204
    scale, 341–48
    urbanization, 205, 348, 367
Ecosystem, 94
Edges, 379–81, 423
Egalitarian society, 198–99
Elasticity, 405–6
Engels, F., 224–25
Engel's law, 534
Energy, 120–36
Energy crisis, 120, 126–31
Energy efficiency, 132
Entropy, 105
Environmental factors, 476
Environmental perception, 158
Equilibrium models, 571
Establishments, 287
European Economic Community (EEC), 531, 539–40, 544
Export earning stabilization scheme (STABEX), 545
Extensive margin, 169

Factor endowments approach, 520
Fagen, R. E., 30 (see also Hall, A. D.)
Fanon, F., 590, 602
Filtering process, 220
Firm-centered economy, 592–93
Fixed costs, 203–4
Fixed input, 167
Food crisis, 112–14
Food resources, 100–14
Frank, A. G., 12, 301, 487, 570, 581, 590

Index

Free, L. A., 561 (*see also* Cantril, H.)
Free trade, 517, 520–22, 563
Freight-on-board (FOB), 412–13
Freight rates, 402–3, 406–7, 411
Fried, M., 199
Friedmann, J., 422, 570, 576–83
Functional region, 248
Functional size, 286
Functional unit, 286–87

Game theory, 431–36, 443
Galbraith, J. K., 7–8, 345–46, 428, 488, 556–57
Galtung, J., 583, 585
Gappert, G., 546
Geertz, C., 592, 602
General Agreement on Tariffs and Trade (GATT), 537, 542
General System of Preferences (GSP), 542–43
Generative cities, 199
George, S., 87, 164
Ghettos, 239
Gilbert, A., 574
Global solution, 459
Goldsmith, E., 92
Good, C. M., 271
Goodwin, W., 328
Gottmann, J., 226
Gould, P., 396, 420, 432, 493 (*see also* Taaffe, E. and Morrill, R.)
Gourou, P., 28
Graph theory, 379, 423
Gravity model, 67
Gray, H., 88 (*see also* Tongri, S.)
Green revolution, 109–11
Griffin, K., 114, 488, 491, 533–37, 540, 557, 559–63
Group of 77, 542–43
Grove, D. J., 271 (*see also* Huzar, L. I.)

Hagen, E., 480–81
Hägerstrand, T., 437–38, 447
Haggett, P., 392
Hall, A. D., 30 (*see also* Fagen, R. E.)
Hall, P., 237
Hardin, G., 85, 113
Harris, C., 217, 222–23, 245, 348 (*see also* Ullman, E. L.)
Hartshorne, R., 29
Harvey, D., 79, 87, 92, 96, 300, 501

Hayter, T., 562, 571
Heckscher, E., 520
Heilbroner, R., 487
Hidden unemployment, 598
Hierarchical marginal good, 254
Hierarchy, 253, 272, 294, 299
Higgins, B., 482
Highest and best use, 181, 208
Hirschman, A., 572–77
Historical dialectical method, 494–501
Horizontal integration, 342–43
Horowitz, D., 557
Horvath, R. J., 184
Hotelling, H., 354–55
Hoyt, H., 217, 221, 223
Hughes, J. W., 225
Hunker, J., 327 (*see also* Wright, A. J.)
Hunt, E. K., 20 (*see also* Sherman, H. F.)
Huzar, L. I., 271 (*see also* Grove, D. J.)

Imperfectly divisible multiples, 340
Imperialism, 11–12, 514, 562–63, 583, 585
Import substitution, 540
Industrial Revolution, 306, 364, 367
Infant industry, 521
Intensive margin, 169
Intermediate technology, 111
International Monetary Fund (IMF), 537
Intervening opportunity, 25–26
Invasion and succession, 220, 224
Involution, 592
Iron law of wages, 7
Isard, W., 267, 318, 332
Isodapanes, 319, 335
Isolated state, 171–72, 177
Isopleths, 158, 319
Isotims, 318, 335
Isotropic plain, 265
Isotropic surface, 20, 22

James, P., 492
Jannelle, D., 419
Jefferson, M., 28
Johnson, E. A. J., 271
Jupplenlatz, M., 599

Kahn, H., 558
Kennelly, R. A., 318
Keynes, J. M., 8, 13, 14
Kimble, G., 478
King, L., 293

Kolars, J., 275 (see also Nystuen, J.)
Kunkel, J., 481

Labor force, 57
Labor-intensive, 160
Labor productivity, 322–25, 334
Labor theory of value, 10
Laissez-faire, 521
Land alienation, 491, 508
Lappé, F. M., 111–14, 140 (see also Collins, J.)
Least-cost-to-build network, 388
Least-cost-to-use network, 388
Leibenstein, H., 573, 479, 493
Lenin, N., 12
Lewis, A., 501, 597–98
Limiting factors, 469
Line-haul costs, 397, 399–400, 408, 412
Linear market, 251–52, 255
Livingstone, I., 557
Local solution, 459
Localized raw materials, 312, 314–18, 323
Location rent, 171–76, 181, 207
Location quotient, 215
Locational cost, 334–36, 367, 372
Locational inertia, 320–21, 324, 328, 357, 361–62, 367
Logan, M., 593 (see also Missen, G.)
Logistic curve, 109
Lomé Agreement, 545
Lord-Ritchie Calder, 85
Lösch, A., 261–67, 293–94, 389, 392, 452
Low labor productivity, 477
Lower circuit, 593, 595, 597–99
Luxemburg, R., 12

McClelland, D., 480–81
MacEwan, A., 129 (see also Ackerman, F.)
McGee, T., 592, 597, 600, 602–3
Mackay, R., 396
Macroeconomics, 3, 19
Maine, H., 589
Malnutrition, 101
Malthus, T., 7, 75–79
Mamdani, M., 87
Man-environment, 3, 27–28, 32
Mangin, W., 600
March, J., 426 (see also Cyert, R.)
Marginal productivity, 164, 167, 169
Market exchange, 198–99, 202

Market linkages, 347
Marketing principle, 255
Maruyama, M., 572
Marx, K., 9–11, 14, 79–80, 486, 589
Massey, D., 307, 372
Massing of reserves, 339
Material index, 357–58
Matrix, 384
Maximum sustainable yield, 99
Meadows, D., 96
Mean information field (MIF), 437–38
Megalopolis, 226
Mercantile model, 267–69
Microeconomics, 3, 19
Minerals, 115–19
Minicity, 235
Missen, G., 593 (see also Logan, M.)
Models (descriptive and normative), 17
Modern-traditional dichotomy, 588–90
Modernization, 493, 588–89
Monopoly, 15
Monte-Carlo model, 447
Monte-Carlo simulation, 451–52, 460
Morgan, W. T., 489
Morrill, R., 269, 300, 420, 447, 450, 452, 454, 457 (see also Taaffe, E. and Gould, P.)
Muller, P., 234
Multinational, 555–59, 612
Multiple-nuclei model, 217, 222, 241
Multiplier effect, 573
Murphy, R., 165
Myrdal, G., 572–77

N-achievement value, 481
Natural increase, 71, 74
Nearest-neighbor analysis, 293
Negative deviations, 389
Net energy, 130
Network change, 420
Networks, 378–96, 420–23
New Economic International Order (NIEO), 546
Non-basic employment, 216
Non-basic firms, 215, 217
Non-recurring source of productivity, 108
Nonrenewable resource, 98, 100, 115
Non-tariff barriers, 539
Notestein, F. W., 92
Nyerere, J., 604–5
Nystuen, J., 275 (see also Kolars, J.)

Index

Official Development Assistance (ODA), 552
Ohlin, B., 520
Oligopoly, 15
Optimizer, 182, 251, 298, 320, 426, 458–60
Optimum population, 97
Organization of Petroleum Exporting Countries (OPEC), 531, 546
Orientation, 308
Overpopulation, 95

Paddock, W. and P., 113
Parasitic cities, 199
Parsons, J., 164
Pelzer, K. J., 28
Peripheral area, 422–23
Peripheral economy, 612
Permanent cultivation, 154
Plantation, 148
Polarization effects, 573
Polarized metropolis, 241
Pollutants, 105
Population composition, 49
Population crash, 95
Population density, 39, 41
Population distribution, 39, 41, 43
Population explosion, 73, 80
Population migration, 63, 65–70
Population pyramids, 49–50, 53
Porter, P. W., 28, 155, 166, 481 (see also de Souza, A. R.)
Positive deviations, 389
Potential surface, 340–53
Poulantzas, N., 13, 570
Pred, A., 271, 328, 428 (see also Berry, B.)
Price, 28
Price instability, 525, 528, 530, 541
Principle of least effort, 264
Private land use decision process, 207
Production costs, 322, 330, 351, 371
Production function, 203
Production linkages, 347
Production-possibilities curve, 518
Productivity theory, 516
Profit-maximizing firms, 204, 207
Profit repatriation, 557
Proletariat, 466, 501, 508
Prothero, R. M., 184
Proto-proletariat, 585, 588, 592–99, 602, 604, 612

Psychic income, 427, 431
Pure competition, 203, 240
Pure raw materials, 312, 314–15, 408
"Push-pull" model, 65

Ralph, E., 266, 300, 301
Range, 251–52, 299
Rank-size rule, 281–86
Rank society, 198–99
Rate-break points, 410
Ravenstein, E. G., 66
Reciprocity, 198–99, 202
Recurring source of productivity, 108
Recycle, 118–19
Redistribution, 198–99, 202
Regional integration, 542, 547
Reilly, W. J., 248
Relative distance, 23
Relative location, 24, 26, 166, 191
Renewable resource, 98–99
Rent gradient, 174–75
Reserve, 97, 116
Resource allocation, 2, 17–18
Resources, 79
    natural, 92–94, 97
Retail gravitation, law of, 249
Ricardo, D., 3–8, 14, 79, 169–70, 517, 520
Riddell, J. B., 493
Robinson, J., 12
Roder, W., 504
Rodney, W., 466
Roepke, H., 436
Rostow, W., 483–87

Saddle-point, 433
Santos, M., 498, 593, 599
Satisficer, 33, 426–27
Saul, J. S., 13, 609 (see also Arrighi, G.)
Scarcity, 79
Schulman, S., 599
Schumacher, E., 96, 156
Scott, E., 271
Sector model, 217, 221, 241
Self-centered economy, 613
Semple, E., 27–28, 328
Service linkages, 347
Settlement-building functions, 286
Settlement-building trade, 246
Settlement-forming function, 286
Settlement-forming trade, 246
Settlement-serving trade, 246

Sex ratio, 53–54
Sherman, H. F., 20 (see also Hunt, E. K.)
Shifting cultivation, 154
Shimble index, 383–84
Shopping good, 295–97
Shortest path, 381
Simmel, G., 589
Simon, H. A., 284
Simulation, 436–39
Singer, H., 589–90
Site characteristics, 156, 191
Skinner, G. W., 271
Slater, D., 498
Smith, A., 3–5, 14
Smith, D., 318, 330, 332, 334
Snell, W., 392
Social dualism, 482
Social surplus, 199
Soja, E., 493
Space-cost curve, 170, 318, 331, 334–36
Spaceship life-style, 93, 137–38
Spatial
    diffusion, 436–40
    interaction, 20, 25
    margins to profitability, 170, 319, 331–32, 335–36, 372
    monopoly, 354
    oligopoly, 354
    organization, 2–3, 27, 29, 32
    process, 20, 25
    structure, 20, 25
Spencer, J., 493 (see also Thomas, W.)
Spread city, 225–27, 235–36
Spread effects, 572, 574, 582
Squatter settlements, 586, 599–600
Stages-of-growth model, 487
Stages of production, 167–69
Statistical index numbers, 467
Steady-state, 95, 251
Stewart, C. T., 285
Stine, J. H., 271
Stratified society, 198–99, 240
Structural rigidity, 535, 537
Subsistence, 79
Suburbs, 225, 229–33, 239
Surplus product, 240
Surplus value, 10–11
Suyin, H., 85
Sweezy, P. M., 12 (see also Baran, P.)
Systems of production, 160–66
Szentes, T., 476–79, 481

Taaffe, E., 420 (see also Morrill, R. and Gould, P.)
Tariffs, 537, 539, 540
Technique, 337–38, 372
Technological index, 467
Technostructure, 346, 428
Teitelbaum, M. S., 81
Terminal costs, 397, 399–400, 408, 412
Terms of trade, 521, 533, 563
Thermodynamics, second law of, 96, 104
Thomas, W., 493 (see also Spencer, J.)
Threshold, 251, 253–54, 289, 299
Thünen, J. H., von, 29, 166–67, 169–74, 177, 179, 181–82, 191, 207, 212–13, 255, 309, 429
Thünen rings, 190
Tiebout, C., 455
Time-space convergence, 419–20, 423
Tongri, S., 88 (see also Gray, H.)
Tonnies, F., 589
Total employment, 216
Total product, 167, 169
Trade, 514, 516
Trade area, 246–51, 288–90
Traffic principle, 257, 262
Transferability, 25–26
Transnational system, 556
Transport costs, 203, 206–7, 397–415, 423
Transport cost surface, 350–51, 353
Trend surface analysis, 333
Trickling-down effects, 574, 576

Ubiquitous raw material, 312, 314–18, 365, 367
Ujamaa, 606, 610, 612–13
Ullman, E., 217, 222–23, 245 (see also Harris, C.)
Underdevelopment, 464, 509
Underemployment, 588
Undernutrition, 101
Unemployment, 587–588
Unilineal evolution, 487
United Nations Conference on Trade and Development (UNCTAD), 533, 542–43, 563
Upper circuit, 593, 598–99
Urban multiplier, 216
Urbanization, 44–45, 47

Value added by manufacturing, 308
Vance, J., 267–69

Index

Variable costs, 204
Variable input, 166
Varignon frame, 317, 333, 362
Veblen, T., 8–9
Vertical integration, 164, 342–43
Vertices, 379–81, 423
Vicious circle, 478–79
Vining, R., 285

Warner, S. B., Jr., 196
Webb, J., 493 (*see also* Broek, J.)
Weber, A., 29, 255, 310, 312, 318–19, 323, 332, 408, 589

Weight-losing raw material, 316–18
Wells, H. G., 197
Williamson, J., 576
Wilson, G. L., 376–77
Wolff, R. D., 501
World Bank, 537, 563
Worseley, P., 590
Wright, A. J., 327 (*see also* Hunker, H. L.)

Zero-sum game, 432
Zipf, G. K., 281
Zoning, 223–24
Zwerdling, D., 111